D1397644

Standard
LESSON COMMENTARY®

2007–2008

International Sunday School Lessons

Edited by
Ronald L. Nickelson

Published by
Standard Publishing
Jonathan Underwood, Senior Editor

Fourteenth Annual Volume

Standard®
PUBLISHING
Bringing The Word to Life

Cincinnati, Ohio

CD-ROM AVAILABLE

The *Standard Lesson Commentary*® is available separately in an electronic format. This compact disk contains the full text of the King James *Standard Lesson Commentary*® and *The NIV Standard Lesson Commentary*®, a variety of preparation resources powered by the Libronix Digital Library System, and a collection of presentation helps that can be projected or reproduced as handouts. Order #06008.

System Requirements: Windows Vista/XP/2000; Pentium 133 MHz processor (300MHz recommended), 64 Meg RAM (128 recommended); 60 Meg Available Hard Drive Space; 2x or better CD-ROM drive.

If you have any questions regarding the installation, registration, or activation of this CD-ROM, please contact Logos **Customer Service** at **(800) 875-6467.**

If you have problems with the CD, *Technical Support* is available by telephone at *(360) 679-4496,* by e-mail at *tech@logos.com,* or online at *www.logos.com/support.*

In This Volume

Special Features

Fall Quarter 2007
God Creates

Writers

Lesson Development...................................Mark S. Krause (1, 3-5), Mark Mangano (2), Walter D. Zorn (6),
....John Nugent (7-9), Wesley Paddock (10-13)
Verbal Illustrations ....Charles R. Boatman
Discovery Learning and Reproducible Activities...........Ronald G. Davis (1-9), Bob & Charlotte Mize (10-13)
What Do You Think?..A. Eugene Andrews (1-9), Ted Simonson (10-13)
Why Teach This Lesson? ....Vicki Edwards

Winter Quarter 2007–2008
God's Call to the Christian Community

Writers

Lesson Development.....................Kenny Boles (1-5), James & Mandy Smith (6-9), Mark S. Krause (10-13)
Verbal Illustrations ....James B. North
Discovery Learning and Reproducible Activities............................Ronald G. Davis (1-5), Alan Weber (6-13)
What Do You Think?...Ken Beck (1-5), Jeff Snell (6-9), Ken Beck (10-13)
Why Teach This Lesson? ....Vicki Edwards (1-5), David Marvin (6-9), A. Eugene Andrews (10-13)

Spring Quarter 2008
God, the People, and the Covenant

Writers

Lesson Development....................................Walter D. Zorn (1-5), John Nugent (6-9), Joe Sprinkle (10, 11),
....Aaron Prohs (12, 13)
Verbal Illustrations ....Charles R. Boatman
Discovery Learning and Reproducible Activities...............Richard A. Koffarnus (1-5), Ronald G. Davis (6-13)
What Do You Think?.........................Vicki Edwards (1-5), A. Eugene Andrews (6-9), Chad Summa (10-13)
Why Teach This Lesson? ....A. Eugene Andrews

Summer Quarter 2008
Images of Christ

Writers

Lesson Development..............................Lee M. Fields (1, 2), Mark S. Krause (3-5), Larry Chouinard (6, 7),
....Rick Allbee (8, 9), William R. Baker (10-14)
Verbal Illustrations ....James B. North
Discovery Learning and Reproducible Activities...........................Ronald G. Davis (1-5), Alan Weber (6-9),
....Charlotte Mize (10-14)
What Do You Think?...........A. Eugene Andrews (1-5, 8, 9), Truitt F. Evans, Sr. (6, 7), Vicki Edwards (10-14)
Why Teach This Lesson? ....Chuck Terrill

Index of Printed Texts, 2007–2008

The printed texts for 2007–2008 are arranged here in the order in which they appear in the Bible. Opposite each reference is the page number on which the lesson that treats the passage begins in this volume.

Cumulative Index of Printed Texts

A cumulative index for the Scripture passages used in *The NIV Standard Lesson Commentary®* for September 2004–August 2008 is presented here for your convenience.

Musings of a Repentant Technophobe
USING MODERN TEACHING TOOLS

by Chuck Terrill

Technology scares me. I don't like it. When 8-track tape players became popular, I stuck with my record player. When cassette players became popular, I traded my record player for an 8-track tape player. When CDs became fashionable, I bought a cassette player. It seems that I have always managed to stay about a decade behind in the area of technological advance.

I have repented, albeit begrudgingly. I exchanged my typewriter for a computer just a few years ago. I don't know much of anything about what makes a computer work, but the computer has changed my life.

In our media driven age, the way we present our lessons is important. You know that you have been faithful in your responsibilities as a teacher. You've studied hard, and God has given you a message to present. You know what the Bible says and what it means. How can you help your students apply biblical truth to their lives?

Start by going to www.standardlesson.com. Then click on the "In the World" link. Once you land on that page, you can bookmark it or put it in your Internet browser's favorites file. That way you can return easily time and time again. I assure you, it is well worth the effort! This resource will give you timely insight into how the message of the Bible relates to us for the week at hand.

There is little relevance in using illustrations or applications that are long outdated. Our students aren't overly concerned about how mankind perceived God one hundred years ago. They are asking, "What is God doing now? How does the Word of God apply to me today?" You will find that "In the World" is always timely and relevant in this regard. You will receive insight and direction that will help apply Scripture to the lives of your students in a meaningful way.

Now here's the best news: "In the World" is free. This is just one of many ministry resources that Standard Publishing makes available to you to help you faithfully teach the Word of God. While you are visiting www.standardpub.com, review their other valuable resources. You might want to read the Daily Devotion or sign up for the free eNewsletter. All of these free resources are made available for your personal growth and development.

Something else that had me scared was the use of multimedia in the presentation of my Sunday school lessons. Maybe you, also, experimented with creating Microsoft PowerPoint® slides at one time, but you determined that the result just really wasn't worth the extra effort. But what if you had your own assistant, who would design and construct a PowerPoint® presentation for you every week? That sounds good, doesn't it?

Standard Publishing is your own, personal PowerPoint® design assistant! If you purchase the *Standard Lesson eCommentary,* the slide presentations are on the CD. You will also find the PowerPoint® presentation on the CD that accompanies the Standard Lesson Quarterly *Adult Resources* packet.

These presentations are skillfully done and are ready to present or project just as they are. If your computer has the full version of the PowerPoint® program, you have the option of editing the presentation. Even if you don't have the full version of PowerPoint®, you can download the free PowerPoint® "reader" at www.microsoft.com/downloads. It will enable you to use (but not edit) Standard Publishing's dynamic presentations.

Statistically, we remember much more of what we both hear and see as opposed to only hearing or only seeing. That's the main reason to use the PowerPoint® presentations. The extra effort will be well worth it.

Standard Publishing has a wealth of resources for teachers of the International Sunday School Lessons. The student book, *NIV® Bible Student,* will help your learners to retain more knowledge as they study in advance. The *Adult Resources* packet contains posters as well as take-home papers that are relevant to the lesson of the day. You might also want to use the on-line lesson at www.christianstandard.com in your preparation time.

Don't be a technophobe. You'll be glad you went online to discover the valuable resources that Standard Publishing has to offer. Your students will rejoice as well.

Fall Quarter 2007

God Creates

(Genesis)

Special Features

Lessons

Unit 1: God Creates a People

Unit 2: God's People Increase

Unit 3: God's People Re-created

About These Lessons

Everyone knows the frustration of trying to follow the plot of a movie after missing the first 10 minutes. Beginnings are vitally important! The Bible itself has a grand "plotline," so to speak. A proper understanding of Christianity has its start with the book of Genesis—the beginning.

Sep 2

Sep 9

Sep 16

Sep 23

Sep 30

Oct 7

Oct 14

Oct 21

Oct 28

Nov 4

Nov 11

Nov 18

Nov 25

Our Heritage

by Walter D. Zorn

Every Christian should become well acquainted with Genesis, the first book of the Bible. Why? Because it is a divine revelation about the beginning of all that we observe—our universe and the people who live on the earth.

Genesis also reveals to us the beginnings of the Hebrew people, who were chosen by God to precede the Messiah. As Christians we trace our spiritual ancestry back to Abraham, who "is the father of us all" (Romans 4:16). This makes the study of Genesis imperative for Christians who wish to be informed about the beginning of our faith. Our beginning as Christians is found not only at Pentecost (Acts 2) but also with Abraham (Genesis 12–25), and before him, with the first human beings, Adam and Eve.

International Sunday School Lesson Cycle
September 2004—August 2010

YEAR	FALL QUARTER (Sept., Oct., Nov.)	WINTER QUARTER (Dec., Jan., Feb.)	SPRING QUARTER (Mar., Apr., May)	SUMMER QUARTER (June, July, Aug.)
2004-2005	The God of Continuing Creation (Bible Survey)	Called to Be God's People (Bible Survey)	God's Project: Effective Christians (Romans, Galatians)	Jesus' Life, Ministry, and Teaching (Matthew, Mark, Luke)
2005-2006	"You Will Be My Witnesses" (Acts)	God's Commitment— Our Response (Isaiah; 1 & 2 Timothy)	Living in and as God's Creation (Psalms, Job, Ecclesiastes, Proverbs)	Called to Be a Christian Community (1 & 2 Corinthians)
2006-2007	God's Living Covenant (Old Testament Survey)	Jesus Christ: A Portrait of God (John, Philippians, Colossians, Hebrews, 1 John)	Our Community Now and in God's Future (1 John, Revelation)	Committed to Doing Right (Various Prophets, 2 Kings, 2 Chronicles)
2007-2008	God Creates (Genesis)	God's Call to the Christian Community (Luke)	God, the People, and the Covenant (1 & 2 Chronicles, Daniel, Haggai, Nehemiah)	Images of Christ (Hebrews, Gospels, James)
2008-2009	The New Testament Community (New Testament Survey)	Human Commitment (Character Studies)	Christ in Creation (Ezekiel, Luke, Acts, Ephesians)	Call Sealed with Promise (Exodus, Leviticus, Numbers, Deuteronomy)
2009-2010	Covenant Communities (Joshua, Judges, Ezra, Nehemiah, Mark, 1 & 2 Peter)	Christ the Fulfillment (Matthew)	Teachings on Community (Jonah, Ruth, New Testament)	Christian Commitment in Today's World (1 & 2 Thessalonians, Philippians)

"Creation"	"Call"	"Covenant"	"Christ"	"Community"	"Commitment"

This quarter's emphasis will be on the covenant people whom God created; but first he had to create a universe that could sustain people made in his image. While the fallen state of humanity is not discussed in this series, it is part of the backdrop as we observe how God chose one man and his wife to be in special covenant relationship with him. Somehow God, through this one family, would create a new people, a nation that would bring redemption to the world.

UNIT 1: GOD CREATES A PEOPLE

SEPTEMBER

Lesson 1 begins with the creation of the universe. But the focus of Genesis 1 is not the entire universe as such. Rather, the focus is on this earth, as God fashioned it and its inhabitants: all kinds of living creatures. Humanity was the crown and climax of creation. This creation of an inhabitable and inhabited earth occurred within a six-day period, with the last three days paralleling the first three days. Not until humanity was created as male and female did God pronounce all his creation to be "very good." Humans were given stewardship responsibility for God's good creation. Believers should experience nothing but awe and wonder in the presence of all creation.

Lesson 2 emphasizes the meaning and importance of humanity having been created in the image of God. There are many opinions as to what this word *image* means, but it clearly relates to the fact that humanity is God's representative on earth and has stewardship over it. It is imperative for us to take care of the earth that God has given us.

Lesson 3 is about God's promise to Abram and Sarai (later renamed Abraham and Sarah) that they were to have a son in their old age. It is through this son that a new nation was to be born. That nation was to bring blessing and salvation to all the peoples of the world. How could an old man and woman, past the age for bearing children, have such a child of promise? Nothing is too hard for God! Eventually Abraham trusted God and "[God] credited it to [Abraham] as righteousness" (Genesis 15:6). Sarah's initial laugh of derision was turned into a laugh of joy. Isaac (meaning "laughter") became, in a sense, God's joke on the world. Abraham did indeed become a "father of many nations" through this one son.

Lesson 4 recounts the story of Ishmael's birth. It really is a story of lack of trust on the part of Abraham and Sarah. They thought they would never have children of their own, despite God's promises. Time was running out, they thought, and so they did the only "natural" thing to do: they produced a child through a surrogate mother, Hagar. In spite of the resulting conflict, God blessed Hagar and Ishmael; thus was born an estrangement between Jews and Arabs. We can learn an important lesson from God's care and concern for Hagar and Ishmael.

The continuation of the covenant promises depended on Isaac's marrying the "proper" wife and having "proper" children. *Lesson 5* is the story of that selection process. Through prayer, a test, and spiritual discernment, Abraham's servant found Rebekah, a member of Abraham's family. Rebekah's kindness proved her to be God's choice for Isaac. Through her the promised seed of Abraham continued.

UNIT 2: GOD'S PEOPLE INCREASE

OCTOBER

Lesson 6 continues the story about Rebekah's marriage to Isaac. They finally had children—twin sons who struggled with each other from before birth. The sibling rivalry created a bitter struggle between two peoples from which the older (Esau = Edom) would serve the younger (Jacob = Israel). Parental favoritism fostered the rivalry, and the results were disastrous. Things worsened when Esau rashly sold his birthright to Jacob. In spite of Jacob's taking advantage of Esau, God worked through Jacob to fulfill his promises.

Lesson 7 examines Jacob's dream at Bethel. This involved a ladder that led to Heaven, with angels descending and ascending on it and God above it. In this vision God restated to Jacob the covenant promises as they were originally given to Abraham. In God's sovereign care, Jacob was promised a land, numberless "seed," and God's own divine presence and assurance of fulfillment. Thus, Bethel ("house of God") became a place of worship, where Jacob committed himself to Yahweh God.

In *Lesson 8* Jacob-the-deceiver was deceived by his uncle Laban. Jacob had been given Leah as a wife instead of Rachel, and he had to agree to work seven more years to earn the right to have the younger daughter as his second wife. God used the deception as an opportunity to expand Jacob's family as promised. God is able to work in disappointing situations to bring about good.

Lesson 9 is the story of a great family reunion and reconciliation. It involved two brothers who had been bitter enemies (see Lesson 6). Although Jacob expected a battle, Esau greeted him with hospitality and signs of forgiveness.

NOVEMBER

UNIT 3: GOD'S PEOPLE RE-CREATED

Lesson 10 is the continuing saga of how parental favoritism can wreak havoc on sibling relationships (see Lesson 6). The fact that Joseph revealed his dreams (which he had a moral obligation to do) made things worse. His brothers reacted by selling him into slavery. Joseph's brothers thus set in motion a series of actions that cascaded in a direction they could not possibly have imagined.

Lesson 11 continues to unfold the mysterious ways of God in the account of Joseph. Joseph not only dreamed, he also interpreted dreams. His interpretation of Pharaoh's dream caused Pharaoh to elevate Joseph to a position of high power. God was the source of the dreams and thus he, ultimately, was the one who elevated Joseph to his position.

The story of Joseph reahces a climax with *Lesson 12*. Joseph's wisdom and oversight over the granaries of Egypt preserved many people, including his own family, the family of promise. Thus, Joseph partially fulfilled the promise to Abraham, for Joseph was blessed to be a blessing. We can say that Joseph was a "type" of Christ in that (1) those closest to him betrayed him and (2) God used the experience to bring about a deliverance.

Lesson 13 draws the patriarchal stories to a close, with Jacob's blessing of Joseph's sons. The uniqueness of this blessing was in the way Jacob crossed his arms and placed his right hand on Ephraim, the younger son, thus giving him the chief blessing. Jacob himself had experienced something similar in the declaration that "the older will serve the younger" in God's plan. Jacob's legacy continued through his sons as well as through his grandsons from Joseph.

FROM THE PAST TO THE FUTURE

God created a universe out of nothing. He placed planet Earth within it. Upon that planet he put the crown of his creation: humanity, created in the image of God. Then sin intervened. To redeem a fallen world, God planned to send his Messiah through a new people created (seemingly out of nothing) just for that purpose. Today, we have a heritage of sin from Adam and a heritage of faith from Abraham. We feel the effects of these two legacies constantly. Through Christ, we know which one wins out in the end!

The World of Abraham circa 2000 B.C.

——— Abraham's Journey to Canaan

Chronology of Genesis

From the Call of Abraham to the Death of Joseph

2167 BC	Abram born	
2092 BC	Call of Abram	Genesis 12:1-5
2081 BC	Ishmael born (Lesson 4)	Genesis 16:15, 16
2067 BC	Isaac born (Lesson 3)	Genesis 21:1-3
2050 BC	Abraham offers Isaac	Genesis 22:1-19
2007 BC	Jacob and Esau born (Lesson 6)	Genesis 25:24-26
1992 BC	Abraham dies at age 175	Genesis 25:7
1930 BC	Jacob flees to Haran (Lesson 7)	Genesis 28:10
1916 BC	Joseph born	Genesis 30:22-24
1899 BC	Joseph sold into slavery in Egypt at age 17 (Lesson 10)	Genesis 37:2, 28
1887 BC	Isaac dies at age 180	Genesis 35:28
1886 BC	At age 30, Joseph interprets Pharaoh's dream (Lesson 11)	Genesis 41:46
1877 BC	Jacob goes to Egypt *Beginning of the Israelites' 430-year stay in Egypt (Exodus 12:40, 41), leading to the exodus in 1447 BC (Lesson 12)*	Genesis 46:5, 6
1860 BC	Jacob dies at age 147 (Lesson 13)	Genesis 47:28
1806 BC	Joseph dies at age 110	Genesis 50:26

THE BEGINNING

LESSON 1

WHY TEACH THIS LESSON?

My daughter attended a Christian school during her early grade school years. Following our family's relocation, she attended public school. Both schools offered field trips to observe nature. After her first public school trip, she noticed one difference: "We looked at the same things, but this time we said, 'Isn't nature wonderful?' instead of 'Isn't God wonderful?'"

The apostle Paul said, "Since the creation of the world God's invisible qualities—his eternal power and divine nature—have been clearly seen, being understood from what has been made, so that men are without excuse" (Romans 1:20). Although the fingerprints of God are all over his creation, some will choose not to acknowledge him.

Your students have a choice to make today. That choice is the same one that every human before us has faced: Will we acknowledge the existence of our creator or not?

INTRODUCTION

A. THE DEBATE OVER INTELLIGENT DESIGN

I recently spoke to a friend I had not seen for years. I knew that he had been adopted as a child, but I did not know that for several years he had been seeking his birth parents. He eventually found he had another "family" of brothers and sisters; he has developed relationships with them. His comment about this to me was, "When I found out more about where I came from, I began to understand much better who I am." We are intuitively curious about our origins!

The book of Genesis is a book of origins, although it speaks of our origins in a much more profound way than the "origins" my friend was concerned with. As we read Genesis, several questions come to mind: Does this book provide reliable scientific data? Should believing Christians engage in scientific research and debate? Is there any room in the public classroom for the story of creation that Genesis provides?

Many people today (even some Christians) would answer *no* to all three questions. Others have long been engaged in the pursuit of *creation science*, an approach that sees Genesis as a certain guide to the origins of the universe and life itself. Creation science, however, has difficulty gaining a wide hearing in the mainline scientific community. Creation science is dismissed as being tied too closely to what is viewed as a pre-modern, superstitious, unscientific worldview.

Recently, a variation of creation science has gained notice: *the theory of Intelligent Design*. This effort is supported by scientists having solid academic credentials. Michael J. Behe, a leading proponent of Intelligent Design, has pointed out that many scientific investigations lead to the observation of "irreducible complexity" in natural phenomena. Behe claims that the physical characteristics of living organisms are too complex to be explained by mindless processes such as natural selection and mutation—thus the necessity of a designer.

DEVOTIONAL READING:
PSALM 8

BACKGROUND SCRIPTURE:
GENESIS 1:1-25

PRINTED TEXT:
GENESIS 1:1-6, 8, 10, 12-15, 19, 20, 22, 23, 25

LESSON AIMS

After participating in this lesson, each student will be able to:

1. List elements of the days of creation.

2. Summarize the method and design of God's creation as presented in Genesis 1.

3. Make a plan for greater stewardship toward one aspect of God's created resources.

KEY VERSE

In the beginning God created the heavens and the earth.
—Genesis 1:1

LESSON 1 NOTES

There is no conflict between the foundational assumptions of the theory of Intelligent Design and the book of Genesis. Intelligent Design demands that we understand a master intellect behind the order of the universe, a designer or creator. This is clearly taught in Genesis.

Yet the theory of Intelligent Design by itself is unable to understand God as more than a master artisan, a superior being who turns out an amazing series of inventions from his workshop. The theory of Intelligent Design cannot lead us fully to the God of the Bible, who not only made us but also continues to have a personal relationship with his creatures. For the fullest understanding of who God is and how we can relate to him, we must turn to the Bible.

B. LESSON BACKGROUND

Genesis in not merely the first book in the Bible. It stands as the first book in a five-book section of the Old Testament we call the *Pentateuch* or the *Books of Moses* (Genesis, Exodus, Leviticus, Numbers, Deuteronomy). This collection was finished long before the end of the Old Testament period; it was already in use during the times of the kingdoms of Israel and Judah, centuries before Christ.

The overall purpose of the Pentateuch is to tell the story of the origins of the nation of Israel. With this purpose in view, we can understand that Genesis serves as an introduction to the great events of nation-birthing found in Exodus. Genesis provides us with the place to start: the beginning, with God's creation of the heaven and the earth. What better place to start could there be?

Included in this account is the creation of the first man and woman. They are the ancestors of all people, not just the nation of Israel. The tragedy of Genesis is that humanity rebelled against its creator. Sin flourished. Later, the story focuses on Abraham, father of the nation of Israel,. because God planned to use one of his descendants (Jesus) to redeem humanity from the bondage of sin.

And so we begin the greatest story ever told. It is the drama of human origins and humanity's eventual deliverance from its self-caused alienation from the creator of the universe. The stage could be no bigger, the stakes no higher.

I. GOD AT THE BEGINNING (GENESIS 1:1, 2)

Where did God come from? You will not find the answer in Genesis. God is uncreated, separate and apart from any created thing. The existence of an uncreated creator is the reason there can be anything instead of nothing. The universe is not self-explanatory. It exists because God upholds it by his powerful word (see Hebrews 1:3).

A. BEGINNING, GOD, HEAVEN, EARTH (v. 1)

1. In the beginning God created the heavens and the earth.

The opening of Genesis has no comment on *God* other than to place him at *the beginning.* However far back in time we can imagine, God was there! This is an understated, yet striking, testimony to God's eternality: *In the beginning, God.*

The text sketches God's creation in broad terms. The use of *the heavens* and *the earth* together may refer simply to the totality of the physical universe. Some think, however, that *heavens* as used here refers to the realm of God and the created angelic beings. That is a domain not normally accessible to humans.

B. EARTH, DARKNESS, SPIRIT, WATERS (v. 2)

2. Now the earth was formless and empty, darkness was over the surface of the deep, and the Spirit of God was hovering over the waters.

Visual for Lesson 1. *Start a discussion by pointing to this visual as you ask, "Why is it important to acknowledge this truth?"*

WHAT DO YOU THINK?

What should our acceptance of the fact that God created the world mean in our lives on a day-to-day basis?

At this point in creation, the future home of humanity is characterized four ways. First, it is *formless* or unfinished; God has yet to mold it into final state. Second, it is *empty;* the living creatures that will inhabit it have yet to be created. Third, it is dark; this is not a limiting factor for God (see Psalm 139:12), but the condition must be changed in order for earth to be a suitable habitation for humans. Fourth, it is watery; there is no solid ground to stand upon. This too is a condition that must be modified in order to give human life a chance for survival.

The text notes the presence of *the Spirit of God.* This is not a separate being from God of verse 1. God's ability to be present is not limited by conditions that allow for his presence. This is an indirect affirmation of the doctrine of God's omnipresence (his presence everywhere).

While this spiritual presence of God is not referred to as the Holy Spirit, the concept is there in part. Holiness refers to more than moral purity. The Bible also understands being holy as being separate. At this point, God clearly is separate from his creation. The created world is not part of God, and he is not part of the created world. They are distinct.

II. CREATION, DAYS 1–3 (GENESIS 1:3-6, 8, 10, 12, 13)

The work proceeds in an orderly fashion. God does not leave the world void and uninhabitable. He has a plan that leads to the final creation of human beings in his image.

This part of Genesis does not describe any creative method of God beyond speaking. The mechanics of this are not revealed to us in any scientific way. We must believe that the word of God is powerful and creative (see Psalm 33:6; Hebrews 11:2, 3). In the New Testament, this creative Word of God is identified with his Son (see John 1:3; Hebrews 1:3).

A. FIRST DAY OF CREATION (vv. 3-5)
3-5. And God said, "Let there be light," and there was light. God saw that the light was good, and he separated the light from the darkness. God called the light "day," and the darkness he called "night." And there was evening, and there was morning—the first day.

God's first day of creation concerns not living creatures but *light.* It is difficult to conceive of life without light, for it is a necessary component of life as we generally understand it. If there were no light, it would be a blind universe.

Notice that *darkness* is not created. Light is separated from darkness, but there is no sense of God "making darkness." This is because darkness has no real existence. It is simply an absence, a lack of light. Darkness is a "without." This is why darkness is an apt metaphor for moral evil and sin, which is living "without God" (our moral light).

Verse 5 establishes the pattern for the days of creation. Each section ends with the statement *there was evening, and there was morning—the . . . day,* indicating a creative cycle has been completed. This is also the source of the Bible way of reckoning days. For most of the Jews of Bible times, the new day does not begin at sunrise but at sundown, because that signals the end of the old day.

B. SECOND DAY OF CREATION (vv. 6, 8)
6, 8. And God said, "Let there be an expanse between the waters to separate water from water. . . . God called the expanse "sky." And there was evening, and there was morning—the second day.

WHAT DO YOU THINK?

How has your belief in God as creator helped you in the difficult times of life?

WHAT DO YOU THINK?

How can the ancient recurring phrase And God said *speak to our lives today?*

HOW TO SAY IT

Abraham. AY-bruh-ham.

Deuteronomy. Due-ter-AHN-uh-me.

Hebrews. HEE-brews.

Judah. JOO-duh.

Leviticus. Leh-VIT-ih-kus.

omnipresence. AHM-nih-PREZ-ence.

Pentateuch. PEN-ta-teuk.

Older versions use the word *firmament* in place of *expanse*. In either case, what the text is describing is the separation of "ground waters" (rivers, lakes, oceans) from "sky waters" (clouds). This is an essential step in transforming the watery void (v. 2) into a place fit for human habitation.

FURNISHING A NEW WORLD

America's space probes to Mars early in this century revealed a barren world. Mars had water on it sometime in the ancient past, although not as much as on the primeval Earth that Genesis describes. Nevertheless, a Florida company called 4Frontiers Corporation has announced plans to establish a high-tech human colony on Mars by the year 2025.

The company plans to begin by developing a replica of the proposed Mars settlement here on Earth and charging admission to tourists (see www.sliceofscifi.com and www.4frontiers.com). Backers say it is necessary to colonize Mars in case disease or a collision with an asteroid should wipe out the human race or if we happen to make Earth uninhabitable through war or pollution.

The 4Frontiers plan sounds only slightly like God's activity in preparing the Earth for human habitation. There are significant differences: God's presence was everywhere in his creation; he had a plan that could see beyond the next 20 years; and he had the power to make his plan work regardless of whatever technical difficulties there were to overcome.

It is good to remember that we humans are creatures, not the creator. In this light we should frame even our most grandiose plans with appropriate humility.

—C. R. B.

WHAT DO YOU THINK?

When God looked at his creation, he said that it was good. How should that influence our attitude toward this world and toward our work?

C. THIRD DAY OF CREATION (vv. 10, 12, 13)

10. *God called the dry ground "land," and the gathered waters he called "seas." And God saw that it was good.*

The organization of the earth continues. Now the *waters* are no longer allowed to dominate, but are confined to appropriate areas. This allows for dry *land*, a prerequisite for plant life.

12, 13. *The land produced vegetation: plants bearing seed according to their kinds and trees bearing fruit with seed in it according to their kinds. And God saw that it was good. And there was evening, and there was morning—the third day.*

Various kinds of plant life appear. This continues the preparation of the earth for human habitation, for now there is renewable sustenance for humankind and for the necessary animals.

The author notes a remarkable thing about the vegetation: it produces *seed* after its own kind. In other words, the seed from an apple produces apple trees, not watermelons. Modern science has explained the mechanics of this, but it was very mysterious to people in the ancient world. If we pause to consider the consistency of this pattern, it is still remarkable today. God makes plant life that is capable of reproduction, and therefore that plant life is not dependent upon his direct creative action for each succeeding generation.

VISUALS FOR THESE LESSONS

The visual pictured in each lesson (example: page 18) is a small reproduction of a large, full-color poster included in the Adult Resources *packet for the Fall Quarter. The packet is available from your supplier. Order No. 192.*

III. CREATION, DAYS 4–6 (GENESIS 1:14, 15, 19, 20, 22, 23, 25)

The author now moves on to describe the creation of the patterns of the earth in relation to other heavenly bodies.

D. FOURTH DAY OF CREATION (vv. 14, 15, 19)

14, 15, 19. *And God said, "Let there be lights in the expanse of the sky to separate the day from the night, and let them serve as signs to mark seasons and days and years, and let them be lights in the expanse of the sky to give light on the earth." And it was so. . . . And there was evening, and there was morning—the fourth day.*

The author's interest is not in astrophysics or the possibility of space travel. Rather, he is explaining how *days* and *seasons* came into being, thus allowing for the growing cycles that result in crop production from the plant life (food) that came in day three.

It is astounding for us to contemplate the perfection and intricacy of God's system! Consider that water can exist in its liquid form only within a very narrow temperature range, namely from 32 to 212 degrees Fahrenheit. This is a tiny slice of the range of temperatures found in our solar system, from the inferno of the sun (27 million degrees Fahrenheit at its core) to the temperature of absolute zero of the outer planets (approaching –459 degrees Fahrenheit).

Yet, because of the precise distance that the earth is positioned from the sun as well as various other factors, water is able to remain liquid over most of our planet. There could be no life as we know it without this precious liquid. Modern scientific knowledge does not negate the majesty of these verses, but only makes them more astounding.

HEAVENLY BODIES

NASA's Deep Impact space probe of 2005 was made to collide intentionally with the comet Tempel 1. The mission's purpose was to create a cloud of comet debris that could be photographed and analyzed by the mother craft orbiting the comet. The debris cloud gave scientists clues about how the solar system was formed at the time of creation that Genesis tells us about.

However, Marina Bai, a Russian astrologer, brought a lawsuit for $300 million against NASA to compensate her for what she called her "moral sufferings." Bai claimed that the experiment deformed her horoscope and violated her life and spiritual values. Bai said that the comet was important to her life because her grandfather had wooed her grandmother by showing her the comet.

While the astrologer's claims can appropriately be ridiculed as silly, her belief in the power of heavenly bodies to control human destiny is a common one today. Even some Christians have an unwarranted, unholy respect for this pseudo-science. Genesis establishes that God put the heavenly bodies in their places as signs of his power, to give light to his creation, and to establish the seasons by which the earth brings forth our food. Other interpretations go beyond (or against) what Scripture teaches. —C. R. B.

E. FIFTH DAY OF CREATION (vv. 20, 22, 23)

20. And God said, "Let the water teem with living creatures, and let birds fly above the earth across the expanse of the sky."

On the fifth day God begins to supply the earth with animal life. This day is devoted to "nonland" creatures: *birds* and aquatic life. Today, we have developed the capabilities to fly and to live underwater. But for most of history, neither of those was feasible.

Thus the birds and aquatic life are creatures that ancient people understand to be fundamentally different from humans. To appreciate these marvels is to begin to understand the wonder of God's created world that permeates this beautiful Genesis account.

22, 23. God blessed them and said, "Be fruitful and increase in number and fill the water in the seas, and let the birds increase on the earth." And there was evening, and there was morning—the fifth day.

WHAT DO YOU THINK?

Separating night from day, seas from dry land, etc., establishes certain boundaries. What significance does (or should) that fact have on your life?

DAILY BIBLE READINGS

Monday, Aug. 27—God the Creator (Psalm 8)

Tuesday, Aug. 28—The First Day (Genesis 1:1-5)

Wednesday, Aug. 29—The Sky (Genesis 1:6-8)

Thursday, Aug. 30—The First Harvest (Genesis 1:9-13)

Friday, Aug. 31—The Sun and Moon (Genesis 1:14-19)

Saturday, Sept. 1—The Birds and Sea Creatures (Genesis 1:20-23)

Sunday, Sept. 2—The Animals (Genesis 1:24, 25)

Mighty and loving creator, the all-wise and all-powerful God, may we stand in awe of your master design and plan for the universe. May we live daily in appreciation of the marvels of your creation, our world, which exists and is sustained through the word of your power. In Jesus' name, amen.

At the time of the writing of Genesis, the total human population of the earth was a tiny fraction of what it is today. Even so, the rivers and oceans of Genesis are full of fish, and the skies are full of a marvelous variety of birds. The few urban varieties of birds that most people are familiar with today are but a small fraction of the avian creatures.

The Lewis and Clark expedition explored the Pacific Northwest of the U.S. some 200 years ago. On that expedition the explorers observed such a heavy migration of salmon that it seemed as if one could walk across the river on the backs of the fish! This abundance now has been reduced, but we can still appreciate God's original provision for *the earth.*

F. SIXTH DAY OF CREATION (v. 25)
25. God made the wild animals according to their kinds, the livestock according to their kinds, and all the creatures that move along the ground according to their kinds. And God saw that it was good.

God's last stage of preparation of the earth for the coming of humanity is to create land animals. The term *livestock* has the meaning of range animals that eat plant life. Later, the author differentiates between domesticated and wild animals of this class (Genesis 3:14).

The *creatures that move along the ground* are probably reptiles and small rodents. Such animals are later considered unclean and generally forbidden as a food source for the Israelites (see Acts 10:12-14, where Peter objects to eating "anything impure or unclean").

The stage is now fully set for the creation of men and women. This will be covered in next week's lesson.

CONCLUSION

Violin players are taught from the first day of lessons that their violins must be tuned every time they play. The longer the violinist waits to retune, the worse the instrument sounds. After Adam and Eve's disobedience, creation ended up being "out of tune" because of sin. The one who created our earth and its heavens intends to return and "retune" it according to his perfect will.

Paul teaches that all creation is anticipating the revelation of God's ultimate purpose (see Romans 8:19-23). Paul even says that "the whole creation has been groaning as in the pains of childbirth right up to the present time" as it waits for its creator (Romans 8:22). The one who created will re-create, and there will be "a new heaven and a new earth, the home of righteousness" (2 Peter 3:13). What a glorious day that will be! Then sin will be no more, and "he will reign for ever and ever" (Revelation 11:15).

As wonderful as this promise is, however, we do not know when God's re-creation of the universe will be. It could be tomorrow. It could be 10,000 years from now. Until that day, this present universe is what we have. Although it is marred by human sin, it retains the pattern and intention of the master designer.

That fact should bring praise to our lips. When science discovers some new intricacy or complexity in nature, we should marvel. When we see the vivid colors of the sunrise on a stately peak, we should stop to ponder the artistry of the maker. When we hear the roar of the ocean, Genesis 1 should come to mind again. When we are high in the mountains on a clear night and see the uncountable stars in all their majesty, we should stand in awe of their creator, for "the heavens declare the glory of God" (Psalm 19:1).

THOUGHT TO REMEMBER
It was God who created.

Discovery Learning

This page contains an alternative lesson plan emphasizing learning activities. Classes desiring such student involvement will find these suggestions helpful. The next page is a reproducible activity page to further enhance discovery learning.

INTO THE LESSON

Put up a sign reading *Unintelligent Design* before class begins. As class begins ask, "What are examples of what has proven to be 'unintelligent design' in the modern world of products and businesses?"

Allow time for response. If the group needs examples, suggest such products as the Edsel, New Coke, and Betamax video. (Be prepared for the argument that the problem with some of these was marketing rather than product design.) Draw upon the lesson's introductory comments to make a transition to the study of the Word.

Alternative: Have one of your learners do a sentence diagram Genesis 1:1 on the board. This should come out as *subject:* God; *action:* created; *object:* the heavens and the earth; *qualifier:* in the beginning (adverbial prepositional phrase). Note both the simplicity of the expression and the profundity of the thought.

INTO THE WORD

Divide the class into six groups (or pairs). Give each a piece of poster board and a broad-point felt-tip marker for writing. One piece of poster board should be labeled "Day One," another "Day Two," etc. Ask each group first to identify what God created on the day listed on its poster board. When they finish, each group is to make a quick list of what needed to be in place for that created entity (or entities) to exist and sustain itself (or themselves). After a few minutes, collect the sheets and post them in numerical order for class viewing.

With a tone of mock arrogance, say, "I just don't think these look good in that order, so I'm going to rearrange them." Then switch two of the sheets and make an appropriate comment. For example, you can switch day two and day five, then ask, "Now, don't you think that will work better?" Wait for a learner to say something like, "Well, that won't work because the flying creatures of day five would have no home without the sky created on day two."

Make other impossible switches as time allows. Then comment, "The order of God's creation is second in importance only to the actual creative acts themselves. In the succession of days, we can see God making preparations for the creative work that follows." (You can also add, "And everything has to be in place and functioning in full unity before God can reach the peak of his work: the creation of humans. But that's next week's study.")

Next, give each learner a sheet of paper. Ask each to number his or her paper from 1 to 16 (or refer your learners to the student books, if you use that resource). Say, "I am going to read a number of truths affirmed in today's lesson text. For each truth, you are to identify a verse number that reveals it. Some truths may be in more than one verse." Then read the following:

1. Oceans are God's way of collecting water to allow dry land to appear. 2. The earth changed in form, at God's directive and control. 3. God announced that an element of his creation was good. 4. There was a beginning for all material elements. 5. Grasses, herbs, and trees were created with reproductive abilities. 6. Water covered the earth at its beginning. 7. When light appeared, darkness was no more. 8. Animals were God's last creation before humans. 9. Eternal God was present when time began. 10. Flying creatures were made on the fifth day. 11. Though God is light, the earth began in darkness. 12. The first things God named were *day* and *night*. 13. Sea creatures were God's first creation of life forms for the earth. 14. The sky was created to contain some of earth's water. 15. Sun, moon, and stars were created to establish seasons and seasonal markers for the earth. 16. The Spirit of God sustained the earth and held it in place until all creation was complete.

After taking responses to all truths, allow time for follow-up comments. These comments may include objections to the manner in which some of the truths are worded.

INTO LIFE

Distribute the words of the hymn, "I Sing the Mighty Power of God," by Isaac Watts from the reproducible page. In addition to the instructions listed in the activity I Couldn't Have Said It Better, suggest that class members use the stanzas for daily devotions in the week ahead. As they do, they can renew their commitments to being good stewards of God's creation. Reflecting on two lines of the hymn per day will offer real challenge and opportunity for praise and submission.

For an alternative or additional devotional and prayer exercise, distribute copies of the I Can't Keep Quiet exercise from the reproducible page.

I Couldn't Have Said It Better

Isaac Watts, the prolific Christian hymn writer, expressed well his attitude toward God's creation in the following poem, usually sung to the tune "Ellacombe."

Verses from Genesis 1
1
2
3
4
5
6
8
10
12
13
14
15
19
20
22
23
25

I sing the mighty power of God, that made the mountains rise,
That spread the flowing seas abroad, and built the lofty skies.
I sing the wisdom that ordained the sun to rule the day;
The moon shines full at God's command, and all the stars obey.

I sing the goodness of the Lord, who filled the earth with food,
Who formed the creatures through the Word, and then pronounced them good.
Lord, how Thy wonders are displayed, where'er I turn my eye,
If I survey the ground I tread, or gaze upon the sky.

There's not a plant or flower below, but makes Thy glories known,
And clouds arise, and tempests blow, by order from Thy throne;
While all that borrows life from Thee is ever in Thy care;
And everywhere that we can be, Thou, God art present there.

Draw circles around words or phrases and run lines from them to the right to connect thoughts with verses in today's text.

I Can't Keep Quiet

Consider each of the following to be the beginning to a prayer in response to God's creative acts in Genesis 1. Complete each with an expression of your own praise and commitment.

"God of creation, I know that all the waters of the earth are by your design. Therefore I will _____."

"God of all power, I know that the dry land is of your hand for our good. Therefore I will _____."

"God who is light, I value the light you have provided for us. Therefore I will _____."

"God of vastness, I marvel at the depth and breadth of your universe. Therefore I will _____."

"God of infinite artistry, I am blessed by the variety of your creatures. Therefore I will _____."

God of grace and plenty, I am awed by the abundance of trees and plants you have made available to sustain and comfort us. Therefore I will _____."

IN THE IMAGE OF GOD

LESSON 2

WHY TEACH THIS LESSON?

Most science classes teach that people are animals—mammals, to be more specific. Perhaps that is an accurate characterization in terms of a specific classification system. However, I never feel good about hearing that I am an animal or a mammal. It's not that I feel bad about being warm-blooded or having hair. It's just that it doesn't address all that I am.

Today's lesson offers your learners much more dignity than the simple science lesson offers. We are the favored creatures, made in the very image of the almighty God. While we can glean important insights from a discussion of what it means to be made in God's image, one thing is clear: it is an honor that sets us apart from all other life on earth.

The weight of this idea should influence every relationship your learners have. Each person they encounter is also created in God's image. Think about how respectfully, gently, and thoughtfully your learners will treat others if the power of this reality saturates their thoughts!

INTRODUCTION

A. FAMILY RESEMBLANCE?

Many people seem to be enthralled with detecting "resemblances." They look at a baby's picture and can't help exclaiming, "He has his father's eyes" or "She has her mother's nose." Some people are able to hire themselves out as celebrity look-alikes for parties. Late-night comedians occasionally even amuse their audiences with pictures of people who look like their dogs!

We may have two eyes, two ears, one nose, etc. as dogs do, but that and any other kind of resemblance between them and us is ultimately superficial. The being we most closely resemble is God. We are created in his image. Parts of the Bible can be thought of as a kind of mirror in this regard. When we look into its pages, we can see descriptions of God—his love, his holiness, etc. As we see those descriptions, we realize that they should be reflected in our own character as well (example: 1 Peter 1:15, 16).

We hasten to add that there are many ways that God is not like us. He is all-knowing and all-powerful, but we are not. His divine nature is not ours. He is ever the creator while we are ever the creature.

Attempts to "be like God" in these ways is satanic (Genesis 3:5). Yet through Christ we put off the old man of sin and "put on the new self, created to be like God in true righteousness and holiness" (Ephesians 4:22-24). That is where the ideal family resemblance lies! When that renewal in Christ happens, the image of God from Genesis 1:27 shines brightly in our lives.

B. LESSON BACKGROUND

God formed light on the first day of creation. God then waited until the fourth day to fill the cosmos with sources of that light. On the second day of creation,

---

DEVOTIONAL READING:
ISAIAH 40:25-31
BACKGROUND SCRIPTURE:
GENESIS 1:26–2:3
PRINTED TEXT:
GENESIS 1:26-31

LESSON AIMS

After participating in this lesson, each student will be able to:

1. Recite Genesis 1:27 from memory.

2. Explain the significance the "image of God" has in terms of his or her relationship to other created things and to other people.

3. Suggest one way for his or her church to treat those of other races with the respect due them as beings created in the image of God.

KEY VERSE

God said, "Let us make man in our image, in our likeness, and let them rule over . . . all the earth." —Genesis 1:26

God formed the sky and established terrestrial waters. God waited until the fifth day to fill that sky with birds and those waters with living creatures. On the third day of creation, God formed the dry land. He waited until the sixth day to fill that land with animals and people.

In six creative days, then, God formed and filled this world to be the theater of his glory. Psalmist and prophet alike proclaim that God's glory is revealed and praised from the east to the west (Psalms 50:1; 113:2, 3; Isaiah 45:6; 59:19; Malachi 1:11). If everything that is exists by the command of God, then the whole creation must give glory to God.

Taking center stage in this theater is humanity, the pinnacle of God's creative activity. The verb *created* occurs three times in Genesis 1:27. This makes clear that here the goal has been reached toward which all of God's creativity from verse 1 onward was directed. Only after the creation of mankind does God judge his work to be "very good" (1:31). Up to that point, he had found all that he had made merely "good" (1:4, 10, 12, 18, 21, 25). The most striking feature of the creation of mankind is that both male and female are created "in the image of God" (Genesis 1:26, 27).

I. GOD CREATES (GENESIS 1:26, 27)

A. IMAGE, PART 1 (v. 26a)

26a. Then God said, "Let us make man in our image, in our likeness,

Genesis 1:26 is the initial verse in the narration of humanity's creation. The shift from *Let there be* to *Let us make* is clue enough that something momentous is being narrated.

But what does God really mean when he says *Let us make man in our image, in our likeness*? Our lesson introduction notes that we "resemble" God in certain ways. Yet we are also very different from him. We have physical bodies and are subject to death; God, on the other hand, is Spirit (John 4:24; 1 Timothy 1:17; 6:16). Furthermore, he does not originate or decay in time (Psalms 90:2, 4; 102:24-28; Isaiah 44:6; 48:12).

Over the centuries, theologians have explored our "resemblance" to God in terms of a group of spiritual qualities. Note how human behavior is based on (or should be based on) the following divine characteristics: *compassion* (2 Corinthians 1:3, 4), *forgiveness* (Colossians 3:13), *holiness* (Leviticus 19:2; 1 Peter 1:14-16; 1 John 3:3), *humility* (Philippians 2:3-11), *kindness* (2 Samuel 9:3), *love* (Ephesians 5:2; 1 John 4:7-21), *mercy* (Luke 6:36), *peacemaking* (Matthew 5:9), and *righteousness* (Ephesians 4:24).

These passages strongly suggest that we resemble (or should resemble) our creator in some vital ways. Let us not forget that as his image-bearers, we represent him. In the ancient world, images of "gods" or kings were viewed as representatives of deity or royalty. Mankind, created in the image of God, is the representative or viceroy of God. We are not God, but other people should be able to see Christ in us. Our holy living should reflect God's majesty.

At this point, we should pause to consider how sin has affected the image of God in us. Has humanity's decision to sin defaced God's image in us or caused the loss of that image altogether? The answer to this question is supplied by three biblical references: Genesis 9:6; 1 Corinthians 11:7; and James 3:9. All three speak of humanity after the fall into sin in terms of humanity before that fall. This suggests that the image of God in us is not lost through sin.

A claim that fallen humanity no longer bears the image of God would compromise our uniqueness. On this view, sinful humans would no longer have

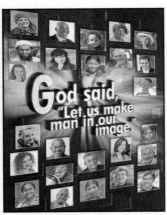

Visual for Lesson 2. *Point to this visual as you ask, "How do we get into trouble when we forget this truth?"*

unique moral, rational, or religious capacities. Our Bible and our experiences tell us otherwise!

Sin clearly does, however, hinder our relationship with God. Sin hinders God's desire that we represent his interests. Accordingly, the New Testament points us to one who can restore our relationship to God.

As the sinner turns to God through faith in Jesus Christ, he or she begins to live for the glory of God, not for self and sin. Upon following the biblical plan of salvation, he or she becomes a member of a different kingdom—the kingdom of God. As such, this person begins to represent the concerns of his or her new king. What a privilege!

B. DOMINION (v. 26b)

26b. ". . . and let them rule over the fish of the sea and the birds of the air, over the livestock, over all the earth, and over all the creatures that move along the ground."

This half-verse reflects the priorities of creation. It shows the hierarchy of God's attention and intention. God lets us *rule* over the earth, and we exercise that dominion (both wisely and not so wisely) every day. That is not to say that we rule over every aspect of existence on earth. No one can predict the exact course of a hurricane or the time of the next earthquake, let alone control them. Being the dominant species on earth has not resulted in the defeat of AIDS or even the common cold. Dominion has limitations.

Having dominion also has implications for ecology. Although the environmental movement often errs on the side of fanaticism, we still have a responsibility for stewardship of the earth's resources. That responsibility is a clear reflection of our mandate to have dominion *over all the earth*. Rulers bear responsibility in the eyes of God for that over which they rule. As we rule the earth, we will answer to God for our deeds (or lack of deeds) in that role.

Being created in God's image is God's acknowledgment that he puts more value on humans than on other elements of creation. Yet this fact does not negate the value of the rest of creation. Our concern for the creation is driven by our love for the creator. We look forward to the day when the ideal of Psalm 8 and Genesis 1:26 will be realized fully (compare Revelation 21:4, 5).

The text before us describes the extent of human dominion. Obviously, domesticated animals, *livestock*, are ruled by people. There is no question about that. But what about the other creatures listed?

Birds and *fish* in ancient times were not particularly subject to humans in any practical sense. Apart from limited hunting and fishing techniques, ancient people had little impact upon such creatures. Perhaps the confidence expressed in this verse is a kind of prophetic hint—a God-given awareness that humanity's future reach will extend to the depths of the oceans and beyond the heights of the atmosphere.

King David was one who was well acquainted with the idea of human dominion, particularly in light of what he wrote in Psalm 8:6-8: "You made him ruler over the works of your hands; you put everything under his feet: all flocks and herds, and the beasts of the field, the birds of the air, and the fish of the sea, all that swim the paths of the seas."

Years before he became king himself, David was a regular in King Saul's presence. David knew that kings may rule countries, but their personal impact on the day-to-day lives of their subjects was often quite limited. Many of a king's subjects lived their lives without ever seeing the king. Yet a king's influence can

DAILY BIBLE READINGS

Monday, Sept. 3—*The Creator of All (Isaiah 40:25-31)*

Tuesday, Sept. 4—*Created in God's Image (Genesis 1:26, 27)*

Wednesday, Sept. 5—*God Provides (Genesis 1:28-31)*

Thursday, Sept. 6—*A Hallowed Day (Genesis 2:1-3)*

Friday, Sept. 7—*God's Glory in Creation (Psalm 19:1-6)*

Saturday, Sept. 8—*Thanksgiving for God's Greatness (Psalm 103:1-14)*

Sunday, Sept. 9—*Remember God's Commandments (Psalm 103:15-22)*

How to Say It

Colossians. Kuh-LOSH-unz.
Ephesians. Ee-FEE-zhunz.
Ezekiel. Ee-ZEEK-ee-ul or Ee-
    ZEEK-yul.
Isaiah. Eye-ZAY-uh.
patriarchs. PAY-tree-arks.
Philippians. Fih-LIP-ee-unz.
taurine. TO-reen.

be felt profoundly through taxation, conscription into military service, etc. A king's dominion is extensive, but it also has limits.

We may draw a similar parallel concerning our dominion over the earth and her creatures. We do not influence directly the daily lives of every bottle-nosed porpoise, sparrow hawk, or giant anteater. Yet human ability that is exercised improperly can result in eventual extinction of various species. As those with dominion over creation, we need to use care.

The Two Sides of Dominion

The human race has condemned itself for despoiling nature, allegedly causing global warming, and abuse of our planet's resources. Some of the accusations are valid. For example, widespread use of DDT and other pesticides almost brought the noble bald eagle and other avian species to extinction. Strip mining once left vast tracts of land as wastelands upon which nothing could grow. Chemical spills poisoned the ground, and oil spills polluted the oceans.

But there is also good news: DDT was outlawed and the bald eagle has made a spectacular comeback. Reforestation, restoration of landforms, and pollution controls on automobiles and industry are all part of a concerted effort to undo the damage done in an earlier, less informed era. A specific example of this turnaround is the whooping crane. Only about 20 were left in 1941; now there are about 475.

There are indeed two sides to our dominion over creation: to be responsible and to be irresponsible. The Bible calls on us to be stewards who use the earth's resources properly, resisting the temptation either to abuse the creation or to worship it. We glorify God when we are good stewards.   —C. R. B.

C. Image, Part 2 (v. 27)

27. *So God created man in his own image,*
in the image of God he created him;
male and female he created them.

All humans are stamped with God's *image*. *Male and female*, old and young, rich and poor—it doesn't matter. Possessing this image means that God expects us to treat each other with the respect and dignity that that image calls for. Yet so often respect is not what we see. The problem is sin.

The New Testament teaches us how sin must be handled: God's image in us must be transformed into conformity with the God-Man, Jesus Christ. The challenge is "to be conformed to the likeness of his Son, that he might be the firstborn among many brothers" (Romans 8:29).

Our conformity to Christ should grow day by day. Full and final conformity to Christ comes at our own death and resurrection. Paul writes, "I want to know Christ and the power of his resurrection and the fellowship of sharing in his sufferings, becoming like him in his death, and so, somehow, to attain the resurrection from the dead" (Philippians 3:10, 11).

Paul also tells us that, "You have taken off your old self with its practices and have put on the new self, which is being renewed in knowledge in the image of its Creator" (Colossians 3:9, 10; compare Ephesians 4:22-24). Could there be any greater privilege than this?

II. God Blesses (Genesis 1:28)

A. Family (v. 28a)

28a. *God blessed them and said to them, "Be fruitful and increase in number; fill the earth and subdue it.*

What Do You Think?

In what ways does being created in the image of God affect your daily living? In what area are you best in this regard? In what area do you need the most improvement?

God gives people the power to reproduce themselves. This mandate should also be seen as a blessing and gift from God. The mandate carries an unspoken promise that God will enable us to fulfill it.

This mandate is repeated to Noah (Genesis 9:1). The patriarchs are reminded of God's part in this divine promise (Genesis 17:2, 20; 28:3; 35:11). The book of Genesis rejoices in the fruitfulness of the human race.

B. DOMINION (v. 28b)

28b. *"Rule over the fish of the sea and the birds of the air and over every living creature that moves on the ground."*

We discussed the meaning of dominion earlier. Here we may add that the Hebrew root behind the verb to *rule* is elsewhere in the Old Testament applied to a king's rule (Isaiah 14:6), to Messiah's rule (Numbers 24:19; Psalms 72:8; 110:2), and to God's rule (Isaiah 41:2). In Genesis 1 the dignity of royal rule is granted to the multitude of humanity. Ezekiel 34:4 implies that proper rule includes strengthening the weak, healing the sick, binding up the injured, and searching for the lost.

The Hebrew root behind the word *rule* occurs 15 times in the Old Testament. This verb carries the idea of some sort of coercion—for example, the subjection of a country through war (Numbers 32:22, 29). It follows, then, that creation will not easily oblige humanity's dominion, especially after sin enters the picture. Humans will have to bring creation into submission through strength or force.

III. GOD PROVIDES (GENESIS 1:29, 30)

A. HUMANITY (v. 29)

29. *Then God said, "I give you every seed-bearing plant on the face of the whole earth and every tree that has fruit with seed in it. They will be yours for food.*

Here we see how God made provision for humanity. People are to have as food the *seed* and *fruit* of plants. God's original intent is for humans to exist on a vegetarian diet. In Genesis 9:3, after the fall and the flood, people will be given permission to eat meat: "Everything that lives and moves will be food for you. Just as I gave you the green plants, I now give you everything."

Much later, Isaiah's expectation will be that one day "the lion will eat straw like the ox" (Isaiah 11:7; compare Isaiah 65:25). This prophecy suggests that a return to the paradise that originally existed in the Garden of Eden is to come.

B. LAND ANIMALS (v. 30)

30. *"And to all the beasts of the earth and all the birds of the air and all the creatures that move on the ground—everything that has the breath of life in it—I give every green plant for food." And it was so.*

God also provides for the animals and birds in the form of *every green plant*. This can imply that there is not yet a predator-prey relationship among the animals at this point in the biblical narrative.

Some students of the Bible propose, however, that to give the animals *every green plant* to eat doesn't necessarily exclude the possibility that the animals also ate each other. If they did, then Adam and Eve certainly would have known what the phrase, "you will surely die," meant, because they actually would have seen death among the animals (Genesis 2:17).

Today, we know that felines (cats) need a substance called *taurine* to survive. This is an amino acid that is found in animal tissue. (You can see taurine listed as an ingredient on a can of cat food.) Did the felines that were created before

WHAT DO YOU THINK?

God could have filled the earth with people all by his own direct, creative power. So why do you think God chose instead to create just two people and tell them to be fruitful and multiply?

WHAT DO YOU THINK?

What does it mean to you personally to rule over God's creation? What cautions do you (or should you) take in this role?

WHAT DO YOU THINK?

How has God been the provider for your life and your church?

humans need taurine? If so, did they get it by eating other animals before humans chose to sin and thus bring about their own deaths? No one knows—the Bible doesn't say.

IV. GOD APPRAISES (GENESIS 1:31)

A. GREAT CREATION! (v. 31a)

31a. God saw all that he had made, and it was very good.

We discussed in the Lesson Background what it means for God to appraise his creation as *very good*. The strong implication is that the creation of mankind is indeed the ultimate purpose of God's creative week. Humanity is not an afterthought in the creation, but is the result of God's intention and good pleasure.

PART OF WHAT MAKES US "VERY GOOD"

When God had finished his creative work, capped by creation of man and woman, he pronounced it "very good." Part of what made it "very good" was the character of life itself that enables us to overcome adversity and see beyond ourselves. We can excel at this trait at times.

An example is Jessica Esquivel. In 1990 she contracted chickenpox when she was six years old. She became gravely ill, with streptococcus bacteria shutting down her organs and cutting off the flow of blood to her extremities. Surgeons eventually had to amputate her legs and arms below the knees and elbows (www.chsd.org).

Twelve years later, her indomitable spirit demonstrated itself as she prepared for her high school prom. Jessica showed off her new "high-heeled feet" that allowed her to wear dressy shoes that evening. Now, as an adult, she works in a hotel chain and aspires to write profiles of people like herself to encourage others to accept the challenge of overcoming life's adversities.

It is this character trait of "getting outside one's self" that reflects God's self-sacrificing nature. It is part of what makes the human spirit "very good." We are indeed "fearfully and wonderfully made" (Psalm 139:14).   —C. R. B.

B. GREAT DAY! (v. 31b)

31b. And there was evening, and there was morning—the sixth day.

The expression *the sixth day* is also fascinating. The previous five days of creation were all referred to indefinitely; translated literally from the Hebrew, they would come out as "day, first," "day, second," etc. However, *the sixth day* in Hebrew is definite—it is "day, the sixth" (as is also the seventh day). Our English translations add the definite article *the* to all the days, but in the Hebrew the definite article is attached only to days six and seven. Days six and seven are thus intended to stand apart from the other five. Day six is the day on which God created us!

CONCLUSION

There is no idea more sinister than philosophical naturalism. Its explanation of human origins devalues us, it leaves us without meaning, it results in despair and misery. Parents, teachers, and preachers should take every opportunity to teach that human value, dignity, purpose, and hope are based first of all in the biblical teaching of creation.

To connect the "created . . . created . . . created" of Genesis 1:27 with the "Holy, holy, holy" of Isaiah 6:3 is tempting! The uniqueness of the latter suggests significance in the former. As the Lord is the super-superlatively holy one, so the human is the super-superlative creature. We stand in a unique relationship with the holy one, who is in our midst!

WHAT DO YOU THINK?

Why do you think God created us last?

PRAYER

Loving Father, we praise you that we are fearfully and wonderfully made. We thank you for the right to represent you and your kingdom. We ask that the Holy Spirit will empower us to reflect you before a watching world.

We thank you for the relationship we have with you through Jesus Christ our Lord. May we be true sons and daughters of you, the creator. In the name of Jesus, the one into whose image we are being transformed, we pray, amen.

THOUGHT TO REMEMBER

Live up to God's image in you.

Discovery Learning

*This page contains an alternative lesson plan emphasizing learning activities. Classes
desiring such student involvement will find these suggestions helpful. The next page
is a reproducible activity page to further enhance discovery learning.*

INTO THE LESSON

Write the following six phrases/clauses on separate slips of paper: "So God created man," "in his own image," "in the image of God," "he created him," "male and female," "he created them." Repeat each as necessary for every learner to have one slip. Hand the slips out randomly as learners arrive.

As class begins, say, "I want you to circulate until you find other class members who have phrases and clauses that form Genesis 1:27—the key verse of today's study. The verse has been divided into six sections." (If the multiples do not work for the number of students typically in attendance, combine some of the segments of Genesis 1:27 to make fewer slips.) Say, "When you have the verse complete, sit together as a group."

INTO THE WORD

Once the groups for the previous activity have formed, give each group a sheet with the following questions. Direct them to read and consider today's text before they answer.

1. In what sense are we made in God's image?

2. In what sense do we have dominion over sea creatures, birds, and land animals?

3. What is the significance of the phrase, "male and female," in its emphatic placement in verse 27?

4. Why would the command to be fruitful and multiply be essential to fulfilling the second part of verse 28?

5. A vegetarian diet for us is the plan of God in verse 29. Why do you think that there is no indication at first for what will later be permitted: people could be meat eaters? (See Genesis 9:3.)

6. Why does God conclude his evaluation of his creation with "very good" rather than the simpler "good" that he had earlier stated?

Your groups will need a significant amount of time to respond; be sure to allow enough time for each group to report its answers. There may be some significantly different conclusions, but a discussion of those differences will be an important part of the study. *Option:* Also distribute copies of the In the Image of God activity from the reproducible page for your faster groups to work on as your slower groups finish the six questions.

Next, say, "Unbiblical views of the nature of humanity are taught both inside and outside the church. Let's see if we can think of four diverse views of people as represented by various worldviews." Give each learner a piece of white paper folded into four equal segments. Provide instructions and scissors for cutting this folded sheet into four connected figures of people; have them do so.

Next, direct your learners (who may be in groups or working individually) to write into the four figures the four diverse views. If they need a start, suggest the view that humans have evolved from apes or a view such as Nazism, which saw one group of humans superior to another.

When students have had time to write down some ideas, ask for the ways in which the views identified contradict the concept of humans being created in the image and likeness of God. For example, the evolutionary view sees no distinction "in kind" between people and the animals that God created for our benefit.

After this activity, suggest that your students carry their cutouts with them for the week ahead. As they do, they can listen and look for inadequate, irresponsible, and unbiblical views of human nature. Tell your learners that the simple cutouts are as inadequate a representation of people as are the views noted on them.

INTO LIFE

Make a transition by saying, "Churches sometimes seem to ignore certain segments of the population in their surrounding community. We almost act as if some individuals and groups are not made in the image of God. Are there groups or types of individuals in our community that our congregation seems to be ignoring? What strategy will help our congregation see that these folks are made in God's image and are worthy of his love?" Allow time for response.

Next, give the following assignment: "As you cross paths with people this week—from family members to people on the street—quickly think this thought: 'You are made in the image of God, in his likeness!' Then consider how any interaction with someone should be tempered by that truth." Then say, "Possibly some of you will have some interesting reflections next Sunday on the impact of that thought on your interpersonal relations. Be prepared to share!" Finally, distribute copies of the Like God? activity from the reproducible page for devotional reflection in the week ahead.

In the Image of God

God occasionally describes himself in human terms—referring to his face, his hands, his feet, his eyes—even though we know that he is altogether spirit. When the Bible says we are made in the image of God, what does that imply? Write in ways we are made in the image of God, using the Scriptures below and other concepts from your own study.

Leviticus 19:2

Matthew 5:9

Luke 6:36

Ephesians 4:24

Ephesians 5:2

Philippians 2:5-8

Colossians 3:13

Like God?

How well are you reflecting God's image and likeness? Rate yourself on the following criteria; use a scale of 1 for "not much at all" to 5 for "very well."

_____ My life is filled with holiness.
_____ My life is filled with love.
_____ I find sin hideous and detestable.
_____ Merciful is my middle name.
_____ I love the company of the righteous.
_____ I treat everyone equally.
_____ I am faithful to my word.
_____ Justice matters to me.
_____ Truth is my watchword.
_____ I work diligently on relationships with others.

If there were a biblical spa where one could go to restore the family resemblance, what services would you check yourself in for?

ABRAHAM, SARAH, AND ISAAC

LESSON 3

WHY TEACH THIS LESSON?

There's a certain irony I've heard about that occurs in corporate meetings: managers who are quick to spend millions of dollars are more deliberate and cautious when the sums drop to thousands of dollars. One explanation for this is that most of us can't properly conceive how much a million dollars is, but since we can understand what a thousand dollars is, we spend it more carefully.

Don't we fall into this problem in faith issues as well? I can say, "God made the universe" without hesitation. I can affirm this anytime, anywhere, with no doubt. But when I stop to think about how I need God's provision for my life, I may hesitate. I ask questions such as, "Will God help me through my current financial dilemma?" Your learners ask themselves this kind of question as well. Such a question requires that they put their faith to a real, concrete test.

Your learners' faith needs to grow beyond knowing that God created the heavens and the earth. It needs to grow to the assurance that God works even on the level of the individual person. That's what this lesson is about.

INTRODUCTION

A. GENEALOGY

Genealogical research attracts much attention these days. Many people yearn to know more about their ancestors and thus their origins. Countries such as the U.S. and Canada are heavily populated by people whose ancestors immigrated. Such folk may try to reconstruct lost information about their family trees from the country of their ancestors' origin.

The quest to regain a connection with the past often yields fascinating stories and details. The resources now available on the Internet have allowed people to do armchair research without visiting courthouses to look at records or tramping through cemeteries to squint at gravestones.

Genealogy is an important subject in the Bible because God's promises often extend over many generations. This week's lesson studies a genealogy that almost ended before it really began.

B. LESSON BACKGROUND

Perhaps the most important ancestor in human history other than Adam is Abraham. Jewish people trace their ancestry back to him through his son Isaac. Many Arabic people see Abraham as their father through his son Ishmael (next week's lesson). While the combined numbers of the Jewish and Arabic people are impressive, Paul taught that Abraham is the father of all Christian believers (Romans 4:16). The book of Genesis tells the story of how God chose Abraham and his wife Sarah to be the ancestor couple for his covenant people.

It is difficult to date the time of Abraham exactly, and even more difficult to understand what society was like in his time. We describe these times as the period of the patriarchs. Abraham was the father/leader of an extended family

DEVOTIONAL READING:
ISAIAH 51:1-5

BACKGROUND SCRIPTURE:
GENESIS 15:1-6; 18:1-15; 21:1-8

PRINTED TEXT:
GENESIS 15:5, 6; 18:11-14a;
21:1-8

LESSON AIMS

After participating in this lesson, each student will be able to:

1. Retell the facts of God's promise to Abraham for offspring.

2. Explain the significance of the miraculous conception of Isaac.

3. Identify one area in his or her life to trust in God's care more fully.

KEY VERSE

Is anything too hard for the LORD? —Genesis 18:14a

and household that included several hundred people. They tended large flocks of animals for their livelihood. This forced them to be seminomadic, as they periodically had to move operations to new grazing areas. The Bible tells us that Abraham lived 175 years—an unusually long life by today's expectations (Genesis 25:7). One educated guess is that he lived 2167–1992 BC.

Abraham first appears in Genesis as Abram, the son of Terah (Genesis 11:31). They were citizens of Ur, a large, sophisticated city in Mesopotamia. Terah, Abram, and their families left that life to travel westward to Canaan. Terah died in Haran, about halfway to the final destination (Genesis 11:32).

At that time, the Lord called Abram to continue the trek to Canaan, giving him a list of promises and blessings. Two of the most important were (1) that Abram would be the father of "a great nation" and (2) that through him "all peoples on earth will be blessed" (Genesis 12:2, 3). This was the beginning of what we call the Abrahamic covenant.

The key to God's covenant with Abraham was his descendants: those who would prepare the way for God's chosen Messiah, Jesus. Yet Genesis records that Abraham and Sarah were not blessed with a child for many, many years. How this major problem was overcome is the marvelous story of this week's lesson.

I. COUNTING STARS (GENESIS 15:5, 6)

Genesis records six occasions during which God appeared to Abraham in order to make or reinforce covenantal promises. These are Genesis 12:1-3, 7; 13:14-18; 15:4, 5, 13-18; 17:1-8; 18; and 22:1-18. Genesis 15, which records the third of the six occasions, begins with God's appearance to Abraham in a vision. Abraham is reminded that the Lord is his "shield" and "very great reward."

Abraham is troubled by this because he is childless and part of God's promise to him involve a large number of descendants. He sees no alternative but to leave his considerable wealth to his chief employee, Eliezer of Damascus (see Genesis 15:2, 3). Yet he quickly learns that this is not God's plan.

A. UNFATHOMABLE HEAVENS (v. 5)

5a. He took him outside and said, "Look up at the heavens and count the stars—if indeed you can count them."

Abraham does not have a telescope. Even so, about 5,000 *stars* are visible to the naked eye. But just try counting them as you look at the night sky! It is almost impossible since it's hard to remember which ones you've already counted and which ones you haven't as you number them off.

Modern technology doesn't seem to make the job much easier. Some researchers estimate that our galaxy, the Milky Way, has 400 billion stars. One educated guess is that the total number of stars in the universe is something like the numeral 1 followed by 22 zeros.

These numbers boggle the mind, and the estimates are just that—estimates. We would not be able to count accurately the stars on a very clear night by hand and naked eye, and scientists come up with estimates that are rounded off in the billions. They cannot count the stars either. (That 400 billion estimate of the number of stars in the Milky Way used to be 200 billion!)

The bottom line is that the number of stars is uncountable. It is a figure known only by the creator of the stars.

5b. Then he said to him, "So shall your offspring be."

This is not just Abraham's own, immediate *offspring*, but the many generations that will proceed from them. All of these are considered as Abraham's seed.

DAILY BIBLE READINGS

Monday, Sept. 10—Listen! (Isaiah 51:1-5)

Tuesday, Sept. 11—Abraham Believed (Genesis 15:1-6)

Wednesday, Sept. 12—Abraham Doubted (Genesis 17:15-22)

Thursday, Sept. 13—Abraham the Host (Genesis 18:1-8)

Friday, Sept. 14—Sarah's Laughter (Genesis 18:9-15)

Saturday, Sept. 15—Sarah's Joy (Genesis 21:1-8)

Sunday, Sept. 16—The Faith of Abraham (Hebrews 11:8-12)

Abraham undoubtedly considers this to be a great gift. God promises a marvelously open-ended blessing to his chosen vessel, Abraham.

B. FAITHFUL ABRAHAM (v. 6)

6. Abram believed the LORD, and he credited it to him as righteousness.

Abraham's earlier attitude could be expressed as, "Don't tell me about thousands of descendants; just show me one!" He undoubtedly has difficulty imagining a large progeny when he does not have even a single child. Yet when God illustrates his promise by means of uncountable stars, Abraham no longer questions. He believes. He trusts that God will keep his promise.

This is a simple act of faith, but it has enormous consequences. Because of his faith, God considers Abraham to be a righteous man. This is the first clear statement in the Bible of the principle of justification by faith. Abraham does not earn God's favor by his deeds. To the contrary, he is given the status of a righteous person by his faith.

As we will see, this is the faith coming from (and resulting in) an obedient heart. Abraham is willing to trust God and follow his directions. The affirmation of this verse is so important that it is repeated in Romans 4:3, 9, 22; Galatians 3:6; and James 2:23.

AMAZING STATISTICS

If you're a baseball fan, you may know the name of Fernando Tatis, but few others do. In the history of Major League Baseball, only 12 players have hit two "grand slam" (bases loaded) home runs in a single game, and Tatis is one of them. But Tatis stands alone in the record books as the only player to hit two grand slams in the same inning!

It happened in the third inning of a game played on April 23, 1999. The first three batters got on base, and Tatis came to the plate and hit a home run. Later, two batters walked and another got on base on an error, loading the bases. After Mark McGwire flied out with the bases loaded, Tatis came to bat and hit his second grand slam of the inning, gaining for himself a unique place in the record book. This obviously was not a good day for the opposing pitcher!

Abraham's place in the record book of history is also unique. He stands alone as the common (or claimed) spiritual ancestor of billions. Abraham casts his shadow across 4,000 years of history. Ballplayers sometimes say, "You gotta believe!" That, in essence, was the secret of Abraham's greatness: "Abram believed the Lord; and he [the Lord] credited it to him as righteousness." It is still as true now as it was 4,000 years ago: without faith, we cannot please God.   —C. R. B.

II. COUNTING YEARS (GENESIS 18:11-14a)

We noted earlier that the Lord appears to Abraham six times in Genesis. The setting now before us is the fifth of those six. Abraham's heart of obedient faith is now to be put to the test. God does not make Abraham's son appear out of thin air. The appearance of a son will involve both Abraham and his wife, Sarah.

A. ABRAHAM AND SARAH LIMITED (vv. 11, 12)

11. Abraham and Sarah were already old and well advanced in years, and Sarah was past the age of childbearing.

At this time Abraham is about 100 years old, and Sarah is 90 (see Genesis 17:17). Physical change has affected their bodies. Sarah has stopped her monthly cycles. People of the ancient world knew, as we know today, that a woman in this stage of her life no longer becomes pregnant.

Chronology of Genesis
From the Call of Abraham to the Death of Joseph

Year	Event	Reference
2167 BC	Abram born	
2092 BC	Call of Abram	Genesis 12:1-5
2081 BC	Ishmael born (Lesson 4)	Genesis 16:15, 16
2067 BC	Isaac born (Lesson 3)	Genesis 21:1-3
2050 BC	Abraham offers Isaac	Genesis 22:1-19
2007 BC	Jacob and Esau born (Lesson 6)	Genesis 25:24-26
1992 BC	Abraham dies at age 175	Genesis 25:7
1930 BC	Jacob flees to Haran (Lesson 7)	Genesis 28:10
1916 BC	Joseph born	Genesis 30:22-24
1899 BC	Joseph sold into slavery in Egypt at age 17 (Lesson 10)	Genesis 37:2, 28
1887 BC	Isaac dies at age 180	Genesis 35:28
1886 BC	At age 30, Joseph interprets Pharaoh's dream (Lesson 11)	Genesis 41:46
1877 BC	Jacob goes to Egypt *Beginning of the Israelites' 430-year stay in Egypt (Exodus 12:40, 41), leading to the exodus in 1447 BC (Lesson 12)*	Genesis 46:5, 6
1860 BC	Jacob dies at age 147 (Lesson 13)	Genesis 47:28
1806 BC	Joseph dies at age 110	Genesis 50:26

Visual for Lesson 3. *Keep this chart posted all quarter to give your learners a chronological perspective.*

WHAT DO YOU THINK?

What are some ways that you have you seen God use elderly people to accomplish his will and advance his kingdom? [Use Exodus 20:12; Proverbs 23:22; 1 Timothy 5:1, 2; and 1 Peter 5:5 to enhance your discussion.]

12. So Sarah laughed to herself as she thought, "After I am worn out and my master is old, will I now have this pleasure?"

Sarah has been a woman of faith, having followed Abraham when he left Haran (Genesis 12:4, 5). At this point, however, her faith falters. Not only does she doubt her body's ability to achieve pregnancy, she doubts her husband's ability to impregnate her.

So Sarah laughs the laugh of derision in her heart. Her chuckle is not from happiness. It is from lack of faith.

B. THE LORD NOT LIMITED (vv. 13, 14a)

13. Then the LORD said to Abraham, "Why did Sarah laugh and say, 'Will I really have a child, now that I am old?'

This skeptical *laugh* in Sarah's heart does not go unnoticed by God. The Lord is well aware of the seeming impossibility of a pregnancy for Abraham and Sarah. *14a. "Is anything too hard for the LORD?"*

The reader of Genesis 1 knows that God created the heavens and earth. Thus to read that God can give a child to an elderly couple seems a small matter compared with what we already know to be true. If we have believed what we read, we can easily answer the question *Is anything too hard for the Lord?* by responding, "Nothing is too hard for [him]" (compare Jeremiah 32:17, 27).

We are reminded of another woman, a very young woman, who will be confronted with a miraculous pregnancy many centuries after the time of Abraham. She will question this too, because of her virginity. She will then be reminded that "nothing is impossible with God" (Luke 1:37). She will give a simple response of obedient faith: "I am the Lord's servant. . . . May it be to me as you have said" (Luke 1:38).

III. COUNTING BLESSINGS (GENESIS 21:1-8)

Sarah's laugh of derision eventually gives way to faith, since a footnote to Hebrews 11:11 tells us that, "By faith even Sarah, who was past age, was enabled to bear children because she considered him faithful who had made the promise."

A. PROMISED SON IS BORN (vv. 1, 2)

1, 2. Now the LORD was gracious to Sarah as he had said, and the LORD did for Sarah what he had promised. Sarah became pregnant and bore a son to Abraham in his old age, at the very time God had promised him.

God is present in Sarah's life to fulfill his promise, and the result is a miraculous pregnancy. This is not a virginal conception, for that is a unique event in human history. But this is still a supernatural event—a conception, gestation, and birth that science cannot explain.

Somehow, God reversed the effects of aging on Sarah. Thus a woman who is some 40 or 50 years past the natural childbearing state is allowed to be as fertile as a 20-year-old wife for the case of this single pregnancy.

B. PROMISED SON IS NAMED (vv. 3-5)

3. Abraham gave the name Isaac to the son Sarah bore him.

In a wonderful bit of irony, the boy is named *Isaac*, which means, "he laughs." This is no longer the laugh of derision or doubt. It is now a laugh of joy.

In this case, God's promise-keeping has the providential side effect of giving an elderly childless couple the joy of their hearts. They have *the son* they must have asked for in prayer for many years.

WHAT DO YOU THINK?

What was a time when you doubted the promises or provisions of God and even laughed at the seeming absurdity of the situation? How did things turn out? How did you grow spiritually as a result?

WHAT DO YOU THINK?

How does Genesis 21:1, 2 help ensure a proper view about God and time?

4, 5. When his son Isaac was eight days old, Abraham circumcised him, as God commanded him. Abraham was a hundred years old when his son Isaac was born to him.

God previously had established the circumcision of all the males in Abraham's household to be the primary sign of his covenant with Abraham. Accordingly, Abraham had applied the circumcision knife to all the men and boys, including his son Ishmael and himself (Genesis 17:23, 24).

We can imagine the joy that Abraham now feels. He is able to apply this sign of the covenant to the one who will fulfill the promise of a multitude of descendants for him.

C. PROMISED SON BRINGS JOY (vv. 6-8)

6. Sarah said, "God has brought me laughter, and everyone who hears about this will laugh with me."

We see a side of Sarah here that should endear her to us. Her original laughter of contempt is reevaluated, and now she is able to see the humor of her situation. She has abandoned any bitterness she may have harbored for her years of childlessness. She is not embarrassed to laugh out loud so anyone who hears can share with her, for her *laughter* springs from a deep joy that God has given to her.

LAUGHING FOR JOY

"Did you hear the one about . . . ?" So goes the opening line of countless jokes. Most of us enjoy a good joke, and if the story is told well, it doesn't even have to be plausible to make us laugh. Some people like side-splitting, belly-laugh-producing jokes; others prefer subtle humor. Whatever our preference, laughter is good medicine. In recent years science has established that laughter is good for our physical, mental, and emotional health. A good laugh relaxes muscles, reduces stress, lowers blood pressure, and enhances the function of the immune system. It even reduces pain.

Sarah's decision to name her child Isaac—meaning "he laughs"—was especially poignant. At first, Sarah laughed at God's "ridiculous" announcement. That was a laugh of derision, and it's hard to see any "good medicine" in it. It was a scornful laugh that originated in the pain of barrenness.

But by the time her child was born, Sarah was laughing for joy. This was a laugh of thanksgiving for a promise fulfilled. If we see God as Sarah came to see him, we will also find our lives filled with delight. Think about it: When was the last time you laughed with joy over something marvelous that God did in your life?—C. R. B.

7. And she added, "Who would have said to Abraham that Sarah would nurse children? Yet I have borne him a son in his old age."

Sarah's situation is startling: an elderly woman nursing a baby who has an old man as the father. It is absurd from a worldly standpoint, but marvelous from the standpoint of faith. Sarah's joy for having a son is mingled with her pleasure at giving her faithful husband this child.

8. The child grew and was weaned, and on the day Isaac was weaned Abraham held a great feast.

The rate of infant mortality in the ancient world is very high. Perhaps 25 percent of live-born babies do not live to see their first birthday. There is nothing more tragic than the death of a baby, but many societies have done things to protect parents from part of the pain this loss can bring. In some cultures, for instance, babies are not named until they are several years old. The idea in that practice is to lessen attachment to the infant in case of early death.

WHAT DO YOU THINK?

What was a time when you experienced an "Isaac moment," a time of joyous laughter at God's provisions? What led up to that moment, and how did things turn out? How was your faith increased?

HOW TO SAY IT

Abraham. AY-bruh-ham.
Abram. AY-brum.
Damascus. Duh-MASS-kus.
Eliezer. El-ih-EE-zer.
Haran. HAIR-un.
Isaac. EYE-zuk.
Ishmael. ISH-may-el.
Mesopotamia. MES-uh-puh-TAY-me-uh.
patriarchs. PAY-tree-arks.
Terah. TAIR-uh.
Ur. Er.

In Abraham and Sarah's world, it is a time for celebration when a baby is *weaned*. This is because weaning is a fairly reliable sign that a child will live to adulthood and not become a casualty of a childhood disease or birth defect.

So they celebrate! The first step in becoming the father of a large nation has now been taken. God has kept his promise, and Abraham's faith has not been in vain.

CONCLUSION

A. THE IMPORTANCE OF ABRAHAM

The promises to Abraham focused on two points: (1) Abraham's posterity was to be made a great nation and be given the land of Canaan as a possession (see Genesis 17:8), and (2) in Abraham (and through Christ) all the families of the earth were to be blessed (see John 8:56-58; Galatians 3:16).

In this light, Genesis 12:2, 3 can be seen as the theme of the entire Bible: God would make a great nation of Abraham, and God would bring blessing to the nations through Abraham and his offspring. We as Christians believe that Abraham is the "father of the faithful" and that Jesus is the true child of Abraham. Everyone in Christ is part of the offspring of Abraham.

Paul's writings are very important for forming our self-understanding as Christians. Paul was a Jewish Christian, and he was extremely knowledgeable about the Jewish Scriptures, our Old Testament. Paul was "a Hebrew of Hebrews" (Philippians 3:5). We may be surprised, then, when we learn who Paul thought was the primary hero of the Old Testament. We may expect this person to have been Moses, the great lawgiver and founder of the nation of Israel. Indeed, Paul had great respect for Moses. But Paul's "leading man" was Abraham. This is because Paul understood Abraham to be the primary example of the person of faith.

In the fourth chapter of Romans, Paul lays out a devastating argument against the necessity of circumcision for Christians. This amounts to a repudiation of the whole idea of being considered righteous because of keeping the Jewish law, an idea that was being debated in the first-century church.

Paul notes that Abraham was reckoned as righteous because of his faith (Romans 4:3-5; compare Genesis 15:6). But in a nice piece of detective work, Paul also notes that this reckoning occurred before Abraham was circumcised (Romans 4:10-12; compare Genesis 17:24). Abraham's right standing with the Lord was not the result of works, but the result of his faith.

This may seem like a complicated argument from the ancient world that has little relevance for us today. But such a conclusion would be to miss Paul's point. It is because of this system of "righteousness through faith" (as opposed to "righteousness through works") that all Christians are saved.

We cannot earn our salvation. It is a gift, given freely by God to those who believe in his Son, Jesus Christ, as they follow the biblical plan of salvation. It is this mighty truth that allows Paul to say, "those who believe are children of Abraham" (Galatians 3:7).

B. ABRAHAM AND YOU

To be a Christian means to be a person of faith. Today's lesson teaches the story of two faithful people, Abraham and Sarah, and how they acted faithfully in spite of various "facts of life." Abraham's heart trusted that God would provide a son even when his mind told him this was impossible. May we examine our own lives and be resolved to live as people of faith, fully trusting God for our current lives and for our eternal future.

Discovery Learning

*This page contains an alternative lesson plan emphasizing learning activities. Classes
desiring such student involvement will find these suggestions helpful. The next page
is a reproducible activity page to further enhance discovery learning.*

INTO THE LESSON

As learners arrive, tie a piece of yarn or string into a bow on a finger of each one. As class begins, have someone recall the meaning of the old practice of tying a string around one's finger as a reminder of something to be done.

Then say, "Today's study is about an occasion to be anticipated with hope and remembered with joy." Have learners keep the strings on their fingers through the Into the Word segment.

Alternative: Buy or borrow one of the large foam hands with the pointed index fingers displayed by sports fans who consider their teams to be "Number 1." Tie a large ribbon into a bow around the finger. Display it and say, "Today's lesson text describes an occasion of which the Bible challenges us over and over, *remember!*"

Assign the following texts (or a sampling of them) to individual readers; all are related to today's lesson text and God's promises to Abraham: Genesis 26:3; 28:4; Exodus 2:24; 6:2-4, 8; 32:13; Leviticus 26:42; Numbers 32:11; Deuteronomy 1:8; 6:10; 9:5; 29:12, 13; 30:20; 34:4; Joshua 24:2-4; 2 Kings 13:23; 1 Chronicles 16:15-18; Nehemiah 9:7, 8; Isaiah 51:2; Ezekiel 33:24; Luke 1:72, 73; Acts 3:25; 7:1-5; Romans 4:18; Galatians 3:6, 7, 29; Hebrews 6:13-15.

Have learners read their verses aloud. Say, "God's promises to Abraham became the watchword of his people. When the church began, the apostles affirmed that Abraham's covenant was fulfilled in Christ's covenant. Christians are children of Abraham."

Option: Put copies of the Miracle Births activity from the reproducible page in your learners' chairs so they can work on it as they arrive.

INTO THE WORD

Call the following activity Ask Abraham. Say, "If we could ask Abraham some questions about the occasion of today's lesson text, the answers would be clear. Read the text and then 'be Abraham' as I ask him questions."

Give the class opportunity to read the lesson text silently, and then ask this series of questions. Remind your learners to "be Abraham" as they respond (answers are in parentheses after each question): 1. When the Lord came to you the third time, where did he tell you to look? *(toward the heavens);* 2. Was it day or night? *(night);* 3. How many stars could you see? *(too many to count);* 4. How many offspring did you have at the time? *(none);* 5. How many offspring did God say you would have? *(as many as the stars);* 6. Did you believe God? *(yes);* 7. How did God respond to your belief? *(called me righteous even though I was a sinner);* 8. At what stage of life were you when God reiterated his promise to give you a son? *(too old to have children; Sarah too!);* 9. How did your wife Sarah react to this latest promise? *(she laughed);* 10. Did God notice Sarah's lack of faith? *(yes, he asked me about it);* 11. Is anything too hard for God? *(no, Sarah and I experienced the "impossible");* 12. How do you account for Sarah's being able to become pregnant? *(the Lord enabled it);* 13. When did this son arrive? *(just when God said he would; about a year after Sarah laughed);* 14. How old were you when Isaac was born? *(100 years old);* 15. Why did you circumcise Isaac? *(because God established that as part of the covenant);* 16. What difference did you see in Sarah's attitude when her son was born? *(her laughter was from joy);* 17. What did you do on the occasion that Isaac was weaned? *(we held a great celebration feast);* 18. What have you learned from all this, Abraham? *(let learners respond openly).*

Then ask one further open-ended question: "How does Abraham's faith apply to today?" To enhance learning, distribute at this point copies of the The Seed of Abraham activity from the reproducible page.

INTO LIFE

Copy and distribute the following checklist (if you do not use the student books, where this activity also is found). Say, "Look at these life situations and check off the ones that convict you most. At the bottom of the page, write your commitment to trusting God more in the one area for which you have the greatest difficulty."

___ I barely make it financially, but God still expects me to be generous with his church and the needy.

___ My schedule is hectic, but God still wants me to make time for study, worship, and service.

___ I'd much rather spend time with godly friends and family, but nonetheless God wants me to cultivate relationships with the ungodly, as a witness to them.

___ Spiritually, I know God has assured me of his presence and a glorious future, but nonetheless my anxieties about the here-and-now often run amok.

Miracle Births

Often people speak of "the miracle of birth," yet we all know that the laws of conception, gestation, and birth are as fixed as any science. But the one who believes God knows that nothing is too hard for him. He can set aside the usual processes of reproduction and do things supernaturally. See if you can match each of these "miracle babies" with the right Scripture without looking up the passage.

__ 1. Isaac   A. Genesis 21:1, 2

__ 2. John the Baptist   B. Genesis 25:21

__ 3. Jesus   C. Judges 13:2, 3

__ 4. Jacob and Esau   D. 1 Samuel 1:5, 20

__ 5. Samson   E. Matthew 1:18, 20

__ 6. Samuel   F. Luke 1:7, 24

The Seed of Abraham

Paul, by the Spirit, clearly affirms, "If you belong to Christ, then you are Abraham's seed, and heirs according to the promise" (Galatians 3:29). If you accept this passage as truth, write your name on the two line below.

_____ , Abraham's descendant

_____ , Christian

1. Is it logically possible to write a person's name on one line but not the other? Explain.

2. Does being Christian result in being Abraham's true seed or is it the reverse? Explain.

ABRAHAM, HAGAR, AND ISHMAEL

LESSON 4

DEVOTIONAL READING:
GENESIS 16
BACKGROUND SCRIPTURE:
GENESIS 21:9-21
PRINTED TEXT:
GENESIS 21:9-21

Sep
23

WHY TEACH THIS LESSON?

Divorce is common in various cultures today. In addition to family strife, we often see infighting in the workplace, and even in the church. In a word, human relationships are messy. What your learners need is a model of right relationships! God himself provides us with such a model. God loves us even when we behave unlovingly to others. God protects and provides, even for those who are not in a relationship with him at the moment.

When faced with conflict, we often put our energy into assigning blame so we can figure out who has the burden of making amends. In today's lesson, we do not see God in the role of cosmic referee in which he tries to undo people's bad choices. Rather, God works with us, through our flaws. This will teach your learners that it's more important that we help others grow into the people whom God wants them to become than it is for us to critique them and choose sides.

INTRODUCTION

A. OUTSIDERS AND INSIDERS

"Call me Ishmael." So begins the famous novel *Moby-Dick*, by Herman Melville. Melville employs many biblical names and images to tell a story of self-destruction of the obsessive Captain Ahab. Ishmael, the narrator, is always the outsider, not quite part of the main drama unfolding around him. His namesake, the Ishmael of Genesis, also ended up being an outsider.

Today, Muslims see Abraham as their father in the faith, much like Jews and Christians do (compare Romans 4:16). Muslims, however, trace their spiritual lineage back to Abraham through Ishmael, the son who was cast out of Abraham's household. According to the Qur'an (or Koran), the holy book of the religion of Islam, Abraham was told by God to take Ishmael and his mother, Hagar, to a far land. They traveled many days until they came to a deserted place.

Unbeknownst to them, so the story goes, this was the spot where Adam had built the first place to worship God. Abraham left Hagar and Ishmael there. When Hagar and Ishmael were near death from lack of water, the Qur'an claims that the youngster began to kick in the sand, and a well sprang up. This became the well Zamzam, and the city that grew around it is known today as Mecca. Muslims falsely believe that a descendant of Ishmael named Mohammed restored true worship of God at this site in the seventh century AD.

Unrest and violence in the Middle East today are partly fueled by different ideas concerning how people are connected to Abraham and his sons. Jews claim the side of Isaac, the child of promise according to Genesis. Muslims believe that their ancestor Ishmael was the primary child of promise blessed by God. Each side sees itself as the "insider" and the other as the "outsider."

LESSON AIMS

After participating in this lesson, each student will be able to:

1. Outline the facts regarding Abraham's dismissal of Hagar and Ishmael.

2. Summarize the significance of God's promise in Genesis 21:13.

3. Suggest some ways for his or her church to reach out to Muslims or other non-Christians with the gospel.

KEY VERSE

[God said to Abraham,] "I will make the son of the maidservant into a nation also, because he is your offspring."
—Genesis 21:13

LESSON 4 NOTES

This religious rivalry, combined with politics and nationalism, has led to instability and war, disrupting the lives of many innocent people. The fundamentalist brand of Islam believes there is no room for accommodation with infidels, those who don't believe as they do and who don't follow the teachings of Mohammed to the letter.

This week's lesson looks at the story of Abraham, Hagar, and Ishmael from the Bible's point of view. It is a sad story of a family broken apart because of foolish behavior and bitterness. We grieve with Abraham as he is forced to choose between his two sons. Many studying this lesson have experienced the pain of family fighting and break-up. Today's text offers hope to us in that we see that God did not curse one side of a family squabble while blessing the other side.

B. LESSON BACKGROUND

Last week's lesson focused on how Abraham and Sarah were able to have a son in spite of advanced age. Regarding Sarah specifically, we learned of many admirable qualities: her faith, her courage, and her sense of humor and joy.

Yet there was another side to Sarah that was not so admirable. Today we see a headstrong woman, who could be jealous and scheming. In the end one of her schemes backfired, and her jealousy caused her to act with cruelty.

Sarah and Abraham lived in a world where it was common for households to include slaves. One of their slaves was an Egyptian girl named Hagar (Genesis 16:3). Hagar was Sarah's personal attendant. When Abraham and Sarah's attempts to produce a child were unsuccessful, Sarah hatched a scheme to remedy the problem: she offered to let Abraham have Hagar as a type of slave-wife, hoping this union would yield a child.

Sarah's logic in this seems strange to us. Why would a wife willingly allow her husband to have an intimate relationship with another woman? This seems to be a recipe for disaster! But the logic of this practice, common at the time, went something like this: "If my slave produces a child, that child will be mine, just like his mother is my property." Sarah thought she could have a son by a secondary way, and thus please her husband.

This plan "worked" (if we can use that word!), and Abraham and Hagar conceived the baby that was to become Ishmael. But the plan backfired on Sarah in two ways. First, becoming pregnant had an unanticipated effect on Hagar: she began to think that she was better than Sarah (Genesis 16:4). Hagar had been successful at becoming pregnant, something Sarah had failed in; this ruined the relationship between the two women and ensured that Ishmael would never be accepted by Sarah. Second, Ishmael himself displayed his own arrogance after Isaac was born. This is where today's lesson begins.

I. HAGAR AND ISHMAEL DISMISSED (GENESIS 21:9-13)

Many people today live in "blended" households. Typically, this involves a woman with one or more children marrying a man with one or more children— the children from previous marriages. Those familiar with blended families will testify that theirs is not an easy situation. There is often conflict, perceived slights, and favoritism. Now imagine a blended family that involves more than one wife! That explosive combination is what we find in Abraham's household.

A. CONFLICT IN THE HOUSEHOLD (vv. 9, 10)
9. But Sarah saw that the son whom Hagar the Egyptian had borne to Abraham was mocking,

Ishmael, *the son* of *Hagar the Egyptian,* is recorded as *mocking.* We don't really know what or why he is mocking. He may be mocking *Sarah* for her old age, or he may be mocking Isaac. This is probably learned behavior, copied from his mother. We also don't know exactly how old the boy is at this time, although Genesis 17:25 indicates that he is at least 13. We can see that he is old enough to poke fun and immature enough not to know that this is a dangerous practice.

10. . . . and she said to Abraham, "Get rid of that slave woman and her son, for that slave woman's son will never share in the inheritance with my son Isaac."

Ishmael's unwise display of haughtiness is the final straw for Sarah. So she demands that Hagar and Ishmael be expelled from the household, where she rules as the supreme mistress. She had once used Hagar as a tool to satisfy her husband's desire for a *son.* That purpose is no longer valid, for Sarah now has her own son, namely *Isaac.*

In her anger, Sarah decides to jettison this embarrassing mistake once and for all. She does this both to soothe her own wounded pride and to protect the rights of the younger Isaac as Abraham's rightful heir.

B. CONFLICT FOR FATHER ABRAHAM (vv. 11-13)

11. The matter distressed Abraham greatly because it concerned his son.

This is not so easy for *Abraham.* Sarah is rejecting his true, biological *son* by another woman. Abraham's blood flows in Ishmael's veins. Abraham, however, was a willing accomplice in the unwise impregnation of Hagar. The fact that he tried to "push" God's timetable in trying to obtain a son now brings him grief.

12. But God said to him, "Do not be so distressed about the boy and your maidservant. Listen to whatever Sarah tells you, because it is through Isaac that your offspring will be reckoned.

In this moment of great distress, *God* does not abandon *Abraham.* God instructs Abraham to go ahead and do what *Sarah* wishes, as curious and cruel as it may seem. God's promises will still be fulfilled through *Isaac.*

Families can be horribly dysfunctional. They can bear the scars of abuse, betrayal, and tragedy. However, God does not abandon us, even in the darkest days. Yet, while God is at work, he does not always restore a family to an earlier state that seemed to be better. The mess that had been created in Abraham's family by several factors is not going to be fixed by God as we may think of *fix* or *repair* in human terms. Instead, we will see God unfailingly love each family member and do what is best to care for him or her.

13. "I will make the son of the maidservant into a nation also, because he is your offspring."

This word of the Lord must surely be a surprise to Abraham. God has plans for Ishmael too! His descendants will become *a nation* also. He too shares in the blessings of being a *son* of Abraham. However, Abraham will experience little firsthand joy in the successes of Ishmael's life, for the expulsion is to proceed.

II. HAGAR AND ISHMAEL SUSTAINED (GENESIS 21:14-19)

Abraham ultimately is driven by his obedient faith. He has been tested many times before. Now he is about to be tested again.

A. ABANDONED BY FAMILY (v. 14)

14a. Early the next morning Abraham took some food and a skin of water and gave them to Hagar. He set them on her shoulders and then sent her off with the boy.

WHAT DO YOU THINK?

What was a wrong-headed (or even sinful) way that you tried to deal with a mistake you made? How did things turn out? What should you have done instead?

[Psalm 51 and 1 John 1:9 can enrich your discussion.]

WHAT DO YOU THINK?

What was a time when God worked amazing things in your family life when the situation seemed hopeless? How did you honor him for his provision?

HOW TO SAY IT

Abraham. AY-bruh-ham.
Beersheba. Beer-SHE-buh.
Canaan. KAY-nun.
Deuteronomy. Due-ter-AHN-uh-
me.
Habakkuk. Huh-BACK-kuk.
Hagar. HAY-gar.
Ishmael. ISH-may-el.
Ishmaelites. ISH-may-el-ites.
Koran or Qur'an. Kuh-RAN.
Negev. NEG-ev.
Paran. PAIR-un.

WHAT DO YOU THINK?

What was a time when God answered you in a way that you weren't expecting? What did this teach you about how God likes to work?

WHAT DO YOU THINK?

In what ways have you seen God provide for his people when all seemed hopeless? Why do you think that God sometimes waits until the need is very severe before he intervenes?

It seems that Abraham's greatest tests are acted out when he rises up *early* in the *morning*. This is the way he had witnessed the horrific destruction of Sodom and Gomorrah (Genesis 19:27). In the next chapter, it will be the setting of his supreme trial: the sacrifice of his son Isaac (Genesis 22:3). We can imagine the grief at this early-morning drama, perhaps so early that no one else in the household is a witness.

14b. She went on her way and wandered in the desert of Beersheba.

We should remember that the land of Canaan is largely undeveloped at this time. Hagar has no place to go, and she heads into the unpopulated *wilderness of Beersheba*. This is in the southern part of Canaan, the beginning of the cruel Negev desert. Abraham later sees Beersheba as a place of worship (Genesis 21:33). Centuries later, it will be the southern extremity of Israel (Judges 20:1).

B. ABANDONING HOPE (vv. 15, 16)

15, 16a. When the water in the skin was gone, she put the boy under one of the bushes. Then she went off and sat down nearby, about a bowshot away,

Hagar has lost hope and is preparing to die. Her location is desolate, but it has enough vegetation to provide *bushes* that are large enough to provide a measure of shade from the relentless sun. The distance of *a bowshot* is about 100–150 yards, still within hearing distance.

16b. . . . for she thought, "I cannot watch the boy die." And as she sat there nearby, she began to sob.

Hagar cannot bear to *watch* her son *die*. The teenage boy does not follow her, so we assume he is incapacitated from lack of water. Now alone, Hagar weeps bitterly. She pours out all her feelings of abandonment. God allows her to reach the utter depths of human despair, but he has not given up on her.

C. SAVED BY GOD (vv. 17-19)

17, 18. God heard the boy crying, and the angel of God called to Hagar from heaven and said to her, "What is the matter, Hagar? Do not be afraid; God has heard the boy crying as he lies there. Lift the boy up and take him by the hand, for I will make him into a great nation."

God now conveys a message to *Hagar*. We can imagine that the last thing she expects to hear in the desert is a voice *from heaven!* Interestingly, *the angel* doesn't say that God has heard her sobbing, but that God has been moved by the sound of *the boy crying*.

Hagar herself will share Ishmael's blessings. She is thus made privy to the promise Abraham has been given: Ishmael too will be the father of *a great nation*. Hagar's life has not been in vain. Her life has great purpose in the plans of God.

19. Then God opened her eyes and she saw a well of water. So she went and filled the skin with water and gave the boy a drink.

The rare watering place in the desert (oasis) is highly prized by the semi-nomadic shepherd people of Abraham's day. *Water* is life. "No water" means rapid death. Hagar and Ishmael are saved by God's miraculous provision of water where there should be no water, *a well* in the wilderness.

TAKING A GAMBLE . . . OR NOT

A California couple decided to spend a few days in Las Vegas on a gambling vacation. The thoughtful pair arranged for a dog-sitter. However, they left their two sons—a nine-year-old and an autistic five-year-old—by themselves at home. The boys' grandmother began to suspect the nature of the situation and called police.

The couple was charged with two felony counts of child endangerment. The emotional charge by the older boy was, "They shouldn't leave us alone. I didn't know who I could call in an emergency. I thought they loved [the puppies] more than they loved us." The boys had reason to question their parents' care for them. A similar event had taken place a few months earlier.

Abraham didn't abandon his son so he could go to Las Vegas in search of a good time. Even so, some may think that Abraham took a gamble on his son's life. But we must not overlook one crucial fact: Abraham acted at God's direction. To follow God's leading is never a gamble. To *believe* that statement is probably fairly easy; to have the godly courage to *live it out* may be another matter entirely!   —C. R. B.

III. HAGAR AND ISHMAEL BLESSED (GENESIS 21:20, 21)

With a secure water supply, Hagar and Ishmael begin to prosper. Later, there is a measure of reconciliation between the two sides of Abraham's clan, for we are told that Isaac and Ishmael together bury their father (Genesis 25:9). Ishmael lives to the ripe old age of 137 and has a large family (25:12-17).

A. ISHMAEL BECOMES A MAN (v. 20)

20. God was with the boy as he grew up. He lived in the desert and became an archer.

To be *an archer* implies that Ishmael rejects the life of a tender of flocks of animals. He is now a hunter, living off the wild game of the *desert*. In this he prefigures a future rejected relative: Esau (Genesis 25:27). One occupation is not superior to another, for God blesses both.

B. ISHMAEL TAKES A WIFE (v. 21)

21. While he was living in the Desert of Paran, his mother got a wife for him from Egypt.

It is difficult to be certain about this location, but ancient *Paran* is probably located near the site of modern Elat on the northern tip of the Gulf of Aqaba. *The Desert of Paran* is the extremely inhospitable region to the west, still largely uninhabited today. The name *Paran* has a rich biblical history. (See Genesis 14:6; Numbers 10:12; 12:16; 13:3, 26; Deuteronomy 33:2; Habakkuk 3:3.)

Since Ishmael's father is not a part of his life, it is up to *his mother* to find him a *wife*. Hagar does so, and the unnamed wife is from her people, the Egyptians. Elsewhere we learn that Ishmael ends up with 12 successful sons (see Genesis 25:12-16). Some of these descendants later figure into other Bible stories as the Ishmaelites. See Genesis 37:25-28; Judges 8:24.

God keeps his promise to Abraham and to Hagar concerning Ishmael and his descendants. While our family structures differ from those of Abraham's time, we learn important lessons about God's care for families in conflict.

UNWELCOME, BUT STILL LOVED

A couple was evicted from their home of many years on Fifth Avenue in New York City. "Pale Male" and "Lola" are red-tailed hawks that had built a nest on a window ledge of an apartment house. Some residents of the building had complained about the carcasses of rats and pigeons that fell from the nest onto the sidewalk below. Thus the eviction.

However, the hawks were invited to return just three weeks later. After the original nest was removed, bird lovers raised a fuss. So an architect designed a new nest to prevent the overflow of uneaten prey that had caused the trouble. The birds were soon back home, raising a family.

WHAT DO YOU THINK?

What can the phrase, "God was with the boy as he grew up," teach us about God's presence during wilderness times in our lives?

[You may find Exodus 2:15; 3:1; Luke 4:1, 2, 42; 5:16; Galatians 1:17; and Revelation 1:9 useful in wrestling with this question.]

Visual for Lesson 4. *Point to this visual as you ask, "What kind of call from God would cause you to be willing to make a move of this magnitude?"*

Hagar and Ishmael had been evicted from Abraham's home because their presence was distasteful to at least one of the residents (Sarah). Then God befriended them and saw to it that they were blessed. Today, those who trace their spiritual descent through Abraham and Ishmael are the Muslims. Many of them have declared Christians to be their enemies. In reaction, at least some Westerners would like to "evict" Muslims and send them somewhere else. How can we demonstrate the truth and grace of Christ to people whom we may find hard to love? —C. R. B.

CONCLUSION

The apostle Paul uses the life and person of Abraham to illustrate the truths of the gospel and its application to the people of the church. In Galatians 4, Paul employs the family troubles of the patriarch to explain our freedom in Christ. You must know the story of today's lesson to make sense of his powerful argument.

Paul's primary agenda in Galatians is to refute the idea that Christians are required to keep the Jewish law. For Paul, this obligation would negate the freedom we have in Christ. One way Paul makes his point is to use a story from the first book of the law (Genesis) to illustrate the importance of freedom in God's plan of redemption.

Paul begins with a contrast of Hagar and Sarah (Galatians 4:22). Hagar is a "slave woman"; Sarah is a "free woman." Paul points out that the child Abraham produced with Hagar was "born in the ordinary way," that is, through natural impregnation and birth. The child produced with Sarah was "as the result of a promise," that is, through supernatural provision to allow the elderly woman to become pregnant (4:23).

Paul goes on to equate the slave woman and her son with the bondage of the law as symbolized by the Jerusalem of his day (Galatians 4:25). This is his way of talking about the stifling, restrictive legalism that some Jewish Christians were trying to impose upon Paul's Gentile converts. To force the law upon these non-Jews would be to bind them by the old covenant and ignore the blessings of the new covenant.

Paul contrasts this with the free woman and her son, whom he equates with the heavenly Jerusalem (Galatians 4:26). His final point in this section is "we are not children of the slave woman, but of the free woman" (4:31). In other words, why would you exchange the marvelous freedom from sin that is possible through faith in Christ for the bondage of the Jewish law? (See 5:1.)

Paul's foundational point here is not directly tied to the teaching points of the Hagar/Ishmael story as found in Genesis (today's lesson), but that should not worry us. Our study of Genesis allows us to see this crucial doctrine of Christian freedom in a striking way. We are free in Christ! Not free to sin, but free to live our lives for the glory of God and in his service.

There is a larger doctrinal point that lies behind both the Galatians illustration and the Genesis account, however. That is that God is a God of promises, and he always keeps his promises. He did not abandon his promise to Abraham when Abraham attempted to keep his line going by having a child with a slave woman. The Lord was still faithful to provide through both Isaac and Ishmael, despite Abraham's foibles.

Likewise, God will not abandon us, even when our families—either our physical family or our spiritual family—are in shambles. God's love for us is proven through his gift of his only Son, Jesus. Even when the animosity among the members of a fractured family runs very high, God's love is constant and unchangeable. In times of personal adversity, we are well reminded to "keep yourselves in God's love" (Jude 21).

Discovery Learning

This page contains an alternative lesson plan emphasizing learning activities. Classes desiring such student involvement will find these suggestions helpful. The next page is a reproducible activity page to further enhance discovery learning.

INTO THE LESSON

Display one or more Muslim (Islamic) symbols around your classroom for learners to see as they arrive. Inexpensive flags with the Muslim crescent moon may be available locally. A copy of the Qur'an by the door should stir interest. Also display a modern map of the Arabic world (Middle East), with Mecca highlighted.

The lesson writer in the Introduction has a good summary on Ishmael's relationship to Islamic belief. Read that section of the introduction, beginning with the sentence, "Today, Muslims see Abraham as their father in the faith" and ending with "Muslims falsely believe that a descendant of Ishmael named Mohammed restored true worship of God at this site in the seventh century AD." The reading will take only about a minute, but it will offer a valuable background to today's study and a valuable insight into the current world situation.

INTO THE WORD

Distribute copies of the following word-search puzzle. (Also found in the optional student book.)

```
S S A R A H H A G A R F
A U B R Y S U O L A E J
S H P A M E I S A I C C
S A C E I L S H R M A O
E A E C R F L G S A R M
R R A N D I I H H A G P
T G A A R S O A A B A A
S R E E A H H R R N A S
I R M G I N S A I A C S
D I S N H E M C A T E I
L S A E R S A H H A Y O
G L O V E S A R A B R N
```

Say, "Look in the puzzle for words that characterize deep feelings. As you find these words, look at the lesson text for verses in which such an emotion must have been felt passionately." The words to be found are: *compassion, distress, dread, grace, grief, jealousy, love, panic, selfishness, superiority,* and *vengeance.*

Allow some latitude for learners' identification of related verses. For example, compassion could characterize Abraham in his providing some sustenance for Hagar and Ishmael as he dismisses them (v. 14); some will see God's compassion as Ishmael cries out (vv. 17, 18).

Note that every study of the Scriptures is directly or indirectly a study of the nature of God. Read aloud the following statements about God. Ask class members to decide what each of the following statements reveals about God's nature. The statements are drawn from events of both today's and last week's lessons.

1. By grace God chose Abraham, a sinner, to be the father of God's special people.
2. God had a plan for Abraham's life that he revealed to Abraham.
3. Even those chosen by God can still go the way of their own will.
4. God sometimes allows bad things to happen in order to realize his will fully.
5. God keeps his promises, even when they appear to have been forgotten.
6. God is everywhere, even in the wilderness.
7. God even loves people who are lost in their own pride.
8. God hears and answers prayers.
9. God sustains, sometimes miraculously.
10. God may do more than he promises, but he never does less.

If the class needs a stimulus, suggest this for the first statement: "God can do as he pleases; he has chosen to use sinners to accomplish his redemptive will."

INTO LIFE

Say, "Paul uses Isaac and Ishmael as figures of those born free and those born to bondage, respectively (Galatians 4:22-31). If Ishmael is a figure for those who are still caught in slavery to law and sin, let's make an 'Ishmael pact' in which we commit to speaking on behalf of Christ to those who are lost in the wilderness of unrighteousness."

Distribute "Hello, my name is . . ." peel-and-stick labels. Ask each to write *Ishmael* on the label and wear it. When asked what the label means, each can respond: "I Speak How My Almighty Expresses Love! John 3:16!" Or make an acronym from the word *Isaac* instead.

Alternative: Have learners complete in pairs the Paul's Lesson from Hagar and Ishmael activity on the reproducible page. Distribute copies of the Can't See the Water activity as learners depart.

Paul's Lesson from Hagar and Ishmael

In Galatians 4:22-26, 28-31, Paul draws an analogy contrasting freedom in Christ to bondage under the law. Look at that text, printed to the right. Then sketch out on the left some details from the story presented in today's lesson text. Draw lines to connect Old Testament facts (left) with New Testament applications (printed text to the right).

> 22For it is written that Abraham had two sons, one by the slave woman and the other by the free woman. 23His son by the slave woman was born in the ordinary way; but his son by the free woman was born as the result of a promise. 24These things may be taken figuratively, for the women represent two covenants. One covenant is from Mount Sinai and bears children who are to be slaves: This is Hagar. 25Now Hagar stands for Mount Sinai in Arabia and corresponds to the present city of Jerusalem, because she is in slavery with her children. 26But the Jerusalem that is above is free, and she is our mother.
>
> . . . .
>
> 28Now you, brothers, like Isaac, are children of promise. 29At that time the son born in the ordinary way persecuted the son born by the power of the Spirit. It is the same now. 30But what does the Scripture say? "Get rid of the slave woman and her son, for the slave woman's son will never share in the inheritance with the free woman's son." 31 Therefore, brothers, we are not children of the slave woman, but of the free woman.

Can't See the Water

Until God intervened and revealed to Hagar a well (an oasis), she and her son were doomed to die. Many in your own daily circle "can't see the water of life." No one has revealed to them that free fountain. Complete the following commitment to be the bearer of living water to some thirsty friend or acquaintance.

> To _____ , who is wandering in a spiritual wilderness, I will reveal Jesus Christ, who is the oasis of life, the living water.
>
> Signed _____

God Creates
Unit 1: God Creates a People
(Lessons 1-5)

ISAAC AND REBEKAH

LESSON 5

WHY TEACH THIS LESSON?

Some have described our life with God as a dance. This "dance of life" can be difficult at times. The sovereign God rightly insists on "leading," although he doesn't act as a puppet master, pulling our strings to get the desired movement. Rather, he guides us, giving us freedom to move.

In the dance of life, some of your learners may want to remain still, taking no action until they think they have a supernatural sign to show them the creator's plan. At other times, your learners make decisions independently, calling on the Lord only after they're in trouble.

Today's lesson will help your learners avoid these two extremes. The servant in today's lesson shows us some great steps for the dance of life: humbly call on God for his wisdom and guidance while doing everything that you know is right to do. Acknowledge and thank God for his help. Share the details of your dance with others. Who knows, your learners may inspire others to join the dance!

INTRODUCTION

A. HOW TO CHOOSE A SPOUSE—OR NOT!

When I was in graduate school, students were surprised when one of our classmates made plans to return to her home country rather suddenly. When asked what the reason was, she said, "My parents have found a husband for me, and I am going to marry!" She was very happy.

To us, this seemed strange. She had never met her future husband. Yet she trusted her parents and the process of arranged marriage. Thus she looked forward to becoming the wife of someone she did not know.

Arranged marriage is still practiced in some places in the world today, but it is becoming rarer. For example, all marriages in Japan were once arranged, but today this has slipped to no more than 10 percent. Western influences have convinced young people all over the world that they should be able to choose their own marriage partners and that marriage should be based on love, not the perceived standards of parents.

A key figure in some societies is the matchmaker, the marriage arranger. This person suggests marriage combinations that will be satisfying and successful. Ironically, a more recent variation of this is online matchmaking services. In this system men and women seeking marriage undergo testing to develop a personality profile. These profiles are matched by a computer, supposedly yielding a higher probability of compatibility. Therefore, we have come full circle and may be returning to arranged marriages, but with a machine doing the arranging rather than parents or tribal elders!

No matter what system is used, there is no "sure thing" when it comes to selecting a marriage partner. People change over time, and circumstances arise that can be allowed to destroy a commitment. The story of Isaac and Rebekah is the record of God's special provision for a blessed marriage. We should not ex-

DEVOTIONAL READING:
PSALM 100

BACKGROUND SCRIPTURE:
GENESIS 24

PRINTED TEXT:
GENESIS 24:34-45, 48

Sep
30

LESSON AIMS

After participating in this lesson, each student will be able to:

1. Tell how God continued the promises to Abraham by providing a wife for his son Isaac.

2. Use the story of Isaac and Rebekah to suggest how God may be guiding his or her life choices today.

3. Seek God's guidance in a particular area through prayer and obedience to his will.

KEY VERSE

I bowed down and worshiped the LORD. I praised the LORD, the God of my master Abraham, who had led me on the right road to get the granddaughter of my master's brother for his son.
—Genesis 24:48

LESSON 5 NOTES

pect God to control our marriage choices today at the same level. But the match of Isaac and Rebekah also involved their parents. Isaac was not left to wander around looking for a wife, dating and hoping. Abraham guided the process.

B. LESSON BACKGROUND

Sarah, Abraham's wife, died at age 127 (Genesis 23:1, 2). Since she was 90 years old when Isaac was born, we assume that Isaac was nearing age 40 when Abraham began the search for that son's future wife (25:20). Sarah's death probably caused Abraham to realize that his own passing was coming, and that he must see to the marriage of his son before it was out of his hands.

This week's lesson is about an arranged marriage that was crucial to the history of Israel. God's promise to Abraham was that he would be followed by many descendants (Genesis 12:2), and that one of those descendants would be a blessing to "all peoples on earth" (Genesis 12:3). We know this person to be Jesus Christ (Galatians 3:16). God had provided Abraham with Isaac. But there would be no descendants unless Isaac had a wife and they produced children. How that wife was provided is the focus of this lesson.

I. MISSION EXPLAINED (GENESIS 24:34-41)

Abraham decided that Isaac should not marry a Canaanite woman (Genesis 24:3). The wisdom of this decision was borne out later in the Old Testament, for marriage to foreign women often resulted in the introduction of paganism into Israel (see Judges 3:5, 6). That led to various disasters.

So in the first part of Genesis 24, Abraham directs a trusted servant to return to Abraham's kindred to find a wife for his son. This is not a small matter! The servant takes 10 camels loaded with goods and provisions for this lengthy trip of approximately 500 miles. When the servant leaves his master, Abraham probably does not expect him to return in less than a year.

The text tells us that the purpose of the journey is fulfilled relatively quickly, as the future wife of Isaac is identified and negotiations for her begin. She is Rebekah, the granddaughter of Abraham's brother Nahor (Genesis 24:15, 48). She is pictured as a beautiful, chaste, and obedient young woman, the perfect wife for Isaac (24:16-18).

We should pause to consider the importance of that name *Nahor.* This is both a personal name and a place name in Genesis. Nahor was the name of Abraham's grandfather (Genesis 11:23-26) and of his brother (11:27). While we know little about this brother, Genesis tells us that Nahor worshiped God as Abraham did (31:53). This means that Nahor and his family practiced the worship of one God as opposed to the worship of multiple gods of the Canaanites and other surrounding peoples. This was undoubtedly a central factor in Abraham's desire to find a wife for Isaac from his own family (24:1-4).

Nahor is also the name of a city in northern Mesopotamia (Genesis 24:10). Although the exact location of this city is unknown today, there is frequent mention of a city called *Nakhur* in the ancient Mari tablets (discovered in 1935, dated eighteenth century BC). This leads us to understand that the extended family of the Nahor clan is well known, prosperous, and influential in this region.

A. GOD'S BLESSINGS (vv. 34-36)

34. So he said, "I am Abraham's servant.

We do not know the name of this *servant.* Some believe it is Eliezer, mentioned as the steward of Abraham's household in Genesis 15:2. This reference to

Eliezer, however, is 40 to 50 years prior to the text in front of us. It is thus likely that he has already died.

The unnamed servant of this story is probably in a similar position to Eliezer's, the senior servant (Genesis 24:2). He is presented as a person whom Abraham trusts without reservation. He is a man of prayer and integrity (see 24:12-14). He is speaking to Laban, Rebekah's brother, shortly after arriving at the town of Nahor (24:10, 11, 28-33).

35. "The LORD has blessed my master abundantly, and he has become wealthy. He has given him sheep and cattle, silver and gold, menservants and maidservants, and camels and donkeys.

Abraham's wealth is measured in the number of animals he owns, the number of servants he has, and the amount of precious metals he has accumulated. In all of these things, God has richly *blessed* Abraham. The servant said that Abraham *has become wealthy* and recognized in his community (compare the description of Isaac's wealth in Genesis 26:14).

36. "My master's wife Sarah has borne him a son in her old age, and he has given him everything he owns.

Abraham's servant provides another important piece of information. Abraham has only one *son* considered to be an heir, and this son will inherit all of Abraham's wealth. This means that the servant is searching for a woman to marry a man who will be very wealthy when his father dies. The fact that Isaac was born in the time of *old age* of his parents implies that Isaac should receive his inheritance in the near future.

B. ABRAHAM'S DESIRE (vv. 37, 38)

37, 38. "And my master made me swear an oath, and said, 'You must not get a wife for my son from the daughters of the Canaanites, in whose land I live, but go to my father's family and to my own clan, and get a wife for my son.'

Although Abraham has prospered in the land *of the Canaanites,* he has been unwilling to assimilate into their culture. This is largely a religious issue. Abraham and his family have a tradition of worship of the one true God. The Canaanite people, on the other hand, practice fertility cults. These involve ritual, temple prostitution and other abominations to the Lord. The conquest of the promised land of Canaan that occurs later, as described in the book of Joshua, indicates that such abominations were still being practiced in Canaan long after Abraham's time (compare Deuteronomy 7:22-26).

C. SERVANT'S OATH (vv. 39-41)

39, 40. "Then I asked my master, 'What if the woman will not come back with me?'

"He replied, 'The LORD, before whom I have walked, will send his angel with you and make your journey a success, so that you can get a wife for my son from my own clan and from my father's family.

The servant is frank about the providential circumstances surrounding this quest for *a wife.* Abraham has lived by faith his entire life (see Hebrews 11:8, 9, 17). The servant has carried out his master's will confidently, believing that God's *angel* has prepared his way.

41. "'Then, when you go to my clan, you will be released from my oath even if they refuse to give her to you—you will be released from my oath.'

The servant is also practical in his negotiations. He does not know what type of reception he will receive from Abraham's kin. They may not be open to sending one of their young women away with an unexpected stranger. If this

Chronology of Genesis

From the Call of Abraham to the Death of Joseph

2167 BC	Abram born	
2092 BC	Call of Abram	Genesis 12:1-5
2081 BC	Ishmael born (Lesson 4)	Genesis 16:15, 16
2067 BC	Isaac born (Lesson 3)	Genesis 21:1-3
2050 BC	Abraham offers Isaac	Genesis 22:1-19
2007 BC	Jacob and Esau born (Lesson 6)	Genesis 25:24-26
1992 BC	Abraham dies at age 175	Genesis 25:7
1930 BC	Jacob flees to Haran (Lesson 7)	Genesis 28:10
1916 BC	Joseph born	Genesis 30:22-24
1899 BC	Joseph sold into slavery in Egypt at age 17 (Lesson 10)	Genesis 37:2, 28
1887 BC	Isaac dies at age 180	Genesis 35:28
1886 BC	At age 30, Joseph interprets Pharaoh's dream (Lesson 11)	Genesis 41:46
1877 BC	Jacob goes to Egypt *Beginning of the Israelites' 430-year stay in Egypt (Exodus 12:40, 41), leading to the exodus in 1447 BC (Lesson 12)*	Genesis 46:5, 6
1860 BC	Jacob dies at age 147 (Lesson 13)	Genesis 47:28
1806 BC	Joseph dies at age 110	Genesis 50:26

Visual for Lesson 5. *Keep this chart posted all quarter to give your learners a chronological perspective.*

WHAT DO YOU THINK?

Isaac was not to marry outside of his culture, his people. How can this ancient principle speak to the people of God today, if at all?

[Hint: Be sure to consider 2 Corinthians 6:14.]

happens, then the servant's obligation is fulfilled, and he is *released* from his *oath* to Abraham.

II. WOMAN IDENTIFIED (GENESIS 24:42-45)

Abraham's servant now recounts for Laban the events that have just happened. The story the servant tells about how he encountered Rebekah must sound very strange to those listening. It seems strange to us too, unless we understand the ways of God. God's promise to Abraham requires that Isaac become a father, and God is ensuring that this will happen.

A. SERVANT SETS CONDITIONS (vv. 42-44)

42. "When I came to the spring today, I said, 'O LORD, God of my master Abraham, if you will, please grant success to the journey on which I have come.

The long *journey* of Abraham's servant ended at the well or *spring* that is mentioned in Genesis 24:11. There the servant expected to meet a suitable woman, as women are the ones who come to draw water. The servant did not leave this to his own discernment, however, but prayed to *God* for the right match.

43, 44. 'See, I am standing beside this spring; if a maiden comes out to draw water and I say to her, "Please let me drink a little water from your jar," and if she says to me, "Drink, and I'll draw water for your camels too," let her be the one the LORD has chosen for my master's son.'

The servant was looking for a young, unmarried woman, all of whom normally would be virgins in that culture. The servant had devised a little test for any woman who might come to the well. He wanted to see if he could find a *maiden* who would be willing to show generous hospitality to a stranger.

To pass the test, however, she needed to go beyond the bare minimum of giving a *drink* to the thirsty man. Abraham's servant wanted someone who would volunteer to *draw* enough *water* out of the well to satisfy his entire entourage (Genesis 24:14). This is many gallons for thirsty *camels*! It is estimated that a camel can drink 25 gallons of water in a few minutes. The woman the servant wanted thus would be committing herself to hoisting perhaps 200 to 250 gallons of water out of the well. At one or two gallons a dip, this would be a commitment to raising and lowering her pitcher for an hour or more.

B. CONDITIONS ARE MET (v. 45)

45. "Before I finished praying in my heart, Rebekah came out, with her jar on her shoulder. She went down to the spring and drew water, and I said to her, 'Please give me a drink.'"

Abraham's servant had come much too far not to carry out his plan. Even though he had arrived at a new place and knew no one, he boldly had proceeded to ask *Rebekah* for a *drink*. She responded just as he envisaged. Then he knew that God had directed him to the right woman to be Isaac's wife.

RIGHT PERSON, RIGHT PLACE, RIGHT TIME

Which statement do you think has greater validity: "The times make the person" or "The person makes the times"? Sometimes it's hard to tell. Sometimes it's a little of both as one reinforces the other.

Take the case of Rosa Parks. It was December 1, 1955, in Montgomery, Alabama, when she refused to give up her seat on a bus to a white man. She was African-American, and she was tired of the injustices inflicted on people of her race through segregation laws.

WHAT DO YOU THINK?

What can we learn from the prayer of Abraham's servant that can apply to the way we pray?

WHAT DO YOU THINK?

What are some ways to respond when God answers our prayers?

Parks was arrested, convicted, and fined. In response, African-Americans boycotted the bus system for 381 days. In 1956, the U.S. Supreme Court banned segregation on public transportation. Parks was just a private person trying to better the lot of her people in a small way. But that day she was the proverbial "right person in the right place at the right time." History was made because of it.

When Abraham's servant approached the well in Nahor, he met a young woman who would do what she could under the circumstances that confronted her. As a result, Rebekah's name has become known to devout people ever since.

We don't know how aware Rebekah may have been of God's leading, but she did what was right in the circumstance. As such, she became a vital link of the blessings that come to us today from the God of Abraham, Isaac, and Jacob. What small thing will you do today that may set in motions ripples through history? —C. R. B.

III. GOD WORSHIPED (GENESIS 24:48)

In Genesis 24:46, 47 (not in today's text), Abraham's servant recounts Rebekah's generosity. The servant is able to taste success for his long mission! God has blessed his efforts and has granted the desires of Abraham.

A. REMEMBERING GOD (v. 48a)

48. "And I bowed down and worshiped the LORD. I praised the LORD, the God of my master Abraham,

Abraham's servant continues to recount the events that have just happened. It is curious that the servant does not say that he approaches God as his own Lord, but as *the Lord, the God of my master Abraham*. This shows that while he is confident, capable, and entrusted with a large, expensive expedition, he is still a humble, devoted man. As he begins to see Abraham's quest fulfilled, he takes joy for his master. His first impulse is to thank God for the success.

We can certainly learn a lesson from this. Prayer is every bit as appropriate in our times of victory and success as in our times of desperation and need.

B. ACKNOWLEDGING DIVINE LEADING (v. 48b)

48b. ". . . who had led me on the right road to get the granddaughter of my master's brother for his son."

The servant does not take credit for the success. He understands that he has been *led* to Rebekah. While we may take this for granted, we can feel a sense of wonder at what has been accomplished. Abraham has been largely out of touch with his relatives "back in the old country." He took a risk to find a wife for Isaac.

This mission could have been thwarted in many ways. The servant could have run away with the camels and their precious loads, and Abraham never would have been able to find him. The caravan could have been attacked by bandits and wiped out. The servant might have been unable to find Abraham's kin in the vast territory of Mesopotamia. The servant could have schemed and conspired with a woman to pose as the right wife for Isaac, thus deceiving Abraham.

Finding Rebekah is something along the lines of finding the proverbial needle in a haystack. From a human standpoint, the odds that this quest would be successful must have been very low. Yet God, who always keeps his promises, works to ensure Isaac gets the right wife. God thus ensures that the line of Abraham will be continued through the birth of God's Son, Jesus Christ.

PRAISING GOD IN GOOD NEWS AND BAD

On January 2, 2006, an explosion in a coal mine near Sago, West Virginia, trapped 13 miners deep underground. The eyes of the world had been on the

---

HOW TO SAY IT

Abraham. AY-bruh-ham.
Canaanite. KAY-nun-ite.
Eliezer. El-ih-EE-zer.
Isaac. EYE-zuk.
Laban. LAY-bun.
Mesopotamia. MES-uh-puh-
   TAY-me-uh.
Nahor. NAY-hor.
Rebekah. Reh-BEK-uh.

WHAT DO YOU THINK?

What lessons for Christian servanthood do we learn from the servant of Abraham?

WHAT DO YOU THINK?

In what ways do you need to honor God for his personal leading in your life?

PRAYER

Ageless and timeless God, you are always faithful and merciful. We acknowledge that you guide your people if they follow your lead. We know that you will never abandon us if we trust in you.

May we be resolved to seek your will and follow your paths in all our decisions, small or great. We pray this in the name of the author of our salvation, Jesus Christ, amen.

situation for nearly two days when the first hint of good news came at 11:50 PM on January 3.

CNN cautiously reported that 12 miners had been found alive. CNN then reported that news as fact some 15 minutes later. Newspapers started printing their morning editions with the good news. The headline of the *Atlanta Journal Constitution* was typical: "Miracle in Mine." As church bells rang, the families waiting at the Sago Baptist Church that night changed their prayers from petition to thanksgiving. They began singing praise songs.

Three hours later the thanksgiving and praise turned to anger when news arrived of a miscommunication. Only one miner was alive. We can understand the feelings of those relatives and friends whose hearts were torn by that terrible mistake in communication.

It's easy to praise God when the news is good. Abraham's servant demonstrated this fact as he praised God for the way his quest was concluded. This is not hard to understand. But the real test of our faith in God is when the news is bad. What do we say then? Can we still thank God for his care even when things do not go the way we want?   —C. R. B.

CONCLUSION

Many believers have thought that life's decisions would be simpler if they could just hear an audible word from God telling them what to do. If only God were like a magic mirror on the wall, which could speak directly into our situation and unambiguously tell us what to do!

But if God were to speak this way, would we listen and heed his voice? We all have been given solid advice by our parents that we ignored. As acts of rebellion and as assertions of independence we shunned this advice.

God has given us loads of "advice" in the form of his Word, the Holy Scriptures. Yet we often disregard this form of divine guidance and think that our way is better. This is to our detriment and loss. We learn hard lessons. We come back to God, ask for forgiveness, and admit that his ways are best for us. Do we really believe that an audible voice of God would keep us from ignoring his direction? On the contrary, just as we heard Mother's warnings and still did the wrong thing, we would be found guilty of disobeying God's direct, personalized counsel.

This has bearing when it comes to finding a marriage partner. It is unrealistic to expect a return to a system of arranged marriages today, but we can learn from this process. The young person would be well served to trust the opinions of his or her parents and other wise family members. The parents would be prudent to consider the best interests and happiness of their son or daughter before they attempt to veto a potential partner.

And all sides would be sensible to act as people of faith, praying fervently for God's guidance and blessing. For parents, such prayer should begin when the son or daughter is very young. That will make it more likely that a pending marriage will be the cause of great celebration and joy, as it was for the servant of Abraham in this lesson.

God's Word should be the guide to the one seeking a spouse and to the parents who provide counsel. While we should not expect to hear God's voice pointing us to marriage partners, we can easily use God's standards to "narrow the field," so to speak (see 1 Corinthians 7; 2 Corinthians 6:14). We can pray persistently that God will lead us to the right person. We can ask others to pray for us. And in all things, whether married or unmarried, we can resolve to be used by God and be joyful in his service.

THOUGHT TO REMEMBER

God still wants to guide our decisions.

Discovery Learning

This page contains an alternative lesson plan emphasizing learning activities. Classes desiring such student involvement will find these suggestions helpful. The next page is a reproducible activity page to further enhance discovery learning.

INTO THE LESSON

Decorate your learning space with wedding reception items such as bells and flowers. Offer wedding cake as learners arrive. Display a "Congratulations" banner.

If your budget allows, send wedding invitations to class members prior to class. One of your learners may enjoy creating these invitations on his or her computer. Consider using an e-mail chain if your class has one.

Use today's lesson text for the information on the invitation: bride and groom's parents' names, bride and groom's names, location (your classroom), and time (class time and date). For a bit of humor, add the note, "Sheep and goat gifts only, please."

INTO THE WORD

As learners walk into class, give each a slip labeled either "bride" or "groom"; in this light, have learners sit either on the "bride" or "groom" side of the classroom, as their slips indicate. Then say, "Today's story is of an arranged marriage between families hundreds of camel-miles apart. What made the marriage untypical was the fact that God was the matchmaker. It was he who intervened and enabled the marriage.

"Nevertheless, there had to be certain qualms, anxieties, and questions for the parents of both Isaac and Rebekah. You have a slip that identifies which perspective I want you to ponder. Here's your task: ask questions you think may well have been in the minds of the parents you are 'thinking for.' I'll write them down as we go. Begin by reading through the entirety of today's lesson text."

Write on the board the headings "Bride's Parents" and "Groom's Parents" to prepare for a two-column list. If groups need examples to get them started, give these: For the bride's parents, "Will we ever see our daughter again?" For the groom's parents, "Will my servant actually bring a bride back?" (If you use the student books, you will find other questions listed there as examples.)

Tell your learners that the questions do not necessarily need biblically precise answers. Learners are free to use their "sanctified imaginations" as long their answers are consistent with human emotions.

Allow a brief time for discussion as you add each item to your two-column list. At an appropriate point, caution your learners that we should not expect God to intervene in our lives in the same way that he did for Isaac. Say, "Isaac had a critical, unique role to play in God's plan to redeem the world through Abraham's lineage. But if you look at how God was able to intervene in the life of Isaac to accomplish God's will, you may see that God has the power to work in your life as well, if you allow him."

Next ask, "How do you see God guiding your own life choices?" If responses come slowly, offer such stimulus questions as, "How may God's hand have been at work in leading you to the job you now have?" "How have you seen God answer your prayers for direction in a specific matter?" "How do your prayers reflect the fact that you are inadequate for some tasks and must depend on God's power and grace?"

Let class members respond freely. Their witness to one another here may have the same effect the servant's testimony had on Rebekah and her family: conviction!

INTO LIFE

Display the phrase, "My next big decision is . . ." Ask your learners to finish that idea, either audibly or in their own minds. Suggest that they ponder such areas as family, job, health, service, and finances. After allowing a moment or two for learners to ponder this issue, dramatically edit your phrase to read, "God's role in my next big decision is . . ." Say, "We are not always careful to consider how God is involved. Look at Abraham's confidence that his decision was being guided by God. Abraham's confidence even rubbed off on his servant."

Provide each learner with a strip of paper 1" wide by 8" long. Ask class members to write on their strips the phrase, "God's role in my next big decision," leaving an exaggerated space between the words *in* and *my*. Make one yourself and then demonstrate a point by holding the strip in view of all and tearing it slowly between the *in* and *my*. Say, "Every decision is made with God either attached or detached. Which will it be for you? Take the slip with you to help you think about your next big decision."

Option: In addition to or instead of the above, have your learners complete, in pairs or small groups, the Secrets of a Successful Marriage activity from the reproducible page. The Secrets of a Successful Life activity is also an additional or substitute exercise.

Secrets of a Successful Marriage

Though the arranged marriage of Isaac and Rebekah is unlike most modern marriages, it was successful and happy. Look at Genesis 24 and decide how each of these potential "secrets" is or is not reflected in that marriage. Write your notes below each one.

Financial security promotes marital success.

The presence of God's blessing promotes marital success.

Love promotes marital success.

The approval of both families (bride's and groom's) promotes marital success.

Earnest prayer promotes marital success.

A willingness to share the burdens of daily life promotes marital success.

Faith in God promotes marital success.

Secrets of a Successful Life

If fame is a part of success, the servant of Abraham—who does all the work in Genesis 24—was not a success! He is not even named, nor does he appear again in the biblical narrative. Yet he demonstrates the secrets of a successful life. He might get a 10 for each of the following achievements. How would you rate yourself on each, from 1 (a definite underachiever) to 10 (a conspicuous success).

_____ The servant earned the confidence and trust of the one to whom he answered (v. 2).

_____ The servant made sure he understood the expectations his boss had of him (v. 5).

_____ The servant carefully planned his strategy for accomplishing his assignment (vv. 9-11).

_____ The servant called on God to do for him what he could not do on his own (v. 12).

_____ The servant used his resources wisely to accomplish his goals (vv. 22, 53).

_____ The servant praised God, who did the "impossible" part (vv. 26, 27, 48).

_____ The servant would not let sentiment impede the completion of his task (vv. 55, 56).

_____ The servant carefully reported the manner of his accomplishment (v. 66).

Look at the list of "Success Secrets." To which one do you need to give the most attention? Write a commitment statement to the Lord here:

God Creates
Unit 2: *God's People Increase*
(Lessons 6-9)

ESAU AND JACOB AS RIVALS

LESSON 6

WHY TEACH THIS LESSON?

Choices. We make them every day. Sometimes we deliberate, seek counsel, and pray before deciding. At other times, a pressing physical or emotional need may seem to overwhelm us, forcing an instant decision.

Today, you may have "an Esau" in your class in this regard. This is someone whose failure to value his or her inheritance in Christ results in affairs, over-spending, overeating, substance abuse, and other false fixes to smooth over momentary discomfort. You may also have "a Jacob" in your class—someone ready to provide the false fix for personal gain.

Such decisions (by either an Esau or a Jacob) can destroy what God wants for us. Such decisions affect not only one's eternal salvation, but also the relationships within families and churches. Today's lesson challenges your learners to be wary of quick solutions that carry long-term cost.

INTRODUCTION

A. SIBLING RIVALRY

I have a sister who is one year and one month younger than I. We were bitter rivals growing up. One might say we fought like cats and dogs! There were no holds barred.

As we grew to be teenagers, I could no longer physically fight my sister, but we continued our battles with our tongues. I felt that Dad preferred my sister; I received several punishments for things I never did.

However, there was one time my sister took my side. I climbed a tree after being told not to, and then I fell and nearly killed myself. I had actually broken my left arm close to the shoulder. I asked my sister not to tell Mom or Dad lest I receive certain punishment. She obliged and "protected" me, helping me hide my broken arm for two weeks. The pain became unbearable, and I had to reveal my predicament.

When I finally confessed, I was taken to the doctor. Despite the fact that my sister went along with my request, I think she enjoyed my agony more than ever. The rivalry persisted even when one was doing the other a favor; each was gleeful at the other's suffering. Such is sibling rivalry.

B. LESSON BACKGROUND

Today's lesson is the opening story of the struggle between close relatives—Jacob and Esau, the twin sons of Isaac. We should not be surprised to read of such a struggle, because Genesis records similar animosities leading up to today's text: between brothers Cain and Abel (4:1-16); within Noah's family (9:18-27); between Abraham and Lot, his nephew (chapter 13); and between half-brothers Ishmael and Isaac (chapters 16, 17, 21). This kind of rivalry did not cease with Esau and Jacob, but continued among Jacob's sons, namely Joseph and his brothers (chapters 37–50).

DEVOTIONAL READING:
1 CORINTHIANS 1:26-31
BACKGROUND SCRIPTURE:
GENESIS 25:19-34
PRINTED TEXT:
GENESIS 25:19-34

LESSON AIMS

Oct 7

After participating in this lesson, each student will be able to:

1. Describe the early rivalry between Jacob and Esau.

2. Compare and contrast the rivalry between Jacob and Esau with rivalries within families and/or churches today.

3. Create a plan for his or her church to help people recognize and defuse destructive tensions that threaten families and/or the church.

KEY VERSE

The LORD said to her, "Two nations are in your womb, and two peoples from within you will be separated; one people will be stronger than the other, and the older will serve the younger."
—Genesis 25:23

LESSON 6 NOTES

Barrenness is also part of our lesson's background. This was a key issue for the story of Abraham and Sarah, as we saw previously. Only God was able to open Rebekah's womb, but not as she expected or perhaps wanted!

Isaac and Rebekah were living somewhere near Beer Lahai Roi (translation: "well of the living one who sees me"; Genesis 25:11). This was between Kadesh and Bered, somewhere south of Beersheba in the Negev (see Genesis 16:14).

I. SIBLINGS STRUGGLE BEFORE BIRTH (GENESIS 25:19-26)

A. FAMILY BACKGROUND (vv. 19, 20)

19. This is the account of Abraham's son Isaac.

Abraham became the father of Isaac,

The phrase *This is the account of* describes an important framework. If a narrative follows this phrase in Genesis, the meaning is something like "family history" or perhaps "story." If a genealogical list follows, the meaning is best understood as "descendants."

After the initial introduction of creation in Genesis 1:1–2:3, there are ten such accounts given. These are the heavens and the earth (Genesis 2:4–4:26), Adam (5:1–6:8), Noah (6:9–9:29), Ham and Japheth (10:1–11:9), Shem (11:10-26), Terah (11:27–25:11), Ishmael (25:12-18), Isaac (25:19–35:29), Esau (36:1–37:1), and Jacob (37:2–50:26). We note that the rest of Genesis is taken up with the stories of Esau and Jacob in this regard, primarily with the latter.

The phrase *This is the account of Abraham's son Isaac* is the title of the eighth of these generational segments in Genesis. The phrase that follows is so abrupt as to be somewhat amusing: *Abraham became the father of Isaac.* He certainly did, but not without great agony, fretting, and even laughter (Genesis 15:2; 16:1-4; 17:17; 18:12-15).

In fact, *Isaac* means "he laughs" in Hebrew. We could say that the conception and birth of Isaac revealed God's sense of humor to the world: only a sovereign God could bring about this birth, because Abraham and Sarah were 100 and 90 years old, respectively, when Isaac was born (Genesis 17:17; 21:5)!

20. . . . and Isaac was forty years old when he married Rebekah daughter of Bethuel the Aramean from Paddan Aram and sister of Laban the Aramean.

Verse 20 gives us more family background. The mention of *Laban* provides hints at the future adventures of Jacob, who will be one of Isaac's sons. The fact that the text informs us that Isaac is *forty years old* when he marries *Rebekah* implies the unusual lateness of Isaac's marriage.

Rebekah, for her part, is the *daughter of Bethuel*; he is a son of Nahor, a brother to Abraham (Genesis 22:20-24; 24:15). Laban is Rebekah's brother, an *Aramean* (or Syrian). That family lives in *Paddan Aram*, located in northwest Mesopotamia (part of modern-day Syria). The name *Paddan Aram* means "Plain of Aram" (see Genesis 28:2-7; 31:18; 35:9, 26; 46:15).

B. BARREN WIFE (v. 21)

21. Isaac prayed to the LORD on behalf of his wife, because she was barren. The LORD answered his prayer, and his wife Rebekah became pregnant.

A *barren* wife is socially despised in ancient times (compare 1 Samuel 1:1-7; Psalm 113:9; Isaiah 54:1). Yet great men are born to mothers who previously had been barren and were desperate for God's help (see Judges 13:2-5 regarding Samson and 1-Samuel 1:11 regarding Samuel the prophet).

Only by God's will and purpose are the sons—soon to be known as Jacob and Esau—conceived. On the surface it seems that God answers Isaac's prayer of supplication immediately. But one must remember that Isaac and Rebekah have been married 20 years by this point (compare Genesis 25:26b with 25:20). Couples in ancient times usually expect children very soon after marriage; thus Isaac and Rebekah have been anticipating children for some 20 years!

Isaac's plea to God thus may cover a rather long period of time—perhaps 15 or more years of pleading. This should teach us to wait on God and be content in his timing. The prayers are answered. God's sovereignty over his creation and creatures is demonstrated in this conception.

C. INQUIRY OF THE LORD (vv. 22, 23)

22. The babies jostled each other within her, and she said, "Why is this happening to me?" So she went to inquire of the LORD.

In this case there are twins—surely unexpected. Just as the case of Isaac brought the laughters of disbelief and joy, so now Rebekah is overwhelmed with the struggle going on *within her*! She is happy for the pregnancy but disturbed about the turmoil within.

The Hebrew word for *jostled each other* usually comes with the idea "to oppress, crush, suppress, smash." The form of the Hebrew in this text means "to struggle together," that is, to kick and shove one another. Rebekah is concerned about what is happening to her: *Why is this happening to me?* Just as Isaac had turned to Yahweh God because of his wife's barrenness, so now Rebekah turns to Yahweh God concerning her difficult pregnancy. So *she went to inquire of the Lord.*

Exactly how and where she does this we do not know. The use of mechanical means, such as the priest's Urim and Thummim for *yes* or *no* answers, is not yet available (see Exodus 28:30). There is no mention of a prophet, priest, or angel to deliver the message. Yet God does respond. As God answered Isaac's prayer, so now he answers Rebekah's inquiry.

23. The LORD said to her,

> **"Two nations are in your womb,**
> **and two peoples from within you will be separated;**
> **one people will be stronger than the other,**
> **and the older will serve the younger."**

Verse 23 lays out the answer in poetic form. The response addresses the destiny of the sons as *two nations,* one to be *stronger than the other.* The statement *the older will serve the younger* suggests that it is the younger who will be the stronger, but not necessarily. At this point, it is possible that the stronger, elder son will indeed serve the weaker, younger son. However, as nations later on, the stronger will be Israel/Judah over the weaker Edom. These are the two nations at issue.

Variations of the theme *the older will serve the younger* are found throughout Genesis. Note the Lord's acceptance of Abel over Cain (Genesis 4:4, 5), Isaac over Ishmael (17:17-21), Joseph over his brothers (37:5-11), Ephraim over Manasseh (48:17-20), and Judah over Reuben (49:3, 4, 8-10). We could add David over his older brothers (1 Samuel 16:1-13) and Solomon over Adonijah (2-Samuel 3:2-5; 1-Kings 1).

"The law of primogeniture" is in effect at this time, and Moses will articulate it more fully centuries later (Deuteronomy 21:15-17). This law requires that every father give his firstborn son a double share as an inheritance. This double share is in line with the eldest son's responsibilities as the family's new patriarch. Yet at times God seems to delight in reversals. Consider that the "many who are first will be last; and many who are last will be first" (Matthew 19:30).

WHAT DO YOU THINK?

What are some ways that people react when God delays granting answers to prayers that they know are in his will? How can we comfort people during those times?

WHAT DO YOU THINK?

What are some areas in your life where you have questioned God because of your own frustrations and uncertainties? Where did your questioning lead you?

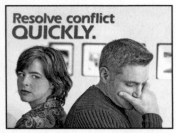

Resolve conflict **QUICKLY.**

Visual for Lesson 6. *Use this visual to start a discussion on conflict resolution. Ask, "What's a good first step to take toward resolving conflicts?"*

God has a specific purpose in mind when he notes that *the older will serve the younger* (see Romans 9:10-12).

DIFFERING PERSONALITIES

Nicola and Stuart Richardson tried for six years to have children. Fertility treatments finally succeeded. At seven weeks a nurse saw two heartbeats on the ultrasound scan. After further scanning, the nurse told Nicola that she could see *four* heartbeats! On January 21, 2002, Nicola gave birth to three boys and a girl. The children have personalities that differ from one another. As their mother describes them, Harry is active, Matthew loves music, Ben charms everyone with his smile, and Anna is content to play alone.

The Richardsons discovered what every parent of more than one child knows: children are different! Rebekah certainly was aware of this, even before her children were born. Her alarm at the struggles of her preborn babies was so great that she felt compelled to ask God, *Why?* The Lord explained the situation in terms of her sons' future relationship with each other, including the lives of their descendants.

Parents today should not expect direct revelations from God concerning their children's future or their relationships with one another. The parents' task is to recognize differing personalities as a fact of life, then shape those personalities so God may be glorified in their lives. —C. R. B.

D. BIRTH OF TWIN SONS (vv. 24-26)

24. When the time came for her to give birth, there were twin boys in her womb.

The original Hebrew of this story includes the exclamation "Behold!" or "Now see!" Thus the story is narrated as if it is a surprise to Rebekah when she discovers she has *twin boys in her womb*.

25. The first to come out was red, and his whole body was like a hairy garment; so they named him Esau.

But the fact that Rebekah is bearing twins is not the only surprise. These boys are as different as night and day—they are definitely not identical twins! The first son born comes out *red* (which sounds like *Edom* in the Hebrew). His appearance is somehow *like a hairy garment*. The parents name him *Esau*, which sounds like the word for *hairy*, though it does not mean the same. Thus, Esau is named for his appearance (compare Genesis 25:30; 36:1, 8).

26. After this, his brother came out, with his hand grasping Esau's heel; so he was named Jacob. Isaac was sixty years old when Rebekah gave birth to them.

While one son is named for his appearance, the other is named for his action: *his hand* is *grasping Esau's heel.* The name *Jacob* sounds like the word *heel* in Hebrew. The verb form means "to defraud." It carries the idea of sneaking up behind someone to betray, hamper, hinder, or even supplant. Figuratively, it means "to deceive." This "heel grabber" will be a deceiver who himself will often be deceived (see Genesis 27:36; 29:25; 31:7, 26, 27).

Jacob will indeed live up to his name. Jacob's pattern of deceit will cause conflict. These brothers are in conflict even before birth. Conflict will follow them and their descendants.

II. SIBLINGS STRUGGLE AFTER BIRTH (GENESIS 25:27-34)

A. DIFFERENCES (v. 27)

27. The boys grew up, and Esau became a skillful hunter, a man of the open country, while Jacob was a quiet man, staying among the tents.

WHAT DO YOU THINK?

What is the meaning and significance of your name? Should you care? Why, or why not?

Esau and *Jacob* are not only born in conflict, they live in conflict. One indication is their differing occupations; this difference ties in to parental preferences (see below). Esau becomes *a skillful hunter, a man of the open country.* He loves the outdoors, especially the hunting of wild game. He certainly looks the part, having a hairy body and perhaps a reddish color to either his hair or skin or both.

By contrast, Jacob is not a man of the fields. He is, rather, *a quiet man, staying among the tents.* The word *quiet* used to describe Jacob probably means "complete" or "self-contained." Thus he is able to live quietly and self-sufficiently. Perhaps he follows the herds as he dwells in the tents.

B. PREFERENCES (v. 28)

28. Isaac, who had a taste for wild game, loved Esau, but Rebekah loved Jacob.

Not only are the boys different in abilities and interests, they are also treated differently by their parents. *Isaac* loves *Esau* for his ability to provide *wild game* from the countryside. Apparently this is the main reason Isaac prefers Esau. *Rebekah,* on the other hand, prefers *Jacob,* but no reason is given. Rebekah may have God's response of Genesis 25:23 in mind as she sides with the younger son.

Psychologically, all this makes for a profound difference in the ways the boys react to circumstances and life in general. Such preferential treatment is bound to cause ongoing conflict within the family. And it does.

C. DISDAINFULNESS (vv. 29-34)

29, 30. Once when Jacob was cooking some stew, Esau came in from the open country, famished. He said to Jacob, "Quick, let me have some of that red stew! I'm famished!" (That is why he was also called Edom.)

It is ironic that a mighty hunter would come in from the field *famished* and weak. Yet, there *Esau* stands, vulnerable before his brother, who apparently has been preparing a *stew* of lentils that looks *red* (see v. 34, below).

As we have already noted, Esau was "red" when he was born; now he begs for some *red stew.* Thus, his descendants will be called *Edom,* which means "red." These words look and sound alike in Hebrew. The play on words emphasizes the foolishness of Esau's action (see Hebrews 12:16, 17).

31. Jacob replied, "First sell me your birthright."

Jacob takes advantage of his brother's vulnerability and immediately tells him what he wants in exchange for the soup: *First sell me your birthright.* No "please" or "I pray thee," just the outright desire of the birthright.

32. "Look, I am about to die," Esau said. "What good is the birthright to me?"

Rationalizing is very easy when we're under stress! There is no doubt that Esau greatly exaggerates his own condition of being *about to die.* But haven't we all said at some time, "I am so hungry I could die" or "I'm dying of thirst"? The point is that Esau despises his birthright as firstborn in order to gratify an immediate felt need of hunger.

33, 34. But Jacob said, "Swear to me first." So he swore an oath to him, selling his birthright to Jacob. Then Jacob gave Esau some bread and some lentil stew. He ate and drank, and then got up and left.

So Esau despised his birthright.

Jacob makes Esau *swear* an oath, thus securing the *birthright* permanently. The older is beginning to serve the younger!

Before bringing our lesson to a conclusion, it is useful to pause and consider verses 29-34 as a whole. The story is told in an "X-shaped" manner to emphasize

---

WHAT DO YOU THINK?

What family principles do we learn from the differences between Esau and Jacob?

HOW TO SAY IT

Abraham. AY-bruh-ham.
Adonijah. Ad-o-NYE-juh.
Aramean. Ar-uh-ME-un.
Beer Lahai Roi. BEE-er-luh-HI-roy.
Beersheba. Beer-SHE-buh.
Bethuel. Beh-THEW-el.
Ephraim. EE-fray-im.
Japheth. JAY-feth.
Laban. LAY-bun.
Manasseh. Muh-NASS-uh.
Mesopotamia. MES-uh-puh-TAY-me-uh.
Paddan Aram. PAY-dan-A-ram.
Reuben. ROO-ben.

the fact in the middle statement. The flow goes something like this, with statement D in that important middle position:

A^1: *Esau came in from the open country* (v. 29).
B^1: *let me have some of that red stew* (v. 30).
C^1: *first sell me your birthright* (v. 31).
D: *I am about to die . . .*
what good is the
birthright to me? (v. 32).
C^2: *he [sold] his birthright* (v. 33).
B^2: *Esau . . . ate and drank* (v. 34a).
A^2: *[Esau] . . . then got up and left* (v. 34b).

Notice that statements A^1 and A^2 are similar or parallel to each other in a certain way. The same is true for statements B^1 and B^2 as well as statements C^1 and C^2. So what does the middle statement D emphasize? The foolish logic people can use to talk themselves into doing the dumbest things!

INSTANT GRATIFICATION

Too bad Esau didn't live in the twenty-first century! When his brother demanded that high price for a bowl of soup, Esau merely could have gunned his SUV down to the ATM, grabbed a quick $40, then gone around the corner to the McTaco-in-the-Box drive-up window. He thus could have satisfied his hunger in a couple of minutes with little fuss and bother.

But on second thought, that hypothetical sequence still may may not have been fast enough for Esau. Think about your computer. In the last two decades, processing speed has increased exponentially. Yet which of us hasn't complained when it doesn't respond as rapidly as we wish?

This mind-set affects us even at church. Some churches have started putting the Sunday sermons on CDs, but to have to wait for a week to pick it up has become too tedious. So some churches now have the CDs ready as church-goers walk out the door!

Movie actress Carrie Fisher sarcastically noted that "instant gratification takes too long." Esau is an easy target for his impatience as well as his deeper problem: his willingness to trade something of long-term value for the instant gratification of his need for food. But in this way Esau is a very modern person. How often in the past month have you trapped yourself with this same immature attitude?

—C. R. B.

CONCLUSION

The rivalry between Jacob and Esau yielded bitter fruit for many years. Their two peoples (the Israelites and the Edomites) would forever be known as enemies (see 1 Samuel 14:47, 48; 2 Samuel 8:13, 14; Jeremiah 49:7-22; Ezekiel 25:12-14; 35; Obadiah; Malachi 1:2-5).

But today's story is really about God's choice—his purpose and will being worked out through the life of a young man who was chosen in spite of himself. The deceiver would be deceived often enough that one day he would learn how to struggle not only with others but with God and prevail (Genesis 32:28). The consequences would change his name (*Jacob* to *Israel*) and his life forever.

Sometimes when God chooses a person, it may not be pleasant—it may be for a life of struggle rather than one of contentment. God sees to it that we all must struggle with him before we can make a significant contribution to his kingdom.

Incidentally, my sister and I have reconciled our bitter rivalry from years past.

Discovery Learning

This page contains an alternative lesson plan emphasizing learning activities. Classes desiring such student involvement will find these suggestions helpful. The next page is a reproducible activity page to further enhance discovery learning.

INTO THE LESSON

Display this fictitious word and its definition as class begins: "sibble *(verb,* 2007): to quibble with a sibling over who is 'number one.'"

Introduce two men (whom you have recruited in advance) to present the following dual monologues representing Jacob and Esau. With a bit of dramatic flair, say, "Now here are Jacob and Esau, the siblings who sibble."

Give your two actors copies of the following script ahead of time to allow each to become familiar with it. The process is simple alternating lines, as given.

ESAU: Mother always did like my brother best.
JACOB: Father always did like my brother best.
ESAU: Mine was the birthright; I *was* born first.
JACOB: Mine was the birthright, by hook or by crook.
ESAU: I became a manly man, a hunter. Un-h-h!
JACOB: I was a Mama's boy, hanging around the tent.
ESAU: Well, we were twins, but we didn't look alike. They called me the hairy one. And we certainly didn't act the same.
JACOB: Well, we were twins, but we hardly acted like twins . . . or looked like twins. My brother's red hair set him apart.
ESAU: I was a man of food. I loved to eat meat from the animals I hunted, as did my father!
JACOB: I was the sensitive one. I learned to cook from my mother. My specialty was bean soup.
ESAU: We were special children, conceived by God's grace. It's simply that I was more special than my brother. Just ask Dad.
JACOB: We were special children, born by God's intervention, just as our father had been. It's simply that God wanted me to be the leader.
ESAU: Did not! *JACOB:* Did too! *ESAU:* Did not! *JACOB:* Did too! *ESAU:* Did not! *JACOB:* Did too!

Interrupt your actors, and ask them to be seated. They can continue to growl and snipe at one another.

INTO THE WORD

Because today's study is about family division and rivalry, designate half of your class as *US* and the other half as *THEM.* (Simply draw an invisible line down the middle.) Say, "In this next activity it's going to be '*Us* versus *Them,*' so hold your animosities and your elbows in! We don't want this to turn into a 'Jacob versus Esau' conflict."

Give the learners time to read through today's text in Genesis 25:19-26. Then say, "The US group can answer my questions with a word or phrase beginning with either *U* or *S.* The THEM group can answer my questions with a word or phrase beginning with either *TH* or *EM.*"

Alternate asking the following questions to US and THEM. Keep score, as an additional source of group rivalry. Give questions one and two as samples. Award points for reasonable answers that are not listed within parentheses.

1. US, what was Rebekah's relationship to Laban? *(sister);* 2. THEM, how old was Isaac when he married? *(thirty plus ten);* 3. US, how do you suppose Isaac and Rebekah felt about being childless after 20 years of marriage? *(sad, unhappy);* 4. THEM, how could one characterize the lengthy state of Rebekah's womb? *(empty);* 5. US, how does God characterize the "one people" in Rebekah's womb in relationship to the other? *(stronger);* 6. THEM, which of the two does God say will serve the other? *(the older);* 7. US, what attitude does verse 24 imply? *(surprise);* 8. THEM, how old was Isaac when the twins were born? *(threescore);* 9. US, how might one describe Esau's newborn appearance? *(unusual);* 10. THEM, what's another word that could be used to describe the boys' birth other than "came out"? *(emerged);* 11. US, what kind of hunter was Esau? *(skillful);* 12. THEM, rather than describe Jacob as plain or quiet, how else might one characterize him? *(thoughtful);* 13. US, how might you say the parents loved the boys? *(unequally);* 14. THEM, how could you characterize Esau's claim he was close to death? *(theatric).*

INTO LIFE

Tell your learners that you want them to suggest principles of "A Parenting Curriculum." It will note elements that must be a part of an effective parenting course of study to be offered by the church. Of course, they will want to consider the successes and mistakes of Isaac and Rebekah. Once you have the list, pass it along to church leadership for consideration. Perhaps your class can sponsor and/or lead such a class.

Options: Use either or both of the activities on the Reproducible Page as additional or substitute exercises.

A Bowl of Soup

In Genesis 25:29-34, a bowl of soup means more to Esau than his birthright. On the bowl of soup, write in some of the near worthless things that Christians sometimes allow to endanger their spiritual birthright.

Now make it personal: What are some of the earthly pleasures that will lure you away from your spiritual birthright if you let them? What is your plan for attacking this problem? Jot your thoughts below:

A Jacob and Esau Church

If Isaac's family constituted the membership of a church, what parallels would you draw? Consider Jacob and Esau as the two factions within that church. Two examples are given to get you started.

THE ESAU SIDE

1. Loves tradition.

2. Wants a bigger building.

3. _____

4. _____

5. _____

6. _____

THE JACOB SIDE

Wants change.

Wants more mission support.

_____

_____

_____

_____

What preventions or cures do you think would solve these kinds of problems? Jot your ideas below.

JACOB'S DREAM AT BETHEL

LESSON 7

WHY TEACH THIS LESSON?

Who among us hasn't been amused, startled, or confused by a dream that occurred during the night? Some dreams are so vivid that we can't get back to sleep. The best response to a dream is usually to have a good laugh, shake it off, and get on with real life.

But not all your learners will take that path. A few will buy one of those speculative books on how to interpret dreams. Some will look at today's lesson as confirmation that since God has spoken through dreams, he can do so again—so they expect him to do so. God certainly can do so, but *can* isn't the same as *likely to*. The fact is that God has spoken to people through dreams in only a handful of instances in the entirety of the Bible.

It is much more important to focus on Jacob's response to God's leading rather than on the procedure God used to provide that leading. Make no mistake: God expects a personal response from each of your learners today. God does not allow us to "hide" withing a larger group—be it a Christian family, a church, or a Christianized nation. The calls are personal, and the responses must be as well.

INTRODUCTION

A. SECOND-GENERATION BELIEVERS

Many of us have been challenged by evangelistic sermons claiming that "Christianity is only one generation from extinction." By this, preachers usually mean no one is automatically born a believer. Although many people have been brought up in Christian homes, this favorable environment is not enough to make one a Christian. At some point each person must respond to the gospel through personal decision, not the decision of the parents. This is why Christians must spread the good news to the next generation.

Our Jewish forefathers also had to make personal decisions. Abraham accepted God's call, Isaac accepted God's call, and in today's passage even Jacob—the deceiver—is invited to continue the faith of his father and grandfather. How does his response apply to us today?

B. LESSON BACKGROUND

Isaac and Rebekah had been living prosperously in Beersheba since Isaac made peace with the Philistines (Genesis 26). Like her mother-in-law Sarah, Rebekah was unable to conceive. So God intervened to keep the promise alive. Unlike her mother-in-law, however, Rebekah gave birth to twin sons. This complicated matters since only one son could be the child of promise.

God foretold that Jacob was to be that child, but Jacob did not wait patiently for God to fulfill this prophecy. Instead, he lived up to (or down to!) his name, which can mean "heel-grabber": he manipulated his brother into surrendering his birthright, and he deceived his father in order to get the blessing that was intended for Esau.

DEVOTIONAL READING:
PSALM 105:1-11
BACKGROUND SCRIPTURE:
GENESIS 27:41–28:22
PRINTED TEXT:
GENESIS 28:10-22

LESSON AIMS

After participating in this lesson, each student will be able to:

1. Recount the contents of Jacob's dream and his reaction to it.

2. Compare and contrast Jacob's dream with "normal" dreams.

3. Explain how he or she will be sensitive to God's leading, balancing clear direction from Scripture with analysis of external circumstances.

Oct
14

KEY VERSE

I am with you and will watch over you wherever you go, and I will bring you back to this land. I will not leave you until I have done what I have promised you.
—*Genesis 28:15*

LESSON 7 NOTES

Esau, of course, was furious about his brother's deception—so much so that he plotted to kill him as Cain did Abel. Aware of these plans, Rebekah arranged for Jacob to escape his brother's fury and marry a woman from Abraham's kin. It was important that the child of promise maintain a pure bloodline by not marrying a Canaanite. So Jacob went to Haran, the hometown of Rebekah's brother Laban.

I. JACOB'S JOURNEY (GENESIS 28:10, 11)

A. HEADING TOWARD HARAN (v. 10)

10. Jacob left Beersheba and set out for Haran.

Haran is located north of the promised land, approximately 550 miles from Jacob's home in *Beersheba*. This journey thus puts plenty of needed distance between Jacob and his brother's wrath, but it is also a risky move in light of family history.

In Genesis 11:31 we are told that Abraham's father, Terah, left his homeland of Ur of the Chaldeans with the intention of arriving in Canaan, the land of promise. Was he called by God to do this? We know that God was recognized as Terah's God (Genesis 31:53), yet Terah also worshiped false gods (Joshua 24:2). The Bible is silent about why he set out for Canaan and why Terah did not complete the trip. He went as far as Haran (about 600 miles northwest of Ur) and settled there. It was up to his son Abram (later renamed Abraham) to finish what he had begun.

Perhaps Abraham remembered his father's failure. So when arranging a wife for his son Isaac, Abraham deliberately sent his servant—not Isaac personally—to Haran to find a wife (Genesis 24:6-8; see Lesson 5). This move ensured that Isaac would not be tempted to stay in Haran as his grandfather had. Rebekah, on the other hand, could not afford to keep her son Jacob nearby. The threat posed by Esau was too great; so Jacob's risky journey began.

B. LAYOVER IN LUZ (v. 11)

11. When he reached a certain place, he stopped for the night because the sun had set. Taking one of the stones there, he put it under his head and lay down to sleep.

Jacob at this point is about 60 miles into his journey. He has run out of sunlight and thus stops *for the night*. We learn in verse 19 that this certain place is called Luz, a region located 20 miles northwest of the Dead Sea.

What is most notable about this place is that it is not noteworthy. Other travelers in Jacob's day may intentionally set up camp near a temple or other holy place in hopes of gaining the favor of their god(s). Jacob, on the other hand, stops at no place in particular. This underscores the fact that Jacob does not attempt to engineer or manipulate the divine blessing he is about to receive, as was the case with the blessing he received in dealing with Esau. The revelation he is about to receive is entirely due to God's gracious initiative.

Christians need to hear this message today. We have not been instructed to orchestrate a divine word from God. It is not a matter of praying the right prayer, meditating the right way, or assuming the right bodily posture. God is not like a vending machine that yields goods automatically when we push the right buttons.

Instead, God speaks to whom he will, when he will, and how he will. In Scripture God sometimes reveals himself to those who have petitioned him with fervent prayer and fasting, but often he does so when humans least expect it.

WHAT DO YOU THINK?

How does Jacob's situation compare and contrast with the times we seek God in the comfort of our worship centers?

"NOWHERE"

"Where are you going?" "Nowhere."

"What are you going to do?" "Nothing."

"Whom are you going to do it with?" "Nobody."

That conversation (or a variation of it) has taken place countless times between parents and teens. Actually, there are lots of places that can be classified as *nowhere* or *nowhere in particular*. As one moves westward across the North American continent, one can find vast expanses of prairie and desert that qualify as nowhere.

Even places that used to be *somewhere* are now *nowhere*. Towns that were once thriving now may be hanging on by a thread; or they may have turned into ghost towns, slowly disintegrating as sun and weather beat upon them.

The place where Jacob stopped was *nowhere*—just a convenient place to sleep. But God met him there. We may think that the great experiences of life must happen in special places. Yet such events often happen in ordinary places that become special because of what happens there. Wherever we meet God is somewhere special! That's what Jacob came to discover.   —C. R. B.

II. JACOB'S DREAM (GENESIS 28:12-15)

A. WHAT JACOB SEES (v. 12)

12. He had a dream in which he saw a stairway resting on the earth, with its top reaching to heaven, and the angels of God were ascending and descending on it.

While sleeping, Jacob dreams of a *stairway* that spans the gap between *heaven* and *earth*. This stairway is not there, however, for Jacob to climb. The one who reached to grab his brother's heel, his brother's birthright, and his father's blessing will not climb this stairway to reach and grab God.

Neither will God descend to meet Jacob face to face. Only God's angels ascend and descend. God is above; Jacob remains on earth. There is a necessary gap between the two. This distance may be for Jacob's protection, or God may simply be teaching him a lesson about holiness.

B. WHAT GOD SAYS (vv. 13-15)

13a. There above it stood the LORD, and he said: "I am the LORD, the God of your father Abraham and the God of Isaac.

God's speech to Jacob is a monologue. Jacob is not invited to converse with God; he is required to hear what God has to say.

God says three things. First, God introduces himself as the God of *Abraham* and *Isaac*. Will he be Jacob's God as well? At this point, it is not clear that Jacob will follow the footsteps of his fathers. The decision to find a wife from Abraham's kin is an important step in the right direction, but Jacob's journey is also driven by his desire to survive Esau's wrath. Yet the way that Jacob responds to this gracious initiative of God will be decisive for how many will come to know God: as the God of Abraham, Isaac, and Jacob (Exodus 3:15).

13b, 14. "I will give you and your descendants the land on which you are lying. Your descendants will be like the dust of the earth, and you will spread out to the west and to the east, to the north and to the south. All peoples on earth will be blessed through you and your offspring.

Second, God affirms that the promise he made to Abraham and Isaac is now extended to Jacob. Using language similar to Genesis 13:14-16, God promises to give Jacob and his descendants the very *land* that Jacob is in the process of leaving, to multiply Jacob's offspring *like the dust of the earth*, to *spread* his family in all four directions, and to bless *all peoples on earth* through them. Despite Jacob's

---

DAILY BIBLE READINGS

Monday, Oct. 8—Remember God's Works (Psalm 105:1-6)

Tuesday, Oct. 9—An Everlasting Covenant (Psalm 105: 7-11)

Wednesday, Oct. 10—The Conflict Deepens (Genesis 27: 41-45)

Thursday, Oct. 11—To Seek a Wife (Genesis 27:46–28:5)

Friday, Oct. 12—Esau Takes Another Wife (Genesis 28:6-9)

Saturday, Oct. 13—God's Covenant with Jacob (Genesis 28:10-17)

Sunday, Oct. 14—The Place Named Bethel (Genesis 28: 18-22)

WHAT DO YOU THINK?

What part will you and your church have in helping fulfill God's intent to bless the world?

WHAT DO YOU THINK?

What do we learn about God as he identifies himself here? How does this knowledge of God help us?

past, despite the threat to his life, and despite his self-imposed exile from the land of promise, God assures Jacob that he is indeed God's chosen man.

15. "I am with you and will watch over you wherever you go, and I will bring you back to this land. I will not leave you until I have done what I have promised you."

Third, God recognizes Jacob's insecurities as one heading for unfamiliar territory. Thus God commits to be *with* Jacob, to protect him in his travels, and to return him to the land of promise.

III. JACOB'S RESPONSE (GENESIS 28:16-22)

A. WITH AWE (vv. 16, 17)

16, 17. When Jacob awoke from his sleep, he thought, "Surely the LORD is in this place, and I was not aware of it." He was afraid and said, "How awesome is this place! This is none other than the house of God; this is the gate of heaven."

Abraham and Isaac each had a chance to obey. Now it is Jacob's turn. How will he respond?

Upon waking from his dream, Jacob reacts to God's threefold speech with a threefold affirmation: (1) *the Lord is in this place,* (2) *this is none other than the house of God,* and (3) *this is the gate of heaven.* We will point out the importance of each of these three below. An important fact to be noticed at this point is that Jacob's threefold affirmation is couched in fear. He had gone to sleep on common turf, but he awakens on holy ground.

Although God's message to Jacob is full of comfort, the awe-inspiring nature of the vision also sounds a clear message: God is no human to be trifled with or manipulated. He stands on high with angels to do his bidding. God proclaims his word; humans must listen and respond. This recognition on Jacob's part is vital in his development as God's man, the man of the promise.

In our day of undisciplined speech about God, we need to be reminded of the healthy fear exemplified by our forefathers in the faith. Men like Jacob, Moses, Elijah, Isaiah, Ezekiel, and Daniel truly respected God's awe-inspiring presence. God is still a consuming fire (Hebrews 12:28, 29). The apostle Paul deems it appropriate to describe God as dwelling in unapproachable light, unable to be seen with human eyes (1 Timothy 6:15, 16).

WHAT DO YOU THINK?

Is Jacob's response to God's presence a model for us today? Why, or why not?

B. WITH A MEMORIAL (vv. 18, 19)

18. Early the next morning Jacob took the stone he had placed under his head and set it up as a pillar and poured oil on top of it.

Rather than immediately resuming his journey, Jacob lingers to commemorate the place where God has met him. He selects the *stone* that functioned as his pillow, sets it upright, and anoints it with *oil*. We should not associate this act with idol worship, as if Jacob believes the stone itself possesses magical, dream-inducing powers. Such a practice will later be condemned as detestable to God (Deuteronomy 16:22).

We should view this instead as an act of reverence, an acknowledgement that Jacob has received God's message loud and clear. Anointing with oil is a common way to set apart particular persons or objects in ancient times. By anointing kings, priests, altars, and garments, the Israelites who come after Jacob will set apart people and things for service on behalf of the one true God.

So Jacob does not regard this rock as special in and of itself. Rather, he considers this particular place to be sacred because God has chosen it for his unique purposes. It is God who gives it meaning—a meaning that Jacob wishes never to forget. This is part one of Jacob's threefold response.

It is fitting for Jacob to use a stone for this purpose. In ancient times, stones serve as witnesses to agreements between parties, especially agreements concerning property boundaries. Years later Jacob will erect another stone to commemorate a boundary agreement between himself and his future father-in-law (Genesis 31:46-53). In setting up this first stone, Jacob may be communicating to God that he accepts God's will for his life, including the boundary lines to the land that God has promised to Jacob's descendants.

REMEMBERING

Sixteen million U.S. citizens served in America's armed forces during World War II. More than 400,000 of them died.

Surprisingly, it took nearly 60 years for a monument to be built in Washington, D.C., to honor those who served in what has been called "the defining event of the twentieth century." Nevertheless, there is now a monument for those who fought in that war. These were common people called upon to make uncommon sacrifices and save the world from tyranny.

Erecting memorials is nothing new. This practice is seen in many cultures of many eras. Centuries ago, Jacob erected a stone memorial as a tribute to the God who turned his life in a new direction. Most war memorials today are constructed at sites far removed from where the events they commemorate took place. Not so with Jacob; he raised his stone at the very site where his life took its turn. It was a reminder of Jacob's vow that his life would be different from that point onward.

Today, God has already done the work of setting up "spiritual remembrance stones," if we can use that terminology. The Lord's Supper provides a frequent reminder of the work of Christ. Baptism is a tangible reminder of a person's decisive turn toward him. How do you use these two "spiritual remembrance stones" to draw ever closer to him?   —C. R. B.

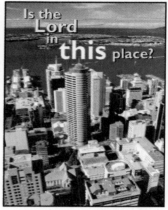

Visual for Lesson 7. *Start a discussion by asking, "How do you associate God's presence with the places you frequent?"*

19. He called that place Bethel, though the city used to be called Luz.

In parallel with the second part of Jacob's threefold affirmation of verses 16, 17, he renames *Luz* to be *Bethel.* The new name means "house of God." The name sticks. Future Israelites will remember its significance. Even God, when he later reappears to Jacob, identifies himself as "the God of Bethel" (Genesis 31:13).

Unfortunately, not all future Israelites will learn the lesson that Jacob learns there. Instead, they will set up idols and establish Bethel as a worship center to compete with Jerusalem. This will gain for Bethel a reputation of transgression (1 Kings 12:28-32; Hosea 10:15; Amos 4:4). How easy it is for later generations to forget! The fear is lost, the awe subsides, and another gift to God degenerates into an agent of idolatry.

C. WITH A VOW (vv. 20-22)

20-22. Then Jacob made a vow, saying, "If God will be with me and will watch over me on this journey I am taking and will give me food to eat and clothes to wear so that I return safely to my father's house, then the LORD will be my God and this stone that I have set up as a pillar will be God's house, and of all that you give me I will give you a tenth."

Jacob's vow is part three of his threefold affirmation of verses 16, 17. This vow may be interpreted in a wholly positive or somewhat negative way. Positively, we notice that Jacob officially accepts his father's God as his own and pledges to give him *a tenth* of all he will acquire, as Abraham did (Genesis 14:18-20). Negatively, Jacob seems to place conditions on his allegiance, saying if God does what he has promised (and more), then Jacob will worship him.

HOW TO SAY IT

Abraham. AY-bruh-ham.
Beersheba. Beer-SHE-buh.
Bethel. BETH-ul.
Canaan. KAY-nun.
Chaldeans. kal-DEE-unz.
Esau. EE-saw.
Haran. HAIR-un.
Laban. LAY-bun.
Luz. Luzz.
Terah. TAIR-uh.
Ur. Er.

PRAYER

"O God of Bethel, by Whose hand / Thy people still are fed, / Who through this weary pilgrimage / Hast all our fathers led.

"Our vows, our prayers, we now present / Before Thy throne of grace; / God of our fathers, be the God / Of their succeeding race.

"Through each perplexing path of life / Our wandering footsteps guide; / Give us each day our daily bread / And raiment fit provide.

"O spread Thy covering wings around / Till all our wanderings cease, / And at our Father's loved abode / Our souls arrive in peace" (Philip Doddridge, 1737).

In Jesus' name, amen.

WHAT DO YOU THINK?

Do you have your own sacred place—your own, private Bethel —where you meet God on a regular basis? What is it like? If you don't have one, what can you do to set one up? Or should you let God take the initiative in this regard?

We see Jacob specifying the elements of *food* and *clothes* along with God's already generous offer of continued blessing. One could construe Jacob's response as a desire to turn God's gracious gift—which is meant to be accepted and appreciated on God's terms—into a negotiation, with two parties jockeying for position.

Such jockeying, if that is indeed what is going on here, would hark back to Jacob's strained relations with Esau and would point forward to Jacob's strained relations with Laban. Indeed, God's later encounter with Jacob will be that of a wrestling match, after which Jacob is renamed *Israel,* meaning "one who wrestles with God."

So—is Jacob's vow the initial round of that wrestling match? Or is it a promising start to a committed, though imperfect, relationship? When Jacob finally arrives at his destination, God certainly uses Laban to teach Jacob a much-needed lesson about Jacob's cunning ways. But should we see that lesson as a response to Jacob's former life before Bethel or to his entire life, including his desire to strike a deal at Bethel?

It is not necessary for us to answer such questions with full confidence. But it is helpful to consider possible answers in light of God's future reflection on the Bethel encounter. Many years later, when it is time for Jacob to leave Haran and return home, God will remind Jacob of the vow he made and the rock he anointed at Bethel (Genesis 31:13). This will remind Jacob of a time of hope and a symbol of promises made and things to be fulfilled. So while it is possible to see Jacob's conditional vow as a symptom of flawed character, one may also see it as a turning point in his life. It is a time when he not only accepts God's gracious invitation but also takes concrete steps to apply it to his own situation.

Today we don't expect direct revelations from God in dreams. Even so, Christians have had "Bethel-like moments." These are times when God awakens us to his claim upon our lives. Can you identify moments like this in your own life?

CONCLUSION

Jacob was born into an important family that was chosen by God to do great things. Jacob knew from an early age that the day would come when he would be called to continue his family's legacy. Yet Jacob was far from perfect. At his best he listened, waited, and obeyed. At his worst he tried to force events along paths of his own choosing via human ingenuity and deceit.

Yet God was able to work through Jacob's worst moments. God showed his love for Jacob at Bethel by extending to him a promise that he did nothing to deserve. Jacob could have responded in all sorts of negative ways. Instead, Jacob recognized that the call was from God and responded with that fact in view.

Through Jesus Christ our Lord, God's invitation to join the people of promise—the church—has been extended to all. It matters not whether we are male or female, slave or free, Jew or Gentile. It matters not whether we grew up in a solid Christian home, in a "Christmas-and-Easter-only" religious environment, or in the belly of paganism. It matters not whether we were a respectful youth, raucous teen, or greedy business person. God's invitation confronts us where we are, regardless of where we have been.

Our past cannot stand in for us, whether good deeds, ideal parents, or worldly achievements. God lays claim to our present life and calls us to an eternity with him. Despite Jacob's imperfections, he responded to that call and took the necessary first step forward. God was certainly not finished working on him, but Jacob welcomed him in to begin that work. So must we.

THOUGHT TO REMEMBER
Respond to God today.

Discovery Learning

This page contains an alternative lesson plan emphasizing learning activities. Classes desiring such student involvement will find these suggestions helpful. The next page is a reproducible activity page to further enhance discovery learning.

INTO THE LESSON

Set up a 5' or 6' stepladder at the front of your class's space. On the rungs, set or attach the following objects: an EXIT sign, an angel figurine or doll, a pillow, a rock, a packet of seeds, a small replica of a crowd of people, a loaf of bread, a candle pillar/pedestal, a garment.

On the top step set a card that says, "Genesis 28:10-22." Say, "All the items here relate in some way to today's text. As the text is read, see whether you can make the associations."

INTO THE WORD

Recruit in advance one of your better readers to read the lesson text aloud. If possible, also recruit someone proficient in American Sign Language to sign the words as they are read; the text is graphically rich and will show itself well in signs.

After the reading, let your learners identify representations they see between the objects and the text. If there are any they cannot relate, use this list to help them: *EXIT sign,* verse 10 (as Jacob leaves his home); *pillow,* verse 11; *stairway,* verse 12; *angel figure,* verse 12; *descendants,* verses 13b and 14 (Jacob's seed spread abroad); *crowd of people,* verse 17 (the house of God); *bread,* verse 20; *candle pillar/pedestal,* verse 22 (the stone pillar set up); *a garment,* verse 20 (expressing Jacob's trusting God for clothes).

Explain, "One basic principle of biblical interpretation is that we must not quickly generalize or spiritualize when reading a Bible story and seeing God's intervention. I am going to make several generalizations related to today's text. I want you to decide whether each generalization is justifiable. Give me your reasoning."

Read each of the following generalizations and allow learners to react positively or negatively. (The activity is included in the optional student book.) 1. Having godly grandparents and godly parents does not make one godly. 2. When God has a special revelation to give, he will give it to you personally in a dream. 3. Angels ascending and descending on a stairway is a picture of Jesus coming to earth. 4. The land of Israel, which Jacob was leaving, was given perpetually to Jacob's descendants. 5. God could speak no sweeter words to a person than, "I am with you and will watch over you." 6. When one realizes that God is somehow meeting him or her, it

is both dreadful and delightful. 7. Setting up and dedicating a shrine to God is the right thing to do when one feels especially touched by him. 8. It is OK to bargain with God in a "something for something" (*quid pro quo*) manner, as Jacob did. 9. Jacob's example of committing a tenth of all that he had to God is a validation of the tithe as the required expectation in Christian giving. 10. God's faithfulness to his promises is never in doubt; ours always is.

INTO LIFE

Say, "The instructions for the direction that our lives should take comes to us in a manner different from God's direction for Jacob. How does God give us direction and assurance for our lives?" Let learners respond, assuming they will mention the Scriptures' primary role, plus open and closed doors of opportunity as secondary.

Comment on the answers. Then say, "Jacob's revelation was a divine intervention that came to him in words and images. In what way or ways is God's revelation to us today similar and dissimilar?" Learners should take note of the priority of God's written Word.

Distribute copies of the following personal-response list (also included in the optional student book). Suggest that learners use it for a time of self-evaluation sometime in their devotional lives in the coming week.

* *Often I find myself running away, as Jacob did, from the consequences of my behavior.*
* *Sometimes my sleep is restless because of conflicts in my interpersonal relationships.*
* *I am always glad to receive reassurances from God's Word regarding my future.*
* *Occasionally, I act as if I were not aware of God's presence where I am.*
* *I need to establish a "pillar" that reminds me of God's presence and blessing.*
* *I should think of every place as Bethel, the house of God.*
* *I have full confidence that God will provide my daily needs for food, clothing, and housing.*
* *I am committed to returning a significant portion of God's material blessings for use in the work of his kingdom.*

Options: If you wish to emphasize the Into Life segment, use either or both of the activities on the reproducible page as time allows.

Separated but Accessible

When God showed Jacob a ladder, it became clear that Jacob was separated from God. But God was making himself accessible in a certain way. On the rungs of this ladder, write in some ways that God has made himself available or accessible to you with all his power and righteousness. A sample is given to get you started.

God has inspired and protected his Word.

Promises, Promises

In Genesis 28:13b-15, God makes grand promises to Jacob when God challenges him to believe and serve him as his father and grandfather did. Rank-order the following from 1 (most important) to 6 (least important) in what you think was their value in Jacob's mind when he heard them.

_____ "I will give you and your descendants the land on which you are lying."

_____ "Your descendants will be like the dust of the earth, and you will spread out to the west and to the east, to the north and to the south."

_____ "All peoples on earth will be blessed through you and your offspring."

_____ "I am with you and will watch over you wherever you go."

_____ "I will bring you back to this land."

_____ "I will not leave you until I have done what I promised you."

Now go back and reorder them as you think Jacob *should* have valued them, based on your own 20/20 hindsight of Bible history. Is there a difference in your ordering? Why, or why not?

Though some doubt God's keeping of his promises (see 2 Peter 3:4), we live with the grand promise of 2 Peter 3:13, a verse worthy of memorization. Find and write that life-sustaining promise here:

_____

_____

_____

JACOB AND RACHEL

LESSON 8

WHY TEACH THIS LESSON?

Think about this saying: "We must learn from others' mistakes. We don't have time to make all the mistakes on our own." Now try this one: "There are two ways to learn things: by wisdom and by experience. Wisdom is when you learn from the mistakes of others; experience is when you learn from your own." Despite these truths, we often fail to learn from the mistakes of others. So we blunder along, to our own hurt. One of those hurts occurs when we we try to bend and manipulate God to our will rather than allowing him to bend us to his.

Your learners need that lesson for their entire lives. In that light, today's lesson offers us a snippet of the agony of one whose "do it my way" lifestyle boomeranged on him. Many learners of your learners will relate to this. The best news from this lesson is that God doesn't give up on us. He disciplines us to shape us.

INTRODUCTION

A. ACTIONS AND CONSEQUENCES

If you want to spark an interesting discussion among Christians, ask people to share testimonies of discipline that may have been divine in origin. I have done this in various settings, and the results are both amusing and instructive.

The essential storyline often goes something like this: "When my coworkers, neighbors, or schoolmates engage in various 'low-profile' sins, whether speeding, shoplifting, or cheating on their taxes, they seldom get caught and often appear to benefit from their choices. For the most part, I resist such practices due to my faith and convictions. But the one time I decided to join their iniquity, I was caught red-handed and had to bear the shame."

I know this to be true in my own life. The one time I lied to my boss, I was exposed. The one time I joined my friends in an act of theft, we all got busted. The one time I drag-raced my buddies, the radar gun nailed me. It is not like I engaged in these activities all the time only to have my actions finally catch up with me. No, these were flukes. They were one-time acts of rebellion, and, without fail, I never got away with them—and it's a good thing too!

Scripture teaches that God disciplines those whom he loves (Hebrews 12:5, 6). God loves us so much that he will not allow us to avoid consequences (immediately or eventually) when we tread sinful paths. We should not be alarmed when we do not escape cleanly from sinful endeavors. We should be deeply concerned, however, if we *do* continue to get away easily.

If discipline is a sign of divine love (and it often is), then God certainly loved Jacob. In today's lesson, God allows Jacob to suffer twice in order to straighten his crooked path.

B. LESSON BACKGROUND

Last week we saw God shower his grace on Jacob by meeting him at Bethel. There God extended the promise he had made to Jacob's grandfather Abraham.

DEVOTIONAL READING:
PSALM 91

BACKGROUND SCRIPTURE:
GENESIS 29

PRINTED TEXT:
GENESIS 29:21-35

LESSON AIMS

After participating in this lesson, each student will be able to:

1. Describe Jacob's family life.

2. Compare and contrast marriage customs of Jacob's time with those of today.

3. Write a prayer committing some disappointing circumstance in life into God's hand and seeking guidance for dealing with the situation in a positive manner.

Oct
21

KEY VERSE

So Jacob served seven years to get Rachel, but they seemed like only a few days to him because of his love for her. —Genesis 29:20

LESSON 8 NOTES

Despite Jacob's legacy of deception, God gave him the honor of being the father of the chosen people through whom God would bless all nations. Jacob accepted this offer. Then he continued his northward journey to escape Esau and to acquire a wife from his mother's household.

In Genesis 29 we learn that Jacob arrived safely in Haran and was graciously welcomed into the household of his uncle Laban. Since Jacob would be staying for a while, working arrangements had to be made. Jacob had fallen for Rachel, the younger and more attractive of Laban's two daughters. So he offered to work seven years in exchange for Rachel's hand in marriage. Typically, the groom was obligated to offer some kind of "bride price" to the bride's family. This would offset the work production the family would be losing by giving their daughter in marriage. In this case, seven years of labor was an agreeable arrangement to both parties, so a deal was made.

Jacob was so enamored with Rachel that the years seemed to fly by (Genesis 29:20). Jacob was then ready to claim his bride, pack his bags, and head back home to the promised land. Things could not have been going better for Jacob, but God was not finished with him. Jacob's character was about to be forged in the fire of divine discipline.

I. JACOB'S DECEPTION RETURNED (GENESIS 29:21-27)

A. JACOB'S INTENT (vv. 21, 22)

21. Then Jacob said to Laban, "Give me my wife. My time is completed, and I want to lie with her."

After Jacob's years of service pass, he seems to demand that his *wife* be given to him. There are at least three ways this abruptness may be understood. First, the author may be summarizing concisely what was actually a much more pleasant exchange. Second, *Jacob* may be showing his eagerness to finally consummate his long-awaited marriage. Third, Jacob's tone may reflect tension that has somehow arisen between him and *Laban*. Perhaps the two of them do not have a healthy working relationship. Whatever the case, the ruse that Laban is about to pull on Jacob certainly indicates that the relationship between the two is about to get worse!

Jacob calls Rachel his *wife* not simply because they are about to be married. In Jacob's day, a woman has the legal status of "wife" during the betrothal period.

22. So Laban brought together all the people of the place and gave a feast.

Ancient Near Eastern weddings are not one-day events. They often involve a week of feasting, attended by the families being brought together in the marriage.

There is no evidence to indicate that Jacob's family back in Canaan is able to attend the wedding or that they even know of the event. This is important. Were Isaac and Rebekah present, Jacob would not be as vulnerable to the deception that *Laban* is plotting. Thus far, however, Jacob is oblivious to Laban's scheme.

B. LABAN'S DECEPTION (vv. 23-25)

23. But when evening came, he took his daughter Leah and gave her to Jacob, and Jacob lay with her.

How, we may wonder, is Laban able to pass off *Leah* for Rachel? Would not Jacob know the truth simply by looking at her?

Two factors may account for Jacob's oversight. The first factor is lighting—or lack thereof. We are told that Laban brought Leah to Jacob in the *evening*. In an age before electricity, the darkness of evening is much more pronounced than what we experience today.

The dim lighting is only compounded by the fact that women often wear veils on their wedding day. In Genesis 24:65 we see Rebekah (Laban's sister) veiling herself lest she be seen prematurely by her groom-to-be, Isaac.

24. And Laban gave his servant girl Zilpah to his daughter as her maidservant.

It is customary for parents, especially those who are wealthy, to give wedding gifts to their daughters. A *maidservant* is certainly a generous gift! This indicates that whatever tension may exist between Laban and Jacob, Laban still loves *his daughter* and seeks to bless her. Our introduction to *Zilpah* is important because Leah later gives her to Jacob for the purposes of bearing additional children (Genesis 30:9-13). Leah's handmaid thus becomes mother to two of the twelve tribes of Israel—no small role for a servant.

25. When morning came, there was Leah! So Jacob said to Laban, "What is this you have done to me? I served you for Rachel, didn't I? Why have you deceived me?"

The next *morning* Jacob discovers that he has been tricked. Naturally, he is appalled. But the reader has a hard time feeling sorry for him. We remember from Genesis 27 that it was Jacob who took advantage of his father's inability to see clearly in pretending to be Esau. The one who had deceived his own father is the one who is now *deceived* himself. Although we cannot approve of the deception practiced by Laban, and we rightly recognize that two wrongs don't make a right, perhaps we see the divine hand at work: God allows Jacob to be deceived. This brings consequences on Jacob in a "what goes around comes around" kind of way. Is this divine payback for Jacob's past behavior?

"IT SERVED HIM RIGHT"

"What goes around comes around." "He had it coming to him." "It served him right." People have various ways of acknowledging the repayment of evil when they think they see it.

But what if you wish to help out with the revenge? Lucky you! A psychic web site offers a "Get Even Voodoo & Revenge Spell" to pay back someone who has done you wrong—all for a mere $39 (plus $7.25 for shipping). Of course, for those times when someone is trying to do the same to you, there is a "Self-Protection Voodoo & Revenge Spell" for the same price.

All of this is based on the faulty assumptions that life is subject to the various whims of forces ruling the universe and that all one needs is a little cash to employ or survive their onslaught. That's quite a stretch from the biblical view of God! It is he who works (or allows) what will ultimately be the best for us. Laban's deception may have "served Jacob right," but it wasn't fictitious karma at work.   —C. R. B

C. LABAN'S JUSTIFICATION (v. 26)

26. Laban replied, "It is not our custom here to give the younger daughter in marriage before the older one.

The irony continues! Jacob, who disrespected the significance of birth order by manipulating Esau into handing over his birthright (Genesis 25:27-33), is now manipulated by *Laban* into honoring the order of birthright. We are not told that Laban knows about Jacob's earlier misdeeds, but here Laban attempts to justify his own actions.

Laban informs Jacob that birth order must not be violated in his land. He is almost saying to Jacob, "Maybe you do that kind of thing down in your country, but up here we keep to our principles." If that's the case, then Laban is tacitly admitting that birth order takes precedence over honesty. In any case, we cannot resist thinking that Jacob recognizes that he is "reaping what he sowed" for deceiving his father and taking advantage of his brother.

WHAT DO YOU THINK?

What was a time when an old sin came back to haunt you? How did God's love and grace see you through that situation?

WHAT DO YOU THINK?

Were you ever guilty of manipulating circumstances or people to achieve selfish desires? How did God enable you to put this kind of sinful practice in the past?

HOW TO SAY IT

Abraham. AY-bruh-ham.

Bilhah. BILL-ha.

Esau. EE-saw.

Judah. JOO-duh.

Laban. LAY-bun.

Levi. LEE-vye.

Naphtali. NAF-tuh-lye.

Reuben. ROO-ben.

Simeon. SIM-ee-un.

Zilpah. ZIL-pa.

BOUND BY TRADITION?

One of the vices of each younger generation is the compulsion to try everything that is new. However, one of the vices of each older generation is the refusal to try *anything* new! Someone has said that the seven last words of the church are, "We've never done it that way before." Many congregations shrivel up and die because they refuse to consider any new way of doing things.

Tradition can be a good thing. It can keep us from hastily jumping on the bandwagon of every new idea that comes along. But tradition becomes the deadly weight of *traditionalism* when we allow it to anchor us in the past. That can prevent us from following God in new paths where he may want us to walk. For example, traditionalism can keep us from singing new music. On the other hand, always doing something different just because it is different results in a kind of traditionalism in and of itself!

Unfortunately for Jacob (and Leah!), Laban allowed a cultural tradition to sacrifice the principle of honesty. Couldn't Laban have mentioned to Jacob the birth-order tradition up front, before Jacob's seven years of service started? Whether we keep traditions or break them, God expects us to base our actions on principles of integrity and holiness. —C. R. B.

D. LABAN'S CONCESSION (v. 27)

27. "Finish this daughter's bridal week; then we will give you the younger one also, in return for another seven years of work."

Laban now makes a slight concession to Jacob. He could demand that Jacob serve him an additional *seven years* first and be allowed to have Rachel only afterward. Instead, he allows Jacob to marry Rachel immediately after Leah's weeklong marital celebration is concluded, with the seven additional years of work to follow. (See Judges 14:12, 17 for an example of another weeklong wedding feast.) This plan may satisfy Jacob's longing for Rachel, but it severely strains Jacob's marital relationships, as future events will demonstrate.

II. JACOB'S FAVORITISM BACKFIRES (GENESIS 29:28-35)

A. LABAN'S ACTION (vv. 28, 29)

28, 29. And Jacob did so. He finished the week with Leah, and then Laban gave him his daughter Rachel to be his wife. Laban gave his servant girl Bilhah to his daughter Rachel as her maidservant.

Laban's deception reveals a flaw in his character, regardless of how he justifies his decision. He does not have to choose between honoring birthright priorities and being forthright with Jacob up front. He could have both (1) informed Jacob of the birthright principle and (2) required him to honor them. Be that as it may, *Laban* does honor this second agreement with Jacob.

As with Leah, Laban gives a *maidservant* to *Rachel. Bilhah*, like Zilpah, is more than a generous wedding gift. She will also become mother of two tribes of Israel, namely Dan and Naphtali (Genesis 30:1-8).

B. GOD'S INTERVENTION (vv. 30, 31)

30. Jacob lay with Rachel also, and he loved Rachel more than Leah. And he worked for Laban another seven years.

Jacob keeps his part of the bargain by serving *seven more years*. Jacob's marriage to *Rachel* becomes official with both the arrangement by Laban and the act of sexual intercourse (he *lay with Rachel also*). Jacob knows that sexual intercourse is the event chosen by God for the two to become one flesh (Genesis 2:24; Matthew 19:4-6).

WHAT DO YOU THINK?

Seven more years! In what areas has love for Christ driven you to go the second mile (or the second year)? What was a time when someone else went the second mile with you or for you?

This means that ideally there is no such thing as premarital or extramarital sex for our forefathers of the faith. All sex is intended to be marital. This is why Paul insisted that the young men in Corinth not sleep with prostitutes. Such men thought they were simply meeting physical needs or desires. But Paul reminded them of the issue of becoming one flesh (1 Corinthians 6:15, 16).

We also see in this verse that Jacob clearly favors Rachel above *Leah*. On the one hand, we cannot blame him for this. He did not choose Leah, but was tricked into marrying her.

On the other hand, however, we recall that the favoritism of his parents contributed to the feuding between Jacob and his brother, Esau (Genesis 25:28). Had Isaac not favored Esau and had Rebekah not favored Jacob—had the two parents loved both children equally—then perhaps Jacob would not be exiled from his homeland while Esau's temper cools. So Jacob continues the unhealthy pattern of favoritism set by his parents. That poor choice warrants divine attention.

31. When the LORD saw that Leah was not loved, he opened her womb, but Rachel was barren.

Leah may be the firstborn daughter, but she is second place in Jacob's eyes. She is *not loved* by her husband, and her physical appearance is somehow inferior to that of her sister (Genesis 29:17). Yet God sometimes chooses to exalt those of whom little is expected. In the case at hand, his intervention favors Leah.

We see this pattern of intervention on God's part again later in Moses, the man who could not speak very well. We also see intervention with Gideon, the least in his family. God does not need "great" people to do his work, and that gives hope to ordinary folks like us.

God's method of blessing in the case at hand is simple: He ensures that Leah is fertile and *Rachel is barren*. Jacob may prefer Rachel as a companion, but he also needs a wife who will give him sons. His future livelihood depends on it, as does the promise that God gave him.

C. LEAH'S SONS (vv. 32-35)

32. Leah became pregnant and gave birth to a son. She named him Reuben, for she said, "It is because the LORD has seen my misery. Surely my husband will love me now."

Reuben is the first of six sons that God will give *Leah*. This is all that a woman in her time and situation can ask for. When God's blessings rain down, they pour!

Notice, however, that the first three sons are given names that reflect her husband's continued neglect. The name *Reuben* is made from two words that mean, "to see" and "a son." With this name she highlights how God has seen her affliction and how she hopes that her *husband* will begin to appreciate her because of this son.

33. She conceived again, and when she gave birth to a son she said, "Because the LORD heard that I am not loved, he gave me this one too." So she named him Simeon.

Apparently Jacob does not show Leah his appreciation, because she names her next son *Simeon*. This name is built from the word meaning "to hear." This name thus reflects her acknowledgment that God has *heard* about how her husband continues to disregard her.

34. Again she conceived, and when she gave birth to a son she said, "Now at last my husband will become attached to me, because I have borne him three sons." So he was named Levi.

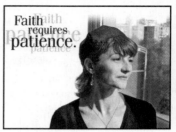

Visual for Lesson 8. *Ask for volunteers to explain why the statement on this visual is true. Follow their response by asking for examples.*

WHAT DO YOU THINK?

How does God continue to show his concern for those the world looks down on? What is your part in meeting the needs of those considered to be "the downtrodden"?

WHAT DO YOU THINK?

What was a time when God blessed you in a time of affliction? What has his blessing meant to you since that time?

God of Abraham, Isaac, and Jacob, we come to you humbly and thank you for your discipline. It can be terribly uncomfortable to be on the receiving end of that discipline, yet there is no place more valuable to be. Thank you for not abandoning us. May we submit to your discipline when you bring it, lest in resisting it we find ourselves resisting you. In Jesus' name, amen.

The second son, Simeon, also is not enough to gain Jacob's favor. So Leah names her third son *Levi*, meaning "joined." By this she expects that her husband will now *become attached* more fully to her emotionally.

35. She conceived again, and when she gave birth to a son she said, "This time I will praise the LORD." So she named him Judah. Then she stopped having children.

With Leah's fourth *son* comes an important shift in tone. Leah feels no longer compelled to name her sons with reference to Jacob's disfavor. Instead, she turns her attention to God's favor. She realizes that although she may never receive her husband's emotional affection, she is clearly loved by God. For this reason, she names her fourth son *Judah*, meaning "praise."

Leah's childbearing days do not end at this point (see Genesis 30:17-21). But this particular phase, marked by the words *then she stopped having children*, ends on a high note. God is praised, and the tribe that descends from Judah will become Israel's royal line from which will come David and Jesus. In retrospect we now see that Jesus descended from a fourth-born son of a neglected wife of a swindling man (Jacob) of a second-born son (Isaac) of a wandering pilgrim (Abraham). Praise God for his marvelous deeds!

CONCLUSION

One may assume—based on the dream at Bethel, the warm reception at Haran, and the immediate identification of a worthy spouse—that Jacob had the world by the tail. All he had to do was wait a few years for Esau to drop his grudge. Meanwhile Jacob would marry the woman of his dreams and return home to claim Abraham's promise.

But just when it seemed that Jacob was free and clear, God allowed events to take an unexpected course. With a level of deception equal only to Jacob's own, Laban taught Jacob a lesson in integrity (although lesson-teaching probably was not Laban's intent). Jacob eventually had to reckon also with the legacy of his parents: the favoritism he inherited from them, which he assimilated into his own marital relationships.

We wish we could say that Jacob "learned his lesson" fully. We wish we could say that he never again deceived or stooped to divisive favoritism. But he did. He later tricked Laban out of livestock (Genesis 30:37-43) and played favorites with Rachel's oldest son (37:3, 4).

But God still refused to abandon Jacob. Instead, he allowed Jacob's bad decisions to blow up in his face (sometimes called *natural consequences* today). Jacob and Laban parted company after a dangerous encounter (Genesis 31). Jacob was forced to bow before the brother who was supposed to serve him (33:3). Jacob's favorite wife died in childbirth (35:16-20). Eleven of his sons deceived him into thinking that his favorite son, Joseph, was dead (37:12-35). Indeed, Jacob lived a long, hard life of wrestling with God and people—thus God's new name *Israel* for him, meaning, "he struggles with God" (32:22-28).

To struggle with God is a gift of grace to us. It means that God has not abandoned us; he is still there for us to struggle with. It means that despite our imperfections God continues to guide and shape us. Divine discipline may not be our preferred means of relating to God, but at least it means the relationship is active.

We should not, however, intentionally provoke divine discipline. Our God is still a consuming fire (Hebrews 12:29); he will not be toyed with. Furthermore, Jacob would not wish his struggles on anyone else. I suspect he would much rather we learn from his mistakes, submit to God, and enjoy more of the blessings that God showers on those who seek to please him.

THOUGHT TO REMEMBER

Receive the Lord's discipline as a gift.

Discovery Learning

This page contains an alternative lesson plan emphasizing learning activities. Classes desiring such student involvement will find these suggestions helpful. The next page is a reproducible activity page to further enhance discovery learning.

INTO THE LESSON

Display this old saying for learners to see as they arrive: "What goes around comes around." Underneath, have these choices displayed: (A) a universal truth, without question; (B) wishful thinking, for the vindictive; (C) an observation of farmers having livestock in corrals or pens; (D) a simple description of seasons and weather patterns, based on Earth's shape and orbit; (E) a matter of divine discipline, both in this life and the next.

Ask your learners to choose which of those labels they think best fits the old saying. After they defend their answers, say, "Today's study is a 'what goes around comes around' story. In this story, the deceiver Jacob is thoroughly deceived by his kinsman Laban. Let's see if there's any legitimate use of the old expression."

Say, "To understand the story in today's text of Genesis 29:21-35, one must know the beginning, found in verses 1-20 of the chapter." Recruit in advance readers for each of these parts: narrator, Jacob, shepherds (one may represent), and Laban. Give them labels to wear around their necks. Each may stand as he reads his part.

Narrator reads verses 1-3.
Jacob reads verse 4a.
Shepherd reads verse 4b.
Jacob reads verse 5a.
Shepherd reads verse 5b.
Jacob reads verse 6a.
Shepherd reads verse 6b.
Jacob reads verse 7.
Shepherd reads verse 8.
Narrator reads verses 9-13.
Laban reads verse 14a.
Narrator reads verse 14b.
Laban reads verse 15.
Narrator reads verses 16-18a.
Jacob reads verse 18b.
Laban reads verse 19.
Narrator reads verse 20.

INTO THE WORD

Next, say, "Now we're ready for today's text. It's a text that has two key players, both of whom were known to play fast and loose with the truth. But first of all, we want to make sure that we ourselves don't play fast and loose with the truths of the story." Give each learner a copy of the statements below. Tell them that these statements include factual errors that they are to find and correct. (Work in teams, if desired.)

1. Jacob asked Laban to give him his wages and health insurance, as he wanted to marry Leah.

2. Laban gathered together all the men of the city and declared a fast.

3. After dark, Laban took Leah, his daughter, and brought her to Jacob with Jacob's full knowledge and consent.

4. In the daylight, Jacob saw that Laban had played a trick, so Jacob reminded Laban that he had served nine years for Rachel.

5. Laban told Jacob that his country never gave the older before the younger.

6. Jacob promised to serve for seven more months.

7. Jacob loved Rachel just as much as Leah, and served Laban for the seven additional months.

8. When the Lord saw that Rachel was loved, he opened her womb, but Leah had to wait.

As learners note the corrections, you will have opportunity to make teaching points from the lesson commentary. *Options:* Use the Nearsighted Scribe activity on the reproducible page in place of the above. Use the Love and Its Consequences activity as an additional exercise if you wish to stress this segment.

INTO LIFE

Gather empty 7-Up® cans for the following application activity, one per learner. Asking around in advance may identify someone who will save the cans for you. Also provide slips of paper that can be rolled and passed through the openings on the tops of the can.

Say, "Jacob worked seven years for the hand of Rachel. He was 'up, up, up' the whole time, because of his deep love for her. Imagine how far 'down, down, down' he fell on the morning he awoke to find Leah beside him. Then he had to think, 'Seven years down, seven years to go' when Laban offered him Rachel.

"Use your 7-Up® can this week to remind you of today's study. For some major disappointment you have had, consider writing it on the slip, rolling it up, putting it in the can, standing the can upside down, and saying, 'Lord, this disappointment has kept me down too long. Help me up by your Spirit.'"

Nearsighted Scribe

Consider the following rendition of parts of Genesis 29:21-31 to be the work of a nearsighted scribe who has failed to include some words. Make all the corrections you can without looking at your Bible. Then check your Bible to see how accurate you are.

Then Jacob said to _____, "Give me my _____. My time is _____, and I want to lie with her."

So _____ brought together all the people of the place and gave a feast. But when evening came, he took his daughter _____ and gave her to _____, and Jacob lay with her. And Laban gave his servant girl _____ to his daughter as her _____.

When _____ came, there was _____! So Jacob said to Laban, "What is this you have done to me? I served you for _____, didn't I? Why have you deceived ___?"

Laban replied, "It is not our custom here to give the _____ daughter in marriage before the _____ one. Finish this daughter's bridal _____; then we will give you the younger one also, in return for another seven _____ of work."

And Jacob did so. He finished the week with _____, and then Laban gave him his daughter _____ to be his wife. Laban gave his servant girl _____ to his daughter Rachel as her maidservant. Jacob lay with Rachel also, and he loved Rachel more than Leah. And he worked for Laban another seven years.

When the Lord saw that Leah was not _____, he opened her _____, but Rachel was _____.

Love and Its Consequences

Here are some sayings. Which of these do you see reflected in Genesis 29? Which do you find to be true in a positive way? Which do you find to be true in a negative way (that is, as warnings)? Which do you find to be untrue altogether? Why?

"When love is deep, time is short."

"True love works hard for the object of that love."

"Love is blind, but lovers aren't."

"Love sometimes gets in the way of in-laws; in-laws sometimes get in the way of love."

"Love is always worth a celebration."

"Love is not deterred by disappointment."

"Lack of attention is a certain sign of lack of love."

God Creates
Unit 2: God's People Increase
(Lessons 6-9)

ESAU AND JACOB RECONCILED

WHY TEACH THIS LESSON?

I watched my neighbor guide her two small children following a dispute over a toy. She told the offender to go to the other child, speak directly to him and say, "I'm sorry." The child obeyed. She then coached the offended child to say, "I forgive you." How I marveled at the latter! For me, those words stick to the roof of my mouth even when sincere apologies flow.

Reconciliation is God's way. Yet this hard truth accompanies reconciliation attempts: There are no guarantees when we try to repair relationships. Apologies and paybacks may be rejected. But in cases where the humility of the wrongdoer meets the grace of the one wronged, the results are priceless.

INTRODUCTION

A. STORIES OF ESTRANGEMENT

A man and his wife have not spoken in days. One too many times she embarrassed him in public, and one too many times he responded harshly. Even though they share the same bed, a cold gap remains between them.

Two coworkers communicate only indirectly through other employees. One too many times an idea was stolen, and one too many times others were recruited to take sides. Though they occupy adjacent offices, genuine collaboration is out of the question.

Tales of wounded pride are all too common. Each of us is familiar with a close relationship that was threatened by an unfortunate conflict caused by one party's lapse of judgment and another party's defensive retaliation. Scripture does not teach us that following Jesus means that Christians will live lives free of conflict. It does show us, however, a way to overcome.

Matthew 18 and other New Testament passages provide principles and procedures for seeking genuine reconciliation. The Old Testament furnishes stories of success and failure that bring these principles to life. Today we consider one such story.

B. LESSON BACKGROUND

The feud between Jacob and Esau began at an early age. Even in the womb, these boys jockeyed for position. The struggle was so intense that their mother, Rebekah, thought it was necessary to ask God for an explanation.

God informed her that two "nations" were in her womb and that the older would serve the younger (Genesis 25:23). This jockeying for position continued at their birth. Although Esau emerged as the firstborn, Jacob was clutching at his heel even as he left the womb. This prenatal rivalry was later compounded by parental favoritism (Genesis 25:27, 28).

DEVOTIONAL READING:
PSALM 133

BACKGROUND SCRIPTURE:
GENESIS 33

PRINTED TEXT:
GENESIS 33:1-11

LESSON AIMS

After participating in this lesson, each student will be able to:

1. Describe the reunion of Jacob and Esau.

2. Identify the facts of Jacob's humility in the reunion story.

3. Make a plan for reconciliation to one person estranged from him or her.

Oct 28

KEY VERSE

Esau ran to meet Jacob and embraced him; he threw his arms around his neck and kissed him. And they wept. —Genesis 33:4

LESSON 9 NOTES

As the boys grew older, the tension mounted. On one occasion, Jacob manipulated Esau into trading his birthright for stew (Genesis 25:29-34). On another, Jacob and Rebekah tricked Isaac into conferring his fatherly blessing on Jacob instead of Esau (Genesis 27:1-40). This was the breaking point in the brothers' relationship. Having been tricked twice, Esau planned to kill Jacob after their father passed away (Genesis 27:41).

This prompted Jacob to flee northward. His relocation gave Esau the time and space he needed to cool off (Genesis 27:42-45). But the plan took much more time than Jacob had anticipated. Laban, his father-in-law, tricked him into staying twice as long as he had planned. Then Jacob stuck around for several more years to gain enough wealth to head back home. So after 20 years of self-exile (Genesis 31:38), Jacob finally began his perilous journey home.

The first obstacle he faced was Laban. The two of them had a falling out, and it took divine intervention to allow Jacob to leave in peace (Genesis 31:29). Then, upon reaching the border of the promised land, Jacob encountered a second obstacle: an angelic messenger who wrestled with him all night (32:22-32). Before leaving, this wrestling angel blessed Jacob by renaming him *Israel*, which means "one who struggles with God." Surviving this heavenly opponent prepared Jacob for his most intimidating human foe: a potentially vengeful Esau.

I. JACOB APPROACHES ESAU (GENESIS 33:1-3)

A. JACOB SEES ESAU (v. 1a)

1a. Jacob looked up and there was Esau, coming with his four hundred men;

By this point, *Jacob* has taken two precautionary measures to increase his chances of surviving the encounter with *Esau*. First, Jacob has sent messengers ahead with gifts of appeasement (Genesis 32:3-5). Second, he has divided his group into two camps (Genesis 32:7); should those in one camp die by the sword, the others might escape.

The sight Jacob now sees must be terrifying. He undoubtedly wonders why Esau is bringing along such a large escort. This is certainly not a typical homecoming party! Is Esau trying to protect himself, or is he planning to attack Jacob? As readers, we experience this episode much like Jacob: we have no clue what Esau will do next.

B. JACOB PREPARES TO MEET ESAU (vv. 1b, 2)

1b, 2. . . . so he divided the children among Leah, Rachel and the two maidservants. He put the maidservants and their children in front, Leah and her children next, and Rachel and Joseph in the rear.

Again Jacob divides his camp, this time according to preference. Those he loves least head the procession. In Genesis 29:30-35 we saw Jacob's greater love for *Rachel* despite Leah's status as first wife and mother of his first sons. This ranking, then, appears to be for protection, since it provides Jacob's favored family members with a head start in case a battle breaks out (32:8). It can also, however, be a matter of protocol: as Jacob introduces his loved ones to Esau, perhaps he wishes "to save the best for last."

C. JACOB BOWS BEFORE ESAU (v. 3)

3. He himself went on ahead and bowed down to the ground seven times as he approached his brother.

Here we see that Jacob is no coward. He could remain with Rachel and Joseph at the end of the procession, but instead he places himself on the front line.

WHAT DO YOU THINK?

What motives do people have for placing some things or certain family members at greater risk? How can we improve our motives and strengthen our faith in this regard?

More importantly, however, Jacob bows before *his brother,* Esau. This action is doubly significant. On the one hand, it stands out as a model for those seeking to initiate reconciliation. Jacob has deeply wounded Esau in the past. Realizing this, Jacob comes humbly, begging forgiveness. Even though Jacob may feel justified in his past actions, and even though 20 years have elapsed, Jacob still comes humbly as if he had committed the offense only the day before. He sets aside pride to prostrate himself before Esau—not just once, but *seven times.* His bowing is not a superficial act, but is an act of complete contrition and submission.

On the other hand, Jacob's bowing stands out in this story because the blessing Jacob stole from Esau seemed to indicate that Esau would be the one bowing before Jacob (Genesis 27:29). To be sure, the Edomites, who descend from Esau, will have to submit (bow) to the Israelites, who descend from Jacob. But between Esau and Jacob personally, this apparently doesn't happen in their lifetimes. Only Jacob does the bowing.

This teaches Jacob (and us) an important lesson about divine promises: the promises God makes concerning his people are not always experienced firsthand by the initial recipients of the promise. Abraham was told that he would become a great nation, that he would inhabit the promised land, and that all nations of the earth would be blessed through him. Yet Abraham did not see this promise realized in his own lifetime.

God knows that Jacob's descendants will become *Israel,* God's special people. God also knows that Esau's descendants will become *Edom,* a less powerful nation that will be made subject to Jacob's descendants (especially David, 2 Samuel 8:14). So, in the long run, the blessing will come to fruition, as will the promise to Abraham. But Jacob "jumped the gun" and tried to force matters down a path of his own choosing. The result of his antics? Jacob bows before Esau.

God's purposes will not be thwarted despite human shenanigans. After 20 difficult years, God brings Jacob and Esau's relationship back into proper alignment. Now that Jacob is "at the bottom," God can use him to do great things.

This verse teaches us three lessons. First, humility may be central to reconciliation. It's not always about who is more right or wrong—it often is about swallowing our pride so God may bring peace. Second, it is dangerous to personalize God's promises strictly. God has made many promises to the church, but not all of us will experience all of them in our lifetimes. Third, those who exalt themselves will be humbled by God (compare Luke 14:11; 18:14). We are to be patient and faithful until God elevates us in his own timing.

FOLLY OF PRIDE, WISDOM OF HUMILITY

In 1980, Robert Graham created the Repository for Germinal Choice—what some came to call the Nobel Prize sperm bank. Graham, the inventor of shatterproof plastic eyeglasses, believed the repository could improve the human race. Women could choose the father of their babies from the genius-level contributors to the repository. However, not many women were interested. In 19 years, only 215 children were born through the repository's efforts.

One outspoken donor and supporter was William Shockley, who had won a Nobel Prize in 1956 for his work on the transistor. He was reputed to be a racist who promoted the idea of tampering with genetics to accomplish his vision. His loud advocacy of both the repository and his racist views brought derision to the organization. It closed in 1999.

Pride—whether in one's accomplishments, genes, or wealth—is evidence of misplaced values. Pride fosters arrogance. Humility is a much better way to relate to God and to others. After pride had forced Jacob and Esau apart, Jacob's humble

"How pleasant it is for brethren to dwell together in unity."
—Psalm 133:1

Visual for Lesson 9. *Point to this visual as you ask, "Why is unity important to the church?" Explore the difference between* unity *and* uniformity.

WHAT DO YOU THINK?

In what areas of your life do you need to come humbly before another, seeking forgiveness? What responsibility do offended parties have to express their hurt?

approach to his brother initiated the reconciliation process. Is there an area of your relationships where a humble approach could work in a similar way?   —C. R. B.

II. ESAU RECEIVES JACOB (GENESIS 33:4-7)

A. BROTHERS EMBRACE (v. 4)

4. But Esau ran to meet Jacob and embraced him; he threw his arms around his neck and kissed him. And they wept.

Like the father in the story of the prodigal son (Luke 15:11-32), *Esau* runs to embrace his "prodigal brother." Jacob cannot imagine a warmer greeting. Emotions pour from them both. We see tears of joy and reconciliation.

But is it all too good to be true? The last man who *ran* out, *embraced*, and *kissed* Jacob was Laban (Genesis 29:13). Laban then proceeded to deal with Jacob in a less-than-honest fashion for 20 years. Jacob certainly appreciates this warm reception from Esau, but the reconciliation is not yet complete.

B. JACOB INTRODUCES (v. 5)

5. Then Esau looked up and saw the women and children. "Who are these with you?" he asked.

Jacob answered, "They are the children God has graciously given your servant."

Esau is the first to speak. He is likely aware that these people are Jacob's family, thus his question is rhetorical. The question gives Jacob an opportunity to introduce his family properly. Note that Jacob refers to himself as Esau's *servant*. This reinforces his own humility.

C. FAMILY BOWS (vv. 6, 7)

6, 7. Then the maidservants and their children approached and bowed down. Next, Leah and her children came and bowed down. Last of all came Joseph and Rachel, and they too bowed down.

Not only does Jacob bow before Esau, the members of his entire entourage humble themselves in this manner. This reinforces the completeness of Jacob's contrition.

III. JACOB AND ESAU RECONCILE (GENESIS 33:8-11)

A. PEACE OFFERING EXPLAINED (v. 8)

8. Esau asked, "What do you mean by all these droves I met?"

"To find favor in your eyes, my lord," he said.

Esau is still in the driver's seat, thus he asks all the questions. Of course, he already knows why Jacob sent the gifts; the envoys Jacob sent ahead relayed that message previously (Genesis 32:4, 5). But Esau also knows it is necessary that he and Jacob have this conversation—a conversation that must take place face to face. Jacob not only submits to this line of questioning, he also defers to Esau as *my lord*. Jacob's intentions are clear: he seeks *favor*, which, in this case, means forgiveness of past wrongs.

B. PEACE OFFERING DECLINED (v. 9)

9. But Esau said, "I already have plenty, my brother. Keep what you have for yourself."

It is difficult to gauge Esau's response. At face value, it appears that he declines the offering because he does not need it and prefers that Jacob use it to meet his own family's needs. But for Jacob, it is crucial that *Esau* accept it. This is Jacob's attempt to clear his conscience and set things right. He has stolen from

Esau, and the two will not be reconciled fully until repayment is made. That being the case, Esau's initial denial is either (1) an effort to keep the power he now holds over Jacob, or (2) a sincere act of generosity, or (3) a cultural practice somewhat along the lines of Genesis 23:7-16. Regardless, Esau's initial response is not acceptable to Jacob.

C. PEACE OFFERING ACCEPTED (vv. 10, 11)

10. "No, please!" said Jacob. "If I have found favor in your eyes, accept this gift from me. For to see your face is like seeing the face of God, now that you have received me favorably.

Jacob desperately needs Esau to accept the peace offering. So he begins to apply pressure. Esau has presented himself as the gracious older brother. He ran to Jacob, hugged him, and kissed him. But for his act of *favor* to be complete, he must set Jacob free from the debt. Esau must allow Jacob a concrete way to express his gratitude for the grace he has received.

To deny Jacob the means to do this will be to withhold forgiveness and subject Jacob to a different form of bondage. It is almost as if Jacob is saying, "If you are truly the gracious man I think you are, and if you are truly pleased with me, then you need to accept these gifts. If not, this is all just a sham and the real Esau is the bitter Esau I left behind who doesn't know how to let go of a grudge."

It is also important to discuss why Jacob compares seeing Esau's face to seeing *the face of God*. There are a few ways we can understand this. One way highlights Esau's graciousness. God is known for his grace, and in this encounter Esau's response to Jacob rises to a level that is pleasing to God. Put differently, Esau receives Jacob so warmly that it is like Heaven smiling down.

Another interpretation highlights Esau's position of judgment. Jacob could be acknowledging that Esau occupies the position of judge—and Esau knows that Jacob is guilty. Esau has heard Jacob's pleas for mercy, and at this point Esau can either grant or withhold pardon for Jacob's sin.

A third interpretation stresses language parallel to that of the previous chapter. Jacob spent all night wrestling with a mysterious, extraordinary man (Genesis 32:24); this man is identified in Hosea 12:4 as an angel. After surviving the fight, Jacob renamed the place *Peniel,* meaning "face of God," because he believed he had seen God face-to-face and lived (Genesis 32:30). So Jacob simply may be comparing the experience he just had with the angel to the experience he is now having with Esau. As Jacob had doubts about surviving the encounter with the angel, so also he now has doubts about surviving the encounter with Esau (although in neither case did Jacob actually see God himself). Under this interpretation, it is almost as if Jacob is saying, "I have stared death in the face and have lived to talk about it" concerning both encounters.

It is difficult to tell which of these interpretations is right. It may be some combination of them.

11. "Please accept the present that was brought to you, for God has been gracious to me and I have all I need." And because Jacob insisted, Esau accepted it.

Like the situation of Abraham's purchase of a burial plot in Genesis 23, Jacob knows he has to pay. He cannot remain indebted to Esau, so he urges Esau until he complies. We see here that genuine reconciliation requires responsibility of both parties. Jacob has to be willing to humble himself, and Esau has to let go of a long-held grudge. This applies to Christians today. Christ has taught us to forgive others' debts as we have been forgiven (Matthew 6:12; 18:21-35). Hanging on to resentment is unhealthy for both parties.

WHAT DO YOU THINK?

What principle can we apply to modern life from Jacob's insistence that Esau accept his gift? Or is that an ancient cultural practice that we can safely disregard? Explain.

HOW TO SAY IT

Abraham. AY-bruh-ham.
Colossians. Kuh-LOSH-unz.
Corinthians. Ko-RIN-thee-unz.
Esau. EE-saw.
Galatians. Guh-LAY-shunz.
Hosea. Ho-ZAY-uh.
Laban. LAY-bun.
Peniel. Peh-NYE-el.

PRAYER

We thank you, Father, for reconciliation through Christ. It is tempting, Lord, to hoard reconciliation, to accept it for ourselves but fail to extend it to others. Prepare us to accept with joy the ministry of reconciliation that you have entrusted to us. In Jesus' name, amen.

WHAT DO YOU THINK?

What does Esau's acceptance of Jacob's gift teach us?

Sometimes reconciliation is a matter of verbal confession and verbal forgiveness. At other times, restitution may need to be made so both parties may truly experience closure. In such cases the party that was wronged must, with a sincere heart, imitate Esau's willingness to accept an offer that has been made, even though he or she may prefer not to.

Notice also the language Jacob uses in this verse. Until this point in the conversation, he has not referred to himself as being a recipient of God's *gracious* blessing, perhaps in order to avoid digging up painful memories of blessing theft (Genesis 27:35, 36). But he approaches Esau and implores him to receive *the present*. It is almost as if Jacob is saying, "Take your blessing back. I don't want it anymore. It wasn't mine for the taking."

If this is so, then the Jacob and Esau saga has come full circle. Jacob surrenders, as best he can, that which he had stolen. Thus he can move forward with only that which God provides for him. Jacob learns to trust in God alone, and that is sufficient to carry him the rest of his journey. He indeed has "overcome" in his struggle "with God and with men" (Genesis 32:28).

BRINGING GIFTS FOR PEACE . . . OR PIECES?

On March 9, 2004, a psychology professor at Claremont McKenna College offered a "gift" of an unusual sort to her campus community. After speaking at a forum on racial tolerance, she filed a police report alleging that her car had been vandalized. It apparently was a hate crime, since racist epithets had been spray-painted on her car. What a perfect gift of an illustration concerning the subject the professor had addressed in her forum!

The next day, administrators gave a "gift" to the students by calling off classes for the day. Thousands of students gladly received the gift of a day free from classes in order to bring their own "gifts" to campus: demonstrations against such a terrible act of racial intolerance.

However, it was soon discovered that the professor had damaged her own car in order to call attention to the issue of racial prejudice. The court then had a "gift" for the manipulative professor: a one-year prison sentence. What the professor hoped to accomplish in terms of fostering racial peace ended up merely shredding her own reputation into pieces (www.sfgate.com).

Jacob had a history of being a manipulator. But when he brought gifts to Esau, they were offered in a genuine spirit. Too often what people bring to resolve relationship problems is not so much a peace offering as it is an attempt to prove themselves right. The frequent result is not peace, but relationships that are in pieces. —C. R. B.

CONCLUSION

Christians can learn valuable lessons from the account of Jacob and Esau. We may find ourselves in the shoes of one or the other at different points, sometimes the offender and sometimes the offended. Our culture encourages us to respond with extremes. At one extreme is inflicting payback. At the other extreme is a kind of quietism, meaning "just try to forget about it and move on with life."

Our Savior, however, does not give us either of those options. He calls us to seek reconciliation actively with those who have offended us (see Matthew 5:23, 24; 18:15; compare 2 Corinthians 5:18-21; Galatians 6:1, 2; Colossians 3:13; and James 5:16).

Those of us who share the blame for being estranged from another person must humble ourselves like Jacob. Those of us who have held grudges against someone who has wronged us need to embrace the offending party, like Esau, as we accept genuine confession, forgiving truly as Christ Jesus has forgiven us.

THOUGHT TO REMEMBER

Reconciliation requires humility and acceptance.

Discovery Learning

This page contains an alternative lesson plan emphasizing learning activities. Classes desiring such student involvement will find these suggestions helpful. The next page is a reproducible activity page to further enhance discovery learning.

INTO THE LESSON

Recruit a pair of learners and ask them to walk back and forth in front of the class, crossing paths. As they do, they are to greet one another in ways typical to a variety of cultures and contexts. Suggest such greetings as (1) a hearty handshake, (2) a simple hug, (3) a bowing of the head to each other, (4) a tip of the hat (which you'll need to provide), (5) an elaborate handshake and hug, (6) a kiss on each cheek, (7) a snappy salute, (8) a friendly wave, (9) a slight nod accompanied by hands positioned palm-to-palm, fingertips-to-the-lips, (10) a sign-language "I love you," and/or (11) others of your choosing and description. Ask the pair simply to cross back and forth quickly, demonstrating the greetings as they use few, if any, words.

When they finish, ask, "What determines the type of greeting you offer and receive?" Expect answers dealing with time and place, the intimacy of the relationship, and culture.

INTO THE WORD

Now ask the pair to demonstrate the manner of Jacob's greeting to his brother Esau according to Genesis 33:3. Ask the class, "What called for that elaborate greeting, and what did it signify?"

To complement your learners' responses to the previous questions, be sure they understand the causes and the depth of the estrangement between the Jacob and Esau. The passage of time (20 years) could have allowed a hardening of hearts and deepening of animosities—or the opposite!

Make two cutouts of biblical men (robed figures) in profile. Set them on a chalkboard rack or attach them to a wall in a nose-to-nose position. Distribute cutout arrows with the following words/phrases on them: *Parental Favoritism, Different Interests and Abilities, Childhood Rivalries, Lying, Cheating, Threats of Murder, Miles and Years, Prosperity.*

Ask those holding the arrows to bring them up and attach them between the brother figures. As they do, they are to move the figures apart the distance of the arrow being used—thus creating a visual of estrangement.

As each arrow is added, ask, "What specifically does this represent that can cause an alienation, a distance between the two brothers?" This will offer an opportu-

nity for a review of the brothers' relationship all the way back to Genesis 25 and Lesson 6.

Now ask seven class members, by name, to come to the front, bow, and remove the arrows one by one, consequently moving the two brother-figures closer together. After seven are moved, one item will be left, with the brothers close, but not "kissably close." Ask, "After looking at today's text, what else is there in Jacob's (or Esau's) behavior that can remove this last barrier to brotherly kindness and closeness?"

Someone will likely say, "Jacob's gift of many animals," "Esau's running, embracing, kissing, and weeping," or "the kind, reconciling words of either brother." If need be, suggest they look at Genesis 32:9-11 or 32:13-15 or 33:4.

Let the class continue to list and explain elements of Jacob's plan to meet Esau in a context of humility, grace, and blessing. As they do, make a list entitled, "Steps and Prerequisites to Reconciliation."

Expect elements such as *giving significant gifts* (Genesis 32:13-15); *setting aside the fears that are intrinsic in estrangement* (32:11); *"wrestling with God" a bit* (32:24, 25); *using intermediary ambassadors to break the ice* (32:16-21); *praying* (32:9-12); *demonstrating personal humility* (33:3); *being willing to show true emotion* (33:4); *affirming the presence of God's grace* (33:5, 11); *having witnesses present* (33:5-7); and *offering hospitality* (33:12). (A similar activity is included in the optional student book. If time allows, use the Reconciliation activity from the Reproducible Page for deeper study.)

INTO LIFE

To move to application, hand each learner a wedge-shaped piece of paper or distribute copies of the Removing Wedges activity from the reproducible page. Say, "All of us have experienced wedges between ourselves and others. Sometimes we create the wedge; sometimes others create it. Is there someone from whom you are estranged—either in your family, church, or at work—with whom you can begin a process of reconciliation? Which of the ideas from our 'Steps' list can you use?"

Direct learners to write down a reconciliation technique they will use to try to remove their "wedge." Indicate that once the wedge is removed, they should tear up the paper or work sheet.

Reconciliation

In Matthew 18:15-17, Jesus offered a procedure for reconciling with someone who has sinned against you. The four-step process goes like this:

1. Talk privately with the offender, clearly describing the offense and your concern for reconciliation.

   If reconciliation does not take place, then . . .

2. Take two or three others along as witnesses to establish the facts of the matter.

   If reconciliation does not take place, then . . .

3. Bring the matter to the church in assembly for full public awareness of the situation.

   If reconciliation does not take place, then . . .

4. Treat the offender as a pagan. That is, make the break definite and permanent.

What would you find difficult about each step in Jesus' process? How do you convince yourself to "do it Jesus' way"?

Removing Wedges

Many behaviors drive wedges between people. As in the case of Jacob and Esau, these can include family members' favoritism, sibling rivalry, lying and cheating, and threats. On the lines between the two figures below, write in practices that help resolve interpersonal conflicts. Note strategies Jacob used in Genesis 32 and 33. Consider the practices to be magnets that draw the two together.

JOSEPH IS MISTREATED

LESSON 10

WHY TEACH THIS LESSON?

Some people are good at planning for the future, sometimes at the expense of the "right now." Others live only for today. God excels at providing for both today and tomorrow.

As a certain writer said, "I have a point of view. You have a point of view. God has view." It is essential for your learners to keep this in mind, especially when they face trials. They need to know that God is the one who has the big picture for our lives. Knowing he has plans for our tomorrows makes it easier to get through the hardships and betrayals of today.

God's plans for us do not guarantee family harmony, pain-free living, or an up-front understanding of what is happening to us. And yet "we know that in all things God works for the good of those who love him, who have been called according to his purpose" (Romans 8:28). Today's lesson shows this idea in action.

INTRODUCTION

A. THE BUTTERFLY EFFECT

Have you ever noticed that something that seemed to be small or insignificant at one point can have a major effect over a longer period of time? One theory of forecasting changes in the weather and the stock market says that small variations in initial conditions can bring about large variations in the long-term behavior of a system.

The idea was originally expressed by Edward Lorenz in 1963 in a paper he wrote for the New York Academy of Sciences. Initially, he referred to the effect as being like the flap of a seagull's wings, but later would use the more picturesque phrase *butterfly effect*. Simply stated, the idea is that the flap of a butterfly's wing in one part of the world could eventually result in a hurricane in another part. (A more scientific description for *butterfly effect* is "sensitive dependence on initial conditions.")

The lesson today about Joseph is a portion of the greater narrative that describes God's movement to bring salvation to the world. Whether or not butterflies can cause hurricanes can be debated. But one thing is certain: the reach through history of the things done to and by Joseph is profound indeed!

B. LESSON BACKGROUND

Jacob eventually returned to Canaan from living in Paddan Aram, where he had married and where most of his children were born (last week's lesson). The livelihood of the family was based on raising livestock. In this relatively dry region, it was necessary to move the flocks and herds around to provide them with daily food. Sometimes the shepherds would have to go long distances to find that food.

Jacob was a very successful shepherd, and apparently he intended for Joseph, his favorite son, to follow in his footsteps. To that end, we see Joseph learning

---

DEVOTIONAL READING:
PSALM 70
BACKGROUND SCRIPTURE:
GENESIS 37
PRINTED TEXT:
GENESIS 37:5-11, 19-21, 23, 24a, 28

LESSON AIMS

After participating in this lesson, each student will be able to:

1. Describe the early relationship of Joseph with his brothers and parents.

2. Explain why Joseph had to tell about his dreams.

3. Make a commitment to share the gospel in a situation where it may not be welcome, and be prepared for the potentially difficult result.

Nov
4

KEY VERSE

His brothers . . . sold him for twenty shekels of silver to the Ishmaelites, who took him to Egypt.
—Genesis 37:28

the family operation. The biblical record tells us that Joseph had eleven brothers and one sister. The nature and significance of Joseph's interaction with his brothers is a vital part of the Genesis account.

I. DREAMER DREAMS (GENESIS 37:5-9)

As we enter into the story of Joseph, around the year 1900 BC, we find a boy at age 17 (Genesis 37:2). Immediately we are introduced to a love-hate triangle consisting of Joseph, his brothers, and their father, Jacob. Joseph's father loved him more than he loved his other sons. This created a burning resentment toward Joseph.

Three things aggravated the situation. First, Joseph had brought a bad report about his brothers to his father, Jacob (also known as *Israel*; Genesis 37:2). Second, Joseph received preferential treatment in terms of a special coat, a colorful one perhaps with long sleeves (37:3, 23). Third, Joseph had been having dreams of personal grandeur. That's where our story opens today.

A. SHEAVES IN THE FIELD BOW DOWN (vv. 5-8)

5. Joseph had a dream, and when he told it to his brothers, they hated him all the more.

For the most part, we discount the possibility of receiving information through dreams today. It is comparatively rare even in the Bible for people to receive revelations from God in dreams. Dreams in the Bible can refer to the normal dreams of sleep (Isaiah 29:7, 8), the imaginary dreams of false prophets (Jeremiah 23:25-32; 27:9, 10), or dreams of revelation (Genesis 41:17; Daniel 2:28).

The dreams of revelation are found primarily in Genesis and Daniel. *Joseph* is one of the few to whom God speaks in this manner. Equally important is the fact that Joseph will later demonstrate the God-given ability to interpret the dreams of others (Genesis 40:12, 13, 18, 19; 41:25-32). This ability will open doors for the family of Jacob to come to Egypt.

As we are introduced to Joseph's dreams, we are also introduced to his brothers' response. For them the *dream* represents an intolerable attitude of superiority.

6, 7. He said to them, "Listen to this dream I had: We were binding sheaves of grain out in the field when suddenly my sheaf rose and stood upright, while your sheaves gathered around mine and bowed down to it."

We are introduced to the style of grain harvest in Joseph's day. Men and women go out with hand sickles and cut the *grain*. As they do, they gather the cut stalks into *sheaves*. The sheaves are stacked in the field to await transport to the place of threshing. (A fuller picture of the process of grain harvesting in Bible times is found in the book of Ruth.)

Older translations of the Bible use the word *obeisance* to describe this bowing. The idea is that of an act of great respect. It signifies that someone else has (or will have) power over the one doing the bowing.

8. His brothers said to him, "Do you intend to reign over us? Will you actually rule us?" And they hated him all the more because of his dream and what he had said.

Joseph's suggestion that *his brothers* will bow down to him infuriates them. As far as they are concerned, Joseph will never *rule* over them.

Though the Bible is silent on this matter, it is very possible that the brothers have already discussed killing Joseph as soon as Jacob is dead (compare Esau's idea in Genesis 27:41). Whether they have or not, Joseph's dream adds fuel to the already burning fire. It is bad enough to have to accept the fact that Joseph is

WHAT DO YOU THINK?

What was a time when you saw speaking the truth cause resentment? How do you handle such a reaction in a godly way?

their father's favorite. But the suggestion that they will bow down before him is too much. The stage is being set for terrible happenings.

We may note at this point that we have a prediction that will be fulfilled in the later years of Joseph. "When Joseph's brothers arrived, they bowed down to him with their faces to the ground. . . . Then he remembered his dreams about them" (Genesis 42:6, 9; compare 43:26, 28; 44:14).

B. SUN, MOON, AND STARS BOW DOWN (v. 9)

9. Then he had another dream, and he told it to his brothers. "Listen," he said, "I had another dream, and this time the sun and moon and eleven stars were bowing down to me."

Some time after the first *dream,* Joseph dreams again. For Joseph, the two dreams provide absolute verification that the message is true, since the two dreams concern the same subject. We may compare this with Pharaoh's two dreams in the same night; those dreams had different images but the same meaning (Genesis 41:25).

Joseph's second dream has implications as serious as the first. It predicts that Joseph's father (Jacob), his mother, and his 11 brothers will bow down to him. The number 11 leaves no doubt about whom these images signify!

DELUSIONS OF GRANDEUR

Jackie Gleason starred as bus driver Ralph Kramden of *The Honeymooners* in the early years of television. Ralph lived with his wife, Alice, in a run-down apartment in the city. He was a blustering big-mouth—a self-appointed "king of his castle"—who went through scheme after scheme in which he dreamed of becoming great, rich, and successful.

Ralph's best friend, Ed Norton, worked for the sewer department. Ed was a more down-to-earth kind of person, yet he also had dreams of grandeur. One observer noted that the men had more ambition than aptitude.

Part of the appeal of these fictional characters was that they represented the mind-set of many watching. Ralph was "everyman," the frustrated plodder whose life was dull despite his daydreams. Joseph also had dreams of grandeur, but these were of a far different type from those of Ralph Kramden and "everyman"! Joseph didn't create his dreams; they came from God. Joseph's dreams were not daydreams, whipped up out of whims of fantasy; they were God's revelation of assured future events.

Some Christians have been known to muse about all the grandiose things they could do for God if only they could win the lottery or some such. Much more productive and pleasing to God would be efforts to strengthen our character and integrity. As time would tell, those were to become hallmarks of Joseph's life. They can be ours as well.   —C. R. B.

II. FAMILY REACTS (GENESIS 37:10, 11)

Joseph usually is the one who can do no wrong in his father's eyes. But this dream offends even his father. The implications are incredible, even to Jacob.

A. JACOB REBUKES (v. 10)

10. When he told his father as well as his brothers, his father rebuked him and said, "What is this dream you had? Will your mother and I and your brothers actually come and bow down to the ground before you?"

It is possible that Joseph's *father* (Jacob) does not know about the first dream regarding the sheaves. Jacob certainly wants his son to be the leader of the fam-

Comparison of Joseph and Jesus

Joseph		Jesus
Genesis 30:22-24	Conceived under miraculous circumstances	Luke 1:26-38
Genesis 37:28	Taken to Egypt under stressful circumstances	Matthew 2:13-15
Genesis 37:5	Rejected by brothers	John 7:5
Genesis 37:11	Hated because of envy	Matthew 27:18
Genesis 37:23	Stripped by enemies	Matthew 27:28
Genesis 37:28 Leviticus 27:5	Sold for the price of a slave	Matthew 26:15 Exodus 21:32
Genesis 39:6b-12	Resisted strong temptation	Matthew 4:1-17
Genesis 39:13-20	Suffered undeserved punishment	Mark 15:25-32
Genesis 40	Associated with two criminals, one who was blessed and one who was not	Luke 23:39-43
Genesis 41:46	Began most important work at age 30	Luke 3:23

Visual for Lesson 10. *After exploring these comparisons, ask your learners if they can think of others.*

ily, but to hear Joseph now declare his authority in this fashion is too much. Is Joseph really arrogant enough to think that his father and *mother* and 11 *brothers* will *bow down* to him? (The mother in view here is not Rachel, who is dead by this time, but Joseph's stepmother, Leah.)

At this moment it appears that Joseph is alone: his brothers hate him, and his father has rebuked him. We should keep in mind, however, that Joseph is being honest about what he experienced. The Bible makes it clear that these dreams are not fabrications on Joseph's part.

B. BROTHERS ENVY (v. 11)

11. His brothers were jealous of him, but his father kept the matter in mind.

The idea that the brothers are *jealous of* Joseph suggests a stronger and more significant passion than even hatred. The emotion of envy magnifies the possibility that their feelings will spill over into violence. This is another signal that the brothers are plotting revenge.

The phrase *his father kept the matter in mind* tells us that Jacob recognizes that this dream does have potential for revelation. Jacob's reaction is similar to that of Mary in the New Testament: "But Mary treasured up all these things and pondered them in her heart" (Luke 2:19).

In any case, Jacob seems unaware of the danger that Joseph is in. This is seen by the fact that Jacob is willing to send Joseph to check on his brothers one more time (Genesis 37:12, 13, not in today's text).

III. PLOT DEVELOPS (GENESIS 37:19-21, 23, 24a, 28)

It is only a matter of time until Joseph is again alone with his brothers. Supposedly they are tending flocks near Shechem, so Joseph goes there first. But a resident of the area tells him that his brothers have moved to Dothan, about 14 miles north of Shechem (Genesis 37:12-17) and perhaps 60 miles from home.

Dothan is a major city in the area, important to two people in the Bible: Joseph and Elisha. Whereas God allows Joseph to be taken to Egypt in slavery from near Dothan, he will miraculously deliver Elisha from the Syrian army in that locale centuries later (2 Kings 6:13-17). The brothers may have moved on to there in order to find better grass for the flocks and herds or because more water is available. There is no suggestion that they are trying to hide from their father.

A. FIRST PLAN: MURDER (vv. 19-21, 23, 24a)

19, 20. "Here comes that dreamer!" they said to each other. "Come now, let's kill him and throw him into one of these cisterns and say that a ferocious animal devoured him. Then we'll see what comes of his dreams."

Here comes that dreamer indicates that Joseph has gained a new nickname that is intended to be an unveiled insult. The brothers' first plan is to *kill* Joseph outright. That will put an end to his *dreams* and free them from this pesky brother! **21. When Reuben heard this, he tried to rescue him from their hands. "Let's not take his life," he said.**

Reuben is the oldest of the brothers. He is the one who accepts responsibility as the firstborn son to save Joseph by suggesting that they cast him into a cistern (Genesis 37:22, not in today's text). For reasons unknown, Reuben apparently leaves Joseph in the care of the other brothers (v. 29, not in today's text). **23, 24a. So when Joseph came to his brothers, they stripped him of his robe—the richly ornamented robe he was wearing—and they took him and threw him into the cistern.**

WHAT DO YOU THINK?

What was a time when you had to tell a truth that turned out to be very unpopular? How did you handle the situation?

WHAT DO YOU THINK?

Was it inconsistent for Jacob to rebuke Joseph but keep the matter in mind anyway? Why, or why not?

WHAT DO YOU THINK?

Does it surprise you that Joseph's brothers conspired to kill him? Why, or why not? What does this situation teach us about dealing with human nature in a godly manner?

WHAT DO YOU THINK?

Why do half-hearted attempts to do right usually fail?

The offensive *robe* has to be removed. The robe symbolizes all the things the brothers hate about *Joseph*. Its existence demonstrates that he is privileged. Stripping Joseph of this article of clothing provides a first taste of revenge. Humiliating this 17-year-old boy brings the brothers cynical pleasure.

The next stage of their revenge is throwing Joseph into a dry *cistern*. This undoubtedly is deep enough for it to be impossible for him to climb out without assistance from outside.

B. SECOND PLAN: SLAVERY (v. 28)

28. So when the Midianite merchants came by, his brothers pulled Joseph up out of the cistern and sold him for twenty shekels of silver to the Ishmaelites, who took him to Egypt.

After casting Joseph into the cistern, it is time for lunch (see v. 25, not in today's text). Before the Midianites arrive, the brothers may enjoy special delicacies that Joseph has brought from their father. It is doubtful that they shared any with their captive!

As they eat, they spot a camel caravan on its way to *Egypt*. Dothan is close to one of the major trade routes to that country. The brothers recognize the opportunity to solve their problem while keeping their hands free of their brother's blood.

It is at the suggestion of Judah that Joseph be sold to the *merchants* (see vv. 26, 27, not in today's text). Reuben planned to save Joseph somehow, but failed. Instead, Judah is the one to step forward and provide a solution that keeps Joseph alive.

We will see this failure-success pattern again. When famine later comes to Canaan and the brothers return from Egypt with food, Reuben will try to convince his father to allow Benjamin to go along on a follow-up trip. That offer will be rejected (Genesis 42:37, 38). Judah then will demonstrate leadership qualities once again by stepping forward to accept personal responsibility for the life of Benjamin. His offer will be accepted (43:8-15).

We may pause to consider the two designations, *Midianites* and *Ishmaelites*. One opinion is that these are different designations for the same group. In favor of this idea, we may compare Genesis 37:36 with 39:1; the former says it is the Midianites who sell Joseph to Potiphar while the latter says it is the Ishmaelites who do so. Much later we find Gideon fighting against "the Midianites" (Judges 7:24, 25; we are told that "it was the custom of the Ishmaelites to wear gold earrings" (Judges 8:24).

On the other hand, some scholars see the caravan as made up of Midianite merchants who act as "middlemen" for the Ishmaelites. Both groups are relatives of Abraham. Ishmael was Abraham's son born to Hagar, Sarah's Egyptian maidservant. Midian was one of the sons of Keturah, Abraham's second wife (Genesis 25:1, 2). Both the Midianites and Ishmaelites are thus blood relatives of Jacob and his family.

The relative value of *twenty shekels of silver* is uncertain. Weighing a total of about 8 ounces, 20 shekels of silver seems to be the going price for slaves in the time of Joseph. Compare Exodus 21:32, where servants (slaves) later are to be valued at 30 shekels of silver. Jesus' life will also valued at 30 pieces of silver when he is betrayed centuries later (Zechariah 11:12, 13; Matthew 26:15; 27:9, 10).

In any case, the sale of Joseph brings monetary profit to the brothers as well as providing the means by which they can be rid of him. The brothers confidently

HOW TO SAY IT

Canaan. KAY-nun.
Dothan. DOE-thun.
Elisha. E-LYE-shuh.
Esau. EE-saw.
Hagar. HAY-gar.
Ishmael. ISH-may-el.
Ishmaelites. ISH-may-el-ites.
Israel. IZ-ray-el.
Keturah. Keh-TOO-ruh.
Midian. MID-ee-un.
Midianites. MID-ee-un-ites.
obeisance. oh-BEE-sense.
Paddan Aram. PAY-dan A-ram.
Potiphar. POT-ih-far.
Shechem. SHEE-kem or SHEK-em.

Family Feuds

Describe the disagreements or fights you are having (or have had) with family members. Rate them in seriousness on a scale of 1 to 5 (with a 1 being mild).

Issue You Disagreed About	How Serious?	Ongoing?
_____	_____	_____
_____	_____	_____
_____	_____	_____
_____	_____	_____
_____	_____	_____
_____		

Spend some time praying about how to reconcile those feuds that are still causing a rift.

Modern Callings

Interview a well-known Christian (or read a biography about one). Make notes on how the person knew he or she was called of God and the path his or her spiritual journey took. Make notes on the notepad below. Pay particular attention to places in the testimony or story concerning times when God's calling became clear only through adversity.

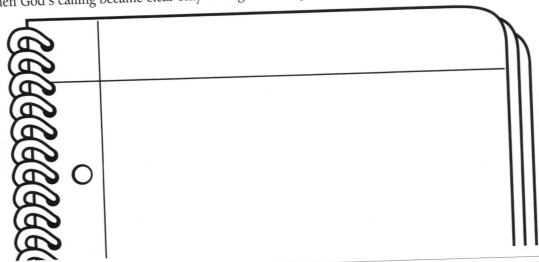

JOSEPH IS EXALTED

LESSON 11

WHY TEACH THIS LESSON?

When betrayed, injured, or overlooked, we can become bitter or depressed. Your learners need to realize that God never wastes their pain. As the biblical record of Joseph's life continues, we see God using Joseph's trials to mature him and to bring about a plan of provision through this faithful servant.

On the other hand, it's easy to feel proud or deserving of our blessings when things go well. In those cases, your learners need to learn not to confuse God's achievements with their own. We know that humility is a trait that makes us useful in the kingdom of God. It keeps us from becoming self-important. It keeps us close to our source of strength.

In good times and bad, it's easy to forget God's behind-the-scenes work. Joseph, though confident of God's ability to work through him, remained clear about his own inability: "I cannot do it" (Genesis 41:16). The challenge is to remain humble and encouraged through all circumstances, realizing that God is shaping us through each frustration and success.

INTRODUCTION

A. RISING ABOVE ADVERSITY

Milos Cols (pronounced Milosh Schultz) is an evangelical minister in Prague, Czech Republic. As a minister there during the Communist era, he experienced a great deal of adversity. The government took away his ordination. He was not allowed to preach in Prague. The intent was to stop his activities by making his life as miserable as possible.

One day Milos was called in by the secret police for questioning. He showed up late, and the interrogator was furious. Milos told him, "I was sleeping so well that I forgot to wake up on time for this meeting." It was a subtle way to say, "You do not frighten me, no matter what you choose to do." The interrogator understood the innuendo and was even more furious. When his tirade ended, he allowed Milos to leave, unharmed.

Communism left Prague in 1989, and Milos is still preaching the Word. God expects his servants to rise above adversity, and he strengthens them to do so. That's just what Milos did.

B. LESSON BACKGROUND

When we last saw Joseph, he was on his way to Egypt and into slavery. His chances for a good life appeared to be very bleak. Joseph probably thought he would never see his family again.

Joseph was purchased by Potiphar, the captain of Pharaoh's guard. Joseph proved to be an excellent worker. Soon he was appointed to be manager over all the administrative affairs of Potiphar's household.

This situation lasted as long as Joseph was able to keep his master's wife away from him. Potiphar's wife lusted after Joseph, creating a major temptation for

DEVOTIONAL READING:
PSALM 105:16-22
BACKGROUND SCRIPTURE:
GENESIS 41:25-45
PRINTED TEXT:
GENESIS 41:25-40

LESSON AIMS

After participating in this lesson, each student will be able to:

1. Explain how God elevated Joseph to a position of power in Egypt.

2. Compare Joseph's experience of hardship resulting in blessing with other biblical or modern examples.

3. Give thanks to God for working all things together for good in his or her own life.

KEY VERSE

Pharaoh said to Joseph, "Since God has made all this known to you, there is no one so discerning and wise as you. You shall be in charge of my palace, and all my people are to submit to your orders. Only with respect to the throne will I be greater than you."
—Genesis 41:39, 40

Nov
11

him. One day she waited for the appropriate moment to try once more. Joseph rebuffed her, but in revenge she accused him of attempted rape (Genesis 39).

Joseph wound up in prison. There he demonstrated his skills as an administrator, and he was soon running the prison. This position lasted for several years. During that time, Pharaoh's cupbearer and baker were thrown into prison. Both had dreams. Joseph interpreted their dreams, and the interpretations proved to be accurate: the butler was restored to his position, and the baker was hanged.

Then Pharaoh had dreams that no one could explain. The cupbearer told Pharaoh about Joseph. Joseph was cleaned up, appropriately dressed, and brought before Pharaoh (Genesis 41:14).

The Egyptians believed that revelation from "the gods" could come through dreams. The dreams of Pharaoh thus provided the avenue for Joseph to be released from prison. Joseph himself had had two dreams (Genesis 37:5-7, 9) and two of his fellow prisoners had dreams as well (40:5-23). Then Joseph found himself confronted with two dreams of Pharaoh to interpret.

WHAT DO YOU THINK?

How did Joseph's experiences in Potiphar's house and in prison serve as preparation for his challenge before Pharaoh? How are Joseph's experiences relevant for us today?

I. DREAMS' EXPLANATION, PART 1 (GENESIS 41:25-27)

A. GOD IS REVEALING (v. 25)

25. Then Joseph said to Pharaoh, "The dreams of Pharaoh are one and the same. God has revealed to Pharaoh what he is about to do.

We are not able to identify with certainty the *Pharaoh* under whom Joseph serves, but we can make an educated guess. Using biblical chronology, we can date Joseph's life to between 1916 and 1806 BC. Joseph enters Pharaoh's service at age 30 (Genesis 41:46). That is about the year 1886 BC. This dating points to Sesostris (also spelled Senusret) II as the Pharaoh in question. His reign occurs during Egypt's Middle Kingdom Twelfth Dynasty (a dynasty that lasts from approximately 1937 to 1759 BC).

This Pharaoh, whoever he is, has had two dreams. Yet *the dreams of Pharaoh are one and the same.* When dreams come in twos, it shows that God is firm about the matter (see v. 32, below). Pharaoh does not understand his dreams, but he is certain that they have a divine source. Any lesser explanation will not satisfy. Joseph confirms his feelings and warns Pharaoh that the dreams contain a serious matter. Joseph does not claim to be the source of the wisdom. Rather, God is the source (see Genesis 41:16). Pharaoh may even be familiar with the name for God of *Elohim*, because the god *el* is well known in that day.

B. FAMINE IS COMING (vv. 26, 27)

26, 27. "The seven good cows are seven years, and the seven good heads of grain are seven years; it is one and the same dream. The seven lean, ugly cows that came up afterward are seven years, and so are the seven worthless heads of grain scorched by the east wind: They are seven years of famine.

The meaning of the dreams is made known: Egypt is to enjoy *seven years* of great harvests followed by *seven years of famine.* The idea of plant life being *scorched* signifies God's judgment (compare 2 Kings 19:26; Isaiah 37:27). An *east wind* can also indicate judgment from God (Exodus 10:13; Psalm 48:7; Jeremiah 18:17; Ezekiel 17:10; 19:12; Jonah 4:8).

II. DREAMS' EXPLANATION, PART 2 (GENESIS 41:28-32)

A. REVIEW OF THE DREAMS (vv. 28-31)

28, 29. "It is just as I said to Pharaoh: God has shown Pharaoh what he is about to do. Seven years of great abundance are coming throughout the land of Egypt,

HOW TO SAY IT

Abraham. AY-bruh-ham.
Czech. Check.
Egypt. EE-jipt.
Ezekiel. Ee-ZEEK-ee-ul or Ee-ZEEK-yul.
Isaiah. Eye-ZAY-uh.
Jeremiah. Jair-uh-MY-uh.
Nathan. NAY-thun.
Pharaoh. FAIR-o or FAY-roe.
Potiphar. POT-ih-far.
Senusret. Sen-OOS-ret.
Sesostris. Sis-OS-tris.

As Joseph reviews the meaning of the dreams, he assures Pharaoh that the message of the dreams is going to come to pass, and that it will happen very soon (*what he is about to do;* see also v. 32, below). This adds to the urgency of the situation.

Joseph is not some sort of magician or fortuneteller who can explain dreams (compare Daniel 2:1-11). He has already proven that he is God's conduit for explaining this kind of revelation (Genesis 40). Joseph correctly recognizes that he is only a tool in the hands of God (Genesis 41:16). If there is an explanation to Pharaoh's dreams, it will come from God.

30. "*. . . but seven years of famine will follow them. Then all the abundance in Egypt will be forgotten, and the famine will ravage the land.*

What Joseph is proposing is almost unbelievable. *Seven years of famine?* Incredible! A prediction of famine must take into account the fact that rain in *Egypt* is rare anyway. The average rainfall along Egypt's coastline is only four to eight inches per year. That is not adequate to support crops, even without a famine. The rest of the country, away from the coastline, may get only one or two inches of rainfall annually. Instead, agriculture in Egypt is tied to the Nile River. The Nile floods annually, bringing a new load of rich silt for the coming year's crops.

What all this means is that the powerful Egyptian "gods" of the Nile are going to fail for seven years. Yet Pharaoh believes that the dreams are true messages from the spiritual world, and Joseph provides him with the explanation. Up to this point no one else can even guess what the dreams are about. Pharaoh does not challenge Joseph's interpretations. This undoubtedly is tied in with Joseph's successful track record in interpreting the dreams of the butler and the baker.

31. "*The abundance in the land will not be remembered, because the famine that follows it will be so severe.*

Joseph is in the role of court prophet similar to that of Nathan in 2 Samuel 7. To bring bad news to a ruler is dangerous, but Joseph must tell the truth: the *famine* will be very *severe.* The famine will affect not only Egypt but surrounding lands as well (Genesis 41:54, 57). The famine *will be so severe* that people will forget the good years when they had plentiful crops. It was famine that brought Abraham, Joseph's great-grandfather, to Egypt (12:10). It will be famine that will drive Joseph's brothers and father to Egypt as well (42:1-3; 43:1; 47:4).

B. REASON FOR TWO DREAMS (v. 32)
32. "*The reason the dream was given to Pharaoh in two forms is that the matter has been firmly decided by God, and God will do it soon.*

The famine to come will be an act of *God.* There is a significant purpose for this famine. Yet even Joseph, with his wisdom and insight, surely is not aware of the primary reason for the upcoming famine.

Remember that *Pharaoh* is not the only one who has had his *dream* repeated or presented *in two forms.* Joseph himself had two dreams that had one and the same meaning (Genesis 37:5-7, 9).

"AN ILL WIND . . ."

People in many places think their own weather is unique in being highly changeable. They like to say, "If you don't like the weather in _____, just wait five minutes, and it will change." Whether or not such a bold statement is true in every location, the western United States is especially subject to drastically changing weather patterns. The *El Niño* phenomenon of one year can bring record rains; the *La Niña* weather pattern that may follow can result in near drought.

WHAT DO YOU THINK?

How can we recognize an approaching famine of God's Word? What corrective action can we take to avoid or reverse such a famine?

Strong winds are common in *La Niña* years. Those *Santa Ana winds,* as they are called, quickly dry out the vegetation. This often results in horrendous wildfires. Government agencies are trying to get better at predicting weather patterns to improve preparedness.

Even with modern forecasting tools and big budgets, no modern governmental agency can beat Joseph in accuracy of predictions and being prepared for a natural disaster! He listened to God and thus saved the lives of many. Yet our job is even more important than Joseph's was. The book of Revelation predicts disaster after disaster that will befall the sinful people of the world. Will we warn them in time?   —C. R. B.

III. JOSEPH'S ADVICE (GENESIS 41:33-36)

A. WISE MAN NEEDED (v. 33)

33. *"And now let Pharaoh look for a discerning and wise man and put him in charge of the land of Egypt.*

Joseph proceeds to give *Pharaoh* advice on how to deal with the coming crisis. This displays boldness on Joseph's part. After all, he is a slave, freshly yanked out of prison. Pharaoh, by contrast, is viewed as a god-king. How dare a mere mortal presume to advise a god-king before that god-king requests him to do so? Yet Joseph plunges forward.

The word *now* shows a transition from the stated facts to the moral conclusion. The word *discerning* deals with the ability to show good judgment. The man for this new position must be skilled in leading people; compassionate, yet firm; and of the highest integrity. Otherwise, the project will fail.

B. SUPPORT TEAM NEEDED (v. 34a)

34a. *"Let Pharaoh appoint commissioners over the land*

The next stage will be for *Pharaoh* to *appoint commissioners over the land* to assist the new "starvation avoidance director" or perhaps "famine relief director" (if we may call him by either of those titles), and to implement the boss's plan. This will be more than just an advisory committee. It is to be a structured, action organization that is controlled by the government.

C. STOCKPILE NEEDED (vv. 34b-36)

34b-36. *". . . to take a fifth of the harvest of Egypt during the seven years of abundance. They should collect all the food of these good years that are coming and store up the grain under the authority of Pharaoh, to be kept in the cities for food. This food should be held in reserve for the country, to be used during the seven years of famine that will come upon Egypt, so that the country may not be ruined by the famine."*

The tax is to be one-fifth of the crops raised in each of *the seven years of abundance.* But if the famine is to be for seven years, then how will collecting only one-fifth per year for seven years be enough for *seven years of famine*? A period of famine doesn't necessarily mean that food production goes all the way down to zero. In any case, Joseph is preparing (under divine guidance) to feed more that just the Egyptians (Genesis 41:53-57). Unknowingly, Joseph is preparing food stores even for his own family.

IV. PHARAOH'S RESPONSE (GENESIS 41:37-40)

A. TOTAL AGREEMENT (v. 37)

37. *The plan seemed good to Pharaoh and to all his officials.*

WHAT DO YOU THINK?

How can we make Joseph's boldness our own in the twenty-first century?

WHAT DO YOU THINK?

In what ways would you say that you are a person of discernment, as Joseph uses the concept? How can you improve?

Pharaoh and everyone around him are duly impressed by what they have seen and heard from Joseph. The man before them appears to have no devious agendas. Rather, Joseph is transparent in the whole matter. Joseph has identified the source of the explanation as God, not himself (Genesis 41:15, 16). He has given sound advice as to how to deal with the crisis. Now the matter is in the hands of Pharaoh.

We are not told how long the matter is discussed. No disagreement or debate is noted.

B. BEST CHOICE (v. 38)

38. So Pharaoh asked them, "Can we find anyone like this man, one in whom is the spirit of God?"

The question *Pharaoh* raises involves whom to appoint to the position of "famine relief director." This will take an unusual person. The most important characteristic will be integrity. The opportunities for graft, bribery, and other misconduct will be enormous. This person will have vast powers and access to great wealth.

Pharaoh is aware that many men are not able to handle such a job without being corrupted by it. Pharaoh has never seen Joseph before. But Joseph has already demonstrated his integrity, first in the house of Potiphar (Genesis 39:5-10) and then in the prison (Genesis 39:20-23). Pharaoh may not be fully aware (or aware at all) of Joseph's integrity in these cases, but God certainly knows.

We need also to remember that Joseph has earned respect by his ability to do what Pharaoh's advisors could not do—namely, interpret the dreams of Pharaoh, the baker, and the cupbearer. For Pharaoh, this is evidence of divine leading in the life of Joseph.

No man could do what Joseph has done if he didn't have divine help. Joseph is thus identified as a man *in whom is the Spirit of God*. The phrase *Spirit of God* is used only twice in Genesis—here and in Genesis 1:2. Pharaoh believes that a divine spirit can empower servants of the deity. Thus Joseph is the ideal man for this important job.

Pharaoh's choice is undoubtedly the result of God's work on his heart. What is happening here is not by chance or coincidence. Pharaoh expected his own advisors to be able to interpret the dreams, but they could not. To their credit, they don't even try to fabricate an interpretation (Genesis 41:8). Now standing before Pharaoh is a man who interprets the dreams without apparent expectation of personal gain.

WISDOM IN LISTENING

In the spring of 2004, a self-styled "prophet" who had a substantial audience among Christians in the San Diego area announced an impending disaster. "God had told him" that he would send a devastating earthquake upon the coastal regions of California during the second week of September that year. Yet not a single earthquake of any significance occurred anywhere in the world during that period!

The following spring, the same man predicted a major disaster for the western coast of the U.S. for the end of August. It could be prevented only if vast numbers of Christians went to the Pacific shoreline and prayed for God to stop the calamity, he claimed. There was no noticeable increase in prayer activity on California beaches, but no catastrophic event occurred either.

Joseph was a much better prophet than this man in California—fortunately for Pharaoh! Despite the fact that Pharaoh was a pagan ruler, it was to his credit that he listened carefully to what the man of God had to say. Pharaoh undoubtedly had

God keeps promises even under the bleakest circumstances.

Visual for Lesson 11. *This sobering visual can bring to mind past tragedies. Ask your learners how they draw on God's promises to cope.*

PRAYER

Heavenly Father, give us the determination to persevere when times are difficult. Help us to use those times to draw closer to you. When we do draw closer, help us to remain close. Help us to thank you for the good times and the blessings you bestow. Give us the integrity that Joseph had. In Jesus' name, amen.

WHAT DO YOU THINK?

How can you cooperate with God in working out his will for your life? What parallels do you see between Joseph's life and yours?

THOUGHT TO REMEMBER

God never forgets faithfulness.

other prophets, but he chose to listen to the one who truly spoke God's message. Are we as wise as Pharaoh in that regard?

—C. R. B.

C. HIGH POSITION (vv. 39, 40)

39, 40. Then Pharaoh said to Joseph, "Since God has made all this known to you, there is no one so discerning and wise as you. You shall be in charge of my palace, and all my people are to submit to your orders. Only with respect to the throne will I be greater than you."

The unbelievable becomes believable. Only a few hours earlier, Joseph had been in prison. He had been there for over two years (Genesis 41:1), with little hope of ever being released.

Yet Joseph had made the best of the situation. Rather than sitting down, folding his arms, and pouting, he had gone to work. As a result, he had risen to become second only to the warden in that prison.

When Joseph left prison to meet Pharaoh, he had no idea what direction his life was going to take. A meeting with Pharaoh! This could have meant either the end of his life, freedom, or merely being thrown right back in prison. It is highly unlikely that the thought of receiving a lifetime appointment to a high government position ever crosses Joseph's mind.

But now he is being made the second most important man in all of Egypt (compare Daniel 2:48; 5:29; 6:1-3). Egypt is one of the most powerful nations in the world at the time. Now Joseph is in charge of *all* of Pharaoh's *people*. Joseph's word is to be the final word in all matters. He is answerable to no one except Pharaoh.

In the text that follows, we find Pharaoh affirming Joseph's high status (Genesis 41:41). Pharaoh does this by giving his personal signet ring to Joseph (Genesis 41:42). This kind of ring is used to make wax-seal impressions on official decrees. That seal impression will be as if Pharaoh himself is issuing the decree.

Joseph is also given linen robes and a gold neck chain. He will also ride in a chariot—the limousine of the day. He is given a bodyguard who is to run before him (Genesis 41:43). People will bow down as his chariot passes by.

But that's not all. Joseph also is given a wife from the family of one of the most important religious figures in the country (Genesis 41:45). We cannot resist speculating at this point that Joseph must recall his early dreams, wondering how they will come to pass. He certainly will recall those dreams a few years later (Genesis 42:9).

CONCLUSION

Joseph is one of the greatest men of the Old Testament. He started out as the special child of his father, but was hated by his brothers. He was sold into slavery by these brothers. Then he was indicted by a vindictive woman for refusing to be unfaithful to God. He was forgotten in prison for a time by a person whom he befriended and for whom he predicted a return to his former position.

Any one of these events could have been enough to send a person into a permanent depression. Joseph had frequent opportunities to sin. Who would care if he did? Potiphar's wife certainly wouldn't have cared! His father thought he was dead. His brothers were far away and didn't know or care where he was. His peers in Egypt were accustomed to sin and degradation. They would not seek to lead Joseph in the right direction morally.

Through exile, slavery, and abuse, Joseph remained faithful to God. After 13 years (from age 17 to age 30), God honored Joseph's faithfulness.

Discovery Learning

This page contains an alternative lesson plan emphasizing learning activities. Classes
desiring such student involvement will find these suggestions helpful. The next page
is a reproducible activity page to further enhance discovery learning.

INTO THE LESSON

Prior to class, make a large poster collage depicting recent natural disasters across the world. This can be a combination of headlines and photos from magazines and newspapers. It can be articles and images downloaded from the Internet. A long sheet of butcher paper could be used in place of a poster board, or the display could be put on a bulletin board. Another alternative is to affix the materials to the board or wall one item at a time as each is introduced.

Have the class discuss these events, including whether national and international response was adequate to meet the needs of the victims in specific instances. Then ask if anyone has experienced a natural disaster. Ask that person or persons to tell how they felt, how they survived, how others reacted, etc.

The discussion may include testimonies of how God provided and protected them during these times of crisis. Do not allow this section of the class to extend very long. The testimonies should be short, highlighting God's providential care.

INTO THE WORD

Have a class member briefly retell the story of how Joseph came to be imprisoned in Egypt. You may wish to call this person early in the week to ask him or her to be prepared. Ask this question for discussion: "Given Joseph's revelatory dreams of leadership, what do you think went through his mind while he was imprisoned?"

Next, divide the class into small groups. Give each group a sheet of paper and ask for drawings of Pharaoh's dreams. Say that you want the drawings to be in comic-strip fashion (stick figures are fine). There should be two series of drawings: one series for the first dream and another series for the second dream.

Call the class back together and ask someone from each group to show and explain their comic strip. Then lead a discussion centered around these questions:

1. Why do you think Pharaoh believed Joseph's interpretation of the dreams?

2. What *events* in Joseph's past prepared him to head up the effort to store food in view of the coming famine?

3. What *characteristics* of Joseph qualified him for the role of "famine relief director"? (This exercise is in the optional student book.)

Write responses on the board; discuss as appropriate. Then say, "Another interpreter of dreams was Daniel." Have someone read Daniel 2:1-30. Write "Joseph and Daniel" at the top of the board. Ask, "What similarities are there between Joseph and Daniel?"

Have a "scribe" list responses on the board. Follow with these questions: "How was God working in each of the two situations to further his plans? Did either man seek this ability or the fame that followed?"

Ask the class to list other Bible characters who suffered while God was working out his plan. (*Option:* Use, in small groups, the God's Preparations Then activity from the reproducible page.)

INTO LIFE

Before class, write the following three questions on a poster (large enough to be seen throughout the classroom). Do not show the poster until you come to this part of the lesson.

1. What was a difficult time in your life that turned positive?

2. What situation in your life right now may be the beginning of something that God is doing?

3. Specifically, how will you respond to God in this situation?

Divide the class into groups of four. Appoint one person in each group who will be in charge of keeping the discussion moving. Have each group discuss the questions sequentially. Ask the leaders of each group to encourage (but not force) everyone to participate. State a time limit before starting the discussions; notify the leaders a few minutes before the time is up, so they can be sure that every question is covered. (You may wish to encourage use of the God's Preparations Now activity from the reproducible page.)

When time is up, ask for volunteers to offer answers to the class as a whole. Be sensitive to the possibility that there may be some who were willing to reply in the previous small-group setting, but who would be embarrassed to do so in front of everyone.

Finally, have a time of silent prayer. Each should pray about how God is working right now is his or her life to produce a great harvest in the future. At the end of one minute, the teacher should close the prayer audibly, thanking God for his work in the lives of the learners.

God's Preparations Then

Take a look at the Bible characters noted in these passages. How were they being molded by God during difficult times?

Passage	Person(s)	Circumstances	What God Was Doing
Exodus 2:11-22			
1 Samuel 23:7-26			
Job 1:6–2:10			
Matthew 26:75			
Luke 22:44			
Acts 16:22-24			
1 Peter 4:12			
Revelation 1:9			

God's Preparations Now

Do you remember the old acronym PBPGINFWMY? It stands for *Please be patient, God is not finished with me yet.* On the notepad below, list some of your current struggles and how God may be molding you through them. What Scriptures help you most?

GOD PRESERVES HIS PEOPLE

LESSON 12

WHY TEACH THIS LESSON?

After gritting one's teeth through a movie or a novel where the leading character suffers injustice after injustice, there is nothing more satisfying than seeing the turning point arrive. That is the moment when the hero or heroine gets the upper hand. It's all a person can do, whether in a crowded theater or at home, not to yell out, "Yes!" Today's Scripture brings us to that moment of truth.

But it will be easy to learn the wrong lesson from the story of Joseph. That wrong lesson is something like, "If you're faithful to God for long enough, he will vindicate you before your earthly enemies in this life." The accounts of godly martyrs within the pages of the Bible say otherwise (examples: Jeremiah 26:20-23; Acts 7:54-60).

The correct "bigger picture," rather, is that God is in control. He is working out his plan. This can be difficult to believe when life seems to be out of control. Yet the God who guided Joseph's destiny is the one who is guiding ours. This is worth relearning as many times as it takes!

INTRODUCTION

A. A STRUGGLING YOUNG MINISTER

A young minister found a church about 200 miles from the seminary he planned to attend. The church at first was very glad to have him. But they had one restriction: he could not attend board meetings.

The young minister was not upset by this restriction because he didn't enjoy board meetings anyway. The agreement stipulated that the employment could be terminated by either party by giving a notice of 30 days to the other.

About a year after the young minister was hired, the church held a special board meeting. The major topic of discussion was this new minister. It was concluded at that meeting that they would fire him, but would wait 30 days before telling him he had been fired. Then he would have to leave immediately.

One conscientious elder came to the young man and told him what had happened. Immediately the young man began to look for another church, and he found one. He would be going back to school in just two weeks, and the new church provided a rent-free parsonage, all the utilities, and a raise in salary. The elder who warned the young minister even gave him the money needed for his next semester's tuition. God still can bring good out of bad situations!

B. LESSON BACKGROUND

When we last saw Joseph, he had become the second most powerful man in Egypt, an unimaginable height of power. Joseph then had two sons—Manasseh and Ephraim—by his Egyptian wife Asenath (Genesis 41:50-52).

The predicted years of plenty passed, and the famine arrived. The Egyptians survived by buying the grain that was stored up from the years of plenty (Genesis 41:53-56). Canaan experienced famine as well (42:5). Word came to Jacob that

DEVOTIONAL READING:
PSALM 85
BACKGROUND SCRIPTURE:
GENESIS 43:1–45:15
PRINTED TEXT:
GENESIS 45:1-12

LESSON AIMS

After participating in this lesson, each student will be able to:

1. Summarize Joseph's speech to his brothers when he revealed his identity.

2. Articulate the importance of seeing the "bigger picture" when viewing the events of life.

3. Write a prayer that asks for God's strength in resisting temptation to seek revenge when wronged.

KEY VERSE

Nov
18

God sent me ahead of you to preserve for you a remnant on earth and to save your lives by a great deliverance.
—Genesis 45:7

DAILY BIBLE READINGS

Monday, Nov. 12—Restoration of God's Favor (Psalm 85)

Tuesday, Nov. 13—Food in Egypt (Genesis 42:1-20)

Wednesday, Nov. 14—Jacob's Difficult Decision (Genesis 43:1-15)

Thursday, Nov. 15—Dining Together (Genesis 43:16-34)

Friday, Nov. 16—Joseph Tests His Brothers (Genesis 44:1-13)

Saturday, Nov. 17—Judah's Plea (Genesis 44:14-34)

Sunday, Nov. 18—Brothers Reconciled (Genesis 45:1-15)

grain was available in Egypt (42:1, 2). So 10 of Joseph's 11 brothers came to Egypt to buy grain. Joseph quickly recognized them, but he did not reveal his own true identity (42:6-8). The brothers knew only that they were dealing with an Egyptian official through a translator (42:23).

The brothers revealed that their father was still alive. Joseph had them arrested as spies and thrown in jail for a time. Reuben concluded that this was their punishment for having sold Joseph into slavery (Genesis 42:22). The brothers were released, given their grain, and sent back home. But Simeon had to stay behind as a hostage (42:24-26). Joseph told them they could buy no more grain if they did not bring back the youngest brother with them (42:33, 34; 43:3-5).

Joseph was age 17 when his brothers sold him into slavery (Genesis 37:1). He was age 30 when he entered Pharaoh's service (41:46). By the time Joseph saw his brothers on their return trip to Egypt, there had been 7 years of plenty and 2 years of famine (45:6). This means that Joseph was about age 39 when the brothers saw him in Genesis 42:6. Thus it was some 21 or 22 years since Joseph had seen any of his family members.

As we pick up today's story, the brothers have returned to Egypt, this time with brother Benjamin, who hadn't made the first trip. It is the second year of the famine (Genesis 45:6). The brothers' second trip to Egypt is recorded in Genesis 43. Our text today follows the test that Joseph devised in Genesis 44. Their return home was cut short as they were forced to return to Joseph's presence (Genesis 44:3-5, 14).

I. JOSEPH'S ANNOUNCEMENT (GENESIS 45:1-4)

A. JOSEPH UNRESTRAINED (vv. 1, 2)

1a. Then Joseph could no longer control himself before all his attendants, and he cried out, "Have everyone leave my presence!"

Joseph wants to be alone with his brothers for the very personal moment to come. It is not the type of moment that Joseph wants to share with his Egyptian associates. Thus he cries, *Have everyone leave my presence!*

Perhaps the Egyptians will consider it a bit strange for Joseph to be associating so intimately with this rag-tag band of foreigners. The Egyptians may also worry that Joseph, their boss, will be more vulnerable. He will have no guards around to protect him if the visitors decide to attack. But privacy will help the brothers respond to Joseph with less fear.

1b. So there was no one with Joseph when he made himself known to his brothers.

The first shock comes when *Joseph* begins to speak to his brothers in their native tongue (exactly what he says is in v. 3, below). Up to this time a translator has stood between them (Genesis 42:23). Joseph has understood what they have been saying all along, and they have not realized it. To them, Joseph has been no more than a powerful Egyptian authority with whom they have to deal.

The second shock will be when he reveals to them who he is. The translator may have referred to Joseph by his Egyptian name, Zaphenath-Paneah. That means something like, "the one who furnishes the sustenance of the land" (Genesis 41:45).

2. And he wept so loudly that the Egyptians heard him, and Pharaoh's household heard about it.

Joseph had *wept* when he first saw his brothers. He also had wept upon seeing his brother Benjamin. But those weepings were done out of sight (Genesis 42:24; 43:30). Joseph is known as a man who is able to exercise great self-control (compare 39:8-10). But now the dam of his emotions bursts. He can suppress his emotions no longer.

Has Joseph waited and prayed for this moment of reconciliation? At this point he has seen his brother Benjamin personally, and he knows his father is still alive. It is a time for tears of joy, a time for great rejoicing.

The weeping is so great that the sound of it penetrates the stone walls; everyone can hear it. This is a moment of raw emotion. This is the third time Joseph weeps for his brothers. He will do so two more times (Genesis 45:14, 15; 50:17).

We have no information of any adverse effect this incident has on Joseph's relationship with Pharaoh. Quite the opposite seems to be the case (Genesis 45:16-20).

B. JOSEPH REVEALS (vv. 3, 4)

3a. Joseph said to his brothers, "I am Joseph! Is my father still living?"

The first thing the brothers hear this Egyptian official speak in their native Hebrew is the startling declaration *I am Joseph*. It makes sense for Joseph to reveal his true name first.

But why does Joseph ask if his *father* is *still living?* Just moments earlier the brothers were expressing their great concern for their father if Benjamin were not to return with them (Genesis 44:29-32). Isn't the issue of the father's being alive already settled? Note that Joseph does not ask about "your father," but *my father.* Joseph is concerned about more than the mere fact that his father is still breathing. He wants more detail.

3b, 4. But his brothers were not able to answer him, because they were terrified at his presence.

Then Joseph said to his brothers, "Come close to me." When they had done so, he said, "I am your brother Joseph, the one you sold into Egypt!"

When *Joseph* reveals who he is, the *brothers* cannot speak because they are *terrified.* The Hebrew word can also mean "disturbed" or "panicked." (This same Hebrew word is used to describe high degrees of alarm in Judges 20:41; 1 Samuel 28:21; and 2 Samuel 4:1.) In their imaginations they may visualize torture, imprisonment, exile, and death. At one time they had power over Joseph's life to do as they pleased. Now the tables are turned. Joseph's further statement *the one you sold into Egypt* is not necessarily said in anger or rebuke. It primarily serves as a reminder of how this whole state of affairs got its start.

WHAT IS LEAST EXPECTED

Gary Tenen and Randy Tufts came upon a hole in the ground in the Arizona desert in 1974. What they really found was a lot more: it was a seven-acre wet, or "living," cavern right there under the arid Arizona surface. Eventually Tufts and Tenen would discover rooms the size of football fields, smaller chambers, and an underground lake. One of the cave's notable features is the second longest stalactite ever found: one-quarter inch wide and 21 feet long! As Tufts said, "We never expected to find anything like this in our wildest dreams."

The two kept their find secret for as long as possible. Eventually they contacted the owners of the land. The owners in turn sold the land to the Arizona State Park system for the cavern's preservation. Today, Kartchner Caverns is a jewel in the state's park system, bringing delight to thousands of visitors each year.

Joseph's brothers went to Egypt only to buy grain. While there, they discovered what they least expected: their long-lost brother. "I am Joseph," he said. The added words, "the one you sold into Egypt," left no doubt. Joseph would prove to be an unexpected treasure to them: he would save their lives! God sometimes brings into

Visual for Lesson 12. *Ask your learners, "How do God's past provisions for you lead you to trust in him for the year to come?"*

our lives a treasure (something or someone) we least expect and creates a wonderful blessing. When that happens, will you be able to recognize God to be the true source?
—C. R. B.

II. GOD'S PURPOSE (GENESIS 45:5-8)

A. WHAT THE BROTHERS SHOULD NOT DO (v. 5a)

5a. "And now, do not be distressed and do not be angry with yourselves for selling me here,

Joseph sees no need for self-blame. Nor does he want a feud to erupt in which each brother blames the others for what they had done more than 20 years previously. The reason for Joseph's challenge is given next.

B. WHAT GOD IS DOING (vv. 5b-8)

5b. ". . . because it was to save lives that God sent me ahead of you.

Joseph comforts the brothers with what is the central issue of the whole drama: *God* has been directing the sequence of events all along. It is God who has now brought them all to this place and point in time.

We do not know when Joseph realizes this bigger picture of preserving life. It may have been when he saw his brothers arrive for food the first time. If they are out of food early in the famine, what will happen to them as the famine drags on?

The bigger picture that Joseph sees is not necessarily a revelation from God. It is more likely the insight of a wise, godly man who is able to put the various pieces of the puzzle together.

6. "For two years now there has been famine in the land, and for the next five years there will not be plowing and reaping.

Here we learn how long the *famine* has lasted thus far. Joseph's information that the famine will last for another *five years* is news to the brothers! Who is this man who knows how long a famine will last? This only adds to the brothers' shock. It is important for the brothers to know that this famine is a long-term hardship, not one that will end shortly. That will influence their decision to return to Egypt with their families.

7. "But God sent me ahead of you to preserve for you a remnant on earth and to save your lives by a great deliverance.

We do not know how much Joseph understands regarding the significance that his extended family will have in the greater plan of *God*. Joseph certainly knows of the promises made to Abraham, Isaac, and Jacob (see Genesis 50:24, where Joseph recites the promise on his deathbed). But it is doubtful that Joseph understands how sweeping and far-reaching God's plans really are!

Abraham's concern was to have a son; Joseph is concerned about placing what family members there are in a place where they will be safe and secure. Security, abundance of food, good living conditions, and a sense of peace may help his extended family to flourish. What is happening to them is all part of a great plan of God. Joseph is simply an instrument in carrying out the plan.

8. "So then, it was not you who sent me here, but God. He made me father to Pharaoh, lord of his entire household and ruler of all Egypt.

Joseph is a man with status—so much so that he is considered to be a *father to Pharaoh*. That status came to him by the power of *God*. Joseph does not claim any great achievements as his own.

Even so, it is important for the brothers to know how great his position is. This is not to frighten or threaten them, but to let them know that he has come a long way. He has the power to save them from the famine. When we consider all

WHAT DO YOU THINK?

How do we see in Joseph the meeting of the spiritual and the practical? Can this be a model for us? Why, or why not?

three descriptors of Joseph's position (*father . . . lord . . . ruler*), we see a powerful person indeed!

This is not merely bluster on Joseph's part, because Pharaoh said much the same things when Joseph was first appointed to his position (Genesis 41:40-43). The brothers are dealing with the man who, more than 20 years earlier, had told them dreams of how he would rule over them. The dreams have come to pass. The brothers end up bowing before Joseph numerous times (Genesis 42:6; 43:26, 28; 50:18).

GOOD NEWS FROM BAD?

The continent of Africa has long been a cauldron brewing with bad news. In recent years, Zambia, Malawi, and Zimbabwe (among others) have seen millions of people suffer malnutrition and starvation. Chronic drought destroys hope of growing sufficient food. Sometimes one faction will use hunger as a weapon against another. HIV/AIDS has taken so many adults in some countries that few are left to work the farms. Political corruption destroys morale.

Can good come out of such evil? If Joseph's situation is an example, the answer is *yes*. His brothers sought to do evil to him, but God turned it into good—to the saving of many lives. Even today, God may step in and turn evil events into an opportunity for good. The leadership of two people has begun to offer hope to Africa. Bono, lead musician of the band U2, is challenging Western society to help the world's neediest people. And Rick Warren, minister of Saddleback Church in California, has started three foundations to provide aid.

But from God's eternal perspective, saving lives won't mean much unless we save souls as well. If the misery of Africa results in taking the gospel for the spirit along with food and medicine for the body, what good news that will be!

—C. R. B.

III. JOSEPH'S INSTRUCTIONS (GENESIS 45:9-12)

A. COME TO EGYPT (v. 9)

9. "Now hurry back to my father and say to him, 'This is what your son Joseph says: God has made me lord of all Egypt. Come down to me; don't delay.

What we see here is a departure from the patriarchal policy of the Old Testament. No longer is Jacob (Joseph's *father*) making the major decisions for his family. Instead that responsibility has shifted to Joseph. This is not Joseph's plan, but God's. Joseph is not making recommendations; he is giving orders.

Joseph is now occupying the position Jacob had envisioned for him except that Joseph is now in charge of even his own father. Jacob will need to be convinced that this move is the will of God—after all, God had given him and his forefathers the land of Canaan. That "divine convincing" will come in Genesis 46:1-4. The words *hurry* and *don't delay* make it clear that this move must be made immediately if the family is to continue to flourish.

B. DWELL IN GOSHEN (v. 10)

10a. "'You shall live in the region of Goshen

All of this information is directed at Jacob, Joseph's father. Jacob needs to know that Joseph has the power to give him and his extended family land in Egypt.

It is important that this land be somewhat separated from where most of the Egyptians live. The children of Israel need to flourish on their own and maintain their own way of life. They should not be seen as a threat to their neighbors

WHAT DO YOU THINK?

Some character qualities of Joseph's servanthood were godliness, responsibility, wisdom, and forgiveness. Why are these four so necessary in the lives of Christians today? What would life be like if we lacked one particular quality, but still had the other three? Or can they really be separated?

[Some passages for discussion are Ephesians 4:32; Colossians 1:28; 2:3, 23; 3:13; 1 Timothy 2:2, 10; 5:8; 6:6; Titus 1:1; James 1:5; 3:17; and 2 Peter 1:3, 6, 7; 3:11.]

THOUGHT TO REMEMBER

God has a plan that is greater than our current situations.

(compare 1 Chronicles 7:21). They need land that will be useful for their herds (Genesis 47:1-4).

Goshen is unknown outside of the Bible. It is also called the "land of Ramses," but that does not help us to know exactly where it is. We believe that it is in the Nile Delta, in the northeast part of Egypt. This gift is from God for his people. Do the travelers know that they and their descendants will be in Egypt for some 400 years (Genesis 15:13)?

10b. "'. . . *and be near me—you, your children and grandchildren, your flocks and herds, and all you have.*

Joseph wants his father and his family to be nearby. He has his own wife, children, and Egyptian associates. But that is not the same as having his extended family around. Joseph has strong feelings for his father. Joseph knows his father feels the same about him. It will be important for them to be close to one another.

There is no evidence that Joseph "takes over" the family after Jacob dies. The children of Israel will exist within Egypt as a subsociety without rulers in the traditional sense. That will change when a new king arises in Egypt, a king who will exert authority over the Israelites in a most forceful way (Exodus 1).

C. AVOID BECOMING DESTITUTE (v. 11)

11. *'I will provide for you there, because five years of famine are still to come. Otherwise you and your household and all who belong to you will become destitute.'*

Joseph wants his father to know about the *five years of famine* that remain. If they fail to respond to Joseph's request, they could lose everything. Perhaps the veiled warning here is that they could die if they stay in Canaan.

IV. JOSEPH'S VERIFICATION (GENESIS 45:12)

12. *"You can see for yourselves, and so can my brother Benjamin, that it is really I who am speaking to you."*

Joseph has been telling his brothers what he wants them to say to their father Jacob. Now Joseph shifts back to addressing the brothers themselves. Do they really need any more evidence to convince them that it really is Joseph who is in their presence?

CONCLUSION

The greatest attribute in the character of Joseph is that of *servanthood*. But the important aspect to this is not Joseph's service to Potiphar, the prison warden, or even Pharaoh. The important thing is his service to God. Joseph's faithfulness to God resulted in the saving of many lives. These included not only those of Egypt and Joseph's own family, but of many in the countries surrounding Egypt.

This is also a special instance of the concept of *the suffering servant* in the Bible. In the early years of his life, Joseph suffered for maintaining his integrity. Those who should have been closest to Joseph were his betrayers; but God used the experience to bring about physical redemption for Jacob's family. In that sense he is a "type" of Christ. Centuries later, God used Christ's obedience to make eternal redemption available to all humanity.

Joseph understood, to some extent, what was happening as part of a larger plan being worked out by God: it was to preserve life. In an even larger sense, God was continuing to fulfill his promises to Abraham that would culminate in the coming of the Messiah.

Discovery Learning

This page contains an alternative lesson plan emphasizing learning activities. Classes desiring such student involvement will find these suggestions helpful. The next page is a reproducible activity page to further enhance discovery learning.

INTO THE LESSON

There are many modern stories of how God has worked in adverse circumstances to bring about good. Find someone in your church or town who can give a testimonial that demonstrates God's providential care in his or her life during a very difficult period. Begin class by letting the person tell his or her story.

If you cannot find a person willing to do this, read to the class the story of the fleas in the barracks from *The Hiding Place* by Corrie ten Boom. If you do not have a copy of this book, the excerpt is easy to find on the Internet.

INTO THE WORD

Have someone (other than the teacher) research the details of how Joseph prepared Egypt for the famine and how the food was distributed when the famine began. Begin this section of the lesson with a report from that individual. Use of visuals such as maps, charts, or drawings will be very helpful in keeping the learners' attention.

Remind the class that Joseph's own family also suffered from the famine. Then ask these questions: "Why did Jacob send only 10 of the 11 brothers to Egypt? Why didn't the brothers recognize Joseph when they arrived in his presence?"

Several answers are possible for the second question. They can include the fact that many years had passed, and Joseph had matured; the brothers were not expecting to find him there, so they would not be looking for him; Joseph was dressed as an Egyptian; Joseph did not speak to them in the Hebrew language; etc.

Ask what Joseph learned from his brothers on this trip. Answers are that his father was still alive as was the younger brother Benjamin (Joseph's full brother). Ask why Joseph imprisoned them before letting them go home and why he kept Simeon when they left. Allow the class to use their "sanctified imaginations" as they think of possible reasons.

Next, assign class members who enjoy drama to play the roles of Jacob and the 11 brothers (or fewer than the 11, depending on your class size). Have them role-play the discussion about returning to Egypt a second time for more supplies. Then ask the class to describe vividly the scene when the brothers came into Joseph's presence after the silver cup was found in Benjamin's bag. What emotions were the brothers feeling before and after Joseph revealed who he was? What clues are there that show the depth of Joseph's emotions?

Then ask, "What was Joseph's summary of the reason for his ordeal in Egypt?" Finally have the class discuss the provisions Joseph made for his family. Explore why Goshen was chosen as a home for Jacob and his sons.

Next divide the class into groups of four (quads). Provide a copy of the Joseph's Life activity from the reproducible page for each group. Ask each quad to fill in the graph showing the progression of Joseph's highs and lows. When groups have completed their charts, draw a composite chart on the board; this will include all the events listed by the groups. There may be some discussion concerning where on the graph to put each event.

INTO LIFE

Write the following Scripture references on the board: Psalm 94:1-3; Nahum 1:2; Hebrews 10:30. Say, "Joseph had every reason to want revenge inflicted on his brothers; however, he did not succumb to the temptation to respond to them that way."

Then have the class as a whole look up the passages written on the board. Ask, "What do those words teach about vengeance or revenge?" Mention that Joseph triumphed in part because he resisted the desire for revenge. Then say, "Suggest ways that vengeance can be destructive both to the one seeking revenge and one(s) against whom revenge is taken." (This activity is in the optional student book.) Ask for reactions to the old saying, "Revenge is a dish best served cold."

Give each learner a sheet of paper. At the top they should write "Revenge." Have them write "Forgiveness" about one-third of the way down the page and "Prayer" about two-thirds of the way down the page. Give these instructions: "Under *Revenge,* list circumstances where you wanted to strike back; under *Forgiveness* make a list of people whom you need to forgive; under *Prayer* write a prayer asking God to help you to forgive with the same spirit Joseph demonstrated." Allow a few minutes of silent work. Ask for volunteers to share answers.

For a take home devotional reflection, distribute copies of the My Life activity from the reproducible page.

Joseph's Life

On the graph below chart the highs and lows of Joseph's life.

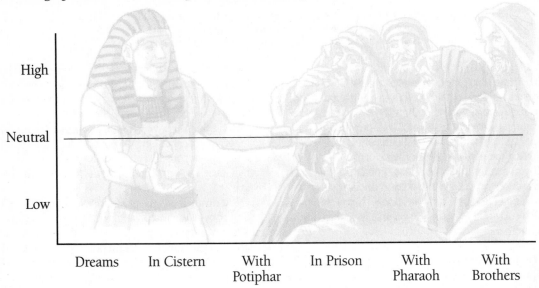

High

Neutral

Low

| Dreams | In Cistern | With Potiphar | In Prison | With Pharaoh | With Brothers |

My Life

List some difficult times in your life. Then write how God turned them into "kingdom good."

| DIFFICULT TIME | HOW GOD TURNED IT TO KINGDOM GOOD |

_____

_____

_____

_____

_____

_____

JACOB BLESSES HIS FAMILY

LESSON 13

WHY TEACH THIS LESSON?

One of the joys of life is that of sharing things with others. Parents know this. Thus they frequently share things with their children. The things they share range from bequests of small amounts of cash now and then all the way up to the transfers of large estates upon the parents' death.

But how many of your learners really grasp the idea of sharing a spiritual inheritance or passing along a spiritual legacy? This should be of even greater joy than that of sharing material wealth. Sharing testimonies has long been a part of what believers do, but do your learners realize that their spiritual legacies include the entirety of their life examples?

All of us can adopt children in the faith (compare 1 Timothy 1:2). Today's lesson will help everyone readjust their thinking about the importance of passing along a spiritual heritage to that next generation of church leaders.

INTRODUCTION

A. PASSING ALONG A HERITAGE

Erskine E. Scates, Sr. (1909–1979) was an outstanding church leader. During his various ministries, he planted or reopened churches in Colorado, New Mexico, Utah, and Wyoming. He also planted a Bible college and led in establishing several youth camps.

Many men and women entered the ministry or went to the mission field because of Scates's influence. One of the key contributions he made was the heritage he passed on to his family. Erskine and his wife, Faith, had several sons. One led successful ministries in New Mexico and Arizona. Two more became career missionaries. Several grandchildren are also involved in ministry, both in the United States and Brazil.

That's what you call leaving a heritage! But as Scates labored in ministry back in the 1930s and 1940s, do you suppose that he had any idea of the kind of heritage he was in the process of passing along?

B. LESSON BACKGROUND

Joseph's brothers followed his instructions concerning their move. They took the wagons Pharaoh gave them, returned to Canaan, and brought Jacob (their father) and the rest of the family to Egypt. All together, 70 souls ended up in the land of Egypt. These included Joseph and his children, who were already there (Genesis 46:27; Exodus 1:5).

It was a stirring moment when Jacob and Joseph met. They clung to one another and wept for a long time (Genesis 46:29, 30). Some of the family even were privileged to meet Pharaoh. At that point Jacob (also known as Israel) was 130 years old (47:9); he lived another 17 years (47:28).

Jacob was nearly blind as he approached the time of his death (Genesis 47:29; 48:10). Like his father before him, Jacob sensed the urgency to settle his

DEVOTIONAL READING:
PSALM 145:1-13

BACKGROUND SCRIPTURE:
GENESIS 48:8-21

PRINTED TEXT:
GENESIS 48:11-19

LESSON AIMS

After participating in this lesson, each student will be able to:

1. Describe Jacob's (Israel's) blessing of Joseph's children.

2. Explain the importance of the heritage passed on from Jacob to his grandchildren.

3. Pass along a spiritual heritage by explaining to someone else his or her own walk with the Lord.

KEY VERSE

Israel said to Joseph, "I never expected to see your face again, and now God has allowed me to see your children too." —Genesis 48:11

Nov
25

affairs (compare Genesis 27:1-4). A primary task was to bestow blessings on his sons and grandsons. This was an intentional ceremony, not a casual after-thought. Joseph, through his two sons Manasseh and Ephraim, received the double portion. Judah received the blessing that stated that the line of the Messiah would pass through his tribe (compare Genesis 49:9-12 with Hebrews 7:14; Revelation 5:5).

Our lesson today looks at the blessing given to Manasseh and Ephraim, Jacob's grandsons. The year is about 1860 BC.

I. UNEXPECTED MEETING (GENESIS 48:11, 12)

A. ISRAEL'S ASTONISHMENT (v. 11)

11. Israel said to Joseph, "I never expected to see your face again, and now God has allowed me to see your children too."

Let's begin by making sure that we don't get confused by names. *Israel* was the new name given to Jacob after he wrestled the mysterious man at Peniel (Genesis 32:24-30). Thus, Israel and Jacob are one and the same person.

The name *Israel* means "one who struggles with God"; this depicts the en-tire life of Jacob. Jacob's original name meant something like "heel-grabber" or, figuratively, "manipulator." Jacob's new name, Israel, is a covenant name. The importance of this name is seen in the fact that the designations *Israel* and *Israelite(s)* appear more than 2,500 times in the Bible!

I never expected to see your face again is Israel's admission of the despair in his life at the loss of Joseph years earlier. Israel had assumed that he would never see Joseph again. We are reminded of the depth of pain Israel felt when the brothers concocted the story that Joseph had been killed by a wild animal. It had seemed like the end of the world for Israel (Genesis 37:33-35).

Perhaps a tremor goes through Israel's body as he thinks of the approximately 22 years of pain he experienced because he believed Joseph to be dead. (It's amazing that his other 11 sons were able to keep "their little secret" all those years!) All of that has now changed. Israel can have the joy of passing on a spe-cial heritage through his favored son.

The phrase *God has allowed me to see your children too* means that not only does Israel have the joy of seeing his son again, he also becomes acquainted with that son's own offspring. The specific children in view here are Joseph's two sons, Manasseh and Ephraim (Genesis 48:1, 5, not in today's text).

This particular meeting probably is not the first time that Israel has seen these grandchildren. We may assume that he saw them with Joseph when Israel first arrived in Goshen (Genesis 46:28, 29).

B. JOSEPH'S REVERENCE (v. 12)

12. Then Joseph removed them from Israel's knees and bowed down with his face to the ground.

Reuben is Israel's firstborn. But because he committed a sexual sin, Israel is giving Reuben's blessing rights to Joseph's sons (Genesis 49:1-4; 1 Chronicles 5:1, 2). Those sons are Manasseh and Ephraim; they are the ones whom *Joseph removed . . . from Israel's knees.*

Elsewhere in Genesis, bowing depicts a greeting to someone worthy of great honor (Genesis 24:52; 33:3; 42:6; 43:26). That is undoubtedly the case here as Joseph shows respect to his father, who is near death. Joseph lives in a world where respect is openly demonstrated. Joseph's respect toward his father is not an act of worship, but of esteem.

WHAT DO YOU THINK?

What was a time in your life when the presence of children drew you closer to God?

WHAT DO YOU THINK?

What are some ways to show respect to parents today that may be different from how respect was shown in Bible times? What are some extremes to avoid?

II. SWITCHED BLESSING (GENESIS 48:13-16)

A. POSITION OF CHILDREN (v. 13)

13. And Joseph took both of them, Ephraim on his right toward Israel's left hand and Manasseh on his left toward Israel's right hand, and brought them close to him.

The next stage of the ceremony is about to begin. *Joseph* positions his children in order to receive *Israel's* blessing. Like his father Isaac before him, Israel in his old age is hardly able to see (Genesis 27:1; 48:10). Yet Israel is not depending on touch to determine which boy is which. Israel knows that Joseph will place the older boy under his right hand and the younger under his left. Joseph places the boys in their proper birth order before Israel so that Israel will give the primary blessing to the older son and the secondary blessing to the younger.

B. POSITION OF HANDS (v. 14)

14. But Israel reached out his right hand and put it on Ephraim's head, though he was the younger, and crossing his arms, he put his left hand on Manasseh's head, even though Manasseh was the firstborn.

Now an amazing thing happens: when *Israel* stretches out his hands, he crosses his arms. In so doing, he chooses *the younger* over *the firstborn*. Israel does this intentionally; this is no accident. Israel undoubtedly remembers his own experience when he was on the receiving end of the blessing, especially since he received the better blessing through his own deception rather than by his father's freewill choice. Israel knows exactly what he is doing, and no one will be able to deceive him.

Perhaps we see a little bit of Israel's former shrewd nature come to the surface one last time. By crossing his arms, Israel may be reminding Joseph that he (Israel) is still the patriarch. Joseph has the highest status possible in Egypt next to Pharaoh. He is accustomed to telling people what to do. When Israel was about to visit Pharaoh, Joseph told him what to say. But the decision as to who will receive the major blessing belongs to Israel, not Joseph.

C. REQUEST OF ISRAEL (vv. 15, 16)

15. Then he blessed Joseph and said,
   "May the God before whom my fathers
     Abraham and Isaac walked,
   the God who has been my shepherd
     all my life to this day,

As Joseph's sons are being blessed, *Joseph* is *blessed* as well. An important aspect of the blessing is for Israel to recall those whom God led and cared for previously, namely his grandfather, *Abraham*, and his father, *Isaac*. These two *walked* in the way of the Lord. James even identifies Abraham as "God's friend" (James 2:23; compare 2 Chronicles 20:7).

The phrase *who has been my shepherd* recognizes the fact that God has cared for Israel all of his life. God cared for him when he fled to Paddan Aram and when he left that place to return home. Had God not intervened, Laban, Israel's uncle and father-in-law, may have killed him (Genesis 31:24, 29). God cared for Israel when he returned to Canaan. God cared for him in his encounter with his brother Esau. God cared for him and his family when Simeon and Levi massacred the men at Shechem (34:25; 35:5).

The last great testimony to that care was when Joseph sent for him to come to Egypt to live. Imagery of God's care is very powerful in the Bible. See Psalm 23 and the picture of Jesus as the good shepherd in John 10:11-18.

WHAT DO YOU THINK?

Is it possible for Christian fathers and grandfathers to bless children today as Israel does here and in Genesis 49? Why, or why not?

HOW TO SAY IT

Boaz. BO-az.
Canaan. KAY-nun.
Ephraim. EE-fray-im.
Ishmael. ISH-may-el.
Israel. IZ-ray-el.
Laban. LAY-bun.
Levi. LEE-vye.
Manasseh. Muh-NASS-uh.
Paddan Aram. PAY-dan A-ram.
Peniel. Peh-NYE-el.
Pharaoh. FAIR-o or FAY-roe.
Shechem. SHEE-kem or SHEK-em.

16. ". . . the Angel who has delivered me from all harm
     —may he bless these boys.
May they be called by my name
     and the names of my fathers Abraham and Isaac,
and may they increase greatly upon the earth."

Putting verses 15 and 16 together, we see a threefold recognition of (1) God in covenant with Israel's *fathers,* (2) God as Israel's own shepherd, and (3) *the Angel* who had *delivered* him.

Many commentators believe that this angel was actually an appearance of God in human form rather being a created angel, as we may normally think. We read of visits by "the angel of the Lord" to various people in the Old Testament. At some point in the narrative the statement may switch from "angel of the Lord" to "Lord." For example, compare Genesis 16:7-12 with 16:13; also compare 22:15 with 22:16. Thus the phrase *angel of the Lord* could be another way of saying *Lord* or *God.* In some cases, however, the angel of the Lord seems to be distinct from God (see 2-Samuel 24:16; Zechariah 1:11-13; Luke 1:11).

With the phrase *bless these boys,* Israel begins the blessing. The phrase *who has delivered me* introduces one of the powerful relationship pictures we have in the Old Testament: that of redemption or deliverance. The Hebrew word that is behind this idea occurs more than 100 times in the Old Testament, and its first usage is right here.

One direction that the concept of deliverance or redemption takes in the Old Testament is that of *kinsman-redeemer.* This is a person who rescues family members who fall into debt or slavery (Leviticus 25:25, 49). The most famous story in the Old Testament regarding a kinsman-redeemer is found in the book of Ruth. As kinsman-redeemer, Boaz takes on the responsibility of marrying Ruth and redeeming the family property.

Israel had no earthly kinsman-redeemer to rescue him from the fury of either his brother or his uncle. Israel recognizes that it was God who had taken on that role, protecting him until he could return again to Canaan. The same could be said about Joseph; indeed, Joseph himself said it (see Genesis 45:5, 8, 9; 50:20). Joseph has no earthly person who stands in for him in times of trouble, but he is delivered again and again by God.

Israel (Jacob) requests two blessings for the boys. The first is an issue of identity: *May they be called by my name and the names of my fathers Abraham and Isaac.* When Moses encounters God hundreds of years later, God will be the God of Abraham, Isaac, and Jacob (Exodus 3:6, 15, 16; 4:5). This threefold identification with Abraham, Isaac, and Jacob is so important that it carries across hundreds and hundreds of years, right into the New Testament (Luke 20:37; Acts 3:13; 7:32).

The second requested blessing is for the boys to *increase greatly upon the earth.* The promise made to Abraham and Isaac (Genesis 22:17; 26:4) is now being passed on to Joseph's sons. Shortly after the exodus begins more than 400 years later, the tribes of Manasseh and Ephraim will number together 72,700 (Numbers 1:32-34)—and that counts only males age 20 and older (Numbers 1:3). Blessings fulfilled!

TELLING THE TRUTH VOLUNTARILY

James Frey got his proverbial "15 minutes of fame" on October 26, 2005, on *The Oprah Winfrey Show.* But his fame had turned to infamy by January 2006. His best-selling book *A Million Little Pieces* was purportedly the true story of his sensa-

---

WHAT DO YOU THINK?

How can we use special occasions in the church to pass along blessings to the generation to follow—that is, to give solemn reminders of and encouragement in the Christian faith?

DAILY BIBLE READINGS

Monday, Nov. 19—Bring *Your Father (Genesis 45:16-20)*

Tuesday, Nov. 20—God's *Reassurance (Genesis 46:1-4)*

Wednesday, Nov. 21—The *Reunion (Genesis 46:28-34)*

Thursday, Nov. 22—A *Blessing (Genesis 47:7-12)*

Friday, Nov. 23—Joseph's *Promise (Genesis 47:27-31)*

Saturday, Nov. 24—A *Grandfather's Blessing (Genesis 48:8-21)*

Sunday, Nov. 25—The *Greatness and Goodness of God (Psalm 145:1-13a)* tionally wretched life. He claimed to have led a thoroughly despicable existence as an alcoholic, drug addict, and criminal. One of his claims involved having a role in a train crash that killed two young women.

Oprah interviewed Frey on her show and recommended his book to her audience. Sales of the book skyrocketed. But then an investigative Web site poked many holes in his story. Soon Frey had to admit to the deception. The truth became clear.

Israel certainly had committed his share of deception in his life! But Israel's acknowledgment near the end of his days was of a wholly different kind from that of Frey. The most important distinction is that Israel's confession was self-initiated and voluntary while Frey's admission was forced from him by an investigation.

Israel's acknowledgment reminded Joseph of the real source of his strength and blessings: the God of their fathers. Israel recognized that it was God's messenger who had redeemed him from the evil he had committed. God wants us all to have this attitude, an attitude of voluntary acknowledgment of the truth that our hope lies in him alone. And it would be a good idea to make this confession before we come anywhere close to reaching Israel's age of 147!   —C. R. B.

"One generation shall praise thy works to another." —Psalm 145:4

Visual for Lesson 13. *How can we make the statement on this visual a daily reality? Ask your learners to list specific ways.*

III. ATTEMPTED CORRECTION (GENESIS 48:17-19)

A. JOSEPH'S DISPLEASURE (vv. 17, 18)

17, 18. When Joseph saw his father placing his right hand on Ephraim's head he was displeased; so he took hold of his father's hand to move it from Ephraim's head to Manasseh's head. Joseph said to him, "No, my father, this one is the first-born; put your right hand on his head."

The second half of verse 16 did not reveal any distinction, on the surface, between the blessings given to *Manasseh* (the older) and *Ephraim* (the younger). Yet Joseph knows the significance of the positioning of *his father's* hands; the *right hand* is the hand of chief blessing.

Joseph is determined that his *firstborn* son will receive the special blessing from Israel. His attempt to *move* Israel's hands indicates his concern. Joseph may assume that Israel has the same wish. When Israel crosses his arms (Genesis 48:14), Joseph perhaps thinks that this is just a blind man's mistake.

Joseph undoubtedly is aware that as soon as the blessing is given, it cannot be altered. The finality of the blessing demonstrates how seriously people in Bible times take such pronouncements. In the incident when Israel (Jacob) received the blessing intended for Esau (by this time many decades in the past), no court papers were served, no lawyers were summoned, no one tried to figure out how to overturn the blessing on the grounds of "false pretenses" or "fraudulent conveyance." The blessing of the patriarch is final; it is not changed even by the patriarch himself (compare Esther 1:19; 8:8; Daniel 6:8, 12).

B. ISRAEL'S REFUSAL (v. 19)

19. But his father refused and said, "I know, my son, I know. He too will become a people, and he too will become great. Nevertheless, his younger brother will be greater than he, and his descendants will become a group of nations."

Using touch, a blind man still can tell the difference between a taller, older child and a shorter, *younger* one. Israel makes it clear that he knows what he is doing. He considers himself to be still in control. Israel will make this one final decision for the family, not Joseph.

So we have another instance of reversed blessing. Traditionally, the oldest son was to receive the greater honor. But Isaac was chosen over Ishmael, and Jacob over Esau. Now it's Ephraim over Manasseh.

WHAT DO YOU THINK?

What was a time in your life when "the customary" was set aside as the Lord led in a new and surprising direction? What was the end result?

He too will become a people indicates that Manasseh still will have tribal status in the land when the Israelites take Canaan. This alone is a great blessing both to Manasseh and to Joseph. There will be no singular "tribe of Joseph" that receives land. But through his sons, Joseph actually will have the share of two tribes.

The words *his descendants will become a group of nations* is a figurative expression that establishes that Ephraim's descendants will be of more significance than those of his brother. "He blessed them that day and said, 'In your name will Israel pronounce this blessing: "May God make you like Ephraim and Manasseh."' So he put Ephraim ahead of Manasseh" (Genesis 48:20).

We see here a demonstration of the faith of the aged patriarch. He knows what God wants him to do, and he will do God's will over the protests of even his favorite son. Shortly after the exodus begins hundreds of years later, the tribe of Ephraim will be about 25 percent larger than the tribe of Manasseh (Numbers 1:32, 34).

Shortly after blessing the children of Joseph, Israel gives blessing and benediction to the rest of his sons (Genesis 49). Jacob then breathes his last and his body is embalmed (50:2). His body is carried back to Canaan and placed in a cave (49:29–50:14).

PASSING THE TORCH

The 2003 *Tour de France* was the centennial event of that famous bicycle race in and around France. Throughout the race, the focus was on Lance Armstrong, who ended up with his fifth consecutive victory. An hour-long celebration of the event's history followed the race. Past winners rode by the cheering crowds.

A poignant moment occurred just before the parade began. An older man on an ancient bicycle was to ride at the head of the parade. By his side was a young boy on a small, modern bike. It was to symbolize the "passing of the torch" from a one generation of cyclists to another. One photograph shows the two riders as they are waiting for the signal to begin the parade. The older man is gently resting his hand on the child's shoulder, as if to encourage him for what was ahead.

Today's lesson allows us to witness part of a passing-of-the-torch ceremony (the rest is in Genesis 49). Sometimes a torch is passed intentionally and voluntarily; sometimes it is forcefully taken; sometimes the passing "just happens" without much thought as people drift through the natural cycle of life. The passing happens in families, in businesses, and in churches. Members of all generations must use godly wisdom as they play out this drama of changing roles.   —C. R. B.

CONCLUSION

How important it is to leave a legacy! Israel (Jacob) had received a legacy from his father, who had received it in turn from *his* father. Then it was Israel's turn to leave it to the following generation. Life goes on a generation at a time. Each generation builds upon (or destroys) what the previous generation leaves behind.

A legacy can be thought of as a kind of inheritance. Usually when we think of an inheritance, we think of cash and various physical assets. A much more important inheritance is a spiritual one. What kind of people will live in and lead the next generation? Very often, people follow the example of those who precede them, whether good or bad. So the example set is vitally important.

Church leaders have a great responsibility in this regard (see 1 Timothy 4:12; Titus 2:7). We are responsible for the legacy we leave behind in life and teaching. Our legacy includes our sense of humility, the way we interact with others, and a holy lifestyle. We will be remembered longest for what we did, not what we said. The condemnation of those who set a bad example will be severe (Mark 9:42).

Discovery Learning

This page contains an alternative lesson plan emphasizing learning activities. Classes desiring such student involvement will find these suggestions helpful. The next page is a reproducible activity page to further enhance discovery learning.

INTO THE LESSON

Prior to class, contact three or four class members and ask them to bring something that has been passed down in their families. At the beginning of class, have each one tell the story (briefly) of the article he or she brought. Ask why that article is important to its present owner. Make a transition by noting that today's lesson is about a spiritual inheritance or heritage; this is something that is far more important than physical memorabilia.

Alternative introduction: Say, "Many people research their genealogies. Genealogies were important to ancient people also. Notice how many times genealogies are included in the Bible. How many of you have someone in your family who has documented a genealogy?" After responses, ask, "Why do you think genealogies are still important—or are they? What about the cautions in 1 Timothy 1:4 and Titus 3:9? Do you consider your own ancestry to be a blessing or a burden? Why?" Allow discussion, but don't let it drag out.

INTO THE WORD

Bring several Bible times-and-customs books to class. (Find these in your church library or the public library.) Write on the board the names of Israel's (Jacob's) 12 sons. Next to Joseph's name, write *Manasseh* and *Ephraim.*

Divide the class into small groups. Ask each group to research and write a brief newspaper article about Jacob's blessings on his descendants. Inform your groups that the bulk of the story should focus on the switched blessings of Manasseh and Ephraim (today's text). The story and its headline can be a bit "sensationalized" to recognize how unusual such a switch was.

Inform the groups that they can work in a passing mention of the blessings of Genesis 49 (not part of today's text) at the end of their articles. Distribute the times-and-customs books as resources for details such as traditional rituals regarding the blessings, deviation from tradition, expected family actions and reactions, etc. (If this assignment is too difficult for your class, ask the groups to write only some possible headlines.)

Allow about 10 minutes, then read each group's newspaper articles to the entire class. Discuss. Ask your learners to list the main point of each son and grandson's blessing (or "antiblessing," as the case may be!),

using today's text along with Genesis 49 as a guide. Write answers beside the names on the board.

Move back to a focused discussion of today's text by pointing out the distinction (or "hierarchy") of blessings of which both Israel and Joseph were aware. Say, "The firstborn normally was to receive the primary or greater blessing. Does this ancient 'hierarchy of blessing' seem like favoritism, or was there good reason for it?"

Point out that Israel (Jacob) certainly had material assets to leave to his descendants, but the blessings focused on issues of a spiritual nature rather than "I leave Ephraim 10 percent of my sheep." Ask your learners to compare and contrast Israel's emphasis in his pronounced blessings with the emphasis we see today on the disposition of material assets in wills. Use this as a transition to the Into Life segment.

INTO LIFE

Say, "Ancestry is significant, but it is beyond our control. It is what it is; it cannot be changed; we cannot pick our parents. What is still within our control, however, is the legacy or heritage we leave to the generation to follow."

Point out that many people have made financial preparations for their children through wills and trust funds. However, the most important inheritance to leave behind is a spiritual legacy. No more important blessing can be left for our loved ones. However, our legacies can be left to our spiritual children and grandchildren, not just to those related to us by blood or legal adoption.

Distribute copies of the Passing the Blessing On activity from the reproducible page. Ask your learners to write a spiritual blessing to each of their children and/or grandchildren. Those who do not have children will write to someone whom they consider to be a son or daughter "in the faith" (see 1 Timothy 1:2) whom they influence. (Those who do have biological or adopted children can write to spiritual children as well.)

Encourage your learners to give or mail the blessings to the people addressed. The experience may be difficult for those who are estranged from family members or whose children have died. Gently suggest that it can be a healing process for them to write the blessing, even if not mailed. Distribute the Your Spiritual Family activity from the reproducible page for devotional reflection.

Your Spiritual Family

Write your name on the trunk of the tree below. On the roots, write the names of people in your "spiritual family" who have helped you (or are helping you) in your Christian growth. On the branches, write the names of people to whom you are leaving a spiritual legacy.

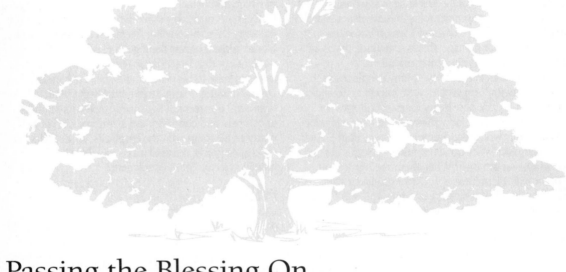

Passing the Blessing On

Write a spiritual blessing for each of your children. Include your intention to be the conduit for those blessings. If you do not have children, write to those whom you consider to be your "spiritual children," that is, a son or daughter "in the faith" (see 1 Timothy 1:2). If you do have biological or adopted children, you can write to spiritual children as well.

My Blessing . . .

_____

_____

_____

_____

_____

_____

Winter Quarter 2007–2008

God's Call to the Christian Community

(Luke)

Special Features

Lessons

Unit 1: God's Call in Christ

Unit 2: Inspired by God's Call

Unit 3: Responding to God's Call

About These Lessons

This quarter we look to the Gospel of Luke to discover how God calls the church to live out her purpose. The requirements are breathtaking in scope! But we have the power of the Holy Spirit to help us put them into action.

Dec 2
Dec 9
Dec 16
Dec 23
Dec 30
Jan 6
Jan 13
Jan 20
Jan 27
Feb 3
Feb 10
Feb 17
Feb 24

God's Call, Then and Now

by Mark S. Krause

This quarter we will look at texts from Luke's Gospel that deal with God's call to his people. One cannot read the Bible without encountering individuals who are called by God to do certain things.

God's Call, Then and Now

God calls the community of Christian faith (the church) to live out the purpose for which she was created. That purpose is summed up in the Great Commission: "Go and make disciples of all nations, baptizing them in the name of the Father and of the Son and of the Holy Spirit, and teaching them to obey everything I have commanded you" (Matthew 28:19, 20). The "everything I have commanded you" includes the lessons that God's Word teaches us this quarter.

Lesson 2

Lesson 7

Lessons 3, 8, 9, 10, 11

Lessons 12, 13

Lessons 1, 5, 6

Lesson 4

Mediterranean Sea

Capernaum

Sea of Galilee

Tiberias

Nazareth

GALILEE

Yarmuk R.

Caesarea

Pella

Jordan R.

Samaria

SAMARIA

Jabbok R.

Joppa

PEREA

JUDEA

Jordan R.

Emmaus

Jericho

Jerusalem

Bethany

Bethlehem

Dead

Sea

Arnon R.

Lessons from LUKE

THE GOSPEL OF LUKE

God's Call to the Christian Community
Unit 1: God's Call in Christ
(Lessons 1-5)

CALLED TO BELIEVE

LESSON 1

WHY TEACH THIS LESSON?

Believers need to be reminded on a fairly regular basis of some realities concerning their faith and the God whom they serve. The most important is that God is God. Psalm 100:3 boldly declares "Know that the Lord is God." Our Lord God is the creator and sustainer of life. Everything flows from him. All creation has come from his hand. All creation continues by his power.

Bad things happen when we lose track of these facts. We begin relying on our own strength. We begin walking by sight rather than by faith. We push God off the thrones of our hearts and put ourselves there instead.

We all drift into that mode at some time or other, don't we? Today's lesson provides the cure. Zechariah received this cure the hard way. But we can learn from his mistake. Today, we shall!

INTRODUCTION

A. TALL TALES

The annual Liars' Contest used to be a popular event within the Pennsylvania German community. Each person would tell a story to see who could go the furthest beyond the reach of credibility. It was all in good fun because no one was expected to believe the outlandish tales.

However, when God tells a person something that is frankly incredible, he expects to be believed. When God warned Adam and Eve that eating the fruit of the forbidden tree would result in their deaths, he meant it. When he told Noah, Abraham, and Moses things that seemed totally impossible, they believed him. Then the time came for Zechariah to take his turn. He was called to believe that God would give him a son and that son would prepare for the coming of the Messiah.

B. LESSON BACKGROUND

Through the centuries of the Old Testament, God spoke to the Jewish people through the prophets at many times and in various ways (see Hebrews 1:1). But by the time we reach Luke 1, it had been 400 years since God said anything at all. So when an angel came from Heaven to announce that God was going to raise up a prophet, it was (or should have been) a stunning development for God's people.

On a more personal level, the announcement was stunning to a priest named Zechariah. Although his name means "God remembers," he and his wife, Elizabeth, could well have thought that God had forgotten them. They were childless because she was barren; in addition, they were "well along in years" (Luke 1:7). Still, they were wholly devoted to serving their God.

As God broke his 400 years of silence, the events would be carefully recorded by Luke, a physician and an associate of the apostle Paul (Colossians 4:14; 2 Timothy 4:11). As Luke explained in the opening verses of his Gos-

DEVOTIONAL READING:
PSALM 66:1-4, 16-20
BACKGROUND SCRIPTURE:
LUKE 1:5-25
PRINTED TEXT:
LUKE 1:8-23

LESSON AIMS

After participating in this lesson, each student will be able to:

1. Describe the meeting between Zechariah and the angel Gabriel.

2. Explain why Zechariah should have believed the angel and why he doubted.

3. Confess one area of life where his or her faith could be stronger.

KEY VERSE

And now you will be silent and not able to speak until the day this happens, because you did not believe my words, which will come true at their proper time.   —Luke 1:20

WHAT DO YOU THINK?

Whom do you know whose life reflects a quiet, faithful walk with Jesus? What impact has that example had on you?

WHAT DO YOU THINK?

What was a time when a certain event or routine in your life proved to be something special for God in a way that was above and beyond your beginning expectation?

pel, he was the recipient of eyewitness testimony and had "carefully investigated everything from the beginning" (Luke 1:3). We can put full confidence in what he wrote. The historical truth of these events teaches us a lesson that Zechariah learned the hard way: we are called to put full confidence in God.

I. ORDINARY SETTING (LUKE 1:8-10)

A. FAITHFUL SERVICE (vv. 8, 9)

8. Once when Zechariah's division was on duty and he was serving as priest before God,

On the surface, the day looks ordinary. The priests are performing their usual service, and people are saying their routine prayers. But something quite extraordinary is about to happen. Little does he (Zechariah) know what God has planned for him on this "ordinary" day.

Zechariah is a member of the priestly course of Abijah (see 1 Chronicles 24:10; Luke 1:5). As one of 24 such divisions of the priesthood (see 1 Chronicles 24:18), his group takes its turn to serve at the temple two weeks of every year. Then they serve with all the other groups during the major festivals.

Zechariah, now an old man (Luke 1:18), can look back over the many years that he has faithfully executed the priest's office. In faithful submission to the will of God, he is like the priests who later become believers in Jesus (see Acts 6:7).

9. . . . he was chosen by lot, according to the custom of the priesthood, to go into the temple of the Lord and burn incense.

When priests and their assistants serve at *the temple,* their responsibilities include sacrificing animals, filling the oil in the lamp stand, and setting out the "showbread" on the sacred table. At special times they also lead the people in prayer and praise to God. According to the custom of their office, the priests cast lots to decide who will do which duty. Casting lots keeps the selection process impartial (compare 1 Chronicles 24:5, 31; 25:8; 26:12-16).

The specific *lot* that falls to Zechariah on this day is to *burn incense* at the altar of incense. This is a wooden box overlaid with gold, standing in front of the Holy of Holies. According to Exodus 30:1-10, incense is to be offered twice daily. Since there are thousands of priests, each is permitted to burn this incense no more than once in his lifetime. Thus Zechariah knows this "ordinary" day is special for him in a certain way. But he does not yet know just how special it will be!

B. EXPECTANT MOMENT (v. 10)

10. And when the time for the burning of incense came, all the assembled worshipers were praying outside.

The scene is typical and ordinary: while the priest goes into the Holy Place, the surrounding courtyards are filled with *worshipers.* But "ordinary" need not imply "unsacred." This is always a sacred moment. The sacredness is about to be enhanced by what God is going to do. A devout priest is serving, the people are *praying,* and God's silence of 400 years is about to be broken.

II. EXTRAORDINARY NEWS (LUKE 1:11-13)

A. STARTLING APPEARANCE (vv. 11, 12)

11. Then an angel of the Lord appeared to him, standing at the right side of the altar of incense.

The altar of incense is next to the giant curtain that separates the Holy Place from the Holy of Holies (also known as the Most Holy Place), the two rooms of the temple (Exodus 30:6; 40:5; 1 Kings 6:22). The fragrance of the burning incense is a sweet aroma in God's presence.

As Zechariah goes about his duties of replenishing the incense, *an angel of the Lord* appears beside the altar. Named later in the narrative as Gabriel (v. 19), this is the same angel who will carry God's message to a young virgin named Mary in a few months.

12. When Zechariah saw him, he was startled and was gripped with fear.

The reaction of Zechariah is not surprising except in its understatement! He is *startled* because he cannot fathom what is happening. In addition, he is *gripped with fear* since the event is clearly supernatural.

SPEAKING TO AN ANGEL, RESPONDING TO GOD

The title of a syrupy love song from the 1950s asks "How Do You Speak to an Angel?" The point of the song is that a young man has met the perfect girl, but he is tongue-tied.

Obviously, the recording artist was using the word *angel* in a figurative way. But if we take the question of the song title literally, Scripture provides insight. Appearances by angels sometimes cause fear (Daniel 8:15-17; Luke 1:12, 29, 30; Acts 10:1-4). In such cases, the angel may speak words of comfort so the human will be able to respond. In other cases, people react to angelic encounters in a rather human-to-human way. See the cases of Abraham, Lot, and Gideon in Genesis 18:1-5; 19:1, 2; and Judges 6:11-13.

Despite the apparent calmness of Abraham, Lot, and Gideon, knowing that an angel was coming from the presence of God would cause any of us to become a bit "startled" at the appearance of such a heavenly being! I don't expect to receive a visit from an angel (none of us should), but if it happened I think I would be terrified. I probably would be just as tongue-tied as the young man depicted in the 1950s song.

However, the fact of ultimate importance is that Zechariah and others who received angelic appearances listened and obeyed. God has much to say to us through the pages of his Word. We need not react with dread at his words, but we must indeed listen and obey.   —J. B. N.

B. STUNNING PROMISE (v. 13)

13. But the angel said to him: "Do not be afraid, Zechariah; your prayer has been heard. Your wife Elizabeth will bear you a son, and you are to give him the name John.

Zechariah does not know what is happening, but the angel does. Gabriel knows both Zechariah and *Elizabeth* by name; he even knows that the faithful priest has been praying for *a son*. Elizabeth is to *bear* a son; his *name* will be *John* (which means, "Yahweh has been gracious").

At certain times in Scripture, God sends angels to deliver news that is simply unbelievable from a human perspective. But people are expected to believe it anyway. Such is the case here. Against the laws of nature, Zechariah is going to have a son! That son will be the one to prepare for the coming of the Christ.

To be childless in the Jewish culture is considered to be a severe misfortune (Luke 1:25). We may assume that Zechariah has prayed year after year for a child, to no (apparent) avail. In his old age he may have begun to pray that *prayer* less and less often. But God has heard, and God has not forgotten. God answers the prayer on his own timetable (compare Genesis 15:1-5; 21:1-7; 30:1, 22). The son of Zechariah and Elizabeth will go on to be one of the most remarkable men in history: John the Baptist.

Visual for Lesson 1. *Keep this visual posted all quarter as a reminder of how our 13 lessons fit together.*

WHAT DO YOU THINK?

What was a time when you prayed for something and you were surprised when God answered your prayer? What did you learn about yourself as a result?

III. EXCEPTIONAL SON (LUKE 1:14-17)

A. His Character (vv. 14, 15)

14. "He will be a joy and delight to you, and many will rejoice because of his birth,

The fear and confusion of Zechariah eventually will be replaced with *joy* and gladness. Like Abraham in his old age, Zechariah is going to have a son!

While the *birth* of a baby is generally a time of celebration and happiness, this birth will be something more. More than just the family and friends, *many will rejoice* at John's birth (compare Luke 1:57, 58). The effects of his birth bring joy even across the centuries to our own time.

15. ". . . for he will be great in the sight of the Lord. He is never to take wine or other fermented drink, and he will be filled with the Holy Spirit even from birth.

Many movie stars, athletes, and politicians are great in the sight of people. But John will grow up to be *great in the sight of the Lord*. It is, after all, the Lord's evaluation that is important! Jesus will later say of him, "Among those born of women there has not risen anyone greater than John the Baptist" (Matthew 11:11).

Like those who took the Nazirite vow to separate themselves to the Lord, John will drink nothing intoxicating (compare Numbers 6:1-3; Judges 13:2-5; Amos 2:11, 12). But John is not just another Nazirite; he is far more special. *He will be filled with the Holy Spirit even from birth.* Three months before he is even born, he leaps for joy, undoubtedly by the Spirit, when Mary comes to see Elizabeth (Luke 1:41).

"He Shall Be Great"

I once knew a man who had a very high opinion of his granddaughter. His view of her was always expressed with highest praise: she was beautiful, smart, and talented. I didn't want to disagree with him, but I thought he overrated her. She was an attractive teenager, but I would not have called her beautiful. She got good grades in school, but I would not have called her exceptionally intelligent. As for her talent, I was equally underimpressed.

As the old saying goes, "Beauty is in the eye of the beholder." I didn't share his estimate of her abilities. But then again, I don't think he had a very wide exposure to people of talent and intelligence with which to compare hers. The girl was outstanding in his eyes. And that's all right; I appreciated his devotion to his granddaughter. Yet if this same estimate had come from an experienced judge of beauty and talent contests, I would have been more inclined to take it at face value.

John was to be "great in the sight of the Lord." The Lord is objective about such things (remember, he "does not show favoritism"; Acts 10:34). He has wide experience in knowing and judging people. Being judged "great" in the Lord's sight certainly puts John in a special category. May God see each of us as "great" as we do our parts to prepare the world for Christ's return!   —J. B. N.

B. His Mission (vv. 16, 17)

16. "Many of the people of Israel will he bring back to the Lord their God.

Gabriel's prediction that John's mission will be to call *the people of Israel* to return to *the Lord* implies that many Israelites have fallen away from God. *Many* eventually will flock to hear John, will repent, and will be baptized by him (Matthew 3; Mark 1:1-8; Luke 3:1-20; John 1:19-28).

17. "And he will go on before the Lord, in the spirit and power of Elijah, to turn the hearts of the fathers to their children and the disobedient to the wisdom of the righteous—to make ready a people prepared for the Lord."

John's mission was also predicted at the end of the Old Testament: "See, I will send you the prophet Elijah. . . . He will *turn the hearts of the fathers to their children*, and the hearts of the children to their fathers" (Malachi 4:5, 6). In this way John is to prepare the people of Judea for the coming of the Messiah. Although John himself may or may not have been aware of his importance as a "type" of *Elijah*, Jesus understood it perfectly (see Matthew 17:10-13).

It is striking that God's closing words in the Old Testament and some of the first words in the New Testament are about John the Baptist. Although there have been more than 400 years of silence between the times of Malachi and Luke, God's plan has not changed. Now John will have a significant role in helping to make that plan a reality. He will be wholly devoted to preparing the way for the Messiah. John will have no regard for his own importance. Right up to the time of his grisly death, he will live only to answer the call of God.

IV. DIVINE CONFIRMATION (LUKE 1:18-23)

A. HUMAN DOUBT (v. 18)

18. Zechariah asked the angel, "How can I be sure of this? I am an old man and my wife is well along in years."

What *the angel* has just said is more than Zechariah can swallow! In his human weakness, Zechariah is reluctant to believe (compare Genesis 18:12). So Zechariah blurts out the thought of his heart: *How can I be sure of this?*

Zechariah needs some kind of proof that such things will be so. After all, he is *an old man* and his *wife is well along in years*. The years have taken their toll on them both. While the unbelief of Zechariah is understandable, we should not make excuses for it.

B. ANGELIC SENTENCING (vv. 19, 20)

19. The angel answered, "I am Gabriel. I stand in the presence of God, and I have been sent to speak to you and to tell you this good news.

The angel now identifies himself. In so doing, he shows why Zechariah should believe what he has just been told. *Gabriel* is the same angel who had carried God's message to Daniel five and a half centuries earlier (Daniel 8:16; 9:21). This exalted being, who regularly *stands in the* very *presence of God*, has come with a message directly from on high. It is God's message, and it is *good news*. So why shouldn't Zechariah believe it? Zechariah surely knows how God opened the womb of Sarah (Genesis 21:1-7)!

20. "And now you will be silent and not able to speak until the day this happens, because you did not believe my words, which will come true at their proper time."

God, in an act of stern kindness, gives Zechariah both punishment and confirmation: he will *not* be *able to speak* for the entire period of Elizabeth's pregnancy. Until the day when these things happen—and they most certainly will—Zechariah will suffer the consequence of his unbelief. God has spoken and Zechariah does not believe. Now Zechariah cannot speak further words of unbelief or any other words at all. God will lift the punishment at the *time* of John's naming (Luke 1:62-64).

C. DIVINE PROOF (vv. 21-23)

21. Meanwhile, the people were waiting for Zechariah and wondering why he stayed so long in the temple.

The crowds pray and wait outside in the temple courtyards. On this day, Zechariah is their closest link to the presence of God, so they are eager to

WHAT DO YOU THINK?

How does God interact with us today? [Hints: John 16:5-15; Acts 2:38, 39; 1 Thessalonians 5:11; James 1:2-4; 5:16; 1 Peter 4:10, 11.] What are some reasons for failing to notice God working in and around our lives?

WHAT DO YOU THINK?

Scripture offers us examples of God-fearing individuals who struggled to understand or believe something that God told them. What Bible passages do you struggle to understand or believe? How do you remain faithful in spite of doubt?

HOW TO SAY IT

Aaronic. Air-AHN-ik.
Abijah. Uh-BYE-juh.
Abraham. AY-bruh-ham.
Judea. Joo-DEE-uh.
Malachi. MAL-uh-kye.
Moses. MO-zes or MO-zez.
Nazirite. NAZ-uh-rite.
Yahweh (Hebrew). YAH-weh.
Zechariah. ZEK-uh-RYE-uh.

PRAYER

Our Father, we thank you for remembering us in spite of our sins and for opening the door of salvation. Thank you for providing all we need to be able to believe in your Son Jesus. He is the one by whom we are saved. In his name we pray, amen.

see him emerge from the sacred building. Usually the stay of a priest in the Holy Place lasts only a few minutes. Then he comes out and pronounces the familiar Aaronic blessing on the people (see Numbers 6:24-26). When Zechariah delays, taking much longer than a priest usually does, they are concerned. What is happening?

22. When he came out, he could not speak to them. They realized he had seen a vision in the temple, for he kept making signs to them but remained unable to speak.

Zechariah finally emerges. He does not say the expected words of blessing on the people; indeed, he is unable to *speak to them* at all! Instead, he uses hand signals to explain what has happened. The fact that he is speechless is proof that the hand of God is upon him.

23. When his time of service was completed, he returned home.

When the two weeks of his ministry in the temple are over, Zechariah returns to his own house in the hill country of Judea (see Luke 1:39, 40). The chief priests and their important assistants have houses in Jerusalem itself, but lesser priests live out in the countryside. There they farm, keep livestock, or work at a trade.

Zechariah's return *home* is not the end of the story; it is only the beginning. After four centuries of silence, God has spoken to his people once again. God's plan of salvation is moving forward!

CONCLUSION

A. ZECHARIAH: "GOD REMEMBERS"

God tells no tall tales; it is impossible for him to lie (see Hebrews 6:18). Throughout history, God has required that people listen when he speaks and that they believe what he says.

God's expectation applied to Zechariah, perhaps especially so. Yet even though he was a faithful priest (Luke 1:6), he stumbled at believing God's "impossible" promise. Since we have the advantage of hindsight of the completed New Testament, we may be tempted to excuse Zechariah's failure because we know some things he didn't. But Zechariah also had hindsight to draw on: he undoubtedly knew of the Old Testament accounts of how God intervened to bring sons to elderly, childless couples. Having hindsight is no guarantee that we will always exercise faith!

God did not intend to leave us in the bondage of sin. From the beginning of our disobedience, when God promised that the seed of woman would crush Satan's head (Genesis 3:15), God had a plan to save us. After many centuries, God still pushes his plan forward. Now we—like Zechariah—are called to believe.

B. JOHN: "YAHWEH HAS BEEN GRACIOUS"

John the Baptist was rightly named. He was living proof of God's graciousness. To Zechariah and Elizabeth in their old age, God extended grace by granting them a son. To the entire human race, God proved his grace by sending his own Son—whose way John the Baptist prepared. As this all unfolded, one thing was clear: Yahweh (God) has been gracious.

As we enter this Christmas season, let us remember again each part of the sacred story. Let us rejoice to hear Gabriel's glad tidings to Zechariah and to Mary; let us echo the multitude of the heavenly hosts praising God. We believe in the baby of Bethlehem; we believe in the Christ of the cross; we believe in the future return of our king. We have been called to believe—and we do!

THOUGHT TO REMEMBER

God yet calls us to believe.

Discovery Learning

This page contains an alternative lesson plan emphasizing learning activities. Classes desiring such student involvement will find these suggestions helpful. The next page is a reproducible activity page to further enhance discovery learning.

INTO THE LESSON

Place a copy of the activity In the Line of Aaron and Levi from the Reproducible Page in chairs for your early learners to work on as they arrive. Prior to class, cut from poster board seven rectangles of about five by eight inches each. Write the following letter pairs on them, one letter pair per rectangle, front and back: D and B, O and E, U and L, B and I, T and E, E and V, R and E. Be certain that the letter on the back of each rectangle is upside down in relation to the letter on the front.

Affix these seven as "flaps" on the wall. The word *DOUBTER* should be showing. Ask the class to guess the letters underneath the letters that are showing. With each correct guess, lift the flap and tape it up to allow the letter to show. Once the second word is fully revealed, say, "That's the challenge of today's study: *Doubter, believe!* The doubter today is Zechariah, but the same challenge comes to all of us." Keep the letter flaps in view to refer to later.

INTO THE WORD

Distribute the following matching activity. Have your learners work in pairs or small teams. Say, "The headings of the lesson outline are given here in alphabetical order. The all-capital headings are the main outline elements; mixed-case headings are subpoints. Use today's text to help you discover the right answer." (This activity is included in the optional student book.)

____ Angelic Sentencing	a. Luke 1:8, 9
____ DIVINE CONFIRMATION	b. Luke 1:8-10
____ Divine Proof	c. Luke 1:10
____ EXCEPTIONAL SON	d. Luke 1:11-13
____ Expectant Moment	e. Luke 1:11, 12
____ EXTRAORDINARY NEWS	f. Luke 1:13
____ Faithful Service	g. Luke 1:14-17
____ His Character	h. Luke 1:14, 15
____ His Mission	i. Luke 1:16, 17
____ Human Doubt	j. Luke 1:18
____ ORDINARY SETTING	k. Luke 1:18-23
____ Startling Appearance	l. Luke 1:19, 20
____ Stunning Promise	m. Luke 1:21-23

Give learners a few minutes to work and then call for answers. As segments and titles are correctly matched, have those verses read aloud.

Next, introduce the following Hard-to-Believe activity. Write on the board this question: How important is this issue to me in believing what someone is stating as truth? Then ask for a silent response to each of the following. The possible responses are a raised fist (that is, with no fingers extended) for no importance; index finger up for very little importance; two fingers up for of some importance; three fingers up for very important.

1. Lack of knowledge about the one making the claim. 2. Personal experience. 3. Being outside the realm of empirical science. 4. The time and setting of the affirmation. 5. The lack of confirming witnesses. 6. Inability to prove the claim immediately. 7. The seemingly low confidence of the one affirming. 8. The person's skeptical, even cynical attitude. 9. The likelihood of being scoffed at or laughed at for believing it. 10. The absence of biblical revelation or biblical precedent for the claim.

Quickly run through the list and ask for responses. Then write this question on the board: How may these factors have had an effect in Zechariah believing or disbelieving the message given to him?

Repeat each element and ask learners to respond. For example, for #1, did Zechariah know Gabriel personally? For #2, were the years and years of Elizabeth's barrenness reason to believe she could not become pregnant? For #3, how would the physical condition of Zechariah and Elizabeth for becoming parents affect Zechariah's reaction? For #10, would not Zechariah know of the Old Testament examples of Abraham and Sarah, Elkanah and Hannah, and others?

Make your way through the entire list in this manner. This will allow you a thorough examination of why Zechariah should have believed and why he doubted. (A similar exercise is in the optional student book.)

INTO LIFE

Distribute copies of the Zechariah's Doubts—And Ours from the Reproducible Page. Work on it as a class or in small groups. Finally, give each learner a strip of paper that is printed with seven blocks bearing the letters D, O, U, B, T, E, R. Ask each to carry the slip for the week. Learners are to pick a time each day to write one letter of the word *BELIEVE* on the back. Tell them this is the daily challenge for the godly: *Doubter, believe!* Refer back to the Into the Lesson activity.

In the Line of Aaron and Levi

Zechariah "was serving as priest before God" (Luke 1:8) in obedience to the Old Testament laws of worship. Look at each of the following texts and jot down some insights concerning Zechariah's service.

Exodus 30:7-10

Exodus 30:34-38

Leviticus 4:7

1 Chronicles 24:6-19

Zechariah's Doubts—and Ours

Knowing of Zechariah's reasons to believe and many, many others, the Christian still finds occasions of doubt in his or her daily walk. What is your level of occasional doubt in each of the following areas? Put from zero up to four Ds to rate your level of doubt beside each belief statement below. At the end add one of your own, an area in which you find yourself occasionally plagued by doubt.

B _____ I believe that God created the world from nothing.
_____ I believe that God answers my prayers.
E _____ I believe that the Holy Spirit empowers my life.
_____ I believe that the Bible is the inspired Word of God.
L _____ I believe that a sinner can change to conform to Christ.
_____ I believe that the gospel is intended for everyone.
I _____ I believe that Christianity is the only religion capable of saving souls.
_____ I believe in the eternal damnation of those outside of Christ.
E _____ I believe that God expects me to worship with other Christians weekly.
_____ I believe that God can use my talents in extraordinary ways.
V _____ I believe that there is life after death and that I am bound for Heaven.
E _____ I . . .

What commitment statement will you make to God to shed any doubts noted above?

God's Call to the Christian Community
Unit 1: God's Call in Christ
(Lessons 1-5)

CALLED TO BE A VESSEL

LESSON 2

WHY TEACH THIS LESSON?

Mary's calling was unique; it was special. There was no calling that had ever been or ever would be again quite like her calling. Mary was called to be the earthly mother of the Messiah. Although she was an ordinary person, the special call of God on her life transformed her from being ordinary to unique with a special purpose. Her place and calling were very important in the kingdom of God and in the world.

Your learners should realize that even though Mary's calling was vitally important, so is theirs. God calls every believer to carry out tasks in the kingdom of God. Every call is unique and important in God's eternal plan. No two callings are just alike. Each called person has an individual purpose and place in God's kingdom. The challenges and difficulties each believer faces will vary depending on the nature of his or her calling. Mary, for example, had to watch in agony as her son died on a Roman cross. But God strengthened her for her task. He will strengthen us in fulfilling our callings as well.

INTRODUCTION

A. PRECIOUS CARGO, FRAGILE VESSELS

New York jeweler Harry Winston bought the famed Hope Diamond from an estate sale in 1949. In 1958, Winston decided to donate the diamond to the Smithsonian Institution in Washington, D.C. Weighing 45.52 carats, the gem was extremely valuable.

So how would the transfer be made? Rejecting armored trucks or elaborate delivery schemes, Winston merely put the diamond in a box and sent it through the U.S. mail! It arrived in good order, without incident.

Are we startled that someone would choose a fragile vessel and an ordinary means of conveyance for such an extraordinary cargo? As we ponder this account, we can recall the fact that God chose a young peasant named Mary to bring his precious Son into the world. When she was called to be a vessel, she agreed. Her willingness to be used by God is the highlight of this week's lesson.

B. LESSON BACKGROUND

As we compare last week's lesson with today's, we see interesting parallels in God's plan to bring salvation to humanity. The angel Gabriel appeared to both Zechariah and Mary, in separate incidents. Each was quite startled at Gabriel's appearance. Gabriel instructed each not to be afraid. Each was promised a child. Each was given a hint of his or her child's future greatness. Each was told what the name of his or her child was to be.

Thus the beauty of God's plan for salvation continued to unfold. Zechariah had been called to believe; then Mary was called to be a vessel. Even though we should not expect angelic appearances today, God continues to issue calls to us through his Word.

DEVOTIONAL READING:
PSALM 40:1-5
BACKGROUND SCRIPTURE:
LUKE 1:26-38
PRINTED TEXT:
LUKE 1:26-38

LESSON AIMS

After participating in this lesson, each student will be able to:

1. Retell the story of Gabriel's appearance to Mary.

2. Give examples of other instances in which God chose "lowly" people to carry out his tasks.

3. Write a prayer that asks God to use him or her in a way that seems impossible to human thinking.

KEY VERSE

"I am the Lord's servant," Mary answered. "May it be to me as you have said." —Luke 1:38

I. GABRIEL'S GREETING (LUKE 1:26-30)

A. IN A REAL TIME AND PLACE (v. 26)

26. In the sixth month, God sent the angel Gabriel to Nazareth, a town in Galilee,

Luke's Gospel is careful to locate events in both time and place. The account is definitely not a "once upon a time" fairy tale! In preparing to send his Son into the world, God makes sure that this angelic announcement is documented.

After *Gabriel* appeared to Zechariah in Jerusalem and announced that Elizabeth would give birth to a son (Luke 1:13), the mute priest returned home to the hill country of Judea (1:23, 39, 40). Elizabeth rejoiced in the knowledge of her pregnancy, but remained in seclusion for the first five months (1:24). Then, in the sixth month of her pregnancy, something of even greater importance takes place.

Gabriel, the *angel* who stands in the presence of God himself (Luke 1:19), is sent to a city of *Galilee* by the name of *Nazareth*. Nazareth is not mentioned anywhere in the Old Testament, but it is situated very close to Sephoris (or Sepphoris), the capital of the district of old Galilee. Nazareth is also close to an important trade route. This city's location is about 17 miles due west of the lower end of the Sea of Galilee (see, for example, www.nazarethvillage.com). A derogatory evaluation of the character of the city comes from Nathanael: "Nazareth! Can anything good come from there?" (John 1:46).

DAILY BIBLE READINGS

Monday, Dec. 3—God's Wonderful Works (Psalm 40:1-5)

Tuesday, Dec. 4—An Unexpected Visitor (Luke 1: 26-29)

Wednesday, Dec. 5—Mary's Son's Future (Luke 1:30-33)

Thursday, Dec. 6—The Miraculous Conception (Luke 1:34, 35)

Friday, Dec. 7—Nothing Is Impossible! (Luke 1:36-38)

Saturday, Dec. 8—Elizabeth Blesses Mary (Luke 1:39-45)

Sunday, Dec. 9—Mary Sings to the Lord (Luke 1:46-56)

B. TO A REAL PERSON (v. 27)

27. . . . to a virgin pledged to be married to a man named Joseph, a descendant of David. The virgin's name was Mary.

This time Gabriel's message of an unexpected birth is not to an elderly man, but to a very young woman who is a *virgin*. Some reject the idea that a virgin can have a child. But Scripture does not shy away from its bold claim: the miracle of the ages is about to happen—to a virgin. If one cannot accept the miraculous, then one cannot accept Jesus.

To be *pledged* means that *Mary* and *Joseph* have already taken the first steps to becoming *married*. To break the relationship at this point requires a legal divorce (compare Matthew 1:19). Thus an ancient pledge is a much stronger concept than the modern idea of being engaged.

The final step of the extended marriage process takes place in a ceremony where the groom calls for his bride and takes her to his home. In the case of Mary, even after Joseph takes her to his home, she remains a virgin until after Jesus is born (see Matthew 1:24, 25).

We are not entirely sure whether it is to Mary or to Joseph that Luke is referring as being *a descendant of David* at this point. Joseph definitely is of that line according to Matthew 1:20 (compare Luke 3:23, 31). Mary's own descent from David would signify that Jesus is of David's line biologically as well as legally through adoption by Joseph. For the Messiah to be of the house of David is an important part of the story line (see 2 Samuel 7:12-16; Matthew 1:1; Luke 1:32; 3:31; 18:38, 39; etc.).

C. WITH REAL GRACE (vv. 28-30)

28. The angel went to her and said, "Greetings, you who are highly favored! The Lord is with you."

Since a young woman is usually betrothed in her teens at this time, it is likely that Mary is quite young when *the angel* greets her. Perhaps she is no more than 15. Even so, she is *highly favored* in the eyes of the Lord. There is no record that the priest Zechariah, for his part, received such a commendation.

Gabriel continues his greeting with words of assurance. The phrase *the Lord is with you* means that God is about to do something good for his people (compare Judges 6:12).

"THE LORD IS WITH YOU"

I grew up in a midwestern state of the U.S., and my entire family, grandparents included, lived within an 80-mile radius. But when I was 12, my maternal grandparents moved to Florida. That Christmas my mother, my sister, and I went to spend Christmas break with them. While we were there, my grandfather took me fishing. I'm not sure I had ever been fishing before or even had been out in a boat.

The whole experience was rather exciting and intimidating at the same time. But as long as grandpa was with me, I had no fear. The water, the rocking of the small rowboat, the sights and sounds—nothing made me afraid. Grandpa was close by, and I felt secure.

Mary was initially troubled at the appearance of the angel, but she was soon told of the Lord's favor. A message of reassurance is also available to each of us. We have the Lord's promise that he is with us at all times (Matthew 28:20). With this realization, we can be as relaxed and confident as a child out on the water with his grandpa.
—J. B. N.

29. Mary was greatly troubled at his words and wondered what kind of greeting this might be.

But *Mary* is confused and *troubled* at the *words* of Gabriel. Angelic appearances can have this effect! Dozens of questions probably flash through her mind in an instant. Why has an angel appeared to her? What do these words signify? So far nothing makes sense, because this event is far beyond anything she has ever experienced.

30. But the angel said to her, "Do not be afraid, Mary, you have found favor with God.

Gabriel recognizes the obvious signs of distress in Mary's countenance. So he assures her with the words *Do not be afraid*. He also calls her by name, a subtle proof that this is no case of mistaken identity. It is indeed *Mary* who has found favor with God; it is she who is the one God has chosen!

The position of women is generally low in the ancient world. But God singles out a woman to be a favored servant. He is going to send salvation to the world through his Son—and his Son will not come out of thin air, but will be born of a woman (see Galatians 4:4). Luke's Gospel and his book of Acts tell of women who were significant in God's plan (examples: Luke 2:36-38; 7:36-50; Acts 16:11-15; 18:1-3).

II. GOD'S MESSAGE (LUKE 1:31-33)

A. MARY'S SON (v. 31)

31. "You will be with child and give birth to a son, and you are to give him the name Jesus.

Gabriel's greeting now gives way to God's message for Mary: contrary to all expectation and all human experience, this virgin will conceive. Gabriel knows the baby's gender in advance. He also announces to Mary (as he had to Zechariah) that God has chosen the baby's *name*. That name is to be *Jesus*. This is the Greek equivalent of the Hebrew name *Joshua*, which means, "the Lord is salvation."

This verse is an obvious fulfillment of the prophecy in Isaiah 7:14. The wording is similar, although the designation of the child is expressed differ-

WHAT DO YOU THINK?

God still invites faithful people to assist with his work. What can you do in the coming week to respond? How might you have to rearrange your priorities to serve him best?

WHAT DO YOU THINK?

What are some limitations that people believe hinder them from serving God? How may God view such limitations?

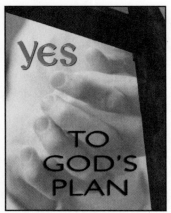

Visual for Lesson 2. *Have this visual on display in the front of the room as you introduce the question at the top of page 137.*

the question at the top of page 137.

HOW TO SAY IT

Ezekiel. Ee-ZEEK-ee-ul or Ee-ZEEK-yul.

Gabriel. GAY-bree-ul.

Galilee. GAL-uh-lee.

Isaiah. Eye-ZAY-uh.

Jerusalem. Juh-ROO-suh-lem.

Judea. Joo-DEE-uh.

Micah. MY-kuh.

Nathanael. Nuh-THAN-yull

Nazareth. NAZ-uh-reth.

Sephoris. SEF-uh-ris.

Zechariah. ZEK-uh-RYE-uh.

ently. In Isaiah the designation is *Immanuel,* which means, "God with us" (see Matthew 1:23). Both designations correctly identify God's Son: *Immanuel* identifies who he is; Jesus tells us what he is going to do. Many other names and titles, such as those prophesied in Isaiah 9:6, also apply to him.

B. GOD'S SON (v. 32a)

32a. "He will be great and will be called the Son of the Most High.

God has a special plan for Mary, but the far greater plan is for her child. Every mother wants her children to be great, but Jesus *will be great* in ways that Mary cannot begin to imagine. Although John the Baptist will be called "a prophet of the Most High" (Luke 1:76), Jesus will be called *the Son of the Most High.*

During Jesus' ministry some 30 years later, people will embrace him gladly as a healer and teacher. The people will shout with excitement at the thought that he is the kind of Messiah for whom they have been waiting. But when Jesus says that God is his own Father, making himself equal with God, they will be angry enough to kill him (see John 5:18). Can Mary accept what the angel declares before Jesus' birth, that he is to be the Son of the Most High?

C. DAVID'S SON (vv. 32b, 33)

32b. "The Lord God will give him the throne of his father David,

Centuries earlier, God had promised David that one day a special descendant of his would rule (again, 2 Samuel 7:12-16). God himself is to establish the kingdom for that son of David. *The throne of his father David* that the *Lord God* will give to this child means that the child will be no less than the long-awaited Messiah.

The eager expectation for this Messiah will be seen later in the expressions that people use when they fervently cry out to Jesus: "Lord, Son of David, have mercy on us!" (Matthew 20:30); "Hosanna to the Son of David!" (Matthew 21:9); "Blessed is the coming kingdom of our father David!" (Mark 11:10). Devout Jews of the time know that the Messiah—whenever he is to come and whoever he is—will be a son of David (see Matthew 22:42-46).

33. " . . . and he will reign over the house of Jacob forever; his kingdom will never end."

The closest Old Testament expression of *and he will reign over the house of Jacob forever* is in 2 Samuel 2:4, where David is anointed to rule "over the house of Judah." God promised David that the kingdom God would establish would be an everlasting *kingdom* (2 Samuel 7:16; also see 1 Kings 8:25; Micah 4:7). The reign of Jesus will extend not just through earthly years, but also through all eternity. We see Messiah's eternal rule expressed in Ezekiel 37:25: "David my servant will be their prince forever."

Furthermore, the good news of the Messiah will be not just for the Jews. As the angel will tell the shepherds on the night when Jesus is born, "I bring you good news of great joy that will be for all the people" (Luke 2:10). God's plan for salvation intends that the inhabitants of Heaven will include those of "every tribe and language and people and nation" (Revelation 5:9).

No End

A challenge that has attracted countless scientists and inventors over the years is the idea of creating a perpetual motion machine. Perpetual motion refers to "a condition in which an object moves forever without the expenditure of any limited internal or external source of energy" (Wikipedia).

Many designs have been attempted over the years, but none has ever worked "perpetually." Some designs depend on magnetism, some depend on gravity. Some designs are known as "Rube Goldberg"-type inventions—complicated in construction, almost whimsical in nature, and apparently more useful for generating chuckles than anything else. The problem is that there is always enough friction that some of the energy is dissipated, and ultimately the motion of the machine stops.

Only God is the source of perpetual energy. And his angel Gabriel announced to Mary that God's kingdom would never end. The Roman Empire lasted for 1,229 years; the Holy Roman Empire lasted for 1,004 years. As I write this, the U.S. government under its current constitution is the longest-lived government in the world (218 years). No one knows how long the United States of America will endure, but the kingdom of God will last forever! The energy of its king will never be exhausted. Where does your primary allegiance lie?   —J. B. N.

III. MARY'S RESPONSE (LUKE 1:34-38)

A. Reasonable Doubt (v. 34)

34. "How will this be," Mary asked the angel, "since I am a virgin?"

Sometimes when God calls someone to do something, that person raises doubts. Moses felt incompetent (Exodus 3); Gideon felt incapable (Judges 6:15); Zechariah was skeptical (Luke 1:18). Mary herself raises a concern: *How will this be . . . since I am a virgin?*

Mary correctly understands that Gabriel does not mean that she and Joseph will eventually have a son after they are fully married. God's plan calls for her to conceive before that marriage is consummated. Thus Mary's question is one of honest bewilderment. By saying *I am a virgin,* Mary states the fact that she has never been sexually intimate.

Thus Mary expresses reasonable doubt that what the angel has said can be possible. She knows that she is a virgin, and who can believe that a virgin can bear a child? Yet she readily accepts the explanation she receives (next verse).

B. Divine Explanation (vv. 35-37)

35. The angel answered, "The Holy Spirit will come upon you, and the power of the Most High will overshadow you. So the holy one to be born will be called the Son of God.

God's intention is that his own *Holy Spirit will come upon* Mary. In that way the miracle of the virginal conception can and will happen. Because Jesus is to be born through God's Spirit and God's *power,* he will be holy, and he will rightly *be called the Son of God.* Through all the years of his life on earth, Jesus will be *holy.* He will be tempted in every point, just as everyone is, yet completely without sin.

The virginal conception is a supernatural event. That is to say, it is an event that goes above and beyond what we know to be the normal laws of nature. To be sure, there were cases in the Old Testament of God's miraculous or providential intervention for children to be conceived (Genesis 18:10-14; 25:21; 30:22; Judges 13:3; 1 Samuel 1:19, 20). The fact that no one else is ever conceived in the way Luke 1:35 tells us does not mean that Jesus could not have been. Instead, the virginal conception proves the uniqueness of God's Son.

36. "Even Elizabeth your relative is going to have a child in her old age, and she who was said to be barren is in her sixth month.

In confirmation of what he is saying, Gabriel tells Mary that God's miraculous plan is already in effect: her elderly relative *Elizabeth* is already in

What Do You Think?

When was a time you struggled to make sense of something that was happening to you? How did your faith grow as a result?

Prayer

Father, may it be unto us according to your will. Help us to follow the example of Mary in humble submission. Most of all, fill us again with joy for the coming of Jesus into the world. In his holy name we pray, amen.

the *sixth month* of her own pregnancy. These two miracles prove that God is intervening in history in a special way.

37. "For nothing is impossible with God."

What a marvelous truth Gabriel now proclaims! This is an echo of Genesis 18:14. Mortals cannot break the laws of nature, but God can. Mortals cannot walk on water or raise the dead, but God can. *Nothing* that is necessary to the plan of God can ever be *impossible* to him. He who ordains the laws of nature is able to suspend them.

When we reflect on the statement for with God *nothing is impossible,* we may ask ourselves, "What about Hebrews 6:18?" That verse says that it is impossible for God to lie. God cannot lie because to do so would violate his holy nature. He can never be divided against himself. But in all that is consistent with truth and holiness, nothing is ever impossible with God.

C. HUMBLE ACCEPTANCE (v. 38)

38. "I am the Lord's servant," Mary answered. "May it be to me as you have said." Then the angel left her.

Mary is to be honored for her humble acceptance of God's call. As *the Lord's servant,* she completely yields herself to God's will. In total surrender, she invites the fulfillment of the angel's message so that everything can take place according to his word. With the message delivered and accepted, Gabriel returns to Heaven.

While Scripture does not teach us to worship Mary or pray to her, it is entirely appropriate to honor her purity, her faith, and her submission. She is aware of the difficulties this pregnancy will bring—with Joseph, with her own family, and with the people of Nazareth. Yet she willingly accepts her role in God's great drama to prepare for the coming of Jesus, on whom the main attention should be focused.

CONCLUSION

Throughout sacred history, God has chosen men and women to be instruments of his will. He chose Abraham to begin the Jewish nation; he chose Moses to be their lawgiver. He chose the kings to rule them; he chose the prophets to instruct them. All of these were chosen and called to play their significant roles in his plan.

As his plan to save humanity neared a critical point, God chose Mary. He called her to be a chosen vessel, to become the earthly mother of his divine Son. She was young, inexperienced, perhaps naïve. But in her virginal purity she was the right vessel to bring Jesus into the world.

The beauty of Mary's story lies in her willing submission to God's plan. Despite the fact that she could not grasp how everything was to happen, she was willing. Regardless of the physical hardships and the social disgrace she would endure, she was willing. Even though there would be "a problem of explanation" with Joseph, she was willing.

Mary's willing response to God's call is an example for all Christians today. God still issues calls to men and women to be used as his holy vessels, and we must respond to those calls. He calls us to accept his Son, to become followers, and then to be proclaimers. He calls us to be his vessels—vessels of his love, vessels of his truth, vessels of his power. "But we have this treasure in jars of clay to show that this all-surpassing power is from God and not from us" (2 Corinthians 4:7).

WHAT DO YOU THINK?

What life circumstances have challenged or enhanced your service to God? How have you dealt with the challenges?

WHAT DO YOU THINK?

The Bible records various responses to God's invitations to join him in fulfilling his plans: think of Moses, Gideon, and Jonah. Which one is most like your own response to something God has invited you to do?

THOUGHT TO REMEMBER

God still calls people to be vessels for him.

Discovery Learning

This page contains an alternative lesson plan emphasizing learning activities. Classes desiring such student involvement will find these suggestions helpful. The next page is a reproducible activity page to further enhance discovery learning.

INTO THE LESSON

Do a Who Am I? activity in which you read the following identification statements. Ask your learners to name the Bible person being described as you complete each description.

1. "Though I was of lowly birth, God picked me for an important role in his redemptive scheme. I was born to slaves in a foreign land, but I was raised by royalty. After working as a shepherd, I was used by God to deliver his people from slavery. Who am I?" (*Moses*)

2. "Though I was of lowly birth, God picked me for an important role in his redemptive scheme. My father had eight sons; I was the youngest. We lived in Bethlehem. From shepherd boy to king of Israel—that was my destiny. God's Messiah was one of my descendants. Who am I?" (*David*)

3. "Though I was a lowly shepherd, God picked me for an important role in his plan of redemption. My task was hard and fearful. I had to pronounce doom on Israel's neighbors, including Damascus, Gaza, Tyre, Ammon, and Moab. I even pronounced doom and exile for Israel herself. My visions involved locusts, fire, and a plumb line. I even predicted the death of Israel's king. My name begins with the letter A. Who am I?" (*Amos*)

4. "Though I was of lowly birth, God picked me for an important role in his plan of redemption. I was an obscure maiden in an obscure village. Who would think my name would become known throughout the world? Who would think I would be chosen by God to give birth to his Son? Who am I?" (*Mary*)

At the conclusion, turn to today's text. (See also the optional student book for this activity.)

INTO THE WORD

Distribute copies of the following puzzle (or use the optional student book, where it is also printed). Say, "Find 13 words that can be used of Mary as she is described in today's text in Luke 1:26-38. As you find and circle each word, identify also the verse that states or implies that description of Mary." If you do not want this to be a "silent" activity, have students work in pairs.

```
M A L R E E C N A I F D
Y C H A A L A A L D E E
D T U O Y E B Z I E D S
A V M E L O S A S E E U
L B B I B E R R R H O F
N L L D T F H E E H A N
I A E E A N D N D A M O
G A I D S L O E N F T C
R H E L I S O G R D C A
I L L W E F E R T I L E
V D E T O L B D E A V E
O B E D I E N T S S E L
```

The 13 words to be found are *angel* (v. 26), *Galilean* (v. 26), *Nazarene* (v. 26), *virgin* (v. 27), *fiancée* (v. 27), *blessed* (v. 28), *confused* (v. 29), *afraid* (vv. 29, 30), *fertile* (v. 31), *royal* (v. 32), *bewildered* (v. 34), *humble* (v. 38), and *obedient* (v. 38). For the last part of the exercise to work, all 13 words must be located.

Next, give this direction: "Look at the puzzle's unused letters. Can you find a message there?" (The unused letters in sequence left to right, top to bottom read: "Mary: called to be a vessel; behold the handmaid of the Lord, called to be a vessel"; those who finish early can work on the Two Special Servants activity from the Reproducible Page while others complete the word search.) The message emphasizes the lesson title, theme, and the desired response to this study.

INTO LIFE

Tell your learners that the next activity is called Impossible Tasks. Ask them to identify the Bible person who was given a seemingly "impossible" imperative by God. 1. Build a massive boat! 2. Cross the sea without a boat! 3. Destroy the walled city! 4. Kill the giant! 5. Have a baby as a virgin! 6. Evangelize the world! Answers are *Noah, Moses, Joshua, David, Mary,* and *the church.*

Ask the class to identify other "impossible tasks" God demanded of people in the Bible. Ask also for examples of what your learners consider impossibilities that were accomplished through the ages by people empowered by God. Conclude by suggesting that each learner ponder a prayer that includes some petition most would deem impossible. (Alternative: use the Impossibility Thinking activity on the Reproducible Page instead.)

Two Special Servants

Last Sunday's study was of God coming to Zechariah; today's study is of God coming to Mary. Many similarities mark the two occasions. Identify Bible verses in Luke 1 for both Zechariah and Mary for the affirmations in the following chart.

Zechariah		Mary
_____	The angel Gabriel is the messenger.	_____
_____	The person visited is devout.	_____
_____	The message is of an unexpected, miraculous birth.	_____
_____	The one visited expresses amazement and confusion.	_____
_____	The angel confirms his message.	_____
_____	The child to be born is a son.	_____
_____	One son will be a prophet of the Most High; the other, the Son of the Most High.	_____
_____	The birth will be an occasion of great joy for many.	_____
_____	God chooses the name for the baby.	_____
_____	The Holy Spirit will play an integral part.	_____

Impossibility Thinking

Undoubtedly, neither Zechariah nor Mary had pondered in advance what God introduced to them through Gabriel. Both reacted with wonder: he with "How can I be sure of this? I am an old man and my wife is well along in years" (v. 18); she with "How will this be, since I am a virgin?" (v. 34). From a human perspective, both conceptions seemed impossible.
But Gabriel affirmed, "Nothing is impossible with God" (v. 37).
Ask yourself the following questions:

Do I believe that statement? Why, or why not?

What "impossibility thinking" have I engaged in?

What impossible thing am I willing to pray for, knowing that it cannot be accomplished apart from God's grace and power?

God's Call to the Christian Community
Unit 1: God's Call in Christ
(Lessons 1-5)

CALLED TO PROCLAIM

LESSON 3

WHY TEACH THIS LESSON?

Shared testimonies can be powerful tools in the hands of the Lord. This is true in cultures all over the world. Shared testimonies draw nonbelievers to Christ; shared testimonies also encourage believers in their faith.

Your learners need to see the great potential of a shared testimony. An important daily goal for believers is to look prayerfully for opportunities to tell of God's goodness and grace at work in their lives and in the world around them. When they ask God to provide such opportunities, they may be surprised when he chooses to do so in unusual ways!

INTRODUCTION

A. RELIGIOUS PHONIES

The Didache, a Christian work written in the second century AD, offers advice on how to spot a false prophet: if a prophet comes to your house and tries to stay more than two days or if he asks for money, then he is a false prophet. Regardless of the validity of this advice, there always has been a need for a way to spot religious phonies, including those who falsely claim to speak for God.

In the Old Testament there were false prophets who predicted peace when God said there would be war and destruction (Jeremiah 14:13-16). In our own times there are those who wrongly predict the time of Christ's second coming. There are also those who prophesy health and wealth—often in exchange for a generous donation. John the Baptist, however, was a true prophet of God. John stands in sharp contrast to false prophets of all eras.

B. LESSON BACKGROUND

A genuine prophet of the Old Testament could prove that he spoke for God by being able to predict accurately what would happen. If a self-proclaimed prophet tried to do this and his prediction did not come to pass, he was to be put to death (Deuteronomy 18:20-22). But God's prophet also had the important task of proclaiming God's call to repentance. In the writings of the Old Testament prophets, this call to righteous living comprises the majority of their content.

Thus, *foretelling* and *forthtelling* were the two tasks of the prophet. John the Baptist came as "a prophet of the Most High" (Luke 1:76). In his predictive, foretelling role, John's main task was to proclaim a message of the coming of the Messiah. His message was that "one more powerful than I will come. . . . He will baptize . . . he will burn up the chaff with unquenchable fire" (Luke 3:16, 17).

In the forthtelling role, John proclaimed God's call to repentance. Like the prophet Nathan rebuking King David (2 Samuel 12) or Elijah condemning King Ahab (1 Kings 21), John confronted King Herod (Matthew 14:4). Like many of the prophets of old, John was finally killed for proclaiming God's truth to someone who did not want to hear it. Jesus said, "Among those born of women there is no one greater than John" (Luke 7:28).

DEVOTIONAL READING:
MALACHI 3:1-4
BACKGROUND SCRIPTURE:
LUKE 1:57-80
PRINTED TEXT:
LUKE 1:59-64, 67-80

LESSON AIMS

After participating in this lesson, each student will be able to:

1. List three elements of praise in "Zechariah's song."

2. Compare and contrast John's role as a "prophet of the Most High" with our responsibility to proclaim Christ.

3. Write a short song or poem of praise for the area of service that God has granted him or her.

KEY VERSE

Immediately his mouth was opened and his tongue was loosed, and he began to speak, praising God.   —Luke 1:64

LESSON 3 NOTES

Unlike the prophets before John, the Bible gives us a tantalizing glimpse of the beginning of his life. Just as the angel Gabriel had promised, Elizabeth gave birth to a son in her old age. The presentation of a newborn child was a community event. So neighbors and relatives gathered in the rural village in the Judean hill country where John's parents lived to rejoice and praise God for this blessing (Luke 1:57, 58).

I. NAMING THE BABY (LUKE 1:59-64)

A. USUAL PROCEDURE (v. 59)

59. *On the eighth day they came to circumcise the child, and they were going to name him after his father Zechariah,*

Circumcision of infant males *on the eighth day* is a sacred duty of Jewish parents (Genesis 17:9-14; Leviticus 12:3; compare Luke 2:21). At this time, those in attendance are determined that the child should be named *Zechariah,* in honor of *his father.* They probably reason that it is an appropriate tribute to the father who finally has a son. The name *Zechariah* fittingly means, "God remembers." Selecting this name for the baby seems the obvious choice!

B. MOTHER'S PROTEST (vv. 60, 61)

60. *. . . but his mother spoke up and said, "No! He is to be called John."*

Sometime during the nine months of pregnancy that followed the angelic appearance, Zechariah apparently informed his wife what the angel had said about the child's name. (He would have had to use some means other than audible words to communicate this, since he is mute even up to this point in the narrative.) Therefore when well-meaning friends and relatives propose the name *Zechariah,* Elizabeth has a firm answer: No! Instead, *John* is to be the name. Appropriately enough, the name *John* means, "Yahweh has been gracious."

61. *They said to her, "There is no one among your relatives who has that name."*

The neighbors and relatives cannot understand such a departure from tradition. They know the family trees of both Zechariah and Elizabeth. They know that there is *no one* named John who is related to either of them.

What those in attendance apparently do not know is the content of the angel's message of nine months earlier: "Do not be afraid, Zechariah; your prayer has been heard. Your wife Elizabeth will bear you a son, and you are to give him the name John" (Luke 1:13).

C. FATHER'S RESPONSE (vv. 62-64)

62. *Then they made signs to his father, to find out what he would like to name the child.*

The people who have gathered to celebrate the circumcision and naming of the baby are puzzled. They can think of no reason why Elizabeth prefers the name *John* to the name of her husband. Therefore, they turn to Zechariah in the expectation that he will have the good sense to overrule his wife.

While the angel had said that Zechariah would be unable to speak (Luke 1:20), the fact that those present make *signs* to him may indicate that he is deaf as well as mute. In any case, those gathered are able to communicate their question to Zechariah.

63. *He asked for a writing tablet, and to everyone's astonishment he wrote, "His name is John."*

The *writing tablet* that Zechariah requests is perhaps a wooden slate with a shallow surface of wax. If so, he can use a pointed stylus for writing in the

WHAT DO YOU THINK?

How would you encourage a person who was experiencing opposition for doing what he or she knew was right? What gives you the courage to say what is right when you're in the minority?

wax. The stylus may be flat on the other end for smoothing out the wax to erase what is no longer needed. Zechariah has had nine months to become proficient with this instrument!

With the writing tablet in hand, Zechariah settles the issue about the name: *His name is John.* In that one short statement, Zechariah demonstrates obedience to God's message as delivered by the angel. All the people gathered for this event, however, are amazed that Zechariah has chosen the same nonfamily name as his wife has. What is going on?

"HIS NAME IS . . ."

What's in a name? that which we call a rose
By any other name would smell as sweet.
—Romeo and Juliet, Act II, Scene 2

What's in a name? A great deal! The name *George Washington* suggests diplomatic skill, graciousness, and selfless service. The name *Adolf Hitler* does not. The name *Marilyn Monroe* suggests blatant sexuality. The name *Mother Teresa* does not. These are more than "just names"; they carry a great deal of emotive force.

Today we give our children names based on a variety of factors, but normally without any particular realization of, or concern for, the original meaning of the name itself. But this has not always been the case. In biblical times, names were often given to carry special significance. Some even were changed to fit the situation. Thus *Abram* ("exalted father") became *Abraham* ("father of a multitude"). *Naomi* ("pleasant") changed her name to *Mara* ("bitter"). *Jacob* ("grasps the heel," or figuratively, "deceiver") had his name changed to *Israel* ("he who struggles with God").

Both Joseph and Mary were told to call Mary's baby *Jesus* ("savior"). Zechariah was told to name his son *John* ("Yahweh has been gracious"). When we follow the biblical plan of salvation, each of us takes on a new name: *Christian* ("of Christ"). Make sure you don't change this name to something else!   —J. B. N.

64. Immediately his mouth was opened and his tongue was loosed, and he began to speak, praising God.

Zechariah regains the power of speech as soon as he demonstrates his obedience. When *his tongue* is *loosed,* his first words are words of praise. All the gratitude and wonder that has been bottled up inside of him for nine months comes pouring out. Even after the people return to their homes, they can't stop talking about this special child (Luke 1:65, 66, not in today's text). Everyone who hears the story is amazed. What must the future hold for this child?

II. PRAISING THE LORD (LUKE 1:67-75)

A. FOR HIS SALVATION (vv. 67-71)

67. His father Zechariah was filled with the Holy Spirit and prophesied:

Earlier, Zechariah was punished for being doubtful (Luke 1:20). Now God is accepting Zechariah back into service fully as he is *filled with the Holy Spirit* and prophesies. This means that he is enabled by the Holy Spirit to say what he could not say on his own, and the words are of great poetic beauty.

While Zechariah's words came from his heart, they are authored ultimately by God's Spirit. The result is a literary splendor that is beyond mere spontaneous speech. Often called the *Benedictus* (from the Latin for *Blessed*), Zechariah's marvelous outpouring has two parts. Verses 68-75 are praise to God for the salvation he is delivering to his covenant people. Verses 76-79 are a pronouncement of the role John will have in preparing for the coming of the Messiah.

HOW TO SAY IT

Benedictus. BEN-eh-DIK-tus.
Deuteronomy. Due-ter-AHN-uh-me.
Didache. DID-uh-kay.
Elijah. Ee-LYE-juh.
Herod. HAIR-ud.
Jeremiah. Jair-uh-MY-uh.
Leviticus. Leh-VIT-ih-kus.
Micah. MY-kuh.
Yahweh (Hebrew). YAH-weh.
Zechariah. ZEK-uh-RYE-uh.

WHAT DO YOU THINK?

What was a time in your life when you received a clear and immediate blessing as a result of honoring or obeying God? Explain.

WHAT DO YOU THINK?

Praise of God is still appropriate for us 2,000 years later. What avenues do you have for praising God? What tends to prevent you from pouring out praise to him? How do you overcome this?

WHAT DO YOU THINK?

Quickly think of three things for which to praise God. What do these three things say about your view of what's most important?

DAILY BIBLE READINGS

Monday, Dec. 10—A Messenger Is Coming (Malachi 3: 1-4)

Tuesday, Dec. 11—Elizabeth Births a Son (Luke 1:57-61)

Wednesday, Dec. 12—His Name Is John (Luke 1:62-66)

Thursday, Dec. 13—God Sends a Powerful Savior (Luke 1:67-75)

Friday, Dec. 14—Preparing the Way (Luke 1:76-80)

Saturday, Dec. 15—Warnings to the Crowds (Luke 3:7-14)

Sunday, Dec. 16—A Powerful One Is Coming (Luke 3: 15-20)

68. "Praise be to the Lord, the God of Israel,
    because he has come and has redeemed his people.

The first words to come from the lips of Zechariah in nine months are spoken with joy. *Praise be to the Lord* is a statement of recognition that God deserves to be praised. The faithful *God of Israel* has not forgotten his people. Now *he has come* to them, which means that he is stepping into human history in an act of divine power. Now he comes to redeem, rescuing his people from their captivity to sin. The day of God's coming is a day of deliverance! However, as Jesus would later say about Jerusalem, "You did not recognize the time of God's coming to you" (Luke 19:44).

69. "He has raised up a horn of salvation for us
    in the house of his servant David

Zechariah's praise for this *horn of salvation* may refer to the horns on the corners of the altar at the temple. A guilty person could cling to them in order to escape death (as in 1 Kings 1:50; 2:28). More likely, however, the *horn* is a symbol of strength and protection (as the horns of an ox). By means of this *horn of salvation*, the enemy will be vanquished and the people will be delivered (compare 2 Samuel 22:3; Psalm 18:2).

Zechariah expects this *salvation* to be *for us in the house of his servant David*, meaning the Jewish people (compare 2 Samuel 7:26; 1 Chronicles 17:24). The mention of David is a strong sign that the promise of a Messiah is about to be fulfilled (compare Psalm 132:11, 12, 17). What will be revealed later is that Christ will be the Savior not only of the Jews, but of all who believe.

70. " . . . (as he said through his holy prophets of long ago),

From the beginning God announced there would be deliverance. To Adam and Eve came the promise of one who would crush the serpent's head (Genesis 3:15). God demonstrated deliverance to Noah, and he promised the coming Messiah to Abraham. In many different generations, he spoke *through his holy prophets.* Zechariah knows these prophecies and is excited that now, at last, they are being fulfilled.

71. " . . . salvation from our enemies
    and from the hand of all who hate us—

In the more than 400 years since the close of the Old Testament, the land of Israel has been subjected to numerous invasions, civil war, and armies of occupation. Israel thus is eager to be saved from her *enemies*, especially the occupying armies of Rome. For too long she has suffered at *the hand of all who hate* the people of God. Zechariah, like most of the people of Israel, may be thinking mostly in terms of a Messiah who will deliver the nation from her political, earthly enemies (Psalm 106:10).

When Jesus comes, the cheering crowds will turn against him when they see that he is not going to be the kind of king they want or expect. Although Jesus will not provide deliverance from Rome, he will provide deliverance from Israel's more important enemies: the hosts of Satan. This spiritual deliverance is the salvation that ancient Israel needs most of all. It is what we need most as well.

SAVED FROM OUR ENEMY

The plotline of "alien invasion" is a staple of science-fiction books. This kind of plot goes back a long way.

The granddaddy of this kind of science-fiction theme is H. G. Wells's famous *The War of the Worlds,* published in 1898. This book tells the tale of a Martian invasion of England. The staying power of this story line is amazing. Orson Welles adapted the tale into a fictionalized documentary that aired on radio on October 30, 1938, as a Halloween feature. (For the American audience, the Martians landed in New Jersey.) The story then became a movie in 1953 and again in 2005.

Whenever a book or movie features an "alien invasion" plotline, there is always a sense of relief at the ultimate demise of the invaders. And the more harm the invaders are seen to inflict, the greater that relief is! Now think about it: is there any nonfictional invader that has ever harmed humans more than the one known as *sin*?

"Salvation from our enemies" was Zechariah's hope. That God did even better by making it possible for all to be saved from the enemy of sin was the result of the cross. Sin is the ultimate enemy of the human race, and God's grace is what allows us to be saved from this mortal foe.   —J. B. N.

B. For His Covenant (vv. 72-75)

**72. " . . . to show mercy to our fathers
    and to remember his holy covenant,**

God had promised in the Old Testament to *show mercy to* his people (compare Micah 7:20). Zechariah expects that the God of all mercy is going to *remember his holy covenant*: if humans will give God their allegiance, he will be their protector. Just as he did not abandon the children of Israel to their slavery in Egypt, he will not now abandon his children in spiritual captivity. The meaning of Zechariah's own name says it well: "God remembers." Perhaps Zechariah himself is remembering passages such as Genesis 17:7; Leviticus 26:42; and Psalm 105:8, 9 as he praises God.

**73, 74. " . . . the oath he swore to our father Abraham:
    to rescue us from the hand of our enemies,
        and to enable us to serve him without fear**

The oath in question is found in Genesis 22:15-18. There God promised *Abraham* that his seed would become a mighty, victorious nation.

Zechariah may be speaking better than he knows. The promised deliverance is not to be the kind often seen in the Old Testament, where Israel was delivered temporarily from oppressors. By the Messiah's deliverance, God's people will be able fully to *serve him without fear,* without the specter of further defeat hanging over their heads. This will be God's gift to his people, a favor that he will grant.

75. " . . . in holiness and righteousness before him all our days."

As a devoted priest, Zechariah knows what it means to serve the Lord. All his life he has been "upright in the sight of God, observing all the Lord's commandments and regulations blamelessly" (Luke 1:6). Now righteous Zechariah eagerly anticipates a day when all God's people will be able to serve him *in holiness and righteousness.* This hope will be partially fulfilled when Christ establishes the church, whose members are "a holy priesthood, offering spiritual sacrifices" (1 Peter 2:5; compare Titus 2:11-14). The fulfillment will come when we serve him in full holiness in Heaven (Revelation 22:3).

III. PREDICTING THE MESSIAH (LUKE 1:76-80)

A. Preparing the Way (v. 76)

**76. "And you, my child, will be called a prophet of the Most High;
    for you will go on before the Lord to prepare the way for him,**

The second part of the *Benedictus* concerns the role of John the Baptist. Speaking tenderly to the infant, Zechariah prophesies the future of his son. John will be not only *a prophet of the Most High,* he also will be widely recognized and *called* as such. In that role, John's job will be *to prepare the way for*

PRAISE
BE TO
THE
LORD

LUKE 1:68, NIV

Visual for Lesson 3. *Point to this visual as you ask, "How and why will you praise the Lord this Christmas season?"*

Our Father, we praise you for your tender mercy. We thank you for the remission of our sins. Loosen the self-imposed silence of our tongues so we can be bold to proclaim your wonders. In Jesus' name, amen.

Jesus (Isaiah 40:3; Malachi 3:1; Matthew 3:3). Some 30 years after Zechariah prophesies the words before us, John will tell the people to repent and get ready for Jesus (Matthew 3:11, 12; Mark 1:1-8; Luke 3:1-18; John 1:19-34). The beautiful words of Zechariah echo the prophecy of Isaiah 40:3-5.

B. PROCLAIMING SALVATION (vv. 77-79)

77. " . . . to give his people the knowledge of salvation
       through the forgiveness of their sins,

After John grows up and begins preaching in the wilderness, he will proclaim a baptism of repentance "for the forgiveness of sins" (Luke 3:3). John's preparatory ministry will be a vital first step for *his people* to learn *the knowledge of salvation.* Through John's ministry the people will learn at least two important things. First, they have sin, of which they must repent. Second, only God can provide *forgiveness of their sins.*

78, 79. " . . . because of the tender mercy of our God,
       by which the rising sun will come to us from heaven
    to shine on those living in darkness
      and in the shadow of death,
      to guide our feet into the path of peace."

When God sends John the Baptist to call people to repentance, it will not be an act of anger. Rather, it will be an act of deepest love, an act of *tender mercy.*

Matthew 4:15, 16 (from Isaiah 9:1, 2) speaks of Jesus as a dawning light (see also Isaiah 58:8, 10; 60:1-3). The promise of the *rising sun* (or dawning of the sun) is a promise that the Messiah will come. What a glorious day when God visits his people! To *those living in darkness* (Psalm 107:10), Christ will come as the light of the world (John 8:12). To those *in the shadow of death,* the promise will be that those who believe in Jesus will live, even though dead (John 11:25). To the lost, Christ will come as the way *to guide* their *feet.* To all who do not know *the path of peace,* Christ will come as the prince of peace. Today, the fulfillments of Zechariah's prophecies are facts of history.

C. GETTING HIMSELF READY (v. 80)

80. And the child grew and became strong in spirit; and he lived in the desert until he appeared publicly to Israel.

Raised in a godly home, young John grows both physically and spiritually. At some point his elderly parents die, and John lives *in the desert* of Judea. Year by year the time for his public appearance approaches. Captive *Israel* is going to hear the message of redemption!

CONCLUSION

John's mother, Elizabeth, stood up against the pressure of popular opinion and insisted that what God said about naming the baby would be carried out. John's father, Zechariah, was faithful as well—once he had learned from nine months of silence. He joyfully proclaimed the praise of God and the salvation of God. Following in his parents' footsteps, John was faithful to his own call to proclaim. To people who trusted their own goodness and ancestry to save them, John proclaimed repentance. To a nation largely unaware that they sat in darkness, John proclaimed the coming of the Lord. He was the prophet—the spokesman—for God.

We can learn from the example of the godly family of today's lesson. God has called his people to proclaim. Let us be faithful to that call.

What are you doing today to live out a life of service to God? How do the seasons of life affect this?

John was called to proclaim. So are we.

Discovery Learning

This page contains an alternative lesson plan emphasizing learning activities. Classes desiring such student involvement will find these suggestions helpful. The next page is a reproducible activity page to further enhance discovery learning.

INTO THE LESSON

Recruit in advance a class member to deliver the following two- to three-minute monologue. Your actor should be dressed as an elderly Jewish priest (Zechariah) of the first century.

"My son. *[dramatic pause]* I never thought I would say those words. God had been good to me and my wife, Elizabeth. We had lived a long time with his blessings. But he had not answered our fervent prayers for a son. In resolute faith we had gone about the service of our God day by day, year by year.

"When I was called from my Judean village to do my regular priestly duties at the temple, I had no idea what God was about to do. He is, indeed, the God of marvelous surprises.

"My temple duty was simple. *[Use hand gestures to illustrate the following.]* I add incense to the fire, to show the prayers of God's people ascending as a sweet aroma to our Father God. All assembled outside pray; the smoke from my incense symbolizes their words rising to Heaven. But on one particular day, suddenly neither the aroma nor the smoke had my attention. For beside me stood God's messenger, Gabriel.

"I was stunned and afraid. I could not believe the angel's words. Elizabeth and I were to have a son, a very special son. My doubt earned my penalty: I became mute until it all came true.

"For nine long, silent months, I could not vocalize my praise nor tell my story. But the day of the naming of my son—ah, the melody of the words *my son!*—I had to write in large letters *HIS NAME IS JOHN* when all my family members were insisting that we name him after me. That was the angel's word . . . God's word. So it had to be mine as well. And the second I lifted my stylus from the writing tablet, I could speak. And I haven't stopped yet . . . as you can readily hear. Glory to God!"

INTO THE WORD

Have incense burning as learners arrive to direct attention to the context for today's study: the incense-burning duty of Zechariah in the temple. (Do not do this if your class includes anyone who is sensitive to strong aroma, if fire codes forbid it, or if it

will set off a smoke detector.) Have two of your good oral readers read Luke 1:5-25, 57-67 aloud to give the whole picture of Zechariah and Elizabeth's story; have your readers alternate reading odd- and even-numbered verses to make it more interesting.

Display the word *PRAISE* written vertically and ask the class to help you prepare an acrostic on the word, based on Zechariah's song in Luke 1:68-79. Suggest the class look for deeds and attributes of God revealed in Zechariah's words. For example, in verse 68, God is Redeemer and God Initiates certain actions. From verse 69, God Saves. From verse 70, God Speaks. From verse 72, God Remembers. From verse 74, God Protects. From verse 75, God Expects things of us (holiness and righteousness). From verses 72 and 78, God Acts mercifully. From verse 67, God Inspires men to speak. From verses 72 and 73, God Plans.

Once your class has its acrostic, stop and ask individuals to offer sentence prayers, praising God for the elements Zechariah noted in his prayer. For example, "O God who speaks, help us to listen to your words." (This activity is also included in the optional student book.) *Alternative:* Distribute copies of the Praise Poem exercise from the Reproducible Page for small groups or pairs to work on as a "sword drill" competition.

INTO LIFE

Make this proposal to your learners: "For Monday through Saturday of this coming week, use Zechariah's praise song for your personal devotional time, two verses each day. For example, on Monday, read verses 68 and 69, personalizing the verses in whatever ways possible, such as substituting *me* for *us* in verse 69."

Prayer thoughts can follow the models of the sentence prayers offered in the preceding activity. For example, Monday's prayer could be something like, "O God of redemption and salvation, thank you for adopting me into the family of your servant David."

The optional student book includes two sections calling for the learner to compare himself or herself first to the elderly Elizabeth and Zechariah, then to Zechariah's son in the matters of serving the Messiah. You may find those to be useful group procedures. Distribute copies of the A Great Light activity from the Reproducible Page for your learners to take home.

Praise Poem

In Luke 1:68-75, Zechariah uses expressions and ideas that occur in other biblical texts. Read the references to the right and match each with an expression from Zechariah's lips.

_____ "Praise be to the Lord, the God of Israel"
_____ "He has come and has redeemed his people"
_____ "He has raised up a horn of salvation for us"
_____ "In the house of his servant David"
_____ "As he said through his holy prophets"
_____ "Salvation from our enemies and from . . . all who hate us"
_____ "To show mercy to our fathers"
_____ "To remember his holy covenant"
_____ "To rescue us from the hand of our enemies"
_____ "To enable us to serve him without fear"
_____ "To serve him . . . in holiness and righteousness"

A.   Joshua 22:5
B.   2 Samuel 22:3
C.   1 Kings 8:16
D.   Psalm 44:7
E.   Psalm 111:9
F.   Ezekiel 16:60
G.   Daniel 6:27
H.   Micah 20:7
I.   Zechariah 12:10
J.   Philippians 1:14
K.   Hebrews 11:1

A Great Light

Isaiah 9:2 pictures the coming of the Messiah as a great light shining "on those living in the land of the shadow of death." That passage concludes with the simple affirmation, "a light has dawned." Fill in the blanks in the affirmation from Zechariah to the right that "borrows" from Isaiah's declaration.

Clip this box and display it in a place where you'll see it many times this week. These verses are ideal for memorizing for your defense arsenal of ready verses.

"Because of the _____ _____ of our God . . . the _____ _____ will come to us from heaven to shine on those _____ in _____ and in the _____ of _____, to guide our feet into the _____ of _____."

—LUKE 1:78, 79

God's Call to the Christian Community
Unit 1: God's Call in Christ
(Lessons 1-5)

CALLED TO REJOICE

LESSON 4

WHY TEACH THIS LESSON?

We know that Scripture calls us to live lives of rejoicing. Consider Philippians 4:4 to "Rejoice in the Lord always. I will say it again: Rejoice!" But often that's easier said than done! How do we maintain lives of joy when circumstances work against us?

The key to being able to live lives of rejoicing is to remember what the Lord has done, what he is doing, and what he will do. What a powerful tool for empowering and stirring up faith! Rejoicing indeed can and should characterize every day of our lives. The God of Heaven who sent his Son to be born in Bethlehem still works in our lives! How could it be otherwise? Does it make any sense to claim that God doesn't really care much about us today even though he sent Jesus into the world to die on our behalf?

The shepherds had joy at Jesus' birth. With all the evidence of the Lord's care we have had since then, how can we not "rejoice in the Lord always"?

INTRODUCTION

A. CLOSE ENCOUNTERS OF A SPECIAL KIND

Thirty years ago, the well-known movie *Close Encounters of the Third Kind* attempted to create the excitement and wonder that would attend the arrival of intelligent creatures from outer space. It is only one of many such movies and TV shows that have tried to imagine an extraterrestrial visitation.

But what of a close encounter, an actual visitation, from the creator himself? What about such an event in real history, not just in science fiction? What would it be like if the greatest being of all came to our planet? What preparations would we make? What excitement would it cause?

Such a visitation, of course, has actually happened. Jesus Christ, through whom the universe was created (John 1:3; Hebrews 1:2), arrived on our planet just over 2,000 years ago. He did not come in an armada of spaceships, nor was his coming greeted by world leaders. He came in a way that no one could have imagined: he made his close encounter by being born into the human race through the most humble of circumstances.

B. LESSON BACKGROUND

Julius Caesar lived from 100 to 44 BC. Before his assassination, he adopted Gaius Octavius as his son. However, the young man had to overcome dangerous foes before he could claim his place as the emperor of Rome. Following the defeat of Antony and Cleopatra in 31 BC, the Roman senate conferred on Octavius the title *Augustus*, meaning "the august one," in 27 BC.

Until his death in AD 14, Caesar Augustus was one of the most powerful of earthly rulers. But earthly glory is fleeting. Jesus' birth was little-noticed when Augustus was famous, but now that birth is world-known while Augustus is all but forgotten.

DEVOTIONAL READING:
PSALM 96:1-6
BACKGROUND SCRIPTURE:
LUKE 2:1-20
PRINTED TEXT:
LUKE 2:1-14

Dec
23

LESSON AIMS

After participating in this lesson, each student will be able to:

1. Recite the story of Jesus' birth from Luke's Gospel.

2. List several evidences of joy or reasons for joy that are found in the text.

3. Read today's text aloud at a family or work Christmas celebration.

KEY VERSE

Today in the town of David a Savior has been born to you; he is Christ the Lord. —Luke 2:11

I. ROYAL DECREE (LUKE 2:1-3)

A. CAESAR'S DEMAND (v. 1)

1. In those days Caesar Augustus issued a decree that a census should be taken of the entire Roman world.

Luke takes special care to show that Jesus is born at a real time, in a real place. Jesus' birth comes about during the reign of *Caesar Augustus,* who serves officially as Roman emperor from 27 BC to AD 14. As ruler of *the entire Roman world* (a phrase that signifies the known area around the Mediterranean Sea), Augustus has the power to decree an official census to assist in collecting taxes.

TAXES

Benjamin Franklin (1706–1790) is credited with the observation, "In this world nothing is certain but death and taxes." Franklin is normally thought of as a smiling, optimistic entrepreneur. But this famous quotation may strike one as being depressing, fatalistic, and negative.

Taxes do seem to be a constant fact of life. People have complained about taxation for centuries. High taxation rates contributed to civil unrest during the era of the Roman Empire. High taxation was one of the factors that resulted in the French Revolution. High taxation rates contributed to the Whiskey Rebellion in Pennsylvania in 1794. But comparatively speaking, modern America does not have it that bad. Residents in some countries of Europe pay much more in taxes as a percentage of their income. Yet Americans still like to complain about taxes!

Joseph and Mary went to Bethlehem to register for their taxes. We may wonder whether those two griped about their taxes while on the way. Do you think that this event shows us God's sense of humor as he integrates Jesus' birth with the all-too-human chore of dealing with taxes?　　　　—J. B. N.

B. PEOPLE'S DUTY (vv. 2, 3)

2. (This was the first census that took place while Quirinius was governor of Syria.)

Luke connects the birth of Jesus to events that are well known to people of the time. Even so, the exact year of Jesus' birth is difficult to determine, and there are various facts to consider. The first is that the birth is during Augustus's four-decade reign (v. 1), but that doesn't narrow things down much! The second fact is that *Quirinius* is *governor of Syria.* This man had been made "Counsel" in 12 BC, with his governorship coming somewhat later.

A third fact to consider is that the birth of Jesus takes place during the lifetime of Herod the Great (Matthew 2; Luke 1:5). We know from secular history that Herod died just before the Passover of 4 BC. When these and other facts are combined, a reasonable calculation places the birth of Christ in 5 or 4 BC.

This calculation may seem curious to us. We naturally may suppose that Jesus would be born in "the year zero" (even though there is no "year zero") just by definition, since BC means "before Christ." The problem is traceable to the work of a sixth-century monk named Dionysius. Our modern calendar is based on his calculations, and unfortunately he made an error of several years.

3. And everyone went to his own town to register.

Every Jewish man has to return to the city of his ancestors to be enrolled. For Joseph this means a long journey in support of a despised Roman tax.

II. HUMBLE BIRTH (LUKE 2:4-7)

A. JOSEPH'S SITUATION (v. 4)

4. So Joseph also went up from the town of Nazareth in Galilee to Judea, to Bethlehem the town of David, because he belonged to the house and line of David.

HOW TO SAY IT

Bethlehem. BETH-lih-hem.

Caesar Augustus. SEE-zer Aw-GUS-tus.

Cleopatra. Clee-oh-PAT-ruh.

Dionysius. Die-oh-NISH-ih-us.

Gaius Octavius. GAY-us Ock-TAY-vee-us.

Galilean. Gal-uh-LEE-un.

Galilee. GAL-uh-lee.

Julius Caesar. JOO-lee-us SEE-zer.

Manoah. Muh-NO-uh.

Mediterranean. MED-uh-tuh-RAY-nee-un.

Micah. MY-kuh.

Nazareth. NAZ-uh-reth.

Quirinius. Kwy-RIN-ee-us.

Solomon. SOL-o-mun.

When *Joseph* first learned that his pledged bride was already pregnant, he decided to give her a quiet divorce (see Matthew 1:18, 19). Only after an angel appeared to him did Joseph agree to keep her as his wife. While Scripture does not state what difficulties he and Mary experienced in *Nazareth,* it is easy to imagine the gossip they endured as Mary began to "show."

Now the decree from Rome gives them an opportunity to leave. Their journey takes them some 70 miles southward. But since they are traveling to an elevation that is about 1,250 feet higher than Nazareth, Scripture says they go *up* from *Galilee* into *Judea.*

Joseph's ancestral home is *Bethlehem* because he is of *the house and line of David.* Bethlehem is the city where David lived as a boy (see 1 Samuel 17:12, 58). Bethlehem means "house of bread." This is a fitting meaning for the birthplace for the one who will be "the bread of life" (John 6:35, 48)!

B. MARY'S SITUATION (vv. 5, 6)

5. He went there to register with Mary, who was pledged to be married to him and was expecting a child.

For *Mary* the trip is probably both a bane and a blessing. The trip is naturally quite uncomfortable given the advanced stage of her pregnancy. But at least this trip takes her away from the wagging tongues in Nazareth. The virgin's baby will be born in another town, in welcome privacy.

In obedience to the angel of the Lord, Joseph had taken Mary as his wife. Since he has not yet had intimate relations with her (see Matthew 1:25), Scripture says they were *pledged to be married.* Mary is now reaching the final days of her pregnancy and so is *expecting a child.*

Thus by a royal decree issued in far-away Rome, these two make their way to Bethlehem. By a divine decree issued five centuries earlier in Micah 5:2, the birth of their child is predetermined to be in Bethlehem. Little does Caesar Augustus know that he is helping to carry out the plan of God!

6. While they were there, the time came for the baby to be born,

Perhaps Joseph and Mary complete the journey to Bethlehem before the ninth month of her pregnancy begins. Scripture simply affirms that while they are there *the time* comes for the delivery of *the baby.* By human appearances it will be just another baby. But in divine reality the son of Mary is the Son of God.

C. BABY'S SITUATION (v. 7)

7. . . . and she gave birth to her firstborn, a son. She wrapped him in cloths and placed him in a manger, because there was no room for them in the inn.

Thus Mary gives birth to her *firstborn* child, which is *a son.* This is not her only child; there will be other sons and daughters in years to come (see Mark 6:3).

In accordance with the custom of the time, Mary wraps the baby in long strips of cloth. This procedure is intended to keep the baby warm and give him a sense of security. An ancient non-biblical work notes that the baby who would later become King Solomon "was nursed with care in swaddling clothes. For no king has had a different beginning of existence" (Wisdom of Solomon 7:4). The opposite of such care is seen in Ezekiel 16:4.

Various interpretations have been offered regarding *the inn* that has *no room* for this family. Perhaps it is a public stopping place with "no vacancy" in the sleeping quarters that are located around the perimeter of the building; therefore, Joseph and Mary can go only to the open feeding area for animals. A tradition dating back to the second century puts the birthplace in a cave.

WHAT DO YOU THINK?

Without overspiritualizing things, when have you noticed God working through the "mundane" events in life? How can we get better at noticing his work around us?

DAILY BIBLE READINGS

Monday, Dec. 17—Sing a New Song (Psalm 96:1-6)

Tuesday, Dec. 18—Joseph and Mary (Matthew 1:18b-21)

Wednesday, Dec. 19—Traveling to Bethlehem (Luke 2:1-5)

Thursday, Dec. 20—Jesus, Firstborn Son (Luke 2:6, 7)

Friday, Dec. 21—Angels Proclaim the News (Luke 2:8-14)

Saturday, Dec. 22—Shepherds Visit the King (Luke 2:15-20)

Sunday, Dec. 23—Judging with God's Truth (Psalm 96:7-13)

WHAT DO YOU THINK?

Jesus set aside great power and majesty to become human. What are some ways we can set aside our own personal power or influence? Under what circumstances should we do so?

Whatever the exact circumstance, it is a humble beginning for the prince from Heaven! The baby Jesus has only a common *manger,* an animal's feed box, for his bed.

III. ANGELIC ANNOUNCEMENT (LUKE 2:8-12)

A. UNSUSPECTING SHEPHERDS (vv. 8, 9)

8. And there were shepherds living out in the fields nearby, keeping watch over their flocks at night.

The scene moves from the manger to the *nearby* countryside. The focus remains on how humble the setting is. In the surrounding area, there are lowly *shepherds* who camp *in the fields* with their sheep. The shepherds are *keeping watch over their flocks* that *night* to protect them from predators and thieves.

9. An angel of the Lord appeared to them, and the glory of the Lord shone around them, and they were terrified.

If there ever was a once-in-a-lifetime experience, this is it! Along with *an angel of the Lord* appears the *glory,* or shining majesty, of God to radiate all *around them.* The shepherds, as simple peasant folks at the bottom rung of the social ladder, are less ready than anyone to be in the presence of majesty. Their fear is understandable. Their reaction may be compared with that of Manoah and his wife in Judges 13:22. After the angel of the Lord spoke to them, Manoah said, "We are doomed to die! We have seen God!"

B. UNPRECEDENTED NEWS (vv. 10, 11)

10. But the angel said to them, "Do not be afraid. I bring you good news of great joy that will be for all the people.

An *angel* is literally a "messenger," and this angel has a wonderful message indeed. First, the angel quickly offers the shepherds reassuring words: *Do not be afraid.* Then comes the threefold message: *good news . . . great joy . . . all the people.* The birth of this child is indeed "good news," the beginning of the gospel. He will bring the world the joy of salvation.

Surprisingly, this salvation will be available not just to those of Israel, but to everyone. Some restrict the phrase *all the people* in this context to mean only the Jews. The reason is that other accounts mention salvation of "his people" (Matthew 1:21) as Jesus reigns over "the house of Jacob" (Luke 1:33). The prophecies of Isaiah, Amos, and others, however, support the view that the pronouncements include Gentiles. God intends salvation to be for Jew and non-Jew alike (Acts 10:34, 35; 11:18).

FOR ALL PEOPLE

The American Civil War was devastating. Approximately 600,000 soldiers died—about 2 percent of the U.S. population. Men fought for various reasons. Some fought to keep slavery; some fought to eliminate it. Some fought for state's rights; some fought to preserve the union. Some fought to protect their families; some fought against their own brothers.

Four months after the pivotal battle of Gettysburg in 1863, U.S. President Abraham Lincoln went to that small Pennsylvania town to dedicate a cemetery for the honored war dead. In his famous address there, he called attention to the fact that the nation "conceived in liberty, and dedicated to the proposition that all men are created equal" was then engaged in a war that was testing whether such a nation could endure. He concluded by urging his hearers to be dedicated to ensuring that government "of the people, by the people, for the people" should "not perish from the earth."

Lincoln's frame of reference was that government belonged to the people—all the people. The ultimate result of that war was that one class of people could not enslave another class. American liberties were to be for everyone. If a human government can choose that ideal as its goal, how much more so when God's will is concerned! God is no respecter of persons and shows no favoritism. The message of the angel to the shepherds was that the good tidings of great joy would be to *all the people*. It still is.   —J. B. N.

11. *"Today in the town of David a Savior has been born to you; he is Christ the Lord.*

When the angel says *to you*, he signifies that this event is directed even to lowly shepherds. The shepherds know that *the town of David* is Bethlehem. This newborn baby will be the rescuer for those who need to be rescued, *a Savior* for those who need to be saved—meaning everyone! While many Jews hope for a Messiah to deliver them from the Romans, God intends that the Messiah deliver them from their sins.

The Savior will be known as *Christ the Lord*. The title *Christ* comes from a Greek word meaning "the anointed one." In Hebrew the word for "the anointed one" is *Messiah* (John 1:41). Anointing with oil was the Old Testament inauguration ritual for prophets, priests, and kings. As God's anointed, Jesus will fill all three offices. As the Lord, Jesus will be master over everyone.

C. UNLIKELY SIGN (v. 12)

12. *"This will be a sign to you: You will find a baby wrapped in cloths and lying in a manger."*

A Jewish commentary on Psalm 23 says, "There is no more disreputable occupation than that of shepherd." The religious leaders certainly would consider shepherds to be unlearned and ignorant (compare the reaction of the religious leaders to Peter and John—fishermen—in Acts 4:13). Yet the only invited guests to witness the newborn Jesus on this glorious night are shepherds!

Knowing that the shepherds can hardly believe their ears, the angel voluntarily gives them *a sign:* when they arrive in Bethlehem they will find the baby *wrapped in cloths and lying in a manger*. The swaddling clothes are to be expected on any newborn baby; the manger as a baby bed is not. The sign is to confirm to them, when they find the baby, that everything the angel says about him is true. Shortly thereafter, they find Jesus just as the angel predicts (v. 16).

IV. DIVINE PRAISE (LUKE 2:13, 14)

A. GLORIOUS MULTITUDE (v. 13)

13. *Suddenly a great company of the heavenly host appeared with the angel, praising God and saying,*

No earthly dignitaries are on hand to welcome the arrival of God's Son. Even if there were, would they know what words to say? So God provides his own welcoming party in the form of a *heavenly host*. This happens *suddenly*, as the one angel is joined by a *great company* of angels. In the Old Testament such words typically identify an army of angels, who serve the Lord of Hosts (Psalms 103:21; 148:2). Scripture does not state whether this host fills the sky or stands on the hills that surround the shepherds.

This host has an additional message. Their voices join to praise God for the great thing he has done. What God had planned from the beginning is taking place. What the prophets had prophesied, even without understanding the

Visual for Lesson 4. *Be sure you have this visual on display as you discuss the phrase, "Glory to God in the highest."*

WHAT DO YOU THINK?

Should we seek signs today? Why, or why not?

[Hint: enrich your discussion by considering Mark 13:22-27; John 4:48; 20:30, 31; 1 Corinthians 1:22, 23; 1 Thessalonians 4:16; and 2 Thessalonians 2:9.]

WHAT DO YOU THINK?

You see in a shopping mall parking lot a festive holiday banner that reads Peace on Earth. *How does the original context of that phrase help us avoid misinterpreting it?*

WHAT DO YOU THINK?

What Christmas tradition causes you to rejoice most in the meaning of the Christmas message?

THOUGHT TO REMEMBER

The gospel is still good news of great joy for all people.

full import of their own words, is being fulfilled. And what the angels have longed to look into (see 1 Peter 1:10-12) is finally coming about. No wonder the heavenly host is summoned to rejoice!

B. GLORIOUS MESSAGE (v. 14)

14. "Glory to God in the highest,
      and on earth peace to men on whom his favor rests."

A primary message of that first Christmas is *Glory to God*. To say this is to proclaim that he who dwells "in unapproachable light" (1 Timothy 6:16) has sole claim to glory. To God alone belong all majesty, radiance, and splendor. He is the Lord of Heaven and earth; he is *God in the highest*. In Heaven, glory is given to God; on earth, *peace* is extended to us.

Peace is more than the mere absence of conflict; it is the presence of everything that is necessary for one's well-being. This peace will come to the world through the prince of peace. Rome had brought a military peace that would later permit the early Christians to spread the gospel. The peace mentioned here, however, is a peace between God and people. For one of the greatest peace pronouncements in the New Testament, see Romans 5:1.

The phrase *on whom his favor rests* indicates that God shows favor to those who accept his grace.

CONCLUSION

A. CLOSE ENCOUNTER IN BETHLEHEM

With their words ringing in the ears of the shepherds, the angels departed and returned to Heaven. No heavenly messenger had ever proclaimed such a glad message. To the world had been born a Savior, Christ the Lord. We should join the humble shepherds in their excitement and amazement. This is a message that calls everyone to rejoice.

The message of the birth in Bethlehem is far more than the mere sweetness of a baby. The real message of Christmas is the coming of the Son of God to live (and give) his life as the Son of Man. "The Word became flesh and made his dwelling among us" (John 1:14). This is the miracle of the incarnation.

Jesus came to have a close encounter, an intimate participation in our world. He came as a baby, helplessly swaddled in tight strips of cloth. He came as a human to face hunger and thirst, temptation and persecution. He wept real tears; he bled real blood; he died a real death on the cross; he gained a real resurrection.

In all this, "he became the source of eternal salvation for all who obey him" (Hebrews 5:9). He "has been tempted in every way, just as we are—yet was without sin" (Hebrews 4:15). Jesus knew what it was to be a man. He came to earth to be Immanuel—"God with us" (Matthew 1:23).

B. CLOSE ENCOUNTER IN HEAVEN

Jesus came to live with us on earth so that one day we can live with God in Heaven. His close encounter with humanity makes possible our close encounter with God later. Revelation 21:3 foretells the day when, "He will live with them. They will be his people, and God himself will be with them and be their God."

Because of the messages of Christmas and Easter, we can look forward to the day when we shall join the angel's praise: "Glory to God in the highest." Christmas calls us to rejoice in the coming of our Savior. Christmas calls us to rejoice in the gift of God's grace.

Discovery Learning

This page contains an alternative lesson plan emphasizing learning activities. Classes desiring such student involvement will find these suggestions helpful. The next page is a reproducible activity page to further enhance discovery learning.

INTO THE LESSON

Put copies of the Summarizing the Text activity from the Reproducible Page in each chair for your learners to work on as they arrive. Recruit in advance a person to play the part of a TV news anchorperson. After your opening prayer, this person enters the classroom, sits at a desk in front of the class, faces a pretend TV camera, and makes the following announcement:

Now some breaking news as our last item. By decree of the president, all citizens must return to the place of their birth for a census and taxing enrollment. All must complete this enrollment by the fifth of January in the year 2008. Failure to comply is not an option. Failure to comply is punishable by imprisonment.

The anchorperson then "signs off," briefly shuffles some papers, and leaves.

Ask, "What kind of burden would that requirement place on you, if any? Would you feel resentful?" After a brief time of sharing say, "Of course, that is much like the Roman decree heard in a remote Galilean village by a young couple, newly married and expecting, whose family hometown was a journey of several days away."

If your class uses the optional student book, you may find the Angel Words exercise there to be a good alternative to the above activity.

INTO THE WORD

Read John 1:14 to your class. In that verse Jesus, the Word become flesh, is said to be full of grace and truth. Point out that Jesus said of himself, "I am . . . the truth" (John 14:6). Distribute paper and pens (or use this activity from the optional student book) and say to your group, "The story in our text today in Luke 2 is a very familiar one, so let's take a true-false quiz on the content. Number your paper from 1 to 15." Then read the following affirmations:

1. The Roman ruler who made the decree for Joseph and Mary to travel to Bethlehem was Julius Caesar.

2. The primary purpose of Caesar's enrollment demand was to have an accurate census.

3. The governor of Syria at the time was Brastius.

4. Joseph needed to travel to Bethlehem, David's hometown, for he was of David's family line.

5. Joseph and Mary traveled to Bethlehem when she was in the late stages of pregnancy.

6. While in Bethlehem, Mary delivered her baby.

7. The baby boy born was Mary's first child.

8. The newborn baby was laid in an animal's feeding trough because that was customary, for comfort and a sense of security.

9. Nearby to Bethlehem, God's angel appeared to shepherds in the night to announce the baby's birth.

10. The angel's glow of God's glory severely frightened the shepherds.

11. The angel indicated that the good news was only for the Jews.

12. The angel clearly called the baby Christ.

13. The directions given to the shepherds for finding the child in Bethlehem included the fact that a star would shine brightly over the place as they approached.

14. A large number of angels joined the first angel with praises and a blessing.

15. It appears that Jesus was born at night.

Answers are: *1. F; 2. F; 3. F; 4. T; 5. T; 6. T; 7. T; 8. F; 9. T; 10. T; 11. F; 12. T; 13. F; 14. T; 15. T.*

After moving through the statements and allowing time for silent response, repeat the statements and let students answer aloud. Ask for confirming verses.

INTO LIFE

Close today's session with an oral reading of Luke 2:1-14. Prepare copies of the text that you have marked for three readers (or groups of readers) to read aloud. For example, consider this division for verse one: (1) "In those days," (2) "Caesar Augustus issued a decree," (3) "that a census should be taken of the entire Roman world." You can simplify the readers' task by putting each segment on its own line.

Next, say, "The biblical texts recording the events surrounding Jesus' birth are read often in this season. Look for an appropriate occasion over the next few days to read today's text aloud in the presence of family, friends, or coworkers." (The optional student book has an activity entitled Ever Feel Like a Shepherd? If you are able to use that resource, draw your learners' attention to it as time allows.) As your learners depart, hand each a copy of A Shepherd's Poem and instructions from the Reproducible Page.

A Shepherd's Poem

During the week ahead, find another person—either adult or child—with whom you can share the following poem about the Bethlehem shepherds visiting God's good shepherd at the manger. Be certain to note the biblical allusions as you share the poem.

The Shepherds and the Shepherd

The shepherds have come to see one of their own;
The babe will soon come to be Shepherd full grown.
They know the cold nights keeping sheep in the fold;
He knows of lost sheep from the Israel of old.
So, shepherds, greet Shepherd: his glory is known!

The angels have told them the Christ is now born:
He lies in a manger, no robe to adorn.
They know the discomfort of sleeping on ground;
He knows that no bed for his rest will be found.
So, shepherds, greet Shepherd: O marvelous morn!

So shepherds return to the sheepfold in joy;
They've seen the Good Shepherd in small baby boy.
They know that their sheep are depending on them;
He knows that lost sheep will stay lost without him.
So, shepherds, greet Shepherd: just call him God's joy!

Summarizing the Text

Look at each verse of Luke 2:1-14 and find two words for each of the following pairs of letters. Look for words that come in order in the verse and in some sense "fit" together. To get you started, the *C A* in verse one is for "Caesar Augustus"; the *N R* in verse 7 should be "No Room."

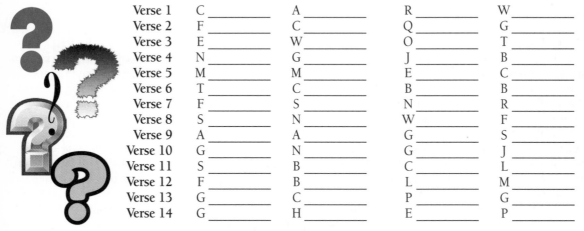

Verse 1	C _____	A _____	R _____	W _____
Verse 2	F _____	C _____	Q _____	G _____
Verse 3	E _____	W _____	O _____	T _____
Verse 4	N _____	G _____	J _____	B _____
Verse 5	M _____	M _____	E _____	C _____
Verse 6	T _____	C _____	B _____	B _____
Verse 7	F _____	S _____	N _____	R _____
Verse 8	S _____	N _____	W _____	F _____
Verse 9	A _____	A _____	G _____	S _____
Verse 10	G _____	N _____	G _____	J _____
Verse 11	S _____	B _____	C _____	L _____
Verse 12	F _____	B _____	L _____	M _____
Verse 13	G _____	C _____	P _____	G _____
Verse 14	G _____	H _____	E _____	P _____

Now look back at your words in sequence and mentally fill in the whole story told in these verses.

God's Call to the Christian Community
Unit 1: *God's Call in Christ*
(Lessons 1-5)

CALLED TO WITNESS

LESSON 5

WHY TEACH THIS LESSON?

Every person who has accepted the Lord Jesus Christ as Savior has become a witness to the story of the gospel. This person has experienced the power of Jesus Christ personally and has tasted the mercy and grace of God firsthand. That's a use of the word *witness* in the sense of *seeing* or *experiencing*.

But *witness* also has the sense of *telling*. Do your students recognize the great opportunity and responsibility they have to tell the story of their salvation? No stories of salvation are exactly the same but each witness story is a lifeline to a drowning world. Simeon in today's lesson is a witness to your students. He will inspire them, in a way, to go forth and do the same.

INTRODUCTION

A. TO WITNESS

When a crime is committed, the police always look for witnesses. When a disaster hits a community, the reporters for the evening news always want to interview a witness on the site. Many times people on the scene can hardly wait to tell what they know. This is a reminder that the verb *witness* has at least two meanings: "to see something" and "to testify about something."

People see and testify not only to crimes and disasters, but also to good things. People who are getting married choose good friends to sign the marriage license in witness. They invite family and friends to witness the happy event. Life has many special moments that are good to witness.

In this lesson we will be introduced to a man who witnessed a great event of history. He was told long in advance of the great day; he spent his life waiting for the moment. The event was the arrival of the Messiah at the temple; the eyewitness was a man named Simeon.

B. LESSON BACKGROUND

A striking element of Luke's account of Jesus' birth is the mention of the man Simeon. While he bore the noble name of one of the tribes of Israel, absolutely nothing is known about him outside Luke's few verses. Of the various things this text says about Simeon, the most important is that "the Holy Spirit was upon him" (Luke 2:25).

While the presence of the Holy Spirit was not a common experience in the lives of the people of Israel, the Holy Spirit has been directly involved since the beginning (Genesis 1:2). In the Old Testament the Spirit came upon people whom God selected to do special tasks. To such people the Spirit gave skill in craftsmanship (Exodus 31:3), wisdom in leadership (Judges 3:10), or phenomenal physical strength (Judges 14:6). As king of Israel, David pleaded with God, "Do not . . . take your Holy Spirit from me" (Psalm 51:11). Most importantly, the prophets were enabled to speak "as they were carried along by the Holy Spirit" (2 Peter 1:21).

DEVOTIONAL READING:
ISAIAH **49:5, 6**
BACKGROUND SCRIPTURE:
LUKE 2:22-38
PRINTED TEXT:
LUKE 2:22-35

Dec
30

LESSON AIMS

After participating in this lesson, each student will be able to:

1. Explain who Simeon was and why his witness to the coming of the Messiah was so significant.

2. Understand that the promises of God are certain, even when they seem to be delayed.

3. Make a commitment to proclaim to others how he or she has seen God fulfill his promises.

KEY VERSE

Simeon blessed them and said to Mary, his mother: "This child is destined to cause the falling and rising of many in Israel, and to be a sign that will be spoken against." —Luke 2:34

LESSON 5 NOTES

As the Gospel accounts begin, it had been more than 400 years since the last Holy Spirit–inspired Scripture was penned (the book of Malachi). Today we will see that Simeon had received, at some point in his life, Holy Spirit–inspired knowledge of the coming of the Messiah. He had a firsthand privilege of seeing the infant Savior.

I. WITNESS BY OBEYING (LUKE 2:22-24)

Our opening verses show several of the ways in which God calls people to be witnesses to their faith. The first is by obedience to his Word. Joseph and Mary demonstrate their respect for God by doing what he says. The purification of the mother and the redemption of the firstborn son are acts of submission to God's law.

A. PURIFICATION (v. 22a)

22a. When the time of their purification according to the Law of Moses had been completed,

According to the Law of Moses, a Jewish woman is ceremonially unclean for 7 days after she gives birth to a son (Leviticus 12:2-4). On day 8 she is to have her baby circumcised (Luke 2:21). Then she is to remain in seclusion for another 33 days. During this period of nearly 6 weeks, she is not to touch any hallowed thing, nor can she go to the temple. When the 40 days of her *purification* are over, it is time for Mary and Joseph to take the baby Jesus to Jerusalem.

B. PRESENTATION (vv. 22b, 23)

22b, 23. . . . Joseph and Mary took him to Jerusalem to present him to the Lord (as it is written in the Law of the Lord, "Every firstborn male is to be consecrated to the Lord"),

As Luke makes clear, there is more than one requirement of the law that Mary and Joseph deal with. One is Mary's purification (Leviticus 12); the other is the presentation and redemption of their son. The two requirements are closely linked. Devout Jews perform this presentation in Jerusalem if at all possible. Once Joseph and Mary reach the city, they go to the temple so they can *present* their firstborn *to the Lord.*

The Law of the Lord gives a specific requirement for *every firstborn male.* Firstborn males belong to the Lord as his holy possession. This applies to both humans and livestock (Exodus 13:2, 12). This law reminds the people that the Lord had brought the Jews out of Egypt by slaying the firstborn of the Egyptians (Exodus 13:15).

The Lord also provided a way by which the newborn male could be redeemed or "bought back" at a price of five shekels (Numbers 18:15, 16). From the very infancy of Jesus, everything in his life is done to fulfill all that the law requires (see also Matthew 3:15; Galatians 4:4).

DEDICATED TO THE LORD

I am not a firstborn child. I am the second son (third child) born to the third son (fourth child) in my grandfather's family. Yet when my mother was pregnant with me, my 70-year-old grandmother (a very devout Christian woman) dedicated me to the Lord. That may seem a bit brazen to some. After all, won't the child grow up to make his or her own decisions about religion or anything else?

My grandmother never told my parents what she had done. She never told me either, as she died when I was only a few months old. She told only my aunt. My aunt did not tell me what my grandmother had done until I was 26 years old. At that time I was already engaged in a preaching ministry, and I was taking advanced studies to prepare for a career in Bible college teaching. It was an uncanny feeling to discover that I had been dedicated to the Lord's service even before I was born!

Long before Jesus was born, he had already been dedicated to his task. His presentation in the temple was the formality that confirmed what God had predicted as far back as the Garden of Eden. Today—right now—you have the opportunity to dedicate yourself (or dedicate yourself anew) to serving God. You need not and should not depend on a parent or grandparent to do this for you. What choice will you make?   —J. B. N.

C. SACRIFICE (v. 24)

24. . . . and to offer a sacrifice in keeping with what is said in the Law of the Lord: "a pair of doves or two young pigeons."

The parents also *offer a sacrifice* to God. In *the Law of the Lord*, the parents are told to offer a lamb as a burnt offering and a turtledove or pigeon as a sin offering (Leviticus 12:6-8). If they cannot offer a lamb because of their poverty, they are permitted to offer *a pair of doves or two young pigeons*. (One of the pair would take the place of the lamb as the burnt offering; the other would be the sin offering.)

The offering of Joseph and Mary serves as a subtle reminder that these people are humble peasants. They do not have the means to offer a lamb as a burnt offering. This fact reminds us that God's Son does not come to live in the palace of a king. He experiences humanity's hardships; he suffers as the Son of Man (see 2 Corinthians 8:9).

II. WITNESS BY BELIEVING (LUKE 2:25-29)

When God speaks, his people accept what he says as true. Thus we bear witness by believing. Although God's promises may seem unlikely or even impossible, they are steadfast and sure. In these verses Simeon bears witness to God's faithfulness by believing that the Messiah would indeed come in his lifetime.

A. LIFETIME OF WAITING (vv. 25, 26)

25. Now there was a man in Jerusalem called Simeon, who was righteous and devout. He was waiting for the consolation of Israel, and the Holy Spirit was upon him.

Simeon is the name borne by a man who encounters Jesus' family in the temple. This is a famous name, the name of the second son of Jacob by Leah; it is thus the name of 1 of the 12 tribes of Israel.

According to the way the world looks at people, there is little that is noteworthy about Simeon. In God's sight, however, Simeon has an important role in identifying the infant Jesus as the long-awaited Messiah. Simeon is a *righteous* man who is *devout* in the practice of his faith. This man is *waiting for the consolation,* or "comforting," *of Israel*. He is part of the faithful remnant of Israel who still expects that God will comfort his people as Isaiah had promised (see Isaiah 40:1, 2; 49:13). *The Holy Spirit*, whom Jesus later will call the Comforter (John 14:16), has a special presence in Simeon's life.

26. It had been revealed to him by the Holy Spirit that he would not die before he had seen the Lord's Christ.

The Holy Spirit has brought consolation into Simeon's life by revealing a wonderful truth: before Simeon dies, he will see *the Lord's Christ*. The Lord God has promised to send his Christ, his Messiah—his Anointed One. Jesus is the one anointed by God to bring deliverance. Many thousands of God-fearing

---

WHAT DO YOU THINK?

What inspiration can we gain from the fact that Joseph and Mary faithfully fulfilled their obligations under the Old Testament law, despite having been shown special, miraculous attention by God?

HOW TO SAY IT

Augustine. AW-gus-teen or Aw-GUS-tin.
Corinthians. Ko-RIN-thee-unz.
Egypt. EE-jipt.
Egyptians. Ee-JIP-shuns.
Galatians. Guh-LAY-shunz.
Isaiah. Eye-ZAY-uh.
Israel. IZ-ray-el.
Leviticus. Leh-VIT-ih-kus.
Simeon. SIM-ee-un.
Zechariah. ZEK-uh-RYE-uh.

Jews have lived and died without seeing the coming of the Messiah. But the Spirit has assured Simeon that he will see this event. How blessed Simeon is!

B. MOMENT OF FULFILLMENT (v. 27)

27. *Moved by the Spirit, he went into the temple courts. When the parents brought in the child Jesus to do for him what the custom of the Law required,*

The Spirit previously has rested upon Simeon to reveal the coming of Christ. Now that same Spirit leads Simeon *into the temple courts.* Today is the day—the great moment has finally arrived!

Guided by the Spirit, Simeon notices a certain young couple who has come to present their child after *the custom of the law.* The Spirit has brought Simeon to this encounter with *the child Jesus.*

HE CAME BY THE SPIRIT

I am not what I call a subjective person, nor easily moved by warm fuzzies. I tend to think of myself as rational, thoughtful, and methodical. Perhaps that is why I am always a bit skittish when I hear people say, "It was a God thing."

I know what they mean: they believe that God led them to a certain action that turned out to be beneficial to themselves and others. Yet I always struggle with the question, "But did God really do it, or was it just coincidence?" It's not that I don't believe that God works in marvelous ways or that he is incapable of direct intervention in our lives to accomplish his will. I just wish there were some kind of objective test I could apply that would guarantee that the event was indeed "a God thing."

Even so, I cannot deny that God has indeed led people throughout history. Centuries ago, he led Augustine to England to begin the conversion of that people to Christianity. He led Boniface to Germany to begin the conversion of the tribes there. He led Luther through the turmoil of the sixteenth-century Protestant Reformation. He led John Wesley into a significant revival in England in the eighteenth century. He led Dwight Moody into revivalism in the century that followed.

Perhaps I just need to have more faith in God's leading. His leading is always better seen in hindsight than in present tense. Regardless, the Spirit led Simeon to the temple for a glorious experience with the incarnate Christ. Where or to whom might the Spirit lead you today?   —J. B. N.

C. WORDS OF BENEDICTION (vv. 28, 29)

28. . . . *Simeon took him in his arms and praised God, saying:*

When *Simeon* approaches the parents, why do Mary and Joseph release their infant into *his arms*? Do they see the reverent joy in his eyes? Does the Holy Spirit also reveal the nature of this event to them? We don't know, but there must be something both commanding and reassuring in Simeon's bearing for the young mother to allow a stranger to hold her baby!

Notice that Simeon's praise is not directed to the child but to *God*, who has brought salvation to his people.

29. *"Sovereign Lord, as you have promised,*
**   *you now dismiss your servant in peace.***

Simeon's words of blessing form a reverent prayer. After untold years of waiting and believing, now he is ready to depart *in peace.* Apparently he is an older man for whom death is imminent. The Christ child has come during Simeon's lifetime, *as* God had *promised.* Everything is just as God said it would be. Following "Mary's Song" (Luke 1:46-55) and "Zechariah's Song" (1:67-79), this begins Luke's third great canticle: "Simeon's Song" (2:29-32).

WHAT DO YOU THINK?

How does the Spirit's leading in our own lives compare and contrast with that of Simeon's? How do we distinguish the Spirit's leading from the impulses of the flesh?

WHAT DO YOU THINK?

Simeon is content for his days on earth to end after he meets Jesus. How have you seen people respond to Jesus in their "golden years"?

WHAT DO YOU THINK?

What was a time when you saw God bring about a blessing after many years of waiting and expecting? What was your reaction?

III. WITNESS BY PROCLAIMING (LUKE 2:30-35)

The ultimate role of a witness is to proclaim what he or she has seen. A witness who sees but fails to speak up has failed to fulfill this function. Simeon gladly speaks out to everyone who will listen: the salvation of the Lord has come!

A. GOOD NEWS FOR ALL (vv. 30-33)

30. "For my eyes have seen your salvation,

As a faithful witness, Simeon is eager to proclaim what he knows. With his own *eyes* he has *seen* the Lord's *salvation*. He has seen the child through whom deliverance will come. Indeed, his eyes have seen the glory of the coming of the Lord (Isaiah 40:5; 52:10)!

Still, it must be admitted that Simeon has seen only a baby. There is nothing remarkable in the appearance of this infant. There is no golden halo over his head. But Simeon sees the baby Jesus through the eyes of faith. He believes what God has revealed through his Spirit. It is in this sense that Simeon can say he had seen the Lord's salvation.

31. ". . . which you have prepared in the sight of all people,

Simeon knows that the arrival of Jesus somehow advances God's plan of salvation *in the sight of all people*. There is important doctrinal truth here: God's salvation is not just for Israel; it is for everyone. God's love is being extended to the whole world. The universality of the gospel is a strong theme in the Gospel of Luke. See the next verse.

32. ". . . a light for revelation to the Gentiles
and for glory to your people Israel."

Simeon gets more specific. This child will be *a light* that will penetrate the pagan darkness of *the Gentiles*, as Isaiah 42:6 and 49:6 promise. This light will also be the shining *glory* of God's chosen *people*. For *Israel*, nothing will be more to the nation's glory than giving birth to the Messiah (Isaiah 46:13).

Christ does not come, therefore, to cast aside either Jews or Gentiles or to set them against one another. When this light penetrates the darkness, there will be illumination for all. In Christ there is neither Greek nor Jew (Colossians 3:11).

33. The child's father and mother marveled at what was said about him.

Simeon has spoken of the child in such glowing terms that Joseph and the baby's *mother* are frankly amazed. While they themselves know special truth about Jesus, they are startled by words spoken by a total stranger. How can he know who this child is? How can he know about the salvation God would bring through him? But Simeon has even more to say!

B. BAD NEWS FOR SOME (v. 34)

34. Then Simeon blessed them and said to Mary, his mother: "This child is destined to cause the falling and rising of many in Israel, and to be a sign that will be spoken against,

Simeon now blesses *Mary* and Joseph, following with a special message for Mary personally. The coming of Jesus is *destined* for both bad news and good. It is the determination of God that it shall be so.

The bad news and good news are expressed in terms of *the falling and rising of many in Israel*. This points to a division within Israel. God has set Christ as the great divide regarding the destiny of every person. While Jesus is the source of salvation for all who obey him (see Hebrews 5:9), he is also the point of spiritual collapse for those who reject him. Though he is himself the *sign* and symbol of God's love, he *will be spoken against* by many of those

Visual for Lesson 5. *Point to this visual as you ask, "In what ways will you be a faithful witness this week?"*

whom he comes to save. Tragically, such opposition is to be especially true of Simeon's own nation (Isaiah 8:14; 1 Corinthians 1:23; 1 Peter 2:8).

C. PAINFUL NEWS FOR ONE (v. 35)

35. " . . . *so that the thoughts of many hearts will be revealed. And a sword will pierce your own soul too.*"

Simeon has yet one more thing to say to Mary. There will be dark moments in her future because of Jesus. The height of her joy at the birth of her son will be matched by the depth of her anguish at the cross. As the nails pierce his hands and feet, and as the spear pierces his side, it will be as if *a sword* were piercing the *soul* of Mary. She will stand at the foot of the cross, staying by Jesus as he dies (see John 19:25).

When Jesus goes to the cross to die, he creates a great moral crossroad. When people see his sacrificial death, *the thoughts* of their *hearts* are *revealed* (Matthew 27:38-43). The idea of the cross is still outright foolishness to many (see 1 Corinthians 1:23). It has been wisely said, "Jesus is the touchstone of human hearts."

CONCLUSION

A. TO WITNESS IS TO SEE

"I was there! I saw it with my own eyes!" Such are the words of a witness. To see, to hear, to feel firsthand—this is what makes a witness. Often a person will take special pride in the fact that he or she was present when some significant event took place. The greater the event, the more important the witness.

The birth of Jesus had been awaited with great anticipation. After so many centuries of preparation, God fulfilled the prophecies and promises. The miracle of the ages came to faithful members of God's community. God chose them for their special roles; they became witnesses of what he had done.

Luke demonstrated how the shepherds were called to witness the newborn Messiah. Then he added Simeon, who had waited much of his life to see God's anointed one. In the verses that follow today's text, Luke also related how Anna, an aged prophetess, gave thanks when the holy family came into the temple.

Other people witnessed Jesus at age 12; still more witnessed him in his ministry. Near the end of the first century, the apostle John would look back and recall Christ, "which we have heard, which we have seen with our eyes, which we have looked at and our hands have touched" (1 John 1:1).

B. TO WITNESS IS TO TELL

When people are witnesses to a big event, they are nearly always eager to tell someone about it. To witness is not only *to see*; to witness is also *to tell*. Joseph, Mary, Simeon—all in their own way became witnesses to the greatness of God. They believed what God said, obeyed what God commanded, and gladly proclaimed what God had done.

At the end of Jesus' life on earth he told his disciples, "You will be my witnesses." The apostles had been eyewitnesses to all he did, so they could testify to what they had seen. Even in the face of persecution they said, "We cannot help speaking about what we have seen and heard" (Acts 4:20). In the words of the apostle John, "We proclaim to you what we have seen and heard" (1 John 1:3).

Christians are also called to be witnesses today. While we are not eyewitnesses to the life of Jesus, we have experienced firsthand the power of his Word in our lives. Witnessing is a vital part of faith, and the world desperately needs to know what we know about Jesus.

Discovery Learning

This page contains an alternative lesson plan emphasizing learning activities. Classes desiring such student involvement will find these suggestions helpful. The next page is a reproducible activity page to further enhance discovery learning.

INTO THE LESSON

Purchase inexpensive birth announcement cards (for a boy) for your class members. Put the following information on the cards: "It's a Boy—the Son of God!"; "Born at Bethlehem, Judea"; "Your Presence (not Presents) Is Requested." You may choose to ask a class member to create these with a computer instead of purchasing them.

If you cannot afford to mail the announcements, simply lay them on the chairs before your learners arrive. As learners react, note that Simeon got an even better birth announcement from God: a special invitation from the Spirit to see the young baby in the temple.

Ask a class member to bring a quality dictionary to class and be ready to read the entries for the word *witness.* Ask students to include the notations that it can be a noun and a verb and that it can be both a transitive verb (takes a direct object) and an intransitive verb (doesn't take an object). Point out today's lesson title "Called to Witness" as you can emphasize the necessity both to see the facts of the story and to repeat the story to others as a testimony. Having witnessed, a witness states his or her witness!

INTO THE WORD

Assign the following Old Testament Scriptures to selected readers: Exodus 13:2, 15; Leviticus 12:2-4; Leviticus 12:6-8; Numbers 3:12; Numbers 18:16. Note the various requirements and conditions as they are read; list them on the board. (These Scriptures are also listed on the activity page of the optional student book in a section titled Birth Rites.) Say, "These passages will help clarify some of the activities of Mary and Joseph in today's text, especially in Luke 2:22-24."

Next, ask your class to prepare an acrostic description of Simeon, as he is seen in Luke 2:25-29. Give each learner a sheet of paper with *SIMEON* written vertically (or direct them to the Simeon Says activity in the optional student book). You can have your learners work in small groups or pairs, depending on class size.

Possible choices (among many) are Spirit-filled, Israelite, Man, Expectant, Old (as Simeon is assumed to be elderly), Noticed (by God). You may wish to tell your class that the words can simply include the relevant letter rather than starting with it (example: devOut).

Alternative #1: Put Simeon on the witness stand. Have an individual dressed as an elderly first-century Jewish man seated in the front of the group. Start right in: "Well, Mr. Simeon, as the prosecution's chief witness in this matter, do you swear to tell the truth, the whole truth, and nothing but the truth?" Let Simeon answer, "I serve the God of truth, so what I report about his dealings with us will be the absolute truth!"

Continue by asking an assortment of questions related to the text or implied by the circumstances of Christ's birth. Let your actor respond as he believes Simeon would. Consider letting the class join in the questioning. Conclude by saying, "Well, members of the jury, you have heard the witness. The choice is yours. Believe, or do not believe!"

Alternative #2: Use the Get Your Witness Here! activity on the Reproducible Page.

INTO LIFE

Simeon's witness in his praise incorporates much doctrine that should be a part of each Christian's testimony. Ask your class to look at Luke 2:30-35 and identify key concepts of God's acts of redemption in Christ.

Write the following concepts on the board. Ask the class to explain how the encounter with Simeon revealed each: 1. Salvation belongs to God. 2. Salvation is available for all, no matter one's ethnicity, gender, or national origin. 3. Salvation is easily likened to light in the midst of darkness. 4. Jesus fulfills the messianic prophecies and thus becomes the glory of all Israel. 5. For incarnation, God provided human parents for his divine Son. 6. Not all will believe the revelation of grace in Christ. 7. Jesus, who brought joy as a newborn, will ultimately bring grief in his death. 8. Jesus will be the great divider of humanity: some will turn their hearts to him, while others will turn their hearts against him.

Let the class suggest connections, but if needed, share these possibilities: #1 with verses 30, 31; #2 with verses 31b, 32; #3 with verses 31, 32; #4 with verse 32; #5 with verse 33; #6 with verse 34; #7 with verse 35a; #8 with verses 34, 35. Challenge learners to compose a personal statement of testimony incorporating as many of these ideas as possible. *Option:* Use the Can I Get a Witness? activity on the Reproducible Page either in place of or as a supplement to this exercise.

"Get Your Witness Here!"

When God reveals marvelous truths to individuals, both in words and in deeds, he expects that person to become a witness to those truths. Simeon was "called to witness," to see God's glory in the baby Jesus and to testify to God's faithful completion of his messianic promises.

Look at the headlines in this hypothetical front page. From Luke 2:22-38 fill in briefly the content related to each idea. At the lower right, describe—or sketch, if your artistic talents are capable—the picture you think an editor would want from the photo journalist for the day's front page. In the last block write the caption appropriate to your "photo."

The Daily Witness

JERUSALEM, JUDEA

Purification Laws Still in Place

Man of Faith Hangs Around Temple

Beautiful New Psalm Overheard

"Can I Get a Witness?"

God's urgent appeal in all ages is "can I get a witness?" How well are you fulfilling your role as a witness of God's revelation in his Word? Look at each of the following "witness-attitudes" as seen in Simeon in Luke 2; respond with *A* for *always*, *U* for *usually*, *S* for *sometimes*, *N* for *never*.

____ I feel confident in the revelation of God regarding the future.

____ I am patiently and expectantly waiting for God's fulfillment in my life.

____ I am unashamed to put myself where God's people gather to worship him.

____ I accept Jesus as the glory of Israel, God's Messiah.

____ I praise and bless God for his faithfulness in promises.

____ I am confident that I can "die in peace" at any time.

____ I believe that Jesus is the dividing line in human destiny.

____ I am ready—in public or in private—to express my commitment to Jesus as God's salvation.

____ "I am not ashamed of the gospel, because it is the power of God for the salvation of everyone who believes: first for the Jew, then for the Gentile" (Romans 1:16).

For any statements for which you could not respond "Always," what commitment will you make to the God of Simeon?

God's Call to the Christian Community
Unit 2: Inspired by God's Call
(Lessons 6-9)

INSPIRED TO INQUIRE

WHY TEACH THIS LESSON?

One way to evaluate what's important to a person is to pay attention to what he or she asks questions about. The more questions, the more interest! A person may sit attentively during a lecture on nuclear physics, but is the person really interested in that presentation? The attentive posture may be just an exercise in politeness. But if the person begins to ask lots of questions when the presentation is over, that's a sure sign that the lecture was important to him or her.

The same is true in church. Hebrews 10:25 tells us "Let us not give up meeting together, as some are in the habit of doing, but let us encourage one another—and all the more as you see the Day approaching." The Lord designed the church in such a way that we grow spiritually as we share our lives and faith with fellow believers. We mature as we interact and ask thoughtful questions.

Your learners need to understand that one blessing of being a part of the body of Christ is the maturity and growth the church enables. Jesus at age 12 provides us an example in his interaction with the religious scholars. If Jesus needed to mature spiritually, who are we to think we don't?

INTRODUCTION

A. PARENTAL CHALLENGES

Parents know what a challenge it is to respond appropriately to the developmental stages in their children's lives. This involves understanding a child's needs at given points. For instance, my four-year-old son has rules geared to his age. "You get three books, a kiss, and a prayer at bedtime," and, "You get to dress yourself, but you may ask for help with the shoes" are examples.

Those are good rules for now, but I have to be ready to make adjustments when he turns five. These will be rules such as, "You can go to kindergarten five days a week," and, "You get a one dollar weekly allowance." He may want the rules for five-year-olds now, but I know the time is not right, so I must resist his requests. Such are the challenges of being a parent!

Now let's try to imagine the parenting challenges that faced Mary and Joseph. How difficult was it for them to understand their son Jesus as he grew? How difficult was it for them to anticipate what his calling signified at the various developmental stages of his childhood? In addition to experiencing the normal physical changes of a boy becoming a man, Jesus was coming to grips with what it meant to be the Son of Man. Our own difficult teenage years provide us with only an inkling of the challenges he faced.

B. LESSON BACKGROUND

The events we read about in this week's lesson witness Jesus in Jerusalem. This is not the first time he has been there (see Luke 2:21-40; also see last week's lesson). It is interesting that the passages describing the two trips end with the same idea: Jesus continued to grow.

DEVOTIONAL READING:
PSALM 148:7-14
BACKGROUND SCRIPTURE:
LUKE 2:41-52
PRINTED TEXT:
LUKE 2:41-52

LESSON AIMS

Jan
6

After participating in this lesson, each student will be able to:

1. Identify the unusual events of Jesus' trip to Jerusalem at age 12.

2. Explain what the story of Jesus as a 12-year-old contributes to our understanding of his life and ministry.

3. Suggest one way to ensure that placing the Father's concerns first is of primary importance in his or her life.

KEY VERSE

After three days they found him in the temple courts, sitting among the teachers, listening to them and asking them questions.
—Luke 2:46

There are two settings for today's lesson. One is the dusty road between Nazareth and Jerusalem (a journey of about 75 miles). The other is the temple in Jerusalem itself. What happened in these two settings will cause us to ask a question that rings true for parents today: What do we make of a child who causes his parents grief when he chooses not to do what he must have known his parents wanted him to do?

I. IMPORTANT TRIP (LUKE 2:41-44a)

A. Faithful Family (vv. 41, 42)

41, 42. Every year his parents went to Jerusalem for the Feast of the Passover. When he was twelve years old, they went up to the Feast, according to the custom.

Why did God select Mary and Joseph to be Jesus' earthly *parents*? This story reveals a primary reason: Mary and Joseph are faithful people. They love God and rear their children to honor him. They are exactly the right kind of people to guide Jesus through childhood.

Jesus' parents regularly attend the annual *Passover* festival. This is a testimony to their faithfulness. Men are expected to attend three major annual feasts in *Jerusalem* (see Exodus 23:14-17; Deuteronomy 16:16). One of these three is the Feast of Unleavened Bread (Exodus 12:17, 18). Although this feast is technically distinct from Passover, the two are right next to each other on the calendar. Thus it is natural to see them as one and the same event (Leviticus 23:5, 6).

It is highly unlikely that each and every Jewish man always attends every major feast annually. But those conscientious in their faith make the effort. That Mary also comes along represents a later development of attendance by women. They attend *according to the custom* (compare 1 Samuel 1:3, 7, 21).

While it is likely that Jesus has been attending Passover with his parents *every year*, this particular one has elevated significance. Jesus is now age 12. Thus he is approaching age 13, when he will take on increased responsibility. The modern ceremony of *bar mitzvah* (literally, "son of the commandment") for Jewish boys who reach age 13 is not practiced in Jesus' day. But as a cultural precursor to that, perhaps Luke tells this story of the 12-year-old Jesus to record the approximate point at which he becomes recognized as having greater status in the religious community.

B. Absent Son (vv. 43, 44a)

43, 44a. After the Feast was over, while his parents were returning home, the boy Jesus stayed behind in Jerusalem, but they were unaware of it. Thinking he was in their company, they traveled on for a day.

For modern readers, it may be difficult to imagine how Jesus' *parents* could "lose" him *for a day* before realizing it. But let's think through what actually happens on such a pilgrimage. The journey of 75 miles between Nazareth and *Jerusalem* is at walking pace, thus it is a trip of at least 3 days. For safety and convenience, those who travel to and from Jerusalem for holy festivals go as groups of families and neighbors. Once they are on the road, they are joined by other groups that are traveling as well.

In this situation, it is natural for the youngsters of the various families to gravitate toward one another and walk together; the adults likely do the same. (We see the same thing at church picnics: the kids prefer to interact with each other rather than with the adults.) Given Joseph and Mary's world of extended families and village life, they naturally assume that Jesus is with others in their traveling party.

What traditions or customs associated with the transition to a new year do you observe in your family? Do any of these help serve to pass Christian faith from one generation to the next? If not, how can you do better?

Regardless of the distance *they* cover by foot, we should consider the time of a day's journey. Imagine traveling all day in your car only to realize you have to turn around and return to your starting point. Whether the travel is by car or foot, it means extra expense, more time away from work, etc. The extra expense of increased worry is our next consideration.

II. STARTLING DISCOVERIES (LUKE 2:44b-47)
A. SEARCH AND RETURN (vv. 44b-46a)
44b, 45. Then they began looking for him among their relatives and friends. When they did not find him, they went back to Jerusalem to look for him.

When Joseph and Mary realize that Jesus is missing, they do not know for certain that he is still *back in Jerusalem.* There is no doubt that they are alarmed by the possibility that something terrible has happened to him. On the return journey they undoubtedly look in desperation for young Jesus all along the way. Even *their relatives and friends* do not know where he is. It is a frightening situation.

IGNORANCE IS BLISS?
An old saying goes, "When ignorance is bliss, 'tis folly to be wise." Ignorance may save us from worry, but it is always best to be informed of actual conditions.

Consider, for example, the case of the Johnstown Flood. Johnstown, Pennsylvania, was built on the flood plain at the juncture of two rivers. A thriving city of 30,000 inhabitants, Johnstown enjoyed the prosperity of the local steel factories. The pressure of its prosperity led the city fathers to narrow the riverbed in order to increase land available for building. Fourteen miles upriver, the South Fork Dam created a large lake on the side of a mountain, 450 feet higher than the city.

On the afternoon of May 31, 1899, following a night of heavy rain, the residents of Johnstown heard a low rumble. The rumble soon turned into a loud roar as the dam broke. A 60-foot wall of water swept downstream, ultimately killing 2,200 people (www.jaha.org). Ignorance of the faulty engineering was not bliss.

Jesus had stayed behind in Jerusalem. Ignorance of that fact definitely did not turn out to be bliss to his parents! Their ignorance of what was happening was accidental, but sadly much ignorance of God's way today is intentional and self-inflicted (Acts 3:17; 17:30; Ephesians 4:18). With the Word of God in our hearts, this need not be so.   —J. B. N.

46a. After three days they found him in the temple courts,
The three-day period in question comprises (1) the first day of travel toward Nazareth before Jesus' parents know he is missing, (2) the daylong journey back to Jerusalem, and (3) a day spent looking around Jerusalem in search of Jesus. The population of modern Jerusalem exceeds 600,000. The population of Jerusalem in Jesus' day is much less, of course. One reasonable estimate puts it at 60,000. Even so, this "normal" population can swell greatly during feast days. So finding a child in such a crowded city naturally proves difficult. The temple precincts themselves, the focal point of the festival, cover an area of many acres.

B. QUESTIONS AND ANSWERS (vv. 46b, 47)
46b. . . . sitting among the teachers, listening to them and asking them questions.
The scene Jesus' parents come across is, at first glance, not an abnormal one: a group of *teachers* discussing the law. What is curious is to see a 12-year-old *sitting* in their midst! Perhaps Jesus simply has found a group and joined the discussion. Or perhaps his impressive interaction with one teacher has attracted the attention of other teachers.

DAILY BIBLE READINGS
Monday, Dec. 31—A Horn for God's People (Psalm 148: 7-14)
Tuesday, Jan. 1—The Passover Feast Instituted (Numbers 9:1-5)
Wednesday, Jan. 2—First Passover Observed (Exodus 12: 11-14)
Thursday, Jan. 3—The Annual Pilgrimage (Luke 2: 39-45)
Friday, Jan. 4—In the Father's House (Luke 2:46-50)
Saturday, Jan. 5—Growing Up in Nazareth (Luke 2:51, 52)
Sunday, Jan. 6—Praise the Lord! (Psalm 148:1-6)

If you had been there, what do you think you would have heard 12-year-old Jesus talking about? What insights from his lips would have astonished the temple crowd? What sayings of Jesus still astonish you today?

47. Everyone who heard him was amazed at his understanding and his answers.

We shouldn't assume that the people are *amazed* because young Jesus actually is doing the teaching. Rather, what is impressive is the way his *understanding* of the discussion allows him to respond and interact. Jesus is clearly performing at a level well above what is normally expected of a child his age. The teachers are genuinely impressed by Jesus, and they naturally are interested in the abilities of a potential pupil.

Earlier in Luke we read that Jesus is God's Son, so perhaps we're not terribly surprised by Jesus' proficiency. But consider him at this point in time. Luke records this story because it marks an important point in Jesus' life. We do not know how much the young Jesus understands about his divinity at this juncture, but he is at the age when a child's ideas on spiritual matters are beginning to form. This occasion, therefore, seems to mark the time when Jesus begins to communicate something about his nature and mission. It also marks the occasion when some Jews begin to recognize that there is something special about him. This is an exceptional moment in history!

III. UNUSUAL DIALOGUE (LUKE 2:48-50)

A. ACCUSATION (v. 48)

48. When his parents saw him, they were astonished. His mother said to him, "Son, why have you treated us like this? Your father and I have been anxiously searching for you."

Imagine that a group from your church goes on a short-term mission trip. As that trip draws to a close, your 12-year-old finds the work to be so meaningful that he begs to stay behind as your group prepares to return home. On one level, you would admire your child's desire to work for the Lord. On another level, you would see this for the youthful zeal that it is.

Yet the case of young Jesus must involve more than youthful zeal. He has come to understand, at some level, that he has a special calling. But at his young age he may not yet understand how best to manage this calling. So he assumes he should stay in Jerusalem without his parents' knowledge or consent. There is a delightful innocence to Jesus' desire to cast aside one set of responsibilities to pursue another. Yet, this is not the time, and his parents have to help him understand this.

So, what do we make of a child who causes his parents grief when he chooses not to do what he must have known his parents wanted him to do? A certain heresy that developed in the second century proposed that Jesus was not really human. People who held this idea could not imagine that Jesus was "like us." Also, some Christians have a hard time believing that Jesus may have been a difficult child at times, even causing his parents anguish, while remaining sinless (Hebrews 4:15).

But here we have an example of the sinless Jesus causing parental anguish in deciding to remain behind. This 12-year-old has enough knowledge to realize something about his mission, but not yet enough experience and patience to push it forward in the best way possible. Indeed, there will come a time when it will be his mother who pushes Jesus to do something even though he realizes that "My time has not yet come" (John 2:4).

We are not told how well Jesus' parents comprehend their son's true nature and role. Mary's Song in Luke 1:46-55 reveals that she is aware that God is going to bring about some kind of fulfillment through her child. Joseph is aware that Jesus somehow is "Immanuel . . . God with us" (Matthew 1:23). When they

bar mitzvah. bar MITS-vuh.
Deuteronomy. Due-ter-AHN-uh-me.
heresy. HAIR-uh-see.
Jerusalem. Juh-ROO-suh-lem.
Leviticus. Leh-VIT-ih-kus.
Nazareth. NAZ-uh-reth.
rabbis. RAB-eyes.

first took Jesus to the temple, Mary and Joseph heard Simeon's understanding of Jesus to be "the Lord's Christ" (Luke 2:25-35). They also heard Anna's understanding of him to be an important part of redemption (2:36-38). But we don't know exactly how Mary and Joseph really interpret all this, even 12 years later.

Thus, the parents' amazement is a little difficult for us to sort out as they see that he is capable of entering into dialogue with the teachers. It appears that this is the first time they see Jesus' abilities in this regard. Yet, Mary is still Jesus' mother, and her concern soon overcomes her wonder.

B. Response (vv. 49, 50)

49. "Why were you searching for me?" he asked. "Didn't you know I had to be in my Father's house?"

The young Jesus is convinced that he belongs in the temple. His answer reveals no concern about the mental state of his parents. His question *Why were you searching for me?* expresses surprise that they would wonder where he is. And when he asks *Didn't you know I had to be in my Father's house?* he expresses how natural it seems to him that this is where he belongs.

The phrase *in my Father's house* is vague in the original Greek. It literally says something like, "about [or in] the ____ of my Father." The translator is left to make an intelligent guess regarding what to put in that blank. The translation *house* is a good choice. An even better choice is *business* (as in the *King James Version*), since it captures an idea that is broader than mere physical location.

Even despite that bit of vagueness, one thing is crystal clear: Jesus has become aware of a personal relationship with God, and it draws him to the temple. Jesus senses that his role in life is not carpentry, but service to the Lord. When Mary speaks of "your father" (v. 48), Jesus responds in terms of his heavenly Father.

Jesus seems to be surprised at his parents' surprise. He thinks that they should have known exactly where he was. Jesus' response signals something of a break between himself and his parents as he announces where his ultimate allegiance lies. Does young Jesus expect to stay at the temple (compare 1 Samuel 1:21-28) while his parents go home? The text doesn't say.

HIS FATHER'S BUSINESS

"Raccoon" John Smith (1784–1868) was a famous evangelists on the Kentucky frontier of the early nineteenth century. An outstanding preacher and minister, he learned the value of a disciplined life as he grew up on that wild frontier.

At age 11, he traveled with his father and brother to south central Kentucky. There they laid claim to 200 acres for the family farm. While his dad and brother began the task of clearing trees from the land, John was sent back 100 miles with a packhorse to get a load of corn for seed and meal.

The idea of sending an unescorted 11-year-old out like this would be unthinkable today! But it was not unusual at the time. John completed his assignment in spite of some distractions, arriving back safely with the corn. Nothing dissuaded him from completing the responsibility given to him by his father.

Jesus at age 12 also felt the weight of responsibility. Thus he tarried in Jerusalem at that tender age. Sadly, some folks never seem to feel the weight of much responsibility at any age. Christian responsibility begins to take hold when we acknowledge that we must be about our heavenly Father's business.   —J. B. N.

50. But they did not understand what he was saying to them.

The parents have been frantically seeking their son. They've been struck with wonder at his abilities in the temple. And now they're hit with a puzzling

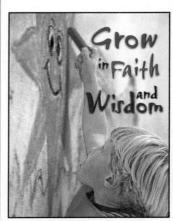

Visual for Lesson 6. *Point to this visual as you ask, "How do you plan to grow in faith and wisdom this week?"*

WHAT DO YOU THINK?

What memories do you treasure, ponder, or savor? What does this say about your own spiritual maturity?

[Be sure to consider Matthew 6:21 and Luke 12:34 as you frame your answer.]

WHAT DO YOU THINK?

Do the aspects of personal growth describing Jesus' life give us a model for spiritual growth in our own lives? Why, or why not?

THOUGHT TO REMEMBER

Make sure to listen to God's desires above your own.

statement. Indeed, one wonders whether they've been able to fathom any of this. Except for the events surrounding Jesus' birth 12 years previously, we assume that life has been relatively "normal" up to this point. This incident means that Joseph and Mary suddenly are faced anew with Jesus' uniqueness. It is all a little too much for them. So they fail to grasp the significance of Jesus' statement.

IV. REVEALED CHARACTER (LUKE 2:51, 52)

A. RETURN AND OBEDIENCE (v. 51)

51. Then he went down to Nazareth with them and was obedient to them. But his mother treasured all these things in her heart.

Even though the young Jesus is surprised by his parents' surprise, he remains *obedient to them.* Jesus realizes that obedience to his heavenly Father means obedience to the parents that his heavenly Father has chosen for him. Jesus never sins, thus he does not violate Exodus 20:12: "Honor your father and your mother."

So he returns with his parents. When we read that Mary *treasured all these things in her heart,* we see her "filing things away" for future reference (compare Genesis 37:11; Luke 2:19).

B. GROWTH AND FAVOR (v. 52)

52. And Jesus grew in wisdom and stature, and in favor with God and men.

This statement reminds us of Luke's comment in 2:40: "The child grew and became strong; he was filled with wisdom, and the grace of God was upon him" (compare 1 Samuel 2:26; Proverbs 3:4). It prepares the reader for what is to come: the story of Jesus' baptism and the official beginning of his ministry.

The account we have just read reveals that the young *Jesus* is coming to grips with how he should live up to his responsibilities both to God and to his parents. Jesus understands that choosing to reject the will of his parents while still under their guardianship is not the behavior of an obedient child. Part of increasing in *wisdom and stature, and in favor with God and men* thus involves obedience to his earthly parents.

CONCLUSION

Jesus had a unique calling. Even so, we can learn some things from his example as we make choices. First, Jesus understood that God would not call him to go against divine principles in order to fulfill God's will for his life. Thus Jesus realized that God's will for him could not involve going against the wishes of Joseph and Mary. Parents have been known to demand that their children do things contrary to God's will, but that was not the case here. So Jesus submitted to his parents' authority. Likewise, we should understand that our choices must not conflict with things we know to be true of God's expressed desires as we daily decide how to live.

Second, we see from Jesus' example that sometimes God says, "Wait—the time isn't quite right." It's easy to get excited about a dramatic plan, claiming that it's God's will to "sell all" (Luke 18:22) and go to a foreign mission field. There indeed are times when we must follow God to challenging, exciting places. But often the harder thing is to stay in the current situation and continue to serve him in an "ordinary" way. After perhaps imagining a life lived in or near the temple, discussing spiritual truths each day, it may have been disappointing for young Jesus to go back to Nazareth and help Joseph carry timber. But that was what God desired at that point in time.

Discovery Learning

This page contains an alternative lesson plan emphasizing learning activities. Classes desiring such student involvement will find these suggestions helpful. The next page is a reproducible activity page to further enhance discovery learning.

INTO THE LESSON

Give each learner a piece of paper that has the outline of a child (photocopy these in advance). Ask each person to identify one of the challenging changes or passages of a child's life and write it on the outline in large letters. You may find it helpful to offer examples by citing transitions such as potty training, learning to tie shoes, or dealing with peer pressure.

After a few moments, ask your learners to share their conclusions and illustrations. In larger classes, ask people to share their conclusions in groups of three or four. After a time of small-group discussion, have groups share their conclusions with the entire class.

Make the transition to Bible study by asking, "Have you ever thought of the boy Jesus experiencing similar childhood transitions? Today's study will focus on one of those transition times in Jesus' life. It will teach us an important lesson about life focus."

INTO THE WORD

Begin the Into the Word section with a brief lecture from the material in the Lesson Background. As you speak, have the phrase *Keyword: Grow* displayed. Your lecture should emphasize the changes and growth experiences in the life of the boy Jesus.

Next, form teams of two to five people for a scrapbooking exercise. Give each team a sheet of letter-sized paper with five photo-frame boxes drawn down the left side. After reading Luke 2:41-52, the teams should list important snapshots they would include of Jesus' boyhood years in the scrapbook they are assembling. They will list these snapshots in the photo frames provided in the handout.

Next, ask students to note down the right side why they feel each snapshot to be valuable for Jesus' scrapbook. Remind the class that God's choice to preserve these images for us in his Word tells us that these snapshots are important. After groups have completed the scrapbook assignment, ask a representative of each group to move to another group and tell why his or her group chose to include their photos.

After the discussions wind down, debrief your class by asking the following questions:

1. What do you think the Lord is teaching about his nature when he says, "Didn't you know I had to be in my Father's house?" (v. 49)? Why did God include that question to Jesus' parents in the Bible?

2. What clues do you see in this text that Mary and Joseph were struggling with Jesus' identity as God's Son, yet also as their own son?

3. Why do you think God also included in the Bible the phrase "and was obedient to them" (v. 51)? What is God teaching us about the nature of Jesus' humanity and divinity?

Alternative: Form small groups to complete the Making the Trip exercise from the Reproducible Page.

INTO LIFE

Tell the class that Jesus, at age 12, was already beginning to focus on his life's mission. He hints of that in verse 49 when he mentions "my Father's house." Suggest that we too must identify our life purpose or mission. Ask, "What do you think is the purpose of humans? Why do we exist? Why did God create us?" Tell them to share their answers by choosing one of the three activities below (reproduce as handouts).

Allow the class to work in the teams formed earlier. Display Genesis 1:26-31 and Micah 6:8 for the groups to refer to.

Option #1 (less difficult): What is the purpose of humans? Post your answer for all to see. After you note this purpose statement, list at least three reasons why your group thinks this. Next, have each person in your group talk about God's specific purpose for his or her own life. What evidence do you have that leads you to believe this purpose actually is of God?

Option #2 (more difficult): What is the purpose of humans? Write a single-sentence answer to the question by creating an acrostic using the word *Purpose.* Start the acrostic with "We Propose that humans . . . " The statement will then use the rest of the letters of the word *Purpose.* Next, have each person in your group talk about God's specific purpose for his or her own life. What evidence do you have that leads you to believe this purpose actually is of God?

Option #3: Complete the Music with Purpose activity from the Reproducible Page.

Allow groups to share their answers. Then close the lesson by thanking God for this reminder to keep life focused on our mission.

Making the Trip

The annual trip to Jerusalem's Feast of the Passover took an unusual twist for Jesus' family in today's text (Luke 2:41-52). Read the text, discover the story's events, and summarize them below.

The Annual Family Tradition (v. 41):

The Scare (vv. 43-46):

The Parental Rebuke (v. 48):

The Surprising Answer (v. 49):

What does Jesus' answer to his parents tell you about his nature?

What does the statement "and was obedient to them" (v. 51) tell us about Jesus' nature?

Music with Purpose!

Let's use music to express our ideal beliefs and behavior. Use the hymnal below to state your views. One example on each side will get you started.

What are some lines from Christian music that reflect what a believer's purpose in life should be?

What are some lines from Christian music that express a person's commitment to fulfill his or her purpose?

1. "What a Mighty God We Serve"

2. _____

3. _____

4. _____

5. _____

1. "I Surrender All"

2. _____

3. _____

4. _____

5. _____

God's Call to the Christian Community
Unit 2: Inspired by God's Call
(Lessons 6-9)

INSPIRED TO LOVE

LESSON 7

WHY TEACH THIS LESSON?

Living a life of love is hard, isn't it? Yet followers of Christ are told to "be imitators of God, therefore, as dearly loved children and live a life of love, just as Christ loved us and gave himself up for us as a fragrant offering and sacrifice to God" (Ephesians 5:1, 2). In other words, believers are told to act like God!

Of course this can only be done when we allow the Lord Jesus Christ, who lives *in* us, to come out and live *through* us. We are to allow his desires to flow through our goals, our actions, our words, and our attitudes. That is what today's lesson will help your learners do. As believers grow and mature in this way, their lives become more effective tools for pointing people to Christ.

INTRODUCTION

A. MY RIGHTS AND MY WRONGS

I know a couple who obviously love each other, but they bicker a lot. Usually a visitor gets drawn into the argument with comments like, "Does your husband watch TV as much as mine?" Before there's time for a response, the grinning husband chimes in, "Do you nag your husband as much as my wife does?" It's just the pattern they have established.

But recently their small group studied *Boundaries,* a popular book written by Henry Cloud and John Townsend. On my most recent visit, I noticed a distinct change in their tone. Instead of their usual bickering, they were heard to say, "You're not hearing my *no,*" and "You don't respect my boundaries." So far so good—but not good enough!

They had come to understand the concept that we are to appreciate the needs of others. But they use this understanding only to have their own needs met. Each is concerned that giving too much to the other means being left with nothing. Each wonders, "If I take care of his or her needs, who will take care of mine?" It's important to have healthy boundaries. But how much should we protect our own interests, and how much should we look out for the interests of others?

Our world is full of messages about "our rights"—as employees, as women or men, as Christians. While our world teaches, "Watch out for yourself because no one else will," Jesus has a different message.

B. LESSON BACKGROUND

This week's passage is an excerpt from Jesus' Sermon on the Plain (Luke 6:17-49). The sermon is dominated by a beatitude section (Luke 6:20-38) that is very similar to that in Matthew 5. It is important to consider the background of the sermon as a whole in order to develop a context for our passage today.

After his baptism (Luke 3:21) and temptation (Luke 4:1, 2), Jesus returned to Nazareth. There he announced the fulfillment of Isaiah 61:1, 2 (Luke 4:18, 19). News about him spread rapidly, and he began to perform miracles to affirm

DEVOTIONAL READING:
PSALM 37:1-11
BACKGROUND SCRIPTURE:
LUKE 6:27-36
PRINTED TEXT:
LUKE 6:27-36

LESSON AIMS

After participating in this lesson, each student will be able to:

1. List several specific acts of love that Jesus commanded in this text.

2. Compare the acts of love in Lesson Aim #1 with the mercy and love of God.

3. Treat one "enemy" in the coming week with the kind of love of which Jesus spoke.

Jan
13

KEY VERSE

Love your enemies, do good to them, and lend to them without expecting to get anything back. Then your reward will be great, and you will be sons of the Most High.   —Luke 6:35

LESSON 7 NOTES

his identity (Luke 4:31-41). Then he selected his disciples. He further affirmed his identity in debates with the Pharisees and by healing people (Luke 5).

Luke 6:1-11 begins to show us that Jesus' understanding of the law was different from that of the Pharisees with whom he debated. Jesus deliberately did things on the Sabbath that certain Pharisees believed to be unlawful. Jesus informed the Pharisees that their understanding of the law was the reverse of what it should be.

This is important because the sermon in Luke 6:20-49 presents the proper way to think about how God expects us to live. Somewhere along the way, religious leaders had begun to teach that godly behavior was based in following minute details of the law. Jesus announced that the details must fit within a bigger picture (compare Luke 11:42).

As Jesus and his apostles came down from a mountain, they were met by a large crowd of people (Luke 6:12-19). They tried to get close to Jesus—to hear him, touch him, and be healed by him. Although the sermon was "in the hearing of the people" (Luke 7:1), we find that Jesus turned and directed his sermon toward the disciples (Luke 6:20). The sermon presented the way to think about the law and what it meant to follow and honor God. Those disciples eventually ended up being leaders of the church. So how did Jesus instruct them on how to live before God?

I. WHAT TO DO (LUKE 6:27-31)

A. GENERAL PRINCIPLES OF LOVE (vv. 27, 28)

27a. "But I tell you who hear me: Love your enemies,

The dominant ethical command in the New Testament is to *love* (Matthew 22:36-40). Modern Christians have numerous ethical issues about which to be passionate: abortion, homosexuality, and stem-cell research are just three. It is troubling, though, for Christians not to be at least as passionate about the rigorous discipline of love.

Love is often considered to be a romantic idea, fit for weak and emotional people. But this sort of thinking ignores the fact that love is "the bottom line" of Christian behavior: the Christian walk begins with love; other ethical ideals follow after that. First John 4:20 is an important text here. In John's view, to fail to love one another is to fail to love God.

As we read through the New Testament's perspective on love, we are alerted to the fact that the kind of love in view is not primarily an emotion. "Dear children, let us not love with words or tongue but with actions and in truth" (1 John 3:18). Love in the New Testament is the practice of self-sacrifice!

The truth is, though, that some are not willing to engage in the sort of self-sacrifice the New Testament stresses. Perhaps we are willing to do some work for someone or give money to a godly ministry in a way that's not too inconvenient. The New Testament, though, sees a love that goes beyond this. The New Testament sees a love that is characterized by allowing one's own needs to be subordinate to the needs of others, even if they despise you (compare Philippians 2:3).

The most difficult form of love required of us is the type of love Christ displayed in his own life. He loved people who hated him, ignored him, and did not even know him. But in practice, how is it possible to love an enemy? To get us started on answering this, we must first get away from the notion that *love* and *like* are the same thing. That is, we must not confuse the command to love with an emotional experience. To love someone is to be willing to sacrifice for that person.

DAILY BIBLE READINGS

Monday, Jan. 7—Trust in the Lord (Psalm 37:1-11)

Tuesday, Jan. 8—Love Your Neighbor (Leviticus 19:17, 18)

Wednesday, Jan. 9—Love Your Enemies (Luke 6:27, 28)

Thursday, Jan. 10—Absorb Injustice (Luke 6:29, 30)

Friday, Jan. 11—Set the Standard (Luke 6:31)

Saturday, Jan. 12—Expect Nothing in Return (Luke 6: 34-36)

Sunday, Jan. 13—Posterity for the Peaceable (Psalm 37: 35-40)

Before we move on, we should pause to note that Jesus' command to *Love your enemies* is nothing new. See Exodus 23:4, 5 and Proverbs 25:21.

27b. " . . . do good to those who hate you,

The normal response to someone who hates you is to hate him or her right back. If people do nasty things to us, we naturally are not very likely to respond by doing things that are genuinely in their best interest! But the life of Jesus provides an example of how love-as-sacrifice reveals itself. By commanding us to *do good to those who hate you,* Jesus is asking us to sacrifice our feelings and indignation on the altar of obedience to him.

We must be careful to note that Jesus is not saying, "Don't hate them back." He is requiring us to go beyond not hating—actually to go so far as to do good for them! Further, the underlying language suggests that Jesus is not talking about just one act of kindness. Rather, he is referring to an entire way of life that is characterized by doing good to those who hate us, as difficult as this may be to implement.

Jesus' command goes against certain elements of the culture of his day. For example, the "Rule of the Community" that is part of the Dead Sea Scrolls calls for love of "all the sons of light" and hatred of "all the sons of darkness."

28. " . . . bless those who curse you, pray for those who mistreat you.

The phrase *mistreat you* refers to abusive treatment. We're still dealing with the same kind of enemy we saw in verse 27, but now Jesus shifts the focus from their attitude to their behavior toward us. Interestingly, in the previous verse we were told to confront hateful attitudes with a good action; here we are commanded to confront hateful behavior with prayer and blessing. That is, Jesus requires us to go even further now and bring an action of love into our private thought world. This speaks to the importance of our inner orientation.

B. CONCRETE EXAMPLES OF LOVE (vv. 29, 30)

29. "If someone strikes you on one cheek, turn to him the other also. If someone takes your cloak, do not stop him from taking your tunic.

The idea in this and the following verse is contrary to the cultural ideal today that we should demand that others observe our personal rights. Once again Jesus is calling us to have a sacrificial attitude. We are commanded to surrender our instinctive reaction toward an enemy for an entirely different response.

Some commentators suggest that the idea here is more of how to respond to religious persecution than to criminal mistreatment. We note, however, that both Jesus and Paul responded sharply when they were struck in the face as acts of religious persecution (John 18:22, 23; Acts 23:2, 3).

Paul noted that the attack against him was in violation of the law. After some dialogue, Paul eventually humbled himself before the Sanhedrin (Acts 23:5). Paul also used the Roman legal system to protect himself from persecution (Acts 22:25; 25:10-12). Clearly, applying Jesus' command as he intends will require much study and prayer! See the next verse.

30. "Give to everyone who asks you, and if anyone takes what belongs to you, do not demand it back.

The commands of Jesus seem severe, don't they? We may ask ourselves how the behavior proposed in this verse is even possible! Is Jesus saying that if someone *asks* me for my home and all of my possessions, then I am to give it all away with a smile to boot?

Keep in mind that Jesus is further developing the idea of love. In so doing, he is saying that our attitude toward our possessions, our sense of entitlement,

WHAT DO YOU THINK?

How do the enemies we face today compare and contrast with the enemies of Jesus' time? What are some ways you have shown love to your enemies?

WHAT DO YOU THINK?

What are some specific ways that we can "do good to those who hate" us and "bless those who curse" us?

should not get in the way of our ability to exhibit Christian love. Christian love cannot work in a context where we privilege ourselves over others.

We may note in passing that to give away our homes and possessions to others merely because they ask may violate 2 Thessalonians 3:10 in that our actions may reward laziness. Such giveaways may also violate 1 Timothy 5:8 if we lose the means to provide for our own families.

C. GOLDEN RULE OF LOVE (v. 31)

31. *"Do to others as you would have them do to you."*

In Jesus' day, there are two forms of this rule floating around: a negative form and a positive form. The negative form is something like, "don't do bad things to others lest others do bad things to you." This form is popular in both Judaism and in the wider Greco-Roman world of the first century.

Jesus stresses the positive form of the Golden Rule. This is the less common but not unknown form at the time. The positive form has a different function: it shifts the focus from self to others. The negative form says, "Keep yourself safe by not stirring up trouble"; the positive form that Jesus uses says, "The way you treat others should be based on how you would like to be treated."

That Jesus uses the less common form demonstrates that he is not just tossing around a popular cliché. Furthermore, the positive form of the Golden Rule reflects the values Jesus has been developing throughout his sermon. In particular, it reflects the idea that our actions toward others cannot be based on how we have been treated so far. Again, we see a reflection of the sacrificial attitude that is required by Christian love.

II. WHY TO DO IT (LUKE 6:32-36)

A. PROPER MOTIVE (vv. 32-34)

32-34. *"If you love those who love you, what credit is that to you? Even 'sinners' love those who love them. And if you do good to those who are good to you, what credit is that to you? Even 'sinners' do that. And if you lend to those from whom you expect repayment, what credit is that to you? Even 'sinners' lend to 'sinners,' expecting to be repaid in full.*

There is an obvious repetition in the structure of these verses as they repeat ideas from earlier parts of the sermon: *love* (v. 27), *do good* (vv. 27, 31), *give/lend* (v. 30). Each of the verses before us contains the phrase *what credit is that to you?* This means something like "why should you get any recognition for doing that?" Returning love for love, good for good, and stuff for stuff is what *sinners* themselves are very capable of doing. That's just natural. But Christians are to go above and beyond this.

When Jesus commands us to live according to the Golden Rule, we should be careful to note that he does not promise that people will respond in kind. The rule is a command from our Lord to act toward others in a specific way, regardless of their response. It is, therefore, not based on a desire to make our lives easier. The single point in these three verses is that the Golden Rule is a norm for *our* behavior and lifestyle. As such, the way we implement this rule is not dependent upon the actions of those whom we are called to love.

WITHOUT REWARD

Servers in restaurants know that the better service they provide, the bigger tip they should receive. We provide Christmas gifts for our mail carriers because packages are left (and will continue to be left) carefully inside our screen

WHAT DO YOU THINK?

Who among those you know is best at living out the Golden Rule? What do you see in that person's life that demonstrates this?

WHAT DO YOU THINK?

In the twenty-first century, what does loving, doing good for, or giving to people who can return the favor look like? How does that contrast with Jesus' example?

doors. It is always a temptation to do things for others with the expectation that they will respond by doing something special for us.

Basil of Caesarea (AD 329–379) set a different example. As an early leader of Eastern Orthodox monasticism, he saw many monks practice lives of extreme self-denial (asceticism). But he thought it was to little purpose other than self-satisfaction. So Basil decided to point monasticism toward a great measure of service outreach with no thought of intrinsic rewards.

As a result, some monasteries became hospitals and took in the sick. Others became educational centers. Many monasteries sent their monks out into the fields to gather the town crops at harvesttime, then return to the monastery and refuse any payment for their work.

Jesus encourages us to give without expectation of receiving in return. Such is the essence of true Christian service. Did Basil of Caesarea understand this better than we do today?   —J. B. N.

B. PROPER ATTITUDE (vv. 35a, 35b)

35a. "But love your enemies, do good to them, and lend to them without expecting to get anything back.

Jesus repeats the threefold theme of *love . . . , do good . . . , and lend.* Tying these to *not expecting to get anything back* again highlights once more a major idea of our passage: don't focus on yourself.

It is tempting for us to agree with Jesus that genuine Christian love does not seek any benefit beyond the opportunity to act in love, then turn to the next verse. But if we stop and think about how Jesus repeats this idea, and if we reflect also upon the fact that love is the dominant ethic in the New Testament, then perhaps we ought to pause to investigate our own intentions carefully.

In all honesty, are we able to act in a way that is self-sacrificing? Can we act in the interests of others with *no* expectation of anything in return? Can we act with no expectation of thank-you cards or pats on the back? God knows our hearts!

LOVE YOUR ENEMY

Dirk Willems was an Anabaptist living in Holland in 1569. The Anabaptists were a persecuted religious minority under the Spanish rulers, who were still trying to enforce a Roman Catholic monopoly in the country. Willems was thrown into prison to await trial as a heretic. The prison diet was inadequate, and Willems lost a considerable amount of weight. Knowing his life was at stake, he made a rope out of knotted rags and lowered himself out of an upper window. Then he ran!

A prison guard saw Willems and pursued. Willems was able to cross over a frozen pond safely; his lightweight, emaciated body did not break through the thin ice. But his pursuer, much heavier, broke through the ice. He tried to get out on his own but was unsuccessful.

Willems heard the man's cries. But Willems knew that if he tried to help the pursuer, he most likely would be caught again. He could not let the man drown. So he returned and helped the man to safety. Then the guard promptly hauled Willems back to prison. Shortly thereafter he was burned at the stake for his "heresy" of being an Anabaptist.

Willems exemplified exactly what Jesus was talking about. Willems loved his enemy to the extent that it cost him his own life. Jesus' words are easily acknowledged, but rarely implemented. Dirk Willems is a marvelous exception. —J. B. N.

35b. "Then your reward will be great, and you will be sons of the Most High,
Here are the ultimate benefits of the kind of love that Jesus has in mind. The stated benefits are a part of a worldview that Jesus is presenting in this

Reflect God's love— love your enemies.

Visual for Lesson 7. *Point to the military uniform as you ask, "How should love for enemies show itself in wartime?"*

WHAT DO YOU THINK?

Without mentioning names, when was the last time you helped someone who absolutely could not repay you? How have you found your motivation to be different when you helped others who could return the favor from when you helped others who could not?

How to Say It

asceticism. uh-SEE-tuh-seh-zum.

Caesarea. Sess-uh-REE-uh.

Greco-Roman. GREH-ko ROW-men.

Judaism. JOO-duh-izz-um or JOO-day-izz-um.

Nazareth. NAZ-uh-reth.

Pharisees. FAIR-ih-seez.

Sanhedrin. SAN-huh-drun or San-HEED-run.

Thessalonians. THESS-uh-LO-nee-unz.

sermon. Jesus clearly is stressing that the ability to love others in a self-sacrificial manner is an important component of our eternal *reward*. This kind of love is a vital part of our identity as *sons of the Most High*.

Thus Jesus' sermon presents the idea that the motivation for living a certain kind of life is not based on "what we can get out of it" in the here and now. Even so, isn't the motivation of an eternal reward at least somewhat selfish in and of itself? The next passage answers this.

C. Proper Example (vv. 35c, 36)

35c. " . . . because he is kind to the ungrateful and wicked.

God's character is our ultimate example. Our desire to please him is our ultimate motivation. The character of God is to love all people, even those who are *ungrateful* and *wicked*.

Jesus introduces this point so that we can understand that the way we're being called to live our lives is not arbitrary. Rather, it is a life that imitates our heavenly Father. So here we have the motivation for achieving the objectives Jesus laid out for us in the earlier part of the sermon.

36. "Be merciful, just as your Father is merciful."

We could restate this as, "Since you have benefited from the Father's mercy, who are you to be unmerciful to others?" That is, the command refers to a kind of behavior (being *merciful*) and a way to measure that behavior (as God *is merciful*).

This idea is repeated elsewhere in the Gospels. Consider the Parable of the Unmerciful Servant in Matthew 18:21-35. Jesus uses the parable to show that God can be endlessly merciful, but that a failure to reflect the very mercy we ourselves are shown is to encounter the wrath of God.

Through all of these verses, the underlying principle is that everything we have is a result of God's love and mercy to us. Thus we are in no position to be unloving, ungracious, or selfish. To do so is to reject God outright.

CONCLUSION

Think of the person you like least. This can be someone you know personally or an infamous public figure. Why do you dislike or fear that person? What would it mean to love him or her as Jesus desires?

This brings us to another question: What does love really look like? It's hard to say, especially when we consider the kind of love Jesus spoke about. Is there such a thing as a loving quarrel? Can a bouquet of flowers be given in hate? Jesus seems to teach that the motive is the deciding factor, not necessarily the action itself. If we argue with an alcoholic sibling in order to convince him that he needs help, it becomes an action of love. If we present an expensive gift in order to be seen as more generous than other guests at the party, it is far from the act of love it would seem to be (compare Matthew 6:1-4).

The love of a mother seems to be a perfect example of the kind of love that sacrifices at each turn. From the moment of conception, she gives over her very body to the needs of the child. The act of bringing her child into the world is one of extreme pain.

As the child grows, the requirement for sacrifice grows, moving the mother to forego sleep to care for him in sickness and to put aside her embarrassment when he causes a scene in a store. In these daily choices, a mother shows her selfless love. Jesus calls us to exhibit that same kind of love, not only to those we hold dear, but also to strangers, even to those who hurt and hate us.

Thought to Remember

Love doesn't always feel good, but love always is good.

Discovery Learning

This page contains an alternative lesson plan emphasizing learning activities. Classes desiring such student involvement will find these suggestions helpful. The next page is a reproducible activity page to further enhance discovery learning.

INTO THE LESSON

Ask two people in advance to prepare a skit that will introduce this lesson. The actors will portray a husband (John) and wife (Mary). The scene will be a dinner-table conversation. John will tell Mary about a sale he had made, but was not present to write it up. A coworker wrote up the sale and put his own name on the sales slip to claim the commission.

John vents his anger and frustration at the dinner table. Mary concludes her comfort by reminding John that Jesus says we must love our enemies. John's response: "Yeah, right! It's absolutely impossible to love that jerk!"

Make the transition to Bible study by asking, "Is that kind of love really impossible as John suggests? Or is it possible to love our enemies? Today, we'll address those questions as we look for practical applications to this difficult assignment from the Lord."

INTO THE WORD

Ask your minister or another speaker to make a video presenting the Lesson Background that is printed in the lesson commentary. Of course, the speaker may add greetings and encouragement to the class during the video presentation. Play the video to the class. Next, do the antiphonal reading that is on the Reproducible Page. Then ask some or all of the following discussion questions (found also in the optional student book).

1. What are the types or descriptions of enemies that Jesus chooses as illustrations in this passage? (*Make a list on the board of students' answers; those answers should draw from the following half-verses: 27b, 28a, 28b, 29a, 29b, 30b.*)

2. What are some practical demonstrations of loving your enemies cited by Jesus? (*Again, make a list on the board of learners' answers; those answers should draw from the following verses and half-verses: 27b, 28a, 28b, 29a, 29b, 30, 31, 35.*)

3. Since the kind of love that Jesus describes in the text is not an emotion, how would you define or describe it?

4. What are some of the obvious benefits to the kind of love at issue in the previous question?

5. What are some possible motives for practicing this kind of love?

6. What are some of the obstacles to expressing this kind of love to those who have been unloving to us?

7. What are some suggestions you would give for developing a discipline to express this kind of love? What habits, emotions, or attitudes need to be developed? (*List the suggestions separately. You will need this list later in the lesson.*)

INTO LIFE

Option #1: Divide the class into "application teams" of three or four. Display this phrase: *Role Play, Mime, or Cartoon.* Each team is to choose one of these methods to demonstrate or illustrate the discipline of showing love to enemies. The demonstration or illustration must represent realistic life situations. Tell them to work quickly because they have only eight minutes to prepare.

Allow each team to share or present its work. Small classes will be able to share each team's presentation. Larger classes may choose to have pairs of teams show their work to one another.

Option #2: Divide the class into "application teams" of three or four. Give each team a piece of poster board and a marking pen. The purpose of these teams is to identify and list the names of persons who have practiced and modeled Jesus' command to love our enemies.

First, each team is to identify at least one person from the Bible, other than Jesus, who demonstrated loving his or her enemies. Then each team is to name one person from history (other than Bible characters) who demonstrated this kind of love.

Finally, each team member is to name one person from his or her personal experience who has demonstrated such a love; if someone thinks it best not to list the name of an individual, he or she may substitute the word *unnamed.* Then have each team share its findings with the rest of the class or with one other team.

Concluding Activity: Ask learners to review the list of suggestions from question #7. Ask, "Which one will be the most helpful to you in developing the skill of expressing love for enemies?"

Ask each learner to write his or her choice on an index card. Each learner can hold it while praying for that skill during the closing prayer time.

Life-Changing Love!

Use today's printed text below as an antiphonal reading.
Ask one half of the class to read the lines marked A.
The other half of the class should read lines marked B.
All class members should read the lines marked All.

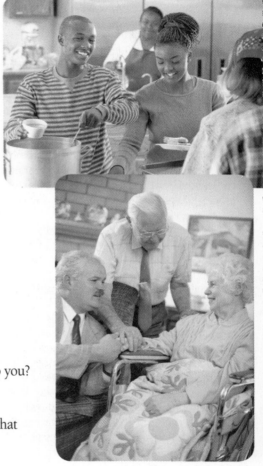

A: But I tell you who hear me:
B: Love your enemies,
All: Do good to those who hate you.

A: Bless those who curse you,
B: Pray for those who mistreat you.

A: If someone strikes you on one cheek,
B: Turn to him the other also.

A: If someone takes your cloak,
B: Do not stop him from taking your tunic.

A: Give to everyone who asks you,
B: And if anyone takes what belongs to you, do not
demand it back.
All: Do to others as you would have them do to you.

A: If you love those who love you, what credit is that to you?
B: Even "sinners" love those who love them.

A: And if you do good to those who are good to you, what
credit is that to you?
B: Even "sinners" do that.

A: And if you lend to those from whom you expect repayment, what credit is that to you?
B: Even "sinners" lend to "sinners," expecting to be repaid in full.

A: But love your enemies, do good to them,
B: And lend to them without expecting to get anything back.

A: Then your reward will be great, and you will be sons of the Most High,
B: Because he is kind to the ungrateful and wicked.
All: Be merciful, just as your Father is merciful.

God's Call to the Christian Community
Unit 2: Inspired by God's Call
(Lessons 6-9)

INSPIRED TO PRAY

WHY TEACH THIS LESSON?

The opportunity to pray and talk to God is a wonderful blessing. It is the chance to be in the presence of the creator of the universe. It gives us the privilege to communicate with our heavenly Father as often as we want to. Our prayer life is like our spiritual cell phone. However, in prayer God is never out of range, his line is never busy, we're not put on hold, and our minutes are free.

But so many seemingly important things can be allowed to squeeze one's prayer life down to nothing. The cure is for your learners to understand the unique place prayer is to have and the consequences for neglecting it. Prayer is to be central to one's life and walk with God. Prayer gives us the chance to allow God to help us to do what we are called to do in his strength. This is obviously better than our trying to do God's will in our own strength. This lesson can help your learners make prayer a top priority.

INTRODUCTION

A. ASKING AND SEEKING

Imagine going to your bank manager to ask for a loan. You sit at his desk and open the conversation with, "You probably won't want to give me a loan. I know you're pretty tight-fisted. In fact, I've heard you never grant loans—especially not to people like me." In spite of your somewhat insulting tone, he continues with the usual process and asks you to present your proof of income. You respond, "Oh, I didn't bother to bring any papers with me, since I expected you probably wouldn't be interested in giving me the loan anyway."

Do you think you'd get the loan? I imagine not; in fact, it would be natural for the flabbergasted bank manager to ask why you even bothered to come to his office if you had no hope that he would give you a loan. Leaving the bank, you tell yourself, "I knew he wouldn't give me the loan," as you blame the manager's hard-heartedness. But would you be right in that assessment of his motives?

When we approach God with a request, how do we assess his motives? Do we assume he's looking for a reason to give us as little as possible? Do we neglect even to approach him when we sense a need because we think he doesn't care? As we'll see today, when it comes to dealing with the one who knows our hearts, motives are as much a factor as the specifics of the request.

B. LESSON BACKGROUND

The passage for today's lesson is the final component of the larger teaching section of Luke 10:25–11:13. In this section, three events give rise to Jesus' description of characteristics of those who wish to follow him. In the first, Jesus is approached by a lawyer and is asked how one could inherit eternal life (Luke 10:25-37); that question gives rise to the Parable of the Good Samaritan. The second is the situation of Martha fussing about Mary (Luke 10:38-42); that gives rise to Jesus' pronouncement that the good disciple seeks Jesus above all else.

DEVOTIONAL READING:
PSALM 28:6-9
BACKGROUND SCRIPTURE:
LUKE 11:1-13
PRINTED TEXT:
LUKE 11:5-13

LESSON AIMS

After participating in this lesson, each student will be able to:
1. Summarize Jesus' teaching on asking, seeking, and finding.
2. Give some examples of the kind of things he or she should and should not ask of God.
3. Create a prayer list of five things or people that he or she will lift up consistently and persistently before God in prayer.

Jan
20

KEY VERSE

So I say to you: Ask and it will be given to you; seek and you will find; knock and the door will be opened to you. —Luke 11:9

LESSON 8 NOTES

The third section (Luke 11:1-13) contains our passage for today (11:5-13). In this section Jesus' disciples asked him how they should pray (11:1). Jesus responded by offering a "model prayer." Then he offered further teachings on the nature of prayer, the teachings with which our lesson is concerned.

Before proceeding, we should take stock of the model prayer, since today's lesson extends from it. The model prayer of Luke 11:2-4 is also located in Matthew 6:9-13 in a fuller form, although the points overlap. In Matthew 6:5-7, Jesus criticizes prayers that are meaninglessly repetitive. He stresses that such repetition is unnecessary since God already is aware of our needs before we pray (Matthew 6:8).

It is this last comment that ties the model prayer as presented in Matthew to this prayer as presented in Luke. In fact, the point of our lesson today is essentially the same as that made in Matthew 6:8: God is already present in our lives, knowing our needs before we pray. Prayer is, on one level, an affirmation of our awareness of God's presence in our lives. The content of this kind of prayer is our need, which God already knows.

I. FRIEND'S REQUEST (LUKE 11:5-8)

A. CONFIDENT EXPECTATION (vv. 5, 6)

5, 6. Then he said to them, "Suppose one of you has a friend, and he goes to him at midnight and says, 'Friend, lend me three loaves of bread, because a friend of mine on a journey has come to me, and I have nothing to set before him.'

Today, not many of us would have the nerve to take a trip and show up unannounced at a friend's door in the middle of the night! Ancient customs of hospitality are different from ours, however. Thus a person *on a journey* might drop in unannounced, especially since in the first century there is no telephone, e-mail, or text messaging with which to do the advance announcing! Such a drop-in visitor might need food, and there are no all-night diners or convenience stores at the time. Thus the need to knock on a neighbor's door *at midnight* to ask for *bread*.

The willingness of the needy neighbor to go to his friend's house to ask for food suggests that he is confident that there will be a positive outcome to the request. He has good reason for this confidence because hospitality is a part of the fabric of the culture. So, based on what is "normal," he expects that the nearby *friend* will oblige (Romans 12:13; 1 Peter 4:9).

Jesus thus is speaking in terms the audience can appreciate. Furthermore, the fact that Jesus opens the parable with the phrase *suppose one of you* brings this story to the level of actual experience. That is, Jesus is using a situation with which he expects them to be able to relate personally. As with other parables, Jesus forces his audience to confront a personal choice; those who hear him have experienced this situation in one form or another.

B. RELUCTANT FRIEND (v. 7)

7. "Then the one inside answers, 'Don't bother me. The door is already locked, and my children are with me in bed. I can't get up and give you anything.'

The response, in short, is "Go away, we're asleep!" And let's be honest: we are not surprised at this response in this situation. However, while we may consider this as somewhat "normal," Jesus actually is using this as an example of ungracious behavior. Having just offered us the example of the model prayer—that we may pray to God for our needs (Luke 11:2-4)—Jesus now implicitly contrasts an ungracious attitude to God's graciousness.

WHAT DO YOU THINK?

What have been your experiences in asking favors from friends? How did the responses affect your friendships? How have you grown spiritually as a result?

WHAT DO YOU THINK?

In what ways have you found God to be different from the one who said, "Don't bother me"?

C. ULTIMATE RESPONSE (v. 8)

8. "I tell you, though he will not get up and give him the bread because he is his friend, yet because of the man's boldness he will get up and give him as much as he needs.

The word *boldness* refers to the courage to make an urgent request. Some may think that this verse means that if we badger God long enough, then he will give us whatever we ask for. To think along this line is to labor under a very dangerous assumption!

Let's do a comparison with the Parable of the Persistent Widow (Luke 18:1-8). That parable describes a widow who keeps asking a wicked judge for relief that he is unwilling to give. However, because she keeps asking and asking, he finally relents: "Yet because this widow keeps bothering me, I will see that she gets justice, so that she won't eventually wear me out with her coming!" (Luke 18:5).

If we leave the text there, we may assume that the point is *persistence pays off.* But as we read on, we find that this is not the point at all. Jesus goes on to explain the parable—and it's always helpful to listen to Jesus' own explanations of his parables before we make our own interpretation! Jesus explains that *in contrast* with the wicked judge, God will respond quickly with his justice (Luke 18:6-8). He will not keep putting people off as the wicked judge does.

The point of the verse in front of us is that Jesus is drawing a contrast between ungracious behavior and the way God acts toward us. This is made clearer in our passage as we read along; the point is that if an ungracious *friend* will eventually live up to his needy neighbor's confidence, how much more so can we expect our heavenly Father to do so.

We have characterized this part of our lesson using the idea of *confidence.* It is important for us, therefore, to draw the connection between *confidence* and *persistence.* Our ultimate interpretation of this passage will be that because of who God is, we can trust that our prayers will be answered. That kind of trust in God leads us to a certain kind of expectation. We observe this kind of confident expectation in the needy neighbor; it lies behind his persistence.

Persistence here is an expression of confidence; the abnormal behavior is not that of the needy neighbor, but that of the reluctant friend. On the basis of this reluctance, Jesus now goes on to make a point about how we can trust God to respond properly in contrast with the reluctant friend.

A CONFIDENT REQUEST

Some years ago I was the interim dean of our seminary. That meant, among other things, that all applications for admission to the school came across my desk for approval. One request came from a potential student who did not have a grade point average that was sufficient to qualify for admission. It wasn't even close. It was easy to turn down her application.

But then the admission department contacted me. "This girl really wants to come," the admission officer said. I explained that her grades were too low. She would never survive graduate school—it was a waste of her money and our time.

The admission counselor contacted the girl and then called me back. "She really wants to come," he insisted. I explained again. "But she really wants to come." In a moment of weakness, I said, "OK, but tell her we think it's a mistake. We can't give her any financial assistance. We'll be glad to take her money, but we think she should stay home and not waste her money on tuition, books, and living expenses here."

But she really wanted to come. So she came. Yet to conclude merely that "persistence paid off" is to look at things superficially. Her persistence was an expression

WHAT DO YOU THINK?

Is this an issue of (a) the friend being ungracious as opposed to God being gracious or (b) the friend reacting "normally" as opposed to God reacting in a way that is "better than normal"? What's the difference, or is there any real difference? Justify your answer.

Visual for Lesson 8. *Use this visual to start a discussion of right and wrong motives in asking, seeking, and knocking.*

WHAT DO YOU THINK?

Why do you think people fail to ask God?

of her confidence. That confidence proved to be well founded three semesters later when she made the dean's honor roll. She ultimately finished two graduate degrees with us. She turned out to be a good student with a compassionate nature, a great sense of humor, and a real desire to learn and serve the Lord. Do you approach your service for God with confidence that he will help you?   —J. B. N.

II. ASK AND RECEIVE (LUKE 11:9, 10)

A. WHAT TO DO (v. 9)

9. *"So I say to you: Ask and it will be given to you; seek and you will find; knock and the door will be opened to you.*

When the statement *Ask and it will be given to you* is read in context, the emphasis shifts away from ourselves and toward God. The result is that we ask because we have confidence that God will give. The two statements that follow, which deal with seeking and knocking, are parallel to this one. Thus we are to be confident that when we ask, *seek*, or *knock* that God indeed will respond.

B. WHY TO DO IT (v. 10)

10. *"For everyone who asks receives; he who seeks finds; and to him who knocks, the door will be opened.*

God is always faithful to respond appropriately to our needs. But let's be honest: are we sometimes too proud to ask God (or anyone else) for help? Do we think we always should try to meet our own needs without God's help? If our answer to these questions is *yes,* then we may have a problem with pride.

Perhaps we think that the old saying, "God helps those who help themselves," is a biblical truth. Actually, it is a quote from Benjamin Franklin's *Poor Richard's Almanack* of 1733 (page 81). The notion expressed in this saying is tied in with the early American ideal of "rugged individualism." Yet God expects us to ask him for our daily bread (Luke 11:3).

Asking requires faith, and God honors faithful people. Jesus is the one who provides a way for us to have confidence that our requests will be heard and fulfilled. We should be wary, however, of the notion that we are the ones who have to get God moving on things, assuming that God won't act unless we push him.

An important point in this and the previous verse is that a specific kind of person is in view here. Recall that today's lesson text occurs within a long teaching section that deals with how Jesus' disciples are to think and behave. Thus when Jesus refers to people who ask, seek, and knock, he is referring to the kind of person who has the sort of relationship with God that Jesus has been describing all along.

In other words, these verses are directed to the kind of people who ask, seek, and knock while having the right kind of motives and goals. This means that the person who asks to win the lottery is not the kind of person Jesus is talking about (compare James 4:3).

III. GIVING FATHER (LUKE 11:11-13)

A. EARTHLY ILLUSTRATION (vv. 11, 12)

11. *"Which of you fathers, if your son asks for a fish, will give him a snake instead?*

All parents have had the experience of their children asking to receive food. The questions that Jesus asks challenge his audience to think through a certain issue in light of their own experiences with their families.

12. *"Or if he asks for an egg, will give him a scorpion?*

The proper response is obvious. That is just the point: the degree to which the right response is obvious is the degree to which we can be confident in placing our trust in our heavenly Father, who meets our needs.

B. HEAVENLY REALITY (v. 13)

13. *"If you then, though you are evil, know how to give good gifts to your children, how much more will your Father in heaven give the Holy Spirit to those who ask him!"*

That Jesus refers to his audience as *evil* does not imply that he is speaking to opponents. Luke 11:1 suggests, rather, that he is addressing his disciples. Jesus is sketching a broad contrast between humans and God. Compared to God, we all are evil (Romans 3:10-18, 23).

Thus, Jesus employs a lesser-to-greater argument: if we ordinary mortals are capable of being nice to our *children,* then God is all the more capable! And if we ordinary mortals are capable of being gracious to our friends, even after a period of ungraciousness (vv. 5-8, above), then God's capabilities for graciousness cannot be doubted.

That Jesus points to *the Holy Spirit* as that which God will *give* us when we pray alerts us to an important fact: Jesus is not referring simply to bettering our material lives through prayer. A popular perception of God says that if you want a bigger car or a better house, all you need to do is ask for it in faith. This theory carries the assumption that God promises us health and wealth. It is a "name it and claim it" view of the gospel.

But there is no such promise in the New Testament. Human expectation of entitlement is just that. Remember that Jesus is teaching us how true disciples understand the nature of God; Jesus is not teaching that we can get from God all we want simply by virtue of persistence.

So, does all this mean that God is not at all concerned about our material situation in life? In next week's lesson, we will see Jesus draw attention to this very issue. We are also instructed by Matthew's version of today's lesson text. Having presented an example of how not to think about prayer (Matthew 6:7), Jesus says that the true disciple understands that the heavenly Father "knows what you need before you ask him" (Matthew 6:8).

The point of the contrast in Matthew is to highlight the difference between how pagans pray and how God expects a believer to pray. The fact that God knows what we need before we pray is to mark the way we pray. True disciples pray for what they need, realizing that God already knows their needs. He knows the distinction between what we really need and what we only think we need.

Luke's account takes this even further by pointing to the giving of the Holy Spirit as being the result of prayer; that is, Jesus frames the issue of need mainly in terms of our relationship with God. The lives of true disciples are focused on serving God. True disciples see that fact as the basis for their prayers.

Moreover, true disciples are confident that God will indeed supply all that they need. Later, Paul will make the point that material possessions are valuable to him insofar as they assist him in his service to God (Philippians 4:11-18). Moreover, Paul's idea of *need* is defined within one's relationship to Jesus Christ. Thus Paul states "my God will meet all your needs according to his glorious riches in Christ Jesus" (Philippians 4:19).

Jesus teaches us that prayer is something to pursue in godly confidence. Doing so reflects our relationship to God through Jesus Christ as we seek greater faithfulness as his disciples.

DAILY BIBLE READINGS

Monday, Jan. 14—Answered Prayer (Psalm 28:6-9)

Tuesday, Jan. 15—Teach Us to Pray (Luke 11:1-4)

Wednesday, Jan. 16—A Friend's Request (Luke 11:5-8)

Thursday, Jan. 17—Ask and Receive (Luke 11:9-12)

Friday, Jan. 18—Persistent in Prayer (Luke 18:1-17)

Saturday, Jan. 19—God's Gift of the Holy Spirit (Luke 11:13; Acts 2:1-4)

Sunday, Jan. 20—Give Thanks to the Lord (Psalm 106:1-3)

WHAT DO YOU THINK?

Was there ever a time when you "gave up" on prayer? What happened? How did you turn this around?

PRAYER

Our good and generous Father, we trust that you love us because of your own goodness, not ours. Help us to ask for those things you want for us and to trust that you will grant them to us. Even as we pray, we know that you will answer in accord with your perfect will. By Jesus' generous work we pray, amen.

HOW TO SAY IT

Philippians. Fih-LIP-ee-unz.
Samaritan. Suh-MARE-uh-tun.

THOUGHT TO REMEMBER

God helps those who forget themselves.

I have a friend who often had to do without things in his youth, although he was not raised in poverty. When he got married and became a father, he determined that his children would not have to go without as he had. Educated and trained as an engineer, he had enough income so that his family did not suffer any deprivation. He was never overly extravagant, but his sons had plenty of toys when they were young, cars when they got older, and all the benefits of his well-intentioned benevolence.

When the sons got married and set up their own housekeeping, they tended to continue the practice of their earlier years. Whenever they saw something they wanted, they bought it, often using credit. The habit of a lifetime was difficult to break. One son finally realized he was in over his head when his credit-card indebtedness reached $30,000.

Jesus says our heavenly Father knows how to give good gifts, just as earthly fathers do. But sometimes earthly fathers go too far. If we stop and think about it, it is undoubtedly a good thing that God does not give us everything we ask for. We could easily become smug, spoiled, satiated, and self-satisfied.

God gives us whatever we really need, but not all that we want. In the process he demonstrates that he is a better Father than earthly fathers. He sustains us, but he also keeps us aware that earthly gadgets don't bring us lasting happiness. Only his grace can do that.   —J. B. N.

CONCLUSION

A friend of mine who is a Bible college professor told me of a certain classroom experience she had had. One day she started the lesson by asking the class to respond to a certain question. The question was, "Are you confident of your salvation?"

She was astonished to find only a few of the 20 students responded in the affirmative. Why the doubt? Perhaps many hesitated to say *yes* for fear of appearing to be prideful. No spiritually mature Christian would dare think, "I'm so good that God couldn't possibly deny my entry into Heaven." Such an approach to salvation focuses on our goodness, not his.

Perhaps the same kind of hesitation shows up in our prayer requests at times. Many of us are aware of the pridefulness of the "name it and claim it" kind of prayers. So we take our prayers too far in the other direction in an attempt to avoid that error.

The result may be that we approach God in a tentative, hesitant way. We may question whether we "deserve" the good things that we request. Such an approach turns the focus away from God and onto ourselves. Avoiding the sin of pride is always a good thing. But being overly self-conscious and introspective in this area brings us right back to the problem of focusing on self!

If we understand just how much God loves us and just how good and generous he is, then our thoughts of our own worthiness (or lack thereof) will not be the main issue in our prayers. A tried-and-true prayer format is summed up in the acronym *ACTS*. These four letters stand for *adoration, confession, thanksgiving,* and *supplication;* they describe a series of steps to follow when we are praying.

Notice that *supplication* (which means asking humbly for something) comes last. The first three steps refer to praising God for who he is, acknowledging the things that hinder our relationship to him, and recognizing what he has already done for us. If we go through those three prayer-steps first, then our supplications are more likely to be offered with right motives.

Discovery Learning

This page contains an alternative lesson plan emphasizing learning activities. Classes desiring such student involvement will find these suggestions helpful. The next page is a reproducible activity page to further enhance discovery learning.

INTO THE LESSON

In the week before this lesson, make a video that surveys 7 to 10 people. Ask for their responses to this question: "What does prayer mean to you?"

You may choose to call church members and video their responses at their homes or conduct this survey at another midweek church meeting or small-group gathering. However, the best survey would be of people on the street. You will probably discover a wide variety of responses.

To introduce today's lesson, tell the class of your survey and play the video responses. Make the transition to Bible study by telling the class that people have varied ideas about the purpose and function of prayer. Many of them are correct. Yet most of us need a clearer definition of prayer's power and purpose.

A variant of the above activity is to ask one of your class members to take some of your learners to the side as they arrive for class. Even a hallway can serve as a videotaping area. Have the videographer ask the same question: "What does prayer mean to you?" Continue taping people's responses right up to the time class begins. Then play the video for the entire class.

INTO THE WORD

Divide the class into study groups as follows:

Group #1. Give this group a copy of Visuals for the Lesson from the Reproducible Page. Ask them to complete it according to the instructions.

Group #2. Give this group one piece of poster board, a marker, and a photocopy of the Lesson Background and the commentary on verses 5-8. Provide the following instructions: "Your task is to read the Lesson Background and the commentary on verses 5-8. Then write out the model prayer (vv. 2-4) and be ready to explain its place in today's study. Also be ready to explain verses 5-8 to the class."

Group #3. Give this group a photocopy of the Introduction and of the commentary on verses 9, 10. Provide the following instructions: "Read the commentary on verses 9 and 10. Then read the Introduction. Your task is to quickly prepare and deliver a skit for the class built on the loan request illustration. Then have a group member explain to the class how this skit illustrates verses 9 and 10."

Group #4. Give this group one piece of poster board, a marker, and a photocopy of the commentary on verses 11-13. Provide this list of questions:

1. How do verses 11-13 clarify or illustrate the intent of verses 9 and 10? 2. What does Jesus mean when he calls his listeners "evil"? 3. What is Jesus' lesson or challenge to us in these verses? Provide also the following instructions: "Read the commentary on verses 11-13. Then write the following questions on the poster board, discuss the questions, and list your conclusions. One of your group members will share your responses with the rest of the class."

Ask each group to summarize its conclusions for the class as a whole.

INTO LIFE

Ask the discussion questions listed below. While asking and discussing the first question, circulate throughout the room as you give each person a colored self-adhesive circle of one-half inch or one inch in diameter. Such circles are commonly available at office supply stores and the stationery section of discount stores. Your church office may have them in supply as well. The circles will be used at the end of the lesson. The discussion questions are as follows:

1. Why does this passage not teach us that God will give us absolutely *everything* we ask at any time?

2. Since *ask, seek, knock* does not mean that God will grant us absolutely everything we ask at any time of our lives, then what does it mean?

3. In terms of persistence, confidence, and motivation, what is Jesus teaching us about prayer? What general truths jump out at you? (List their answers on a large piece of poster board.)

Next, say, "Now, make this lesson personal. Look at the answers we've just listed. Which truth or lesson especially touches you today? Bring your adhesive circle over to the poster board and place it right next to the truth you've just selected."

Close the class by placing the poster on the floor or a table in the center of a prayer circle. With heads bowed, give each of your learners a chance to express a prayer of thanks for the truths listed. Distribute copies of The A.S.K. Club from the Reproducible Page as learners depart.

Visuals for the Lesson

Let's imagine you are preparing a PowerPoint® presentation for Jesus' lesson in Luke 11:5-13. Help build the lesson outline by filling in the blanks.

Lesson for Today: "Inspired to Pray"

I. Confidence in my _____ (vv. 5-8)

II. Joining the A. S. K. club (vv. 9, 10)

    A _____

    S _____

    K _____

III. Warm snapshots of our H _____ F _____ (vv. 11-13)

IV. A wonderful gift of the H _____ S _____ (v. 13)

Fill in the blanks:

Friend,
Ask,
Seek,
Knock,
Heavenly
Father,
Holy Spirit

The A.S.K. Club

As a member of the A.S.K. club (see above), you have a wonderful invitation from the Lord (verses 9, 10). What does this invitation teach you about your relationship with your God and his relationship with you? Jot your ideas below:

God's Call to the Christian Community
Unit 2: Inspired by God's Call
(Lessons 6-9)

INSPIRED TO TRUST

LESSON 9

WHY TEACH THIS LESSON?

At least some of your learners are burdened with worry. Yet worry is wrong because it is a form of unspiritual fear. When believers worry, they are not trusting God. Worry is a sin.

Yet Christians can learn to trust God. Even during times of spiritual storm and other extremely difficult situations, God can be trusted. God created sun, moon, stars, planets, and all living things by his mighty power. If he can do all this, is he not able to handle our problems? This lesson offers Jesus' decisive thoughts on this issue.

INTRODUCTION

A. ADORNMENT OR BURDEN?

Once upon a time there was a wealthy king. He sat in his palace on his throne of solid gold, dressed in the finest silk and furs, and wept. He wept because he didn't have a crown. Oh, he had a plain little thing, of course. But it wasn't the kind of crown befitting a king of his stature. And so he set off on a journey to find the most exquisite jewels in the world in order to transform his plain crown into the grandest ever seen.

First his journey took him to Burma for the purest rubies. Once there, he piled hundreds of rubies onto his plain crown. Then he set his camel toward Russia. There the king acquired the finest emeralds, also heaping them onto his crown. Finally, he turned toward South Africa to find the largest diamond in the world. The king's camel eventually brought him to the jeweler who could provide that diamond. The king's eyes lit up when he saw the enormous jewel. The end of his mission in sight, he balanced it on the very top of his bulging crown.

The king then proudly climbed onto his camel to set off for home, the king's neck straining under the weight of the fantastic headpiece. But once atop the poor beast, there was a swooshing sound as camel, king, and crown disappeared into the desert sands, never to be seen again. The adornment had become a fatal burden!

A nice children's fantasy, isn't it? But when we think of all the people today who sink under the burden of many worldly "adornments"—including the burdens of debt and worry—it may not be such a fantasy after all!

B. LESSON BACKGROUND

Our lesson text occurs within one of the major teaching sections in Luke's Gospel, namely Luke 12:1–13:21. It is set during Jesus' later Judean ministry. This particular teaching section follows a segment that notes increasing friction between Jewish leaders and Jesus.

Many Jewish religious leaders (Pharisees, scribes, etc.) had become very hostile toward Jesus. Just prior to today's text, Luke presents Jesus' teaching against some Pharisees (Luke 11:37-54). Jesus' main criticism was that they

DEVOTIONAL READING:
PSALM 31:1-5
BACKGROUND SCRIPTURE:
LUKE 12:22-34
PRINTED TEXT:
LUKE 12:22-34

LESSON AIMS

After participating in this lesson, each student will be able to:

1. Identify some physical and spiritual treasures listed in today's text.

2. Interpret what it means to receive the kingdom in light of his or her need to trust God.

3. Describe how he or she will trust God more fully for one of the items listed under Lesson Aim #1.

Jan
27

KEY VERSE

Do not be afraid, little flock, for your Father has been pleased to give you the kingdom.
—Luke 12:32

were hypocritical, having evil intent on the inside while posturing godliness on the outside (examples: Luke 11:39, 44).

Hypocrisy presents us with two problems. First, it is simply dishonest since it involves pretending to be something that one is not. Second, and worse, it assumes that God looks only on the surface when evaluating a person's activities. Thus after Jesus left the Pharisees (11:53), he warned his disciples to be wary of the yeast of the Pharisees, "which is hypocrisy" (12:1).

This transition is important to note because it is the basis of the theme throughout the section Luke 12:1–13:21. That is, Jesus' primary point throughout is for his disciples to grasp the difference between the present world and the Father's spiritual kingdom. If the disciples were capable of placing their values in the latter, then the temptations and "adornments" of the present world—which Jesus' enemies loved so much—would not shake them from their future with the Father. Thus, the point is to not fear the threats or temptations of this world, because God has far greater power. In this way, Jesus prepared his disciples for the difficulties they would face as leaders of the church (Luke 12:11, 12). The Parable of the Rich Fool (12:13-21) also deals with attachments to this world. Today's lesson further develops this theme.

I. DON'T WORRY (LUKE 12:22-26)

A. What Not to Worry About (v. 22)

22. Then Jesus said to his disciples: "Therefore I tell you, do not worry about your life, what you will eat; or about your body, what you will wear.

The word *therefore* links our passage to the Parable of the Rich Fool in Luke 12:13-21. But Jesus now shifts the focus away from the desire to amass wealth and toward the general concern of having sufficient material possessions. This problem is more widespread than the one faced by the rich fool; we may not be inappropriately attached to wealth as such, but we likely have a strong attachment to a "regular" comfortable life.

The challenge to *not worry about your life* is startling! Is Jesus speaking in an exaggerated way to achieve a shocking effect? Or does he mean precisely what he says? When our instinct is self-preservation, how can we *not* care for our own lives? The parallel verse at Matthew 6:25 is helpful. Whereas Luke has recorded the verse before us right after the Parable of the Rich Fool, Matthew has recorded it directly after the teaching that a person cannot serve two masters. This is summarized as, "You cannot serve both God and Money" (Matthew 6:24). Obviously, Matthew and Luke see Jesus' idea the same way. The rich fool of Luke 12:13-21 puts his material life above God. In Matthew 6:19-24, material well-being either rules in your life or God does; both cannot rule at the same time.

Thus in referring to one who does *not worry about . . . life,* Jesus has in mind the kind of person who should prefer Heaven over earth. This is the true disciple. The question now becomes this: How we can embrace Jesus' command in a meaningful way? The challenge is to investigate our lives to figure out the nature of our attachments to this world. As we shall see, the issue is a matter of our salvation (compare John 12:25).

We may conclude that Jesus is not calling us to rid ourselves of earthly attachments altogether, but to rid ourselves of spiritually unhealthy ones. If we had "no attachments" to the material world in an absolute sense, we could not function! Thus, our challenge is to determine whether we are being spiritually honest in the way we approach our material possessions. (Such wrongheaded attachments not only involve stuff that we *already* own, but also things that we *want* to own.)

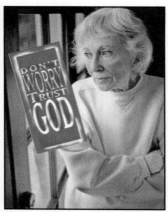

Visual for Lesson 9. *Point to this visual as you introduce the question on page 194.*

B. WHY NOT TO WORRY (vv. 23, 24)

23. "Life is more than food, and the body more than clothes.

When we focus on our material needs, we negate an important reality: the *life* of a true disciple extends beyond the physical to the eternal. The fact is, though, that we are a combination of both physical and spiritual. Thus Jesus does not say we should totally ignore *food* and *clothes*. These are important, but they deal only with the physical aspects of life. We are to see such things as physical means to spiritual ends. If we make them the point of life, then we subordinate our spiritual life to the physical (compare Philippians 3:19).

Paul argues in 1 Corinthians 6:19, 20; 7:23 that Christians must understand themselves to have chosen to relinquish "ownership" of their bodies. That is, with the blessing of salvation comes the sacrifice of our worldly interests. *The body* belongs to the Lord. To use the body to achieve worldly interests at the expense of spiritual ones is to reject Christ's sacrificial purchase of body and spirit.

24. "Consider the ravens: They do not sow or reap, they have no storeroom or barn; yet God feeds them. And how much more valuable you are than birds!

In the overall context of this teaching section, Jesus instructs the disciples how to live according to God's interests while still being in this world. Because the world is hostile to God's interests (see John 15:18, 19), true disciples will experience a conflict of interests while living for him on this fallen planet. Thus Jesus arms the disciples with a way to understand God. The ability to fend off the anxiety that leads us to latch onto this world's interests lies in appreciating how much God cares for us (see also Psalm 147:9).

C. WHERE WORRY DOESN'T LEAD (vv. 25, 26)

25. "Who of you by worrying can add a single hour to his life?

Living a healthy life in terms of diet and exercise may increase one's life expectancy. But *worry* sure won't! If worry leads to ulcers, just the opposite may be the case.

The *King James Version* translates this verse as "And which of you with taking thought can add to his stature one cubit?" Whether it's an issue of adding hours to life or inches to height, the point is the same: worry won't do it.

BODY BUILDING

We live in a time when many are trying to alter their shape. Some want to increase their shape, most want to reduce it. I have a friend who is beginning to lift weights so that he can "bulk up" and show off some real muscle when he wears T-shirts in the summer.

On the other hand, I met a man recently who said that two years ago he weighed 538 pounds. After weight reduction surgery, he lost over 300 pounds. Diet fads are big business, and the public spends billions of dollars every year to try to lose weight.

While we may try to put on or lose weight, nothing practical can be done to increase one's height. Better nutrition over the last century has apparently increased average heights, but a person cannot "think" or even "work" himself or herself into a taller stature. So the question bears repeating: Why should we worry about anything that's beyond our control?   —J. B. N.

26. "Since you cannot do this very little thing, why do you worry about the rest?

This very little thing refers to extending our lives by one hour in verse 25. The phrase *the rest* is probably a reference to "other concerns of this world." With these phrases, Jesus concludes the point from the previous verse: since

WHAT DO YOU THINK?

Why do some people obsess over things like fashion or cuisine? How can we help them see how foolish that is?

DAILY BIBLE READINGS

Monday, Jan. 21—Trust God (Psalm 31:1-5)

Tuesday, Jan. 22—Valuable to God (Luke 12:22-24)

Wednesday, Jan. 23—Worry Won't Help! (Luke 12:25, 26)

Thursday, Jan. 24—Clothed by God (Luke 12:27, 28)

Friday, Jan. 25—God Knows Your Needs (Luke 12:29-31)

Saturday, Jan. 26—Receive the Kingdom (Luke 12:32-34)

Sunday, Jan. 27—Trust God, Not Princes (Psalm 146:1-7)

HOW TO SAY IT

Corinthians. Ko-RIN-thee-unz.
Judean. Joo-DEE-un.
Pharisees. FAIR-ih-seez.
Philippians. Fih-LIP-ee-unz.
Solomon. SOL-o-mun.
Thessalonians. THESS-uh-LO-
   nee-unz.

WHAT DO YOU THINK?

Why do you think some Christians worry, despite Jesus' promise that God will take care of us? How can we help lift one another out of his or her worries?

anxiety does not work in terms of the issues of verses 24 and 25, why worry about anything else? How much better it is to focus on our eternal lives through service in the kingdom of God! Thus Jesus continues to teach his disciples how to think of the eternal while living in the physical world.

II. TRUST GOD (LUKE 12:27-31)

A. SIMPLE EXAMPLE (v. 27)

27. "Consider how the lilies grow. They do not labor or spin. Yet I tell you, not even Solomon in all his splendor was dressed like one of these.

Jesus continues to make his same point. The splendor of Solomon is noted in 1 Kings 10:14-29 and the parallel account 2 Chronicles 9:13-28. The glory of what he created for himself does not compare with the glory that God creates in simple lilies, however. The importance of this fact is demonstrated in the next verse.

B. GRACIOUS GOD (v. 28)

28. "If that is how God clothes the grass of the field, which is here today, and tomorrow is thrown into the fire, how much more will he clothe you, O you of little faith!

Anxiety is fruitless because it fails to grasp who God is and what we mean to him. True disciples, therefore, are not anxious since they trust God to care for them.

Jesus simply says that we need only to consider God's ability to sustain the world around us to confirm God's ability to sustain us. Since he does sustain the world, and we are worth more than plants, then to be anxious is to forget God's love for us. The problem is that of having little faith. At its heart, this is an unwillingness to let go of this world and cling to God.

C. WHAT THE PAGANS DO (vv. 29, 30)

29. "And do not set your heart on what you will eat or drink; do not worry about it.

This verse summarizes the previous section, restating that we ought not to focus on things that give rise to anxiety. Jesus' statement here prepares the disciples to consider what they should concern themselves with (v. 31, below). We cannot allow ourselves to worry about even the small things of our physical lives, since this reveals a lack of trust in God.

30. "For the pagan world runs after all such things, and your Father knows that you need them.

Jesus likens anxiety about daily needs to the things done by those who don't know God (the pagan world). He then contrasts that mind-set to reality: God does know what you need in order to live. We can trust that since God does know what we need, he is able to provide.

D. WHAT YOU SHOULD DO (v. 31)

31. "But seek his kingdom, and these things will be given to you as well."

Up until now, Jesus has been telling us what to avoid doing. Now he reveals what we should do. This verse can be taken several ways, especially if read out of context. In context, the command to seek his kingdom is contrasted with the things that Jesus has been warning us about: material benefit and blessing.

If we busy our lives exclusively with physical concerns, we shift our attention away from that which is most important. In so doing, we risk our relationship with God. The point, though, is not about whether or not we get material needs, but on where we look for our values. When we look at the effort we put into life, is it spent securing spiritual blessings or material blessings?

We should also caution that Jesus is not teaching that true disciples will always have a guarantee of food and water. Faithful Christians die of starvation and thirst. This has been so since Jesus' time. Yet if God wants us to continue to live on this earth and serve his kingdom, then he will enable us to do so through his provision of life's necessities.

Kingdom-seeking is profoundly more important than worrying about material needs in any case. A lifestyle focused on God's kingdom does not place much value in the world's material concerns. This is an extremely difficult concept for those who live in materialistic, consumer-driven cultures. But this doesn't change what Jesus is saying; it just throws things into sharper contrast.

III. DON'T FEAR (LUKE 12:32-34)

A. GOD'S PLEASURE (v. 32)

32. "Do not be afraid, little flock, for your Father has been pleased to give you the kingdom.

The hope of the future is brought to bear upon the concerns of the present. If we focus on God's promises for the future, then we are able to deal with problems in the present—problems that can prevent us from reaching that future reality. To live in anxiety is to fail to grasp who God is and how much we matter to him.

If, however, we do grasp who God is and how much he loves us, then he is sure to *give* to us *the kingdom*. If we can embrace the truth of Jesus' teaching here, then we have all we need to make the leap from a life governed by material concern to a life governed by our eternal membership in the kingdom of God. In doing so, we make sure of our salvation and participation in kingdom blessings.

B. OUR RESPONSIBILITY (v. 33)

33. "Sell your possessions and give to the poor. Provide purses for yourselves that will not wear out, a treasure in heaven that will not be exhausted, where no thief comes near and no moth destroys.

Jesus clarifies the underlying exhortation from the previous verses. We can summarize the verse in contemporary language: "Let go of this temporary world and grab hold of the eternal."

The idea of selling what we have is consistent with what Jesus teaches elsewhere (compare Luke 18:22). Jesus' ministry exhibits a concern for the material needs of the poor, and today it may be through our hands that their needs are met as we *give to the poor* (compare 1 John 3:17). This leads us to conclude that material needs are understood by Jesus to be basic to life. Continual effective living for God does require that basic needs be met.

NO THIEVES

The problems of modern urban living are hard to escape. In a city where I once lived, our home was burglarized twice. Several items of value were stolen, as well as personal items of little worth but of great nostalgic significance. I was very irritated that people had done this to us. I wished for a return to the olden days of trust and security, when a person's belongings were safe—days when people would never lock their houses.

WHAT DO YOU THINK?

How do you recognize those who seek the kingdom of God? How will others recognize you as someone who is seeking the kingdom of God?

WHAT DO YOU THINK?

How would you respond if someone at church suddenly sold everything she owned and gave the money to the poor? Why would you respond that way?

PRAYER

Our Father, you have given us so much. Help us use your gifts for you. Help us to see how we can use finite things for eternal good. In Jesus' name we pray, amen.

But then I realized that perhaps those golden-olden days were not always so safe. Crime has always been a problem. This has been true whether in the year 1900, 1800, 1500, or earlier. In the days of the Roman Empire, many places simply were not safe—either for life or property. That's why Jesus could easily call attention to the issue.

But crime is not a problem in Heaven since there is no sin there. Neither are there any moth-eaten bags that fail to safeguard what they're intended to protect. If we know all this to be true, then why are we still so fascinated with our earthly possessions?

—J. B. N.

C. END RESULT (v. 34)

34. "For where your treasure is, there your heart will be also."

Here it is helpful to consider the comments made to the rich young ruler later in Luke 18:18-22. The man seems to be good disciple-material since he claims to have kept the law. He asks how to have eternal life. Jesus replies that adherence to the external requirements of discipleship must be accompanied by releasing his attachment to material things. Ultimately, the man fails to have salvation because of an unspiritual attachment to earthly possessions.

Many today make the same error. What gives value to our behavior is the intention of our hearts. Being a "good" person, going to church, and praying do not count as acts of discipleship if they are products of a *heart* that is attached to the material world. Thus Jesus challenges the young man: Are you a true disciple?

A disciple's inner life is oriented toward the interests of God's kingdom rather than material concerns. Our lesson concludes with this basic principle. Jesus stresses that attachment to the material world is not a small choice, but a matter of our own salvation. Both those who are and those who are not able to let go of material concerns know where their hearts lie. We should keep this in mind the next time we begin to fret over our pension plans, Social Security, IRAs, and 401(k)s!

WHAT DO YOU THINK?

When you look at your own life, what tells you where your heart and your treasure are truly located?

CONCLUSION

One of the dangers we face when we discuss material issues is to think that Jesus' cautions apply only to the superwealthy, such as Donald Trump. Biblically, though, "rich" includes a certain mind-set. The "rich man" in the Bible is the one who relies on wealth more than on God. The modern Christian who lives in a prosperous Western democracy is certainly not immune from this danger!

We know that our lives shouldn't revolve around acquiring the latest car and the finest clothing. But how should we, as Christians, approach material interests? In a way, it would be easier to live in a hut and wear an old sack than to figure out how to have a three-bedroom home, two cars, and a closet full of nice clothes while not actually caring much for those possessions.

However, Jesus doesn't require us to run away from our lives, but to make choices daily that honor him. We are faced with the challenge of working to provide for our daily needs (2 Thessalonians 3:10) without placing too much value on those things for which we work so hard.

So—how can we be members of an affluent culture without being wrapped up in our material possessions? Is it possible to see a house as a spiritual thing? Perhaps, if one fills it regularly with those who need a roof or a meal. Is it possible to "sell all" and live in a cave yet still be attached to the world? Perhaps, if you do so in order to call the world's attention to yourself and your piety. Only you and God can judge where your treasure really lies.

THOUGHT TO REMEMBER

An eternal perspective is the cure for materialism.

Discovery Learning

This page contains an alternative lesson plan emphasizing learning activities. Classes desiring such student involvement will find these suggestions helpful. The next page is a reproducible activity page to further enhance discovery learning.

INTO THE LESSON

As learners enter the classroom, give each a piece of paper with one of the following four words printed in large letters vertically on it: *WEALTH, WORRY, TREASURE,* and *TRUST.*

Print these instructions on the top of each handout page: "Please make an acrostic out of the word listed below. You may choose to use the letters in the acrostic to begin a word, to end a word, or to serve as one of the other letters of a word. However, the words you choose for the acrostic should describe or define the word assigned."

Learners may begin the assignment immediately. However, be sure to allow latecomers a few minutes to build their acrostics at least partially. Then ask for volunteers to share one acrostic for each word. Make the transition to Bible study by telling the class that the four words you distributed point to key concepts in today's study. The principles behind them were contemporary when Jesus spoke of them, and they continue to speak to us today.

INTO THE WORD

Before class, affix seven pieces of poster board to the walls of your learning area. Each poster board is to have one of the following seven headings:

1. Thinking About Life (vv. 22, 23)
2. Raving About Ravens (v. 24)
3. Lengthening Our Lives (vv. 25, 26)
4. Lilies and Kings (vv. 27, 28)
5. Pagan/National Goals (vv. 29-31)
6. Ahhh, Peace! (v. 32)
7. Sell? Really? (vv. 33, 34)

Depending on class size, appoint a study team or an individual for each poster. Give each team a marker for writing on its poster. (Make sure the posters are thick enough that the ink doesn't bleed through onto the wall.) You may also choose to give each team a photocopy of the lesson commentary of the verse or verses assigned to that team.

Ask the teams to study the assigned verses and commentary. The teams are to make notes on the posters of key points in their assigned texts. They should focus on applying Jesus' teaching to modern life.

After completing the project, each team or individual will explain its conclusions to the class. (A similar activity is included in the optional student book.)

INTO LIFE

Try to make time to do all three of the following activities. Each is unique and important in applying today's text. Depending on the size of your class, you may choose to use small groups. (Activities similar to #1 and #2 are also included in the optional student book.)

Activity #1: Discussion Questions: Interpretations and Applications. What does Luke 12 tell us about how Christians should approach material possessions? How can Christians "provide purses . . . that will not wear out" (v. 33)? How can Christians exist in an affluent society without being wrapped up in material possessions?

Illustrate your answer to each question with a specific, real-life application. Also, give examples of Christians who are living these principles out daily.

Activity #2: Getting Personal. Ask each learner to reread today's text, looking for a word or phrase that stretches or challenges his or her life priorities or lifestyle. Ask learners to circle their words and phrases either mentally or physically. Then ask each person to jot his or her word or phrase on an index card, followed by a brief note about how he or she will try to be like the ideal expressed by the word or phrase.

Activity #3: Looking Outward. Tell your class that the principles about material possessions in this passage apply not only to individuals, but also to groups such as your class. Ask your learners to discuss class-project ideas that demonstrate material unselfishness.

As an example, mention the possibility of your class serving as a work crew to help someone in a way that costs the class money or material assets, not just time. This may involve handyman projects around someone's house or automobile maintenance.

List the ideas on the board as they are presented. You may wish to use a brainstorming format: do not allow discussion until after many ideas are offered. Then ask the class to decide on a project and appoint leaders to spearhead it.

Close with prayer. Then distribute copies of the Word Search on Worry! exercise from the Reproducible Page to learners as they leave.

A Word Search on Worry!

In the blanks below, write Jesus' words concerning worry and treasures found in Luke 12:22-34. Then find these words in the grid below. Be sure to look across, up, down, and diagonally. (The answers are printed below.) If you're not good at this sort of thing, don't worry about it!

Then Jesus said to his disciples: "Therefore I tell you, do not _____ about your life, what you will eat; or about your _____, what you will wear. Life is more than _____, and the body more than clothes. Consider the _____: They do not sow or reap, they have no _____ or _____; yet God _____ them. And how much more _____ you are than birds! Who of you by worrying can add a _____ hour to his life? Since you cannot do this very little thing, why do you worry about the rest?

Consider how the _____ grow. They do not _____ or _____. Yet I tell you, not even _____ in all his _____ was dressed like one of these. If that is how God _____ the _____ of the field, which is here today, and tomorrow is thrown into the fire, how much more will he clothe you, O you of little _____. And do not set your _____ on what you will eat or drink; do not worry about it. For the _____ world runs after all such things, and your _____ knows that you need them. But _____ his _____, and these things will be given to you as well.

Do not be afraid, little _____, for your Father has been pleased to give you the kingdom. Sell your _____ and give to the poor. Provide _____ for yourselves that will not wear out, a treasure in heaven that will not be exhausted, where no _____ comes near and no _____ destroys. For where your _____ is, there your heart will be also.

```
V R Q N I P S R H D H I Y D U E I
N X N R O D N E L P S W S W N K X
U P B J K M D V A L U A B L E J D
M O O R E R O T S J O P F Y V N X
H S S A J U I L T Q P T R S L D D
Y X M X B A R N O B Z R F F L C Y
M T B C L O T H E S O L H A S V Z
T H I E F E E D S W O D B I N N Y
R S H A G A K H V C O O Y T O D A
E M E K B R T F K O R K K H I N Z
A X X U I O A H F H N U N S S Q U
S P N P M N N S E I L I L N S Y X
U X H U S D G A S R O A B E E Y Q
R Q Q R Y G R D G E F U B V S P X
E P D S T T L E O A E W W A S Z Q
N Z B E X J M Y T M P K Z R O J J
X E E S S I N G L E Y Q Q Z P O A
```

God's Call to the Christian Community
Unit 3: Responding to God's Call
(Lessons 10-13)

CALLED TO LABOR

LESSON 10

WHY TEACH THIS LESSON?

In the kingdom of God, there are no "spectator-only" believers. God calls all Christians to be participating actively and faithfully in the work that builds and advances his kingdom. To sit in a monastery doing nothing but singing and praying is not an option!

God has invested in each believer certain spiritual gifts. Our task is to be sensitive to the Spirit's leading regarding how to use those gifts. We hone this sensitivity through Bible study and prayer. As we do, we come to know Christ better, growing in our knowledge of his calling on our lives. Each of your learners needs a clearer understanding of his or her calling. Today's lesson will help them realize that Jesus does indeed call his disciples to do his work. If we don't answer the Lord's call, then who will?

INTRODUCTION

A. TWENTY-FIRST CENTURY MISSION STRATEGY

The work of the church in the nineteenth and twentieth centuries was marked by a great interest in foreign missions. To be a missionary in that era often was a life commitment—a commitment to be trained for service, to leave one's home country, and to take up permanent residence in a foreign land.

The risky nature of these ventures was shown in the requirement of some missionary agencies for their people to take caskets with them when they went out. This was because of the high likelihood that they would die on the mission field. Yet there are many success stories from this era, and nations such as South Korea and the Philippines, as well as many African countries, were left with a permanent Christian witness.

Christian missionary endeavors boomed after World War II, as military veterans came home with a clear understanding of the need for the gospel in foreign lands. As new technology emerged, it was often incorporated into mission work. This included airplanes to reach remote regions and radio broadcasts to penetrate areas closed to missionaries. Later came computers to assist with Scripture translation as well as e-mail and Internet access.

When we speak of *missions* in a technical sense, we mean more than occasional or random opportunities to share the gospel. *Missions* is intentional, strategic, cross-cultural evangelism. It does not happen accidentally. Crossing cultural boundaries to bring the gospel to others requires planning.

One of the most dynamic developments in Christian missions in the last few years is the rise of short-term missionary trips. These have allowed Christians with little training or experience to travel abroad and engage people with the gospel. Admittedly, some short-term mission trips are more productive than others (as is also the case with long-term missions). But the short-term trips have brought a renewed excitement in many congregations concerning the need for worldwide evangelism. Some believers who would

DEVOTIONAL READING:
PSALM 78:1-4
BACKGROUND SCRIPTURE:
LUKE 10:1-20
PRINTED TEXT:
LUKE 10:1-12, 17-20

LESSON AIMS

After participating in this lesson, each student will be able to:

1. Summarize the mission of the 72.

2. Compare and contrast Jesus' sending of the 72 with modern mission work.

3. Give greater support to the evangelistic and missionary efforts of his or her church in one specific way.

Feb
3

KEY VERSE

He told them, "The harvest is plentiful, but the workers are few. Ask the Lord of the harvest, therefore, to send out workers into his harvest field."
—Luke 10:2

LESSON 10 NOTES

never be candidates for full-time mission work have experienced spiritual growth in ways that may not have happened otherwise.

Today's lesson is about a mission trip. It was *intentional,* because it came from Jesus' directives. It was *strategic* because it involved advance planning and sought to accomplish a larger goal. It may have been even a little *cross-cultural* in that the missionaries were going to places where they were not known. (We do not know if those whom Jesus sent out ventured into non-Jewish environments.)

We may be surprised, though, to realize that this was a short-term missions project. Perhaps some of these disciples became "career" missionaries at a later date, but probably most did not. Yet as is true with short-term missions today, the participants engaged in important tasks.

B. LESSON BACKGROUND

Luke 9:51 begins a new section of Luke's story of Jesus. Here we are told that, "As the time approached for him to be taken up to heaven, Jesus resolutely set out for Jerusalem." So Jesus and his group departed from Galilee to visit the holy city.

Some commentators refer to this section (which extends from Luke 9:51 to 13:21) as "the later Judean ministry." This section contains many great teachings of Jesus (example: The Good Samaritan, Luke 10:30-37) as well as his interactions with some interesting people (example: Mary and Martha, Luke 10:38-42).

As we know, it was in Jerusalem that Jesus fulfilled his earthly destiny: the cross. His arrival in the Jerusalem precincts to fulfill that vital part of God's plan (which would be his final trip to Jerusalem) did not happen until Luke 19:29, some 10 chapters later. At least part of the reason Jesus sent out the 72 disciples (Luke 10:1) was to prepare the way for that final trip.

Earlier, Jesus had initiated a similar "sending out" project that was limited to the 12 chosen disciples (Luke 9:1-6). They had been sent out with the authority to cast out demons, the power to heal diseases, and the responsibility of preaching the gospel. The word used to describe the act of sending in Luke 10:2 is related to the word *apostle.* Indeed, when they returned from their mission, the 12 were called *apostles,* for they had been sent out (Luke 9:10).

I. SENDING OF THE SEVENTY-TWO (LUKE 10:1, 2)

A. PREPARING THE WAY FOR THE LORD (v. 1)

1. After this the Lord appointed seventy-two others and sent them two by two ahead of him to every town and place where he was about to go.

Occasionally, the Gospel accounts give us a glimpse of the fact that Jesus was accompanied by a large band of followers. Here we learn of at least 72 disciples, beyond the initial 12 apostles, whom Jesus chooses for special service.

The alert reader may notice that while the *New International Version* says 72, other versions of the Bible and a footnote to the *New International Version* say 70, both here and at Luke 10:17. This is because both the numbers 70 and 72 are found in old copies of Luke.

Both 70 and 72 are significant numbers in the Bible. The number 70 is associated with God's timing in years (see Genesis 11:26; Daniel 9:2) and with the number of Israel's elders (Exodus 24:1). The number 72 is 12 multiplied by half of 12. The number 12 is significant because of the previous mission of the 12 in Luke 9:1-10.

There is more strategy involved here than first meets the eye. The large group of 72 is divided into pairs and *sent* to specific places that Jesus plans

---

HOW TO SAY IT

Corinthians. Ko-RIN-thee-unz.
Ezekiel. Ee-ZEEK-ee-ul or Ee-
    ZEEK-yul.
Jerusalem. Juh-ROO-suh-lem.
Samaritan. Suh-MARE-uh-tun.
shalom (Hebrew). shah-LOME.

WHAT DO YOU THINK?

What is the value in conducting ministry in teams today?

to visit *(where he was about to go)*. Thus they, in some sense, prepare those places for Jesus' arrival.

B. WORKING THE HARVEST FOR THE LORD (v. 2)

2. He told them, "The harvest is plentiful, but the workers are few. Ask the Lord of the harvest, therefore, to send out workers into his harvest field.

The harvest is the multitude of potential believers who have not yet heard the good news about Jesus. *The Lord of the harvest* is not someone controlling who believes and who does not. Rather, he is God, to whom those who believe owe their allegiance.

The workers are no more than that. They are not building their own empires or reputations. They are working for the Lord of the harvest, God, and bringing glory to him (compare John 4:35).

LOST HARVEST

I once worked with a church located in the heartland of the American Midwest. While I was there, the senior minister told me a story that he had heard. It seems that a windmill salesman had passed through that farming area in the early part of the nineteenth century. This was long before the days of electrification, and windmills provided the power to draw the needed water. The windmill salesman was quite skilled; he took hundreds of orders.

Unfortunately, the factory he worked for could not produce enough windmills to keep up with his orders. So they fired him. Unwilling to make the adjustments necessary to meet demand, they found it easier simply to get rid of the successful salesman who was putting such pressure upon their factory schedule. A great "harvest" thus was lost!

We chuckle at such shortsightedness. Couldn't the factory simply have added more workers, putting on a second shift? We may ask the same question about the church. Christ still needs messengers to convey the good news about his kingdom.   —J. B. N.

II. TESTING OF THE SEVENTY-TWO (LUKE 10:3-12)

A. TRAVELING IN FAITH (vv. 3, 4)

3. "Go! I am sending you out like lambs among wolves.

No missionary endeavor is without glitches. Such glitches cause participants to be tested in their patience and their faith. Jesus seems to be designing the mission of the 72 to ensure that such testing will take place.

The metaphor *lambs among wolves* indicates that the 72 disciples will be people of peace thrown against violent opposition. Jesus does not raise up an army of warriors to do battle with physical weapons. They are defenseless in this respect.

4. "Do not take a purse or bag or sandals; and do not greet anyone on the road.

A *purse* is a small leather bag to hold coins; thus the 72 are to go without money. A *bag*, carried over the shoulder, is made of cloth or leather; it holds general traveling accessories, such as a change of undergarments. *Sandals* are their footwear, of course; Jesus prohibits any of the 72 from taking along an extra pair. They must travel light.

To *greet* involves stopping and talking with a person going the opposite direction. The teams are to stick to their purpose and not dilly-dally along the way. Jesus gave similar instructions to the 12 apostles when he sent them out earlier: "He told them: 'Take nothing for the journey—no staff, no bag, no bread, no money, no extra tunic'" (Luke 9:3; compare 2 Kings 4:29).

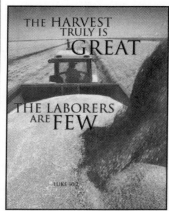

Visual for Lesson 10. *Point to this visual as you introduce the question above.*

B. PARTNERING IN PEACE (vv. 5-7)

5, 6. "When you enter a house, first say, 'Peace to this house.' If a man of peace is there, your peace will rest on him; if not, it will return to you.

To say *Peace to this house* is to offer a blessing (Hebrew *shalom*) upon a household. This means to ask for God's prosperity to rest upon the family in question. If the man of the house is a *man of peace*, a fellow "lamb" seeking God, then this blessing will *rest on him*. If the householder rejects the team, however, there is no harm done because the blessing will be withheld by God to *return to you*.

7. "Stay in that house, eating and drinking whatever they give you, for the worker deserves his wages. Do not move around from house to house.

The teams are to accept with graciousness whatever meals are provided. The idea that *the worker deserves his wages* does not mean that if the home offers low quality food and drink, then that is all the laborers are worth. The quality of ministry is not measured by the level of compensation. Instead, the assumption is that those who minister should have their physical needs taken care of by those to whom they minister (compare 1 Corinthians 9:6-14; 1 Timothy 5:18).

The instruction *do not move around from house to house* is similar to the directive given to the 12 in Luke 9:4. "Staying put" will help eliminate the distraction of always seeking better accommodations.

C. BLESSING WHEN RECEIVED (vv. 8, 9)

8. "When you enter a town and are welcomed, eat what is set before you.

When accepting hospitality, we should be careful not to offend because of our personal pickiness (compare 1 Corinthians 10:27). What may seem unappetizing to you may be considered an expensive delicacy to others. Hospitality is a reciprocal relationship, involving courtesy on both sides. Ultimately we must trust God to provide our daily bread (Matthew 6:11, 25, 26).

EAT WHAT IS SERVED

One health condition I have is a tendency for cholesterol buildup, even when the cholesterol numbers themselves are in the normal range. The result has been two experiences with angioplasty to open up some coronary arteries. A further result is that I am now on a diet restricted in saturated fats. I can live with it easily. I have lost some weight, and in general I feel fine.

However, I also go to East Europe each summer to teach some classes in a mission situation. To my dismay, I have discovered that most people in that area do not understand the meaning of the phrase *low-fat diet*. Sausage, cheese, and other foods high in cholesterol and saturated fats are standard fare.

So I have a dilemma. The people want to honor me as their guest, and they serve me their finest—things I should not eat. For me to refuse would be to insult them.

So I go ahead and eat. I try to be careful, but when a low-fat meal is not possible, I just indulge (moderately). I figure that I am in East Europe for the Lord's business, so the ball is in his court. If he can turn water into wine, he can turn saturated fat into fiber. One night I was served a five-layer torte. I mentally said, "Thank you, Jesus," and I ate it. See 1 Timothy 4:3-5.   —J. B. N.

9. "Heal the sick who are there and tell them, 'The kingdom of God is near you.'

As with the mission of the 12, the 72 are given power over disease (compare Luke 9:1). In the Jewish villages of Jesus' day, this is seen as a sign of God's visitation. This is most clearly demonstrated in the person of Jesus himself (see Luke 11:20), who plans to visit these villages.

DAILY BIBLE READINGS

Monday, Jan. 28—*Instruct the Believers (Psalm 78:1-4)*

Tuesday, Jan. 29—*The Twelve on a Mission (Luke 9: 1-10)*

Wednesday, Jan. 30—*The Seventy-two Go in Pairs (Luke 10:1-3)*

Thursday, Jan. 31—*Travel Lightly in Peace (Luke 10:4-7)*

Friday, Feb. 1—*Proclaim God's Kingdom (Luke 10:8-12)*

Saturday, Feb. 2—*They Returned with Joy (Luke 10: 17-20)*

Sunday, Feb. 3—*See God's Work (Psalm 66:5-12)*

D. DENOUNCING WHEN REJECTED (vv. 10-12)

10, 11. "But when you enter a town and are not welcomed, go into its streets and say, 'Even the dust of your town that sticks to our feet we wipe off against you. Yet be sure of this: The kingdom of God is near.'

If a team is rejected (is *not welcomed*) by a village, that team is to waste no time there. Symbolically, the team members are to wipe the *dust* of that place from their *feet*, indicating that they had received absolutely nothing from the residents (compare Acts 13:51; 18:6). In such a case, the arrival of *the kingdom of God* will not be good news because the villagers rejected the ministry of the 72 disciples.

12. "I tell you, it will be more bearable on that day for Sodom than for that town."

The ancient city of *Sodom* is infamous both for its immorality and for its lack of common hospitality (see Genesis 18:20, 21; 19:5; Ezekiel 16:49, 50). Jesus promises here that that vile city will receive more mercy on the Day of Judgment than the villages that reject the 72 and their mission! (Compare Matthew 10:15; 11:24.)

III. REJOICING OF THE SEVENTY-TWO (LUKE 10:17-20)

A. VICTORY OVER DEMONS (v. 17)

17. The seventy-two returned with joy and said, "Lord, even the demons submit to us in your name."

This mission is for a limited time and includes a planned report-back session. This will be a time for the teams to share their experiences and relate them to Jesus. Jesus will use the information in some way as he continues to plan his itinerary in his travel toward Jerusalem.

Whatever the levels of success, the teams return *with joy*. They have received personal blessing from this experience. The thing that amazes them the most, though, is the reception they had received from *the demons* they had encountered. Those evil spirits had recognized the delegated authority of Jesus in the 72. The devils had been driven out.

B. VICTORY OVER SATAN (vv. 18-20)

18. He replied, "I saw Satan fall like lightning from heaven.

Some see this verse as a reference to a prehistoric event, namely the rebellion of *Satan* in *heaven* and his expulsion to earth. However, this interpretation has more in common with John Milton's *Paradise Lost* than with the information we have in the Bible. The Bible has little information about the origin of Satan and his authority on earth (compare Job 1:6, 7; 2:1, 2; John 12:31; Revelation 12:8, 9).

Jesus' comment indicates that he sees the success of the 72 as a grave blow to the power of Satan. The prince of demons had been able to operate freely in some of the villages, but he is now being fenced in by the power of the coming kingdom of God. The claims of the gospel and the power of Jesus' name are always threats to the people and places controlled by Satan.

Many missionaries today experience unexpected spiritual resistance to their work. In such cases we must believe that the Holy Spirit is more powerful than evil spirits, which are controlled by Satan (compare Acts 13:6-12; 16:16-18).

19, 20. "I have given you authority to trample on snakes and scorpions and to overcome all the power of the enemy; nothing will harm you. However, do not rejoice that the spirits submit to you, but rejoice that your names are written in heaven."

WHAT DO YOU THINK?

How should we respond when our message is not accepted?

The truth that Jesus' missionaries will be protected from the poison of snakebites is shown when Paul survives such an attack (Acts 28:3-6). This is not a blanket promise that those who preach the gospel will never suffer physical harm, even death. The history of missions is full of accounts of martyrs for the cause of Jesus.

Ultimately, though, physical well-being is not of paramount importance. The greatest danger comes from God's authority to consign souls to Hell (Luke 12:5). When we are believers and thus assured that we are not headed for Hell, we truly can say in faith, "nothing can hurt me." Even in the times of greatest trial, we should find joy in knowing that our *names are written in heaven,* in the Lamb's book of life (Revelation 21:27). There is nothing Satan can do to take this away from us.

CONCLUSION

Experiencing and understanding God's call to service is one of the most perplexing issues facing church members. Most assume that "calls of God" are reserved for career preachers, missionaries, etc. Yet we are all called to be faithful and to serve God as the Bible teaches us. This is a universal call, and we should rejoice in it. The more specialized calls to ministry come to relatively few believers. This does not make them elite or specially privileged. It just means they are chosen by God for certain tasks.

I have spent a quarter of a century preparing people for the various ministries of the church. At the same time, I have preached in over 150 local churches. These experiences have caused me to observe two great tragedies.

First, I have found people in ministry positions who were never called by God to be in that ministry. This has caused them to doubt their vocation, act in a tentative manner, and generally cause damage to the people they work with. Ministry training alone does not make a minister.

Second, I have encountered Christians—some who were in their twilight years—who knew they were called by God into ministry *but did not respond to the call.* Such people may have been successful in business and may have lived rich, productive lives. But they have lived regretfully, knowing in their hearts that God intended them to be preachers or missionaries.

In counseling many people through the process of evaluating God's call to ministry, I have found two principles that seem always to apply. First, if God is calling you to ministry, the call does not go away. It is not a one-time invitation. It is not the stirring of the heart at an emotional moment that disappears after a good night's sleep. If God is calling you to be a missionary, for example, that desire will be etched on your heart until the day you die.

Second, if God is calling you to ministry, you will never be satisfied doing anything else. If you are called to be a preacher, circumstances may require you to take a job selling cars or delivering mail at particular points in your life. But you will not be happy doing just that. Your call will cause your heart to yearn for the ministry to which God has appointed you.

Participation in limited ministry experiences is a good way to explore a possible call to ministry. Many churches organize short-term mission trips. Have you ever considered going along on one of these? Such an experience may help you explore the possibility of God's call. Even if God is not calling you to be a career missionary, perhaps he intends that you become an annual mission-trip participant. Maybe he has some other plans for you. In all things, however, we should be guided by Scripture and open to the leading of God's Holy Spirit.

Discovery Learning

This page contains an alternative lesson plan emphasizing learning activities. Classes desiring such student involvement will find these suggestions helpful. The next page is a reproducible activity page to further enhance discovery learning.

INTO THE LESSON

Read an account (or show a very brief video) of a missionary relating how he or she developed an interest in that area of Christian service. The best way to obtain such a testimony is probably via direct e-mail contact with a missionary. You may be able to obtain missionary e-mail addresses from your church office. Make the transition to Bible study by saying, "Today's lesson text shows us how Jesus called and trained missionaries during his time on earth."

Alternative: From the video *End of the Spear,* play the scene where the missionaries are killed. Make the transition to Bible study by saying, "Martyrdom is the ultimate sacrifice that a missionary may be called to make. Of course, there are also other sacrifices. When Jesus called disciples to a short-term mission trip, he cautioned about the sacrifices they would make."

INTO THE WORD

Tell your learners that they will teach portions of the lesson to the entire group. Four teams of 2 to 5 people each are ideal. For classes smaller than 8, double up the tasks; for classes larger than 20, assign the same task to more than one team. Each team is to answer questions about an assigned section of today's text and share its findings with the entire class.

Give each team enough copies of its assignments for each person to have a copy (see below) plus one photocopy of the lesson commentary on its assigned passage. Team 3 will also need a poster board and a marker. (This activity is also in the optional student book.)

Team 1: The Two-Man Teams (v. 1). 1. Why did Jesus send out the new missionaries in teams of two? 2. What value do you see in this team approach? 3. What does this model say to missionary endeavors today, if anything?

Team 2: The Pep Talk (vv. 2-4): 1. Why did Jesus use the metaphor, "lambs among wolves"? 2. What does this metaphor teach missionaries today, if anything? 3. What was the purpose of traveling light? 4. Why did Jesus make the comment about not greeting anyone?

Team 3: The Approach to the Villages (vv. 5-12): 1. What general principles do you find that someone going to the mission field could apply today? (List these on the poster board.) 2. How would you re-phrase this text to be instructions for twenty-first century missionaries?

Team 4: Missionary Reports (vv. 17-20): 1. Given that the reports of the missionaries implied a successful and encouraging trip, why do you think Jesus tempered their celebration by saying that they should focus on their eternal reward? 2. What is the meaning and modern application of Jesus' promise in verse 19?

Allow the teams to report their conclusions.

INTO LIFE

Before class, affix four poster boards to different walls of the room. Write one of these four headings on each poster: *Short-Term Mission Trips, Long-Term Missionaries, Community Outreach Strategies, My Personal Mission Field.* Assign a team to sit near each poster. Distribute these instructions:

Short-Term Mission Trips Team: Make two columns on your poster board. List in the first column the blessings of taking short-term mission trips. In the second column, list a few challenges of these trips. Be ready to share ways to encourage church members to participate in such trips.

Long-Term Missionaries Team: List the names of some missionaries supported by your church or mission board, or list the names of one or more famous missionaries of the past. Then list reasons why those mission works are (or were) important. (Note: This task requires a certain level of knowledge that not everyone in the class may have; you should assign members to the team with this fact in mind.)

Community Outreach Strategies Team: List some ways your church can reach individuals and families in your area with the good news of Jesus. Be ready to tell the class how and why the chosen strategies would be effective.

My Personal Mission Field Team: Each person in your group is to identify one person or group of persons he or she would like to introduce to Jesus. After each such identification, all other group members are to discuss various ways or approaches that could be successful.

Ask one person from the group to summarize his or her team's conclusions to the class. *Alternative:* use teams to complete the Picturing and Practicing Missions activity from the Reproducible Page instead.

Picturing and Practicing Missions

The short-term mission trip exercise that Jesus assigned his followers in Luke 10:1-20 highlights missions today. Your first task: identify missionaries you know (or know of) in various parts of the world. Write those names and the name of the country they serve on the map or margins of the map. Your second task: answer the four questions below.

What does verse 2 teach you about your prayers for the world?

How does verse 3 shape your prayers for missionaries?

What does verse 4 teach you about responsibilities to missionaries?

What sacrifices do missionaries make for their work?

God's Call to the Christian Community
Unit 3: Responding to God's Call
(Lessons 10-13)

CALLED TO REPENT

WHY TEACH THIS LESSON?

So often, people find it very easy to see the faults in other people's lives. Yet they are quick to overlook or ignore faults that lie in their own lives. It appears that there is a built-in self-patience and self-love that causes people to overlook even extreme flaws and wrong actions on their part. It appears that sometimes human beings will go to great trouble to place blame anywhere but on themselves.

Your students need to recognize the importance of daily examining and reexamining their own spiritual lives. Failing to do this can result in believers missing great areas of wrong and disobedience to the Word of God. Today's lesson can allow the Word of God to shine light on their lives and hearts in this regard. As areas of disobedience become apparent, believers' responses must be to make a turnaround. Getting rid of sin starts with repentance.

INTRODUCTION

A. REPENTANCE IN THE BIBLE

"If I have offended anyone by what I did, I'm sorry." In today's world, we often hear this type of apology. While this may be sincere, these words express no regret or remorse for the *actions* that offended. The only regret is that someone *was* offended. This is a far cry from apologizing by saying, "I'm sorry for what I did. It was wrong, and I regret my actions and the damage they have caused. Will you forgive me?" The difference between these two kinds of apologies is *repentance*.

Repentance is a major topic throughout the Bible. Sin is rebellion against God; it is disobedience to his will and commands. Because God is merciful, his primary reaction to our sin is not to punish immediately, but to call for repentance. A constant refrain of God's Old Testament prophets was, "Turn now, each of you, from your evil ways and your evil practices" (Jeremiah 25:5).

A prayer of Solomon describes the first step in repentance: "We have sinned, we have done wrong, we have acted wickedly" (1 Kings 8:47). Repentance begins with recognition of sin. We should not assume that we can determine what is sin by our feelings. The Bible contains many clear statements as to what constitutes sinful behavior.

A second aspect of repentance is to experience a deep-seated sense of sorrow and regret for our sin. This is much more than regret at being caught or sorrow that comes as a result of disastrous sin. It is, rather, a soul-searching realization that our rebellious actions and attitudes constitute a slap in the face of our loving Father in Heaven. Paul describes this as being "sorrowful as God intended" (2 Corinthians 7:9).

A third aspect of repentance is replacing sinful actions with righteous actions. "If a wicked man turns away from his wickedness and does what is just and right, he will live by doing so" (Ezekiel 33:19). John the Baptist

DEVOTIONAL READING:
PSALM 63:1-6
BACKGROUND SCRIPTURE:
LUKE 13:1-9
PRINTED TEXT:
LUKE 13:1-9

LESSON AIMS

After participating in this lesson, each student will be able to:

1. Tell what Jesus said about repentance in light of tragedy and the need to bear fruit.

2. Articulate the biblical connections between sin, repentance, and spiritual fruit.

3. Address one area of his or her life in which repentance and/or the bearing of more fruit is needed.

Feb
10

KEY VERSE

I tell you . . . unless you repent, you too will all perish.
—Luke 13:3

called this the fruit of repentance (Matthew 3:8). True repentance will have tangible results in our lives.

The New Testament uses two concepts to express the idea of repentance. The first is the idea of a change in thinking processes, a renewal of mind (see Romans 12:2). A second way of expressing the idea of repentance is to use the metaphor of the physical act of turning around. The principle is that we cannot be chasing sin and pursuing God at the same time. Paul expressed both of these ideas when he reported that the Gentiles had repented and turned to God (Acts 26:20).

In our world today, repentance seems to be a sadly lacking and increasingly rare commodity. Today's lesson gives us insights into the high level of importance that Jesus placed on repentance. As his followers, we should hear his words carefully.

B. LESSON BACKGROUND

Today's passage from Luke is set during what has been called "the later Judean ministry" of Jesus. Combining Luke 10:1–13:21 with John 7:11–10:39 will give us the fullest picture we can have of this particular facet of Jesus' work. The Gospels of Matthew and Mark do not record Jesus' work during this period.

A theme of Jesus in the two chapters immediately preceding Luke 13 is the need for spiritual preparedness. He taught the necessity for living lives of light, not darkness (Luke 11:35). He exhorted the crowds to realize that they could not hide sin from God (Luke 12:2, 3). He warned of the sin that could not be forgiven (Luke 12:10). He promised strength and words from the Holy Spirit in the time of trials before the religious authorities (Luke 12:11, 12). He illustrated the folly of a man who cared more for his wealth than for his soul (Luke 12:16-21). He instructed his followers to be ready for any coming crisis (Luke 12:35).

There is no more significant aspect to spiritual preparation than repentance. The fruitful spiritual life cannot be found without consistent self-examination and purging of sinful attitudes. We cannot love sin and God at the same time; he will not stand for it. God is a jealous God (Deuteronomy 4:24), one who will have nothing to do with the devotion of his people to fictitious gods.

Jesus understood the preaching of repentance to be at the core of his ministry (see Luke 5:32; 24:47). The thirteenth chapter of Luke contains important teaching on repentance. Here we find the words of our Savior on this matter, a man who needed no repentance because he was without sin.

I. SIN, TRAGEDY, AND REPENTANCE (LUKE 13:1-5)

When a great tragedy occurs, is it God's punishment for sin? Is catastrophe God's way of bringing people to repentance? These are two very different questions. The assumptions behind them are the focus of this section.

A. PILATE AND THE GALILEANS (vv. 1-3)

1. Now there were some present at that time who told Jesus about the Galileans whose blood Pilate had mixed with their sacrifices.

The message Jesus receives comes from *some* of those who are accompanying him on his way to Jerusalem (but they are not necessarily his disciples). They relate the report of a recent atrocity in Jerusalem, where the Roman governor, Pontius *Pilate*, had slaughtered some Jewish *Galileans* within the

---

HOW TO SAY IT

Babylon. BAB-uh-lun.

Deuteronomy. Due-ter-AHN-uh-me.

Ezekiel. Ee-ZEEK-ee-ul or Ee-ZEEK-yul.

Galileans. Gal-uh-LEE-unz.

Isaiah. Eye-ZAY-uh.

Jeremiah. Jair-uh-MY-uh.

Nehemiah. NEE-huh-MY-uh.

Pontius Pilate. PON-SHUS or PON-ti-us PIE-lut.

Siloam. Sigh-LO-um.

Siloamites. Sigh-LO-uh-mites.

Solomon. SOL-o-mun.

Zechariah. ZEK-uh-RYE-uh.

sacrificial areas of the temple. Pilate is known to have little hesitation in using Roman military personnel to crush any resistance to his rule.

The incident is offensive in two ways. First, the brutality of a Roman massacre of Jews is a reminder of the fact that the Jews are not free; they are captives in their own land to the Roman overlords. Thus it is a political outrage. Second, the fact that the incident took place within the temple is a sacrilege, possibly involving the presence of Gentiles (the Roman soldiers who did the killing) in forbidden parts of the temple. Thus, it is also a religious outrage.

2. Jesus answered, "Do you think that these Galileans were worse sinners than all the other Galileans because they suffered this way?

Jesus responds by turning the focus from the perpetrator (Pilate) to the victims (these Galileans). Jesus wants his listeners to consider why this incident happened. Were the victims more sinful than the general population, thus deserving of God's punishing wrath? Were the Romans being used as an instrument of God's justice? The issue thus ceases to be a political question. It is now a doctrinal question.

3. "I tell you, no! But unless you repent, you too will all perish.

Jesus answers his own question. He tells the audience that this is not a matter of the level of sinfulness found among the massacre victims. All men and women are sinners. All unrepentant sinners will eventually perish, for the only eternal reward for sin is death (Romans 6:23).

B. Siloamites and the Tower (vv. 4, 5)

4. "Or those eighteen who died when the tower in Siloam fell on them—do you think they were more guilty than all the others living in Jerusalem?

Jesus now moves to another incident: the collapse of a certain *tower* in *Jerusalem* that had killed 18 people. We have no other details about this tragedy. Some theorize that this tower was part of the wall of the city near the pool of *Siloam*. This pool is located about 600 yards south of the temple precincts in Jesus' day. Jesus' point is that the tower catastrophe was not God's way of punishing its victims.

The mention of Siloam brings out an interesting connection to the story of the man born blind that is found in John 9. This event is in the past as Jesus now speaks. Some in the crowd may know that this man was healed when he washed in the pool of Siloam (John 9:7). The disciples of Jesus thought this man's blindness was the result of sin (John 9:1, 2). Jesus did not accept their "sin causes blindness" conclusion there. And he does not tolerate the "sin causes catastrophe" argument here.

5. "I tell you, no! But unless you repent, you too will all perish."

The language of this verse is identical to Jesus' statement in Luke 13:3, above. The point is the same: sin is not a comparison game where we attempt to point fingers at who is the worst. The need for repentance is universal. The alternative is eternal death. As Paul phrased it, "death reigned" (Romans 5:14) because of the widespread nature of unforgiven sin and unrepentant sinners.

Comparing Sins

Humans seem to have such a knack for making biased comparisons and drawing self-justifying conclusions! The fictional Henry Higgins in *My Fair Lady* reveals this trait nicely when he sings, "Why Can't a Woman Be More Like a Man?" In the song he admits that men have their minor flaws, but when all is said and done, it is men who should be imitated by women and not the reverse.

What Do You Think?

What are some areas in which we as individuals need to repent? What about as a church? What will happen when we do?

What Do You Think?

What is the danger of seeing all tragedies as direct punishments for sin? How do we correct this problem?

What Do You Think?

What are we often tempted to do instead of repenting? How do we overcome this?

Visual for Lesson 11. *Have this visual on display as you ask your learners about spiritual U-turns they have made.*

That kind of comparison makes for a humorous movie script, but it is deadly when it evolves into a game of comparing sins. We all know of people who we think commit more sins than we do. The temptation is both to count their sins and to rank-order those sins (on a scale of mild to horrible). The end result of this comparison game is to conclude that we personally are "not really that bad." Won't God be gracious to us because we are such nice people?

Jesus' words confront those guilty of such smug self-satisfaction. Instead of self-justifying comparisons, we need the constant reminder to repent. We are all sinners. And the penalty for all unrepented sin is eternal destruction. The best time to repent is always now.   —J. B. N.

II. REPENTANCE, FRUIT, AND PATIENCE (LUKE 13:6-9)

If personal tragedy and pain are not God's ways of punishing sin, then why do we suffer? Does God ever use our misfortunes to accomplish his purposes? These are the questions that Jesus now explores in his Parable of the Barren Fig Tree.

A. TREE WITH NO FRUIT (v. 6)

6. Then he told this parable: "A man had a fig tree, planted in his vineyard, and he went to look for fruit on it, but did not find any.

It may seem confusing to find *a fig tree* in a *vineyard* rather than an orchard, but we should not be surprised. Farmers in the ancient world plant several kinds of crops to guard against disaster if a single crop fails. Planting several crops also provides a variety of food for their own families.

The language here does not imply that the farmer himself planted the fig tree, but simply that he owned a vineyard where a fig tree had been *planted*, perhaps by a previous owner. This may be a single tree intended to produce figs for the farmer's family, whereas the surrounding grapevines produce grapes to be sold.

Vineyards are planted in patches of ground that are especially fertile. A fig tree will "use up" the ground where at least one grapevine (and perhaps more) can be cultivated. Thus, the farmer is anxious to gauge the productivity of his tree. We see this concern as he comes to seek *fruit on it.*

B. OWNER AND HIS PATIENCE (vv. 7, 8)

7. "So he said to the man who took care of the vineyard, 'For three years now I've been coming to look for fruit on this fig tree and haven't found any. Cut it down! Why should it use up the soil?'

The task of the hired laborer or servant charged with the *care of* the *vineyard* is to maximize the field's productivity. As we will learn, he is well acquainted with the unproductive *fig tree* and has faith in its potential for bearing fruit.

Some who read this lesson will know far more about fruit trees than this lesson writer does! I can say this much, though. Flanking the entrance to my driveway are two apple trees, one on each side. They are of different (but unidentified) varieties. Some years they both produce fruit. Some years neither one produces fruit. Some years the west tree produces fruit and the east tree doesn't (or vice versa). Why is this? I don't know.

When neither tree had more than a couple of apples in one particular year, I contemplated replacing them with ornamental cherry trees. I decided to wait, though, and the next year they each had a bumper crop. But to wait *for three years*? No way! After three years of no apples, I would declare them lost causes.

8. "'Sir,' the man replied, 'leave it alone for one more year, and I'll dig around it and fertilize it.

The one tending the vines and the tree pleads for his tree. He offers to carefully *dig around it* (aerate the soil) and *fertilize it*. We are not told why, but we see something that can only be described as love in his care for the barren fig tree.

This imagery helps unfold the meaning of the parable. The owner of the vineyard and the tree is God himself, the Lord God of Israel. The barren fig tree is the nation of Israel; this reminds us of Isaiah's parable of the vineyard, which casts Israel as the field that produces an unacceptable crop (Isaiah 5:1-7). The one tending the tree is Jesus.

In context, the owner (God) had shown extraordinary patience with his unproductive tree (Israel), tolerating three years of failure. The standard procedure is to remove the tree after the second year of no fruit. But now the caretaker (Jesus) pleads for a fourth year. He desperately hopes his tree (Israel) will begin to bear fruit that is pleasing to God (compare Luke 6:44).

C. FRUIT OF REPENTANCE (v. 9)

9. "*If it bears fruit next year, fine! If not, then cut it down.*"

The owner agrees to give the tree one more year, one last chance. The stakes are high, though. If there is no *fruit* for a fourth straight year, the tree will be cut down. It will have little potential use except as firewood (compare Luke 3:9). Although fire is not mentioned here, Jesus' hearers know that this is the inevitable result for unproductive fruit trees.

In the Old Testament, Israel's lack of repentance resulted in the national disaster of the destruction of Jerusalem and the captivity in Babylon (see Zechariah 7:8-14). A second destruction, this one by the Romans, will occur in AD 70, only some 40 years after Jesus tells this parable. Sadly, the tree of Israel will indeed be cut down.

The application to individuals is obvious. There is no question but that God is incredibly patient with his unrepentant sons and daughters (compare Nehemiah 9:30). God wants all to come to repentance (2 Peter 3:9). God's *patience,* however, is not the same thing as *permanent tolerance*. God awaits our repentance. God watches for evidence (fruit) of our changed, repentant hearts. Yet at some point, at a time determined by God alone, this period of patience will end. This will seem sudden and unexpected to us, "like a thief" in the night (2 Peter 3:10). If we ignore repentance, we will not be ready for this "day of the Lord."

EXPECTATIONS

Figs are one of the earliest domesticated fruits. Secular records from about 2500 BC refer to figs, as do some of the earliest narratives of the Old Testament. The Spanish brought figs with them when they established a mission at San Diego in 1769. The most common variety of fig was called the *Mission* because of its association with the Spanish missions in California. More variety in figs eventually arrived, including the *Sari Lop,* from Smyrna, Turkey.

But early attempts to grow the Sari Lop in California were a failure. The trees, for some reason, did not produce. As a result, many of the trees were torn up and disposed of as worthless. But some people were not willing to give up on the newcomer. As later discovery proved, it was an issue of pollination. Once that was figured out, the Sari Lop trees were a great success in California (www.nafex.org/figs.htm).

We like reading success stories! But it is safe to assume that if the pollination issue could not have been resolved with the Sari Lop, then the patience of the orchard owners would have run out. A tree that bears no fruit is not worth

WHAT DO YOU THINK?

What can we learn about the caretaker (Jesus) that should serve as a model for us as we interact with those caught in lives of sin?

WHAT DO YOU THINK?

In what ways do you bear fruit to demonstrate that you truly have repented? Or is it prideful to point out your own fruit? Why, or why not?

PRAYER

Merciful Father, we confess our lack of repentance. We confess that there are areas in our lives that we have not totally allowed to come under your control.

Most of all, we confess that your patience with us is far more than we deserve. Your mercies are everlasting. Your steadfast love endures forever. Through your power and presence, give us hearts of repentance and grant to us the capacity to produce fruit in our lives. We pray this in the name of the one who bore the guilt of our sins on the cross, Jesus Christ, amen.

the space it takes up in the orchard and is certainly not worth the caretaker's time. Does this warning sink in?   —J. B. N.

CONCLUSION

Why do bad things happen to good people? Some may think that Christians should be entitled to a special, protective relationship with God that exempts us from personal pain and tragedy. Yet the people of Christ's church live with heartbreak on a continual basis. The joy of childbirth is changed into the grief of crib death. A family's normal existence is shattered by a drunk driver. Financial stability is lost due to unemployment. The list goes on.

A few years ago, a good friend's house was destroyed when a windstorm caused a tree in his neighbor's yard to fall on it. Fortunately, no one was hurt, but there was no way he could have foreseen or avoided this accident. He is a fine person, a leader in his church, a faithful husband, and a wonderful father. Why did this happen to his family?

When we evaluate such tragedies, there are two big mistakes we are likely to make. First, some believe that God causes such events as direct punishment for some type of hidden sin. Today's lesson is a rebuttal to this way of thinking. We are all sinners. If God were constantly punishing sin with tragic consequences, we should be suffering the unspeakable on a daily basis. To believe that God immediately punishes sin with pain is to misunderstand his patient desire for us to repent.

Second, some think that God is unable to prevent our misfortunes and doesn't really care about our suffering. It is easy to feel abandoned when we are in the deepest abyss of sorrow or fear. But this also misunderstands the nature of God. God is sovereign, the master of the universe. Nothing is beyond his control. God is loving, the Father who sacrificed his own Son for us. He will not abandon us in the time of trial. "For the Lord your God is a merciful God; he will not abandon or destroy you or forget the covenant with your forefathers, which he confirmed to them by oath" (Deuteronomy 4:31).

In the end, we may not completely understand the *why* of tragedy, except to remember that we live in a sinful, rebellious, and imperfect world. There is no simple answer, because sin can have both direct and collateral damage to our lives.

Is it possible, however, to understand that God sometimes *uses* tragic events to bring people to repentance? Almost all people will eventually suffer in a way that rocks them to their emotional core. Will we respond by shaking our fist in anger at God? Or will we better understand our utter dependence on him and turn our wayward hearts toward home? Will we accept the reality of life's pain and turn to the one who gives comfort? "You will keep in perfect peace him whose mind is steadfast, because he trusts in you" (Isaiah 26:3).

Yes, we cry when our friend dies because it hurts us deeply. But we must hold on to our eternal hope. We have "a faith and knowledge resting on the hope of eternal life, which God, who does not lie, promised before the beginning of time" (Titus 1:2). We are to be in constant self-examination for those actions and attitudes that separate us from the one who will comfort us the most. This is the fruit of repentance.

The words of the prophet Joel are particularly eloquent for bringing this lesson to a close: "Rend your heart and not your garments. Return to the Lord your God, for he is gracious and compassionate, slow to anger and abounding in love" (Joel 2:13).

THOUGHT TO REMEMBER

God awaits life-changing repentance.

Discovery Learning

This page contains an alternative lesson plan emphasizing learning activities. Classes desiring such student involvement will find these suggestions helpful. The next page is a reproducible activity page to further enhance discovery learning.

INTO THE LESSON

Give each of the first eight learners who arrive a sheet of paper with one of the following words printed on it in bold lettering: *Unless, you, repent, you, too, will, all, perish.* Ask the learners to work together to unscramble the words to make a well-known Scripture statement. If necessary, they may look in Luke 13:1-9 to find these words.

Ask your learners to display the words by standing in front of the class in the correct order. Tell the class that this verse is part of the thrust of today's lesson. The lesson deals with two major issues: God's expectations of his followers and the problem of bad things happening to people thought to be good.

INTO THE WORD

Activity #1. Give each student an index card with one of these letters printed on it: *R, E, P, E, N, T.* Also write the word *repent* vertically down the center of the board.

Tell the class that together you will build an acrostic of this word. Give these directions: "For the letter you have received, identify a descriptive word in today's text that characterizes issues of repentance. The letter assigned to you may be any part of the word you choose. An example: You may use the word *sinners* for the letter *R.* Then be ready to tell why you selected that word." (For classes larger than six students, repeat the letters. A similar activity is found in the optional student book.)

As students report their chosen words, write the words on the board as part of the acrostic. Start by writing one word for each letter. After each letter has an associated word, go back and write additional words beside the appropriate letters. Be sure each student explains why he or she chose each word.

Activity #2. Early in the week, recruit two people to participate in research-and-report activities. The task of the learner delivering *report A* is to help the class understand the concept of *repentance.* The learner is to read ahead of time Luke 13:1-9 and a photocopy of the lesson Introduction. Then the learner is to prepare a brief presentation for the class. This presentation should use visuals to help the class grasp (1) the different kinds of repentance found in everyday apologies and (2) the steps in the process of biblical repentance.

Introduce this segment of the lesson by telling your learners that the class needs some background on the word *repentance* as used in the Bible. Then allow your presenter to explain the results of the research.

Activity #3. The second learner you recruited (see above) will deliver *report B.* This report will help the class understand why bad things happen to people thought to be good. The learner doing this research is to read ahead of time Luke 13:1-9 and a photocopy of the lesson's Conclusion. Then he or she is to prepare visuals to help the class understand (1) the issue and (2) the big mistakes people often make in coming to grips with this issue.

Before *report B* is delivered, read aloud Jesus' statement in verses 1-4 from today's text. Explain that these words raise the question that some ask about why bad things happen to people thought to be good. After *report B,* you may wish to conclude this part of the lesson by asking class members to identify and pray for people who have experienced tragedies in their lives.

INTO LIFE

State: "Let's talk about bearing fruit and repentance. If the church is to bear fruit, where do you think our church does well? And where does it need to repent (change directions) and focus more of her energy?" You may wish to write these questions on the board. (Similar questions are included in the optional student book.)

While the class discusses the question, circulate throughout the room, distributing index cards. Say, "We will now focus on our personal lives. Each person is to identify an area of life where he or she feels a need to bear more fruit for the kingdom of God. Some ideas may include more time in service, winning a family member, or having a stronger testimony at work."

Ask your learners to write just one word on the top of the index card that will remind them of this need. Then they are to write a prayer thanking God for patience as they grow and for increased commitment to the task they have identified.

Alternative: have your learners complete instead the Everyday Issues with Eternal Significance activity from the Reproducible Page. They can work in pairs or small teams. Distribute copies of the Patience and Urgency exercise from the Reproducible Page as learners depart.

Everyday Issues with Eternal Significance

In today's text (Luke 13:1-9), Jesus raises practical and pointed issues and principles for everyday living. Read the verses that include the words printed below. Then write a note in the thought bubble identifying the issue or principle for living that is raised for everyday life.

Patience and Urgency

At some point in time, determined by God alone, his patience will end. Who do you know who needs to repent of sin and accept the Lord's grace? It may even be yourself. Write a two-sentence prayer for that person, including a commitment to help that one understand the importance of his or her decision.

_____

_____

God's Call to the Christian Community
Unit 3: Responding to God's Call
(Lessons 10-13)

CALLED TO BE HUMBLE

LESSON 12

WHY TEACH THIS LESSON?

If we get the wrong idea of what humility is, think of what could happen. We may end up in a state of self-debasement, putting ourselves down. We may end up walking around with our eyes to the ground, refusing to look up. Believers need to know that Christian humility is simply faithful obedience to the Word and Spirit of God. It is being willing to obey God fully no matter what the cost. It is following God's Word and will wherever that may lead as we give him the credit. The Lord Jesus Christ fully obeyed God, even to the point of going to the cross. Through Christ's humble obedience, salvation came to the world.

Believers who grasp the full significance of humility will obey the Lord faithfully in every area of their lives. This brings about the will of God in the world and builds the kingdom of God. Today's lesson offers us help on this very issue.

INTRODUCTION

A. AWARDING OURSELVES

Across the street from my office is a small business that started as a trophy shop. For years it supplied the community with bowling statuettes, trophies for Little League, and engraved paraphernalia for sports tournaments.

Recently, though, it has become an awards business, supplying companies with plaques, engraved paperweights, and other gear to be used as motivational tools for employees. This part of the business is based on the belief that ongoing praise for employee performance will result in higher levels of sales, service, and profits.

That this approach is often effective serves as a commentary on our world today. We have become a society that craves recognition and praise. We value being honored. This is not new or unusual. What is sad, though, is that this overshadows the satisfaction that comes from humble service to others.

One can rarely surf the channels of cable television these days without encountering some type of awards show. Awards are given by academies. Honors are bestowed by virtue of the people's choice. The voting is often controversial, and this just adds to the appeal of the show. Some wags think that we'll eventually see *The Awards Show Channel*, where those who like this type of programming will be able to watch it continually!

Our fascination with watching others receive awards is related to another strong trend in today's world: rewarding ourselves. One commercial for a builder of expensive houses says that we should purchase one of their homes "because life has its rewards." It is the oldest marketing trick in the book: getting us to believe that we *deserve* to be rewarded (or to reward ourselves).

Should Christians participate in this practice of self-indulgent rewarding? If we do good things and end up being recognized and honored, isn't that a positive thing? Are we less than whole if we are not praised? Today's text reveals the teachings of Jesus on this subject.

DEVOTIONAL READING:
PSALM 25:1-10
BACKGROUND SCRIPTURE:
LUKE 14:1-14
PRINTED TEXT:
LUKE 14:1, 7-14

LESSON AIMS

After participating in this lesson, each student will be able to:

1. Identify the marks of humility and lack of humility in today's text.

2. Paraphrase Jesus' illustration of the banquet for the twenty-first century.

3. Make a plan to meet a need without expectation of repayment.

Feb
17

KEY VERSE

For everyone who exalts himself will be humbled, and he who humbles himself will be exalted.   —Luke 14:11

B. LESSON BACKGROUND: JESUS' "REPUTATION"

Luke 14 is set within a period of time that some call "the later Perean ministry" of Jesus. Luke 13:22–19:28 is the most comprehensive of the four Gospel accounts in documenting this period of time. In Luke 14, Jesus stopped for Sabbath-day dinner at the home of an unnamed Pharisee, an important religious leader in his community. As we read the chapter, we realize that this was not a simple matter of hospitality. The Pharisee and his comrades were testing Jesus.

Two years earlier, Jesus had challenged the Pharisees on two important points. First, he had been willing to share meals with people the Pharisees saw as unacceptable (see Luke 5:30). Second, Jesus had shown that laws regarding the keeping of Sabbath were not to be understood absolutely (see Luke 6:2). More recently, Jesus had denounced the practices of the Pharisees and other religious leaders in no uncertain terms (Luke 11:37-52).

As a result, the Pharisees began "to oppose him fiercely and to besiege him with questions, waiting to catch him in something he might say" (Luke 11:53, 54). The Pharisees had labeled him as a Sabbath-breaker, one who followed the Jewish law in a careless, casual manner (see Luke 13:14). In short, they saw Jesus as one who ran with a bad crowd and had no respect for the law.

C. LESSON BACKGROUND: SYMBOL AND SHAME

Two hallmarks of the ancient world are important for putting today's lesson in context. The first is the symbolic power of table fellowship. Today we might sit in a fast-food restaurant and "share" a meal with anyone who sits nearby. We don't know of their character, and we don't care. But for the Jews of Jesus' day, to eat with someone signified tacit approval of that person and his or her behavior.

By contrast, to refuse to eat with someone was a sign of disapproval and rejection of that person. Jesus' willingness to eat with some disreputable characters was both a source of consternation for the Pharisees and a sign of his acceptance of those people (see Luke 15:1, 2; 19:7).

Second, people in the ancient world were very mindful of the concept of *shame*. Today it is hard to find a person concerned about shame. The media parades shameless public leaders and celebrities in front of us daily. Many behaviors once thought shameful now pass as normal. The recognition received for outrageous public behavior is seen as a positive thing—"a good career move"—for some celebrities.

But in the tight-knit communities of Jesus' day, to be shamed had long-term consequences. If a shameful act were exposed, the shame would fall upon the entire family and perhaps upon an entire village (compare Matthew 1:19; Luke 13:17). To act purposely in a shameful manner was unthinkable. Avoidance of shame was every bit as strong a motivation as the quest for honor. This understanding of shame and honor is a key to understanding Jesus' Parable of the Wedding Banquet.

I. HUMILITY THROUGH WATCHING JESUS (LUKE 14:1)

1. One Sabbath, when Jesus went to eat in the house of a prominent Pharisee, he was being carefully watched.

The exact location of the event that is about to unfold is not specified. All we know for sure is that it occurs at the home *of a prominent Pharisee*, probably a well-known leader and teacher (compare Luke 11:37). The Pharisees were a "lay" movement, meaning they all had other professions and did not make their living from being Pharisees. Some lived in small, out-of-the-way places.

Jesus has been invited to this man's *house* on the *Sabbath*. This is a banquet-style meal with many guests. Luke lets the reader know that this meal is not intended to honor Jesus or to hear him teach. It is a contrived situation where the Pharisees watch Jesus closely. In other words, they are testing him in order to find a flaw. This may be "payback" for the recent event where they had been shamed by Jesus (Luke 13:17 or John 10:22-39). But instead of finding an inconsistency in Jesus' words and actions, they are about to learn a powerful lesson in humility.

II. HUMILITY THROUGH CHOICE (LUKE 14:7-11)

A. SEEKING HONOR (vv. 7-9)

7. When he noticed how the guests picked the places of honor at the table, he told them this parable:

To choose *the places of honor* speaks to the strict traditional codes when it comes to seating at such a banquet. The head of the household (in this case the prominent Pharisee of v. 1) is the host; he takes a seat at the center of the head table. The place of greatest honor is the seat that is at the host's right hand. The honor associated with other seats is in relationship to a seat's distance from the host. This is partly based on the assumption that the most important conversations and the best food are found in proximity to the host.

The Jews of Jesus' day do not really sit in chairs at a table as we do. They instead recline on low benches or couches around a table. They use their left arms to prop themselves up, thus freeing their right hands to take food from common bowls or platters. The places of least honor may not be around the table at all, but involve sitting on the floor.

The most foundational meaning of the word *parable* is "comparison." Here, Jesus does not tell a story-parable, but gives a comparison between the jockeying for position around the table and God's call in people's lives for humility in actions and service.

There must be some controversy among the guests over seating arrangements for Jesus to notice and make comments. Perhaps a guest of great honor has arrived unexpectedly and late, causing a chain reaction of demoting people to less honorable seats.

In any case, there is some type of scrambling for seats based on individual desire for respect (compare Matthew 23:6). Jesus seizes upon this mini-chaos as a teaching opportunity.

8. "When someone invites you to a wedding feast, do not take the place of honor, for a person more distinguished than you may have been invited.

The host is master in his own home, and he has unquestioned authority to determine seating order. This is his opportunity to honor those whom he wants to honor and, perhaps, dishonor those whom he thinks are taking advantage of his hospitality. It undoubtedly will be embarrassing to be bumped from one of the most honorable seats!

9. "If so, the host who invited both of you will come and say to you, 'Give this man your seat.' Then, humiliated, you will have to take the least important place.

Losing a seat of honor may involve more than just "going down a level." For example, if there were a banquet with 50 guests and the host determined that the guest in seat #3 did not deserve that much honor, it does not mean that that guest would be pushed down to seat #5 or #8. It may mean that that guest would be sent to the *least important place*: seat #50—probably a seat on the floor. This would be a public indignity and an opportunity for

WHAT DO YOU THINK?

In what ways are people watching us as Christians? Why are they watching? How do you conduct yourself with these realizations in mind?

WHAT DO YOU THINK?

In what ways have you been guilty of jockeying for position at work and at church? How have you made progress in correcting this problem?

WHAT DO YOU THINK?

What are some ways that higher and lower seats present themselves in modern culture? Do you find it difficult to take the lower seat instead of the higher seat? Why, or why not?

HOW TO SAY IT

Deuteronomy. Due-ter-AHN-uh-me.

Perean. Peh-REE-un.

Pharisees. FAIR-ih-seez.

Philippians. Fih-LIP-ee-unz.

quid pro quo. kwid-pro-KWO.

laughter and derision from the more honored guests. It would be a moment of shame not quickly forgotten.

PRIDE AND PLACE

The American Civil War provides numerous illustrations of human characteristics. Some are good, some are bad, many are somewhere in between. An interesting study in contrasts is that of the personal demeanors of Generals George A. Custer and Ulysses S. Grant.

Custer graduated from West Point in 1861 and was immediately sent off to war. He went through the ranks of second lieutenant to major general in less than four years. When he assumed command of his brigade in 1863, he was dressed in a showy uniform of black velveteen, gold braid from his elbow to his wrist, a blue sailor shirt with silver stars sewn on, and a red necktie. He was never accused of humility.

By contrast, General Grant was never accused of flamboyancy. Also a West Point graduate, he served in the Mexican War of 1846–1848, left the army, but came back in 1861. Victorious in several battles in the western theater, he came east in 1864 and ultimately forced Robert E. Lee to surrender in 1865. At the surrender, Grant wore the mud-splattered uniform of a private, with shoulder straps the only indication of his rank.

Custer dressed to impress; Grant (who later became president) cared only to succeed. Custer wanted to be noticed; Grant wanted only to win. If they both had been invited to a wedding banquet in the first century, one wonders who would have pushed up to the head table and who would have drifted to the back.   —J. B. N.

B. SEEKING HUMILITY (vv. 10, 11)

10. "But when you are invited, take the lowest place, so that when your host comes, he will say to you, 'Friend, move up to a better place.' Then you will be honored in the presence of all your fellow guests.

Jesus presents an alternative scenario of being asked to *move up* from a common seat to a place of honor. Yet what Jesus is teaching is nothing new; see Proverbs 25:6, 7.

We may imagine a host looking around and seeing humble Bob in the corner, sitting on the floor. The host may think, "That Bob is a solid guy; he deserves better." He then calls Bob publicly to sit next to him, and thereby honors him in the eyes of everyone present. Rather than embarrassment and snickers from the other guests, they are thinking, "Bob is a lucky guy. I wish I were sitting where he is." Bob *will be honored* by receiving the respect of his *fellow guests.*

11. "For everyone who exalts himself will be humbled, and he who humbles himself will be exalted."

Moses taught Israel that the one *who exalts himself* has done so by forgetting God (Deuteronomy 8:11-14). If praise and honor are rightly given to God, we have no right to take them upon ourselves. God will shame the one who seeks honor at God's expense (see Psalm 35:26).

The flip side of this is that God is not unmindful of people who live lives of intentional humility. There is no need to toot our own horn to get God's attention for our humble deeds of service (compare Matthew 23:12; Luke 18:14).

We may ask ourselves what it means to seek humility. Is this just a sick way of attempting to receive honor through self-abasement? No. True humility is not concerned with honor at all. No task is too degrading. No person is unimportant. No personal pleasure is so enticing that it cannot be postponed or lost. Service motivated by humility has its own rewards.

he that **humbleth** himself **shall be** exalted

Visual for Lesson 12. *Use this visual as a discussion starter on ways to serve those who can't repay us.*

III. HUMILITY THROUGH SERVICE (LUKE 14:12-14)

A. SELF-SERVING BANQUET HOST (v. 12)

12. Then Jesus said to his host, "When you give a luncheon or dinner, do not invite your friends, your brothers or relatives, or your rich neighbors; if you do, they may invite you back and so you will be repaid.

Jesus now directs his attention to the banquet *host*, the unnamed Pharisee. Jesus draws the man's attention to four groups that are typical guests at social meals: *friends* (social peers, often those someone has grown up with), *brothers* (immediate family members), *relatives* (extended family members), and *rich neighbors* (those who may be able to offer financial benefits).

There is nothing inherently wrong with entertaining these people. Rather, Jesus finds fault with the motive for hospitality: the expectation of being *repaid*. Such a *dinner* is not a lavish social event given for the enjoyment of all who attend. It is, rather, a calculated attempt to obligate the attendees. In the future, they must bless the host in some way in return.

B. OTHER-SERVING BANQUET HOST (vv. 13, 14)

13, 14. "But when you give a banquet, invite the poor, the crippled, the lame, the blind, and you will be blessed. Although they cannot repay you, you will be repaid at the resurrection of the righteous."

Jesus now offers a markedly different foursome of potential guests for a private *banquet*. Why not invite those who are seen as social misfits and outcasts? Why not make up the guest roster from the village's *poor, crippled, lame,* and *blind*?

No socially respectable person like the Pharisee would consider allowing such people into his banquet hall. If this were the entire guest list, then the host would even have to place a person who is *poor* or handicapped in the place of honor at his right hand!

Jesus uses somewhat exaggerated language here to make a point. He is not saying that we can never feel right about having a family dinner unless we include some homeless people. His point is that we should not consider ourselves to be practicing true hospitality if we serve only those who can return the favor. Service that is pleasing in God's eyes is service that helps those who cannot help us in return.

To do this is necessarily a humbling process. We are willingly acting as servants for those who may be many rungs beneath us on the social ladder. It is not a false humility, but a practical, legitimate humbling of oneself in favor of the needs of other people. It is to be judged by one thing: can those whom you are serving *repay you*? Are you expecting to get some tangible benefit out of this act? Or are you willing to wait and meekly trust God to reward your selflessness?

"You scratch my back, and I'll scratch yours" is a common ethic. The fancy term for this is *quid pro quo* (literally, "something for something"). In this way of doing business, there is no such thing as a gift without strings attached. The idea is that if I do something that benefits you, you can be sure that I will expect a benefit in return.

While this may be a necessary part of the normal conduct of business, Jesus does not teach this to his disciples as a way to treat others. Is a man truly a generous host if he expects his generosity to be repaid? Is a woman actually practicing humility if she expects her service to be recognized and honored?

The Bible teaches that there will be reward and honor in Heaven (see Matthew 5:12; 6:20; 1 Peter 4) and hints that there will be levels of reward (Luke 19:11-19). We do not understand this fully, and we must caution

WHAT DO YOU THINK?

What are some practical ways we can care for the poor and needy? What cautions are we to be aware of?

WHAT DO YOU THINK?

How can we guard against seeking quid pro quo *in our lives or in the church?*

PRAYER

Lord, give us hearts that seek to serve without a desire for honor or recognition. Give us hearts that are satisfied with the pleasures of doing your will and receiving praise from you. Give us hearts that are humble and pliable to your will. We pray this in the name of the great servant, Jesus, your Son, amen.

ourselves to remember that we are not granted eternal life in Heaven on the basis of our works. However, we can take hope in the promise that God does not overlook our dedication to service and humility. He has plans to reward us appropriately at the *resurrection of the righteous*.

DELAYED COMPENSATION

Frank Capra's 1946 film *It's a Wonderful Life* is a classic, often seen on TV during the Christmas season. It tells the story of George Bailey, who has given up his dreams in order to run the family-owned lending institution. When thousands of dollars are misplaced and his business is about to be shut down, George considers suicide because his life apparently has been so worthless.

Then Clarence, George's guardian angel, intervenes. Clarence shows him how the entire town would have been different in George's absence. Rather than being worthless, George's life has been a blessing to the town. One thing leads to another, and many friends give him money. Even the crusty bank examiner, moved by the town's love for George, puts his own money into the hat.

The fictional George Bailey was a selfless "giver." In the end he experienced a reward that he could not have imagined. Our heavenly Father is willing and able to reward us in the end. Any blessings we have been denied on earth will be compensated in ways that we surely cannot now imagine! —J. B. N.

CONCLUSION

Have you ever been surprised to find out that certain people have led secret lives of service? Have you ever noticed what unexpected things you learn at memorial services?

In my city I recently learned that the prominent owner of a car dealership had been taking one afternoon a week to read stories to critically ill patients at our children's hospital. He had done this for over 30 years. Another time I became aware that a coworker of mine, a single professional woman, had been funneling her money to needy college students. Over the years, she gave away thousands of dollars anonymously, even though her salary was minimal.

While visiting a certain church, I learned that its quiet but steady head usher had passed away that month. The preacher of the church told me that this man had faithfully come early every Sunday morning to turn on the furnace and warm up the building. He then had stayed to hand out bulletins to those entering the sanctuary. He was a very quiet, shy man, but he had found a way to serve without drawing attention to himself. He had done this for nearly 50 years.

Acts of generosity and service that are designed to garner public attention can do a great deal of good. However, Jesus teaches us that such behavior ultimately is self-serving, and we should not expect God to reward us for them. Nor should we expect to be rewarded by those we serve. Service driven by a humble spirit will persevere, even in the face of ingratitude. True, a thank you makes this path easier to travel, but even this reward should not be expected.

Our greatest example of a humble servant is Jesus himself. Paul tells us that before Jesus' incarnation, he shared equality with God the Father. Yet Jesus did not consider this something to be hoarded or protected. Instead, Paul writes, Jesus assumed a human likeness, the form of a servant. Although a rightful king, Jesus humbled himself and went to the cross obediently, taking on the sins of the world as a sacrifice (Philippians 2:5-8). The result of this is God's exaltation of Jesus above all others (Philippians 2:9). Although we will not be exalted in this way, God promises to reward us too—if we choose the life of a humble servant.

THOUGHT TO REMEMBER

God honors humble service.

Discovery Learning

This page contains an alternative lesson plan emphasizing learning activities. Classes desiring such student involvement will find these suggestions helpful. The next page is a reproducible activity page to further enhance discovery learning.

INTO THE LESSON

Before class prepare the front and back of four poster boards. On the front side, each poster board will have identical headings over three columns. Over the first column on each write *Chosen last (or nearly last) for* . . . Over each of the second columns write *Why?* Over each of the third columns write *I Felt* . . . Write one each of these headings on the backs of the posters: *Practicing Humility at Church, Practicing Humility at Home, Practicing Humility at Work, Practicing Humility in the Community.*

When you are finished, each poster will read the same on the front, but differently on the back. Affix the posters to the wall. Be sure to place them far enough apart to allow several people to view and work on the posters simultaneously. Large classes may need more poster boards, in multiples of the four described.

As learners enter the room, hand each a marker. Encourage each person to write one answer in each of the three columns. Each learner is to identify an activity from childhood for which he or she was chosen last (or nearly last) and the associated feelings. (A similar activity is included in the optional student book.)

To begin the class, review a few of the remarks listed on the posters. Then tell the class it is natural not to want to be last. There is prestige and honor in being chosen first. Even in adult years, we desire the honor of being seated at "the head table." Jesus, however, uses this instinct to teach a lesson in how he prefers us to behave and how to think of others.

INTO THE WORD

Deliver a brief lecture from the Lesson Background. Outline your mini-lecture in the following way:

    I. The Context
    II. The Symbolic Power of the Table
    III. The Sense of Shame and Honor

You may wish to write this outline on the board as you speak.

Next, read today's printed text aloud before asking the following questions. 1. What character trait is Jesus teaching us for 2008? (*expected answer: humility*). 2. What is humility? Define or describe it. 3. What behavior does humility often inspire in life? (*expected answer: service*). 4. If we were to throw a banquet like Jesus described in verse 13, whom would we invite, and how could we fulfill Jesus' wishes literally? (*if needed, give an example of a banquet for nursing home residents who seldom get out; rent vehicles capable of transporting the handicapped*). 5. Why do you think humility is important? 6. Why does Jesus encourage this trait and behavior?

INTO LIFE

Ask your class to think back to a Christian memorial service or funeral service. What specific traits and behaviors were mentioned about the deceased? What stories or testimonials do you remember from the memorial services?

List on the board the traits or behaviors mentioned by class members. If your learners need an example, tell the story from the lesson Conclusion of the quiet, shy man who served by faithfully coming to church early every Sunday to warm up the building and hand out bulletins. This life of service was remembered after he died.

After listing these traits and behaviors, ask learners to recall how often service to other people, the community, and the Lord are mentioned and valued at Christian funerals and memorial services. We as the Lord's people value what he values. Worldly measures of success are seldom mentioned at Christian funerals and memorials.

Next, turn over the four poster boards used in the Into the Lesson segment and reaffix them to the wall. Ask class members to move among the posters, writing practical ideas for demonstrating humility in each context. For example, "parking at the very back of the church parking lot" is an act of humility because it allows others to park closer to the door. (A similar activity is included in the optional student book.)

Quickly review a few of the ideas written on the posters. Then ask each learner to select something on the lists that he or she has seldom or never done before and commit to doing it. To conclude the lesson, ask the class members to do a "neighbor nudge" and share what they have chosen to do to demonstrate humility this week. Ask your learners to form pairs to pray for one another in closing.

Distribute copies of the Hidden, but Not Secret exercise from the Reproducible Page to learners as they depart. This will reinforce today's lesson.

Hidden, but Not Secret

Read Jesus' teaching in Luke 14:1, 7-13. Then for each of the following clues from that text find a word in the grid that answers it. The answers are inverted below.

1. The day of this event: _____.
2. The status of the host among his colleagues: _____.
3. Within Judaism's religious parties, the host was a _____.
4. On this day, Jesus was being carefully _____.
5. The guests picked their place of _____ at the table.
6. The parable's setting was at what kind of feast? _____
7. Jesus cautions about seat selection, "A person more _____ than you may have been invited."
8. The person who may ask you to switch seats: _____.
9. The host may say, "Give this man your _____."
10. When #9 happens, you will be _____.
11. Jesus suggests taking the _____ place for a seat.
12. Then the host may call you _____.
13. Whoever exalts himself will be _____.
14. He who humbles himself will be _____.
15. When you give a _____ or _____, do not invite your friends, brothers, _____, or _____ neighbors.
16. Instead, invite the _____, _____, _____, and the _____.
17. By doing #16, you will be _____ and repaid at the resurrection of the _____.

```
P K S H M K D L D I W A H U X G J J M N
O D Z V M S I P N I G K O Z N N B M M J
Y N T Z C E O E P E S J Y I I Y X I T Q
T O N A D C W K A D E S D V O Q K D Y K
A D G A R T T D G X D D T Q Z J D D C Y
V H R N O V J C B L E S S E D N I L B M
R T C U H W V R D W I N D W X N Z C G N
R N B I B O Y I I S L Q D E M A L J G N
E E S I R A H P N A G B G N D Q L I Q G
L N F E N C O P N U H Z U W J J J T X Y
A I S C A O G L E G O P K F C N J T E A
T M P C R T L E R M S Z Q D R O N O H D
I O H K E W Q D I S T I N G U I S H E D
V R D E H C T A W P J G Q L O W E S T G
E P I N G R C N O E H C N U L R U N V V
S R I G H T E O U S W G H U M B L E D O
U S A B B A T H U M I L I A T E D K Y T
J N T G A Y J U T W T D K M E K G V B M
X V X N Q B O T H T I K Z O Y O B E T K
Z M T Z T V T K M V T Y N X Q Y V U Z X
```

Answers: Sabbath, prominent, Pharisee, watched, honor, wedding, distinguished, host, seat, humiliated, lowest, friend, humbled, exalted, luncheon, dinner, relatives, rich, poor, crippled, lame, blind, blessed, righteous.

God's Call to the Christian Community
Unit 3: Responding to God's Call
(Lessons 10-13)

CALLED TO BE A DISCIPLE

LESSON 13

WHY TEACH THIS LESSON?

Simply put, a disciple is one who knows the Lord Jesus Christ and obeys him. To follow Christ is to discipline oneself in certain ways and concerns in life in order to carry out the Lord's will effectively. Believers must decide over and over again, day after day, to follow Christ.

Your learners should know that decisions and spiritual disciplines determine destiny. Their decisions to follow Christ do not mean that they now simply have a title of honor—that of *disciple*. It means that they will live a life of deciding daily to follow the Lord. They will practice three key spiritual disciplines as they make prayer, the study of God's Word, and obedience to God's Word top priorities in their lives.

It is through disciplines such as these that Christians are able by God's grace to fulfill the call of God on their lives. So believers need to have a clear understanding of the characteristics of a disciple of Christ. That's what today's lesson is all about.

INTRODUCTION

A. LEADERS AND FOLLOWERS

"Lead, follow, or get out of the way!" That old slogan may seem trite, but it is based on a great truth in organizations: many people are neither leaders nor followers. They are uncommitted, uninvolved, and disinterested in the success of the institution. Sadly, this is true in many churches. Churches may have qualified leaders, but not enough committed followers to move forward.

The leader-follower relationship requires two elements. First, there must be a leader, the one in front. Second, there must be a follower, someone not in front, but moving in the same direction as the leader. This simple model means that *following* describes a relationship of subservience.

Followers yield themselves to the direction of the leader. It also means that following requires a living relationship. We do not talk about one rock following the lead of another rock in a rock garden. If nothing is moving, then there is no leader-follower relationship.

A central demand of Christianity is that we be followers of Jesus. This does not imply that we are on some kind of group tour. And it is much more than being a member of a certain family. To follow Jesus is an individual, personal choice. It is both a life commitment and a daily decision.

Because Jesus is not a physical presence in our lives, following him is an act of faith. We believe in him; therefore we follow him. To do this is to acknowledge him as our Lord and Master. To follow Jesus is to be his disciple. Jesus leads us all. We in the church submit ourselves to the lordship of Jesus. It is his church—he paid for it with his blood (1 Corinthians 6:20).

But Jesus also calls some in the church to act as leaders on his behalf. Effective, vibrant churches have committed leaders and followers. Ineffective

DEVOTIONAL READING:
PSALM 139:1-6
BACKGROUND SCRIPTURE:
LUKE 14:25-33
PRINTED TEXT:
LUKE 14:25-33

LESSON AIMS

After participating in this lesson, each student should:

1. Identify some marks of disciples that set them apart from non-disciples.

2. Compare and contrast the cost of discipleship in the first century with the cost in the twenty-first century.

3. Give up one habit, belief, or possession that is distracting him or her from full discipleship.

KEY VERSE

Anyone who does not carry his cross and follow me cannot be my disciple.
—Luke 14:27

Feb
24

churches have a large percentage of bystanders, those who choose neither to lead nor to follow. Such churches become like the rock garden. They may have people in place, but nothing ever changes. No progress is ever made.

This is why *discipleship* is such a crucial issue for the church. The church is to be made up of followers (disciples) of Jesus. They are committed to making more disciples. To do this is to carry out the Great Commission of Matthew 28:19, 20.

B. LESSON BACKGROUND

Church folks are very familiar with the term *disciple*. When we study the New Testament, we quickly encounter the disciples of Jesus. Some of these are later described as *apostles*, and their names are familiar to us: Peter, John, Andrew, etc. It is easy to assume, therefore, that *disciple* is the title of some type of specially qualified follower of Jesus.

To go no further than this is to misunderstand who a disciple was in the world of Jesus. In Jesus' day, the term *disciple* was drawn from the type of educational system they practiced. A disciple was simply the student of a chosen teacher. The teacher in Jesus' Jewish world was known as a *rabbi*. In the New Testament, this term is used many times as a title for Jesus (example: John 3:2). A rabbi had students who followed him and learned from him.

There were other traveling rabbis (teachers) at that time besides Jesus. John the Baptist was also called *rabbi* and had disciples (John 3:26; compare Matthew 9:14). There is a question as to who chose the disciples in the ancient world. Some believe that disciples were hand-selected by the teacher (that is, by invitation only). Others think that potential disciples attached themselves to a teacher by mutual agreement, but that the initial contact was made by the student.

Both ways probably were used. Paul was sent at a young age to study under the famous Jerusalem rabbi Gamaliel (Acts 22:3). This was probably the result of Paul's father's choice and Gamaliel's agreement.

While this relationship existed, Paul was Gamaliel's disciple. The Gospels show Jesus inviting individuals to discipleship with the simple call, "Follow me" (example: Luke 5:27). We also see a time when disciples of Jesus were offended by his message and chose to follow him no longer, thus ending the teacher-disciple relationship (see John 6:66).

Luke 14 is part of Jesus' later Perean ministry. The chapter opens with a challenge to Jesus for healing a man on the Sabbath. Such incidents became occasions for Jesus to give instructions to his disciples and to the crowds. In today's lesson, Jesus addresses the crowds with teachings on the nature of discipleship.

I. COMMITTING OUR ESSENTIALS (LUKE 14:25-27)

A. OUR RELATIONSHIPS (vv. 25, 26)

25. Large crowds were traveling with Jesus, and turning to them he said:

Here we see that the traveling group is more than just Jesus and his original 12 disciples. To be *with Jesus* does not necessarily mean these are all his followers. Yet that does not prevent Jesus from seizing the opportunity to do a little teaching.

In the verses that follow, Jesus begins his teaching by noting two conditions for following him. According to Jesus, failure to meet either one of these conditions means that a potential follower "cannot be my disciple."
26. "If anyone comes to me and does not hate his father and mother, his wife and children, his brothers and sisters—yes, even his own life—he cannot be my disciple.

WHAT DO YOU THINK?

How does Jesus' approach to the multitude differ from the response some churches have toward large crowds? What can churches do better to follow Jesus' example?

This seems to be a very hard saying. Is Jesus truly, literally commanding his disciples to *hate* their closest family members? Is a follower of Jesus required to despise one's *own life* in a very literal sense as well?

A key to understanding today's lesson is to appreciate a practice in speaking and writing known as *hyperbole*. Hyperbole is a technique widely used in the ancient world. It is still used often today. Hyperbole is defined as deliberate exaggeration for the purpose of emphasis. Therefore, hyperbole should not be taken literally.

For example, one may say, "He talks on his cell phone constantly." We would not understand this to mean, "He uses his cell phone every second of every day." What this means is, "He uses his cell phone a lot—much more than most people." Hyperbole thus is not intended to be deceptive. Those who use hyperbole make their point by using a deliberate exaggeration that they expect people to recognize as such.

Jesus uses hyperbole frequently. Sometimes this is very easy to detect. For example, Jesus did not really think that people walked around with literal planks of wood stuck in their eyes (Luke 6:41, 42). To take such statements literally is to misunderstand what Jesus says. In other places, though, identifying hyperbole is not as easy. Today's lesson offers some statements of hyperbole, and this verse is one of them. We must be careful to understand such statements as Jesus intends.

To take the verse before us literally is to miss the nature of discipleship. What Jesus is stressing is that his disciples cannot have divided loyalties (compare Luke 16:13). He or she cannot play the role of *disciple* only when it is convenient. Commitment to Jesus demands that a disciple will choose to follow him in even extreme circumstances. If someone is forced to choose between obeying Jesus or obeying his or her *father and mother,* then that person must choose Jesus (compare Deuteronomy 33:9; Matthew 10:37, 38). If the demands or expectations of our spouses would lead to violation of our commitment to Jesus, then we must choose Jesus.

This is not a call to abandon family relationships as a part of Christian discipleship. Christians can still be the best husbands, sisters, sons, and mothers possible. We can still love our families and cherish our relationships. But we cannot allow family loyalty to override our devotion to Jesus and his teachings.

Sadly, some new believers are forced to make this very choice. To be the only Christian in one's family may result in enormous pressure to compromise one's faith or to live a life of conditional discipleship. Right here is where the fellowship and support of the church becomes vital to successful discipleship.

FAMILY OR DISCIPLESHIP?

Anthony (AD 251–356) is considered to be the father of monasticism—a way of life characterized by voluntary poverty and solitude. He sold the family farm he had inherited from his parents, gave away the proceeds, and went to the desert to become a monastic hermit.

Anthony's activities became typical for many of the monks who followed him, monks who became known as *the Desert Fathers.* These monks lived alone in individual mud huts, content to spend their time in prayer and contemplation. They abandoned all semblance of family life and all association with family members. These early monks took the words of Jesus literally in this regard.

One exception, however, was a monk named Abraham. He had a brother who died, leaving an orphan daughter. Abraham took the 7-year-old girl and

Visual for Lesson 13. *Use this visual to review the unit themes of the quarter and how our 13 lessons fit together.*

WHAT DO YOU THINK?

What are some things you need to hate in order to follow Jesus?

WHAT DO YOU THINK?

Why are there many Christians who seem not to have counted the cost of discipleship? How has the church contributed to this problem? How can the church contribute to a solution?

placed her in an outer room in his cell, communicating with her only through a small window. With the passage of time, he taught her in the ways of monasticism—a life of prayer, praise, and self-restraint.

The monk Abraham did the right thing in providing for his young orphaned niece. But in so doing, we must conclude that he violated a literal interpretation to hate family members. One wonders how he reconciled the conflicting ideals!

—J. B. N.

B. OUR FREEDOM (v. 27)

27. "And anyone who does not carry his cross and follow me cannot be my disciple.

As with verse 26, this saying also ends with *cannot be my disciple*. In this case Jesus uses an even more enigmatic image to portray discipleship: carrying *his cross*. We should remember that the cross at this point in time is not a Christian symbol suitable for jewelry. Rather, it symbolizes the execution of a criminal. A Roman cross represents death. What does Jesus intend by this startling declaration? Does he mean that all true disciples will be asked to give up their lives for the sake of Jesus?

To be a Christian martyr is to die for one's faith in Jesus. When forced to choose between either death or renouncing Christ, the Christian chooses death. Martyrdom is a sad yet noble part of the history of the church. But this verse does not teach that we are less than true disciples if we are not slaughtered for the faith.

This is clarified when we compare the verse with Luke 9:23. There, Jesus equates taking up his cross daily with denying oneself (compare Matthew 16:24; Mark 8:34). We die to self when we accept Jesus' call to discipleship. As Paul puts it, we are crucified with him and he now lives in us, taking control of our lives (Galatians 2:19, 20).

II. ESTIMATING THE EXPENSE (LUKE 14:28-33)

A. COMPLETING A PROJECT (vv. 28-30)

28. "Suppose one of you wants to build a tower. Will he not first sit down and estimate the cost to see if he has enough money to complete it?

Jesus continues his address to the crowds by using some simple analogies to illustrate the *cost* of discipleship. The first one involves a building project. A *tower* is some kind of commercial building, perhaps a guard tower for a valuable vineyard or olive orchard. It is intended to enhance or protect the revenue of the owner in some way.

Many of us have witnessed construction projects that began well, but then languished with half-built edifices that served no one. The cause may have been lack of funds to finish the building. This is why a bank will not lend money for new construction unless it is sure there will be *enough money to complete* the project. A half-completed building is of no use to anyone. It costs a lot of money with no return on the investment.

29, 30. "For if he lays the foundation and is not able to finish it, everyone who sees it will ridicule him, saying, 'This fellow began to build and was not able to finish.'

There can be several community reactions to an unfinished construction project, but Jesus chooses this one: *ridicule*. In Jesus' day, no one would be overly concerned about the ugliness or waste of the failed construction. Instead, neighbors would immediately reflect on the foolishness of a builder who underestimated his final costs and ran out of money.

Despite centuries of hard lessons in this regard, this still happens. In the 1970s, a well-known televangelist began to build a very expensive office tower. His ministry went bankrupt before it was finished.

How foolhardy it is to make a commitment without counting its cost! If one signs a contract to buy a house without any idea how it will be paid for, disaster probably will follow. If one joins a club but can never attend its meetings and cannot afford to pay its dues, expulsion is inevitable. Discipleship is not bought and sold like a commodity, but it has a great cost. This cost must be taken into account before the commitment is made.

WHAT DO YOU THINK?

What is an area in your life that you have not been able to finish? What about in the life of your church? What have you learned from these experiences?

B. WINNING A WAR (vv. 31, 32)

31. "Or suppose a king is about to go to war against another king. Will he not first sit down and consider whether he is able with ten thousand men to oppose the one coming against him with twenty thousand?

Jesus' second analogy for the cost of discipleship involves warfare strategy. History tells us that the number of troops is not always the most important factor in winning battles. For example, Julius Caesar was known to have won important battles with armies that were smaller than those of his enemies. Even so, the rule of thumb for wartime is the more troops available, the better. Most generals are leery of engaging another army with equal forces. To wage war with an army outnumbered two to one is extremely risky. The likely outcome is not just defeat, but the total annihilation of the smaller army.

32. "If he is not able, he will send a delegation while the other is still a long way off and will ask for terms of peace.

The wise king knows when he has no hope for victory. In such circumstances, the best course of action is to seek favorable terms for surrender by sending *a delegation*. With his own army intact, he will still pose a threat to the more powerful king, so he may be given some concessions. But if he fights the battle and loses his army, he will be in no position to expect favorable terms. The terms will be dictated to him.

C. LIVING A LIFE OF DISCIPLESHIP (v. 33)

33. "In the same way, any of you who does not give up everything he has cannot be my disciple."

The point of the analogies in verses 28-32 is that there is a personal cost involved in Christian discipleship. In the verse before us, Jesus again uses hyperbole to reinforce his point. By *give up everything,* he does not mean that anyone who becomes a Christian must liquidate all personal assets, give the proceeds to the church, and take a vow of poverty. Rather, the idea is that to be Jesus' disciple, you must love him more than any material wealth or possession.

In the final analysis, we cannot let our attachments to anything hinder our obedience to Jesus and his demands on our lives. These attachments may include families, personal ambitions, investments, and new cars. Jesus comes first.

WHAT DO YOU THINK?

What is one habit, belief, or possession that is distracting you from full discipleship to Jesus? How can your fellow class members help you overcome this problem?

COST AND BENEFIT ANALYSIS

Otto von Bismarck (1815–1898) was a statesman who united northern Germany into a confederation under Prussian control in the 1860s. But he wanted southern German states to join as well. He decided that one way to make this happen was to maneuver the French into declaring war on Prussia. The southern German states would then join Prussia against this aggressive move, and Bismarck would have his united Germany.

God, our Father, you have demonstrated your commitment to us by sending your Son to pay the price for our sins. You have asked us, through Jesus, to be committed to you and obedient to your will.

This is not always easy, Father. May you continue to bless our desire to seek and follow your will. May our lives continue to be conformed to your will by the power of your Word and your Holy Spirit. We pray this in the name of our master, Jesus Christ, amen.

HOW TO SAY IT

Deuteronomy. Due-ter-AHN-uh-me.

Dietrich Bonhoeffer. DEE-trick BON-huh-fur.

Gamaliel. Guh-MAY-lih-ul or Guh-MAY-lee-al.

hyperbole. high-PER-buh-lee.

Jerusalem. Juh-ROO-suh-lem.

Julius Caesar. JOO-lee-us SEE-zur.

monasticism. mah-NAS-tuh-si-zum.

Perean. Peh-REE-un.

rabbi. RAB-eye.

THOUGHT TO REMEMBER

Full commitment still required!

France became a hapless tool in this plan. Spain offered her throne to a German prince, and the French protested. One thing led to another, and the French declared war in 1870. The Prussian army then overwhelmed the French in a series of battles, in one event even capturing Emperor Napoleon III. The Prussians ended up besieging Paris, which experienced several months of famine.

In the ensuing peace agreement, France had to pay hefty war reparations, and she lost most of the provinces of Alsace and Lorraine. France paid a high price to initiate a war she was ill prepared to fight; losing that war cost even more.

The cost of discipleship is itself very high. But this is a struggle that we *cannot* lose as long as we remain faithful. The reward at the end will be worth any price we pay now. Yet Jesus wants us to count the cost in advance nonetheless. When we do, we are less likely to lose heart during those times when that cost seems high.

—J. B. N.

CONCLUSION

Does the cost of following Jesus ever become too great? Are we willing to let Jesus be Lord in some area of our lives but not in others? The Gospels teach that the earliest disciples of Jesus gave up *everything* to follow him (see Mark 10:28; Luke 5:11).

To be a disciple of Christ means that we may be asked to give up ownership of the most private and precious things we have. This means that anything and everything is on the table, especially material possessions and relationships. To hold back in any area means we have not totally yielded to Jesus' lordship, and we are not truly his disciples as he defines that term (Matthew 16:24; Mark 8:34; Luke 9:23).

Jesus does not want people to commit to being his disciples without understanding the depth of that commitment. Discipleship must be more than try it, you'll like it. Jesus is looking for fully devoted followers.

One of the great martyrs of the twentieth century was a German minister named Dietrich Bonhoeffer (1906–1945). During the rise to power of the Nazis in Germany, Bonhoeffer published an important book entitled *The Cost of Discipleship* (1937). In this he challenges Christians to understand that being a follower of Jesus requires full commitment of one's life under any circumstance.

A few years later, Bonhoeffer had these principles put to the test. He was arrested by the Gestapo (the Nazi secret police) for treason and sent to a concentration camp. There he ministered to his fellow prisoners under extreme pressure. His commitment to Jesus allowed him to go to his own execution calmly, secure in his relationship with his Lord.

Jesus' teachings in today's lesson offer us the opportunity to reexamine our commitment to him. Would an outsider describe you as a disciple of Jesus Christ? Does anyone look at your life and see a fully devoted follower of Christ? What or who is more important to you than your relationship with Jesus? Such questions of self-reflection are important in our attempts to evaluate our commitment.

In Revelation 3:16, Jesus offered a different type of comment on this same issue: "So, because you are lukewarm—neither hot nor cold—I am about to spit you out of my mouth." This is a comment about discipleship and commitment. Jesus is not pleased with those who serve him a little. He does not seek our lukewarm commitments. He desires men and women to be his disciples who will count the cost of commitment and then pay the price—whatever the price.

Discovery Learning

This page contains an alternative lesson plan emphasizing learning activities. Classes desiring such student involvement will find these suggestions helpful. The next page is a reproducible activity page to further enhance discovery learning.

INTO THE LESSON

Write the following two headings on the board: *Volunteer Activities* and *Sacrifices Made*. Begin class by asking your learners where they have volunteered their time for service. What are the causes, secular or Christian, for which they have served without pay? Expect answers such as tutoring learners, being a mental health advocate, or teaching Sunday school. List responses in the first of the two columns.

Next, ask, "What are some of the things you gave or sacrificed for these causes or organizations?" List responses in the second column. After completing this exercise, ask the learners, "Why did you make these sacrifices or commitments?" Expect answers that affirm that the sacrifices were important to the causes.

Make the transition to Bible study by reminding learners that the word *disciple* comes from the word *discipline*. Jesus' cause is the greatest of all causes. And he has disciplines he expects of us, his disciples.

INTO THE WORD

Use the commentary to deliver a very brief lecture that you outline this way:

    I. Following Jesus Is Expected
    II. Discipleship Defined
    III. Hyperbole

Write the outline on the board as you speak. Then divide the class into three or more study teams. Give each team a photocopy of the lesson commentary of the passage assigned to that team and a copy of its assignment (below). Some teams will duplicate the assignments if you use more than three teams. Also, give teams B and C poster board and markers. (Questions similar to those below are also in the optional student book.) Team assignments are as follows:

Team A: Read Luke 14:25-27 and the lesson commentary on these verses. Discuss the following questions and be ready to report your answers. 1. Are Jesus' commands in verses 26 and 27 to be taken literally or to be considered as hyperbole? Why do you think so? 2. What is the lesson Jesus wants us to learn in terms of hating our families? Give an example. 3. What does it mean to bear his cross? Explain and illustrate.

Team B: Read Luke 14:28-33 and the lesson commentary on these verses. Then compare and contrast the cost of discipleship in the first century with the twenty-first century. Make two columns on the poster board and jot your ideas in the columns. Be ready to explain your conclusions to the class.

Team C: Read Luke 14:25-33. Then read the lesson commentary notes on verse 33. After reading those notes, identify some marks of disciples of Jesus that set them apart from non-disciples. Decide how you will summarize these to the class. One idea is to make two columns headed *Disciple* and *Non-disciple* on the poster board. List characteristics and behavior traits (or lack thereof) in the columns.

Allow each group to report its conclusions.

INTO LIFE

Brainstorming. Tell the story of Dietrich Bonhoeffer from the Conclusion of the lesson commentary. Then ask, "What characteristics or behavior patterns should an outsider see in fully devoted followers of Jesus Christ?" As the class members brainstorm answers, note these on the board.

Next, remind your learners that Jesus intends this lesson to be personal to each of us. He calls us to examine our commitment and walk as his disciples or followers continually.

Getting Personal. Ask each class member to identify one of the behaviors or characteristics from the brainstorming activity that he or she would like to develop or improve for Jesus' sake. Then ask each to write an acrostic prayer using the word *DISCIPLE* stating a commitment or asking for help. Show this example from a person who wishes to quit swearing:

> **D**ear Lord,
> **I** want to quit
> **S**wearing. As your
> dis**C**iple
> **I**
> **P**romise that I
> wil**L** try to honor you
> in my sp**E**ech.

(You can find this activity in the optional student book as well.)

Alternative: substitute the two activities on the Reproducible Page for the *Getting Personal* segment.

Leaders and Followers

Today's text calls people to be disciples or followers of Jesus. Let's take some time to identify traits of people who are leaders and followers. Unfortunately, in today's church many are neither. Include some of the traits of those who are neither leaders nor followers.

Leaders!

Jesus Christ is not only our redeemer and friend, he is also our leader. List a few of his characteristics that make him a leader worth following.

Followers/Disciples

List some of the characteristics of a good disciple of Jesus.

A PLAN:

Of course we know that moving from the category of "neither" to becoming an effective disciple must come from the heart of the individual. However, there must be a few things we can do to encourage that growth. Name three or four things you can do to help someone else become a devoted disciple of Jesus.

Neither

Now, identify some of the traits of people who are neither leader nor follower in today's church.

Becoming a BETTER Disciple

I know I can become an even better follower or disciple of Jesus if I will give up the following habit, belief, or possession: _____. Plus, I know I can become a better disciple of Jesus if I practice the following discipline: _____.

Dear Lord, I hereby promise to attempt to make the above change in my life. Please help and guide me so that I may be a blessing to you and your church. Amen.

Signed: _____

Spring Quarter 2008

God, the People, and the Covenant

(Chronicles, Nehemiah, Daniel, Haggai, and Luke)

Special Features

Lessons

About These Lessons

A contrarian is someone who chooses to "go against the grain," often doing the opposite of what the world expects. We will meet some contrarians this quarter. Perhaps we will meet ourselves in the process.

Mar 2

Mar 9

Mar 16

Mar 23

Mar 30

Apr 6

Apr 13

Apr 20

Apr 27

May 4

May 11

May 18

May 25

Our Covenant Relationship with God

by Joe M. Sprinkle

The glorious message of the Bible is that God has taken the initiative to establish a personal relationship between himself and his people. The covenants between God and his people establish the relationship. The lessons of this quarter focus on one of God's covenants. The people are to be faithful to their covenant with the Lord, who in turn faithfully keeps his covenant promises.

MARCH

UNIT 1: SIGNS OF GOD'S COVENANT

Lesson 1 draws our attention to the ark of the covenant as a symbol of God's presence among his Old Testament people. **Lesson 2** stresses that one of the most important covenants in the Bible is God's covenant with David. God ultimately kept his covenant promises by raising up Jesus Christ to assume David's throne. Part of the Davidic covenant involved David's son building God's house, as **Lesson 3** establishes. **Lesson 4** offers an example of God fulfilling his promises as Solomon builds and dedicates the temple. Yet sometimes covenants are broken and relationships need to be restored. That's where **Lesson 5** comes in as the book of the law is rediscovered in the days of Josiah.

APRIL

UNIT 2: THE COVENANT IN EXILE

Lesson 6 teaches us about Daniel and his friends remaining faithful to the covenant while in exile as they maintain a distinctive diet in conformity with their Jewish convictions. In **Lesson 7**, Shadrach, Meshach, and Abednego say *no* to idolatry and are willing to die for their convictions, although God honors their faithfulness by saving them. In **Lesson 8** Daniel is condemned to death for refusing to compromise his prayer habits, but God saves him too. Prayer is an essential element for remaining in a covenant relationship with God, as **Lesson 9** demonstrates.

MAY

UNIT 3: RESTORATION AND COVENANT RENEWAL

In **Lesson 10**, Haggai shames his fellow Jews for making personal comfort their priority over rebuilding the temple. Just as the terms of the covenant had warned in Deuteronomy 28, disobedience means forfeited blessings. Moving to **Lesson 11** we see Nehemiah, a courageous and godly leader who steps out on faith to restore God's work among his people. Nehemiah's most visible act of faith in restoring God's work in Judah is the rebuilding of Jerusalem's walls in the face of opposition, as **Lesson 12** reveals. **Lesson 13** shows us Ezra the priest assisting Nehemiah in furthering God's work by reading and explaining God's Word (the law) to the people.

WHO WILL BE FAITHFUL?

God was faithful to his covenant people Israel during the monarchy, during the exile, and after the exile. David, Solomon, Josiah, Daniel and his friends, Haggai, Nehemiah, and Ezra each played a role in helping Israel be faithful to God's covenant. May their actions and words continue to inspire God's people to maintain, deepen, and restore their new-covenant relationships with their Lord.

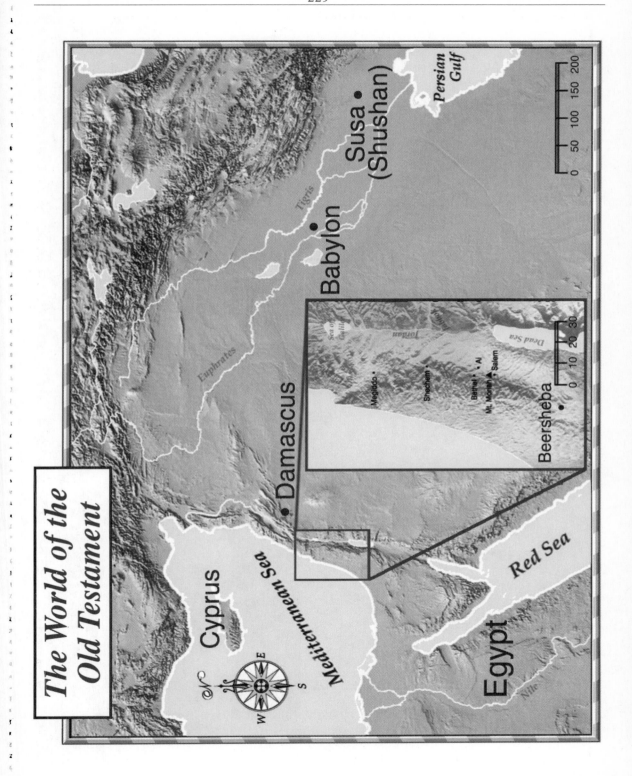

The World of the Old Testament

Persian Gulf

Susa (Shushan)

Babylon

Tigris

Euphrates

Damascus

Cyprus

Mediterranean Sea

Egypt

Nile

Red Sea

Beersheba

Sea of Galilee

Jordan

Dead Sea

Megiddo

Shechem

Bethel

Ai

Mt. Moriah

Salem

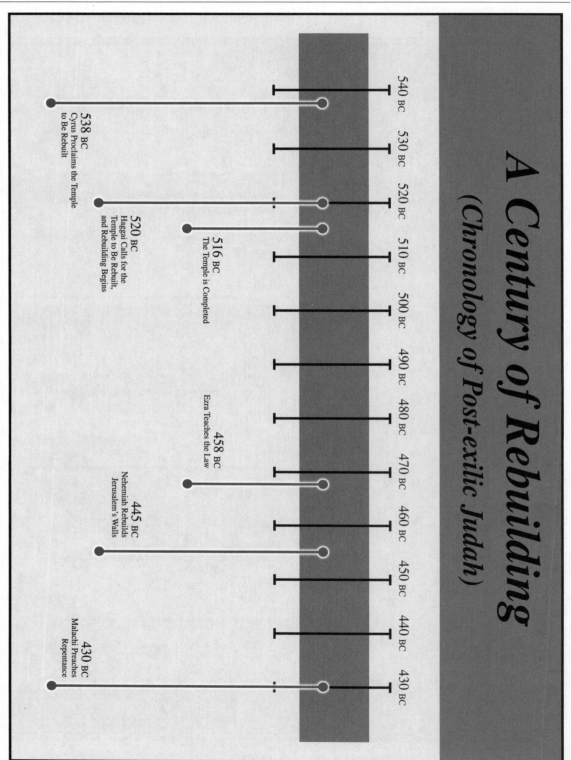

A Century of Rebuilding
(Chronology of Post-exilic Judah)

540 BC

530 BC

520 BC

510 BC

500 BC

490 BC

480 BC

470 BC

460 BC

450 BC

440 BC

430 BC

538 BC
Cyrus Proclaims the Temple
to Be Rebuilt

520 BC
Haggai Calls for the
Temple to Be Rebuilt,
and Rebuilding Begins

516 BC
The Temple is Completed

458 BC
Ezra Teaches the Law

445 BC
Nehemiah Rebuilds
Jerusalem's Walls

430 BC
Malachi Preaches
Repentance

God, the People, and the Covenant
Unit 1: Signs of God's Covenant
(Lessons 1-5)

THE ARK COMES TO JERUSALEM

LESSON 1

WHY TEACH THIS LESSON?

The use of symbols is a vital part of who we are as Christians and as a church. Many churches use symbols to reflect their beliefs and/or practices. Of course, many incorporate the cross in their building design, as this is a key symbol of the church. Others make use of the basin and towel to signify that it is a church that serves in the name of Jesus. One man said the symbol of his church was the covered dish because fellowship meals were the main thing his church was known for!

The secular world knows all about symbols too. Their symbols try to get us to *do something*—namely, buy their products or buy into their ideas. Company logos scream, "Look who we are! Try us!" Evolutionists put feet on the Christian symbol of the fish in an attempt to persuade people against the idea of creation. So we are surrounded by competing symbols. The information overload in this regard can lead us in the wrong path if we are not careful.

As you prepare to teach this lesson, consider what symbol or symbols might be (or should be) used to characterize your church as it gathers for worship. Also, consider what symbol might signify a personal relationship with Christ and what adjustments your learners need to make in that regard.

INTRODUCTION
A. SYMBOLS OF GOD'S PRESENCE

I once visited a certain church to conduct a Bible study. The building was functional, practical, and not "showy." But eight stained-glass windows in the sanctuary overwhelmed me with their messages. On the left were four Old Testament symbols: the tree of life, a rainbow with Noah's ark, a burning bush, and a pillar of fire. On the right were four New Testament symbols: a stable (for Jesus' birth), a cross, an empty tomb, and a dove descending. The impact of these eight beautiful windows has never left me.

These symbols clearly communicate God's presence or promise. As long as Adam and Eve had access to the tree of life, they could live forever in God's presence. Every time we see a rainbow, it reminds us of God's promise never to flood the earth again. Moses knew he was in God's presence when he approached a burning bush. The pillar of fire was a clear demonstration of God's presence in the midst of the Hebrew people.

On the New Testament side, the symbols are just as powerful. The stable symbolizes that the Word of God became flesh. The cross has always been a symbol of God's promised forgiveness. Of course, without the empty tomb of the resurrection there would be no salvation for the world; the resurrection assures us that God is still here. Finally, the dove is a symbol of God's Spirit, which is present

---

DEVOTIONAL READING:
PSALM 150

BACKGROUND SCRIPTURE:
1 CHRONICLES 13; 15

PRINTED TEXT:
1 CHRONICLES 15:1-3, 14-16, 25-28

LESSON AIMS

After participating in this lesson, each student will be able to:

1. Describe the sequence of events that David initiated to bring the ark of God to Jerusalem.

2. Compare and contrast the worship practices of ancient Israel with worship practices today.

3. Determine one way to worship with greater enthusiasm in private or corporate worship experiences.

KEY VERSE

David assembled all Israel in Jerusalem to bring up the ark of the LORD to the place he had prepared for it. —1 Chronicles 15:3

within every Christian. Today's lesson focuses on another important symbol of God's presence for Old Testament believers: the ark of the covenant.

B. LESSON BACKGROUND

The ark of the covenant was ancient Israel's most precious symbol of God's presence. The construction of the ark is recorded in Exodus 37:1-9. That happened in about 1446 BC. Within the ark of the covenant eventually were placed the testimony, a gold jar of manna that the Israelites had gathered during their time in the wilderness, and Aaron's budded rod (Exodus 40:20; Hebrews 9:4).

Four gold rings were fastened to the ark. Poles were inserted through these rings for transporting it. The ark was never to be carried in any way other than by Levites with those poles on their shoulders (Exodus 25:13-15; 37:5; 1 Chronicles 15:2, 15). Since the ark was top-heavy, using a cart to carry it was dangerous (1 Chronicles 13:7-10). Indeed, the top cover itself (called *mercy seat* or *atonement cover*) was made out of gold—an extremely heavy substance (Exodus 25:17).

The ark of the covenant symbolized the throne of God (see 1 Samuel 4:4; 2 Samuel 6:2; 2 Kings 19:15; 1 Chronicles 13:6; Psalm 80:1; 99:1). Perhaps more precisely, the space between the cherubim on the atonement cover represented the "footstool" of God (see 1 Chronicles 28:2; Psalm 99:5). Atonement for sin was made by sprinkling the blood of bulls and goats before the mercy seat (Leviticus 16:11-16). The importance of the ark of the covenant to the Hebrew people cannot be overstated!

After the ark was built and placed in the tabernacle, it stayed with the Israelites throughout their wilderness wanderings. Eventually it was placed in Shiloh, about 30 miles northeast of Jerusalem, after the conquest of the promised land (Joshua 18:1). Through an unusual series of events, the ark ended up in a private residence, where it remained in obscurity for some time (1 Samuel 4:4–7:2). The tabernacle that had housed the ark was located elsewhere at that time, separated from the ark (1 Chronicles 16:39; 21:29; 2 Chronicles 1:3, 13). It was under these conditions that David sought to bring the ark to Jerusalem and place it within a specially prepared tent (1 Chronicles 13:5; 15:1).

Today's background texts of 1 Chronicles 13 and 15 must be understood as part of a literary unit, namely chapters 13–17. This unit brings us to an important stage in the establishment of Jerusalem as both a political and religious center for the newly united kingdom under King David. This stage began when David brought the ark to Jerusalem (chapter 13) and concluded when God gave his promise concerning David's dynasty (chapter 17; see Lesson 2).

By the time David became king, more than 400 years had elapsed since the ark of the covenant had come into being. First Chronicles 13 recounts the first attempt at bringing the ark to Jerusalem. That attempt ended in failure. Someone, either David or the priests, made a serious mistake by appointing the wrong people to move the ark (1 Chronicles 15:13a).

Another mistake was in transporting the ark in the wrong manner (1 Chronicles 15:13b). The result was a tragedy that halted the process (2 Samuel 6:1-7; 1 Chronicles 13:1-10). David was despondent: "How can I ever bring the ark of God to me?" (1 Chronicles 13:12b; compare 2 Samuel 6:9). For three months the project languished until everyone, including David, recognized that God had blessed the household of Obed-Edom, where the ark was housed temporarily (1 Chronicles 13:13, 14).

The author of Chronicles arranged his material to show that David's first major decision and act as king of a united Israel was to bring the ark to Jerusa-

DAILY BIBLE READINGS

Monday, Feb. 25—Let Everything Praise the Lord (Psalm 150)

Tuesday, Feb. 26—The Ark of God (1 Chronicles 15:1-3, 11-15)

Wednesday, Feb. 27—Music, Joy, and Celebration (1 Chronicles 15:16-24)

Thursday, Feb. 28—Bringing the Ark of the Covenant (1 Chronicles 15:25-29)

Friday, Feb. 29—Ministering Before the Ark (1 Chronicles 16:1-6)

Saturday, Mar. 1—A Psalm of Thanksgiving (1 Chronicles 16:7-36)

Sunday, Mar. 2—Worship Before the Ark (1 Chronicles 16: 37-43) lem. Our printed text picks up the story of King David's second attempt at this project.

I. ARRANGEMENTS FOR THE ARK (1 CHRONICLES 15:1-3)

A. DAVID'S PREPARATIONS (v. 1)

1. After David had constructed buildings for himself in the City of David, he prepared a place for the ark of God and pitched a tent for it.

The *city of David* is, of course, Jerusalem. Before David attempts to bring up *the ark*, he improves that city's infrastructure in certain ways (*constructed buildings; see also* 2 Samuel 5:9-11; 1 Chronicles 14:1). This is entirely appropriate, as the population of Jerusalem probably numbers only around 2,000 at the time in an area of no more than 12 acres.

Part of this city-improvement plan involves preparing *a place for the ark of God.* We are not certain where this is, but it is likely the highest place in the area, later to be known as Mount Zion (see Psalm 132:13). Today one observes the Dome of the Rock mosque close to that location.

With the tabernacle still located in Gibeon, David must devise a special *tent* for the ark (2 Samuel 6:17; 1 Chronicles 16:1, 39; 21:29). We may speculate that the tent is patterned in some way after the tabernacle. The tabernacle proper will not be brought to Jerusalem for many years (2 Chronicles 1:6, 13, 5:5).

When God revealed instructions to Moses for building the tabernacle and its furnishings (Exodus 25–31:11; 35:4-40), the ark of the covenant was the first article to be described (Exodus 25:10-22). It was the most important item because it was precisely between the two cherubim on top of the ark where God met with Moses and gave his commands for the Israelites (Exodus 25:22; Numbers 7:89).

WHAT DO YOU THINK?

What symbols have you found to be helpful in reminding you that God is near? Under what circumstances can a symbol be harmful?

B. LEVITES' TASK (v. 2)

2. Then David said, "No one but the Levites may carry the ark of God, because the LORD chose them to carry the ark of the LORD and to minister before him forever."

David's statement *no one but the Levites may carry the ark of God* seems to be reflected in Deuteronomy 10:8; 18:1-5. A certain violation of this rule contributed to the death of Uzzah that marked the first attempt to move it (1 Chronicles 13:7-10; 15:13). Even though he seems to have been a Levite, he apparently was not one of the lawful ones to transport the ark, considering the improper manner in which the first attempt was made (see Numbers 7:1-9, especially v. 9). That mistake involved both *how* as well as *who* in moving the ark.

WHAT DO YOU THINK?

What was a time when one of your plans failed because of poor execution even though your heart was in the right place? How did you grow spiritually as a result of that experience?

C. ISRAEL'S GATHERING (v. 3)

3. David assembled all Israel in Jerusalem to bring up the ark of the LORD to the place he had prepared for it.

This is a good summary of all that David originally tried to do regarding the first attempt to bring the ark *to Jerusalem* (1 Chronicles 13:1-5). This second gathering is thus a natural continuation of this all-important project. In 1 Chronicles 15:4-12, 17-24 (not in today's text), the author gives details regarding whom *all Israel* includes.

II. BRINGING OF THE ARK (1 CHRONICLES 15:14-16)

A. SANCTIFICATION (v. 14)

14. So the priests and Levites consecrated themselves in order to bring up the ark of the LORD, the God of Israel.

WHAT DO YOU THINK?

What can we do to prepare ourselves for drawing near to God? [Hint: Psalm 46:10; 100; Proverbs 15:29; Matthew 5:23, 24; 1 Peter 3:7, 12; and 1 Corinthians 11:27-29 may be useful in guiding this discussion.]

A good description of what it means to consecrate oneself can be found in Exodus 19:10-15. For the priests and *Levites* it means at least washing the body, changing clothing (to fine linen; see 1 Chronicles 15:27), and abstaining from sexual relations. Since Levites have to stay away from the common and the profane, then fasting and prayer may be part of the process, but this is not certain (see also Exodus 29; 30:17-21; 40:30-32; Leviticus 8:5-36).

B. TRANSPORTATION (v. 15)

15. And the Levites carried the ark of God with the poles on their shoulders, as Moses had commanded in accordance with the word of the LORD.

We have already mentioned that the issue of transporting *the ark of God* includes issues of both *who* and *how.* Perhaps those who initially put the ark on a cart in 1 Chronicles 13:7 were ignorant of the implications of Exodus 25:10-15; 37:1-5. *The Levites* must carry the ark by putting its *poles on their shoulders.* The rings for the poles are a permanent part of the ark for this very purpose. No one is to touch the ark on penalty of death (again, see 2 Samuel 6:6-8; 1 Chronicles 13:9-11; 15:13).

THE RIGHT PEOPLE FOR THE JOB

You may have seen the following humorous description of what happens as we age: "A very weird thing has happened. A strange old lady has moved into my house. I have no idea who she is, where she came from, or how she got in." The piece goes on to describe how, when the writer looks in the mirror, the stranger is hogging the view and obscuring the writer's youthful face and body. The stranger puts things in places where the writer can't find them and turns the TV down low so it can't be easily heard.

Most of us over "a certain age" have seen that stranger in the mirror. The person in the mirror is no longer "the right person"—that youthful person we imagined we would be for the rest of our lives.

Being "the right person" is important in many areas of life. That seems to have been the case when the ark was being moved. The first time it was moved, apparently the right people weren't carrying it and/or they had gone about it in the wrong way. That provides a lesson for us: being the person God wants us to be for carrying out his work is more important than who we would like to be.

God chose Levites for holy tasks; today, he chooses Christians for the holy tasks of the church. He uses his Word and our life experiences to prepare us for the work he has called us to do. Those wrinkles and gray hairs can be the evidence that God has been at work in us for a long time, preparing us to do things reserved for those of greater spiritual maturity.   —C. R. B.

C. AUTHORIZATION (v. 16)

16. David told the leaders of the Levites to appoint their brothers as singers to sing joyful songs, accompanied by musical instruments: lyres, harps and cymbals.

With the ark in Jerusalem, the city will become a center for worship. Hence the need for musicians and *singers* from among *the Levites.*

To this end David delegates *the leaders of the Levites to appoint* those with such abilities to sing and to play musical instruments (see 1 Chronicles 15:17-24, not in today's text; see also 2 Samuel 6:5). The three mentioned instruments—namely, *lyres, harps,* and *cymbals*—are three of the most common listed in the Chronicles (1 Chronicles 16:5; 25:1, 6; 2 Chronicles 5:12; 29:25). Nehemiah 12:27 lists these important instruments as they came to be used hundreds of years later.

WHAT DO YOU THINK?

Which songs bring you into a worshipful state of mind? Why?

III. WORSHIPING BEFORE THE ARK (1 CHRONICLES 15:25-28)

A. ARK RETRIEVED (v. 25)

25. So David and the elders of Israel and the commanders of units of a thousand went to bring up the ark of the covenant of the LORD from the house of Obed-Edom, with rejoicing.

God had blessed Obed-Edom's household over the three months that *the ark of the covenant* was in his *house* (1 Chronicles 13:14). This fact gives courage to David to make a second attempt at bringing the ark to Jerusalem (2 Samuel 6:12). In 1 Chronicles 14, the author indicates that God also is blessing David in all that he does. So *with rejoicing* David and all the leaders of Israel go to Obed-Edom's house to *bring up* the ark to the high hill above David's palace. Things are looking up!

Visual for Lesson 1. *Keep this map displayed the entire quarter to give your learners a geographical perspective.*

B. SACRIFICES OFFERED (v. 26)

26. Because God had helped the Levites who were carrying the ark of the covenant of the LORD, seven bulls and seven rams were sacrificed.

This verse tells us about the sacrifices that are made at the beginning of this trip. First Chronicles 16:1 tells us about offerings made as the trip concludes. Second Samuel 6:13 adds to the richness of the imagery: "When those who were carrying the ark of the Lord had taken six steps, he sacrificed a bull and a fattened calf."

C. LINEN WORN (v. 27)

27. Now David was clothed in a robe of fine linen, as were all the Levites who were carrying the ark, and as were the singers, and Kenaniah, who was in charge of the singing of the choirs. David also wore a linen ephod.

At first glance, *David* may appear to be improperly dressed, for he is wearing garments reserved for *Levites*, especially the *linen ephod*. This is a tightly fitted white undergarment that is sleeveless. It usually comes down only to the hips. It is worn by those serving at the tent of meeting (see 1 Samuel 2:18; 22:18).

In a sense, David is acting in a priestly mode in bringing the ark into Jerusalem as he offers sacrifices and blesses the people (1 Chronicles 16:2). His actions are not without precedent when we consider Psalm 110 and the "priest-king" Melchizedek (also see Genesis 14:18-20). It is possible we are viewing David, in a sense, as a priest-king (compare Zechariah 6:9-15; also see Acts 2:29, 30, which refers to David as a prophet).

D. JOY EVIDENT (v. 28)

28. So all Israel brought up the ark of the covenant of the LORD with shouts, with the sounding of rams' horns and trumpets, and of cymbals, and the playing of lyres and harps.

Ancient Israelite worship music is culturally different from what is called "contemporary worship" today. But there is one thing the two have in common: they are both loud (compare Ezra 3:13; Nehemiah 12:43; Psalm 150). The louder the better! By the use of percussion, wind, and string instruments, the gathering crowd of Israelites and their gifted musicians make a tremendous joyful noise to the Lord.

We may be able to imagine how loud this worship is by counting the number of musicians in 1 Chronicles 15:19-22. There we see three musicians on *cymbals*, eight on *lyres*, and six on *harps*. The number of singers is unknown. But 1 Chronicles 15:5-10 reveals hundreds of Levites to be present, all singing.

WHAT DO YOU THINK?

First Chronicles 15:25-28 describes an all-out worship celebration. What would an all-out worship celebration look like today? How would we know if such a celebration had gone "too far"? Or is it even possible to go "too far"? Explain.

PRAYER

Our Father, may we see Jesus this day as he is in all his love and compassion for us. May we discern the unity of the body of Christ, the church. Help us to see Christ in those we serve. Take away all selfishness and greediness in our hearts. May we reflect your righteousness, generosity, and compassion as your image-bearers. Be glorified in your people. In Christ we pray, amen.

HOW TO SAY IT

cherubim. CHAIR-uh-bim.

ephod. EE-fod.

Gibeon. GIB-e-un (G as in GET).

Kenaniah. Ken-uh-NEE-uh.

Levites. LEE-vites.

Melchizedek. Mel-KIZ-eh-dek.

Obed-Edom. O-bed-EE-dum.

Philistines. Fuh-LISS-teens or FILL-us-teens.

Shiloh. SHY-low.

Uzzah. UZ-zuh.

Zechariah. ZEK-uh-RYE-uh.

THOUGHT TO REMEMBER

Rejoice in the symbols of God's presence.

"A WAY TO GLORIFY GOD"

A few years ago, having someone's house "flocked" or "flamingoed" was a popular method by which churches raised money for missions or other congregational projects. A church member would give perhaps $25 to the project, and a crew would place 50 plastic pink flamingoes on another member's front lawn. That person then would have to pay the same amount to have the awful-looking things removed or placed on another member's lawn.

One church in Florida used this idea to raise $1,200 for outreach projects such as feeding and clothing the poor. At one time they had a month-long waiting list for their flightless flock. The coordinator of the project said, "It's a way to glorify God. It's good for the church and good for the community."

What do you think of this method of raising money for the Lord's work? Love it or hate it, it certainly was creative! One Christian's idea of what glorifies God can be different from another's. This is certainly true of our worship music. Some Christians don't like any instrumental music at all; others believe a pipe organ is best; others—most often young people, it seems—would be happy listening to David's worship band making a loud noise. (Some older Christians might say that's *all* it was!) The main challenge is to make our worship become a more heartfelt and meaningful way to glorify God. Remember: he is our audience.

—C. R. B.

CONCLUSION

The ancient Israelites rejoiced greatly, for they had placed on Zion the symbol of God's presence that was initiated by God himself. The ark itself symbolized God's throne, or at least his footstool. The status of the Israelites as God's people was based in large part on their receiving and keeping the Ten Commandments, located within the ark. God's gracious provision for his people during the wilderness wanderings was symbolized by a jar of manna, also within the ark. The God-given leadership of Moses and Aaron was signified by Aaron's budded rod, within the ark as well.

For the Christian, the greatest physical symbol of God's presence is found in the Lord's Supper. Jesus said, "This is my body, which is for you." To symbolize his shed blood Jesus said, "This cup is the new covenant in my blood; do this, whenever you drink it, in remembrance of me" (1 Corinthians 11:24, 25). The Gospel of John makes it clear that God's spiritual presence today is his own Holy Spirit (John 16:5-15; compare Acts 5:32; Ephesians 1:13).

Look around you the next time you worship with fellow believers. What symbols of God's presence do you see? Certainly the cross is a good one. The Bible, as the revelation of God's Word, is another. But keep looking! Some of the greatest symbols of God's presence are all around you. These are the men and women who worship alongside us. God has created every human being in his image (Genesis 1:26, 27). It is we and not the animals who can reflect who God is in love, graciousness, and compassion. Compare Psalm 111:4, 5: "He has caused his wonders to be remembered; the Lord is gracious and compassionate. He provides food for those who fear him; he remembers his covenant forever."

More vital symbols of God's presence are the hungry we feed, the thirsty to whom we give drink, the strangers we welcome, the naked we clothe, the sick we look after, and the prisoners we visit. Jesus himself said, "Whatever you did for one of the least of these brothers of mine, you did for me" (Matthew 25:40b). God is present in those we serve. To serve them is to serve Jesus; to fail to serve them is to fail to serve Jesus.

Discovery Learning

This page contains an alternative lesson plan emphasizing learning activities. Classes desiring such student involvement will find these suggestions helpful. The next page is a reproducible activity page to further enhance discovery learning.

INTO THE LESSON

Collect in advance large pictures of the following from magazines or the Internet: A. a diploma or cap-and-gown for graduation; B. a TV; C. wedding rings; D. a hard hat; E. balance scales; F. a football; G. a piggy bank; H. a recreational vehicle. Label each picture with its letter and display them together on a wall of your classroom.

Distribute these instructions (but don't distribute the answers): For each activity or institution listed below, identify a common symbol from the images displayed. 1. Savings; 2. Justice; 3. Education; 4. Work; 5. Marriage; 6. Vacation; 7. Recreation; 8. Entertainment. *Answers: 1, G; 2, E; 3, A; 4, D; 5, C; 6, H; 7, F; 8, B.* Have volunteers share their answers and discuss other symbols that could have been used.

Next, display or distribute images of these Christian symbols: A. a lion; B. a dove; C. a cross; D. a fish; E. Noah's ark. Explain to your class that each of these symbols was used by the early church to represent some special person, event, or doctrine of Scripture.

Ask your students to match those symbols with these possible answers: 1. The Holy Spirit; 2. Baptism; 3. Jesus (two answers); 4. Forgiveness of sin. *Answers: 1, B (Luke 3:22); 2, E (1 Peter 3:18-21); 3, A & D (Revelation 5:5; the Greek word for fish, ichthus, was used by Christians as an acrostic for "Jesus Christ, Son of God, Savior"); 4, C (1 Peter 2:24).*

Once again, have volunteers share their answers and discuss other symbols the early church used. Then tell your class that today's lesson involves ancient Israel's most precious symbol of God's presence.

Alternative: The Common Symbols exercise from the Reproducible Page conveniently features smaller pictures of the above items. You may wish to distribute copies of this instead of displaying the large pictures.

INTO THE WORD

From the Lesson Introduction and Lesson Background, develop a brief lecture to explain the symbolism of the ark of the covenant, its importance to the Hebrew people, and the historical background of today's lesson.

Then ask three learners to read these verse sections aloud, one volunteer per section: 1 Chronicles 15:1-3, 14-16, 25-28. After a section is read, use the lesson commentary and the questions below to discuss it. (The questions are reprinted in the optional student books.)

First Chronicles 15:1-3: Where would David most likely have prepared a place for the ark in Jerusalem? Why were the Levites the only ones allowed to carry the ark?

First Chronicles 15:14-16: What was involved in the process by which a priest sanctified himself? Why did the priests carry the ark on their shoulders?

First Chronicles 15:25-28: Who normally wore linen robes? (See 1 Samuel 2:18.) What did David's robe signify? (See Zechariah 6:9-15.) How do you imagine the worship sounded, according to verse 28? Why were the Israelites so joyful?

INTO LIFE

Divide your learners into small groups for the two exercises below. If your class is small, you can do the exercises as a class. The first exercise is printed also in the optional student book. If you don't use that resource, distribute copies of the instructions below.

Exercise #1: Their Worship, and Ours. Ask someone in your group to read aloud Psalm 150. Based on what you have heard in today's text (including 1 Chronicles 16:1, 2) and in Psalm 150, make a list of similarities and contrasts between worship practices in ancient Israel and in our congregation today. Answers should be organized into the following categories: 1. Types of worship activities; 2. Types of musical instruments used (if any); 3. Things for which God is praised; 4. Religious symbols used; 5. Involvement of the congregation.

After groups finish their work, discuss their conclusions as a class. When you address the fifth category, ask your learners how they think your congregation compares with Israel in its enthusiasm in worship. Discuss the benefits and possible problems of that level of enthusiasm.

Exercise #2: Passionate Praise. Within your small group, discuss ways to use more Christian symbolism in our worship services. Brainstorm several ways to make your worship more enthusiastic. The bottom of the Reproducible Page includes some spaces for students to write their ideas.

Common Symbols . . .

For each activity or institution listed below, identify at least one common symbol from the images displayed.

. . . of Western Society

1. Savings ___
2. Justice ___
3. Education ___
4. Work ___
5. Marriage ___
6. Vacation ___
7. Recreation ___
8. Entertainment ___

a

b

c

d

e

f

g

h

. . . of Christianity

1. The Holy Spirit ___
2. Baptism ___
3. Jesus ___ & ___
4. Forgiveness of sin ___

a

b

c

d

e

Passionate Praise

Use the space below to (1) list ways to utilize more Christian symbolism in your worship services and (2) list several ways to make your worship more enthusiastic.

Symbols

Enthusiastic Worship

_____   _____

_____   _____

_____   _____

God, the People, and the Covenant
Unit 1: Signs of God's Covenant
(Lessons 1-5)

GOD MAKES A
COVENANT WITH DAVID

LESSON 2

WHY TEACH THIS LESSON?

Many today live in neighborhoods that have protective covenants. These deal with such things as where you can park your car, the color of the exterior trim, or the placement of lawn ornaments and trash cans. We like the idea of having covenants to control our neighbors' behavior; we are not as fond of covenants when it comes to conforming our own behavior to them.

As a Christian you are part of the new covenant in Christ. But has that fact changed your behavior? In teaching this lesson of the covenant God made with David, take time to ask your learners that question. Point out no matter which biblical covenant we're talking about, they all carry certain expectations from God. Today's lesson can cause each of us to think of at least one specific area in which we are not being faithful to the new covenant. What will it take to correct that situation?

INTRODUCTION

A. COVENANT MAKING

When I was growing up, I had a second cousin who was like a brother to me since I had no brother and only one sister. We were the same age and played together as often as we could. When we were in about the third grade, we made a covenant with one another. We even pricked our fingers to "exchange" our blood in this special relationship. (We had seen Indians do this in the movies.)

What was our covenant? *To never get married!* We announced this covenant to all family members and to as many others as we could. This, of course, was in our prepuberty days, and girls were our natural enemies. We actually held each other accountable to the covenant for a number of years. But eventually we broke the covenant. Charles married after he had graduated from high school, and I married at the end of my graduate studies. No one was surprised that we broke our covenant.

Western culture has a problem with the term *covenant*. We know what a *contract* is, but the word *covenant* has fallen into disuse for the most part. Also, the concept of living under a covenant relationship (such as marriage) is antiquated and unthinkable to many because of secular cultural influences. It is no wonder that even many Christians in Western democracies have a difficult time understanding the concept of covenant as the Bible presents that idea. But try we must.

B. OVERVIEW OF OLD TESTAMENT COVENANTS

A *covenant* is an agreement between two parties in which various promises, obligations, and conditions are expressed or implied. The terms of the covenant

DEVOTIONAL READING:
PSALM 78:67-72

BACKGROUND SCRIPTURE:
1 CHRONICLES 17

PRINTED TEXT:
1 CHRONICLES 17:1-4, 6-15

LESSON AIMS

After participating in this lesson, each student will be able to:

1. List the most important features of God's covenant with David.

2. Compare and contrast God's covenant with David and with God's covenant with Christians.

3. Suggest one specific way to demonstrate that he or she is living under the covenant promised to David and fulfilled in Christ.

KEY VERSE

I have been with you wherever you have gone, and I have cut off all your enemies from before you. Now I will make your name like the names of the greatest men of the earth. —1 Chronicles 17:8

depend on the parties and their interests. Many covenants in the Bible are between people. These include covenants of friendship (example: 1 Samuel 18:3; 20:8), the institution of marriage (example: Malachi 2:14), and agreements between rulers or authority figures (example: Genesis 21:27; 31:44; 1 Kings 15:19). The latter includes agreements in which the more powerful ruler may dictate terms to the weaker (example: 1 Samuel 11:1, 2).

The above examples are interesting, but it is the covenants that God has made with his people that we want to focus on. Some think that the first covenant in the Bible is found in Genesis 1 and 2—what has been called *the Edenic covenant*. Here God is seen to obligate humans to have dominion over the earth. One prohibition is given: "But you must not eat from the tree of the knowledge of good and evil" (Genesis 2:17).

The Adamic covenant follows in Genesis 3. There God promises to bring some form of hope in the midst of curses for disobedience to the provisions of Genesis 2:17 in the Edenic covenant. "And I will put enmity between you and the woman, and between your offspring and hers; he will crush your head, and you will strike his heel" (Genesis 3:15).

The third covenant has been called *the Noahic covenant*. Noah and his sons were blessed by God and told to, "Be fruitful and increase in number and fill the earth" (Genesis 9:1). They were given dominion over all living things upon the earth, even the flesh of animals for food. Capital punishment for murder was instituted to acknowledge the sanctity of human life (9:6). The sign of the rainbow assured Noah and his family that God would never again flood the earth (9:15, 16).

The fourth covenant is *the Abrahamic covenant*. God promised to Abraham land of his own, seed that would become a great nation, and blessing (both materially and spiritually) by God's presence. Somehow all peoples of the earth were to be blessed through Abraham (Genesis 12:1-3). This promise was confirmed by the slaughter of animals (Genesis 15:9-21). God obligated himself to the promise of land, seed, and blessing. Abraham's part was to be faithful to God's instructions. The sign of this covenant was to be in the flesh of every male descendant of Abraham (Genesis 17:11-14).

The fifth covenant in the Bible is called *the Sinaitic covenant* or *the Mosaic covenant*. God had delivered the Israelites from Egypt, and at Mount Sinai he bestowed a special position to Israel (Exodus 19:5, 6a). A key part of obeying God's voice was the obligation to keep the Ten Commandments (Exodus 20:1-17). Blessings and curses were pronounced, depending on the Israelites' behavior (Leviticus 26). After the rebellion of the Israelites in the desert, Moses renewed this covenant as he prepared to die on Mount Nebo (Deuteronomy 32–34). The entire book of Deuteronomy is patterned in the shape of a covenant renewal treaty. See also Joshua 8:30-35; 24; 1 Samuel 12; and Nehemiah 8–10.

The prophet Jeremiah spoke of "a new covenant" because Israel had broken the Sinaitic covenant time and again throughout her history (see Jeremiah 31:31-34; Hebrews 8:8-12). But before that new covenant came into being, God instituted *the Davidic covenant*, the subject of today's lesson.

HOW TO SAY IT

Abrahamic. Ay-bruh-HAM-ik.
Adamic. Uh-DAHM-ik.
Davidic. Duh-VID-ick.
Edenic. E-DEN-ik.
Jebusites. JEB-yuh-sites.
Mosaic. Mo-ZAY-ik.
Noahic. No-AY-ik.
Philistines. Fuh-LISS-teens or
    FILL-us-teens.
Sinaitic. Sin-ee-AT-ik.

C. LESSON BACKGROUND

According to 2 Samuel 5 and 6, David ultimately became king over a united Israel. This happened approximately 1000 BC. After conquering the Jebusites and their city of Jerusalem, David made that city the capital of the newly united kingdom. Then he defeated the Philistines (2 Samuel 5:17-25). Afterward, he brought the ark of the covenant into Jerusalem and placed it on Mount Zion under a tent (last week's lesson). This move made Jerusalem both the political and religious capital of the kingdom.

The author of Chronicles, writing much later than the author who writes the parallel account in 2 Samuel, used a combination of psalms to illustrate David's attitude of thanksgiving: compare Psalm 105:1-15 with 1 Chronicles 16:7-22; Psalm 96 with 1 Chronicles 16:23-33; and Psalm 106:1, 47, 48 with 1 Chronicles 16:34-36. It is at this point in the Chronicles account that God made his eternal promise to David—today's text.

I. WHAT DAVID NOTICES (1 CHRONICLES 17:1, 2)

A. KING'S NOBLE DESIRE (v. 1)

1. After David was settled in his palace, he said to Nathan the prophet, "Here I am, living in a palace of cedar, while the ark of the covenant of the LORD is under a tent."

Apparently *Nathan* is a court *prophet* who lives in Jerusalem. As such, he has ready access to King David. The parallel account of 2 Samuel 7 also mentions Nathan. David conveys to Nathan his embarrassment at his personal surroundings of a beautiful *palace of cedar* (see 2 Samuel 5:11; 1 Chronicles 14:1) in contrast with the mere *tent* covering he has provided for *the ark of the covenant* (1 Chronicles 16:1). The implication of David's statement of contrast is his desire to build a better, more permanent structure for God's ark.

B. PROPHET'S RASH RESPONSE (v. 2)

2. Nathan replied to David, "Whatever you have in mind, do it, for God is with you.

We may be inclined to think of the great men of old, such as the Old Testament prophets, as superspiritual. They are indeed very holy, yet they can still make mistakes. What we see here is that Nathan's line of thinking is the same as David's. *Nathan* also equates his own thoughts with the will of God. As a result, Nathan replies, *"Whatever you have in mind, do it, for God is with you."* This statement proves to be rash, as the next verse shows. Nathan jumps the gun.

II. HOW GOD REACTS (1 CHRONICLES 17:3, 4, 6-8a)

A. HISTORICAL REVIEW, PART 1 (vv. 3, 4, 6)

3, 4. That night the word of God came to Nathan, saying:

"Go and tell my servant David, 'This is what the LORD says: You are not the one to build me a house to dwell in.

That very *night*, before anything can be done to advance David's dreamed-of building project, *the word of God* comes *to Nathan* in a vision or "revelation" (see v. 15, below). God gives specific words to Nathan to relate to *David*. What God has to say is rather lengthy, as we shall see.

The first sentence of God's communication is quite pointed: *You are not the one to build me a house to dwell in.* The unmistakable effect of this declarative statement is the negation of David's desire.

6. "'Wherever I have moved with all the Israelites, did I ever say to any of their leaders whom I commanded to shepherd my people, "Why have you not built me a house of cedar?"'

Verse 5 (not in today's text) emphasizes the fact that God has dwelt in a tent ever since the exodus, some 400 years in the past by this time. Yet tents are not durable over such a long period. Materials wear out due to normal wear and tear, exposure to the elements, and destruction by insects. This realization is

WHAT DO YOU THINK?

How is it possible to give something back to the one who owns all things and gives us all things? How do you do this in your own life?

WHAT DO YOU THINK?

What are some ways that God has guided you up to this point in your life?

undoubtedly part of David's desire to improve this situation. Yet has God ever said a word to any of Israel's leaders throughout their history about wanting *a house* to dwell in?

We should pause to note a certain play on words in Hebrew that occurs throughout this chapter. So far the Hebrew word for *house* has had two meanings: it is translated in verse 1 as "palace" but it has the meaning of "temple" in verses 4-6. In verse 10 (below), it will take on a third meaning. This is a major literary device both here and in 2 Samuel 7.

B. HISTORICAL REVIEW, PART 2 (vv. 7, 8a)

7. *"Now then, tell my servant David, 'This is what the LORD Almighty says: I took you from the pasture and from following the flock, to be ruler over my people Israel.*

God, through Nathan, reminds *David* of his humble beginnings. David, the youngest of eight brothers, had been a shepherd boy in Bethlehem (1 Samuel 16:1-12). He had not been allowed even to fight alongside his brothers in battle (1 Samuel 17:14, 15, 28).

By divine providence David killed Goliath, the Philistine hero. This was an important milestone in David's road to kingship. David's days as a shepherd with a sling and staff had prepared him for killing the Philistine giant. Those same shepherd days also prepared him to be king over God's people. The word *shepherd* could be used to describe the role of kings (see Isaiah 44:28; Ezekiel 37:23, 24; Zechariah 11:16). The word also describes God (Psalm 80:1) and Jesus (Hebrews 13:20; 1 Peter 2:25; 5:4).

8a. *"'I have been with you wherever you have gone, and I have cut off all your enemies from before you.'"*

God's presence with David has been constant. Passages such as 1 Samuel 16:13; 17:45-47; 23:2, 14; 24:10; 26:12; 30:23; 2 Samuel 5:10, 23-25; 6:21 bear this out. In this David is unlike his predecessor King Saul. The Spirit of the Lord was with Saul for a while, but eventually departed from him (1 Samuel 16:14; 18:12).

III. WHAT GOD PROMISES (1 CHRONICLES 17:8b-14)

A. DAVID'S NAME (v. 8b)

8b. *"'Now I will make your name like the names of the greatest men of the earth.*

The terminology we see here reminds us of God's covenant promise to Abraham: "I will make your name great" (Genesis 12:2). The fact that it is God who has made David's name great is also reflected in the parallel passage of 2 Samuel 7:9. Ancient rulers get themselves in serious trouble when they assume that their greatness is due to their own efforts rather than to God (see Daniel 4:28-33; Acts 12:19b-23). David does not tread this path!

B. ISRAEL'S SECURITY (vv. 9, 10a)

9, 10a. *"And I will provide a place for my people Israel and will plant them so that they can have a home of their own and no longer be disturbed. Wicked people will not oppress them anymore, as they did at the beginning and have done ever since the time I appointed leaders over my people Israel. I will also subdue all your enemies.*

God is now bringing to fullness his promise of Genesis 15:13-21 to Abraham: that his *people Israel* can have a peaceful *home of their own*. The word *provide* suggests "to put, place, or set." *Wicked people* (Israel's *enemies*) will be subdued, just as God has subdued and will continue to *subdue* all of David's personal enemies.

I HAVE BEEN WITH *thee* WHITHERSOEVER THOU HAST *walked*
—1 CHRONICLES 17:8

Visual for Lesson 2. *Turn this visual into a discussion question: "What was a time when God was with you?"*

The time of the judges (about 1380 to 1050 BC) had seen great oppression of God's people because of unfaithfulness. In God's ideal plan, this shall be no more! Indeed, Israel is to be planted as a vine in an orchard (see Psalm 80:8-11; Isaiah 5:1-7; Jeremiah 2:21; Ezekiel 19:10-14; compare John 15:1-5).

WHAT A DIFFERENCE IN COVENANTS!

Police in Klamath Falls, Oregon, uncovered a bizarre covenant in February 2005. A man had been using the Internet to entice people to participate in a mass suicide that was to take place on Valentine's Day of that year. The plan was for participants to commit suicide while logged onto the Internet with others who had agreed to do the same.

Fortunately, the pact was discovered before it could be acted upon. Someone alerted authorities after learning that a woman planned to kill her children before committing suicide. The man who tried to set up the mass suicide had been promoting his "suicide ideology" for several years.

The covenants God has made come from his loving heart, not from a twisted mind. His covenants are for our benefit. He has no hidden agenda. His covenants have promised life, not death. They have been offered to people with ears to listen. God's promise to David is a vital precursor to the new covenant we have in Christ. Through Christ, we share in God's promise to David. —C. R. B.

C. DAVID'S DYNASTY (vv. 10b-14)

10b, 11. "'I declare to you that the LORD will build a house for you: When your days are over and you go to be with your fathers, I will raise up your offspring to succeed you, one of your own sons, and I will establish his kingdom.

Within the phrase *the Lord will build a house for you* we see the third meaning of *house* that we mentioned in the commentary to verse 6 (above). This word now signifies the dynasty of David. David is promised that his sons shall reign in his stead after his death. A dynasty of Davidic sons will rule over God's people. God himself will build this house (dynasty).

A DIFFERENT KIND OF DYNASTY

What image does the word *dynasty* bring to your mind? In some countries, people may think of a powerful family that rules (either with benevolence or oppression) for generation after generation. Sports fans may speak of a dynasty when a particular team wins two championships in a row. Americans over the age of 35 may recall the tawdry TV show of the 1980s named *Dynasty*. The show involved schemes and feuds for wealth and power in an oil-rich family. In this respect, that TV program portrayed people much like many to be found in real-life political dynasties.

The producers of that program seem to have zeroed right in on the darker side of human nature. The public's taste for the schemes that made the characters of *Dynasty* rich and strong is seen in the fact that there are Web sites devoted to the episodes and characters in the program. Power-at-any-cost can be a strong fantasy.

When God promised David a dynasty, he had something much different in mind! God, not any man, created that dynasty. David himself was the first king in the dynastic line, and his son Solomon was the second. But by far the greatest and ultimate Son in the royal line would be Jesus. His kingdom is one of righteousness, a far cry from the political and TV-show kingdoms of this world. Our righteous lives demonstrate whose kingdom we are subjects of. —C. R. B.

12. "'He is the one who will build a house for me, and I will establish his throne forever.

DAILY BIBLE READINGS

Monday, Mar. 3—God Chose David (Psalm 78:67-72)

Tuesday, Mar. 4—No House for God (1 Chronicles 17:1-6)

Wednesday, Mar. 5—God's House for David (1 Chronicles 17:7-10)

Thursday, Mar. 6—A House of Ancestors (1 Chronicles 17:11-15)

Friday, Mar. 7—Great Deeds of God (1 Chronicles 17:16-19)

Saturday, Mar. 8—A House of Israel (1 Chronicles 17:20-22)

Sunday, Mar. 9—The House of David (1 Chronicles 17:23-27)

We know from the way that history unfolds that the *he* in this verse refers to one of David's sons—namely, Solomon. *He is the one who will build for* God a *house* (temple); the delay of building the temple from the time of David to the time of Solomon thus will be more than 30 years. In the passage of time, God will establish Solomon's kingdom (*his throne*) too (see 1 Kings 2:46b; 8:15-21; 9:5; 10:4-9, 23-25).

13, 14. "I will be his father, and he will be my son. I will never take my love away from him, as I took it away from your predecessor. I will set him over my house and my kingdom forever; his throne will be established forever."'

The phrase *I will be his father, and he will be my son* is adoption terminology (compare 2 Samuel 7:14; Psalm 2:7; 2 Corinthians 6:18). God, as the ruling Father, has adopted this person as a son to be ruler with his approval.

The word *love* should be understood to signify "covenant loyalty." God will not take away his covenant loyalty from David or his descendants as he took it away from Saul (the first king). Note that the author of Chronicles leaves out mention of possible punishment if any of David's sons should sin against God as we see in 2 Samuel 7:14b. This does not mean that the author of Chronicles is ignorant of that. Rather, he wishes to present Solomon in the best possible light (see Lesson 3).

Note also that the author of Chronicles emphasizes God's part in this covenant promise by saying *my house* and *my kingdom* rather than "your house" and "your kingdom," as we see in 2 Samuel 7:16. It is a dynasty, a *kingdom*, a *throne* that will be established forever at the initiative of God (compare also Psalm 89:3, 4, 20-37). While some may think that this never happened, ultimately God does fulfill this promise as he does with all his promises (see Luke 1:32, 33).

IV. WHAT NATHAN DOES (1 CHRONICLES 17:15)

15. Nathan reported to David all the words of this entire revelation.

Nathan is faithful in delivering *this entire revelation* to *David* word for word. While these are joyful *words* to deliver, Nathan will later have to be the bearer of bad news for David (2 Samuel 12:1-12). Nathan will live long enough to be the prophet to anoint David's son Solomon as king (1 Kings 1:34).

CONCLUSION

It is clear that there were all kinds of covenants in the world of ancient Israel. But one of the greatest covenants was God's covenant of an eternal promise to David that his throne would be forever. It was an unconditional promise in the sense that God would somehow fulfill his promise regardless of the behavior of David's descendants.

History tells us that David's royal descendants did sin—grievously. God did punish those descendants, even to the point of cutting off the Davidic dynasty for a long while (see 2 Samuel 7:14; 1 Chronicles 28:7 [next week's lesson]; Psalm 89:19-49). Many years later, a Davidic Son would appear to whom God would give David's throne (see Luke 1:32, 33). Thus this promise was fulfilled at Jesus' resurrection and ascension to God's right hand (see Acts 2:33-36; 13:34).

Just as God is a covenant-keeping God for his people, we need to be a covenant-keeping people for God. Those who accept Christ and follow the biblical plan of salvation enter into God's new covenant. We need to renew our commitment to that covenant daily. Every step we make, every word we speak, every breath we take is to be made in light of our covenant with God. May we keep covenant with God!

Discovery Learning

This page contains an alternative lesson plan emphasizing learning activities. Classes desiring such student involvement will find these suggestions helpful. The next page is a reproducible activity page to further enhance discovery learning.

INTO THE LESSON

Say to your learners, "Imagine that you are part of a building committee in charge of negotiating with a contractor to construct a new addition to the church facilities. Your committee must draft a contract between the church and the builder that is fair to both parties. What would be some of the key elements of that contract?"

As learners share the answers, record their responses on the board for the whole class to see. Some of the key elements would include the names of the parties to the contract, a definition of terms, the terms of payment, the scheduled completion of the project, and provisions for correcting problems in the building.

When you have compiled a sizable list, tell your class that God has made a number of special contracts or "covenants" with people in the Bible. Today's lesson deals with one of those covenants: the one between God and David.

INTO THE WORD

Using the Lesson Introduction, review briefly the various covenants that led up to the Davidic covenant. Then use the commentary to explain the first five verses of today's lesson text.

Just before moving into a consideration of 1 Chronicles 17:6, distribute copies of the following true-false quiz (the quiz is also printed in the optional student book). Say, "Read 1 Chronicles 17:6-15 to find the correct answers."

T F 1. God promised to treat King Solomon differently from how he treated King Saul.

T F 2. God had not yet commanded Israel to build a permanent structure for him.

T F 3. God promised to build David a beautiful palace.

T F 4. God promised David that one of his sons would build the temple.

T F 5. God never claimed to have made David famous.

T F 6. God promised to establish the throne of David's son forever.

T F 7. God reminded David of his humble beginnings before God made him king of Israel.

T F 8. Part of God's promise to David was that Israel would be a nomadic people forever, continually moving from place to as they did under Moses.

Answers: 1. T (v. 13); 2. T (v. 6); 3. F (v. 10, the promise was to create a dynasty of David's descendants); 4. T (vv. 11, 12); 5. F (v. 8); 6. T (v. 12); 7. T (v. 7); 8. F (v. 9). Go over the correct answers as a class.

Inform your learners that distinct sections may be discerned in Old Testament covenants. Distribute handouts that list those sections as follows (or direct attention to the optional student book, where the list is reproduced):

1. The historical prologue: a review of events leading up to the covenant under consideration.

2. The stipulations: statements of the terms of the covenant, including what God promises to do for those who obey them.

3. The sanctions: warnings against breaking the covenant and a description of penalties for doing so.

4. The oath: a pledge to keep the covenant.

Next, divide your learners into small groups. Ask groups to scan 1 Chronicles 17 and 28:2-10, then write a brief summary of what the Davidic covenant included in terms of the four features. When you review their answers, you will find that section one is covered in 17:1-7; 28:2, 3; section two in 17:7-14; 28:4-9; section three in 28:9; section four in 17:23-27.

(To allow more time for the Into Life segment, you can put the answers on the handouts before you distribute them. This will allow you to summarize them quickly, skipping the small-group research at this point.)

INTO LIFE

Remind your class that we live under the new covenant, mediated by our Lord Jesus Christ. Distribute copies of the Our New Covenant exercise from the Reproducible Page. Ask your small groups to study and summarize each of the following Scriptures, then categorize them under the four covenant section headings of *prologue, stipulations, sanctions,* and/or *oath:* Matthew 28:18-20; John 3:14-18; Acts 2:38; 1 Corinthians 11:23-26; Galatians 3:23–4:7; Ephesians 2:8-10; 1 Timothy 6:11-14; Hebrews 1:1-3; 3:1–4:1; 6:13-20; 9:13-15; 10:19-31.

When groups have finished their work, discuss findings as a class. Ask for volunteers to suggest specific ways to demonstrate that one is living under the covenant promised to David and fulfilled in Christ.

Our New Covenant

Read and summarize each of the following Scripture passages. Then categorize your summaries under the four covenant section headings listed below:

Matthew 28:18-20

John 3:14-18

Acts 2:38

1 Corinthians 11:23-26

Galatians 3:23–4:7

Ephesians 2:8-10

1 Timothy 6:11-14

Hebrews 1:1-3; 3:1–4:1, 6:13-20; 9:13-15; 10:19-31.

1. The HISTORICAL PROLOGUE: a review of the past events leading up to the covenant, including God's blessings upon those who enter into the covenant with him.

2. The STIPULATIONS: a statement of the terms of the covenant—what God promises to do for those who covenant with him and what he expects in return.

3. The SANCTIONS: warnings against breaking the covenant and a description of penalties for doing so.

4. The OATH: a pledge to keep the covenant.

God, the People, and the Covenant
Unit 1: *Signs of God's Covenant*
(Lessons 1-5)

GOD CALLS SOLOMON TO BUILD THE TEMPLE

LESSON 3

Mar
16

WHY TEACH THIS LESSON?

Jealousy can be an infectious sin in the life of the church. Some are jealous of those who are especially gifted in music. Others are jealous of those who have special talents in speaking and teaching. David could have been jealous because God chose someone else to build the temple. But David recognized that the temple was God's idea. As the great architect, God knew best who should carry out the task of leading in the construction of this magnificent structure.

The church is also God's idea. He is the designer and foreman of the building of this magnificent spiritual structure. He knows who functions best in the different aspects of the building of his church. The cure for jealousy is encouragement. When we see a fellow Christian using his or her giftedness in the areas of music, teaching, etc., our encouragement of that person can drive feelings of jealousy far away! Today's lesson provides an example of encouragement from King David.

INTRODUCTION

A. CHOSEN FOR A SPECIFIC TASK

One day my dad decided to add a bedroom and porch to the back of our small house. It was a good idea, because my sister and I were reaching our teenage years, and we needed separate bedrooms.

The only problem was that Dad was not a builder. He was a very good sawmiller and mechanic, but he was not a builder. Yet we could not hire people to do such work because we were poor by the standards of America in the 1950s. So we did it ourselves.

When we were finished, it looked good. But the first substantial rain proved all visual satisfactions to be false security. That roof never stopped leaking. So Dad covered the entire back part of the roof with tar, tar, and more tar. That finally stopped the water leaks, but in really hot weather it leaked tar!

Neither my dad nor I ever became builders in the fullest sense of that word. Today I can safely say that God has called me to be a teacher and preacher, and I try to utilize every facet of my abilities in those directions. It is very satisfying. The few times I have tried to remodel our house have ended in frustration. So now whenever I have such a project to do, I hire others to do it. I know my limitations and my calling.

King David recognized that God had called him to carry out certain tasks, but the task of building the temple was reserved for his son Solomon. King David's limitation was not (unlike mine) one of skill, but one of divine restriction (last week's lesson). David thus encouraged his son to complete the task of building the temple. David had an important calling to fulfill, but building the temple was not part of that calling.

DEVOTIONAL READING:
PSALM 132
BACKGROUND SCRIPTURE:
1 CHRONICLES 28
PRINTED TEXT:
1 CHRONICLES 28:5-10, 20, 21

LESSON AIMS

After participating in this lesson, each student will be able to:

1. Summarize David's charge to Solomon.

2. Compare and contrast the attitudes and behavior David challenged Solomon to display with the attitudes and behaviors the New Testament commands for Christians.

3. Encourage one other person in the coming week to be strong in Christian faith and service.

KEY VERSE

Consider now, for the LORD has chosen you to build a temple as a sanctuary. Be strong and do the work. —1 Chronicles 28:10

LESSON 3 NOTES

DAILY BIBLE READINGS

Monday, Mar. 10—*God's Promise to David (Psalm 132: 1-12)*

Tuesday, Mar. 11—*God Chose Solomon (1 Chronicles 28:1-5)*

Wednesday, Mar. 12—*David Advises Solomon (1 Chronicles 28:6-8)*

Thursday, Mar. 13—*Wholehearted and Willing (1 Chronicles 28:9, 10)*

Friday, Mar. 14—*David's Plan for the Temple (1 Chronicles 28:11-19)*

Saturday, Mar. 15—*God Is with You (1 Chronicles 28:20, 21)*

Sunday, Mar. 16—*For God's Chosen (Psalm 132:13-18)*

B. LESSON BACKGROUND

In the first two lessons of this quarter, we have seen our texts from 1 Chronicles paralleled in 2 Samuel. But today's lesson text from 1 Chronicles 28 has no parallel in 1 Kings 1–2, where we would expect to find such a parallel if it existed. The reason seems to be that the author of Chronicles had a particular interest in recording the beginnings of the temple that the author of Kings did not have. We see much emphasis in Chronicles on the skilled craftsmen who participated in this project.

God had chosen Solomon to see this task through (see 1 Chronicles 28:5, 6, 10; 29:1). No other person was to launch this project. Even though David wanted to build the temple and had collected materials for it, God forbade him because he had been a man of war and had shed blood (1 Chronicles 28:3).

David undoubtedly was aware of the divine choices that God had made through the centuries. Judah had been elevated above his brothers (see Genesis 49:8-10), and David himself had been elevated above his own brothers as well (1 Chronicles 28:4). In a sense, Solomon was elevated above his father, David, in being privileged to build the temple. The temple had to be built by a man of peace, which is the meaning of Solomon's name. Solomon's lengthy reign was characterized by peace (1 Kings 4:24, 25).

I. DAVID'S PRONOUNCEMENTS (1 CHRONICLES 28:5-7)

A. SOLOMON CHOSEN TO BE KING (v. 5)

5. *"Of all my sons—and the LORD has given me many—he has chosen my son Solomon to sit on the throne of the kingdom of the LORD over Israel.*

David had six *sons* born from six different wives during his seven and one-half years in Hebron (2 Samuel 3:2-5; 1 Chronicles 3:1-4). When David made Jerusalem his capital, he took more concubines and wives, and more children were born (2 Samuel 5:13-16; 1 Chronicles 3:5-9; 14:3-7). Indeed, God gave David *many* sons. But of all these it is *Solomon* (who is not David's firstborn) who is chosen to sit on David's *throne*. This is a major theme in this text.

David is very conscious of God's promise to him of an everlasting dynasty (see 2 Samuel 7:16; 1 Chronicles 28:4a). David was overwhelmed by this promise when it was given many years before (2 Samuel 7:18-29). It is through the Davidic dynasty that God chooses to accomplish his plan for the world. Somehow God's reign in Heaven is to be expressed through this *kingdom* on earth.

So God's throne in Heaven and the Davidic throne on earth are interconnected. The author of Chronicles uses an unusual phrase to communicate this idea: *the throne of the kingdom of the Lord over Israel.* This throne is "the faithful witness in the sky" (Psalm 89:37); and even though one day God will "cast [David's] throne to the ground" (Psalm 89:44), he will never take away his promise concerning David's everlasting dynasty. Perhaps David may think that Solomon is the "Lord" to sit at God's right hand until all his enemies are made a footstool for his feet (see Psalm 110:1; compare 1 Kings 5:3). We now know that only Jesus fulfilled and fills that role and position (see Luke 1:32, 33; Hebrews 5–7).

B. SOLOMON TO BUILD THE TEMPLE (v. 6)

6. *"He said to me: 'Solomon your son is the one who will build my house and my courts, for I have chosen him to be my son, and I will be his father.*

Even though the author of Chronicles does not mention it, there has been a long and bitter struggle among David's sons to attain the kingship. It took great court intrigues to have *Solomon* anointed king (see 1 Kings 1–2).

It was by divine direction that David announced Solomon as his successor (1 Chronicles 22:5-13) and the future builder of the temple that David himself so much wanted to build (1 Chronicles 22:7, 8). The wording *chosen him to be my son, and I will be his father* emphasizes Solomon's election by God. It also emphasizes an adoption by God in terms of kingship (compare 2 Samuel 7:14a). The verse before us essentially is a covenant statement to reveal a special relationship between God and Solomon, the son of David.

The word *house* signifies "temple." The addition of the word *courts* (as in "courtyards") will be important to the future pilgrims who will arrive in Jerusalem to celebrate the festivals. They will savor the moment when they enter into the courts of the temple (see Psalm 84:2; 100:4; Isaiah 62:9).

C. SOLOMON'S REIGN TO BE CONDITIONAL (v. 7)

7. "'I will establish his kingdom forever if he is unswerving in carrying out my commands and laws, as is being done at this time.'

This verse echoes the original promise in 2 Samuel 7:13-15. But the author of Chronicles decides not to mention the potential punishment of 2 Samuel 7:14b: "When he does wrong, I will punish him with the rod of men." Even without this, however, the author of Chronicles emphasizes the conditional nature of Solomon's reign by using the little word *if*. If Solomon will obey God's commands, then *his kingdom* (dynasty) will last *forever* (compare 1 Chronicles 22:12, 13).

At the time Chronicles is written centuries after Solomon, there is no Davidic king on a throne in Jerusalem. By that time the remnant in Jerusalem knows the conditional nature of the Davidic dynasty because of the destruction by the Babylonians in 586 BC. The people will hold out hope that God will restore Israel's fortunes by an anointed one like David to bring about a return to the golden age of David. Surely God will fulfill his promise to David that his kingdom will be forever! History proves that Solomon became disobedient toward the end of his life. As a result, the Davidic dynasty suffered. That little word *if* packs a big punch!

Before we move on, we should stress also the unconditional element that we brought out in last week's lesson. In the course of time, God places Jesus on David's throne in a spiritual sense (Luke 1:32, 33). God does this despite the sinful behavior of David's descendants.

THE BIG IF

Operation Overlord marked a turning point in World War II. That was the code name for the Allied invasion of Europe, which took place on June 6, 1944. The success of that operation contributed greatly to the eventual defeat of the Nazis.

Several factors helped the invasion succeed. First, General Eisenhower, Supreme Allied Commander, gambled on a break in the weather. Second, Allied planes dropped bombs well north of the invasion area in an attempt to deceive the Germans into thinking the invasion would come elsewhere. Third, Allied airborne troops delayed German reinforcements so the seaborne invasion would have time to establish a beachhead. *If* the weather improved and *if* the deception worked and *if* the delaying action went as planned, then the invasion might succeed. It did.

But what if any one of those *ifs* had fallen through? It is much more likely that the invasion would have failed, with history taking a different turn. *If* is such a little word, but it has profound implications. Most of us have played the "what if?" game with ourselves, if not with others.

David's instruction to Solomon was, in effect, "Serve God with a faithful heart. If you do, then you will be blessed; but if you do not, then God will turn away from you." The principle still stands. *If* is a big word, isn't it?   —C. R. B.

WHAT DO YOU THINK?

What work has God called you to do? If you have not discovered how you can contribute to the kingdom work, what can you do to discover your role?

HOW TO SAY IT

Davidic. Duh-VID-ick.
Deuteronomy. Due-ter-AHN-uh-me.
Gershon. GER-shun.
Kohath. KO-hath.
Levites. LEE-vites.
Merari. Muh-RAY-rye.
shalem (Hebrew). SHAY-lem.
shalom (Hebrew). shah-LOME.

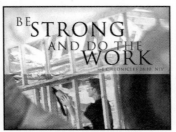

Visual for Lesson 3. *Point to this visual as you ask, "What was a time when God strengthened you for your work?"*

II. DAVID'S CHARGES (1 CHRONICLES 28:8-10)

A. CHARGE TO THE PEOPLE (v. 8)

8. "So now I charge you in the sight of all Israel and of the assembly of the LORD, and in the hearing of our God: Be careful to follow all the commands of the LORD your God, that you may possess this good land and pass it on as an inheritance to your descendants forever.

Those whom David addresses are listed in 1 Chronicles 28:1. In short, they are Israel's leaders and bravest warriors. David concludes his address to them by presenting two witnesses to his words: *of all Israel and of the assembly of the Lord* and *God* himself. The people are charged to obey the Lord's *commands* in order to *possess this good land and pass it on as an inheritance* for their *descendants* permanently. This charge bears a strong resemblance to that given by Moses centuries before (Deuteronomy 32:46, 47).

By the time Chronicles is written, Judah has lost her territory once, and only a remnant populates the land. The people have to learn the hard way that disobedience means the loss of land, just as predicted (see Deuteronomy 31:14-18). For the ancient Israelites, keeping the land is always conditioned on obedience.

B. CHARGES TO SOLOMON (vv. 9, 10)

9. "And you, my son Solomon, acknowledge the God of your father, and serve him with wholehearted devotion and with a willing mind, for the LORD searches every heart and understands every motive behind the thoughts. If you seek him, he will be found by you; but if you forsake him, he will reject you forever.

David charges *Solomon* to *acknowledge the God of your father.* To know or acknowledge God is a covenant concept (see Jeremiah 22:16; Hosea 6:6; Philippians 3:8-10). To know God is to serve him faithfully in covenant relationship. Solomon is to do this with *wholehearted devotion* The Hebrew word for *wholehearted* is *shalem,* which can also be translated "perfect" or "complete." This may be a play on Solomon's name, which is similar to *shalom*—meaning "peace." The words *shalem* and *shalom* look the same without vowels, which is how Hebrew is written. The idea of *wholehearted devotion* is a favorite of the author of Chronicles (compare 1 Chronicles 12:38; 29:9, 19; 2 Chronicles 15:17; 16:9; 19:9; 25:2).

When we add heart to *mind,* we see that Solomon is being charged to know and serve God with every fiber of his being. This is equivalent to the command, "Love the Lord your God with all your heart and with all your soul and with all your strength" (Deuteronomy 6:5).

The fact that God can search all human hearts and minds, understanding even the imaginations of our thoughts, is remarkable from a human standpoint. For God, however, it is reality. That is why God alone is our judge. For that we should be thankful (see Psalm 139:4).

The charge to Solomon here could become a motto for all: "If we seek God, then we will find him; but if we forsake him, then he will cast us off." No great task can be done *for* God unless one first comes to terms *with* God himself. One must *know* the Lord first before one can *serve* faithfully. The building of the temple—indeed, the success of Solomon's entire reign—is contingent upon a personal and covenantal relationship with God by Solomon.

10. "Consider now, for the LORD has chosen you to build a temple as a sanctuary. Be strong and do the work."

The Hebrew word for *consider now* is sometimes translated *see* in the *New International Version* (examples: Deuteronomy 1:21; 11:26). It is like saying, "Be alert to God's call upon your life!"

WHAT DO YOU THINK?

Why do you think that our relationship with God is more important than our work for God? Or is it our work for God that reveals the quality of our relationship with God? Explain.

[Hint: Psalm 51:16, 17; Matthew 15:8; 23:1-36; and 1 Corinthians 13 can enrich your discussion].

God is the one who has *chosen* Solomon *to build a temple* on Mount Zion. The pages of Scripture tell us that it is not an easy life to be handpicked by God. God calls his servants to all kinds of tasks, but this temple-building task for Solomon is a major challenge. And so David charges his son to *be strong and do the work*. Don't we all need someone to provide this kind of encouragement at times?

III. DAVID'S EXHORTATIONS (1 CHRONICLES 28:20, 21)

A. REGARDING CHARACTER (v. 20)

20. David also said to Solomon his son, "Be strong and courageous, and do the work. Do not be afraid or discouraged, for the LORD God, my God, is with you. He will not fail you or forsake you until all the work for the service of the temple of the LORD is finished.

Solomon has heard this before in a private setting before David (see 1 Chronicles 22:13). Now the exhortations are given to Solomon in public.

The kind of public assembly taking place is described in 1 Chronicles 28:1. The nature of this assembly may be compared with that of other assemblies after Israel becomes a monarchy (see 2 Samuel 5:1; 1 Kings 8:1) and after the exile (see Ezra 10:1, 5; Nehemiah 8:1; 9:1). The exhortation *be strong and courageous* is very similar to those found in Joshua 1:6, 7, 9, 18.

One of the covenantal promises that Solomon receives is that of the presence of God himself. He will be there to strengthen and inspire Solomon. Solomon has been chosen for a huge task, and it cannot be done alone. God must be with him. God will see the task to its completion and beyond.

B. REGARDING WORKERS (v. 21)

21. "The divisions of the priests and Levites are ready for all the work on the temple of God, and every willing man skilled in any craft will help you in all the work. The officials and all the people will obey your every command."

We have already mentioned that 1 Chronicles 23–26 is a listing of all those who will participate in the building and maintenance of the new temple. The *priests and Levites* are especially important in this regard.

The author of Chronicles gives some interesting statistics and information concerning the Levites. Only those 30 years old or older are counted, and they number 38,000. Of these, 24,000 are to supervise the construction of the temple while 6,000 are to be "officials and judges." The gatekeepers will number 4,000. Another 4,000 are to play musical instruments as part of a praise orchestra (1 Chronicles 23:3-5).

Organizationally, the Levites are divided into three groups corresponding to the sons of Levi: Gershon, Kohath, and Merari (1 Chronicles 23:6-23). They will be in charge of the service of the temple of the Lord upon its completion (1 Chronicles 23:24-32). For the origin and history of the Levites, see Genesis 29:34; 46:11; Exodus 6:16-25; Numbers 1:47-53; 3:5–4:49; 8:5-26; 35:1-5; etc. Duties in the temple include singing (1 Chronicles 15:16, 17; 25:1-7), oversight of the treasuries (26:20-28), and various other things (26:29-32).

We should recall that while all priests are Levites, not all Levites are priests. Priests are defined in terms of descent from Aaron's sons Eleazar and Ithamar (Exodus 6:23; 28:1; Numbers 3:2-4). David had given the priests an organizational structure (1 Chronicles 24:1-19).

All these people are to be at the disposal of Solomon, especially *every willing man skilled in any craft*. Just as God provided Spirit-filled men to build the tabernacle (Exodus 31:1-11), so God now provides such skilled and willing laborers

WHAT DO YOU THINK?

Tell of a time when you encouraged someone else to a service in God's kingdom. When did someone encourage you to a kingdom task? How did things turn out?

WHAT DO YOU THINK?

There is a saying, "God doesn't call the equipped; he equips the called." Do you agree with this saying? Why, or why not?

for the awesome task at hand (see 1 Kings 5–6). Just as God showed Moses the plans for building the tabernacle (Exodus 25–30), so now David shows Solomon the plans for building the temple; it is a plan inspired by the Spirit of God (1 Chronicles 28:11-19). What Solomon must do now is execute the plan.

CREATING SOMETHING BEAUTIFUL

Question: What is the most complex piece of handmade machinery in the world? *Answer:* A grand piano. Both the question and the answer come from Miles Chapin's book *88 Keys: The Making of a Steinway Piano* (New York: Clarkson Potter, 1997).

The construction of a grand piano takes several years. Little wonder, since each one has 12,000 parts, including "tiny levers, springs, pins, screws, knobs, plates, bushings, bearings, hinges, and flanges," to use Chapin's words. The process involves more than 500 craftsmen who possess skills in mechanical engineering, cabinet-making, wood finishing, and metallurgy.

This complexity makes a grand piano begin to sound like Solomon's temple. The process needed to create both amazes us. People in Solomon's day were given the opportunity to use their gifts and skills to create something of great beauty, and everyone had to work together in harmony. Carrying out the ministries of the church also involves many people and their spiritual gifts coming together. What is your part?   —C. R. B.

CONCLUSION

Solomon had a rare calling: to be ruler over God's people and to build a temple of staggering size and quality. It's safe to say that God will not call anyone today to repeat this role since the church is not ruled by earthly kings, and it is our bodies, not structures of stone, that serve as temples (1 Corinthians 6:19; 2 Corinthians 6:16; Ephesians 2:19-22).

Even so, God still calls us to serve by using the spiritual gifts he has granted (Romans 12:4-8; 1 Corinthians 12; Ephesians 4:11-13). When we recognize what our spiritual gifts are, then we are able to move forward in serving God in specific areas.

However, some people become frustrated when they discover that they are unable to make a living doing what God has called them to do. In other words, they must work at a job in order to make an income that allows them to do what they feel called to do. That situation may be a sign that they have misinterpreted what they thought to be their calling; on the other hand, it may be a sign that even though they have correctly interpreted their calling, God wants them to "go slow" for a while—perhaps to allow time for growth in patience and maturity.

Let me encourage you to listen to God's calling as you discover your spiritual giftedness. When you do, you will find a need in the world you can fill for Christ. Even in retirement, many senior citizens have been given new life by finding such a calling and fulfilling it.

If you wish to make a great contribution to the kingdom of God, first you must have a spiritually healthy attitude concerning who and whose you are. As a child of God, you should have no problem accepting yourself as God's most prized treasure (compare Exodus 19:5).

Second, you need to realize that great achievements require great struggle. Third, expect that great struggle will yield discouragement at times. That is what forces us to lean on God's Spirit to accomplish the task. No one can accomplish great tasks alone. That thought has kept me in the fray when giving up would have been easy. Choose now to make a difference for Christ in the world.

Discovery Learning

This page contains an alternative lesson plan emphasizing learning activities. Classes desiring such student involvement will find these suggestions helpful. The next page is a reproducible activity page to further enhance discovery learning.

INTO THE LESSON

Prepare the following two lists on a sheet of paper; make a copy for each learner. Down the left side, list the occupations *policeman, judge, physician, teacher,* and *minister.* Down the right side, list the character traits or skills of *honesty, courage, wisdom, patience, faith, logic,* and *humor.*

At the bottom of the sheet, print "Which character traits are *E* (for essential), *H* (for helpful), or *U* (for unnecessary) to be successful for each occupation listed?" Distribute copies as your learners enter the classroom (or ask them to turn to the same exercise in the optional student book).

Learners can work on this activity in small groups. Notice that the 5 occupations multiplied by the 7 character traits or skills means that there will be 35 answers. To make this activity go faster, you may wish to assign only 1 occupation to be evaluated per group of learners.

After a few minutes, call on volunteers to share and explain their opinions. Ask what other traits would be essential for each profession. Tell your class that today's lesson will allow comparing and contrasting the attitudes and behavior David challenged Solomon to display with the attitudes and behaviors the New Testament commands for Christians.

INTO THE WORD

Use the Lesson Background and the commentary on 1 Chronicles 28:5-7 to familiarize your learners with today's text. Then divide your class into pairs to work on the following exercise. (This exercise is also printed in the optional student book.)

Solomon's Mission, and Ours. With your partner, study 1 Chronicles 28:5-10, 20, 21 to review the task assigned to Solomon and the character traits he would need to complete that task. Then give brief answers to these questions:

1. What condition did Solomon have to meet in order for God to bless and maintain Solomon's kingdom forever? What conditions do Christians meet in order to be part of God's eternal kingdom?

2. Who would be a witness to make sure Solomon kept God's commandments? Who is our witness in keeping God's commandments?

3. What do you think David meant when he said Solomon should serve God "with wholehearted devotion and with a willing mind"? How can we have such a heart and mind today?

4. Why would Solomon need strength and courage to complete the temple? In what way do we need strength and courage to complete the work on the temple of our bodies (1 Corinthians 6:19; 2 Corinthians 6:16; Ephesians 2:19-22)?

5. Who was to assist Solomon in his work? Who assists us in ours?

After your pairs complete their assignments, review their findings with the entire class. What similarities did they see between the duties of Solomon and the duties of Christians? What essential traits would each need to complete their ministries?

INTO LIFE

Make a transition by asking about the character traits and skills that are essential for missionaries to accomplish their tasks. Write these questions on the board:

1. How are the traits missionaries need to accomplish their tasks different (if at all) from the traits needed by non-missionary Christians? 2. What is our congregation doing to develop the traits that people will need before going to the mission field? 3. What more could each of us be doing to develop the traits and skills that people will need before going to the mission field?

Turn your attention to the lesson conclusion. The author says a Christian desiring to make a contribution for God's kingdom needs one thing and should expect two other things. Write these on the board:

1. A spiritually healthy attitude
2. An expectation of struggle
3. An expectation of discouragement

Discuss each of these points with the class. If the discussion is slow getting started, use these questions as prompts: How do we know when we have a spiritually healthy attitude and when we don't? How do we grow through struggle? Does *expectation* mean the same as *looking forward to it*? Why, or why not?

Alternative: Use The Calling skit from the Reproducible Page. At the end of the skit, ask your learners how they go about evaluating and acting on what they think may God's calling on their lives.

The Calling

For this skit you will need three chairs arranged in a row at the front of the class, facing the back of the classroom. The scene opens with Bob and Karen sitting together in Sunday school class, sipping coffee and munching donuts. George enters, carrying a cup of coffee and his Bible.

KAREN: Good morning, George! You're looking awfully happy today. What's up?

GEORGE: I feel great, and thanks for asking. I just got a terrific offer for my insurance business, and I've decided to sell.

BOB: Wow! That is big news. What does Michelle think about all this?

GEORGE: Michelle and I have been talking with a financial planner. He crunched all the numbers and said we have enough saved so that she can take an early retirement, and we can live comfortably on our investments.

KAREN: So what are you two going to do with all your free time? play golf? travel around the world?

GEORGE: Actually, we've been talking about becoming missionaries. We wouldn't have to raise any support, Michelle has lots of experience traveling in foreign countries, and we both have skills we think could be useful in the right mission setting.

BOB: George, are you serious? That's a BIG commitment you're talking about. Somehow, I can't see the two of you living in a grass hut, eating bugs and stuff.

GEORGE: Not all mission fields are in third world countries. We were thinking about the Far East, maybe Taiwan or China. Michelle already speaks some Chinese.

KAREN: George, those countries are full of Buddhists and Confusionists!

GEORGE: Do you mean "Confucionists"? That's exactly why we want to go there, to offer them an alternative: the good news about Jesus.

BOB: George, they have strange diseases there, like Scars, and they eat boiled cats and stuff. Are you sure you and Michelle are up to all that?

GEORGE: Well, we won't know until we try, will we? And we think God wants us to try.

KAREN: It sounds like you're really committed to this. We'll be praying for you, won't we, Bob? And who knows, maybe some day we'll join you—for a short-term mission trip, that is.

God, the People, and the Covenant
Unit 1: Signs of God's Covenant
(Lessons 1-5)

GOD FULFILLS HIS PROMISES

LESSON 4

WHY TEACH THIS LESSON?

It has been said by some cynics that promises are made to be broken. Unfortunately, we do see promises broken much too often. A couple stands before God and a group of family and friends promising to remain faithful to each other until death should separate them. Then a difficulty arises in the marriage and the promise is broken. Divorce rates attest to this. Politicians run for office making various promises to a diverse constituency to garner votes. But when elected, the promises are too often forgotten.

Frequent promise-breaking by others can make us cynical. We may begin expecting the worst from people instead of the best. Worse, we may begin thinking that keeping our own promises is "optional." To keep any of this from happening, we lift our eyes to the promise-keeping God. That's what today's lesson requires us to do. The lesson will cause us to meditate on God's promises to us. As we do that, we will find ourselves challenged to keep our own promises to him and to others. God is our great role model for keeping promises!

INTRODUCTION

A. PROMISES

People have been known to make promises they didn't keep. When people do keep promises, especially to us personally, it makes us trust them more. The same is true for God. The God we worship is a promise-keeping God. The Scriptures declare that God has kept every promise he ever made and continues to do so. But what about promises we make to God?

I remember making a bold promise to God once. It happened when I was about eight years old. My father was an alcoholic, and our family suffered the usual consequences. My mother was often frustrated with the weekend drinking bouts, and arguments continued throughout the evening on a regular basis. One night my father hit my mother and slammed her against the bedroom wall so hard it shook the house. I saw it happen.

Feeling helpless and hopeless, I ran out of the house to the back lot and jumped into the middle of briars and thistles. There in my "wilderness" surroundings in the middle of the night I prayed. I was not a Christian at the time, but I prayed this prayer anyway: "God, if you are there, please don't let my dad hit my mom again. I will give you my life if you will do this." That was perhaps a rather brazen offer to make. But to my knowledge my parents never fought like that again, although it would be another 13 years before my father would conquer his alcoholism.

Does this kind of bargaining mean anything to God? I felt I had made a promise to God. And if God answered my prayer, I was certainly obligated to keep my promise. He did, and I did! I did not become a Christian until age 14, but my experience at age 8 was the beginning of my life dedicated to full-time Christian ministry. May we all keep our promises. God sure does!

DEVOTIONAL READING:
PSALM 135:1-5
BACKGROUND SCRIPTURE:
2 CHRONICLES 6; LUKE 24
PRINTED TEXT:
2 CHRONICLES 6:12-17; LUKE 24:44-49

Mar 23

LESSON AIMS

After participating in this lesson, each student will be able to:

1. Restate Solomon's words of dedication and Jesus' words of challenge.

2. Compare and contrast the promises of God recognized by Solomon with the promises of God affirmed by Jesus.

3. Tell how he or she would explain the fulfilled promise of Christ's death and resurrection to an unbeliever.

KEY VERSE

This is what I told you while I was still with you: Everything must be fulfilled that is written about me in the Law of Moses, the Prophets and the Psalms.
—Luke 24:44

B. LESSON BACKGROUND I: 2 CHRONICLES 6

Today's text of 2 Chronicles 6:12-17 closely follows the parallel of 1 Kings 8:22-26. A broad look at 2 Chronicles 6 reveals three separate addresses. First, Solomon prayed to God (2 Chronicles 6:1, 2). Solomon did this again as he faced the temple, acknowledging God as present in "a dark cloud" (compare Exodus 19:9, 16; 20:21; Deuteronomy 4:11; 5:22).

Second, Solomon turned from facing the temple toward the congregation in order to bless them (2 Chronicles 6:3-11). The content of this blessing was to praise God for fulfilling his promises to David (see v. 10, a major theme of this chapter). Solomon, David's son, had become king over David's house, the fulfillment of one promise. Another promise was fulfilled when God allowed Solomon to build the temple (vv. 10, 11).

Third, Solomon resumed his prayer to God as he stood on a specially built platform (v. 13) before the altar in the courtyard. Much of today's text is in this third section, with the dedication occurring in about the year 959 BC. The focus is on gratefulness for promises kept and anticipation of the keeping of promises in the future.

C. LESSON BACKGROUND II: LUKE 24

Luke 24 is the resurrection chapter of that Gospel. Here Luke records an appearance of Jesus that is not included in the other Gospel accounts: that of the resurrected Lord to Cleopas and his friend (vv. 13-35) as they walked seven miles from Jerusalem to Emmaus.

Before today's text from Luke 24 opens, Jesus taught those two disciples from Scripture that the Messiah had to suffer before he entered into his glory (Luke 24:26, 27). After recognizing Jesus during the breaking of the bread (vv. 30, 31, 35), they reported their encounter to the disciples in Jerusalem.

Jesus then appeared to them while they were all together. They were so amazed and disbelieving that Jesus resorted to eating a piece of broiled fish in their presence to convince them that his resurrection was real (vv. 41-43)! No doubt the group had experienced this type of meal with Jesus many times before his crucifixion. This is where the second part of today's lesson picks up. Talk about a promise kept!

I. SOLOMON'S PRAYER (2 CHRONICLES 6:12-17)

A. PLACE AND AUDIENCE (VV. 12, 13)

12, 13. Then Solomon stood before the altar of the LORD in front of the whole assembly of Israel and spread out his hands. Now he had made a bronze platform, five cubits long, five cubits wide and three cubits high, and had placed it in the center of the outer court. He stood on the platform and then knelt down before the whole assembly of Israel and spread out his hands toward heaven.

As our text begins, we see Solomon in the third posture that he takes in this ceremony of dedicating the temple of God. (See Lesson Background I for a description of the first two postures.) It is logical to presume that Solomon is in the temple's outer court where the people are, yet he has oriented himself toward or *before the altar.* Why the altar? Because it is the place where sacrifices are made and forgiveness is to be found. The need for forgiveness is a major theme of the prayer to follow in 2 Chronicles 6:22-39 (not in today's text).

The parallel account of 1 Kings 8 does not mention this *bronze platform.* It is an interesting touch added by the author of Chronicles. Converting the *cubits* to modern measurements, the platform is seven to eight feet square and four to five feet high. The use of platforms for special occasions is attested to in other cultures of the ancient Near East.

The purpose of this platform is for Solomon to be seen by the crowd (compare Nehemiah 8:4, 5). This allows the full impact of the occasion to have its effect on the people when Solomon kneels with his hands outstretched *toward heaven* (compare Exodus 9:29, 33; Ezra 9:5; Job 11:13; Psalm 44:20). The setting is dramatic.

The parallel account of Solomon's prayer in 1 Kings 8:22-61 makes for an interesting comparison. That account begins by noting Solomon to be standing; much later, it notes that Solomon rises from where he has been kneeling (v. 54). Thus at some point Solomon has moved from standing to kneeling during his prayer. But the 1 Kings 8 account by itself does not allow us to know exactly when Solomon makes that transition. The account in 2 Chronicles 6 fills that gap: Solomon kneels right at the point we see in 2 Chronicles 6:13, which comes between verse 22 and verse 23 of 1 Kings 8.

B. PRAISE AND RECOGNITION (vv. 14, 15)

14. He said:

"O LORD, God of Israel, there is no God like you in heaven or on earth—you who keep your covenant of love with your servants who continue wholeheartedly in your way.

In the *New International Version* (as in many other translations), the word LORD as rendered in capital letters reflects the Hebrew word *Yahweh*. The stately phrase *Yahweh, God of Israel* occurs three times in our printed text (2 Chronicles 6:14, 16, 17). The exact phrase *there is no God like you* is found in the Bible only here and in the parallel of 1 Kings 8:23. A similar idea (though not the exact wording) occurs in Deuteronomy 4:39; 2 Samuel 7:22; and elsewhere.

Thus does Solomon introduce his praise to God for being a covenant-keeping God. When God keeps a covenant with his people, he shows covenant loyalty to them. To keep the covenant going, God forgives sins against him; without this forgiveness the covenant would collapse. Even so, God still expects us to *continue wholeheartedly* in our walk with him.

15. "You have kept your promise to your servant David my father; with your mouth you have promised and with your hand you have fulfilled it—as it is today.

It is on the basis of covenant-faithfulness and mercy that God kept his promise to *David* to allow his son Solomon the task of building the temple (see 2 Chronicles 6:8, 9). Solomon also anticipates that God will keep his promise that the Davidic dynasty will be forever (compare 1 Chronicles 17:12-14, 23, 24; 22:10; 28; 2 Chronicles 6:10; 13:5; 21:7; 23:3). Solomon thus interprets the completion of the temple and his enthronement as king over Israel as a continuing fulfillment of God's past promises.

C. REQUEST AND REVIEW (vv. 16, 17)

16. "Now LORD, God of Israel, keep for your servant David my father the promises you made to him when you said, 'You shall never fail to have a man to sit before me on the throne of Israel, if only your sons are careful in all they do to walk before me according to my law, as you have done.'

Solomon now looks to the future of the Davidic dynasty. He petitions Yahweh to not allow the dynastic line to *fail.* The fact that the author of Chronicles is writing many years after the apparent failure of David's line in 586 BC makes this request all the more significant.

WHAT DO YOU THINK?

Do most people you deal with "keep covenant" in doing what they say they will do, or is that more the exception than the rule? How does (or how should) this affect you?

WHAT DO YOU THINK?

In what ways has God protected and provided for you?

Solomon, speaking in about 959 BC, knows that the promise of an enduring dynasty is conditional in a sense. That is, the people as well as the king are to *walk before me according to my law* (see also 1 Chronicles 28:7). The Hebrew word translated *keep,* used to refer to God's keeping his promises to David, is the same Hebrew word that challenges the Israelites to *walk* according to God's law.

Interestingly, the parallel passage 1 Kings 8:25 lacks the phrase *to walk . . . according to my law* that the author of Chronicles includes. While Solomon prays for God's promise of an eternal dynasty, the author of Chronicles can hope only for a Davidic Messiah to come in the future. For the author of Chronicles, writing centuries before Christ, the promise is still to be fulfilled. This author has seen how badly the people have sinned in rejecting God's law.

KEEPING PROMISES

General Douglas MacArthur (1880–1964) uttered one of the most famous promises in American history. When Japanese forces overran Allied troops in the Philippines in 1942, President Roosevelt ordered MacArthur to withdraw. MacArthur publicly vowed, "I shall return."

The tide of the war eventually turned, and the Philippines were liberated. As Supreme Commander of Allied forces in the Southwest Pacific Area, MacArthur accepted the Japanese surrender on September 2, 1945. Historians still debate the character of MacArthur in certain regards. He could be flamboyant and arrogant at times. But no one can doubt that he kept his promise.

When Solomon dedicated the temple, he placed the focus where it belonged: on God's faithful fulfillment of his promises. There is no debating the character of God on this matter—he takes his promises seriously and exhibits no flaws in doing so. This fact is both a blessing and a challenge. We are blessed to serve a God who is faithful to his people. We are also challenged by this fact to replicate that divine characteristic in our own lives. Can others count on us for that kind of integrity?

—C. R. B.

17. "And now, O LORD, God of Israel, let your word that you promised your servant David come true."

Solomon certainly wants God's promise to *come true.* This is similar to David's own request in 2 Samuel 7:25-29. The verification can come only as each succeeding king takes his place on the throne of Israel and as each king remains faithful to God's law.

The fact that most of the Davidic kings end up being unfaithful to God according to his law may leave the author of Chronicles wondering how God will fulfill his promise that David's dynasty will last forever. Yet the author of Chronicles hopes for the future. Christians know that God has fulfilled this important promise through the person and work of Jesus the Christ.

II. JESUS' PRESENCE (LUKE 24:44-49)

A. PROPHECY AND FULFILLMENT (vv. 44, 45)

44, 45. He said to them, "This is what I told you while I was still with you: Everything must be fulfilled that is written about me in the Law of Moses, the Prophets and the Psalms."

Then he opened their minds so they could understand the Scriptures.

Solomon reigned between about 970 and 930 BC. Thus we jumped forward almost 500 years to reach the day of the author of Chronicles, whether the author was Ezra or someone else. Now we jump almost another 500 years to Jesus' day in the first century AD. How grand is the sweep of history!

After Jesus' resurrection from the dead, he appeared to various people. In the text before us, Jesus stands in the presence of his apostles (*them*) in their hiding place. Luke has prepared us for verse 44 by reporting at the beginning of his Gospel what the angel Gabriel said to Mary: "The Lord God will give him the throne of his father David, and he will reign over the house of Jacob forever; his kingdom will never end" (Luke 1:32b, 33). That time has come!

Here Jesus reminds his stunned disciples how *everything* that was *written about* him had to be *fulfilled*. The prophecies cover the entire Hebrew Scriptures, described here as *the Law of Moses, the Prophets and the Psalms*. These three designations sum up the totality of the Hebrew Bible, which we call the Old Testament.

Today, our Bibles arrange the Old Testament in a 5-12-5-5-12 format. This means that there are, in order, 5 books of law, 12 books of history, 5 books of wisdom literature, 5 books by "major" prophets, and 12 books by "minor" prophets. But that is not the arrangement of Jesus' day, although the text then and now is the same. The first-century Jews use the simpler arrangement of law, prophets, and psalms. The designation *psalms* is used rather loosely to signify all the inspired Old Testament books that are not properly classified as books of law or prophets.

Other New Testament passages refer to what the law and the prophets say about Christ (see John 1:45; Acts 28:23; Romans 3:21). Jesus uses the Psalms extensively to refer to himself during his ministry (examples: compare Matthew 21:16 with Psalm 8:2; Matthew 21:42 with Psalm 118:22, 23; Mark 15:34 with Psalm 22:1; and Luke 20:42, 43; 22:69 with Psalm 110:1).

B. PROCLAMATION AND WITNESS (vv. 46-49)

46, 47. He told them, "This is what is written: The Christ will suffer and rise from the dead on the third day, and repentance and forgiveness of sins will be preached in his name to all nations, beginning at Jerusalem.

The disciples had had great trouble with Jesus' teaching about his going to Jerusalem to *suffer* and die (see Matthew 16:21-23; Mark 8:31, 32; Luke 18:31-34). But surely Jesus had spoken to them of the suffering servant of Isaiah 53! (Compare Luke 22:37, which quotes Isaiah 53:12.) Jesus' teaching had included the other servant songs of Isaiah (compare Matthew 12:18-20 with Isaiah 42:1-4; Acts 13:47 with Isaiah 49:1-6; etc.). Such texts include Jesus' teaching about *repentance and forgiveness of sins* and Messiah's mission to the Gentiles (*all nations*). And Jesus is unlikely to have left out Isaiah 25 and 26 when discussing his own resurrection (compare John 2:22)!

48. "You are witnesses of these things.

We see the fact of Jesus' resurrection confirmed again in Acts 2:25-28, where the apostle Peter uses Psalm 16:8-11 as an argument for the resurrection of Jesus. Peter was a witness to this fact of history. Peter acknowledges his own status as witness by saying this of David: "But he was a prophet and knew that God had promised him on oath that he would place one of his descendants on his throne. Seeing what was ahead, he spoke of the resurrection of the Christ, that he was not abandoned to the grave, nor did his body see decay. God has raised this Jesus to life, and we are all witnesses of the fact" (Acts 2:30-32).

In an early cleansing of the temple, Jesus had encountered the authorities (John 2:13-18). They had demanded a miraculous sign from him to establish his authority for doing what he did. The sign Jesus offered was unexpected: "Destroy this temple, and I will raise it again in three days" (John 2:19).

WHAT DO YOU THINK?

Jesus opened his followers' minds to the Scriptures. What was a time when you had an "Aha!" moment in God's Word?

Visual for Lesson 4. *Use this visual to introduce the discussion question above.*

The Jews were astonished by this, for the only temple they were familiar with was still being built after 46 years (John 2:20)! Yet Jesus had been talking about himself (John 2:21)—the place of God's dwelling, "the Word became flesh" (John 1:14). From the beginning of Jesus' ministry, his resurrection was uppermost in his mind. The disciples had been witnesses of all this, although full comprehension was delayed.

USELESS CURIOSITIES

Susanne Kaplan has studied landscape architecture. So it's no wonder that she finds intriguing what a former owner of her house did to the front yard. Buried there is what Kaplan calls her "little history museum." It is actually a bomb shelter, built in 1961.

A 30-foot spiral stairway leads down to a room that holds 8 bunk beds, a generator, bathroom, and kitchen. The shelter is typical of thousands that were built during the nuclear war scares of the 1960s—the Cold War era.

Kaplan, like many other homeowners with similar shelters in their yards, is unsure what to do with it. She finds it claustrophobic, and the spiral staircase makes it difficult to use as storage space. Many owners say theirs are havens for vermin and are nothing more than useless curiosities.

Jesus also spent time in an underground space. The fact that Jesus' tomb is empty is a vital fact of Christianity. But the fact God has not chosen to preserve it for us demonstrates that it too is a useless curiosity (wherever it is). Why look for Jesus in a place where he is not to be found?

The gospel message of Jesus' resurrection brings with it the important fact that all graves eventually shall lose their usefulness! The Law, the Prophets, and the Psalms had all pointed toward this truth, but the gospel message finally made it clear.   —C. R. B.

49. "I am going to send you what my Father has promised; but stay in the city until you have been clothed with power from on high."

With Christ's resurrection comes the fulfillment of Old Testament prophecies. However, a more recent promise remains to be fulfilled at the time Jesus speaks the words of verse 49. It is the promise of the Spirit (see John 14:15-31).

Just a short time later, on the Day of Pentecost, the apostles indeed will be *clothed with power from on high* (Acts 2). After Pentecost, each Christian becomes a witness to the power of the indwelling Holy Spirit as well as a witness to the God who keeps promises (Acts 2:38, 39).

CONCLUSION

The concept of *temple* is one of the most important images for the church's mission in the world today. The Old Testament temple was a symbol of covenant made, kept, and broken. God was pleased to put his glory in Solomon's temple (1 Kings 8:11; 2 Chronicles 5:14). Because of the sins of God's people and their kings, God withdrew his glory (Ezekiel 10). The temple was destroyed in 586 BC. Ezekiel envisioned a perfect temple for the future (Ezekiel 40–48).

Jesus visited the temple that Herod was building and called it "my Father's house" (John 2:16). But he also identified himself as the temple, the place of God's dwelling (John 2:19-21). With the arrival of Jesus on earth and his subsequent resurrection, the promise of God's new covenant became reality (Jeremiah 31:31-34; Hebrews 8:8-12; 10:16, 17). The question now is, will we keep that covenant or will we break it? Will we learn lessons from Old Testament history about the faithfulness of God and the tendencies of sinful human nature?

WHAT DO YOU THINK?

How will you be a witness to the power of the Spirit within you this coming week?

THOUGHT TO REMEMBER

God makes promises. God keeps promises.

Discovery Learning

This page contains an alternative lesson plan emphasizing learning activities. Classes desiring such student involvement will find these suggestions helpful. The next page is a reproducible activity page to further enhance discovery learning.

INTO THE LESSON

Distribute copies of the following quiz as your learners arrive. (The quiz is also printed in the optional student book.) Ask learners to match each famous promise with the person who made it. Then decide if the promise was kept or broken.

Promises: 1. "I shall return." 2. "Whether you like it or not, history is on our side. We will bury you." 3. "Read my lips: No new taxes." 4. His "last territorial demand" in Europe would be the Sudetenland. 5. "The Jets will win [Super Bowl III] on Sunday, I guarantee it."

Promise Makers: a. Adolf Hitler, 1938; b. Douglas MacArthur, 1942; c. Nikita Khrushchev, 1956; d. Joe Namath, 1969; e. George H. W. Bush, 1988.

Answers: 1. b. Kept. MacArthur led American troops back to the Philippines in 1944; 2. c. Broken. Far from burying capitalism, Soviet Communism collapsed in 1991. 3. e. Broken. In 1990, President Bush signed into law a major tax increase. 4. a. Broken. After that 1938 promise, Hitler went on to attempt the conquest of all of Europe. 5. d. Kept. Namath led the New York Jets to victory in Super Bowl III.

Discuss the quizzes together. Tell your class that today's lesson deals with some of God's greatest promises fulfilled through Solomon in the Old Testament and Jesus in the New. (*Option*: Use the Action and Reaction, Part 1 exercise from the Reproducible Page to add depth to this discussion.)

INTO THE WORD

Use the Lesson Background to introduce today's text. Then divide your class into small groups; give each a copy of the questions below. Each group will study 2 Chronicles 6:12-17 and Luke 24:44-49. (Answers are in parentheses, but do not distribute those. The questions also appear in the optional student books.)

1. Where was Solomon in Jerusalem when he prayed in the presence of all Israel? (*before the altar of the Lord*); 2. According to David, what sets God apart from false gods? (*He keeps his covenant of love with his servants*); 3. The condition upon which God keeps his covenants is what? (*the people continue wholeheartedly to walk in his ways*); 4. What promise did God make to David? (*an enduring dynasty*); 5. Jesus said which sections of the Old Testament contained prophecies about him? (*the Law*

of Moses, the Prophets, the Psalms*); 6. Jesus commanded the disciples to preach what message? (*repentance and forgiveness of sins*); 7. The disciples were to wait in Jerusalem until they received what? (*power from on high*)

Use the questions and answers to guide your discussion of today's text. Follow each answer by asking, "Why is this important?"

INTO LIFE

Make, photocopy, and distribute copies of the following two-column chart. Down the left-hand side of the page, put the entries that are under the heading *Promise That Messiah Would*. Down the right-hand side, put the entries that are under the header *As Fulfilled in Jesus*. Make each entry on the left-hand side exactly even with its counterpart on the right-hand side.

Promise That Messiah Would . . .

1. come from Judah
2. begin ministry in Galilee
3. preach the good news
4. enter the temple
5. be a prophet
6. die for our sins
7. rise from the dead
8. conquer death for us
9. preserve David's dynasty
10. be a light to the Gentiles

. . . As Fulfilled in Jesus

1. Micah 5:2; Matthew 2:3-6
2. Isaiah 9:1, 2; Matthew 4:12-17
3. Isaiah 61:1; Luke 7:22
4. Malachi 3:1; Matthew 21:12, 13
5. Deuteronomy 18:15; Acts 3:22, 23
6. Isaiah 53:4-6; 1 Peter 2:24, 25
7. Psalm 16:8-11; Acts 2:30-32
8. Isaiah 25:8; 1 Corinthians 15:54, 55
9. 1 Chronicles 22:10; Luke 1:32, 33
10. Isaiah 49:6; Acts 26:23

Allow a time of reaction to the chart. Ask your learners to suggest ways to use this chart as a resource for explaining Christ to unbelievers. (*Option*: Use the Action and Reaction, Part 2 exercise from the Reproducible Page for learners to list their reactions.) Encourage learners to keep the chart in their Bibles for that purpose.

Action and Reaction, Part 1

The five promises we noted from Bush, Hitler, Khrushchev, MacArthur, and Namath (whether kept or broken) are not of equal importance. In the blanks below, rank-order them from most important (#1) to least important (#5). Then see if you can provide a biblical reason for putting them in the order that you did. Discuss.

1. _____

2. _____

3. _____

4. _____

5. _____

> The biblical basis I have for putting the promises in this order is:

Action and Reaction, Part 2

Our "Promise that Messiah would . . ." exercise showed us 10 promises fulfilled in Jesus. How can you use those fulfilled promises to explain Christ to others? As you listen to your classmates' suggestions, jot them in the spaces below.

Good ideas! I can definitely use these:

I am uncertain about these ideas:

God, the People, and the Covenant
Unit 1: Signs of God's Covenant
(Lessons 1-5)

JOSIAH RENEWS THE COVENANT

LESSON 5

WHY TEACH THIS LESSON?

Spiritual renewal has been a popular topic in Christianity over the past several years. Most people may think along the lines of subjective experience when this topic comes up. If so, then renewal may be thought of as a personal matter, with heavy emphasis on positive thinking, introspection, and psychology. The way to renewal is said to be through the use of the arts and music. Group retreats and personal time alone with God are encouraged as helpful ways to find renewal.

These things may be effective tools for seeking renewal, but only if accompanied by a serious study of the Word of God. The text for today's lesson provides the proper basis for spiritual renewal in this regard. Renewal based on God's Word is renewal that focuses on doing things God's way. After this lesson your learners will be more open to allowing God to convict them in areas where they are not living in accord with his Word.

INTRODUCTION

A. MENDING A BROKEN RELATIONSHIP

When I became a Christian at age 14, I knew I had entered into a covenant relationship with God through Jesus Christ. I believed that relationship was sustained by the power of God's Spirit abiding in my life, though I had no means of biblically analyzing the relationship at such a young age.

At age 18 I found myself working at a service station in East Point, Georgia, in 1961. The Civil Rights movement was gaining momentum in the Deep South, and Southern whites who were in businesses that served the public were on edge, fearful of an all-out rebellion. The owner of the service station, the father of a good friend of mine, had given me a job as a gesture of kindness. He was essentially a decent man. But like many Southerners, he held a racial prejudice that considered whites to be superior.

After I had worked for almost three months, my boss trusted me with running the station whenever he went to the bank to deposit money. On one occasion, he said to me as he was leaving, "Don't let any blacks use the whites-only restroom." African-Americans only were allowed to use the same restroom the workers used, which also remained dirty most of the time!

Almost as soon as he left, a large Cadillac pulled into the station. A young black family emerged, and the father asked me to "fill it up with high test." In the process, the mother gathered her two young children to take them to the restroom.

Without thinking or searching my conscience, I parroted my boss's warning and told them they couldn't use the whites-only restroom. Immediately I knew I had made a serious mistake. The father ordered me to stop filling the tank

DEVOTIONAL READING:
PSALM 119:25-40
BACKGROUND SCRIPTURE:
2 CHRONICLES 34
PRINTED TEXT:
2 CHRONICLES 34:15, 18, 19, 25-27, 29, 31-33

Mar 30

LESSON AIMS

After participating in this lesson, each student will be able to:

1. Tell what Josiah did upon learning of the discovery of the book of the law in the temple.

2. Explain why humility is necessary to be in a right relationship with God and his law.

3. Make a public or private renewal of his or her commitment to obey Jesus.

KEY VERSE

The king stood by his pillar and renewed the covenant in the presence of the LORD—to follow the LORD and keep his commands, regulations and decrees with all his heart and all his soul, and to obey the words of the covenant written in this book.
—2 Chronicles 34:31

with gas. He paid me for the gas I had put in to that point, and then the parents rushed their children into the car and sped off.

Why did I have to be so morally weak? I had sinned against God as well as against that family. I fell on my knees underneath the canopy of the station and prayed out loud to God, "O God, forgive me! Take this vile prejudice from my heart forever and never let me be a part of this sinful system again. Give me opportunities to make it up to this family that I have greatly harmed. I beg you, in Jesus' name."

From that day on I dropped the racial prejudice that had been instilled in my life by my parents and my culture from the time I was a child. God tested me on many occasions, giving me many opportunities to help African-Americans who faced formidable roadblocks as they sought an education through a Bible college or a place of service among the churches.

Only after many years of faithful service and direct obedience to God's will in this area of my life could I feel that I had mended a broken relationship with God. Some people seem to require a stunning confrontation with the reality of sin to be obedient fully to the will of God as revealed in his Word. I think that is what happened to King Josiah.

B. LESSON BACKGROUND

Second Chronicles 34 is the story of the reforms of godly King Josiah. Josiah ruled the southern kingdom of Judah from about 640 to 609 BC. Josiah's two predecessors, namely Manasseh and Amon, were evil. Their evil permeated Judah for nearly 60 years. This meant that Josiah had a lot of work to do to turn things around spiritually for his nation.

Second Chronicles 34 offers us interesting parallels to 2 Kings 22 and 23. It is important to study both accounts for the fullest picture. Some information that the author of Chronicles gives us is unique, not being mentioned in 2 Kings 22 and 23.

One such piece of information is that in the eighth year of Josiah's reign (about 632 BC) "he began to seek the God of his father David" (2 Chronicles 34:3a). Perhaps the preaching of Zephaniah of the time had some influence upon the young Josiah (age 16). The ministry of the prophet Jeremiah, which began about 626 BC (see Jeremiah 1:2), may have had some influence as well. Another piece of information in 2 Chronicles but not 2 Kings is that Josiah began to purge the land of idolatry when he was 20 years old (2 Chronicles 34:3b).

Before today's lesson text opens, those accounts tell us that we are in the eighteenth year of King Josiah's reign (2 Kings 22:1, 3; 23:23; 2 Chronicles 34:1, 8), with the king at age 26. At that time he undertook to repair the temple, since it had not been attended to during the reigns of previous kings. Throughout the story one can perceive the author's emphasis on the Levites' part in the repairs (2 Chronicles 34:9, 12, 13, 30; absent from 2 Kings).

After Josiah began his reform in Jerusalem and Judah, he moved into the northern territory. Then, "he went back to Jerusalem" (2 Chronicles 34:6, 7). That holy city is the setting for today's lesson.

I. PROGRESS OF REFORM (2 CHRONICLES 34:15, 18, 19)

Josiah sought to repair the temple in his eighteenth year as king, as noted above. In the process of paying money to the workers and their overseers, "Hilkiah the priest found the Book of the Law of the Lord that had been given through Moses" (v. 14).

A. Finding the Book of the Law (v. 15)

15. Hilkiah said to Shaphan the secretary, "I have found the Book of the Law in the temple of the Lord." He gave it to Shaphan.

We may be amazed to read that *Hilkiah*, a priest, has *found the Book of the Law in the temple*. Isn't that where it's supposed to be? And how can such an important thing ever get "lost"?

The answers lie in the neglect of decade after decade by evil Kings Manasseh and Amon. Whatever godly priests continued to exist during their evil reigns probably were inclined to hide such a precious document from destructive hands. As most of us know to our embarrassment, we can be so good at hiding something for "safekeeping" that we end up forgetting where we hid it!

Another issue also presents itself: Exactly which book is this? Many scholars think that it is probably the book of Deuteronomy. Several facts support this conclusion. First, the phrase "the Book of the Covenant" in 2 Chronicles 34:30 can fit the entirety of Deuteronomy, since it is in the form of a covenant renewal treaty. (We also recognize, however, that the phrase "the Book of the Covenant" is used in Exodus 24:7, most likely to describe the material in Exodus 20–23.)

Second, the emphasis in Deuteronomy 12 on worship in one place is consistent with Josiah's reforms. Third, the purging of the land of pagan cultic places is found also in Deuteronomy 12. This could make a big impression on Josiah, since that is exactly what he is doing even before the Book of the Law is found. Fourth, the reference to "curses" in 2 Chronicles 34:24 could point to the extended curses spelled out in Deuteronomy 27:9-26; 28:15-68. Fifth, the celebration of Passover in 2 Chronicles 35 is similar to the commands of Deuteronomy 16:1-8.

A final argument that Deuteronomy is the book that is found is its emphasis that keeping the land depends on obedience to the covenant. Reading Deuteronomy 29 alone would be enough to cause Josiah to tear his clothes in anguish in this regard (compare 2 Chronicles 34:19, below).

B. Reading the Book of the Law (v. 18)

18. Then Shaphan the secretary informed the king, "Hilkiah the priest has given me a book." And Shaphan read from it in the presence of the king.

Shaphan is part of the group given responsibility to repair the temple (2 Chronicles 34:8). As a *secretary* or scribe, Shaphan naturally has a keen interest in this *book*. So *Hilkiah the priest* delivers the book to him in order to get it to King Josiah as quickly as possible. We may speculate that Shaphan reads the entire book of Deuteronomy to *the king*.

C. Tearing of the King's Robes (v. 19)

19. When the king heard the words of the Law, he tore his robes.

To tear one's clothes is to communicate remorse, humility, and repentance (see Isaiah 36:22; 37:1). King Josiah already has been busy ridding the land of the trappings of idolatry. The anguish that Josiah now demonstrates shows that his heart truly matches those actions. He instinctively knows that outward reform in terms of smashed pagan idols will not necessarily mean inward reform or true repentance on the people's part.

We may note here in passing that Josiah's reaction is in marked contrast to the later reaction of King Jehoiakim (Josiah's son). Evil Jehoiakim will exhibit a brazen contempt for the Lord's message that comes through Jeremiah by cutting up the prophet's scroll, casting it into the fire, and refusing to tear his clothes (Jeremiah 36:22-24).

How to Say It

Amon. AY-mun.
Hilkiah. Hill-KYE-uh.
Jehoiakim. Jeh-HOY-uh-kim.
Jeremiah. Jair-uh-MY-uh.
Jerusalem. Juh-ROO-suh-lem.
Josiah. Jo-SIGH-uh.
Manasseh. Muh-NASS-uh.
Shaphan. SHAY-fan.
Zephaniah. Zef-uh-NYE-uh.

What Do You Think?

Josiah tore his clothes as a way to express his grief over sin. What might a Christian do today when confronted with national or personal sin? [Make sure to consider Psalm 51:17 and Joel 2:13 in your discussion.]

What Do You Think?

What was a time when you set out to improve an area of your life, only to discover that you were in worse shape than you had originally thought? How did you react to the discovery? How did you grow spiritually as a result?

REKINDLING THE SPARK

Everett and Pauline Carl got married the first time in 1936. They eloped to Arizona where it was legal for 17-year-olds to get married. But after 12 years of marriage and three daughters, Everett and Pauline allowed financial problems to sink their marriage, so they divorced. Each married someone else. Years later, both their spouses died. The daughters then planned a family cruise and invited their widowed parents. Everett and Pauline accepted the invitation, and aboard ship the old spark of romance was rekindled. Just after the cruise ended, the couple remarried, having divorced 56 years earlier.

The story of God's people is somewhat parallel to that of the Carls. The Bible often uses the marriage analogy to describe the relationship between God and Israel. However, God divorced northern Israel after she let her fascination with other gods lead her astray (Jeremiah 3:8). God eventually turned away from southern Judah for the same reason (Ezekiel 23:18). But as Josiah was repairing the neglected temple, the lost book of the Law was found, and the relationship with God was rekindled, at least temporarily.

"The Book" still tells us of God's continuing love. Though we might wander, the relationship can be rekindled if we will return to God. May the church continue to present herself as the bride of Christ in all her purity!   —C. R. B.

II. DELAY OF CURSES (2 CHRONICLES 34:25-27)

Josiah's anguish moves him to action: he sends Hilkiah and a delegation to inquire of Huldah the prophetess, who lives in Jerusalem (vv. 20-22, not in today's text). Her response is not reassuring: the curses of the book will indeed fall upon the people and the land (v. 24, not in today's text). The reason is given next.

A. REASONS FOR THE CURSES (v. 25)

25. "'Because they have forsaken me and burned incense to other gods and provoked me to anger by all that their hands have made, my anger will be poured out on this place and will not be quenched.'

The people are violating the key prohibition in Deuteronomy: they are following *other gods* (see particularly Deuteronomy 13). This mind-set has become ingrained in the people over a period of nearly 60 years since evil King Manasseh (Josiah's grandfather) began to reign (2 Chronicles 33:1-9). Burning incense as an act of worship is reserved for the one true God (Exodus 30:1-10; 40:26, 27; Luke 1:9). The prophet Jeremiah, whose ministry overlaps the reign of King Josiah, also speaks out on this issue (Jeremiah 1:16; 7:9; 11:13; etc.).

Hundreds of years before, God promised to pour out his *anger* should his people follow fictitious gods (Deuteronomy 5:7-9; 6:14, 15; 8:19, 20; 31:16-21). God's anger, which will result in the destruction of Jerusalem, is 36 years away, given the time frame of the verse before us.

B. REACTION OF THE LORD (vv. 26, 27)

26, 27. "Tell the king of Judah, who sent you to inquire of the LORD, 'This is what the LORD, the God of Israel, says concerning the words you heard: Because your heart was responsive and you humbled yourself before God when you heard what he spoke against this place and its people, and because you humbled yourself before me and tore your robes and wept in my presence, I have heard you, declares the LORD.'"

The wrath of God that is coming upon the land is certain (see 2 Kings 21:10-15; no parallel in 2 Chronicles). But now the prophetess Huldah speaks

WHAT DO YOU THINK?

Most of us are very comfortable discussing God's love. On a scale of 1 (low) to 10 (high), what is your comfort level when discussing God's anger? Explain.

personally of Josiah, *the king of Judah,* in light of that certainty. Because Josiah is *responsive* to God's Word, God has *heard.* The Lord notices godly humility yet today (James 4:6; 1 Peter 5:5, 6).

III. RENEWAL OF COVENANT (2 CHRONICLES 34:29, 31-33)

In verse 28 (not in today's text) Huldah prophesies that Josiah will go to the grave "in peace" and that his eyes will not see any of the evil coming upon the land and the people. This prophecy may give Josiah a bit of false hope, for he may interpret it to mean that he will live a full life and that disaster is not near. Little does he realize that he will live only another 13 years.

Josiah will die in 609 BC because of a questionable decision to engage the Egyptians in battle (see 2 Chronicles 35:20-25). He goes to his grave "in peace" in the sense that Judah is still a viable nation at the time. Truly Josiah's eyes will not see the destruction of the land because he will die early. What irony the prophetess speaks! Josiah reigns for 31 years (640–609 BC), but lives only 39 years (being born about 648 BC).

A. PUBLIC CALLING (v. 29)

29. Then the king called together all the elders of Judah and Jerusalem.

The *elders* represent all the leadership *of Judah and Jerusalem.* Verse 30 (not in today's text) sketches this gathering further as including "the men of Judah, the people of Jerusalem, the priests and the Levites—all the people from the least to the greatest."

The parallel account in 2 Kings 23:2 mentions prophets instead of Levites, so both groups are included. Both the authors of Kings and Chronicles want to emphasize that all the leadership is there with a huge crowd of people, which includes both "the least" and "the greatest."

B. PUBLIC RECOMMITMENT (vv. 31, 32)

31. The king stood by his pillar and renewed the covenant in the presence of the LORD—to follow the LORD and keep his commands, regulations and decrees with all his heart and all his soul, and to obey the words of the covenant written in this book.

The place where Josiah stands is beside a *pillar* (see the parallel in 2 Kings 23:3). To make *a covenant* may involve sacrificing an animal, although this is not explicitly stated. Perhaps animal sacrifices are not needed for this ceremony. In any case, the king shows his leadership qualities by setting a public example. Further, Josiah will see to it that many animals are sacrificed during his renewal of the Passover celebration, also in this same year (2 Chronicles 35:1-9). Other covenant renewal ceremonies can be found in Joshua 8:30-35; 24; 1 Samuel 12; and Nehemiah 8–10.

32. Then he had everyone in Jerusalem and Benjamin pledge themselves to it; the people of Jerusalem did this in accordance with the covenant of God, the God of their fathers.

It is not just Josiah who renews a commitment to *the covenant* while the others remain spectators. No, Josiah causes the people to recommit themselves as well.

The mention of *Benjamin* adds a bit of color to the narrative that is not found in the parallel of 2 Kings 23:3. Benjamin has always been considered to be a part of Judah as opposed to the northern kingdom of Israel (in exile by his time). Thus Benjamin belongs to the southern tribes (compare 2 Chronicles 25:5; 34:9; Ezra 1:5; 4:1; 10:9).

Visual for Lesson 5. *Start a discussion with this visual as you ask, "What steps can you take this week to renew your life in Christ?"*

WHAT DO YOU THINK?

What practical advice would you offer a new believer to help him or her draw closer to God?

PRAYER

Our Father, you have revealed to us your will through holy Scripture and through your Son, the incarnate Word. Forgive us for breaking covenant with you. Today we renew our covenant with you. Help us to walk in your ways with all our heart, soul, and strength. May your Word bring renewal to our lives so that our relationship with you will be restored. In Jesus' name, amen.

WHAT DO YOU THINK?

As Josiah removed abominations from the land, so we too must "take out the trash" in our lives in order to renew our walk with God. How do you do this in your own life?

THOUGHT TO REMEMBER

Renewal always begins with repentance.

"I PLEDGE ALLEGIANCE . . ."

Americans are flag-wavers. After the 9/11 terrorist attacks, people who hadn't flown an American flag in years hoisted the Stars and Stripes in pride and defiance. Flags flew on poles and radio antennae; they were pasted in windows and painted on the roofs of buildings.

Patriotic symbols were seen everywhere. Much was made in the media about a "rebirth of patriotism." Yet Americans also can be fickle. It wasn't too long before many of the flags came down and people went back to life as usual.

One U.S. senator said that patriotism should be a love of ideals—the values that inspire the nation. A love of godly ideals was what inspired Josiah to lead his people in renewing their pledge of allegiance to God and his covenant. For centuries the people of God had vacillated between serving God and serving idols. The captivity of northern Israel in 722 BC and the Assyrian invasion of 701 BC probably were something like "9/11 experiences" for Judah: first came alarm, then resolve, and then it was back to business as usual.

The text in front of us shows the people once again pledging their allegiance to God. Yet again it wouldn't last. Their attention would again drift elsewhere. Times change, but human nature doesn't seem to!

—C. R. B.

C. PUBLIC PURGE (v. 33)

33. Josiah removed all the detestable idols from all the territory belonging to the Israelites, and he had all who were present in Israel serve the LORD their God. As long as he lived, they did not fail to follow the LORD, the God of their fathers.

This is a summary statement by the author of Chronicles of all that Josiah does to bring reform to the people of God. It also functions as what is called an *inclusio* since it comes full circle where the story of Josiah began: "And [Josiah] did what was right in the eyes of the Lord and walked in the ways of his father David, not turning aside to the right or to the left" (2 Chronicles 34:2).

This speaks highly for a young king who follows two of the most wicked kings ever to rule the southern kingdom of Judah. Unfortunately, Josiah will not live very long. His reforms and renewal will turn out to be "too little, too late," as subsequent events show.

CONCLUSION

I have taught for over 30 years, in two Bible colleges. My emphasis in all my Bible classes has been *teach the people!* How will they ever know the Lord without a mature and full knowledge of his Word?

There is a desperate need in our churches for renewal. We can change worship styles or add programs to help our churches grow, but what we absolutely need is greater biblical literacy.

Only a recommitment to God's Word as divine revelation can avert a coming disaster. Submission to the Word's authority in terms of obedience is vital. Churches are in danger of losing their heritage, identity, and roots. We have whole generations that know little of the Bible, and what little they know is often misinterpreted. A fresh discovery of the Word of God can mend broken relationships with God as well as with others. It is possible to become (again) "a people of the Book"!

One person can make a difference in the life of a congregation by encouraging a recommitment to Bible study. This will take time and effort, but mature study over a long period of time will make all the difference. Let us seek to restore our covenant relationship with God through a renewed effort to understand God's Word.

Discovery Learning

This page contains an alternative lesson plan emphasizing learning activities. Classes desiring such student involvement will find these suggestions helpful. The next page is a reproducible activity page to further enhance discovery learning.

INTO THE LESSON

Make and distribute copies of this quiz for your learners to work on as they arrive. (The quiz also appears in the optional student books.) Learners are to match each famous discovery with the date when it was made.

1. Bedouin goatherds discover the Dead Sea Scrolls; 2. James Marshall discovers gold at Sutter's Mill, Coloma, California; 3. Columbus discovers the new world; 4. Marie Curie discovers radium; 5. Heinrich Schliemann discovers the ruins of the city of Troy, in Turkey; 6. Searchers discover the wreck of the Titanic; 7. William Harvey discovers the human circulatory system; 8. Alexander Fleming discovers penicillin; 9. Francis Crick, James Watson, Rosalind Franklin discover the structure of DNA; 10. Hilkiah, the Jewish priest, discovers the Book of the Law.

A. 622 BC; B. 1492; C. 1628; D. 1848; E. 1870; F. 1898; G. 1928; H. 1947; I. 1953; J. 1985. *Answers: 1. H; 2. D; 3. B; 4. F; 5. E; 6. J; 7. C; 8. G; 9. I; 10. A.*

After you have graded the quizzes together, ask which items on the list were discovered only after having first been "lost" or forgotten. (Items 1, 5, 6, and 10 can fit this description in various senses.) Use this fact to lead into today's lesson, which deals with #10.

INTO THE WORD

Use the Lesson Background to prepare a brief introduction of the events that led up to the discovery of the Book of the Law, where today's text begins. Briefly review 2 Chronicles 33 as you explain how Josiah's grandfather (Manasseh) and father (Amon) had led Judah into idolatry.

Next, divide your class into small groups of three to five. Give each group copies of the following two activities (or direct them to the same activities in the optional student books). Ask your groups to follow the instructions printed on the exercises.

Exercise #1—Recipe for National Revival. Josiah's great reform program in 2 Chronicles 34 had four steps to it: (1) research the law (vv. 15, 18, 20-25); (2) repent of past sins (vv. 19, 26-28); (3) renew the covenant with God (vv. 29-32); and (4) remove pagan influences from society (v. 33). Write a brief summary of Josiah's actions under each of the four steps. Be prepared to share results with the rest of the class.

Exercise #2—Prescription for Church and Personal Revival. How can we apply Josiah's reform program to ourselves? What New Testament passages will help us do so?

After about 10 minutes, have volunteers share their answers. Responses for Exercise #1 may look something like this: 1. When Josiah heard the Word read, he sent the priests to the prophetess Huldah to learn what the Lord wanted them to do; 2. Josiah tore his robes as a sign of repentance for Judah's failure to keep the law; therefore, God promised to spare Josiah from the disaster he would bring on Judah; 3. Josiah brought all the people together to pledge themselves to keep the covenant God made with their ancestors; 4. Josiah had idols removed from the land, so Judah could focus on serving God.

Responses for Exercise #2 may look something like this: 1. Research the Word (1 Corinthians 10:11; 2 Timothy 3:16, 17; etc.); 2. Repent of past sins (2 Corinthians 2:5-11; Revelation 2:5, 16; etc.); 3. Renew the covenant with God (1 Corinthians 11:23-32; etc.); 4. Remove pagan influences from oneself and from the church (1 Corinthians 5; 10:7-10, 14-21; etc.).

INTO LIFE

Make a transition by saying, "Now that we've worked through a recipe and a prescription, let's try to see how this could apply today."

Modern Revival (use the Reproducible Page). Say, "Imagine that you are the spiritual advisor to a political leader. Your job is to help him or her bring moral or spiritual reform to the people. Keeping in mind the constitutional rules governing the interaction of religion and government in our society, what changes or actions would you recommend in terms of Josiah's *Four Rs* reform program?" Have groups brainstorm their ideas and then share them with the class. Ask, "How difficult would it be to carry out these reforms?"

Alternative activity: Interview with a Reformer. Have one of your learners take the role of a TV reporter who is interviewing a modern-day Josiah, who is trying to reform society. Recruit in advance the two who will play these roles so they can work up a dialogue beforehand. If you prefer to do this as a small-group exercise, use the Interview with a Reformer activity on the Reproducible Page.

Modern Revival

Imagine that you are the spiritual advisor to a political leader. Your job is to help him or her bring moral or spiritual reform to the people. Keeping in mind the constitutional rules governing the interaction of religion and government in our society, what changes or actions would you recommend in terms of Josiah's *Four Rs* reform program?

1. Research the Word of God:

2. Repent of past sins:

3. Renew the covenant with God:

4. Remove pagan influences from society:

Interview with a Reformer

You are part of a team of crack TV reporters. You intend to interview a modern-day Josiah who is trying to reform society. Write out a list of questions you would ask in your interview.

1. _____

2. _____

3. _____

4. _____

5. _____

_____

6. _____

_____

HOLDING TO CONVICTIONS

LESSON 6

WHY TEACH THIS LESSON?

It's not easy to row against the currents of the river of life. Trying to paddle upstream is a frustrating thing to do, especially when we see so many others flowing easily with the currents. In our text for today, we will see Daniel and his friends willing to go against the current. They were willing to face the difficulties and pressures of being different—of being holy.

The call to discipleship is a call to be different, to row against the current of popular thinking. Christians many times follow one of two extremes in the Christian life. Some immerse themselves into the popular culture of the day, hoping to be a witness or influence for Christ in the midst of culture. Others become radically separate from the culture, not wanting to be stained in any way. Neither of these approaches is a viable option for being a witness for Christ.

This lesson will challenge your learners to consider where they may be guilty of conforming to the ways of the world. How can they be *in* this world but not *of* this world? This struggle is not new. Daniel and his friends will show us the way.

INTRODUCTION

A. MAINTAINING IDENTITY

In 2005, a new church sought to rent space in a certain public school building. There was nothing unusual about this fledgling church. Countless churches have rented similar facilities for identical purposes. Yet after this church secured a contract, the news went public and the response was startling.

Based on pure speculation, the church was accused of being a terrorist organization seeking to infiltrate the school system to plant bombs in students' desks. The church was required to pay for a security guard to protect school premises from potential terrorist activity. As I write this, a legal battle is being waged over whether it is appropriate for this church, or any other, to rent state-owned facilities.

Christians increasingly are deemed a threat to societal progress. Being Christian is indeed challenging when Christianity is not the norm. For many, these developments seem new and unnerving. But God's people have held minority status quite often throughout history. Scripture has much to say about what it takes to protect our identity in hostile cultures. In Daniel 1, we learn that this requires costly intentional effort. God empowers such effort and blesses those who remain committed to him.

B. LESSON BACKGROUND

Working through Kings David and Solomon, God built Israel into a mighty nation. Israelites occupied an impressive stretch of land, they were ruled by their own kings, and smaller nations paid tribute to them. By the end of Solomon's reign (about 930 BC), the Israelites had come a long way since the Egyptian bondage of some 500 years previous.

DEVOTIONAL READING:
PSALM 141:1-4
BACKGROUND SCRIPTURE:
DANIEL 1
PRINTED TEXT:
DANIEL 1:8-20

LESSON AIMS

After participating in this lesson, each student will be able to:

1. Describe how and why Daniel, Hananiah, Mishael, and Azariah avoided self-defilement.

2. Explain how the example of Daniel, Hananiah, Mishael, and Azariah is helpful to Christians as they face challenges from an ungodly culture.

3. Make a plan to resist one unholy cultural trend.

Apr
6

KEY VERSE

But Daniel resolved not to defile himself with the royal food and wine, and he asked the chief official for permission not to defile himself this way.—Daniel 1:8

But prosperity went to their heads. The Israelites began worshiping the gods of other nations, mistreating the poor, and trusting human power rather than God. The Israelites, whom God called to be distinct from other nations, became like the nations they dispossessed. Through prophets, God warned his people that he would punish them if they refused to reform their ways. The Israelites did not repent permanently, so God used the Assyrians and the Babylonians to conquer his people.

Jerusalem was quite a distance from Babylon—some 900 miles. For the Babylonians to maintain control of the territory of Judah was a challenge. The Babylonians could establish a large military presence in Judah, but the costs would be high and soldiers undoubtedly were needed elsewhere in the empire.

So King Nebuchadnezzar of Babylon chose a different strategy: he crippled Judah's ability to revolt by relocating the most educated and skilled Jews. This way the king of Babylon could benefit from their abilities while the Jews who were left behind would lack the leadership to rebuild. The word we normally use for such forced relocation is *exile*.

In Daniel 1:1-7, we learn that Daniel, Hananiah, Mishael, and Azariah were among those gifted Jews who were taken into exile (about 605 BC). Being of royal blood, they were selected to serve in Nebuchadnezzar's royal court in Babylon. Such service required preparation. So for three years these men were given the finest education Babylon could offer.

Yet such an education raised questions for exiled Jews. How much could they immerse themselves in Babylonian culture before they ceased being Jews? How could they survive among the pagans without becoming just like them? As recent events have taught us, these questions apply not only to ancient Jews, but also to modern Christians. Let us therefore pay careful attention to the answers of Scripture.

I. FAITHFULNESS TO GOD (DANIEL 1:8-13)

A. DANIEL'S REQUEST (v. 8)

8. But Daniel resolved not to defile himself with the royal food and wine, and he asked the chief official for permission not to defile himself this way.

Our text begins with Daniel's heartfelt conviction that partaking of *the royal food and wine* will lead to defilement. It is not clear, however, what it is about the king's royal food that may *defile* Daniel. Jewish law forbids eating certain kinds of meat, but other kinds are perfectly acceptable. Wine is not forbidden (Numbers 6:20; 18:12; 1 Samuel 1:24; Psalm 104:14, 15; etc.), although it is spoken of in negative terms when excess is involved (Isaiah 28:7; 5:11, 22; Proverbs 20:1).

Daniel may be avoiding food and drink associated with pagan temple offerings and thus idolatry (compare 1 Corinthians 8). But under this theory, the vegetarian alternative he proposes in verse 12 would be equally suspect, since flour is also offered to pagan idols.

Perhaps Daniel thinks it inappropriate to eat festive food such as meat and wine during Israel's time of exile—a time of Jewish mourning. This suggestion, however, does not account for Daniel's concerns about defilement. Another theory is that Daniel refuses to be dependent upon a foreign ruler; however, he does not reject extensive training or later appointments to high positions in the king's court.

One further possibility should be considered. Daniel knows that even in exile the Jews need to maintain a distinct identity. They cannot simply blend in with the surrounding cultures. To adopt every and all foreign practices is to

HOW TO SAY IT

Abraham. AY-bruh-ham.

Assyrians. Uh-SEAR-e-unz.

Azariah. Az-uh-RYE-uh.

Babylon. BAB-uh-lun.

Babylonians. Bab-ih-LOW-nee-unz.

Egyptian. Ee-JIP-shun.

Hananiah. Han-uh-NYE-uh.

Judah. JOO-duh.

Mishael. MISH-a-el.

Nebuchadnezzar. NEB-yuh-kud-NEZ-er.

Solomon. SOL-o-mun.

defile themselves and forsake their Jewishness. Daniel knows, however, that one can learn about the ways of other people without accepting those ways. That's probably why he doesn't object to learning the Babylonian language and literature (v. 4).

Food, however, is different in light of God-given dietary laws for Old Testament Jews. The Jews had been set apart by diet. Daniel has to make choices regarding what will compromise his Jewish identity and what won't. To compromise on the food issue will mean that he and his friends are becoming full-fledged Babylonians rather than Jews that happen to live in Babylon.

Regardless of the specific reason for his decision, Daniel is not content to keep his conviction to himself. He sticks his neck out and tells the king's official that he wishes to avoid being defiled by the king's food. What a bold statement! Daniel publicly declares that the king's chosen food is unacceptable.

B. OFFICIAL'S RESISTANCE (vv. 9, 10)

9. Now God had caused the official to show favor and sympathy to Daniel,

The official can respond in more than one way. A mild response would be to demote Daniel. If delicacies enjoyed by the king's closest attendants are not acceptable to Daniel, then perhaps he should join lower-level servants who eat lesser food. More severely, an underling who insults the king's graciousness can be executed. Yet neither of these fates befalls Daniel because *God had caused the official to show favor and sympathy to Daniel.*

10. . . . but the official told Daniel, "I am afraid of my lord the king, who has assigned your food and drink. Why should he see you looking worse than the other young men your age? The king would then have my head because of you."

Although the official does not respond harshly, neither does he immediately grant Daniel's request. Instead, he expresses fear that his own life will be at risk should he agree to Daniel's plan. Perhaps the king will notice a difference in appearance between those who abstain from the food he supplies and those who don't. The official thus makes what appears to be a compelling case for why Daniel's suggestion should be denied.

A person of lukewarm convictions would eat whatever the king sets before him. A bold Jew would go one step further and venture a request like we see in verse 8. But only the most conscientious Jew would persist in his request after being rebuffed like Daniel is here in verse 10.

THOSE WHO ARE DIFFERENT

The Netherlands has a long-standing reputation for cultural "tolerance." The freewheeling drug and sex culture of the late twentieth century seemed to indicate the nation could tolerate anything and still flourish. However, large numbers of Muslim immigrants who settled there did not assimilate into the prevailing culture. The Muslim ghettos became breeding grounds for unrest and, many feared, potential terrorism.

One fearful response has been legal repression, such as outlawing Muslim attire. Similar concerns and responses can be found throughout the world as migration increases in the twenty-first century.

Such circumstances may help us to understand better the situation in which Daniel and his friends found themselves. The Babylonian king, like modern governments, was wary of a cultural minority in his land. As Christianity becomes or remains a minority religion in many lands, we may find ourselves under increasing suspicion as well. The question for Christians is, how will we present ourselves to a culture that is hostile to the truth of Christ?   —C. R. B.

WHAT DO YOU THINK

In what ways have you sought to avoid defiling yourself with the things of this world? How can you do better?

[Hint: Make sure to consider 1 Corinthians 6:18 and 1 Timothy 6:11 in this discussion.]

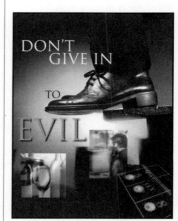

Visual for Lesson 6. *Point to this visual as you ask, "What kind of temptation gives you the most trouble?"*

WHAT DO YOU THINK

What are some areas in which you can prove your faithfulness as well as demonstrate the faithfulness of God?

WHAT DO YOU THINK

How can partnerships be of value when making spiritual commitments today?

[You may find Ecclesiastes 4:12 and Hebrews 10:25 useful in this discussion.]

C. DANIEL'S INSISTENCE (vv. 11-13)

11. Daniel then said to the guard whom the chief official had appointed over Daniel, Hananiah, Mishael and Azariah,

Hananiah, Mishael, and Azariah were introduced earlier in Daniel 1:6. Now we learn that they too share Daniel's convictions. The words "among these" in verse 6 indicate that other Jews besides these four are also in the king's palace. But they apparently make different choices about diet and Jewish identity. We are not told that God judged these other Jews, but as the story unfolds it is clear that God blesses the most conscientious.

12, 13. "Please test your servants for ten days: Give us nothing but vegetables to eat and water to drink. Then compare our appearance with that of the young men who eat the royal food, and treat your servants in accordance with what you see."

Daniel does not give up. Since the official is nervous about the future physical appearance of these four, Daniel proposes a test. He requests *water* instead of wine and *vegetables* instead of meat. This diet resembles what God gave humans to eat in the Garden of Eden (Genesis 1:29) and corresponds to what many nutritionists recommend today.

We must be careful, however, not to read too much into such connections. In Genesis 9:3, God granted that humans also could eat meat. We also should be mindful that what it means to look healthy differs from culture to culture. In modern Western cultures, a slim figure is a sign of health, and a vegetarian diet is one way for overweight people to trim down. In ancient cultures, however, a slim figure may indicate poverty while plumpness indicates the presence of a robust diet and the wealth necessary to have it.

II. FAITHFULNESS FROM GOD (DANIEL 1:14-20)

A. GOD GRANTS SUCCESS (vv. 14-16)

14, 15. So he agreed to this and tested them for ten days. At the end of the ten days they looked healthier and better nourished than any of the young men who ate the royal food.

Here we see God's hand at work in two ways. First, as in verse 9, the official continues to have a favorable view of Daniel. So when Daniel boldly yet respectfully counters the official's reservations, the official does not receive it as an affront to his authority, but as an idea worth trying.

Second, it may be that God blesses these four so they will gain more weight than their peers. Experience teaches us that under normal circumstances those who drink water and eat vegetables lose weight, whereas those who eat meat and drink wine tend to gain. But the exact makeup of the diet, which is unknown to us, may result in the opposite here.

16. So the guard took away their choice food and the wine they were to drink and gave them vegetables instead.

The king's official is now comfortable enough to remove their portions of *wine* and *choice food* altogether. Perhaps for a while he has set these items alongside their vegetables just for show. If so, this procedure is no longer necessary, since the superior appearance of the four Jews now testifies to the validity of their diet. Thus is removed any threat to the official's life.

B. GOD GRANTS BLESSING (v. 17)

17. To these four young men God gave knowledge and understanding of all kinds of literature and learning. And Daniel could understand visions and dreams of all kinds.

God's blessings do not end with the favor and health of *these four*. God does not bless them for mere survival. He wants to bless them with abundant life. Such blessing is central to God's promise to Abraham (Genesis 12:1-3) and covenant with Israel (Deuteronomy 28:1-14).

Such blessing, however, comes with conditions. God's people have to serve God alone and follow his instructions diligently. If not, they will experience curses (Deuteronomy 28:15-68). This is why Jerusalem is destroyed in 586 BC (less than 20 years in the future from the time of the incident we are considering now).

Judah's failure to honor God's Word is the reason these four young Jews now find themselves serving a foreign king in Babylon. The book of Daniel teaches us, however, that even in exile God wishes to bless those who remain true.

C. GOD GRANTS WITNESS (vv. 18-20)

18. At the end of the time set by the king to bring them in, the chief official presented them to Nebuchadnezzar.

The time period in view with the phrase *at the end of the time set* is not the 10-day test we saw earlier, but the three years of training introduced in verse 5. All the trainees are brought before King *Nebuchadnezzar*, not just the four Jews we have been talking about.

19. The king talked with them, and he found none equal to Daniel, Hananiah, Mishael and Azariah; so they entered the king's service.

The king spends time with his new recruits, interviewing them and selecting them for various administrative posts. Like his official, Nebuchadnezzar is impressed with *Daniel, Hananiah, Mishael, and Azariah*. They are therefore given high positions near the king himself; that's what *entered the king's service* signifies.

20. In every matter of wisdom and understanding about which the king questioned them, he found them ten times better than all the magicians and enchanters in his whole kingdom.

God has so blessed Daniel and his rookie friends that they are vastly superior to the king's veteran counselors. Those other counselors are described in such a way as to highlight the source of their so-called wisdom. Unlike Daniel and his friends, who owe their *wisdom* to the one true God, these rivals rely on various tricks and the movements of the stars. (Sound familiar?)

This verse is the starting point for two themes that become increasingly important as the book of Daniel moves along. First, God blesses his people, not just for their own sake, but for the sake of the nations. His will is that all nations worship him. God has exalted these Jews in Nebuchadnezzar's eyes because he wants Nebuchadnezzar to exalt God in the eyes of all Babylon. This begins to happen in chapter two.

Second, we will see that when God's people are exalted in foreign lands, foreigners are not pleased. Imagine how the native Babylonians feel as their positions of power and influence fall under the supervision of Jewish outsiders! Competition and jealousy will arise, and this will pose an additional threat to God's people.

"YOU CAN'T FIGHT CITY HALL"

"You can't fight city hall" is an old sentiment. It is uttered by those who are frustrated with government practices.

Take, for example, the doctrine of eminent domain, which says government may condemn private property for a greater public good. The U.S. Supreme Court ruled

WHAT DO YOU THINK

What are some ways that God has blessed you beyond what you have asked or imagined?

WHAT DO YOU THINK

How can our faith influence our actions and thereby influence the course of history?

PRAYER

We thank you, God, for set-
ting us apart. We thank you for
calling us to the adventure of
following you. This adventure
is never dull and always entails
making tough yet life-giving
choices. Empower us the way
you empowered Daniel and his
friends to make the right deci-
sions. Forgive us when we have
preferred simply to blend in. Give
us the courage to stand out so
that you may use our witness to
draw others unto you. In Jesus'
name, amen.

in 2005 that a city could exercise eminent domain even in cases where a private developer would profit substantially if it were to result in an enhancement of local tax revenues. The high court said this could be done even if the property were not blighted (one of the usual reasons for exercising the doctrine).

This was a case of fighting city hall and losing. But some people decided to continue fighting anyway. Since Justice David Souter had agreed with the majority opinion, someone proposed to use the doctrine to take Justice Souter's farmhouse and turn it into the *Lost Liberty Hotel* with a *Just Desserts Café* on the premises. It was probably a tongue-in-cheek gesture, but it demonstrated frustration with what was perceived to be bureaucratic arrogance.

The four Hebrews in today's lesson decided to "fight city hall," and they won! Of course, it was with God's help, not that of a lawyer. God honored their trust in him and caused them to be elevated to prominent positions in Babylon's government. The "good guys" don't always win in the way the world defines winning. The most important thing is to make sure you're on God's side of the issue before the battle starts.

　　　　　　　　　　　　　　　　　　　　　　　　　　—C. R. B.

CONCLUSION

In adopting an alternative diet, Daniel and his friends reminded themselves daily that they were different from the Babylonians. Remaining God's people meant remaining visibly distinct from the nations.

Christ said that his followers are not of the world, but are sent into it as ones who are set apart (John 17:14-19). We live in the world (1 Corinthians 5:10); yet the apostle Paul cautions us not to be yoked with unbelievers, but to come out and be separate from them (2 Corinthians 6:14-18). The separation is not one of physical isolation, but of maintaining a pure spiritual identity. According to James, pure religion entails, in part, keeping oneself unstained by the world; those who befriend the world become God's enemies (James 1:27; 4:4).

Peter ties these themes together with Israel's Old Testament witness by referring to Christians as strangers in this world (1 Peter 1:1, 17; 2:11) and calling us to be holy as God is holy (1:14-17). So while the cross of Christ has removed barriers between believers—whether of race, gender, age, ability, or social status—our distinctively holy way of life continues to set us apart from those who do not believe. We must never forget, however, that this difference is not for difference's sake. We are different for the sake of witness, so that others may be drawn to God (1 Peter 2:9).

The nonbelievers we know at work, at school, and in our neighborhoods should notice that we are different. If this is not clear to them, then perhaps we, like Daniel and his friends, need a symbolic reminder of our unique identity. They chose diet as their reminder, but that won't work today (see Mark 7:17-19). So we choose other ways to remember and announce our set-apart status. Some wear certain rings to remind themselves of the need for sexual purity. Some wear WWJD bracelets. Others wear necklaces with crosses. Some remove the TV from being the focal point of the living room.

Christians do such things because they believe that symbolic practices can be meaningful if used properly. When Jesus washed his followers' feet, he did not significantly improve hygiene in Palestine. Nor did he change the way kings and governors rule. Rather, he created a symbol for his disciples so they would not forget that leadership in his kingdom is not about worldly power, but about service. How will you remember your unique identity in Christ this week?

THOUGHT TO REMEMBER

Make your unique identity in
Christ known.

Discovery Learning

*This page contains an alternative lesson plan emphasizing learning activities. Classes
desiring such student involvement will find these suggestions helpful. The next page
is a reproducible activity page to further enhance discovery learning.*

INTO THE LESSON

Display the phrase *The Cultural Dilemma of the Godly.*
Also display these scrambled words: AADEIILMSST
and ACDEFIINST.

Let your class ponder the possibilities for a time. If
they need some help, write A_____ED and S_____ED
on the board. If they still struggle, give them the second
letter of each or the third letter from each end. *ASSIMI-
LATED* and *SANCTIFIED* are the words. Briefly note
that the godly person always has a choice: either to be
assimilated or to be sanctified in relation to his or her
culture—to go along or to stand apart, to disappear or
to be conspicuously holy.

INTO THE WORD

Daniel was a man of conviction and action. Ask your
class to look at Daniel 1:8-20 to identify the verse or
verses where Daniel did each of the following as you
read them aloud. Provide paper and pen for this activity
and the next. Possible answers are noted in italics. Allow
alternate responses if there is a reasonable explanation.

1. Daniel challenged *(v. 8).*
2. Daniel understood *(v. 17).*
3. Daniel excelled *(v. 19).*
4. Daniel led *(v. 8).*
5. Daniel endeared himself *(v. 9).*
6. Daniel impressed *(v. 15).*
7. Daniel dieted *(v. 12).*
8. Daniel purposed *(v. 8).*
9. Daniel requested *(v. 8).*
10. Daniel wagered *(v. 12).*

Note that when the king questioned Daniel and his
friends, he found them superior to all the advisors in his
kingdom. Say, "I'm going to question you to see how
superior your knowledge is. Use the entirety of Daniel 1
to answer the following questions."

1. How did Daniel and his friends end up in exile?
2. What valuable objects had the king also brought
from Jerusalem—objects that would play an important
role in another story given in Daniel 5?
3. What type of young men did the king choose for
his government-training program?
4. What was the curriculum of the young men's
program?
5. How long did the academic program last?

6. What names did Ashpenaz give to the four
young men from Judah?
7. What did Daniel find offensive about the king's
planned regimen?
8. Why was the official hesitant to permit Daniel's
request?
9. How long did the four young Jews have to demonstrate the effects of a special diet?
10. What was the "secret" of the young men's success in physical health and mental acumen?
11. On what basis did the king make his final judgment regarding the men to be appointed to places of
administrative leadership?
12. How much better did the king find the Hebrew
men to be in comparison to his other advisors?
13. How long did Daniel remain in a position of authority in Babylon?

Let learners respond in writing as you read the questions or as you reveal them on an overhead. At the end,
go back and have learners respond orally. They should
be able to note verses where the answers are found.

INTO LIFE

Prepare and duplicate strips of paper having a row of
10 1-inch circles. Put the letters *GP* in each of the first 5
circles; put the letters *SC* in each of the other circles.

Give seven strips of circles to each learner, one for
each day of the week ahead. Explain that the GP stands
for *God's Person* and the SC stands for *Society's Child.*

Say, "That is the choice we all have daily: being God's
person and living life in holiness or being society's child
and resembling the culture around us. Carry a new strip
of paper for each day of the week. As you catch yourself
obviously being either *God's Person* or *Society's Child,*
mark off an appropriate circle. At the end of the week,
do a bit of biblical introspection regarding how you did.
Make a commitment to God to look more like his person than simply another child of our wayward society."
Alternative: Use the format for this exercise from the
Reproducible Page rather than the strips of paper.

Go back to the two words with which you started
today's class: *ASSIMILATED* and *SANCTIFIED.*
Point out the relationship of these words to this closing
activity. Distribute as a take-home handout the Defiled
activity from the Reproducible Page.

Being God's Person or Society's Child

Decide in each of the following matters how much you are God's Person (GP) and how much you are Society's Child (SC). Fill in the segments of the circle based on what degree you see yourself as one or the other. Label each segment as GP or SC or use two different colors of highlight markers for the two types.

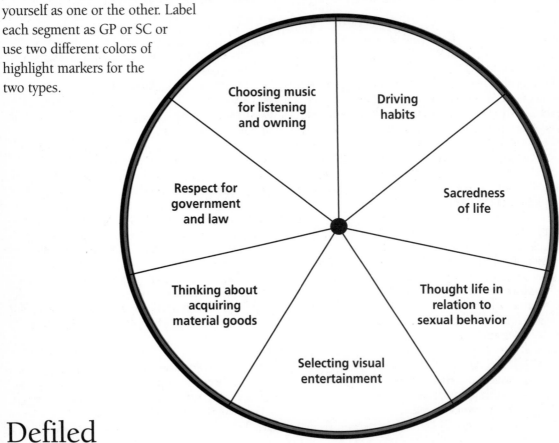

Defiled

Defile is not a word most of us use today. Purity and defilement are not a contrast that we consider often. Personalize and fill in the following paraphrased version of today's key verse, Daniel 1:8.

I, _____ , resolve not to defile myself with _____ or with _____ . So I will inform _____ of my decision not to defile myself in this way.

TAKING A STAND

LESSON 7

WHY TEACH THIS LESSON?

To state the obvious, risk-taking is risky business. Whether it is performing a high-wire act, driving a race car, or eating raw fish, there are possibilities for disaster. Pushing the extremes in risk-taking seems to be a popular thing to do. A whole genre of sports, known as *extreme sports,* has been created to satisfy people's taste for risk.

Many of us are just the opposite, however. We avoid risk. Even so, we recognize the truth in statements such as "no risk, no reward." Companies realize that there are risks that need to be taken at times. But these are calculated risks, done under the guidance of someone holding the title of *risk manager.*

In one sense, taking a stand for God is risky. The three men in our text today understood the risk. They also knew that the reward outweighed any negative consequences. In another sense, however, taking a stand for God is not risky at all! To fail to take a stand is the real risk—a risk of inviting the wrath of God. This lesson will teach your learners to reevaluate their idea of risk. When they do, they will step out on faith.

INTRODUCTION

A. LEARNING TO SAY NO, PART 1

Not long ago, a television cartoon mocked the popular Christian animation series *Veggie Tales.* A friend alerted me to this spoof because of its sick portrayal of the Christian faith. I will not go into all the details, but imagine the cast of *Veggie Tales*—now called the *Religetables*—looking at pornographic material, killing infidels during the crusades, hanging innocent "witches" in Salem, molesting children, etc., while singing pious songs with their cute veggie voices.

Sadly, this warped depiction of Christianity (or at least parts of it) is the image many nonbelievers have of Christian faith. Yet it should not surprise us that unbelievers would portray Christianity in this light. The name of Christ has been slandered from the beginning. What is surprising, however, is how common it is for Christians to enjoy watching programs that routinely belittle Christ and his church.

This incongruity reveals the inability of many Christians to say *no* to various activities. We may feel justified in participating in it as long as we do not let its bad parts affect us. We fear that saying *no* to such activities will make us appear to be puritanical legalists.

This line of reasoning may sound valid, but is it? In Daniel 3, three young Jews faced a similar question. Their answer is instructive.

B. LESSON BACKGROUND

Last week we learned that Hananiah, Mishael, and Azariah were among the young Jewish nobles who were taken into exile during the early days of Babylonian domination of Judah. Daniel 1:7 notes the change of their names to

DEVOTIONAL READING:
PSALM 121
BACKGROUND SCRIPTURE:
DANIEL 3
PRINTED TEXT:
DANIEL 3:10-13, 16-18, 21, 24-26

LESSON AIMS

After participating in this lesson, each student will be able to:

1. Retell the story of Shadrach, Meshach, and Abednego and the fiery furnace.

2. List some challenges that believers face in which they are threatened with harm if they do not go along with popular thinking or behavior.

3. Take a stand against one ungodly law or cultural practice.

Apr 13

KEY VERSES

If we are thrown into the blazing furnace, the God we serve is able to save us from it, and he will rescue us from your hand, O king. But even if he does not, we want you to know, O king, that we will not serve your gods or worship the image of gold you have set up.   —Daniel 3:17, 18

Shadrach, Meshach, and Abednego. Following Daniel's lead, they boldly stood out by choosing their own diet over the king's rations. God honored their stance by exalting them in the king's court and kingdom.

The situation changes in Daniel 3. Independent of Daniel's leadership, these young men face a new challenge. King Nebuchadnezzar erected a giant statue approximately 90' high and 9' wide. Bizarre dimensions notwithstanding, this monument to human greatness, like the tower of Babel in Genesis 11, was a farce in God's eyes.

In Nebuchadnezzar's eyes, however, this statue played a critical role in the stability of his empire. He had relocated droves of foreigners to his capital city, and it was necessary to keep everyone on the same page. Nebuchadnezzar needed to make it clear that there was only one law, one king, and one empire—and that it all revolved around him. This is why he sent a decree to "peoples, nations, and men of every language" that when the king authorized the imperial music to play, they all had to worship the statue (Daniel 3:4, 5).

Failure to comply meant fiery execution. The statue was a symbolic reminder that the Babylonian kingdom was undivided despite its diversity. From an earthly, imperial perspective, it all made perfect sense. But from a godly perspective, it was riddled with problems. In today's text we see how three faithful Jews handled this situation.

I. RESISTANCE (DANIEL 3:10-13)

In verses 8, 9, certain Babylonians (Chaldeans) approach Nebuchadnezzar to remind him of a decree he has established. Yet their agenda is not merely informative. They intend to accuse God's people of violating this decree.

A. KING'S DECREE (vv. 10, 11)

10. *"You have issued a decree, O king, that everyone who hears the sound of the horn, flute, zither, lyre, harp, pipes and all kinds of music must fall down and worship the image of gold,*

What a diversity of musical instruments! Stylistically, it is worth noting that much of Daniel 3 consists of lists of related but distinct items and people, many repeated several times (Daniel 3:3-5, 7, 10, 12-16, 19-23, 26-30). Repetition is a trademark of Hebrew storytelling. The repetition produces a poetic feel with a certain cadence.

We may be curious about the exact form the *image of gold* takes. Is it an image of the king himself? a Babylonian god? some other national or religious symbol? In chapter two, Daniel tells Nebuchadnezzar that he, the king, is the golden head of a statue that he has dreamed about. So perhaps his inflated ego has prompted him to build a golden statue of himself.

On the other hand, the accusations against the Jews in this chapter are that they will not heed the king, serve his gods, or *worship* the statue (vv. 12, 14, 18). Is this list intended to indicate different, distinct offenses, or does the list merely indicate different aspects of the one offense of not bowing to the statue? Again, the text is silent.

Not identifying the precise nature of the statue may be the author's way of saying that what matters most is that the king's decree is violated. What is at stake is the king's authority to dictate what his citizens must do, even if it violates their faith convictions.

11. *". . . and that whoever does not fall down and worship will be thrown into a blazing furnace.*

HOW TO SAY IT

Abednego. Uh-BED-nee-go.
Azariah. Az-uh-RYE-uh.
Babylon. BAB-uh-lun.
Babylonia. Bab-ih-LOW-nee-uh.
Chaldeans. Kal-DEE-unz.
Hananiah. Han-uh-NYE-uh.
Meshach. ME-shack.
Mishael. MISH-a-el.
Nebuchadnezzar. NEB-yuh-kud-NEZ-er.
Shadrach. SHAY-drack or SHAD-rack.
Urijah. Yu-RYE-juh.

WHAT DO YOU THINK?

In what ways does our culture challenge us to bow down to "golden images"? How do we resist?

The penalty for disobedience is severe indeed! But what is the nature of this *furnace*? We do not know for sure, but it may be made of metal and shaped like a beehive with an open top out of which smoke can escape. Additionally, it probably has some kind of side door for removing ashes and monitoring the burning process. Another theory is that it is made of brick and shaped like a tunnel with a similar access door on the side.

B. JEWS' REFUSAL (v. 12)

12. "But there are some Jews whom you have set over the affairs of the province of Babylon—Shadrach, Meshach and Abednego—who pay no attention to you, O king. They neither serve your gods nor worship the image of gold you have set up."

The accusers finally get to the point. The very ones whom Nebuchadnezzar has *set over* his *affairs* refuse to *serve* the king's *gods* and *worship the image of gold*. This verse does not help us discern if the image is associated with the gods, but it is abundantly clear that failure to serve the gods and honor the image is interpreted as a failure to regard the king. The charge is insubordination; the evidence behind the charge involves both gods and the statue.

This passage bookends the denunciation that begins in Daniel 3:8. Verse 8 specifies that the accusers are "astrologers," but a better translation is "Chaldeans" (natives of Babylonia), as in the footnote in the *New International Version* at that verse. Then, in verse 12, the accusers highlight the fact that the king has set Jews over the affairs of Babylon. The repeated use of these ideas suggests that "the locals" are jealous. (We probably see jealousy also in Daniel 6:1-5.) After all, the Babylonian natives have long served loyally, and now these immigrants have been elevated to positions higher than theirs.

So now it is payback time. When the accusers inform the king how these foreigners are ignoring his decree, he will surely punish them and return the locals to their rightful positions of power and influence.

SCAPEGOATS

Finding scapegoats to explain whatever is wrong has a long history. It started in the Garden of Eden (see Genesis 3:12). Modern politicians are especially adept at this. Is the economy in trouble? It's because of the policies of the other political party. Is there too much crime? It's because the previous administration did not crack down on "those people" who are different from us—in skin color, religion, etc.

Name a trouble spot anywhere in the world, and someone can name a scapegoat for why things are the way they are. For Hitler, it was the Jews; for many Arab countries, it's America; in the case of natural disasters in the U.S., blame FEMA. The list goes on.

For Nebuchadnezzar's advisers, the problem to be solved was personal. They were loyal Chaldeans, but their king had placed capable Jews in positions of authority. Those Jews had taken jobs that the Chaldeans probably thought belonged to them. So "they played the race card," and the king fell for it. (We will see this same problem play out in next week's lesson.) The nature of their charge was almost beside the point—it was a convenient launching point for an attempt at payback. It still happens.   —C. R. B.

C. KING'S RAGE (v. 13)

13. Furious with rage, Nebuchadnezzar summoned Shadrach, Meshach and Abednego. So these men were brought before the king.

The accusers' plan succeeds, and *Nebuchadnezzar* takes the offense personally. He may have taken a lot of flak already for his decision to exalt foreigners, and

WHAT DO YOU THINK?

Have you ever been accused of something by people who had a devious intent or a hidden agenda? How did things turn out? How did you grow as a result?

now it blows up in his face. Nebuchadnezzar has been gracious in offering these foreigners education, food, and positions. They have every reason to be grateful, but in Nebuchadnezzar's mind they respond with ingratitude.

II. FAITHFULNESS (DANIEL 3:16-18)

Although Nebuchadnezzar is furious, he does not act rashly. He invites Shadrach, Meshach, and Abednego in and allows them to explain themselves. He gives them a second chance (Daniel 3:14, 15, not in today's text).

A. JEWS' PERSISTENCE (v. 16)

16. Shadrach, Meshach and Abednego replied to the king, "O Nebuchadnezzar, we do not need to defend ourselves before you in this matter.

In response to the king's questioning, the young men begin their response by saying that they *do not need to defend* themselves in the *matter.* They are responding with a firm *no* to the second chance they are being offered. The force of this *no* needs to be felt by Christians today.

We may note that the king's request is not as drastic as it could be since he is not asking these Jews to stop worshiping their own God altogether. He is "merely" asking them to make a certain addition to their worship practice. Is this not the least they can do to pay him respect?

Yet the modern habit of rationalizing questionable practices is nowhere to be found in Shadrach, Meshach, and Abednego. They know that the God of Israel is not to be worshiped alongside other gods. God has no equal, and he will not tolerate being treated as such (Deuteronomy 4:35, 39).

Any action that grants uncontestable allegiance to a sovereign other than God is idolatry. That's what bowing before the statue would do. It is one thing to work for the king and show him the basic respect that is due to those in authority. It is another thing entirely to acknowledge someone or something as a rival to God.

Today, respect also is due to presidents, governors, bosses, elders, and parents (Mark 7:10; 1 Timothy 5:17). But they do not have blanket permission to lead in such a way that they eclipse God. The prophet Jeremiah commanded the Jews to submit to the Babylonian Empire (Jeremiah 27), and the apostles taught Christians to submit to the Roman Empire (Romans 13:1; 1 Peter 2:13-17). But God's people are never to interpret such commands as unconditional support for any and all actions of earthly rulers (example: Acts 4:18-20).

B. JEWS' RESOLUTENESS (vv. 17, 18)

17, 18. "If we are thrown into the blazing furnace, the God we serve is able to save us from it, and he will rescue us from your hand, O king. But even if he does not, we want you to know, O king, that we will not serve your gods or worship the image of gold you have set up."

These three Jews express faith in *God* in two ways. First, they acknowledge that God is *able to save* them from both the *blazing furnace* and the *king* who thinks he has absolute power. They do not worship a weak god or a distant god who is unable to intervene in events on earth. They worship Israel's God, who has proven his ability and who desires to work for the good of those who love him (Deuteronomy 7:9; Romans 8:28). So too Christians today rightly pray for God's intervention. Those who seek to live on their own strength, to muscle their own way out of the tough spots in life, and to avoid faith decisions that require divine assistance have marginalized Father, Son, and Holy Spirit.

WHAT DO YOU THINK?

When have you been guilty of rationalizing actions to avoid being harmed or to avoid doing God's will? How have you grown spiritually through repentance of your shortcomings in this regard?

DAILY BIBLE READINGS

Monday, Apr. 7—God's Protection Forevermore (Psalm 121:1-4)

Tuesday, Apr. 8—King Nebuchadnezzar's Golden Statue (Daniel 3:1-7)

Wednesday, Apr. 9—The Refusal to Worship the Statue (Daniel 3:8-15)

Thursday, Apr. 10—Brought Before the King (Daniel 3:16-23)

Friday, Apr. 11—Not a Hint of Fire (Daniel 3:24-27)

Saturday, Apr. 12—A New Decree (Daniel 3:28-30)

Sunday, Apr. 13—God Will Keep You (Psalm 121:5-8)

Second, these three Jews are firm in their worship of God to the point that they refuse to bow, whether God chooses to intervene or not. God's nonintervention is a strong possibility. In his larger plan, God does not always choose to intervene, as the deaths of Urijah (Jeremiah 26:20-23) and James (Acts 12:1, 2) establish.

Yet true believers are those who faithfully serve God regardless of the negative consequences they may suffer. Christians continue to die for their faith in many parts of the world. Others have lost jobs, housing, and other necessities. Unfortunately, there are also those who claim to be Christians who show that they actually are idolaters because of the compromises they make for the sake of pride, position, property, popularity, or power.

THE PRESSURE OF A PROFANE CULTURE

Ginny Foster spent $10,000 four years ago on T-shirts and bumper stickers that expressed opposition to the deluge of dirty language that surrounds us. Talk about trying to resist culture! Sadly, she gave up the project within two years, saying she no longer had the fire within her to fight this battle. After she appeared on a Showtime TV show, her Web site received hundreds of e-mails full of abusive curses.

Americans do indeed live in a profane culture. An Associated Press opinion poll found that 74 percent encounter profanity frequently or occasionally, while 59 percent admit to cursing a few times a month. Listen carefully and you may even hear profanity among Christians. Certain profane words are so commonly used that those who *really* want to curse may soon have to come up with some new terms!

This is just one of many ways secular culture affects (and infects) godly people. Shadrach, Meshach, and Abednego set a good example by being careful not to compromise with the pagan culture in which they lived. We each may be tempted to sin in different ways, but watchfulness is a trait all Christians should cultivate.

—C. R. B.

III. DELIVERANCE (DANIEL 3:21, 24-26)

Verses 19 and 20 (not in today's text) tell us that Nebuchadnezzar will not accept *no* for an answer. So the three are to be executed in a furnace heated to seven times its normal level. Some of the king's strongest men are assigned the task of binding Shadrach, Meshach, and Abednego.

A. JEWS' PUNISHMENT (v. 21)

21. So these men, wearing their robes, trousers, turbans and other clothes, were bound and thrown into the blazing furnace.

The three Jews are threatening the unity of the king's empire. If Nebuchadnezzar allows them to walk free, he will appear to be weak and indecisive. So the king has to honor his decree and toss them into the fire. Not only that, but he decides to make an example of them by cranking the fire up so high that the men who throw them in die for coming so close (v. 22, not in today's text).

It is interesting to note what kind of religion the Babylon Empire is willing to tolerate. In Daniel 2:47, Nebuchadnezzar acknowledges Israel's God as the God of gods. Presumably this means that it is OK for Jews to worship their God while others worship Babylonian gods. Nebuchadnezzar thus appears to be a tolerant religious pluralist. His subjects can worship whatever and whomever they wish as long as they remain devout citizens who do what is asked of them. This includes "adjusting" one's religious beliefs when the king deems it necessary. Worship of any deity who authorizes worshipers to deny the king's policies is not acceptable.

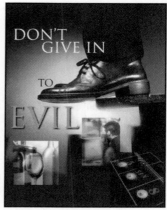

Visual for Lesson 7. *Continue last week's discussion: "What kind of temptation gives you the most trouble?"*

WHAT DO YOU THINK?

How should Christians respond in the face of a pluralistic culture?

B. KING'S ASTONISHMENT (vv. 24, 25)

24, 25. Then King Nebuchadnezzar leaped to his feet in amazement and asked his advisers, "Weren't there three men that we tied up and threw into the fire?"

They replied, "Certainly, O king."

He said, "Look! I see four men walking around in the fire, unbound and unharmed, and the fourth looks like a son of the gods."

As Shadrach, Meshach, and Abednego believe, God is able to spare them. Moreover, God actually does spare them from the flames. It is a miracle that the men are *walking around* alive and well.

Our only clue as to how all this happens is *the fourth* person, this *son of the gods*, who walks among the flames. We should not assume that this fourth person is an Old Testament appearance of Jesus, although we cannot rule out this possibility. The description *son of the gods* is given from the perspective of Nebuchadnezzar, not from one of the devout Jews.

The most probable reading of our verse is that this is an angel. God may be sending an angel to comfort these Jews or to provide a sign to the king and his counselors. Either way, God gets the king's attention!

C. GOD'S PRAISE (v. 26)

26. Nebuchadnezzar then approached the opening of the blazing furnace and shouted, "Shadrach, Meshach and Abednego, servants of the Most High God, come out! Come here!"

So Shadrach, Meshach and Abednego came out of the fire.

It is a mystery how the king can draw close enough to the fire to speak over the roaring flames without being consumed like the men who threw Shadrach, Meshach, and Abednego in! His message nonetheless is communicated, and the Jews walk out unharmed. Not a hair is singed, and their garments bear no scent of smoke according to verse 27. When God delivers, he does so in a convincing manner!

Nebuchadnezzar is certainly convinced. He refers to the Jews as *servants of the Most High God.* This praise culminates in a royal decree that protects those who worship Israel's God (Daniel 3:29). The point is clear: God is indeed the Most High God, and his will always prevails in the end. Those who worship him alone do so with this ultimate end in sight, regardless of short-term suffering.

CONCLUSION

Shadrach, Meshach, and Abednego teach us that it sometimes is necessary to say *no* even when an activity can be rationalized. They could have bowed down to the statue out of gratitude for the king's generosity to them. They could have bowed down to preserve their influential positions in order to use them to do good for other people. They could have bowed down for the sake of their witness, lest Jews gain a bad reputation for being uptight, intolerant, narrow-minded, or unpatriotic.

There were many seemingly good reasons why they could have participated in compromising actions under the pretense that they were not affected by them and were not exchanging Israel's God for the gods of Babylon. Yet these Jews knew better. They knew that no action leaves one unaffected, and that one's willingness to compromise means one has already begun worshiping a lesser god. Their ability to say *no* was their witness, and their story continues to be told because they risked it all to remain faithful. The same is true of Daniel—but that's next week's lesson.

Discovery Learning

*This page contains an alternative lesson plan emphasizing learning activities. Classes
desiring such student involvement will find these suggestions helpful. The next page
is a reproducible activity page to further enhance discovery learning.*

INTO THE LESSON

Cut a large *NO* from poster board. Affix the two letters to the wall near the entrance where learners arrive. Put *No* on large, colorful sheets of paper and display them randomly throughout the room. To begin, ask, "Is it possible for a person to have too many *no's*?" and "Do most people say *no* too much or too little? Why?"

If a church music leader can provide it for you, play the song "Know When to Say No" from the children's musical *It's Cool in the Furnace* (© Word Music, 1973). This musical deals with the early chapters of Daniel.

INTO THE WORD

Recruit three good oral readers. Label them Shadrach (S), Meshach (M), and Abednego (A). Tell the class these three are going to recall the events of today's text. The class's task will be to give verse numbers to the remembrances in terms of Daniel 3, where each idea appears.

Give each reader the statements below. Verse numbers are indicated here, but they should not be included in the reading. The readers can move straight through the list, taking turns as indicated (the statements are already randomized). Allow verse answers after each "remembrance."

S: "I remember our stand: 'even if we must die, we will not worship idols.'" (*v. 18*)

M: "I remember being marched to the furnace fully clothed." (*v. 21*)

A: "I remember how angry King Nebuchadnezzar became at us." (*v. 13*)

S: "I remember the accusations of our enemies." (*v. 12*)

M: "I remember the first foot I stepped out of that furnace, never looking back." (*v. 26*)

A: "I remember being thrown into the fire . . . and receiving no harm!" (*v. 21*)

S: "I remember the king's astonishment when he saw us walking in the fire unscathed." (*v. 24*)

M: "I remember the day we were assigned government responsibilities." (*v. 12*)

A: "I remember our expression of faith in God's ability to save us." (*v. 17*)

S: "I remember hearing the king calling our names and crying, 'Come out!'" (*v. 26*)

M: "I remember all the instrumental music, a regular symphony." (*v. 10*)

A: "I remember the fear produced by the threatened punishment of fire." (*v. 11*)

S: "I remember when the king signed the decree regarding the golden statue." (*v. 10*)

M: "I remember when our heavenly friend materialized with us in the fire!" (*v. 25*)

Optional activity #1: Making a Choice. Reproduce the following multiple-choice quiz. Distribute for learners to work on individually or in pairs. (The quiz also appears in the optional student book.)

1. The stimulus for worshiping the king's statue was (A) the full moon, (B) sunrise, (C) sound of musical instruments; 2. The penalty for failing to obey the king's decree was (A) being thrown to the lions, (B) being burned alive, (C) being beheaded; 3. Shadrach, Meshach, and Abednego were accused of ignoring the king's authority and (A) not worshiping the golden image, (B) stealing from the king's treasury, (C) praying to the God of Heaven; 4. Nebuchadnezzar's attitude when he heard of the disobedient Jews was (A) violent rage, (B) disbelief, (C) forgiveness; 5. Shadrach, Meshach, and Abednego affirmed God's ability to save them, but (A) dared the king to try to kill them, (B) expressed doubt that God would save them, (C) affirmed their faith in God even if he did not save them; 6. The three were thrown into the furnace with (A) copies of their Bible scrolls, (B) copies of the king's decree, (C) all their clothes on; 7. When Nebuchadnezzar looked into the furnace, he saw (A) nothing but flame, (B) three men praying, (C) a fourth man walking with the three thrown in. *Answers: 1. C; 2. B; 3. A.; 4. A; 5. C; 6. C; 7. C.*

Optional Activity #2: Have learners complete the Sign Language exercise from the Reproducible Page.

INTO LIFE

Say to the class, "Laws are still being written that make life difficult for the person of God. Some are laws that forbid; some are laws that permit. What are some of those laws that you find yourself bumping up against?" Make a quick list as learners answer.

Ask the class to explain how each complicates their lives and witness. Ask also for ideas for resolving the complications. (The optional student book lists some examples.) Then have learners finish by completing the Walking in the Fire exercise from the Reproducible Page.

Sign Language

Take a look at each of the following images. How does each represent saying "No"? What might be being refused in each case? Why?

Walking in the Fire

Consider the factual story of Shadrach, Meshach, and Abednego. The incident that involved their being thrown into the roaring fire can be seen as a symbol of any godly person's being thrown into an unholy culture. On the flames below, write in some of the lessons learned by and taught by the three Hebrew men in Babylon. For example, one might note that "no godly person walks in the fire alone."

REFUSING TO COMPROMISE

LESSON 8

WHY TEACH THIS LESSON?

Just hearing the term "man-eating lion" is enough to put fear into us. Lions have 30 teeth designed for tearing flesh. These teeth include large canines to grab and kill prey, smaller teeth to scrape meat from bones, and—well, you get the idea. Being *thrown to the lions* is a figurative expression for being put into a situation for which one is totally unprepared. It is a picture of abandonment to certain destruction or failure.

Your learners may feel as if they have been thrown to the lions on occasion (or, worse, they have compromised on something in order to avoid being thrown to the lions). But we take heart in realizing that the lions to which we are thrown in Western democracies are never literal lions! Our "lions" are potential losses of jobs, etc., when we take a stand for Christ. If Daniel could face his literal lions, then surely we can face our figurative ones. That fact should give your learners great courage in their faith walk.

INTRODUCTION

A. DREAM JOB?

"Thank you for applying at Dream Job, Inc. I'm sure you've read our literature and are familiar with our six-figure salary and deluxe benefits package. Having reviewed your application, we believe you are the one best qualified for this job. There are only a few minor wrinkles to iron out.

"In your application you expressed a strong desire not to work on Sundays. Unfortunately that is one of our busiest days, so we've put you down to work Sunday every other week. You also expressed a desire to be home on Wednesdays by 7:00 PM to attend Bible study. Typically we knock off work by 5:30 PM, so that should not be a problem—but your desire does raise a red flag for us. We want to be sure you are not one of those people who hang crosses in the office, give Bibles to coworkers, and starts prayer groups over lunch.

"Now don't get us wrong, we have no problem with people who are Christians privately; we simply ask all our workers to check their faiths at the door. You can worship whomever you wish before and after work, but in our facilities we do not say words like *Jesus, church, grace,* and *salvation.* I am sure you understand. Did I mention we provide free child care?"

Should a Christian accept an offer like this? Is it appropriate to suspend one's faith temporarily for "the greater good" of one's family or country? The familiar story of Daniel and the lions' den can help form answers to such questions.

B. LESSON BACKGROUND

In Daniel 5 we learn that there has been a regime change. The Babylonian Empire, which carried many Jews into exile, has come to an end. The famous handwriting on the wall of Daniel 5:25-28 predicted that collapse. The year was about 539 BC.

DEVOTIONAL READING:
PSALM 119:57-64
BACKGROUND SCRIPTURE:
DANIEL 6
PRINTED TEXT:
DANIEL 6:4-7, 10, 16, 19, 21, 22, 25, 26

LESSON AIMS

After participating in this lesson, each student will be able to:

1. Retell the story of Daniel and the lions' den.

2. Explain why Daniel could not pray with the window closed, and compare that with situations in which Christians must take their faith public in spite of opposition.

3. Give thanks to God for the strength to resist idolatrous practices and trends.

Apr
20

KEY VERSE

Now when Daniel learned that the decree had been published, he went home to his upstairs room where the windows opened toward Jerusalem. Three times a day he got down on his knees and prayed, giving thanks to his God, just as he had done before. —Daniel 6:10

With this change in regime came a new foreign policy. The Persians believed in sending exiled people home and helping them reestablish their old ways of life. That included religious practices and local governance. As long as those being resettled maintained the peace and paid regular tribute to the Persians, they could govern themselves somewhat independently.

Not all Jews accepted this invitation to go home. Daniel apparently was among these. In fact, Daniel seemed to be prospering even more under Persian rule. We learn in Daniel 6:1-3 that Daniel proved superior to all others as Darius the Mede began appointing local rulers. Daniel was on the verge of becoming second-in-command.

Daniel's status as an exile from a distant land probably strengthened his position. As the new regime settled in, the leaders probably wanted to avoid having Babylonian sympathizers occupying positions of power that could be used as a launching pad for revolt. Perhaps Darius sought to appoint Daniel over such rulers because Daniel could be trusted to keep them in line and would not be swayed by bribes. In any case, the local rulers felt threatened by the prospect of Daniel's promotion (Daniel 6:1-3). So they sought to do away with him.

I. OFFICIALS TRAP DANIEL (DANIEL 6:4-7)

A. OFFICIALS SCHEME (vv. 4, 5)

4. At this, the administrators and the satraps tried to find grounds for charges against Daniel in his conduct of government affairs, but they were unable to do so. They could find no corruption in him, because he was trustworthy and neither corrupt nor negligent.

Daniel's rise to power means less power for everyone else. An uncorrupt boss also means less chance of getting away with graft. So whether due to racism, jealousy, greed, or expectation of "entitlement," the local rulers are determined to eliminate Daniel. Their obstacle is Daniel's impeccable character. He is a man above reproach.

5. Finally these men said, "We will never find any basis for charges against this man Daniel unless it has something to do with the law of his God."

What a compliment! *These men* know that Daniel will not compromise when it comes to faith. His weak spot (to their way of thinking) is not pride, power, or prosperity, but devotion to God's laws. This chapter offers a picture of laws at battle. Whose law is final, God's or Persia's?

An important question to ask is how Daniel earned such a reputation. What personal practices send such a clear message about his priorities? What patterns of speech communicate his single-minded commitment? Could people say the same thing about us that Daniel's enemies say about him? If not, why not?

B. OFFICIALS MANIPULATE (vv. 6, 7)

6. So the administrators and the satraps went as a group to the king and said: "O King Darius, live forever!"

Notice that these men do not appoint a representative to advocate their case before *the king*. Instead, they join together *as a group* to flex their numerical muscle. They begin their act of deceit by complimenting the king and promoting his well-being by wishing him long life. There is nothing out of the ordinary about such an address in royal settings (1 Kings 1:31; Nehemiah 2:3; Daniel 2:4; 3:9; 6:21), so the king's suspicions are not raised.

7. "The royal administrators, prefects, satraps, advisers and governors have all agreed that the king should issue an edict and enforce the decree that anyone

HOW TO SAY IT

Abednego. Uh-BED-nee-go.

Babylonian. Bab-ih-LOW-nee-un.

Darius. Duh-RYE-us.

Jerusalem. Juh-ROO-suh-lem.

Kiev. KEE-ef or KEE-ev.

Meshach. ME-shack.

Nebuchadnezzar. NEB-yuh-kud-NEZ-er.

Shadrach. SHAY-drack or SHAD-rack.

Solomon. SOL-o-mun.

Zoroastrianism. Zor-eh-WAS-tree-eh-nih-zem.

who prays to any god or man during the next thirty days, except to you, O king, shall be thrown into the lions' den."

Now these men falsely claim that *all* rulers have endorsed their idea for a *decree* that is to state that no one may pray *to any god or man during the next thirty days, except to you, O king.* It is obvious that Daniel—who is one of those rulers—has neither seen nor approved it. Thus the idea for such a decree is set before the king with great cunning: it appeals to the king's ego while being a threat only to those whose faith will force them to violate it.

Notice that the proposed decree does not ask the citizens to deny their faith outright or to change their way of life permanently. It merely will instruct people to modify temporarily one practice—that of making requests—and to do this only for a brief period of time. Even so, it will be a symbolic reminder that whatever human or divine being the king's subjects normally petition for daily sustenance, the king is their ultimate source of well-being. This one-month hiatus is designed to affirm the priority of the king over all other benefactors.

It is also important to note the nature of royal decrees in Persia. The Persians pride themselves on ruling humanely. They do not go about torturing subjects to keep them in line, but generously provide for their well-being. The famous Cyrus Cylinder, made of baked clay, sets forth religious tolerance, abolition of slavery, and freedom of choice as hallmarks of Persian rule.

Yet the Persians still need to maintain order and respect. So they establish a strict legal system. Royal decrees cannot be broken—not even by the king. This policy not only deters potential law-breakers but also limits corruption among the officials. Since the king himself keeps these laws, the officials may not bend them for selfish gain. Esther 3 records a Persian edict for the destruction of the Jews. That order could not be rescinded, even by the king himself. But the king could issue a separate decree to allow the Jews to defend themselves.

II. DANIEL REMAINS FAITHFUL (DANIEL 6:10)

10. Now when Daniel learned that the decree had been published, he went home to his upstairs room where the windows opened toward Jerusalem. Three times a day he got down on his knees and prayed, giving thanks to his God, just as he had done before.

Daniel can protect himself in various ways. One possible strategy is secrecy. He can shut his *windows* and pray privately. Or he can leave his windows open but alter his posture so others will not be able to tell he is praying (example: praying silently in bed at night).

A third potential strategy is simple abstinence from prayer for the 30 days. Daniel can merely acknowledge Darius's divine appointment as governor and submit to his authority (compare Romans 13:1-7). After all, Daniel is not being asked to deny God out-and-out. The Law of Moses does not require Jews to pray *three times a day.* So Daniel can take the month off and make up for it next month. As wise as Daniel is, he easily can find some kind of "faith loophole" to keep the king's decree without technically violating God's decrees.

Yet another potential strategy is political change. Daniel can use his favor with Darius to expose the agenda of the officials and undermine the law they have forced into effect, as in Esther 8:5-8. This temptation may be the strongest one Daniel faces, but he resists it as well. Instead of viewing persecution as an ill to be avoided, he sees it as an opportunity for witness. How will the Persian world ever learn that there is a God in Heaven worth serving wholeheartedly if his followers do not publicly live out his claim on their lives?

WHAT DO YOU THINK?

How does our culture ask us to suspend our faith temporarily? How have you resisted doing so?

WHAT DO YOU THINK?

What are some "faith loopholes" you have used to try to avoid being honest about your beliefs with others? How have you learned to avoid using such loopholes?

Visual for Lesson 8. *Point to this visual as you say, "But I thought the art of compromise was a good thing! What do you think?"*

So Daniel goes home and kneels by his open window. We may be tempted to fault Daniel here in light of Jesus' teaching that people should not pray publicly in order to be seen (Matthew 6:5, 6), but that would be a mistake. The kind of public prayer Jesus is condemning is one that is self-serving and hypocritical. Daniel is neither of those. He is displaying his faith publicly with right motives (compare Matthew 5:14-16).

The practice of praying three times daily is not commanded in Scripture, although it is reflected in Psalm 55:17. The practice likely develops independently as a method for Jews in exile to remind themselves of their identity. Facing Jerusalem while praying in captivity was a practice predicted by Solomon centuries before (see 1 Kings 8:46-53). Solomon asked God to answer the prayers of his people should they ever be in that situation. This is the best context for understanding Daniel's prayer.

SPIRITUAL TECHNICALITIES

Human endeavors have sets of rules by which they operate. These rules contribute (or should contribute) to the betterment of society. For example, neighborhood associations have their CC&Rs—covenants, conditions, and restrictions —to protect property values.

Each sport naturally has its own set of rules as well. One unusual rule was established by a Houston-area amateur softball league: a player who hits a home run is *out*. The reason for the rule was that just past the outfield fence were some expensive houses that were getting their windows broken by home runs. Most of the players agreed that the rule was necessary.

But it seems that where there is a rule there is also a "rules lawyer" who will try to find a way around the rule through a technicality. Sadly, there are rules lawyers in Christianity too. They think, "Here's a loophole; I can still do this and be a Christian." That was not Daniel's approach. He simply asked himself, "What is the best way to act to demonstrate faithfulness to God?"   —C. R. B.

III. GOD DELIVERS DANIEL (DANIEL 6:16, 19, 21, 22)

A. DARIUS IS RELUCTANT (v. 16)

16. So the king gave the order, and they brought Daniel and threw him into the lions' den. The king said to Daniel, "May your God, whom you serve continually, rescue you!"

Daniel 6:11-15 (not in today's text) shows us the conspirators going to *the king* to tattle on Daniel. After doing all he can do to spare Daniel's life, Darius's commitment to his decree requires him to throw Daniel *into the lions' den.*

It is interesting to note that the means for capital punishment have changed since the incident involving the fiery furnace in Daniel 3. This may reflect a different religious practice. By this time the Babylonian empire of Nebuchadnezzar has fallen to the Persians. According to Zoroastrianism, the official religion of Persia, fire is sacred. Thus it may be inappropriate to use it for executions.

Note also the king's address to Daniel. First, he acknowledges that Daniel serves his God *continually.* In other words, the king knows that Daniel is unwilling to put his faith on hold temporarily. If God is a God worth praying to, then he is a God worth praying to without ceasing (compare 1 Thessalonians 5:17).

Second, the king holds out the possibility that Daniel's God may come to Daniel's rescue. Perhaps he has heard about Daniel's miracle diet (chapter 1), the fiery furnace involving Daniel's friends (chapter 3), and/or Daniel's ability to interpret revelations from God (chapters 4 and 5). It is also possible to take these words sarcastically: the king may be mocking Daniel for foolishly thinking his God can save him. But the king's sympathy toward Daniel throughout this chapter makes this unlikely.

B. DARIUS IS IN A HURRY (v. 19)

19. At the first light of dawn, the king got up and hurried to the lions' den.

After a night of sleeplessness and fasting (v. 18, not in today's text), the king heads straight *to the lions' den* to see how Daniel has fared. This seems to indicate a certain level of faith on Darius's part. He does not send a cleanup crew to deal with Daniel's remains; rather, he has a glimmer of hope that Daniel has survived.

C. DANIEL IS ALIVE! (vv. 21, 22)

21. Daniel answered, "O king, live forever!

Daniel's first words in this narrative are remarkable. Like Darius's officials in verse 6, he wishes the *king* long life. Despite the fact that it was the king who had thrown him to his anticipated death, Daniel pays him respect. In disobeying the king's decree, Daniel does not wish the king ill. Rather, Daniel rightly believes that the best way to honor the king is to show him that God alone is to be feared. Daniel rejects the lie that says that the best way to honor the king is to follow him blindly wherever he leads.

Likewise, the best way for Christians today to honor our rulers is by disallowing them to compromise our faith for some supposed "common good." We realize that we are to obey our governing authorities (Romans 13:1-7). But we also realize that obedience has its limits (Acts 4:19; 5:29). Christians realize that they ought not give governing authorities a "blank check" to rule as they please, and we rightly critique unbridled patriotism. But it is also wrong to swing in the complete opposite direction and become antiauthority or anticountry. Daniel teaches us to give proper respect within limits. He exemplifies 1 Peter 2:17: "Fear God, honor the king."

22. "My God sent his angel, and he shut the mouths of the lions. They have not hurt me, because I was found innocent in his sight. Nor have I ever done any wrong before you, O king."

Again *God* is the source of deliverance. Previously, God had sent an *angel* to protect Shadrach, Meshach, and Abednego (Daniel 3:25). Now we see that God also sent an angel to protect Daniel by shutting *the mouths of the lions* (compare Psalm 91:9-13; Hebrews 1:14). In so doing, God affirms Daniel's innocence. And in his innocence, Daniel can truly claim to have done the king no harm.

It can never be said of God's people that they are doing what is wrong toward others when they remain faithful to him. Others may perceive it as wrong, and we may suffer because we refuse to defy God. But it is always in the long-term interest of all parties for God's people to remain faithful to him. This does not mean that the innocent will always survive. According to Hebrews 11:32-40, Israel's hall of fame includes both those who escaped death at the hands of enemies and others who died courageously.

TEMPTING OR TRUSTING?

It is said that history repeats itself. Sometimes it does, sometimes it only comes close. An example of the latter happened at the municipal zoo in Kiev, Ukraine, on June 5, 2006. While visitors swarmed the zoo, a man lowered himself by rope into the lion enclosure. He took off his shoes and shouted to the crowd, "God will save me, if he exists." Then he walked toward the lions. A lioness knocked him down and killed him.

WHAT DO YOU THINK?

What are some ways that God may use the demonstration of your faith for good?

[Hint: Matthew 5:14-16; 7:17; John 13:35; 15:8 can enrich your discussion.]

WHAT DO YOU THINK?

Why is it important that we testify before others of God's deliverance?

PRAYER

Living God, thank you for giving us your laws and showing us abundant life through Christ. Thank you for making us a people whose spiritual prosperity does not depend on the ebbs and flows of the nations among which you have scattered us. Make us, like Daniel, a people who never hide our faith nor justify retreat with clever arguments. Instead, may we shine like stars in the universe. In Jesus' name, amen.

WHAT DO YOU THINK?

How are some in positions of authority today guilty of domesticating God's law or making Christianity into a subset of national life? How should we react when we see this happening?

THOUGHT TO REMEMBER

True followers of Christ never suspend their faith.

There are significant differences between the man in the Kiev zoo and Daniel in Darius's den of lions. For one thing, Daniel was not there because he decided to be; the same cannot be said for the man in Kiev. Also, Daniel was not mentally unbalanced; the man in Kiev may have been.

The most important difference, however, was motive. Daniel had no doubts about God's existence. Daniel knew God would do what was right regardless of the consequences for him personally. Daniel was not challenging God to prove his existence. Is Daniel's faithfulness ours as well?
—C. R. B.

IV. DARIUS HONORS GOD (DANIEL 6:25, 26)

A. WHAT EVERYONE MUST DO (vv. 25, 26a)

25, 26a. Then King Darius wrote to all the peoples, nations and men of every language throughout the land:
  "May you prosper greatly!
  "I issue a decree that in every part of my kingdom people must fear and reverence the God of Daniel.

God uses Daniel's witness to make a believer out of *Darius*. Thus Darius sets forth a new *decree*, this one legislating *fear* of Daniel's God.

B. WHY EVERYONE MUST DO IT (v. 26b)

26b. "For he is the living God
    and he endures forever;
  his kingdom will not be destroyed,
    his dominion will never end."

The king's decree is an incredible statement about Israel's God. God has proven that he is powerful by defending his people despite the fact that their land was conquered and they remain under foreign control. Since this heavenly king does not depend upon the well-being of his people in their land for his power, his *dominion* can *never end*.

Of course, this decree does not necessarily reveal an understanding by Darius that every earthly ruler is subject to Israel's God. Also, Darius seems to be ignorant of the fact that faith cannot be legislated. A decree cannot change a person's innermost beliefs. Earthly kings may come close to understanding God's ways, but often they don't quite get it!

CONCLUSION

Christianity once met with widespread appreciation in the Western world. That time, however, is over. Christians are being asked daily to choose between their faith and their jobs, social standing, etc. We began this lesson by asking whether Daniel could teach us anything about whether it is ever appropriate to suspend our faith temporarily. To put faith on hold at the king's request is to fear the king more than God.

While thinking about how to honor Christ in the secular workplace, we should recall that Daniel went home before he offered his prayer for all to see. He didn't take an "in your face" stance while at work in the king's palace. Your boss has the right to tell you, "Please take that picture of Jesus off your cubicle wall." The boss has the right to say what can and cannot happen on company property, within the bounds of law and decency. Few, if any, companies have a policy against bowing one's head in prayer over a meal eaten in the company cafeteria! Openly witnessing for Christ is still possible in many situations.

May we continue to demonstrate by the choices we make that we worship the same God whom Daniel worshiped.

Discovery Learning

This page contains an alternative lesson plan emphasizing learning activities. Classes desiring such student involvement will find these suggestions helpful. The next page is a reproducible activity page to further enhance discovery learning.

INTO THE LESSON

Check your local library to see if you can borrow a sound effects disc that includes the sound of a roaring lion. You can also find this sound effect on the Internet. Have the sound playing as learners arrive.

Before class, give the following monologue to one of your learners to practice in advance. Introduce the monologue by saying, "We are fortunate to have a translation of the lion's roars, for this is none other than one of the lions that wanted to eat Daniel but could not!"

Monologue: "Grrrood morning! My name is Grrregory. Once I thought I was grrrroing to have a tender politician for dinner, Daniel by name. But just when I grrrowled in delight, lockjaw set in. And my paws began to feel like tree trunks, anchored to the grrrround. Oh, the frustration! Oh, the disappointment. It was grrrawful!

"All night long, there sat a juicy meal looking like *he* was saying grrrace. The next thing I knew, I heard the voice of the king. My food jumped up—something I couldn't do—and was pulled out of our den, leaving us starved for protein and calcium. But that diet was soon provided by the king once again."

Say, "Well, that gets us to the end of our story, but we need to start at the beginning."

INTO THE WORD

Ask the class to offer text support for each of the following generalizations as you read them aloud. (This activity is also included in the optional student book.) Possible ideas and verse numbers are given in parentheses, but these should not be included in your reading.

Generalizations: 1. Faith, to be true faith, must be expressed. (*Daniel prayed in full view of his accusers, v. 10.*) 2. Sometimes the godly person must be disagreeable; he must disagree with sin. (*Though Daniel knew the law was in place, he prayed anyway, v. 10.*) 3. It is possible to sound religious and patriotic with ulterior, sinful motives. (*The political leaders suggested a religious devotion to the king, but their intention was to see Daniel dead, vv. 4-7.*) 4. Anyone, even a pagan king, can believe in the power and mercy of God. (*Darius expressed confidence that Daniel's God could save him, v. 16.*) 5. Respect for authority is a necessity if one would be godly. (*Authority is by God's design, and Daniel greeted the king respectfully even after the king sent him to a night surrounded by lions, v. 21.*)

6. Never look for other explanations when it is obvious God did it. (*Daniel credits God for his salvation, v. 22.*) 7. A personal claim of innocence is always appropriate . . . if one is innocent! (*Daniel reaffirms his innocence after being rescued, v. 22.*) 8. Even when people in authority agree on a matter, their decision does not necessarily make it right. (*Many officials colluded for the law proposed to the king, but it's still a bad, even immoral, law, vv. 4-7.*) 9. Capital punishment is the discretionary choice of a government, but death for praying hardly fits the crime. (*Governments, by God's design, are responsible for punishing evildoers, in ancient Persia as today, but God expects appropriate penalties for lawbreakers, vv. 7, 16.*) 10. A servant of God must never let fear overwhelm faith, for fear denies God's power, love, and grace. (*Fear of grisly death would not even give Daniel pause regarding his worship practices, v. 10*).

INTO LIFE

Ask your class to consider the issues below. Say, "Most of us are tempted at times to put our faith on hold by certain events and circumstances. Rate the following as occasions you personally are challenged to leave your faith on hold. Use a scale of 0 to 4, with 0 meaning *not tempted to put faith on hold at all* and 4 for *a real temptation to put faith on hold.* (These are included in the optional student book.)

___You are offered free tickets to a very popular and thought-provoking R-rated movie known to be filled with nudity and sexual activity.

___The office Christmas party has a reputation for drunkenness and crudity. The boss says, "We'll see you there!"

___Your professional association is having its annual convention in Las Vegas. The keynote speaker is someone you have always wanted to hear, but the hotel is best known for its vices.

___You are asked to judge the creative products at a community arts and crafts show. Several of the participants are good friends and fellow church members.

Alternative: Use the A Pillar exercise from the Reproducible Page instead.

As you dismiss class, distribute copies of the Dare to Be a Daniel song from the Reproducible Page as a take-home exercise.

A Pillar

From the list of adjectives and characteristics following, circle the one in each row that you think best describes Daniel, a firm pillar among God's holy people.

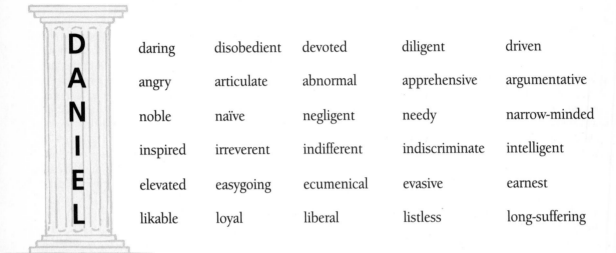

daring	disobedient	devoted	diligent	driven
angry	articulate	abnormal	apprehensive	argumentative
noble	naïve	negligent	needy	narrow-minded
inspired	irreverent	indifferent	indiscriminate	intelligent
elevated	easygoing	ecumenical	evasive	earnest
likable	loyal	liberal	listless	long-suffering

Look again at what you've circled.
Which characteristics of Daniel do you need in your own life? Discuss.

Dare to Be a Daniel

Standing by a purpose true,
Heeding God's command,
Honor them, the faithful few!
All hail to Daniel's band!

Many mighty men are lost
Daring not to stand,
Who for God had been a host
By joining Daniel's band.

Standing by a purpose true,
Heeding God's command,
Honor them, the faithful few!
All hail to Daniel's band!

Many mighty men are lost
Daring not to stand,
Who for God had been a host
By joining Daniel's band.

Refrain:

Dare to be a Daniel,
Dare to stand alone!
Dare to have a purpose firm!
Dare to make it known.

Philip P. Bliss wrote this song in 1873 for his Sunday school class. Look at the words closely to identify their relationships to the story studied today.

Memorize the simple refrain as a daily personal challenge to **dare to be a Daniel.**

God, the People, and the Covenant
Unit 2: The Covenant in Exile
(Lessons 6-9)

PRAYING FOR THE PEOPLE

LESSON 9

WHY TEACH THIS LESSON?

As we have studied through the book of Daniel, we have seen repeatedly the righteousness of that man. Yet in our lesson today we see Daniel including himself in confessing the sin of the nation of Israel.

How different this mind-set is from today! Many of us live in cultures of blame and accusation. Many see themselves as victims; thus they do not take personal responsibility. It's always someone else's fault. We do this in the church too. It is less convicting personally to feel that others are responsible for "sin in the camp" (see Joshua 7).

Undoubtedly, some of your learners are caught up in this "them, not me" blame game. But if godly Daniel can include himself as "part of the problem," then who are we not to do likewise? Your learners need a soul-searching challenge in this regard. Today's lesson provides it.

INTRODUCTION

A. LEARNING HOW TO PRAY

We know that prayer is central to healthy faith. The New Testament instructs us to pray (example: Romans 12:12). It also provides examples of people who made prayer a priority. Jesus left the crowds to speak to his heavenly Father (Matthew 14:23). The apostles were committed to prayer (Acts 6:4), as was the earliest church (Acts 2:42).

Sometimes, however, we are curious about what people actually said while praying because we find ourselves wondering about what to say when we pray. Jesus' model prayer (Matthew 6:9-13) and unity prayer (John 17:20-26) are great places to start. Luke 22:42 and Acts 1:24; 7:59 provide more examples of the specific content of prayers in the New Testament. But the nature of those particular prayers, given the situations in which they were offered, may leave us hungering for even more insight.

The Old Testament is extremely helpful in this regard. The book of Psalms contains a rich supply of prayers that cover a wide range of topics and situations. In addition, the narrative portions of the Old Testament contain many lengthy prayers. By studying how our ancestors in faith prayed through their situations, we can learn how to pray in the situations we face.

Think about Daniel's situation. In his lifetime, Daniel had seen God begin to fulfill his promises for his people, but this fulfillment caused Daniel to be confused. Part of the confusion and distress concerned the length of time involved in fulfillment, as we shall see. Many of us experience the same thing in our lives and the lives of our churches—things just (to our understanding) take too long!

So how do we go about praying when we long for God to intervene and "hurry up" to finish the good work he began in our lives? Daniel's prayer in chapter 9 is a helpful place to start.

DEVOTIONAL READING:
PSALM 130
BACKGROUND SCRIPTURE:
DANIEL 9
PRINTED TEXT:
DANIEL 9:1-7, 17-19

LESSON AIMS

After participating in this lesson, each student will be able to:
1. List the elements of confession and supplication in Daniel's prayer.
2. Explain why confession is an important prerequisite to supplication in prayer.
3. Write an intercessory prayer that includes adoration, confession, and supplication elements.

Apr 27

KEY VERSE

Now, our God, hear the prayers and petitions of your servant. For your sake, O Lord, look with favor on your desolate sanctuary. —Daniel 9:17

B. Lesson Background

Daniel, a Jew, served as a captive in the king's palace in a foreign land. Daniel spent most of his life there, from about 606 BC (Daniel 1:1) until at least 538 BC (1:21). More than one foreign ruler esteemed him highly (2:46-48; 5:29; 6:1, 2). More importantly, Daniel was highly esteemed by God (9:23; 10:11, 19).

Daniel 1–6 focuses on key events in the lives of four Jewish men who remained faithful to God while exiled in Babylon. Daniel 7–12 focuses on the future from Daniel's perspective, particularly how God was to restore his people after subduing those who had oppressed them. We are concerned with how Daniel responded to the plight of his people and how his prayer can teach us to pray.

I. CAUSE FOR CONCERN (DANIEL 9:1-3)

A. The Time (v. 1)

1. In the first year of Darius son of Xerxes (a Mede by descent), who was made ruler over the Babylonian kingdom—

This verse supplies the first clue as to why Daniel is praying the prayer that begins in verse 4 (below). That clue is the year and what it signifies. During Darius's *first year*, the Babylonians (also called Chaldeans) are defeated by the Persians. That is 539 BC. Subsequently, the Jews are released from exile to return to their land.

It need not concern us that historical research has identified Cyrus—not *Darius*—as the ruler who took over the realm of Babylon (2 Chronicles 36:22, 23; Ezra 1; Isaiah 44:28; 45:1, 13). Cyrus did not reign alone.

Daniel 6:28 may imply that Darius and Cyrus reigned right alongside one another. Under this theory, Darius (also known as Gubaru) is thought to lead the Persian army that captures Babylon in 539 BC, and Cyrus, his king, rewards him with a regional kingship. Another theory is that Daniel 6:28 implies that Darius and Cyrus are two names for the same person.

B. The Insight (v. 2)

2. . . . in the first year of his reign, I, Daniel, understood from the Scriptures, according to the word of the LORD given to Jeremiah the prophet, that the desolation of Jerusalem would last seventy years.

This verse provides a second clue concerning why Daniel prays the prayer that follows: Daniel's prayer is prompted by his reading of *Jeremiah the prophet.* The specific prophecy in question is presented briefly in Jeremiah 25:11, 12 and more extensively in Jeremiah 29:10-14. According to this prophecy, Babylon's domination ends after 70 years, and God's people return from captivity to experience peace and prosperity.

But why mention this prophecy in light of the first year of Darius's reign? The answer is found in 2 Chronicles 36:22 and Ezra 1:1-4. The context of these two passages indicates that Cyrus's takeover of Babylon has already occurred in fulfillment of Jeremiah's prophecy as we read the text before us. That being the case, one may assume that Daniel's prayer to follow will be one of praise and thanksgiving. At last, mighty Babylon has fallen! Now God's people can be restored! But this is not how Daniel prays, as we shall see.

C. The Reaction (v. 3)

3. So I turned to the Lord God and pleaded with him in prayer and petition, in fasting, and in sackcloth and ashes.

Before our text gives us the actual content of Daniel's prayer, the author is careful to note Daniel's state of mind: Daniel is in distress. The actions he takes before praying have something to teach Christians today about how to approach God.

Apparently, Daniel is aware of a problem. At this point, we don't really know what the problem is. We'll have to dig into Daniel's prayer below to discover that. But whatever it is, Daniel begins by turning *to the Lord God*. Daniel does not remain fixated on the problem. He can stare at Jeremiah's prophecy until he turns blue in the face, but focusing only on the problem (whatever it is) is not going to help. He must turn to God.

So Daniel turns to God in order plead *with him in prayer and petition*. This shows us Daniel's great faith in God's willingness and ability to act. Then Daniel supports his prayers with behavior. Daniel is not simply paying lip service to God. He demonstrates his concern through the self-denial of *fasting*. The *sackcloth and ashes* demonstrate that Daniel truly grieves. We may compare these signs of mourning with passages such as Nehemiah 9:1; Esther 4:3; and Psalm 35:13.

In our day, sackcloth and ashes are not staples of mourning practices in the Western world. But throughout the ages Christians have remained committed to fasting, that is, abstaining from food or other activities to focus on God (Acts 13:2, 3; 14:23). Indeed, there are countless symbolic gestures by which we can convey to God that our prayers are sincere.

DOING OUR PART

Half a century of rule by the atheistic Communist Party left China with a serious ethical gap. China has embraced capitalism to an extent, but without the Christian perspective that provides the ethical structure that keeps Western capitalism in check. The result is an epidemic of corruption in China. Increasing numbers of both government and business personnel are being prosecuted for graft, bribery, extortion, and even murder.

Another sobering trend in China is a widespread loss of the respect for the elderly that had been a hallmark of Chinese culture. The government has started publicly shaming—even imprisoning—people who neglect their aged parents.

Godly people do not need the threat of punishment to force them into doing right. This was certainly true of Daniel. He was concerned about his fellow Jews. He pled with God for the prophecies of national restoration to be fulfilled. Then he did what he could to confirm his seriousness: he donned sackcloth and ashes and began fasting. The situation was beyond Daniel's control, yet he took the steps he could to show God where his heart was. Small gestures are yet significant today.

—C. R. B.

II. CONFESSION OF SIN (DANIEL 9:4-7)

A. JUDAH'S GOD (v. 4)

4. I prayed to the LORD my God and confessed:

"O Lord, the great and awesome God, who keeps his covenant of love with all who love him and obey his commands,

Daniel demonstrates that he truly knows the God to whom he is praying: he is praying to *the Lord*, the God of Israel. He is praying to the God who beckons us to petition him, but who is also worthy of being feared. This God holds life and death in his hands, so we dare not address him flippantly.

Even so, this *awesome God* is gracious. He *keeps his covenant* with his people and shows them covenant *love*. Here Daniel helps us understand two aspects of

WHAT DO YOU THINK?

What are some specific areas of your life where you need to set your face on the Lord and pray? How can you support these prayers with action?

WHAT DO YOU THINK?

Are there ever times when you approach God with less than proper reverence? How do you keep this from happening?

God that we may have difficulty holding alongside one another. Daniel does not shy away from either attribute, but prays to the God who is both gracious and awesome simultaneously.

This is the God we must fear as we seek his love—the God whose loving mercy we must seek even when we fear him most. These attributes are not somehow in competition with one another inside of God. Rather, they reflect the unique nature of the God we serve.

God demonstrates his mercy especially to those who *love him and obey his commands.* We should not think of commandment-keeping as an outdated Old Testament principle that has somehow been superseded by grace. In John 14:15, Jesus says, "If you love me, you will obey what I command." See also 1 John 2:3; 3:22, 24; 5:3; Revelation 12:17; 14:12.

B. JUDAH'S SIN (vv. 5, 6)

5. ". . . *we have sinned and done wrong. We have been wicked and have rebelled; we have turned away from your commands and laws.*

Instead of offering a prayer of thanksgiving for fulfillment of Jeremiah's prophecy, Daniel begins by confessing sin (here and in v. 6). The sinner's proper response to God is confession. We remember that the Babylonian captivity had come about because of sin. Daniel realizes that Judah's restoration is to be accomplished by repentance.

It is important to note how Daniel identifies with the sin of the people. We know from prior accounts that Daniel is a man of exceptional character and devotion to God. Yet Daniel knows that God's people rise and fall together. So he prays *we have sinned* because he knows something important about God's purpose in the world.

In forming the nation of Israel, God was not trying to create merely a bunch of righteous individuals. Rather, he was creating a holy society. The laws he gave were not only about personal piety, but also about social justice and communal witness. The Israelites are to bear witness to God's purposes in all aspects of their lives. If Israel produces only a few righteous individuals, then it fails. The communal life of God's people must shine like stars in the sky (Daniel 12:3; Philippians 2:15). But Daniel knows that his fellow Jews have failed in this regard, and he does not consider himself to be above them.

6. "*We have not listened to your servants the prophets, who spoke in your name to our kings, our princes and our fathers, and to all the people of the land.*

Daniel also knows that Judah has had every chance to remedy the situation of unholiness. God has not left Israel alone to slip into sin without realizing it. God has sent *prophets* to warn them. These prophets went to all strata of society, from king to commoner, to communicate God's message. But neither the northern kingdom of Israel nor the southern kingdom of Judah heeded them.

C. JUDAH'S LOT (v. 7)

7. "*Lord, you are righteous, but this day we are covered with shame—the men of Judah and people of Jerusalem and all Israel, both near and far, in all the countries where you have scattered us because of our unfaithfulness to you.*"

As Daniel wraps up the confession part of his prayer, the contrast between God and his people comes into sharp relief. God is *righteous,* and all his people are (or should be) ashamed of themselves because they have sinned.

We can now summarize the features of Daniel's confession. First, Daniel knows to whom he is praying. Second, Daniel knows how he stands in relation

---

WHAT DO YOU THINK?

Are there specific sins you need to confess to God? Do you need to confess these sins to others? How will you get started doing this?

WHAT DO YOU THINK?

Why do Christians find it hard at times to listen to God's servants?

to God. Third, Daniel knows he must pray not only for himself but also for others. Fourth, Daniel accepts responsibility for the sin of God's people, not just for his own. Fifth, Daniel confesses sin to God, neither hiding nor ignoring it. Sixth, Daniel acknowledges that the sin of *Judah* and *Jerusalem* and *Israel* has a history. Part of that history is God's consistent warning.

These six features have obvious application to our prayers today. Having established all six, Daniel is in the right frame of mind to make his request.

AN OPEN SHAME

The secular world was delighted just a few years ago when the child abuse scandal rocked the Roman Catholic Church. Similar crimes take place in secular society, but the fact that they were taking place in a religious institution made the news especially "juicy."

Perhaps the more important aspect of the crime was the fact that the church stonewalled when accusations were made. *The Boston Globe,* right in the Catholic Church's backyard, so to speak, reported, "For decades church leaders kept horrific tales of abuse out of the public eye through an elaborate culture of secrecy, deception, and intimidation" (www.boston.com).

The world was appropriately shocked, and the church hierarchy should have been. As months went by, more stories began leaking out. Gradually, the harsh glare of publicity forced the church to confess its corporate sin of covering up the private sins of some of its priests.

The Catholic Church's difficulties with this sin demonstrate how hard it can be to confess sin, especially when the confession needs to be a public one. Daniel's confession in his prayer was done privately, but he was praying on behalf of the Jewish people, whose unholiness was "an open shame." Are there other open shames in the body of Christ that the church overlooks?   —C. R. B.

III. PETITION FOR HELP (DANIEL 9:17-19)

A. INTRODUCTION OF PETITION (v. 17)

17. "Now, our God, hear the prayers and petitions of your servant. For your sake, O Lord, look with favor on your desolate sanctuary.

Verses 8-16 (not in today's text) offer Daniel's lengthy recounting of the sins of God's people. The wrap-up of the prayer is verses 17-19. These two segments build upon one another in ways that involve repetition.

Central to Daniel's request is that God *hear* and respond. Daniel knows that God does not have to heed his petition. God is not obligated. His people have practically disowned him, and he warned them long ago that disobedience on their part would result in rejection on his part (Leviticus 18:28: "If you defile the land, it will vomit you out as it vomited out the nations that were before you"; see also Deuteronomy 28:15-68).

But Daniel also knows that God is merciful and will listen to his earnest prayer. So he asks for a response. He petitions God to show favor upon God's own *sanctuary* for God's own *sake.*

A cynic may read this passage as slick salesmanship on Daniel's part: Daniel wants something from God, so Daniel presents his request as if God is the one who stands to gain. A better reading, however, is that Daniel is acknowledging what has been true all along: the temple sanctuary belongs to God, but the people have acted as if it were theirs to do with as they pleased. Their track record is centuries long in this regard. Similarly, they forget that they exist to fulfill God's purposes in the world, not their own. The future of the Jewish people depends on their recognizing this.

Visual for Lesson 9. *How has prayer changed the lives of your learners? Point to this visual as you ask for examples.*

WHAT DO YOU THINK?

How can you and your church pray more effectively for the Lord to bless his work?

O God who hears our prayer, teach us to pray like Daniel. Like him, we are often baffled by your timing. We cannot see the big picture, and we get hung up on the details. Please give us the faith to wait for you. We confess to you our sins, we submit to you our unworthiness, and we call upon your mercy. Hear us when we pray, for your name's sake and for the sake of your world, in Jesus' name, amen.

How to Say It

Babylonians. Bab-ih-LOW-nee-unz.

Chaldeans. Kal-DEE-unz.

Cyrus. SIGH-russ.

Darius. Duh-RYE-us.

Gabriel. GAY-bree-ul.

Gubaru. Goo-BAHR-roo.

Jeremiah. Jair-uh-MY-uh.

Leviticus. Leh-VIT-ih-kus.

Medes. Meeds.

Philippians. Fih-LIP-ee-unz.

Xerxes. ZERK-seez.

Thought to Remember

Petition God humbly and urgently.

B. Basis of Petition (v. 18)

18. "Give ear, O God, and hear; open your eyes and see the desolation of the city that bears your Name. We do not make requests of you because we are righteous, but because of your great mercy.

Daniel intensifies his petition before submitting its basis. He asks God not only to *hear* his request but also to *see* for himself the *desolation of the city* of Jerusalem. This city, like the temple, is attached to God's *name*. Forgetting this fact led to Judah's demise (1 Kings 11:36; 2 Kings 23:27).

Daniel comes before God knowing that Judah is empty-handed in terms of righteousness. Nothing Judah has done or will do can earn God's favor. Daniel cannot appeal to Judah's holy accomplishments as bargaining chips. The ultimate basis of Daniel's appeal is God's *great mercy*. It can be ours as well.

C. Urgency of Petition (v. 19)

19. "O Lord, listen! O Lord, forgive! O Lord, hear and act! For your sake, O my God, do not delay, because your city and your people bear your Name."

Daniel concludes his prayer with a sense of urgency as he entreats God four times. He asks God to *hear, forgive,* and *act,* doing these quickly (*do not delay*). Notice that Daniel does not make his petition because the Jews are weary of their affliction or worthy of intervention. Rather, Daniel asks God to act because God has an important mission for his *people* to accomplish, and God's reputation in the world is connected to that people.

God took a risk by attaching his *Name* to Israel. By their actions his name is either lifted high or dragged through the mud. In closing his prayer by drawing attention to God's name, Daniel acknowledges that the Jews now remember (or should remember) why they exist. Their task is to live up to their namesake.

CONCLUSION

A. Daniel's Prayer Answered

While Daniel was still praying, God sent the angel Gabriel to answer the prayer (Daniel 9:20-27). In short, Gabriel told Daniel that the punishment had been multiplied by 7. So instead of being restored fully after 70 years, God's people were to be restored after "seventy weeks" (or "seventy 'sevens'"). There is some debate over how to interpret this number, but we can at least say that it involved the distant future from Daniel's perspective. This was not an arbitrary punishment by God. In Leviticus 26:18, God warned Israel that he would punish her sevenfold for disobedience.

B. Daniel's Prayer Applied

We are to remind ourselves, as Daniel did, that God's purposes for us are not complete. Though the power of sin was defeated on the cross, it still rears its ugly head in our lives. Christ is the fulfillment of our hope, but we await a day to experience the fullness that God has in store for us in the heavenly Jerusalem.

Until then, we can follow Daniel's lead in prayer. We draw near to God not only in speech but also in action. Fasting and signs of contrition can help as we own up to individual and corporate sins, confessing them to God and one another. We must renounce all thoughts of entitlement, as if God were obligated to answer our prayers to our liking. We must commit ourselves to him and remain true to his purpose for us in this world, for it is the Christian who bears the name of Christ. We were saved not for comfort, but for God's mission for the church. Daniel prayed like this, and God answered him. Let us pray likewise.

Discovery Learning

This page contains an alternative lesson plan emphasizing learning activities. Classes desiring such student involvement will find these suggestions helpful. The next page is a reproducible activity page to further enhance discovery learning.

INTO THE LESSON

As learners arrive, hand each a copy of the following list of Bible references and directions: "The Bible records many great prayers. Look up these references and figure out who is praying and what the occasion is for each." Genesis 18:23-32; Exodus 32:11-13; 1 Samuel 2:1-10; 1 Kings 8:22-53; 1 Kings 18:36, 37; Nehemiah 1:5-11; Psalm 51; Psalm 73; Daniel 9:4-19; Matthew 6:9-13; Acts 4:24-30; Ephesians 1:15-23.

As an alternative and less time-consuming approach, simply give one reference to each learner along with the same directions. As you discuss these prayers, ask your learners if they see any patterns.

INTO THE WORD

Reproduce and distribute the following list of statements. (They are also printed in the optional student book.) Say, "Daniel's prayer and the prelude to his prayer in Daniel 9 reveal much about God. List a verse from today's text that reveals the truth of each of the following." You may have your learners work in pairs or small groups if you wish.

1. The God of Daniel and of today knows the future: ___.

2. The God of Daniel and of today can provide for human needs: ___.

3. The God of Daniel and of today is the Lord: ___.

4. The God of Daniel and of today welcomes repentance: ___.

5. The God of Daniel and of today is awesome: ___.

6. The God of Daniel and of today keeps his covenants: ___.

7. The God of Daniel and of today shows love: ___.

8. The God of Daniel and of today reveals his expectations: ___.

9. The God of Daniel and of today is offended by sin: ___.

10. The God of Daniel and of today has expressed his will for human behavior: ___.

11. The God of Daniel and of today sends spokesmen to speak to his people: ___.

12. The God of Daniel and of today can hear the prayers of his people: ___.

13. The God of Daniel and of today can give or withhold blessings: ___.

14. The God of Daniel and of today sees our condition: ___.

15. The God of Daniel and of today answers prayer because he is good, not because we are: ___.

16. The God of Daniel and of today can forgive: ___.

17. The God of Daniel and of today can be claimed as "my God": ___.

18. The God of Daniel and of today gives his name to his children: ___.

Possible answers: 1. verse 2; 2. verse 19; 3. verse 4; 4. verse 3; 5. verse 4; 6. verse 4; 7. verse 18; 8. verse 6; 9. verse 5; 10. verse 6; 11. verse 6; 12. verse 17; 13. verse 18; 14. verse 18; 15. verse 18; 16. verse 19; 17. verse 19; 18. verse 19. Accept other answers with reasonable explanations.

INTO LIFE

Make a transition by asking your learners to look at the attributes and actions of God from the exercise of the Into the Word segment. Ask, "How do the truths you see here and in Daniel's prayer affect your own prayer life?" Discuss.

Alternative: Reproduce and distribute the list of questions below. (These are also printed in the optional student books). Say, "A common Christian affirmation is that prayers should include (among other things) adoration, confession, and supplication. This may suggest to us not only content but also sequence. Consider the following questions."

1. Should adoration of God precede personal confession? Why, or why not?

2. Should adoration of God precede supplication for needs? Why, or why not?

3. Should confession of personal weakness precede asking for God's help? Why, or why not?

4. Should supplication be the last concern in our prayers? Why, or why not?

5. Is this sequence the way you usually pray? Why, or why not?

6. What changes do you need to make to your prayer life, if any?

Depending on the time that is available, have your learners work in pairs, small groups, or as a class. Finally, distribute copies of the two activities on the Reproducible Page as take-home exercises.

Great Prayers of the Bible

Find and examine each of the following Bible references of great prayers of the Bible. Complete the activity as part of your Bible study this week.

Who is praying?
What's the occasion?

What kind of prayer is it?
Circle one or more.

Exodus 32:11-13 _____ **Adoration? Confession? Supplication?**

1 Samuel 2:1-10 _____ **Adoration? Confession? Supplication?**

1 Kings 8:22-53 _____ **Adoration? Confession? Supplication?**

Nehemiah 1:5-11 _____ **Adoration? Confession? Supplication?**

Psalm 51 _____ **Adoration? Confession? Supplication?**

Matthew 6:9-13 _____ **Adoration? Confession? Supplication?**

Acts 4:24-30 _____ **Adoration? Confession? Supplication?**

Ephesians 1:15-23 _____ **Adoration? Confession? Supplication?**

Daniel's Prayer as Mine

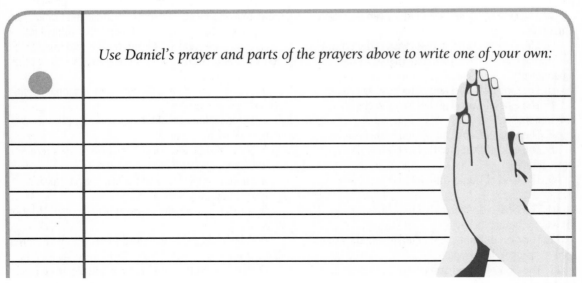

Use Daniel's prayer and parts of the prayers above to write one of your own:

SETTING PRIORITIES

LESSON 10

WHY TEACH THIS LESSON?

If you think about it, much of what we do daily is a repeat of what we did on previous days. Our morning preparations, our workaday world, and our after-work or after-school schedules involve lots of repetition. We are comfortable with routine. And that's not really such a bad thing. Routine gives a certain coherence to life.

But God has ways of forcing us to reexamine our routines. He may be especially inclined to do so when our spiritual routines, disciplines, and priorities are defective. Today's lesson will give your learners a certain "shock treatment" in this regard. The Lord still calls us to seek first his kingdom (Matthew 6:33). That little word *first* carries with it the idea of priorities. When God's Word convicts us in this area, our behaviors and priorities will change.

INTRODUCTION

A. PRIORITIES

There is not enough time in life to do everything that we would like to do, and some things in life are crucial to do, like it or not. For example, if we put off paying our electric bill long enough, the utility company will shut off the power. Paying that electric bill becomes an increasingly high priority as time goes by.

So how does a busy person make sure that the most important things actually get done? One efficient way is to write out a priority list. Of the things that could be done today, what is the most important one? That goes at the top of the list. Then come the second, third, and fourth most important items, and so on.

Once the list is made, one goes down the list and tries to accomplish as many items as time allows. Those things that cannot be accomplished then go on the next day's list. Low priority items at the bottom of the list may never get done, but this system makes sure that the most important things do get done.

But many times I do not operate in this efficient way. I start not with what is most important, but with what I want to do—no matter how trivial. I desperately need to pay the bills, but I watch the news or surf the Internet instead. As a result, some things that absolutely needed to be done that day may have failed to get done. The problem was that my priorities in action did not correspond with the real priorities in my life.

The same problem comes in the spiritual life. The Christian should have the things of God as a priority in life. But all too frequently other matters, both important and trivial, crowd out the things of God. The book of Haggai reminds us that we need to make God and his service our priority.

B. LESSON BACKGROUND

King Solomon began to build the temple around 966 BC. After its completion, it stood for nearly four centuries as the grand religious monument of Solomon's reign.

DEVOTIONAL READING:
PSALM 84:1-4

BACKGROUND SCRIPTURE:
HAGGAI 1; EZRA 5

PRINTED TEXT:
HAGGAI 1:1-10, 12-15

LESSON AIMS

After participating in this lesson, each student will be able to:

1. Describe how the cultural, economic, and religious climate in Haggai's day worked against the rebuilding of the temple.

2. Give a modern example of misplaced priorities that is parallel to the situation of Haggai's day.

3. Suggest a plan to correct one misplaced priority in order to obey God more fully.

May
4

KEY VERSE

"Go up into the mountains and bring down timber and build the house, so that I may take pleasure in it and be honored,"
says the LORD. —Haggai 1:8

The temple replaced the tabernacle as Israel's focal point for worship. The Israelites came to the temple for three annual feasts (Deuteronomy 16:16). Standing as the symbolic dwelling place of God in the midst of his people, the temple had a fond place in the hearts of pious Israelites. For example, in Psalm 84:1-4 the psalmist expresses some sentimental jealousy for the sparrows that built nests in the temple's structure, longing like them to remain always in its courts.

But a catastrophe befell the temple during the reign of Zedekiah. In 586 BC the Babylonians devastated Jerusalem. The temple was looted and burned (2 Kings 25). The period that followed is known as *the Babylonian exile,* a time in which large numbers of Jews were deported from Judah to live in Babylon.

The exile came to an end shortly after Cyrus, king of Persia and Media, conquered Babylon in 539 BC. In late 539 or early 538 BC, Cyrus issued a decree allowing Jews who so wished to return to Judah and rebuild the temple (Ezra 1:1-4). About 50,000 went back.

The Jews who returned from exile were eager to take advantage of Cyrus's decree and rebuild the temple. They succeeded in rebuilding the altar and began once again to conduct sacrifices (Ezra 3:1-6). They even succeeded in laying the foundations for a new temple (Ezra 3:7-13), but opposition forced a halt (Ezra 4:24). As a result, the temple proper remained unfinished for the better part of two decades after Jewish exiles had returned with plans to rebuild it.

After this long time of inactivity, the prophets Haggai and Zechariah preached in the year 520 BC about the need to rebuild the temple (Ezra 5:1, 2). These are the same prophets who wrote the books of the Old Testament that bear their names. The book of Zechariah gives an account of his prophetic encouragement regarding the rebuilding of the temple (see Zechariah 1:16; 4:9). The book of Haggai gives that prophet's perspective on how he preached in this regard and how the people responded to his message.

The book of Haggai consists of four prophetic messages, dating from August to December of 520 BC. Each prophecy begins with the declaration "the word of the Lord came" (Haggai 1:1; 2:1, 10, 20). Today's lesson takes us to the first of these four.

How to Say It

Babylonians. Bab-ih-LOW-nee-unz.

Cambyses. Kam-BYE-seez.

Haggai. HAG-eye or HAG-ay-eye.

Jehoiachin. Jeh-HOY-uh-kin.

Jehozadak. Juh-HOE-zuh-dak.

Jeshua. JESH-you-uh.

Jozadak. JOZ-uh-dak.

Pedaiah. Peh-DAY-yuh.

Shealtiel. She-AL-tee-el.

Zechariah. ZEK-uh-RYE-uh.

Zedekiah. Zed-uh-KYE-uh.

Zerubbabel. Zeh-RUB-uh-bul.

I. TEMPLE NEGLECTED (HAGGAI 1:1-4)

A. CONTEXT (v. 1)

1. In the second year of King Darius, on the first day of the sixth month, the word of the LORD came through the prophet Haggai to Zerubbabel son of Shealtiel, governor of Judah, and to Joshua son of Jehozadak, the high priest:

The date of Haggai's first prophecy is very specific as to the year, month, and day of Darius's reign. This particular *Darius* is the third emperor of the Persian Empire; he follows Cyrus and Cambyses to the throne. Darius reigned from 521 to 486 BC. This Darius is not to be confused with the very different King Darius of the book of Daniel.

The *sixth month* in the Jewish religious calendar is called *Elul* (see the exact use of this designation in Nehemiah 6:15). Because the dates of Persian kings are known with certainty, the *second year* and *sixth month* and *first day* of Darius converts precisely to August 29, 520 BC.

Shortly after returning from exile, two leaders emerge. The first is *Zerubbabel,* the *governor,* who is *son of Shealtiel* (compare Ezra 3:2, 8; 5:2). Shealtiel himself is the son of King Jehoiachin. We know this from 1 Chronicles 3:17-19. That passage says, however, that Pedaiah was Zerubbabel's father rather than Shealtiel. This can be harmonized by realizing that Zerubbabel may have become Shealtiel's son legally through adoption after Pedaiah died (compare Deuteronomy 25:5-10). Zerubbabel is of Davidic descent and, as it turns out, an ancestor of Jesus Christ (Matthew 1:12).

The other leader is *Joshua,* who is the *high priest* (compare Zechariah 6:11). Note that in Ezra 3:2, 8; 5:2, the spelling "Jeshua son of Jozadak" is slightly different from *Joshua son of Jehozadak* here, although this undoubtedly is the same person.

Shortly after returning from exile, Zerubbabel and Joshua led the people in rebuilding the altar of the temple. This allowed renewed sacrifices and celebration of festivals. Nonetheless, the temple itself was not rebuilt (Ezra 3:1–4:5, 24). Haggai addresses the political and religious leaders of Judah to exhort them to finish what they started.

B. RATIONALIZATION (v. 2)

2. This is what the LORD Almighty says: "These people say, 'The time has not yet come for the LORD's house to be built.'"

Sometimes we try to discern the will of God by circumstances. If we try something and things go poorly, then we may be tempted to think, "This must not be God's will." On the other hand, if things do go well, then we may be tempted to think, "This must be God's will." However, such reasoning may not be a reliable guide to discerning God's will!

The plans to rebuild the temple had not gone well for the returned exiles. They had good plans and good intentions to start (Ezra 3:7-13). But political opposition arose that brought the project to a halt (Ezra 4:1-5, 24). Thus the average Jew may well be thinking, "it must not be God's will to rebuild his house at this time." The problem is that this kind of thinking has been going on for more than 15 years! Haggai is anxious to correct this false conclusion.

"I SIMPLY HAVEN'T HAD TIME"

"I decided to quit procrastinating, but I just couldn't get around to starting the project."

Not everyone sees the humor in jokes about procrastination. There are numerous Web sites dealing with procrastination, and one of them carries this blog: "The jokes about procrastination infuriate me. This is not a funny problem—not if you are suffering from true, chronic procrastination."

Procrastination has been defined as "doing something—anything—except what one should be doing at the time." As one Web site says, "Procrastination is the grave in which opportunity is buried." Needless to say, procrastination can be a disruptive tendency.

The Jews who had returned from exile may have been procrastinators. However, they may have been suffering from a spiritual problem: they simply didn't care whether God's house ever got rebuilt, as long as their own living conditions were comfortable. Either way, they found it easy to rationalize not doing what God wanted them to do. Surely none of us have ever had that problem!   —C. R. B.

C. CONFRONTATION (vv. 3, 4)

3, 4. Then the word of the LORD came through the prophet Haggai: "Is it a time for you yourselves to be living in your paneled houses, while this house remains a ruin?"

The message of *the prophet Haggai* that follows is probably the same prophecy mentioned in Ezra 5:1. The failure of the Jews to finish rebuilding the temple is quite understandable up to a point. They had indeed made a start with all

Visual for Lesson 10. *If your learners have personal copies of the* Standard Bible Atlas, *they will find this chart on page 23.*

WHAT DO YOU THINK?

What are some things you have started for the Lord but have not completed? How will you go about making sure you finish?

good intentions. But life undoubtedly was difficult for the Jews when they first returned from exile to begin a new life in Judah. When opposition to rebuilding the temple arises several years before Haggai prophesies, it just becomes easier to let survival take priority.

But most of the returnees are well settled now, a decade and a half after the initial return. It's past time to make God's ruined *house* rather than their own *houses* their priority. Allowing God's temple to remain in ruins is a disgrace and an insult to God. Haggai shames them for this.

II. BLESSINGS FORFEITED (HAGGAI 1:5-10)

A. THINKING IT THROUGH, PART 1 (VV. 5, 6)

5, 6. Now this is what the LORD Almighty says: "Give careful thought to your ways. You have planted much, but have harvested little. You eat, but never have enough. You drink, but never have your fill. You put on clothes, but are not warm. You earn wages, only to put them in a purse with holes in it."

Those who had returned from exile had not prospered materially. Crops of grain for food and grapes for *drink* and flax for clothing had been insufficient to satisfy the needs. Money seemed to disappear, as if leaking from a ripped *purse.*

Haggai indicates that this is no coincidence. Rather, this is happening because the people are giving no thought to the status of God's house. Apparently, people have been thinking, "Because the economy is bad, we can't afford to build the temple." What they should be thinking is, "The reason the economy is bad is because we haven't built the temple."

Behind Haggai's statement is the teaching of Deuteronomy 28. That passage instructs that God will bless his people if they obey him, but he will curse them if they disobey. The lack of material blessing among those who have returned from exile is thus a consequence of their failure to obey God's call to rebuild his temple.

B. THINKING IT THROUGH, PART 2 (VV. 7-10)

7, 8. This is what the LORD Almighty says: "Give careful thought to your ways. Go up into the mountains and bring down timber and build the house, so that I may take pleasure in it and be honored," says the LORD.

The solution to the disobedience is to repent and obey. In this case that means bringing *down timber* so work on the temple can begin again.

Forests exist in the hill country of Judah in ancient times, but the best wood comes from the mountains of Lebanon (compare 2 Kings 19:23). Solomon had imported cedar and other woods for his temple from there (1 Kings 5:6; 7:2; 2 Chronicles 2:8, 16). The text before us probably implies doing the same for Zerubbabel's temple, since that was the original intent of the returning exiles (Ezra 3:7). Thus the people should *go up into the mountains* in Lebanon to acquire the best wood, as is fitting for God's house.

Rebuilding the sacred space of the temple will bring God *pleasure.* Furthermore, the temple will be used to glorify God since it will be a place of worship. Today our bodies are meant to be the temples where God is glorified or *honored* (1 Corinthians 6:19).

9, 10. "You expected much, but see, it turned out to be little. What you brought home, I blew away. Why?" declares the LORD Almighty. "Because of my house, which remains a ruin, while each of you is busy with his own house. Therefore, because of you the heavens have withheld their dew and the earth its crops."

WHAT DO YOU THINK?

What are some personal priorities that you have allowed to displace God's priorities? How do you stay alert to this danger?

WHAT DO YOU THINK?

What causes God to withhold blessings from us today? How do we avoid overspiritualizing in this regard—seeing God blessing or withholding blessing in every action or lack of action on our part?

Because people fail to give attention to God's *house* while they are looking to their own houses, God has decided not to bless them materially. In particular, rains have not come in a timely way, so the *crops* are meager (see also v. 11, not in today's text). But obedience will mean that God will reverse that according to the promises of blessings in Deuteronomy 28.

III. WORK STARTED (HAGGAI 1:12-15)

A. PEOPLE'S OBEDIENCE, (V. 12)

12. Then Zerubbabel son of Shealtiel, Joshua son of Jehozadak, the high priest, and the whole remnant of the people obeyed the voice of the LORD their God and the message of the prophet Haggai, because the LORD their God had sent him. And the people feared the LORD.

The response to prophets in Old Testament times often is not good. Isaiah's audience was blind and deaf to his message (Isaiah 6:9, 10). Jeremiah was beaten and imprisoned (Jeremiah 20:1, 2). But in this case, *the whole remnant of the people*—that is, those who have returned from exile, led by the governor *Zerubbabel* and the high priest *Joshua*—respond positively and prepare to rebuild the temple. This response is also recorded in Ezra 5:1, 2, which indicates that the prophet Zechariah supports Haggai in encouraging the Jews in this rebuilding.

The people *feared the Lord* in the way that Abraham showed that he feared God. Abraham proved he feared God by demonstrating his willingness to obey God's command to sacrifice Isaac (Genesis 22:12). This kind of fear is the awe or respect for God that leads one to turn from sin and obey his commands no matter what. Those who do not obey God do not in fact fear him.

B. LORD'S FAVOR (v. 13)

13. Then Haggai, the LORD's messenger, gave this message of the LORD to the people: "I am with you," declares the LORD.

In response to the people's willingness to build the temple, Haggai conveys God's promise: *I am with you*. What better words can one hear? A sense of God's presence is meant to provide the assurance of God's protection (Genesis 26:24; Isaiah 43:5; Jeremiah 1:8).

Trials and opposition lie ahead. Even after the rebuilding begins, Persian officials will threaten to stop the project (Ezra 5:3-17). But God will see them through to the project's completion (see Ezra 6:13-15; Zechariah 4:8, 9). Christians have a similar assurance of Jesus' presence as we seek to make disciples of the nations and baptize them in his name (Matthew 28:18-20).

C. EVERYONE'S WORK (vv. 14, 15)

14. So the LORD stirred up the spirit of Zerubbabel son of Shealtiel, governor of Judah, and the spirit of Joshua son of Jehozadak, the high priest, and the spirit of the whole remnant of the people. They came and began to work on the house of the LORD Almighty, their God,

Behind the outward act of beginning to rebuild the temple is an inward, invisible movement of God in the spirits *of the people* and their leaders. God often works through human messengers to stir hearts (example: Acts 2:37). In this case the prophets Haggai and Zechariah are used by God to compel action (again, Ezra 5:1, 2).

Other leaders besides these two prophets are important as well: the political leader *Zerubbabel* and the religious leader *Joshua* the *high priest* put this

WHAT DO YOU THINK?

What responses can we expect when we share something from God's Word? How do such responses affect our thoughts on whether or not we were "successful"?

DAILY BIBLE READINGS

Monday, Apr. 28—In God's House (Psalm 84:1-4)

Tuesday, Apr. 29—Time to Rebuild the Temple (Haggai 1:1-11)

Wednesday, Apr. 30—The Work Begins (Haggai 1:12-15)

Thursday, May 1—Rebuilding the Foundation (Ezra 3:8-13)

Friday, May 2—Help Rejected (Ezra 4:1-4)

Saturday, May 3—The Rebuilding Questioned (Ezra 5:1-5)

Sunday, May 4—The Decree of King Cyrus (Ezra 5:6-17)

movement of God's Spirit into the practical effect of temple building. Leaders are still important in the way God stirs his people to action today.

WAKING UP

The First Great Awakening (about AD 1720–1740) came about in reaction to increasing secularism on both sides of the Atlantic Ocean. The secular, rationalistic spirit that preceded the awakening had been itself a reaction to an often-unthinking piety that emphasized emotion more than sound principles of biblical interpretation. So, as usual, the pendulum had swung too far and correction was needed.

The awakening's revitalization of Christian piety had a powerful effect on American culture in the years leading up to the American Revolution. But an educated ministry was needed to teach the large numbers of people turning back to faith, and numerous seminaries for the training of ministers came out of the awakening. We know several of these today as Ivy League colleges. Originally founded as Christian institutions, the Ivy League colleges eventually became secular institutions as the pendulum swung back the other way.

Old Testament history seems to be all about pendulum swings! As Haggai began to prophesy, the Jews had once again fallen away from God's ideal. However, the prophet's powerful preaching brought renewal, revival, and action. Do you think something similar is taking place today? If not, does it need to?   —C. R. B.

15. . . . *on the twenty-fourth day of the sixth month in the second year of King Darius.*

The date mentioned here can be calculated to be September 21, 520 BC. Thus the work begins only 23 days after Haggai had begun preaching on the need to rebuild the temple (Haggai 1:1, 2). In a little over 3 weeks, things start to turn around. God's people begin the task God wishes for them to undertake. The task will not be easy, since the temple will not be completed until March 12, 515 BC (Ezra 6:15). But God will be with them during those four and one-half years.

CONCLUSION

Although God is not calling us to build him a temple of stone and wood, he certainly calls us to worship and serve him. Often, however, we fail to make God and the things of God a priority in our lives. It is easy to fall into laziness, selfishness, or a life of comfortable self-indulgence.

The book of Haggai reminds us of the need to put God first, not ourselves. It exhorts us to be willing to make the sacrifices and the effort necessary to glorify God and further his work in the world. That sometimes involves the bricks and mortar of building physical buildings, such as churches or housing for the poor. Or it can take the form of building God's spiritual building, the church, by evangelizing and making disciples. Both kinds of work require putting God's priorities above our selfish desires.

For larger tasks on behalf of God, there is also the importance of good leadership. Had the prophets Haggai and Zechariah not stepped up to preach and exhort others to action, no temple would have been built. If the people refused to follow the leadership of their governor, Zerubbabel, and their high priest, Joshua, the temple would not have been built.

Each of us has a role to play. God calls some to lead and others to follow in order that greater works can be accomplished for him. Part of our setting priorities is determining what God is calling us to do as individuals: to lead or follow others whom God has raised up. Then our priority must be to live out that calling.

Discovery Learning

*This page contains an alternative lesson plan emphasizing learning activities. Classes
desiring such student involvement will find these suggestions helpful. The next page
is a reproducible activity page to further enhance discovery learning.*

INTO THE LESSON

Write this sentence on the board: "First _____, then
_____." Ask your class to fill in the blanks. Expect a
variety of responses, both serious and humorous. For
example, "First the chicken, then the egg"; "First God,
then others"; "First wash, then dry"; "First birth, then
death"; "First believe, then obey."

Accumulate ideas for a few minutes, and then ask,
"Which of our responses are matters of priority rather
than simple sequence?" Comment, "Today's study is
one of priorities. But sometimes sequence implies priority; for example, giving to Christ's church and her ministries should be first in one's financial planning."

Alternative: Put in each chair a copy of the Can't Get
It Done word-search exercise from the Reproducible
Page for class members to work on as they arrive.

INTO THE WORD

Display the title *Haggai the Unknown*. Comment:
"Haggai is one of those Bible people whose name we
barely know. Today our study offers an opportunity to
change that, as it focuses on the prophet, his task, and
his success."

Prepare 13 large flash cards, each having one of the
following nicknames for Haggai. Show them one at a
time randomly and affix them to the wall or board as
you proceed. Say, "Look at these nicknames for Haggai. Explain how each is an appropriate title for God's
prophet." (After each nickname a brief explanation is
given in parentheses for the teacher's use; do not put
those on the flashcards.)

Nicknames: 1. Haggai the One of Two (*he served at
the same time as the prophet Zechariah*); 2. Haggai the
Temple Prophet (*his message was largely about restoring
the temple*); 3. Haggai the Easily Dated (*Haggai 1:1 gives
a very precise date for Haggai's call to prophesy*); 4. Haggai
the Festive One (*his name means "festive"*); 5. Haggai the
Listener (*he spoke only what the Lord told him to speak*); 6.
Haggai the Timekeeper (*his complaint—actually God's—
was that the people had lost track of the right time to build
the temple: now!*); 7. Haggai the Challenger (*he came to
challenge the people to action*); 8. Haggai the Observant
(*verses 5-7 reveal that God—and Haggai— saw what
happens when people ignore God's work*); 9. Haggai the
Financial Adviser (*he knows what happens to money when
God is not in the picture; see verses 7, 9, 10*); 10. Haggai
the Obeyed (*verse 12 records the result of his message: the
governor and the high priest and the people obeyed*); 11.
Haggai the Comforter (*when the people obeyed, verse 13,
Haggai spoke God's great words of comfort, "I am with
you"*); 12. Haggai the Effective (*the temple was rebuilt
because of the response to his message; see verse 14b*); 13.
Haggai the Hurrier (*verse 15 reports that work began only
about three weeks after he started preaching*).

INTO LIFE

Make a transition by saying, "Haggai challenges the
people to consider their ways. I'd like for you to consider the following questions silently as you carefully
think of your own behavior." Make copies of the following list of questions and distribute. (The list also appears
in the optional student book.)

1. Are there things your church leadership wants to
do but you are standing in the way? 2. Are there repairs
and improvements needed in the church property that
you would never ignore or delay at home? 3. Are you
unsatisfied in your quest for more things? 4. Do you get
the feeling your money disappears without explanation?
5. Are you actively seeking to bring God pleasure and
glory? 6. Do you ever consider natural disasters, such as
famine, to be God withholding his blessing? 7. Do you
stand alongside leaders when they listen to God's Word
and obey? 8. Do you remind God's people that he is
with them when they obey his will?

Alternative exercise. Reproduce the following "op-
posites" on a sheet of paper and distribute copies:
*praying/chatting idly; reading about missions/reading about
celebrities; studying God's Word/watching TV; corporate
worship/recreation; caring for church property/caring for
personal property; church giving/luxury spending; teaching
God's Word/teaching hobbies; visiting the lonely/going shopping.* Put long lines of dots in place of the slant marks so
that the two elements in each pair are on opposite sides
of the page.

Say, "Within each pair, which one is a priority? Draw
small stick figures along the lines to indicate where you
stand. Consider both intent and time spent." (This activity also appears in the optional student book.)

Distribute as take-home work copies of the Haggai
and I exercise from the Reproducible Page.

Can't Get It Done

For every project—church, family, nation, or individual—there is a long list of excuses why one "can't get it done." The Jerusalem Jews of Haggai's time used them all. Find and circle nine excuses that could have been made then (and may still be made now). Responses may be one word or two- or three-word phrases.

```
M S I L A I R E T A M N
E X S C U S T E E E O O
X C E U S O M E E I X T
C U C E O I E X T E C G
U S R B T E E A X G C O
U S U T E E L X C A U D
S S O E E E X C U R S S
Y N S E V X C U S U E W
X C E E S E E X C O U I
T I R I P S F O K C A L
S O O R E D A E L O N L
N E N X C U S E E N X C
```

Haggai and I

If God sent Haggai to you, what would he have to say about misplaced priorities? Ponder your lifestyle and write in several of the balloons provided. Start each with your name.

Excuses: **not time, too busy, no leader, no resources, materialism, not God's will, no revelation, no courage, lack of spirit**

FOLLOWING A VISIONARY LEADER

LESSON 11

WHY TEACH THIS LESSON?

I frequently have an opportunity to be a guest speaker at churches. When I arrive I often take on the persona of a first-time visitor. I look at the facilities from the standpoint of someone who is unfamiliar with the church. I also observe the interpersonal dynamics. To say the least, many churches simply are not "visitor friendly," and the facilities are uninviting. But the members do not see this because they have become familiar with things and thus blind to the needs.

The problem is twofold. First, there may not be a visionary leader to nudge (or shove) the congregation to change. Second, there may not be folks who are willing to follow such a leader. God does not choose everyone to be a Nehemiah. But God *does* expect everyone to support the leaders he sends. Your students are either "part of the solution" or "part of the problem." Today's lesson will require that they choose. As in Nehemiah's day, there is no middle ground.

INTRODUCTION

A. TAKING RISKS, EXERCISING FAITH

Most people are aware of the theme parks and movies of the Walt Disney Company. Many are unaware, however, of the difficulties that Walt Disney (1901–1966) faced in achieving his success. When Disney returned from France after World War I, he had a vision of creating a company that would focus on the new art medium of animation. He started a company called Laugh-O-Grams for that purpose. But it went bankrupt in 1923.

Disney then went to Hollywood with only his baggage and twenty dollars to restart his business. His first series of short cartoons flopped. He had to borrow money from his brother and set up shop in his uncle's garage to keep his animation business alive. But his business slowly grew. When he invented Mickey Mouse, who first appeared on screen in 1928, his company was on its way.

Walt Disney's success came by having a vision and being willing to risk failure. Typically, it is that kind of person who accomplishes great things in business. The same is true in the spiritual life. Those who accomplish great things for God tend to be risk takers (although we may question whether it is proper ever to think of work for God as "risky"). Those who walk by great faith have a vision of what God would have them to do and the courage to attempt things that others would avoid. Nehemiah was that kind of visionary leader.

B. LESSON BACKGROUND

Nehemiah, whose name means "the Lord comforts," was a devout Jew who lived in the fifth century BC. That was the period of the Persian Empire. This empire came to prominence when Cyrus conquered Babylon in 539 BC.

DEVOTIONAL READING:
PSALM 137:1-7; 138:1-5

BACKGROUND SCRIPTURE:
NEHEMIAH 1:1–2:20

PRINTED TEXT:
NEHEMIAH 2:1-8, 11, 17, 18

LESSON AIMS

After participating in this lesson, each student will be able to:

1. Describe how Nehemiah made spiritual, political, and practical preparations for the task of rebuilding Jerusalem's walls.

2. Explain how good preparation is important for getting good results in ministry.

3. Plan a service project following Nehemiah's example.

May
11

KEY VERSE

I also told them about the gracious hand of my God upon me and what the king had said to me.

They replied, "Let us start rebuilding." So they began this good work.   —Nehemiah 2:18

Nehemiah served as cupbearer to Artaxerxes I, the Persian king who reigned from 464 to 424 BC in an area that is now southwest Iran. Artaxerxes was the son of the biblical Xerxes (Ezra 4:6, also known as Ahasuerus), who was the husband of Esther. The kingdom of Xerxes stretched "from India to Cush" (Esther 1:1). Artaxerxes I came to the throne after his father was assassinated. As cupbearer to Artaxerxes, Nehemiah had direct, personal access to this powerful Persian emperor.

In November or December of 445 BC, Nehemiah learned from a fellow Jew named Hanani that those who had returned from exile to Jerusalem were in distress. It had been more than 90 years since the first exiles had returned to the holy city, and the place was still a ruin (Nehemiah 1:2, 3). This news, which Nehemiah found surprising, may be a reference to the destruction of Jerusalem by the Babylonians in 586 BC. Yet this was old news by Nehemiah's day. Instead Hanani may have been referring to some more recent catastrophe.

The wider backdrop may be as follows. During the years 460–455 BC, Artaxerxes was involved in putting down a revolt in Egypt. This helps explain why in 458 BC he cooperated with the Jew Ezra (see Ezra 7:1-7; Ezra appears alongside Nehemiah in Nehemiah 8). Artaxerxes gave Ezra permission to appoint magistrates who knew the law of Ezra's God (Ezra 7:25, 26). Artaxerxes perhaps hoped to win support in his western province of Judea by allowing the Jews to incorporate more of their own legal traditions into the local administration of justice. In this way he may have hoped to discourage the Jews from joining Egypt in insurrection.

Ezra 4:8-16 records a letter from certain Persian officials to Artaxerxes reporting that the Jews were rebuilding the walls of "rebellious" Jerusalem, undoubtedly seen as a prelude to revolt. Artaxerxes responded by giving those officials permission to stop that rebuilding (4:17-23). It is possible that the Persian authorities not only stopped construction of new walls (4:23) but also ended up tearing down Jerusalem's walls that had been rebuilt previously (4:12). This state of affairs may be what Hanani and his colleagues described later to Nehemiah (Nehemiah 1:2, 3). Whatever the cause, Nehemiah began praying and considering over a period of four months what he could do to help his fellow countrymen in Judea (1:4-11). His prayers culminated in asking God to grant him favorable reception by "this man," meaning King Artaxerxes (1:11).

How to Say It

Ahasuerus. Uh-haz-you-EE-rus.
Artaxerxes. Are-tuh-ZERK-seez.
Asaph. AY-saff.
Geshem. GEE-shem.
Hanani. Huh-NAY-nye.
Nehemiah. NEE-huh-MY-uh.
Sanballat. San-BAL-ut.
Shushan. SHOO-shan.
Tobiah. Toe-BYE-uh.
Xerxes. ZERK-seez.

I. SADNESS NOTICED (NEHEMIAH 2:1-3)

A. NEHEMIAH'S POSITION (v. 1a)

1a. In the month of Nisan in the twentieth year of King Artaxerxes, when wine was brought for him, I took the wine and gave it to the king.

The month of Nisan in the twentieth year of King Artaxerxes is March or April of 444 BC. When we compare this date with Nehemiah 1:1, we see that about four months have passed since Nehemiah heard the news about Jerusalem's distress. Thus Nehemiah has a lot of time in which to think, weep, and pray before his encounter with the king (Nehemiah 1:4-11).

Nehemiah comes before King Artaxerxes in Nehemiah's capacity as cupbearer (Nehemiah 1:11). Cupbearer is an important office (Genesis 40:21; 1 Kings 10:5). According to one ancient Greek writer, the cupbearer tastes the king's wine for poison and guards the royal apartment. Such a trusted person can become a confidant and informal counselor of a king and so could influence the king's decisions. Like Esther in the book that bears her name, God had placed a Jew at the right place and time in order to help his people.

B. NEHEMIAH'S SADNESS (VV. 1b, 2a)

1b, 2a. I had not been sad in his presence before; so the king asked me, "Why does your face look so sad when you are not ill? This can be nothing but sadness of heart."

One's face can divulge what a person is feeling. The fact that Nehemiah has *not been sad in* the king's *presence* means that Nehemiah has been able to disguise his feelings over the past several months—putting on a happy face, as it were. But on this particular day, his anguish over his people's condition shows.

The king seems to show genuine concern over the emotional state of his cupbearer. This may say something about the king's capacity for empathy. It also says something about the character of Nehemiah, that he is the sort of person about whom the king is concerned.

Yet the king may have had another motive for asking his question. A gloomy appearance may be evidence of a plot against the king. The courts of ancient kings are hotbeds of intrigue (1 Kings 16:8-10; Esther 2:21-23). Indeed, the king's own father had been assassinated by a member of the court. So a king has good reason to be suspicious of changes in mood among his servants.

"PUT ON A HAPPY FACE"

The lyrics to the song "Put on a Happy Face" from the 1960s musical *Bye, Bye Birdie* reflect a deeply ingrained aspect of American culture. There is even a Christian Web site where the words of the song are accompanied by the tune, some cheery animation, and Scripture quotations such as Psalm 35:9, which says "my soul will rejoice in the Lord."

The pursuit of happiness is one of those "unalienable rights" mentioned in the U.S. Declaration of Independence. However, one curmudgeon says the phrase is "toxic stupidity entirely unworthy of [its author] Thomas Jefferson." He acknowledges the source of his concern: bleak Christmas celebrations in his childhood when his family got drunk in a futile pursuit of "happiness."

Neither this unhappy person nor Nehemiah would likely be cheered up by the sight of the "happy face" symbol we see so often. However, Nehemiah had a better reason for the anguish of his heart: he was consumed by the knowledge that his people were suffering in the ruined city of Jerusalem. There are times when it is entirely inappropriate to "put on a happy face," in spite of our culture's insistence on it!

—C. R. B.

C. NEHEMIAH'S COURAGE (VV. 2b, 3)

2b, 3. I was very much afraid, but I said to the king, "May the king live forever! Why should my face not look sad when the city where my fathers are buried lies in ruins, and its gates have been destroyed by fire?"

Nehemiah's apprehension about saying why he is *sad* is not unreasonable. Artaxerxes has the power of life and death. If indeed the *gates* of Jerusalem had been burned in conjunction with a real or imagined revolt against Persian authority (see the Lesson Background), then the showing of sympathy for Jerusalem may be taken by *the king* as treason. Nehemiah is putting his life in jeopardy by discussing this matter with the king.

Courage is not necessarily a lack of fear. Courage means acting bravely in spite of fear. Later Nehemiah's courage will be shown in continuing the work on the wall despite the opposition and threat by the forces of Sanballat, Tobiah, and Geshem (Nehemiah 2:10, 19; 4:7, 8).

We should pause to note that while Nehemiah is courageous, he is no fool. He says nothing of the reasons why Jerusalem's gates came to be burned

DAILY BIBLE READINGS

Monday, May 5—A Lament for Jerusalem (Psalm 137:1-7)

Tuesday, May 6—Weeping and Fasting (Nehemiah 1:1-4)

Wednesday, May 7—Nehemiah's Confession (Nehemiah 1:5-11)

Thursday, May 8—Permission to Return (Nehemiah 2:1-10)

Friday, May 9—A Secret Inspection (Nehemiah 2:11-16)

Saturday, May 10—Determination to Rebuild (Nehemiah 2:17-20)

Sunday, May 11—Giving Thanks to God (Psalm 138:1-5)

BE A LEADER
. . . OR FOLLOW
A GOOD ONE

Visual for Lesson 11. *Point
to this visual as you ask your
learners to name good leaders
they have followed.*

WHAT DO YOU THINK?

*Why should we take risks
for God? Or is it ever proper to
think of service for God as risky?
Explain.*

(whether originally in 586 BC or more recently). Instead he emphasizes the fact
that the tombs of his ancestors are *in ruins.* This fact may tug at the king's emotions. Often the way a matter is presented determines how it is received.

II. OPPORTUNITY SEIZED (NEHEMIAH 2:4-8)

A. KING'S QUESTION (v. 4a)

4a. The king said to me, "What is it you want?"

Artaxerxes responds by offering a royal favor to help Nehemiah. This is exactly
what Nehemiah has been praying for (Nehemiah 1:11). Now it appears that God
is granting an answer to his prayer.

B. NEHEMIAH'S PRAYER (v. 4b)

4b. Then I prayed to the God of heaven,

Before Nehemiah makes his request, he prays. Obviously, this is not a long
prayer. Rather, it must be what is sometimes called "an arrow prayer"—a brief
prayer shot up to Heaven as fast as an arrow. Such a prayer likely consists of little
more than a quick whisper of, "Help me, Lord!"

C. NEHEMIAH'S REQUEST (v. 5)

*5. . . . and I answered the king, "If it pleases the king and if your servant has
found favor in his sight, let him send me to the city in Judah where my fathers
are buried so that I can rebuild it."*

Nehemiah's previous prayer in Nehemiah 1:11 culminated in asking God for
success before "this man," meaning Artaxerxes. This suggests that Nehemiah
already has a plan in mind. He is ready to propose that plan if he ever has opportunity to raise the matter to the king. So when the right time arrives and
Artaxerxes offers Nehemiah royal assistance, Nehemiah already knows what to
request: he wants to return to *Judah* in order to rebuild Jerusalem. The boldness
of this request should again be emphasized! It was by a royal decree of Artaxerxes
in Ezra 4:17-22 that the building up of Jerusalem had been stopped forcibly.

D. KING'S QUESTIONS (v. 6)

*6. Then the king, with the queen sitting beside him, asked me, "How long will your
journey take, and when will you get back?" It pleased the king to send me; so I set
a time.*

Artaxerxes and Nehemiah hash out the details of Nehemiah's leave of absence. The king evidently considers Nehemiah a valuable person in his service,
so the king negotiates that Nehemiah will return after a certain length of time.

The text does not tell us how Nehemiah replies other than *I set a time.* But his
absence ends up being 12 years (see Nehemiah 5:14; 13:6). His stay probably
extends beyond the original estimate!

E. NEHEMIAH'S REQUESTS (vv. 7, 8)

*7, 8. I also said to him, "If it pleases the king, may I have letters to the gover-
nors of Trans-Euphrates, so that they will provide me safe-conduct until I arrive
in Judah? And may I have a letter to Asaph, keeper of the king's forest, so he
will give me timber to make beams for the gates of the citadel by the temple and
for the city wall and for the residence I will occupy?" And because the gracious
hand of my God was upon me, the king granted my requests.*

Nehemiah goes on to request *letters* permitting him to travel through the
empire. Nehemiah in essence is making himself the governor of *Judah* in asking

for travel papers. Such papers will provide the royal permission needed to travel through regions of other *governors.*

Nehemiah knows he will need construction material. So he asks for *timber* to be provided by a certain *Asaph,* the official in charge of *the king's* western *forest.* Asaph is a Jewish name. An earlier Asaph was a Levite musician who wrote several psalms at the time of David (1 Chronicles 16:5; see the superscriptions of Psalms 50; 73–83). The king generously grants Nehemiah's requests.

III. TASK INITIATED (NEHEMIAH 2:11, 17, 18)

A. TRAVEL AND REST (v. 11)

11. I went to Jerusalem, and after staying there three days . . .

The text does not describe what certainly is an arduous journey of nearly 1,100 miles from Shushan *to Jerusalem.* Naturally, Nehemiah's first priority is to get some rest upon arrival. It is unwise to undertake a great task when one is exhausted.

But no doubt Nehemiah already is planning what he will do. After the three-day rest, he obtains an animal to ride. During the night, when no one will recognize him, he inspects the walls around the city (Nehemiah 2:12-16; not in today's text). Thus before he brings up the matter to the local officials, Nehemiah is making plans concerning how best to proceed.

B. OBSERVATION AND CHALLENGE (v. 17)

17. Then I said to them, "You see the trouble we are in: Jerusalem lies in ruins, and its gates have been burned with fire. Come, let us rebuild the wall of Jerusalem, and we will no longer be in disgrace."

After inspecting the walls and formulating his plans, Nehemiah now makes a public announcement. His audience is the priests, nobles, officials, and "any others" according to verse 16. Up to this time, they have not been told why Nehemiah has come to *Jerusalem.* We wonder how shocked the audience must be to hear Nehemiah now exhort them to join in his great task of rebuilding the walls of Jerusalem.

City walls in ancient times are very important. The most obvious reason is physical security. But there is an important emotional reason too: the city is an object of derision and mockery (a *disgrace*) in its current state (compare 2 Chronicles 7:20; Psalm 44:13, 14). Jerusalem is supposed to be the holy city, the site of God's temple. It should be maintained in a way appropriate to this distinction.

We should also note the power of symbols. The biggest danger for the Jews is that of assimilation into the surrounding pagan culture. The successful rebuilding of Jerusalem's walls will be a symbol that God has not forsaken his people.

THE POWER OF SYMBOLS

What is the most important symbol in your life? In a materialistic culture, many things can vie for top symbolic meaning. Luxury cars, yachts, and Rolex® watches can be on such a list.

Many scoff at such symbols of "conspicuous consumption." Yet material symbols are not always bad. Note the challenge Nehemiah presented to his fellow Jews: "Let us rebuild the wall of Jerusalem, *and we will no longer be in disgrace.*" The important question for us to ask is, "Who was being disgraced?"

Jerusalem with its temple was supposed to be a symbol of God's presence among a certain people of the time. The implication is that the city's disrepair was

WHAT DO YOU THINK?

With the life of Nehemiah as a guide, what should we do when preparing for a project? Is there anything about Nehemiah's life that should not be used as a guide for today? Explain.

WHAT DO YOU THINK?

Why and when is it important to take rest? What have been your experiences (good and bad) in this regard?

a symbolic disgrace to the God of the Hebrews as the one true God. When we apply this outlook to the way we "build" our lives for God, we may be embarrassed at our prideful thinking! People will take notice of the symbols with which we surround ourselves, because those symbols indicate what we value. More importantly, God will notice.   —C. R. B.

C. AUTHORIZATION AND REPLY (V. 18)

18. I also told them about the gracious hand of my God upon me and what the king had said to me.

They replied, "Let us start rebuilding." So they began this good work.

Nehemiah rallies the people around him by giving a stirring testimony of how God already has worked providentially in bringing him to Jerusalem. Nehemiah demonstrates that God is behind this plan to rebuild the walls of Jerusalem. This testimony helps inspire the Jews to help with the project.

CONCLUSION

Nehemiah comes across as an ideal leader of God's people. First, Nehemiah was concerned for others. Though he himself was a worldly success, having risen to an important office in the service of the Persian state, he remained concerned about his countrymen who were less well off. When he heard of the distress of his people in distant Jerusalem, he began to look for an opportunity to help. The New Testament likewise calls us to help others (see 1 John 3:17; etc.).

Second, Nehemiah was willing to step out on faith. By showing concern for his people before the Persian king, Nehemiah jeopardized his own rank and privileges. The New Testament calls us to do likewise (see Mark 10:29, 30).

Third, Nehemiah was willing to make sacrifices. He voluntarily stepped down from his position in the royal court and traveled an enormous distance to serve God's people. The New Testament does not call every Christian to travel to a foreign land, but we are to live lives of sacrifice (Mark 12:43, 44; Acts 2:45).

Fourth, Nehemiah was a man of prayer. As a godly Jew, he was concerned about the fact that the holy city of Jerusalem, symbol of God's presence among his people, was in disarray. When his opportunity before King Artaxerxes presented itself, he first sent up an arrow prayer to God. But months of prayer by Nehemiah had prepared the way for his request before the king. And Nehemiah clearly saw that the unfolding opportunity was from the hand of God. Great Christian leaders are people of prayer, even when they are also people of action (Acts 20:36).

Fifth, Nehemiah took time to plan things out. He waited months for just the right time before making a request to the king about rebuilding. When he made the request, he knew just what he needed to ask for because he had thought things through. When he arrived in Jerusalem, he took time to think and plan before speaking to others about his dreams. Planning ahead is not a failure to walk by faith, as Nehemiah's example shows us. Paul's work reveals him to be a man of planning (2 Corinthians 8:16–9:5).

Sixth, Nehemiah knew how to motivate others. He had no power by himself to build the wall of Jerusalem. He needed help and cooperation. But without manipulation he skillfully mobilized the people behind his plan. The fact that the community of faith joined him was confirmation that God had in fact raised up Nehemiah for this purpose. Today as then, God does not call all of his people to be super-duper motivational leaders as Nehemiah was. But we all can be good followers. Whether a leader or a follower, the prelude to action is personal holiness (1 Peter 1:13-16).

WHAT DO YOU THINK?

When have you found it helpful to recall God's dealings from the past?

PRAYER

Lord, thank you for godly leaders like Nehemiah who have the vision to see the tasks you would have them do and the courage to carry them out. Help us to have the same kind of passion. May we have Nehemiah's zeal and wisdom to accomplish what you would have us do. In Jesus' name we ask this, amen.

WHAT DO YOU THINK?

What were the qualities and characteristics in Nehemiah that made him such an effective leader? How can you develop these in your own life?

THOUGHT TO REMEMBER

God still honors courage.

Discovery Learning

This page contains an alternative lesson plan emphasizing learning activities. Classes desiring such student involvement will find these suggestions helpful. The next page is a reproducible activity page to further enhance discovery learning.

INTO THE LESSON

Display a simple sketch of a block wall, with each block large enough for writing a word or phrase. Across the top of the wall, write *What Does It Take to Build a Wall?* Let learners suggest elements as you write suggestions in the blocks.

Encourage responses to include not only tangible elements (such as bricks and mortar) but also intangibles (such as initiative and planning). (A similar activity is included in the optional student book.) Discuss.

INTO THE WORD

Use the completed activity above to make a transition into a study of today's text by asking the class to note the ways the named elements formed parts of Nehemiah's plan. For example, Nehemiah secured wood for his task as part of the king's decree (tangible), and Nehemiah surrounded his job with prayer (intangible). Ask your learners also to discuss this question: "How does Nehemiah's procedure reflect the maxim *An ounce of preparation results in a pound of production?*"

After discussing that maxim, say, "Nehemiah did certain things as he demonstrated wisdom in leadership. As I read the following, identify a verse or verses in Nehemiah 1 and 2 that reveal each." (A similar activity is included in the optional student book.)

1. Prayed and planned for months. 2. Revealed his true feelings—had no hypocrisy. 3. Boldly expressed his concerns to the one who could help him do something. 4. Prayed spontaneously for God's help. 5. Agreed to his superior's requests. 6. Stated his requests clearly and thoroughly. 7. Credited God for his successes. 8. Rested before initiating a long and difficult job. 9. Solicited the help of others. 10. Maintained clear-cut goals and noble purposes.

Your learners should easily relate these actions and characteristics to the verses of today's text and other verses in the first two chapters of Nehemiah. *Potential answers: 1. 1:1; 2:1; 2. 2:1, 2; 3. 2:3; 4. 2:4; 5. 2:6; 6. 2:7, 8; 7. 2:8; 8. 2:11; 9. 2:17, 18; 10. 2:17, 18.*

Wrap up this task with this question: "How do you see these actions and attitudes in the lives of contemporary leaders, both in business and in the church?" (To keep the conversation from turning negative, you may wish to ask for positive examples only.)

To highlight Nehemiah's prayer life, say, "The picture of Nehemiah's request and the king who granted it tell us something about the power of prayer. Consider the following list of features of Nehemiah's request and the nature of the responses. Note first how it is seen in today's text; then note how it can characterize our prayer life with God the Father." (A similar activity is included in the optional student book.)

1. Request comes in the midst of faithful service and submission; 2. Request is made to a caring, sensitive superior; 3. Request is made in reverential fear; 4. Request is made only after praise to the one asked; 5. Request is both bold and specific; 6. Request is not selfish, but for the welfare of God's people; 7. Request is graciously granted; 8. The grace involved in the request granted is told to others.

Here are examples of observations your learners may offer: for 1, *Nehemiah earned the king's trust by years of careful performance of his duties, and the more we demonstrate our faith and commitment to God, the more he trusts and honors our petitions;* for 8, *to the people of Jerusalem, Nehemiah revealed the way the king had honored his requests (v. 18), and we need to tell others when God graciously honors our petitions, as a witness to him.*

Suggest that each learner use these as criteria for evaluating his or her own prayer life.

INTO LIFE

Divide your class in half. (If the halves are more than five people each, make smaller groups.) Give one of the halves copies of the Holy Hands activity from the Reproducible Page and the other half the Make a Face exercise. Allow six minutes to complete. Ask each group to be ready to share their results with the class.

As learners depart, distribute a half-page copy of a block wall sketch similar to that used in the introductory activity. Label it *What Does It Take to Build a Life?*

Say, "Nehemiah was not concerned solely with building a wall. He was concerned about building lives into a strong nation for God. Take this wall home with you this week and reflect on the important components in building one's life to be a part of the church that is able to defend itself from enemies and prepared to assemble for worship in unity." You can suggest that your learners bring their walls back to class next week for sharing.

Holy Hands

Our hands do God's work. Describe an example of each of the following as "holy hands."

Hands of praying

Hands of healing

Hands of friendship

Hands of welcome

Hands of teaching

Hands of generosity

Hands of creativity

Hands of comfort

Which of the preceding have your hands accomplished in the last month? Which will you commit your hands to in this next month?

Make a Face

Nehemiah's face revealed his deep sadness at the state of affairs among God's people in Jerusalem (see Nehemiah 2:1, 2). If the depiction to the left could represent your face at the state of affairs among God's people in the twenty-first century, what features must you add? Why?

Is this a face that truly represents your concern for God's kingdom? Why or why not?

God, the People, and the Covenant

Unit 3: Restoration and Covenant Renewal

(Lessons 10-13)

FINISHING THE TASK

WHY TEACH THIS LESSON?

There is no shortage of naysayers. From those who spoke of Fulton's steamboat as *Fulton's Folly* to those who told the Wright brothers that powered flight was impossible, the detractors are ever with us. Neither is there any end to those who will try to discourage your learners from living the Christian life. Some of your learners already have felt the sting of this kind of criticism. Churches face criticism from those in the community who do not want those churches to exist.

This lesson will give your learners confidence in the face of criticism in two ways. First, they will come to realize that criticism of God's people and work is nothing new; it goes back to Nehemiah and before. Second, your learners will grow in their ability to step out on faith and courage because they will realize that they are not alone—God is there.

INTRODUCTION

A. PERSEVERANCE THROUGH OPPOSITION

Jason was a young Christian who had a vision to reach youth. He worked hard to organize a rally as a means to bring the gospel to them. His enthusiasm was certainly not lacking as he called others to join him in his vision of winning his peers to Christ.

Although there were many who supported Jason's work and shared in it by giving of their time, finances, and prayers, Jason quickly learned that with any worthy cause comes opposition. Jason heard the comments firsthand. "This is never going to work." "I don't believe anybody will attend, even if it gets organized." Some questioned his integrity—"Jason just wants to be the boss" or "he has to be in the limelight."

After hearing these comments, it didn't take very long for Jason to begin doubting whether he should continue to try to launch this outreach rally. Then came the other disappointments. People said they would help and then would not show up. Rumors spread that the rally had been canceled due to lack of interest. The posters, which had already been mailed out, had the main speaker's name misspelled.

Jason, however, continued to pray. He continued to seek support from those who shared his vision. He pressed forward despite opposition and doubts, and the rally was held as scheduled. There have been many more rallies in Jason's community since that first one, each having some sort of opposition and each being used by the Lord to further his kingdom.

Stories similar to Jason's are being acted out all over the world by God's people, because with every good work of God there are those who will try to stop it. Unfortunately, not all good works end with victory. Many works cease because the worker was not prepared for the opposition—the discouragement was just too much. Today we are going to discover biblical principles that will strengthen us to continue the Lord's work in spite of opposition.

DEVOTIONAL READING:
PSALM 71:1-6

BACKGROUND SCRIPTURE:
NEHEMIAH 4–6

PRINTED TEXT:
NEHEMIAH 4:1-3, 6-9, 13-15; 6:15

LESSON AIMS

After participating in this lesson, each student will be able to:

1. Describe how Nehemiah overcame opposition in rebuilding Jerusalem's walls.

2. Give an example of faith that overcomes adversity.

3. Make a plan to identify, take charge of, and complete a project or ministry that is facing opposition.

KEY VERSE

So we rebuilt the wall till all of it reached half its height, for the people worked with all their heart.

—Nehemiah 4:6

May 18

B. LESSON BACKGROUND

The Judeans returned from the Babylonian captivity in 3 waves. The first wave, of about 50,000 returnees, was in 538 BC, as led by Sheshbazzar (Ezra 1:1, 11). The second wave, of less than 2,000 men, was led by Ezra 80 years later (Ezra 7:1-9). The third wave was 13 or 14 years after the second. It was led by Nehemiah, although we don't know how many Judeans accompanied him (Nehemiah 2:11).

Although the returned exiles were able to complete the rebuilding of the temple by 515 BC, the walls of the city remained in their ruined state. The walls had been destroyed by the Babylonians (Chaldeans) in 586 BC.

As we saw last week, Nehemiah was the cupbearer of King Artaxerxes of Persia (reigned 464–424 BC). When Nehemiah heard about the condition of the city and its gates, he prayed to God and approached the king to seek permission to return to Jerusalem to rebuild. Artaxerxes granted his request. As God's chosen man, Nehemiah arrived to inspect the ruined walls and lead the people in a campaign to rebuild them.

I. OPPOSITION (NEHEMIAH 4:1-3)

Nehemiah 3, which occurs between last week's text and today's, shows us Nehemiah and his work crew in action. Great progress is made in building the wall, despite the anger of some neighboring officials. But the opposition is about to kick things up a notch!

A. SANBALLAT (vv. 1, 2)

1. When Sanballat heard that we were rebuilding the wall, he became angry and was greatly incensed. He ridiculed the Jews,

We first meet *Sanballat* in Nehemiah 2:10. He is governor of Samaria. The Samaritans are located just to the north of Judah. They are of mixed origin, composed of the descendants of Israelites who intermarried with foreign colonists brought in by the king of Assyria after the northern kingdom's deportation in 722 BC (2 Kings 17). The Samaritans had offered to help rebuild the temple earlier, but were rebuffed (Ezra 4:1-5). Do we detect some smoldering resentment?

Opposition toward what is good and right starts in the heart. Nehemiah's arrival in Jerusalem to promote "the welfare of the Israelites" (Nehemiah 2:10) draws Sanballat's initial displeasure. As the work to rebuild the walls proceeds, his displeasure turns to great anger. He does not want the city of Jerusalem to be strengthened, possibly because he wants to be governor of Judea as well as Samaria.

When we are engaged in God's work, we should not be surprised when opposition comes. The enemies of God will be angry at attempts to build Christ's kingdom (John 15:20; 2 Timothy 3:12).

2. . . . and in the presence of his associates and the army of Samaria, he said, "What are those feeble Jews doing? Will they restore their wall? Will they offer sacrifices? Will they finish in a day? Can they bring the stones back to life from those heaps of rubble—burned as they are?"

As is often the case, opposition includes mocking. Personal attacks on the character of someone who chooses to do what is right are common even today. Here we see Sanballat using a series of rhetorical questions to call into question the character of the workmen.

Sanballat's earlier mocking was intended for the ears of the Judeans themselves, to discourage them directly (Nehemiah 2:19). The same is true here since

WHAT DO YOU THINK?

Why should we expect opposition when working for God? How has God strengthened you to overcome opposition?

Nehemiah 4:5 describes the insults as being thrown "in the face of the builders." But now the mockery is also for the ears of *his associates and the army of Samaria.*

If Sanballat's cronies take his word to heart, they will be emboldened in their opposition. Thus Sanballat's mocking serves not only as an attempt to discourage the Jews, but also as a kind of pep talk to his buddies. "These silly Jews actually think they can carry through with this project with the few resources they have!" The one thing that Sanballat is unable to see is that God is with the Jews, that he is their supply and support.

B. Tobiah (v. 3)

3. Tobiah the Ammonite, who was at his side, said, "What they are building—if even a fox climbed up on it, he would break down their wall of stones!"

The opposition and mockery from *Tobiah the Ammonite* now builds on what we see from him in Nehemiah 2:10, 19. Ammon is to the northeast of Judah. The Ammonites are longtime enemies of the Jewish people.

Faithful workers for God will have not only their character ridiculed, they will also see the work they are doing scorned. That's what we see Tobiah doing here. "What quality of workmanship can this be if even the weight of a mere *fox* will cause their *wall* to collapse?" There is no part of the Lord's work that will not be looked on with contempt by his enemies.

Mocking is one of the easiest things to do and one of the favorite weapons of opposition. If God's worker is not prepared when it happens, it can cut deep. It may leave a broken heart and a crushed spirit that may be difficult to endure (Psalm 89:50; Jeremiah 20:7; etc.).

II. DETERMINATION (NEHEMIAH 4:6-9)

Between verse 3 (above) and verse 6 (next) is a prayer of Nehemiah against the enemies. We notice in this prayer that Nehemiah directs his reaction to God, not to the enemies. The prayer looks like what we see at Jeremiah 18:23.

A. Having a Mind to Work (v. 6)

6. So we rebuilt the wall till all of it reached half its height, for the people worked with all their heart.

Despite the anger and mocking of their enemies, the Jews continue their work. They get to the point where they have built up *half* the *wall.* Because they *worked with all their heart,* they do not allow the attempted distractions to stop them from achieving their mission. They continue to move forward, setting their hearts on completing the work God has given them instead of wallowing in their difficulties.

We can see the value of teamwork as God's people join together in a single-minded work. Everyone does his or her part, and no part of the wall is left undone. Cooperation means that the wall goes up at a rapid pace.

B. Having a Mind to Hinder (vv. 7, 8)

7, 8. But when Sanballat, Tobiah, the Arabs, the Ammonites and the men of Ashdod heard that the repairs to Jerusalem's walls had gone ahead and that the gaps were being closed, they were very angry. They all plotted together to come and fight against Jerusalem and stir up trouble against it.

We now see more enemies mentioned, namely *Arabs* and *men of Ashdod.* The Arabs probably are to the south, while the Ashdodites are to the east. Counting Samaria and Ammon, Judah is surrounded by enemies!

WHAT DO YOU THINK?

What was a time when you saw mockery succeed in discouraging Christians in their work for God's kingdom? How do we guard against this tactic?

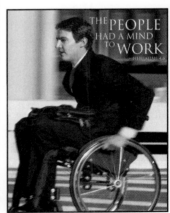

Visual for Lesson 12. *Use this visual as you discuss verse 6. Ask, "What are some things we allow to distract us?"*

The progress that Nehemiah and the workers make on *Jerusalem's walls* does not cause the opposition to cease, but instead makes the opposition even more determined to *stir up trouble against* the completion of the project. It has become obvious to *Sanballat* and *Tobiah* that their attempts to discourage through ridicule are not slowing the workers down. So these two increase their efforts by drawing in neighboring people to join their plot to hinder the work by force.

C. HAVING A MIND TO PRAY AND WATCH (v. 9)
9. But we prayed to our God and posted a guard day and night to meet this threat.

While the enemy conspires, Nehemiah prepares to face the opposition by combining faith in God with action. The faith and action take the forms of praying and posting *a guard.*

Before Nehemiah does anything else, he seeks God's protection and guidance. (See how Nehemiah prays in Nehemiah 1:5-11; 4:4, 5; 5:19; 6:9b, 14; 13:14, 22, 31.) Having confidence in God's protection and favor does not rule out the obligation that the godly person has to watch out for the traps of the enemy. The Scriptures match together the ideas of watching and praying (see Matthew 26:41; 1 Peter 4:7).

God will protect those who watch as well as pray. It has been said that prayer without watchfulness is presumption and watchfulness without prayer is sinful self-confidence. The two truly work together to enable the worker to keep going in the face of opposition.

WILLINGNESS

In America's Great Depression of the 1930s, vast numbers of people were desperate for work. So when construction of the Empire State Building began in 1930, some 3,400 men counted themselves fortunate to get jobs. Their bleak circumstances gave them "a mind to work." And work they did: it took only 410 days to complete the task.

The building of the 1,453-foot tower was called one of the most remarkable feats of the twentieth century. It stood as the tallest building in the world until 1972. The building demonstrated what concerted and cooperative human effort could accomplish, a symbol of "what we were capable of," as architectural historian Carol Willis said.

In a sense, Nehemiah was also an architectural historian. His description of the rebuilding of Jerusalem's walls shows us what God's people were able to do in spite of fierce opposition as they toiled together with a common purpose. They were willing to work, they cooperated with others who shared with them in the task, they committed the project to God in prayer, and they watched carefully for anything that might hinder their work.

This is still a good formula for projects that God's people labor to complete. What project is your church attempting that needs this kind of dedication?

—C. R. B.

III. VICTORY (NEHEMIAH 4:13-15; 6:15)

The enemy's mocking does not discourage the workers in and of itself. But when the threat of force is added, the people began to lose heart (vv. 10-12, not in today's text). So Nehemiah takes action to reverse this morale problem.

A. STRENGTHEN THE WEAK AREAS (v. 13)
13. Therefore I stationed some of the people behind the lowest points of the wall at the exposed places, posting them by families, with their swords, spears and bows.

WHAT DO YOU THINK?

Are the steps Nehemiah took to overcome ungodly opposition still valid today? Why, or why not?

HOW TO SAY IT

Ammonites. AM-un-ites.
Ashdodites. ASH-duh-dites.
Babylonian. Bab-ih-LOW-nee-un.
Chaldeans. Kal-DEE-unz.
Ezra. EZ-ruh.
Nehemiah. NEE-huh-MY-uh.
Samaria. Suh-MARE-ee-uh.
Sanballat. San-BAL-ut.
Sheshbazzar. Shesh-BAZ-ar.
Tobiah. Toe-BYE-uh.

Nehemiah shows his shrewdness in military tactics and human nature. He sees certain areas that need to be strengthened, and he does so. He supplies the weapons necessary for defense. Positioning those with weapons *by families* provides another reason to work and defend the city together.

GUNS AND BUTTER?

Earlier, we discussed the construction of the Empire State Building that was part of America's attempt to put people back to work in the 1930s. In 1933, Nazi Germany initiated its own public works program. Government spending increased sixfold in 6 years. Unemployment dropped from 6 million (34 percent) to nearly zero, with 1 million of those being drafted into the military. Many of the newly employed began working on armaments. Thus began the military buildup that led to the tragedy of World War II.

This militaristic approach to recovery from economic depression came to be called "guns, not butter" or sometimes "guns before butter." The idea is that people must forego personal comforts while fighting (or preparing to fight) a war. Once the war is won, the implied promise is that the good times will roll. But we all know the result of Nazi lies.

When Nehemiah established an armed force, he was not creating an army of conquest that would bring back booty for everyone to enjoy. The arming of the Jews was for defensive purposes only. Their "butter" was the protection of their families (v. 14, below) and a renewed, secure city for the glory of God. And that was "butter enough" for them to keep working! God still calls his people to work and to vigilance. The distribution of earthly "butter" will not always be what we think is fair. But God's eternal reward will make it all worthwhile.   —C. R. B.

B. REMEMBER WHOM YOU WORK FOR (v. 14a)

14a. After I looked things over, I stood up and said to the nobles, the officials and the rest of the people, "Don't be afraid of them. Remember the Lord, who is great and awesome,

Any large task can be tiring. There are pressures that cause disappointment and discouragement. It is probable that as Nehemiah looks things over he can see the enemy making preparations to attack. The appearance of the opposition may be overwhelming, with the thought of defending the city and finishing the wall hard to contemplate. Yet Nehemiah knows that the cure for fatigue, fear, and discouragement is to *remember the Lord, who is great and awesome*. The sight of the enemies may seem great and terrible, but in comparison to the living God, they are not nearly as intimidating. Reminding the people of this truth, Nehemiah tells his workers not to *be afraid of them* (compare 2 Kings 6:13-17).

C. REMEMBER WHAT'S AT STAKE (v. 14b)

14b. ". . . and fight for your brothers, your sons and your daughters, your wives and your homes."

When up against opposition, it is easy to think more about what is happening to us and what it is going to cost us rather than who will be affected by our actions. Here Nehemiah reminds the workers that they are fighting for a noble cause. If these men became too discouraged to fight, their families will be ravaged and destroyed by the enemy. That's motivation!

D. REMEMBER WHO'S IN CHARGE (v. 15)

15. When our enemies heard that we were aware of their plot and that God had frustrated it, we all returned to the wall, each to his own work.

DAILY BIBLE READINGS

Monday, May 12—A Cry for Help (Psalm 61:1-5)

Tuesday, May 13—Mocking Enemies (Nehemiah 4:1-6)

Wednesday, May 14—A Plot to Confuse the Builders (Nehemiah 4:7-11)

Thursday, May 15—The Plot Is Foiled (Nehemiah 4:12-15)

Friday, May 16—Always at the Ready (Nehemiah 4:16-23)

Saturday, May 17—Attempts to Stop the Building (Nehemiah 6:1-14)

Sunday, May 18—The Wall Is Finished (Nehemiah 6:15-19)

The planned surprise attack by Nehemiah's *enemies* is no longer a surprise. So the enemies abandon their plan. It is difficult to assault a fortified position when the defenders are expecting an attack and are prepared to fight back. The sight of God's people standing strong on the partially rebuilt wall, prepared to defend themselves against an attack, is enough to discourage the opposition.

Nehemiah's tactics succeed, but he gives credit to God. This is not the first time God has caused his enemies to despair (Exodus 15:14-16; 23:27, 28; Deuteronomy 2:25). The focus of this and other texts is on what God achieves within a community of believers. It is evident that God is working through the people's prayers and actions to protect and strengthen them. Knowing that God is working through them and that he has brought the enemies' plan to nothing leads the Jews to return to *work.* They have confidence in God's protection and provisions.

E. TAKE NOTE OF THE RESULT (6:15)

15. So the wall was completed on the twenty-fifth of Elul, in fifty-two days.

The enemies said it couldn't be done! "They are too feeble." "It will never work." "If a fox jumps on it, it will break down." When the ridicule doesn't work, the enemies contemplate using force, planning to attack the Jews. Their plan is frustrated and *the wall* is now *completed.* What a hectic 52 *days* it has been! The short time is a testimony to the power of God and the zeal of the workers.

The month *of Elul* corresponds with the latter part of August and the beginning of September on our calendar. The year is 444 BC. Nehemiah's vision has become a reality—and we are less than halfway through the book of Nehemiah at this point! Despite opposition that comes both from within and without (6:14), Nehemiah never loses sight of his mission and for whom he is working. Nehemiah will continue to seek the guidance of God through prayer. Nehemiah will continue to encourage his fellow workers all the way.

CONCLUSION

The fruit of the efforts by Nehemiah and the workers brought glory to God (Nehemiah 6:16). The efforts resulted in emotional and physical security for the Judeans. Undoubtedly there was joy at accomplishing a task against tremendous odds (compare Ezra 3:10-13).

We have a wonderful example of godly and devout leadership in Nehemiah. He was a man of prayer who had his heart in God's work. We see Nehemiah engaging in self-denying labor while inspiring others to do the same. He was steadfast in his work, not easily sidetracked. He depended on God and was ready to give him the glory.

God has called the church to a tremendous task of strengthening its members and taking the gospel to a lost and dying world. It is important that the church be led by people who exemplify the characteristics of Nehemiah. There will be opposition—there always has been—but as God's men and women join together with the same goal in mind, we will be able to accomplish great things for the glory of God.

What has God called you to do? Whatever it is, do not let the size of the task or the amount of time it will take to complete it keep you from setting your heart and hand to it. No job is too big and no problem is too great when we are following God every step of the way. God has called us and equipped us to finish the tasks of the church despite the opposition.

Discovery Learning

This page contains an alternative lesson plan emphasizing learning activities. Classes desiring such student involvement will find these suggestions helpful. The next page is a reproducible activity page to further enhance discovery learning.

INTO THE LESSON

Wrap several small boxes in gray paper so that the boxes resemble stones (or use brick-colored paper, if available). Each box is to be empty except for the word *GOD* written on a small slip of paper inside. Begin class with the boxes stacked in view of your learners.

Say, "In today's text, the enemies of God's people looked at Nehemiah's wall and were amused. They said, 'You don't even have enough boxes for a good wall!' and 'I could crush those blocks with one hand.'" (Take a small, flimsy box and do so.) "Why, I'll huff and I'll puff and blow the whole thing down!" (Do so.)

Then remark, "But those enemies didn't see what was inside that wall." Hand boxes to several learners and say, "Look inside." Have someone tell what's in the box. Then continue, "Nehemiah's enemies saw only rocks and half-armed soldiers. They never realized that Almighty God was in the project. Today's study is a confirmation of this truth: *When God is in it, expect success!*"

INTO THE WORD

Prepare half-sheets of paper with one of the following affirmations and verse numbers printed on each. Establish study pairs or small groups; give each pair or group one of the sheets. (If your class is small, give more than one sheet to each group.) Include the following directions on each sheet: "Think about the maxim printed below in two ways. First, what is its relationship to today's Bible text? Second, what is its relationship to godly living in any time and place?" Give the pairs or groups a few minutes, then call for short responses.

Affirmations and texts: 1. Evil becomes easier in bad company (vv. 1, 3, 7, 8); 2. A mind to work beats a mind to meddle every time (v. 6); 3. Being armed with prayer may not be enough. Better be armed with practical wisdom too (v. 9); 4. Families that defend together, depend together (vv. 13-15); 5. Realizing that God is against you deflates the boldest mischief (4:15); 6. Anger is a poor foundation for action (vv. 7, 8); 7. Nothing pops the mocker's balloon better than the sharp pin of success (6:15). (These statements are also printed in the optional student book.)

To help impress the class that these were real people in a real struggle, tell them you're going to read some "could-have-been quotes" from the occasion. You want them to identify who would have said it and in what verse of the text. Quotes are given here in random order; the answers, which you should not reveal right away, are in parentheses.

Could-have-been quotes: 1. "I'll defend my family and my city!" (*a soldier guarding the lower places, v. 13*); 2. "It's a poor excuse for a wall!" (*Tobiah, v. 3*); 3. "God, help us finish!" (*Nehemiah and others, v. 9*); 4. "Let's push to get it halfway." (*the builders, v. 6*); 5. "Let's go get 'em!" (*Tobiah, Sanballat, and their allies, v. 8*); 6. "Silly Jews!" (*Sanballat, v. 2*); 7. "We're too late!" (*the enemies, 6:15*); 8. "Why fear men when God is on your side?" (*Nehemiah, v. 14a*); 9. You can't build a wall out of gravel!" (*Sanballat, v. 2*); 10. "You're not fighting to defend a wall; you're fighting to defend your family and friends!" (*Nehemiah, v. 14b*).

You may wish to ask this at the end: "What else do you hear the people of today's text saying?" Let learners respond freely and imaginatively. Some possibilities: "So soon?" (*an enemy at the completion of the wall*) or "Glory Hallelujah!" (*one of the builders on the fifty-second day*).

INTO LIFE

Refer to the title of today's study: "Finishing the Task." Say, "Many of the tasks the church needs to accomplish face opposition and simply fizzle out. What are some such projects that fit this description?" Let the class identify some. Possible responses include underfinanced building repairs, benevolent projects that some believe unnecessary, and complicated strategies for new church work in what some deem to be "impossible" places. (Caution: the possibility exists for the discussion to become very negative if your church has had recent problems in such areas.)

After a list is suggested, challenge your learners to consider one such unfinished task that they can help complete. Make the matter a prayer emphasis as class is concluded. Consider sending all your learners a postcard or e-mail reminder this week with this simple message: *Finish the Task!*

Alternative: Distribute copies of the Surrounded exercise from the Reproducible Page to small groups or discussion pairs. Discuss results as a class as time permits.

As each learner departs, give him or her a copy of the Victory Plan exercise from the Reproducible Page.

Surrounded

Nehemiah and his associates were surrounded by those who did not want the work on Jerusalem's wall to be completed. For you to finish the work of the gospel that you have committed yourself to, what opposition must you overcome? Write an opposer or opposing force in each circle.

Make Nehemiah's words your defense statement for each enemy of your faith and mission. Choose either Nehemiah 4:14b or Nehemiah 6:3b and write it in the space below. Plan a memorization scheme for this coming week.

"Opposition? Ha! I say: _____

_____

Victory Plan

Nehemiah 4:13-15 may be summed up as a four-step plan for victory against opposition. How do you see these steps as a part of your personal victory over opposition? Jot your ideas below:

4. Remember Who's in Charge (v. 15)

3. Remember What's at Stake (v. 14b)

2. Remember Who You Work For (v. 14a)

1. Strengthen the Weak Areas (v. 13)

RENEWING THE COVENANT

LESSON 13

WHY TEACH THIS LESSON?

"What one does is more important than what one says." "Actions speak louder than words." These two statements are true in all areas of life, whether the issue concerns a husband who tells his wife he loves her, yet never demonstrates that love, or a doctor who smokes while counseling his patients to practice a healthy lifestyle. We have a derogatory way of describing what's going on in those examples. We call it *paying lip service.*

What an easy pattern to fall into! How often have we said things just to get someone else "off our backs," never intending to take action? One woman said of her boss, "You can sit down and have a nice, congenial conversation with him. He's very pleasant to talk with. But when the conversation is over, he won't do anything, even though you are expecting him to."

If we behave that way in our daily lives, we will behave that way with God too. Christians live under the new covenant, but we fool ourselves if we think that once under it we will never need renewal. Christians *do* backslide. Christians *do* drift into lip service with God. Continuous renewal is needed, and the primacy of Scripture is the answer. That's why today's lesson will change lives.

INTRODUCTION

A. THE WONDERFUL WORD

A survey of history quickly reveals the great influence the Word of God has had on people and nations. One example is the Old Testament revival under King Josiah (2 Kings 23), which was spurred on by finding and reading the book of the covenant to the king. We also note the time of reform under King Hezekiah, who "held fast to the Lord and did not cease to follow him; he kept the commands the Lord had given Moses" (2 Kings 18:6).

The church age has also experienced times of great revival, with expressions of reliance on and obedience to the wonderful Word of God. Many of these revivals pushed themselves forward with slogans such as "the Scriptures alone" and "no book but the Bible."

Just as those who are devoted to the Word will experience revival and continued spiritual growth (2 Timothy 3:14-17), those who neglect the Word will fall into backsliding and spiritual apathy (Hebrews 2:1). As has been said, "Either the Bible will keep you from sin, or sin will keep you from the Bible." The Bible is the reference point for faithful, obedient living. This is because of the nature of its contents and its ultimate author.

Notice some of the things the wonderful Word addresses: the attributes of God, the origin of humanity, the condition of humanity, the way of salvation, the destiny of the unsaved, the destiny of the saved, light for direction, and wisdom for decisions. The Word of God is authoritative and instructive. As has been pointed out, "It is the traveler's map, the pilgrim's staff, the pilot's compass, the soldier's sword, and the Christian's charter."

DEVOTIONAL READING:
PSALM 27:11-14; 19:7-14

BACKGROUND SCRIPTURE:
NEHEMIAH 8

PRINTED TEXT:
NEHEMIAH 8:1-3, 5, 6, 13, 14, 17, 18

LESSON AIMS

After participating in this lesson, each student will be able to:

1. Retell the event of Ezra's public reading of the law, including preparations made and some results.

2. Explain the importance of reading Scripture in public worship.

3. Plan a program or event that will challenge others to be more regular in Bible reading and study.

KEY VERSE

He read it aloud from daybreak till noon as he faced the square before the Water Gate in the presence of the men, women and others who could understand. And all the people listened attentively to the Book of the Law.
—Nehemiah 8:3

May
25

What a blessing and privilege it is for us to have such a gift of love as the wonderful Word of God! Let us be thankful and attentive to it as we consider how others viewed the Word in centuries past.

B. LESSON BACKGROUND

In last week's lesson, we studied Nehemiah's leading of the people in building the wall of Jerusalem. There were serious challenges to overcome. Between the end of that lesson in Nehemiah 6:15 and the opening of today's lesson, we read of more challenges that continued to confront Nehemiah. He had to deal with spies in his midst (Nehemiah 6:17-19). While dealing with those people, Nehemiah had to ensure that the completion of the wall did not mean a return to "business as usual."

Completing the wall was just a start. That wall also needed gates and watchful guards (Nehemiah 7:1-3). Nehemiah also noticed that Jerusalem was underpopulated and there was a problem with a lack of quality housing. "Now the city was large and spacious, but there were few people in it, and the houses had not yet been rebuilt" (Nehemiah 7:4). So Nehemiah relied on a genealogical list to move toward a solution (Nehemiah 7:5-73; compare Ezra 2). But before that solution was reached (Nehemiah 11:1), some important events intervened.

I. FIRST DAY: ATTITUDE OF REVIVAL (NEHEMIAH 8:1-3, 5, 6)

A. ASSEMBLY GATHERS (VV. 1-3)

1. All the people assembled as one man in the square before the Water Gate. They told Ezra the scribe to bring out the Book of the Law of Moses, which the LORD had commanded for Israel.

As verse 2 will show us, it's only been about a week since the walls were finished (last week's lesson). Thus the excitement of that accomplishment has not yet worn off. This is a perfect time, then, to read *the Book of the Law of Moses.* The people are eager to have God's Word brought to them, so they voluntarily gather and ask *Ezra* to read it in their hearing.

This is the first time that Ezra is introduced into the narrative of the book of Nehemiah. He came to Jerusalem about 13 or 14 years before Nehemiah to teach and enforce the law of God (Ezra 7–10). Thus he is an old hand at leading public assemblies and dealing with the people. During the time of the exile, God preserved his Word through men like Ezra. As a *scribe,* Ezra not only studies the law of God, but also helps preserve it.

The assembly gathers *before the Water Gate,* which is probably on the southeast side of the city. The temple and the newly formed walls are in sight as Ezra reads the law of God (see also Nehemiah 3:26; 8:3, 18; 12:37).

2. So on the first day of the seventh month Ezra the priest brought the Law before the assembly, which was made up of men and women and all who were able to understand.

The reading of *the Law* is to both *men and women.* The phrase *all who were able to understand* indicates that young people are present too. Everyone needs instruction and encouragement from God's Word! The importance of teaching children was recognized hundreds of years earlier, in the time of Moses (Exodus 12:26, 27).

The wall is finished "on the twenty-fifth of Elul" (Nehemiah 6:15), which is the sixth month of the Jewish religious calendar. The events in the verse before us take place on *the first day of the seventh month.* The year is not given, but the common inference is that it is the same year that the wall is finished.

How will you show your desire for God's Word today? What will be the outcome when you do?

This puts the events of today's lesson beginning about a week after the completion of the wall.

The seventh month is an important festival month. The first day of this month is to be "a day of rest, a sacred assembly commemorated with trumpet blasts" (Leviticus 23:24). The Day of Atonement is to be observed on day 10 (Leviticus 23:26-32), and the Feast of Tabernacles is to occur on days 15 to 21 (Leviticus 23:33-36). We will see why this is important in this context a bit later.

3. He read it aloud from daybreak till noon as he faced the square before the Water Gate in the presence of the men, women and others who could understand. And all the people listened attentively to the Book of the Law.

How hungry *the people* are for the Word! *From daybreak till noon* is several hours, probably five or six. The desire to seek God is seen in an eagerness to listen for this length of time.

We cannot help but pause and reflect on how indifferent many are who gather for worship today. We must come prepared and eager to hear. If we come expecting nothing, that is probably what we will get. But God blesses the gathering of his people and the instruction of his Word; therefore we should be taking measures to receive the most from his blessings.

A WORD FROM BEYOND

Actress Shirley MacLaine made *channeling* a household word in the 1980s with her book and TV miniseries *Out on a Limb*. MacLaine claimed to speak to a person who had been a contemporary of Jesus. This person "revealed" to MacLaine that she cocreated the world with God, supposedly proving MacLaine's earlier claim that she is God! How nice for her self-esteem.

MacLaine is much enamored with a channeler named J. Z. Knight, who claims to speak on a regular basis with a 35,000-year-old Cro-Magnon warrior named Ramtha. Knight fetches up to $1,000 per person at seminars where people hear her mouth Ramtha's insights such as "[we must] open our minds to new frontiers of potential" (http://skepdic.com).

Ironic, isn't it, how people will pay more attention to charlatans such as these than they will to God? Ezra's people were anxious to hear something "from beyond," and they listened eagerly for hours to God's Word!

At least two things stand out in this incident. First, the people sought their message from a trustworthy source: God's law. Second, they had a trustworthy guide who brought God's Word to their attention. What applications can we make to modern life? —C. R. B.

B. ASSEMBLY REACTS (VV. 5, 6)
5. Ezra opened the book. All the people could see him because he was standing above them; and as he opened it, the people all stood up.

Ezra is standing on a wooden platform (v. 4, not in today's text), which elevates him *above* all the people. Thus they are able to hear and see him (compare 2 Chronicles 6:13). Several others are up on the platform with Ezra, including the prophet Zechariah. We do not know what role they play in helping Ezra.

The *book* that Ezra opens is not like a modern book, but is a long strip of parchment rolled on a stick at either end. Such a document is also referred to as a "scroll" (Isaiah 8:1; 34:4).

Signifying their reverence for the law that is about to be read, the people rise to their feet. The Jewish custom is to sit when listening (Luke 10:39; Acts 13:14) and to stand while in prayer (Luke 18:11-13), although they occasionally stand to show honor to the person speaking or to the occasion (Job 29:8; Ezekiel 2:1;

WHAT DO YOU THINK?

What was a time when you were eager for the Word? How did you satisfy your hunger?

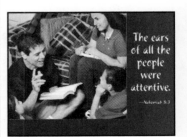

The ears of all the people were attentive. —Nehemiah 8:3

Visual for Lesson 13. *Have this visual on display as you introduce the question on page 334.*

Matthew 13:2). To stand up is an act demonstrating a willingness to listen, believe, and obey what is about to be heard.

To stand in awe and tremble at God's Word is the proper response for one desiring to know the Lord's will. "This is the one I esteem: he who is humble and contrite in spirit, and trembles at my word" (Isaiah 66:2). God's Word is living, active, and powerful (Hebrews 4:12). It therefore should be opened, read, heard, and heeded with reverence.

6. Ezra praised the LORD, the great God; and all the people lifted their hands and responded, "Amen! Amen!" Then they bowed down and worshiped the LORD with their faces to the ground.

The importance of the Bible is based on the author from whom it comes: *the great God,* the all-wise and sufficient one, the holy and eternal one. His attributes are too many and too great for us to comprehend.

It is an amazing thought to ponder that God has spoken to us. As Psalm 8:4 asks, "What is man that you are mindful of him?" Yet the great God has indeed taken the initiative for us to know him and his will. God has put his thoughts in the form of words, which allows us to grasp them. In the case before us, everyone recognizes the importance of the source of what they are about to hear.

Ezra begins by praising *the Lord.* Leaders of God's people should be the first to recognize the greatness of God and the greatness of the work to which he calls them. Such leaders help the people of God understand their dependence on God. Such leaders also understand that what people need is God. So Ezra brings out the words of God (v. 2), opens the book of God (v. 5), reads the Word of God (v. 3), teaches the Word of God (v. 7), and leads the people in praising and worshiping God (v. 6).

As a good priest, Ezra's focus is on God. Ezra's intentions are to get others focused on God as well. "For Ezra had devoted himself to the study and observance of the Law of the Lord, and to teaching its decrees and laws in Israel" (Ezra 7:10). The aim of all preachers today should be to set forth God's truth clearly. Faithful exposition of God's Word is the way to bring people to (or back to) God. "Consequently, faith comes from hearing the message, and the message is heard through the word of Christ" (Romans 10:17).

The response of the people is threefold. First is their cry of *Amen! Amen!* which means "truly, truly" (compare Nehemiah 5:13). Second, the people lift *their hands* to demonstrate need for God and openness to him (compare Ezra 9:5; Psalm 28:2; 134:2). The third reaction is to bow *down* in reverent worship. This bowing is further specified as worshiping *with their faces to the ground* as in Genesis 19:1; Judges 13:20; and 2 Chronicles 7:3; 20:18.

II. SECOND DAY: ACTION OF REVIVAL (NEHEMIAH 8:13, 14, 17, 18)
A. LEADERS GATHER THEMSELVES (V. 13)

13. On the second day of the month, the heads of all the families, along with the priests and the Levites, gathered around Ezra the scribe to give attention to the words of the Law.

The first day had ended with a celebration (Nehemiah 8:12). Now, *on the second day,* the leaders gather to consider what they have heard. When God's Word is heard with an attitude of attentive reverence, it produces a hunger and a thirst for more words of life. So *the heads of all the families, along with the priests and the Levites* desire *Ezra* to instruct them further.

The humility of the leaders is seen in their desire to search for greater understanding. With the readiness of the people to hear and respond to *the words of the*

HOW TO SAY IT

Elul. EE-lull *or* EH-lool.

Ezekiel. Ee-ZEEK-ee-ul *or* Ee-ZEEK-yul.

Ezra. EZ-ruh.

Leviticus. Leh-VIT-ih-kus.

Moses. MO-zes *or* MO-zez.

Nehemiah. NEE-huh-MY-uh.

Nun. NONE.

Zechariah. ZEK-uh-RYE-uh.

Law, it is necessary for the leaders to be instructed on how to direct the people. So instead of being content with only what they heard the day before, they press further. They probably want to discern application and learn how they can better instruct those who are under their charge.

Revival does not happen without action. And right action cannot take place without understanding. A wise and sincere person does not give up on the search for truth and proper application. When leaders and followers in the church decide to settle for nothing less than to understand and apply the whole counsel of God to the best of their ability, their spiritual growth and the growth of the kingdom will not be in doubt.

THE SEARCH FOR UNDERSTANDING

Sigmund Freud died in 1939, yet his influence lingers. He is known as "the father of psychoanalysis" because he launched the modern quest for understanding the human psyche.

It is Freud to whom we owe much of our vocabulary for talking about human behavior. If we have trouble admitting to some negative personal trait, we are *in denial*. If we offer lame excuses for an expensive impulse purchase, we are *rationalizing*. Errors in action or word that supposedly are caused by the unconscious mind are *Freudian slips*. Freud spawned a whole new way of trying to fix personal problems. Where would filmmaker Woody Allen be without him?

In recent years, Freud's method of lengthy self-analysis by expensive therapists has given way to more user-friendly counseling techniques. No one can doubt that the counseling profession has helped multitudes of troubled people. Counseling based on Christian principles has found a place among the ministries offered by many churches.

Ezra was a prophet and a scribe, but perhaps we can think of him as a godly counselor as well. Notice what he did: he led his people to right thinking and right behavior by showing them what God said. Our search for spiritual health will be most successful if we consult the first and greatest psychiatrist: God Almighty!

—C. R. B.

B. LEADERS NOTE REQUIREMENTS (V. 14)

14. They found written in the Law, which the LORD had commanded through Moses, that the Israelites were to live in booths during the feast of the seventh month.

The leaders discover that the Jewish people are required to hold a certain *feast* during the *seventh month*. The feast in question is the Feast of Tabernacles (also called Festival of Booths or Feast of Ingathering), and it is to be observed for a week beginning on the fifteenth day of this month (Exodus 23:16; Leviticus 23:33-36; Numbers 29:12-38; Deuteronomy 16:13-15).

On the first day of the observance, the Israelites are to construct *booths* from tree branches. The Israelites are to *live in* the booths during the entire festival (Leviticus 23:39-43; Nehemiah 8:15). Dwelling in these booths is to be a reminder of the wilderness wanderings their ancestors had experienced after God had delivered them from Egypt. Jesus attends the Feast of Tabernacles in his day (John 7).

C. EVERYONE BUILDS BOOTHS (V. 17)

17. The whole company that had returned from exile built booths and lived in them. From the days of Joshua son of Nun until that day, the Israelites had not celebrated it like this. And their joy was very great.

*Sidebar:*

WHAT DO YOU THINK?

Do you think it would be a good idea for a person just to read the Bible on his or her own, skipping all the commentaries and instructions from others? Why, or why not?

WHAT DO YOU THINK?

What part of Scripture have you been guilty of setting aside? What corrective action have you taken (or will you take)?

The leaders learn about the Feast of Tabernacles on the second day of the month (v. 13, above). Since the feast is to start on the fifteenth day, everyone has only 13 days to get the word out and prepare. So the actions of revival continue as the people are obedient to what they have heard from the law of God.

To make the *booths* and stay in them certainly can be considered to be a great inconvenience. But the people have a heart to obey! Their heart is seen in the fact that they celebrate this festival in a way that has not been seen since *the days of Joshua son of Nun*, some 1,000 years before.

To be sure, this festival had been celebrated in various ways since Joshua's time (see 1 Kings 8:2, 65; Ezra 3:4). But this celebration is different somehow. The difference seems to be in the specific connection of the booths with the wilderness wanderings *(that had returned from exile)*. What a powerful visual aid of God's providential care!

The verse before us causes us to recall that the purpose of proclaiming, reading, and hearing the Bible is to apply the truth that is uncovered. "Do not merely listen to the word, and so deceive yourselves. Do what it says" (James 1:22).

The attitude and actions of the people result is *joy* that is *very great*. People who seek to know and do the will of the Lord will experience the joy that comes from knowing and serving the great God. Rejoice in the Lord!

D. EVERYONE HEARS THE LAW (v. 18)

18. Day after day, from the first day to the last, Ezra read from the Book of the Law of God. They celebrated the feast for seven days, and on the eighth day, in accordance with the regulation, there was an assembly.

The people continue in their obedience as they observe *the feast for* all *seven days* as mandated. They conclude *on the eighth day* with *an assembly* as required by Leviticus 23:36, 39 and Numbers 29:35-38. While they are participating in the feast, Ezra continues to *read* and expound *the Book of the Law of God* daily. This reading reminds us of Deuteronomy 31:9-13. Thus the people continue to receive instruction as they celebrate and worship.

CONCLUSION

There is nothing like God's Word, desired and applied, to bring about revival. The result of the reading of the Word in today's lesson was that the people entered into a formal covenant of renewed devotion to the law and service to God. It was signed by Nehemiah, the leaders, the princes, and the priests. They promised to keep the law of Moses, pay their tithes, support the temple, and keep the Sabbath. They bound themselves under a curse to keep this covenant (Nehemiah 9:38–10:39). The people were serious about following God.

As we have seen in this lesson, there are attitudes and actions that will lead to revival and spiritual growth. We too should continue to grow in our knowledge and observance of the Word of God because of the infinite value of the things written in it.

A careful and continuing search of the Bible will produce many great rewards. We will find truths and promises that will encourage and give strength. We will discover instructions to correct wrong thinking and conduct. We will find comfort and joy in knowing true fellowship with God.

If you are in need of restoring your covenant relationship with the Lord, you will find that he is willing and ready to receive you with open arms. Commit yourself to learn from, obey, and worship the Lord as a sign of your renewed relationship with God. You too will experience great gladness in returning to him.

Discovery Learning

This page contains an alternative lesson plan emphasizing learning activities. Classes desiring such student involvement will find these suggestions helpful. The next page is a reproducible activity page to further enhance discovery learning.

INTO THE LESSON

Recruit one of your congregation's best oral readers to stand on a step stool at the beginning of class to read the following series of texts about the marvelous Word of God: Joshua 1:8; Job 23:12; Psalm 119:18, 163; Isaiah 40:8; 55:11; Matthew 24:35; Luke 11:28; John 14:23; Hebrews 4:12; 1 Peter 1:23. Your reader may decide to include surrounding context of personal choice. The order does not need to be in biblical sequence.

At the end say simply, "If all of that is true about God's Word, a person would be foolish to ignore it. Today's text describes an occasion where the people of God listened to the Word of God and then obeyed it. May we be so wise."

Option: Put a copy of the A Little More, or a Lot More? exercise from the Reproducible Page in each learner's chair. Class members can work on this as they arrive.

INTO THE WORD

Use the following statements as discussion starters for today's text. Verse numbers are noted in parentheses for the teacher's use. (These statements also appear in the optional student book.)

1. When people gather together in unity to hear the Word of God and to worship, then powerful blessings take place (*v. 2*); 2. Anyone who hungers to know the will of God must go to the Word of God, where his will is revealed (*v. 3*); 3. Faithful exposition of God's Word is the way to bring people back to God (*v. 6*); 4. When God's Word is heard with an attitude of attentive reverence, it produces a hunger for more words of life (*v. 13*); 5. Revival cannot happen without action, and right action cannot take place without understanding (*v. 13*); 6. The purpose of proclaiming, reading, and hearing the Bible is to apply the truth (*v. 17*); 7. Because of the infinite value of the Word of God, we should continue to grow in our knowledge and observance of the things written in it, determined to take every advantage of the privileges we have to study God's Word (*v. 18*).

Next, inform your class that you are going to describe behaviors that reflect positive attitudes, and you want them to note where in Nehemiah 8 the people demonstrated these. The verse numbers noted in parentheses at the end of each statement are for the teacher's use and should not be revealed until the learners have had a chance to answer. The statements below are given randomly.

1. Shouted "Amen! Amen!" (*v. 6*) 2. Stood attentively for hours on end. (*v. 3*) 3. Stood in respect as the book was opened. (*v. 5*) 4. Expected their family heads and national leaders to help them understand. (*v. 13*) 5. Immediately obeyed long-forgotten commands. (*vv. 14, 17*)

(The optional student book also contains an activity with these statements.)

INTO LIFE

Have one of your better readers make a recording of the lesson background texts for the upcoming summer lessons. (The *King James Version* has no copyright restrictions; for copyrighted versions, such as the *New International Version*, seek written permission from the holder of the copyright.) Duplicate the recordings onto audiocassettes or CDs, and give one to each class member.

Provide these directions: "Listen to the recorded texts for the upcoming summer lessons as you are working at home or traveling. Begin a habit of hearing the texts several times before Sunday's study session." Tell your learners that this is a way to begin to give regular and diligent attention to God's Word.

End the lesson by pointing out that the writer of Psalm 119 affirmed his own attitude toward the Word of God in various ways. Reproduce and distribute copies of the following for your learners to initial if they concur (also included in the optional student book).

___ "I delight in your law" (v. 70).
___ "Your word is a lamp to my feet" (v. 105).
___ "I will meditate on your precepts" (v. 78).
___ "I will always obey your law, for ever and ever" (v. 44).
___ "May my tongue sing of your word" (v. 172).
___ "I will never forget your precepts" (v. 93).
___ "I have hidden your word in my heart that I might not sin against you" (v. 11).
___ "At midnight I rise to give you thanks for your righteous laws" (v. 62).

As you dismiss class, give each learner a copy of the Psalm 119 and Me exercise from the Reproducible Page as take-home work.

A Little More, or a Lot More?

Consider the following practices and attitudes regarding Scripture. For each, decide how much more you and your congregation need to be doing. Mark the scale of pluses based on your decision.

	Doing well already	Need much more
Public reading of Scripture	++	
Listening to the Word patiently	++	
Vocal affirmation of the Word	++	
Attendance in Bible study groups	++	
Consulting Scripture for guidance	++	
Obedience to the Word	++	
Joy from knowing God's Word	++	

Now complete the following three responses to establish how you intend to allow God's Word to help you improve:

I can, with God's help and the direction of his Word, . . .

I can, with the blessing of his Spirit and the truth of the Scripture, . . .

I can, motivated by a desire to see his Word known and obeyed, . . .

Psalm 119 and Me

The psalmist who penned our Psalm 119 extols the Word of God in all 176 verses. In typical Hebrew parallelism, the author emphasizes by repetition in each verse his joy in God's Word. Read through that psalm and identify five verses that strike you for their beauty and value. Commit yourself to memorizing these five verses. Record the date you accomplish the task of memorizing each one.

Psalm 119: _____   Date memorized ____ / ____ / ____

Psalm 119: _____   Date memorized ____ / ____ / ____

Psalm 119: _____   Date memorized ____ / ____ / ____

Psalm 119: _____   Date memorized ____ / ____ / ____

Psalm 119: _____   Date memorized ____ / ____ / ____

Summer Quarter 2008

Images of Christ

(Hebrews, Gospels, James)

Special Features

Lessons

About These Lessons

Images are all around us. Some we see clearly and directly. Some we see indistinctly, as distorted reflections. Some are harmful to look at (example: pornography). Some are beneficial to behold (example: Psalm 19:1). No images are more important than those of Christ—this quarter's lessons.

Jun 1

Jun 8

Jun 15

Jun 22

Jun 29

Jul 6

Jul 13

Jul 20

Jul 27

Aug 3

Aug 10

Aug 17

Aug 24

Aug 31

A Thousand Words

by Lee M. Fields

I enjoy looking at photographs of my children. I marvel at how they have changed physically over the years. Yet, the photos do not record the growth of my children spiritually and emotionally. Words are necessary for that. This quarter's material treats the theme *Images of Christ* in a powerful way. The images are word pictures. They record sharply the real person and work of Christ. Following images from Hebrews and the Gospels, James presents images to help us put hands and feet to our faith.

JUNE

UNIT 1: IMAGES OF CHRIST IN HEBREWS

Hebrews was written to Jewish believers undergoing persecution. The author writes to bolster their faith by presenting images of who Jesus really is. **Lesson 1** stresses the uniqueness of God's Son. He is of the same essence as the Father. Christ's priesthood (reality) is both different from and superior to the Levitical priesthood (shadow), as **Lesson 2** drives home. In **Lesson 3**, we see the author of Hebrews contrasting the earthly and heavenly temples. This strengthened the original readers, who were undergoing persecution. **Lesson 4** offers us a picture of Christ as the best example of enduring under wrongful suffering. **Lesson 5** leaves no doubt that Christ's nature ought to affect our relationships with other Christians, our commitment to truth, and our praise to God.

JULY

UNIT 2: IMAGES OF CHRIST IN THE GOSPELS

Each of the next four lessons comes from a different Gospel account. The writers are careful to present accurate pictures of Jesus. In **Lesson 6**, Jesus is the master teacher—one able to confront successfully both spiritual and earthly opponents. Jesus is the powerful healer in **Lesson 7**; his power as healer confirms the truth of his message. **Lesson 8** asks a question: if Jesus can wash his disciples' feet, how can we not follow his example of serving one another? **Lesson 9** recounts Peter's great confession. It also gives us a foretaste of the suffering the Messiah had to undergo.

AUGUST

UNIT 3: IMAGES OF CHRIST IN US

Instead of looking at Jesus from the outside as we would watch a movie, James allows us to see Jesus from inside of us, as though we were actors in the movie. It is quite a vista to see Jesus inside us, changing us to be more like him. For example, **Lesson 10** stresses that when Christ lives in us, the Father is able to help us become more like him in attitudes, speech, and service. Christ was no respecter of persons, as **Lesson 11** establishes, and neither should we be. **Lesson 12** offers us James's thoughts regarding areas in which our speech must be wise. As Christ works in us, may our words be used for the benefit of others. **Lesson 13** leaves no doubt that we should be godly servants in both attitudes and actions. Jesus expects us to correct a condemning judgment of others. The subjects of patience and prayer as the correct approaches to handling our desires wrap up our quarter in **Lesson 14.**

In the course of studying these lessons, let us study the word pictures of Jesus. Let us also take before and after photographs of ourselves. As we become more like him, I dare say we will marvel at the change.

GOD'S SON

LESSON 1

WHY TEACH THIS LESSON?

Everyone needs something to believe in, and most people seem to believe in angels. People of many religious backgrounds engage in discussions about angels. Protestants, Catholics, Jews, proponents of the "New Age," Jehovah's Witnesses, Mormons, and Muslims all share a belief in angels. Magazines dedicated exclusively to angels are now in vogue. Books continue to be written on the subject. Angelic figurines adorn countless Christian homes. Think about it: haven't you spoken of "a guardian angel" at some time in your life?

Some of your students may be overly interested in angels and angelology to the neglect of Jesus Christ. Though there are many angels, there is only one holy Son of God. This lesson will draw your students' attention back to Christ, who is far superior to any angelic being. The lesson will warn your students against an undue fascination with angels, thus helping your students avoid idolatry.

INTRODUCTION

A. ANGELS

Some folks have an intense fascination with angels. Print and electronic media are filled with stories of angelic visitations. Talk of angels is welcomed, because with angels people can have religious experiences without Jesus Christ.

The problem is that biblical teachings about angels get mixed in with unbiblical ideas. Angel stories are not necessarily bad; angels do exist and do God's bidding. But angels from God never distract from him. We must be careful never to leave the master for the servant.

B. LESSON BACKGROUND

The book of Hebrews is a bit unusual. It ends with greetings like an epistle (Hebrews 13:20-25), yet the beginning is unlike a normal letter (contrast the opening verses of Hebrews with those of Colossians, etc.). Even so, the author refers to this work as "a short letter" in Hebrews 13:22.

Hebrews 1:1-4 is the introduction that contains the starting threads of the key themes of the book. These themes are woven into the fabric of the entire work. Hebrews 1:4, the last verse of this introduction, leads into the author's first point, which actually extends through 2:4.

The original readers of the book of Hebrews were Jewish believers who had been undergoing some persecution (Hebrews 10:32-34). They were tempted to give up true Christianity for something false (10:35-39). Jews of the first century had a pervasive fascination with angels. We see evidence of this in some of the nonbiblical writings that come into being between the Old and New Testaments (called *the intertestamental writings*).

We can almost hear the original readers' questions that prompt our author to write chapter 1: "We know about angels; is Jesus as strong as they? He died; is he powerful enough to save?" The author of Hebrews has clear answers.

DEVOTIONAL READING:
PROVERBS 8:22-31
BACKGROUND SCRIPTURE:
HEBREWS 1
PRINTED TEXT:
HEBREWS 1:1-12

LESSON AIMS

After participating in this lesson, each student will be able to:

1. Describe how the Son is superior to the angels.

2. Tell something about why Jesus' superiority to the angels is important.

3. Prepare a response to a charge that the Son is one of the created angels.

KEY VERSE

The Son is the radiance of God's glory and the exact representation of his being, sustaining all things by his powerful word.
—Hebrews 1:3

I. GOD'S COMMUNICATION (HEBREWS 1:1, 2a)

A. FORMER REVELATION (v. 1)

1. In the past God spoke to our forefathers through the prophets at many times and in various ways,

In the past God communicated indirectly. The Greek word translated *at many times* means literally "in the manner of many parts." Considering that the Old Testament is God's revelation through many writers over the course of many centuries, we understand what the author means. *Various ways* refers to the fact that God spoke after Moses by various means, such as dreams and visions (Numbers 12:6-9).

The phrase *to our forefathers* refers to Jewish ancestors, the recipients of Scripture. The instrument God used to speak was *the prophets*. Naturally, we think of Isaiah, Jeremiah, etc., as prophets. We expand our understanding when we realize that Moses, Samuel, and David are considered to have been prophets as well (Deuteronomy 18:18; 1 Samuel 3:20; 2 Samuel 23:2-7; Acts 2:30).

B. LATTER REVELATION (v. 2a)

2a. . . . but in these last days he has spoken to us by his Son,

This verse makes two contrasts with verse 1. The first is between "the past" of verse 1 and *in these last days* here. The last days began with the first coming of Christ. We have been living in the last days for two millennia (1 John 2:18).

The second contrast is between "through the prophets" of verse 1 and *by his Son* here. More specifically, this contrast is between the prophets as mere human mouthpieces for God and one who has the quality of divine sonship. When God speaks through his Son, he cannot be more direct! To see Jesus is to see the Father (John 14:9). People who long for more revelation from God need simply to look to the Son. There is no greater nor clearer revelation of God.

NEW AND IMPROVED

We have all seen the ads for "new and improved" versions of various products. These range from automobiles to can openers, from toothpaste to gee-whiz washing machines.

Producers of computer software are constantly upgrading their products. I have an antivirus package on my computer that gets upgraded frequently. Even books get improved. I have one writing style manual that is currently in its 14th edition. How do they expect us to write in good English if they keep changing the rules?

I often wonder, however, if the result is really improved. The most recent product may indeed be new, but is it improved? And if it is really improved, what does that say about the previous model? Doesn't that mean that the previous one was inferior? E. S. Ames tells the story about being in his vacation cabin in the Michigan woods and noticing one day the potbellied stove that provided heat for the building. It had a brand name, and then the inscription *Perfection No. 42*. "If it is 'perfection,'" he mused, "then why did it take 42 versions to get to this point?"

Sometimes the more recent products are not really improvements. But sometimes they are. That's what the writer of Hebrews means. God had previously spoken to us through the prophets. But now he has spoken to us through his Son. That's an improvement!   —J. B. N.

II. GOD'S SON (HEBREWS 1:2b-4)

A. SON'S INHERITANCE (v. 2b)

2b. . . . whom he appointed heir of all things, and through whom he made the universe.

Deity is described in seven ways in verses 2, 3. The first two descriptions, here in the second half of verse 2, are related to the actions of God. The last five, in verse 3, are related to the nature and actions of the Son.

First, God appointed the Son as *heir of all things* (compare Matthew 21:38). As God's heir, the Son has divine authority and ownership, far more than any created being. *All things* means, naturally, everything that exists. In Matthew 28:18, Jesus made known that at that time he had this authority over all.

Second, God *made the universe* by means of the Son. The Greek word translated as *universe* usually refers to time, but it is used here to refer to all that goes on or exists in time. Hence, *the universe* is a good translation. The Son not only owns the universe, he was also involved in creating it (John 1:3; Colossians 1:16).

B. SON'S GLORY AND IMAGE (v. 3a)

3a. The Son is the radiance of God's glory and the exact representation of his being,

We now move to the first two of the five descriptions of the nature of the Son. The Father has *glory* of his own, of course. At the same time, the Son also has actual light—brightness or *radiance*. Thus the Son is not reflected light, as we see coming from the moon, but has light himself, as we see from the sun.

Moreover, the Son bears the image of God. The term for *exact representation* is used of the imprint stamped on coins. *Being* refers to God's real essence. These two terms make clear that this Son, though distinct as a person from the Father, is of the same divine nature as the Father. Whatever the "stuff" is that makes the Father to be God also makes the Son to be God. The writer of Hebrews could not be clearer. How vital this truth is to the readers! Despite their doubts, they have made the right decision to follow Jesus as the Christ.

C. SON'S WORK (v. 3b)

3b. . . . sustaining all things by his powerful word. After he had provided purification for sins,

Third, the Son bears or sustains *all things.* Deuteronomy 33:27 speaks of the arms of God holding the dwelling place of Israel. The Jews refer to God as the one who carries his world, citing Isaiah 46:4, where God will carry his people and deliver them. The Son uses his word to do this; *his powerful word* refers to a power that is limited to God alone (2 Corinthians 4:7). The Son's role as sustainer is that which only the divine one can fill.

Whereas the third description of Jesus (above) is of something that continues for all time, the fourth description is that of an occurrence at a specific point in history. The Son brought about the *purification,* or cleansing, from *sins* when he died on the cross. It was the Son (and nobody else) who made the purification through his blood on the cross (Hebrew 9:14).

This fact does not signify that the cleansing is applied to everyone automatically without condition. Rather, the idea is that purging of sin is available through the Son's sacrificial act.

D. SON'S POSITION (vv. 3c, 4)

3c. . . . he sat down at the right hand of the Majesty in heaven.

Fifth, the Son *sat down.* This expression might not catch the attention of those who live in places without kings. This is an official, ceremonial occasion, drawing on Psalm 110:1. The *right hand* of a king signifies a place of honor and

Visual for Lessons 1, 6, & 10. *Use this visual to open a discussion on the various titles or descriptions of Jesus.*

WHAT DO YOU THINK?

How does (or how should) knowing that your sins have been purged by Christ affect your daily life?

DAILY BIBLE READINGS

Monday, May 26—*From the Beginning (Proverbs 8:22-31)*

Tuesday, May 27—*Appointed Heir (Hebrews 1:1-5)*

Wednesday, May 28—*In the Beginning (John 1:1-5)*

Thursday, May 29—*The Firstborn (Hebrews 1:6-9)*

Friday, May 30—*The Work of God's Hands (Hebrews 1: 10-12)*

Saturday, May 31—*Full of Grace and Truth (John 1:14-18)*

Sunday, June 1—*Heir of All Things (Hebrews 1:13, 14)*

WHAT DO YOU THINK?

What significance does (or should) the Father/Son relationship hold for your life in practical ways?

---

prestige (1 Kings 2:19) as well as power for punishment, support, and deliverance (Exodus 15:6; Psalm 18:35; 138:7). The term *the Majesty in heaven* refers to the Father.

4. So he became as much superior to the angels as the name he has inherited is superior to theirs.

In all these ways the Son is as *superior to the angels* as his *name* is *to theirs*. What names? *Son* versus *angel*. Whereas an angel is a created messenger, the Son is the divine, uncreated creator. The difference is infinite. With this lead-in our author moves to the first topic.

III. SON'S SUPERIORITY (HEBREWS 1:5-7)

A. JESUS IS THE SON (v. 5)

5a. For to which of the angels did God ever say,
   "You are my Son;
      today I have become your Father"?

In the following argument, the author presents a chain of Scriptures intended to demonstrate truths about the Son's superiority to *angels*. Our task is to understand each quotation in its original context, then see how the author of Hebrews is using it.

Here in verse 5, the phrase *You are my Son; today I have become your Father* is from Psalm 2:7. It is used here to make a vital point: no angel is called *my Son*. That is a title reserved for the unique *Son* of God, as described in verses 1-4. Though the promises made by the Lord in Psalm 2:8, 9 might apply in part to David, they can apply fully only to Jesus.

5b. Or again,
   "I will be his Father,
      and he will be my Son"?

This quotation is from 2 Samuel 7:14. The quotation comes from the passage that is establishing the Davidic covenant. David wished to build a temple for the Lord. Through Nathan the prophet, the Lord explained that he did not need a special house. Instead, the Lord was to establish a house for David.

In 2 Samuel 7:12-16, the Lord says he will raise up David's "offspring" and will establish his kingdom. It is that offspring or descendant who will build his house; the offspring, ultimately, is the Lord's Son. King Solomon did build a temple, but it was destroyed. Solomon governed a nation in a golden age, but that kingdom split at the time of his death and eventually ended.

The true fulfillment of the Davidic covenant is in the descendant that came after Solomon—the Messiah. The Old Testament teaches this (Jeremiah 23:5; Zechariah 6:12), and the New Testament records this as fulfilled in the first coming of Jesus (Luke 1:32, 33).

In this one verse the author of Hebrews has carefully proven that there is one Son of God. Christ is he, not any angel.

B. JESUS IS TO BE WORSHIPED (vv. 6, 7)

6a. And again, when God brings his firstborn into the world, he says,

Paul Ellingworth reasons that the word *brings* refers to Jesus' heavenly enthronement after his resurrection. In this case, *the world* would refer not to the earth, but to the heavenly world. This conclusion best fits the context given the following quotes about the actions of angels. *Firstborn* is another term for Son; the element "first-" emphasizes the Son's supremacy over creation, picking up from Hebrews 1:1-4.

6b. "Let all God's angels worship him."

The location of this quotation is the first issue. Some say it comes from the end of Psalm 97:7, which reads, "*worship him, all you gods*" (where *gods* may be used loosely to mean *angels*). However, the wording is not exactly the same as Hebrews.

More likely the author is quoting from Deuteronomy 32:43 in the Septuagint, which is the ancient Greek translation of the Old Testament. Most translations of Deuteronomy 32:43, including the *New International Version,* do not contain the phrase *and let all the angels of God worship him* because the Hebrew text does not have it. Perhaps your edition of the *New International Version* has a footnote at Deuteronomy 32:43 and Hebrews 1:6 that explains this.

Deuteronomy 32 is a song that Moses recited before the assembly of Israel about the Lord's judgment on the wicked. In the Septuagint, the song includes a call for the heavens to rejoice and for the angels of God to worship "him." The author of Hebrews identifies the speaker as the Father and *him* as the Son, the object of worship. In doing this, our author is also attributing to the Son the great deeds of the Lord mentioned in Deuteronomy 32.

The point is clear: since *God's angels worship* the Son, he is superior to them.

7. In speaking of the angels he says,
   "He makes his angels winds,
      his servants flames of fire."

The author now quotes Psalm 104:4 to define the glorious function of *angels.* They are powerful spiritual beings who are servants of God. To describe them as *flames of fire* reminds us of passages such as Genesis 3:24 and Exodus 3:2. Our author's point is simply that the angels are *servants.* They do not have the authority of the Son that we see in the next verse.

IV. SON'S POSITION (HEBREWS 1:8-12)

A. Authority (vv. 8, 9)

8, 9. But about the Son he says,
   "Your throne, O God, will last for ever and ever,
      and righteousness will be the scepter of your kingdom.
   "You have loved righteousness and hated wickedness;
      therefore God, your God, has set you above your companions
      by anointing you with the oil of joy."

These two verses quote Psalm 45:6, 7. The ancient title to Psalm 45 calls it "a wedding song." Though Psalm 45:2 may be addressed to an earthly king (and verses 10-15 do seem to celebrate the wedding of an earthly king), the author of Hebrews indicates that some verses are addressed to someone else.

This someone else is "O mighty one" (Psalm 45:3), who defeats the king's enemies (Psalm 45:5). Further, Psalm 45:6 addresses this mighty one as God, yet as one who is somehow distinct from God in Psalm 45:7b ("therefore God, your God"). Who else can this divine and mighty king be but the Son of God?

The point is that Jesus' *kingdom* lasts forever. This can be said about no angel, much less about any earthly king.

B. Permanence (vv. 10-12)

10-12. He also says,
   "In the beginning, O Lord, you laid the foundations of the earth,
      and the heavens are the work of your hands.

Resources for These Lessons

The visual pictured in each lesson (example: page 339) is a small reproduction of a large, full-color poster included in the Adult Resources packet for the Summer Quarter. That packet also contains the very useful Presentation Helps CD for teacher use. The packet is available from your supplier. Order No. 492.

What Do You Think?

What are some ways you have been guilty of failing to worship Christ properly? What have you done to improve?

What Do You Think?

How do you follow the Lord in loving righteousness and hating wickedness?

What Do You Think?

Why is it important that we see Christ as one who never grows old?

"They will perish, but you remain;
   they will all wear out like a garment.
"You will roll them up like a robe;
   like a garment they will be changed.
But you remain the same,
   and your years will never end."

The author of Hebrews now quotes from Psalm 102:25-27. The key issue is the identity of the speaker of the words recorded here in Hebrews 1:10-12. In the Hebrew of Psalm 102, the speaker throughout the psalm is the psalmist, and the one being addressed is the Lord. But our author uses the word *also* in verse 10 to connect this quotation to the introduction in verse 8: "But about the Son he says, [quotes Psalm 45:6, 7] . . . He also says, [quotes Psalm 102:25-27]." Thus our author clearly identifies the speaker as the Father and the addressee as the Son.

Our author does not doubt the superiority of the Son over the angels, and neither should we. The Son is the Lord God. He is the eternal, unchanging creator of all. When we are under crushing pain or stress, we might be tempted to follow something or someone other than the Son. At all times, but especially during dark days, we do well to remember the infinite magnificence of the person and power of the Son.

Here to Stay

Ira and George Gershwin comprised one of the greatest duos in American popular music. They were at their peak during the 1920s and 1930s. They wrote numerous Broadway shows, including the musical *Porgy and Bess*. Among the many classic songs they composed are "I Got Rhythm," "Embraceable You," and "Someone to Watch Over Me."

"Our Love Is Here to Stay" also stands tall as one of the best-loved songs of that era. The intent of the song was to declare that although cultural modes, features of the earth, etc., may change, "our love" is eternal. A nice, sentimental thought, but surely containing poetic exaggeration and embellishment.

The writer of Hebrews, however, makes a similar statement. The foundations of the earth and the very heavens shall perish, become old like a garment, and ultimately be folded up and put away. But the Lord God will ever remain the same. All else will change, but his years will not fail. What should this fact lead us to do?

—J. B. N.

CONCLUSION

In the 2002 movie *Spiderman*, there is a scene with a girl trapped inside a burning building. The flames are so intense that the police and firefighters are unable to save her. Spiderman, wanted by the police for being a suspected criminal, arrives. At the scene, Spiderman is arrested. He offers to go get the girl. The policeman, though obligated to hold him, suddenly lets him go. Why? Because only Spiderman is able to help. They need the amazing Spiderman to do what they could not.

But that's fiction, and there is no Spiderman. Yet humans do indeed live in a burning building: death. This is because of sin. We need someone who can rescue us because we cannot overcome or escape on our own. Whom will we trust to do this? A guardian angel? The author of Hebrews has a better answer: trust Jesus! He is stronger than any angel (or any other created being).

Our superhero is the very Son of God. He alone is able to save. He is not a comic book character. He is real.

Thought to Remember

When we listen to Jesus, we listen to God.

Discovery Learning

*This page contains an alternative lesson plan emphasizing learning activities. Some of these activities
are also found in the helpful student book,* NIV Bible Student. *The next page
is a reproducible activity page to further enhance discovery learning.*

INTO THE LESSON

Display a collection of angel figurines, ceramic and otherwise, in your study space. You may be able to borrow these from a class member who collects them. This will be a useful visual aid as you examine the contrasts between the Son and the angels in today's text. A suggestion in the Into Life section also utilizes these angelic representations.

Use the following "coded" messages to introduce not only today's study but also the first five lessons in this unit of study from the epistle to the Hebrews. Prepare 5 strips of paper, each strip 2½" high. Put creases across each strip 1" up from the bottom. Fill the top 1½" of each strip (from the top edge down to the crease) with the following descriptions, one per strip: GOD'S SON, INTERCESSOR, REDEEMER, LEADER, ETERNAL.

Fold up each strip on its crease and tape lightly so that the bottom half of each word is covered. Display each, one at a time. Ask the class to "decipher" the word that is only half seen.

After all are identified, say, "For these next five weeks, we will be looking at texts that reveal images of Christ in Hebrews, lessons that affirm Jesus to be God's Son, our only intercessor, our perfect redeemer, our trustworthy leader, and our eternal Christ." Leave these five posted throughout the five sessions.

INTO THE WORD

Create ahead of time four sets of 4" by 6" cards: seven cards that each say NO!; seven cards with the letters and exclamation B, E, T, T, E, R, ! (one each per card); five cards with J, E, S, U, S (one letter each per card); five cards with A, N, G, E, L (one letter each per card).

To begin, post these two labels side by side: GOD'S SON and ANGELS. Then post the following labels underneath GOD'S SON: (1) appointed heir of all things, (2) made the universe, (3) the radiance of God's glory, (4) the exact representation of his being, (5) sustains all things by his powerful word, (6) provided purification for our sins, and (7) sat down at God's right hand. Turn to the ANGELS column. At each line, ask, "Can this be said of any angel?" Post a NO! card as each question is answered. After you post all seven, read verse 4 and say, "In every way, the Son is better."

Now have learners read verses 5-7 in unison. Remove the NO! cards and post the following labels under ANGELS: (1) never referred to as sons, (2) never recorded as calling God "Father," (3) never an object of worship, (4) made by God, (5) simply servants of God to do his bidding.

When all five are in place and related to the text, take your B-E-T-T-E-R-! cards put them letter by letter to the left—under GOD'S SON—on each line to spell BETTER! (If you have the capability, consider preparing the preceding activity as a PowerPoint® presentation.)

Next, divide your class into groups of 5 or 6, or at least 2 groups if you have fewer than 10 learners total. Give each group a set either of the J-E-S-U-S cards or the A-N-G-E-L cards. Ask your groups to write a statement for each card using the letter in some significant way in the statement. Here are some examples: for U, a group could write "I am Jesus; the creation of the universe was in my hands"; for A, a group could write "I am an angel, an ambassador to do my Master's will."

Give groups time to complete all statements. Then ask them to reveal their decisions to the entire class. As they do, ask, "How do you see that truth in today's text?" You can use either the Jesus Is Speaking! or the Jesus Is Superior! activity (or both) from the Reproducible Page at this point.

INTO LIFE

Display some angel figurines (see the Into the Lesson idea). Ask the class to keep a tally of angel images and references they see and hear of in the coming week. Say that you will ask for a report at the beginning of next week's study. Suggest they consider why people collect and display angel figures and why they make such remarks as, "I guess my guardian angel was watching out for me" and "There are angels everywhere at work."

Some people believe in angels but do not believe in Jesus' sonship. Ask the class, "How could we respond to someone who holds such a belief?" Note that the response should emphasize the superior care, presence, and power of the Son. Anticipate that learners will note some of Jesus' superior attributes in today's text and study. Recommend that they listen for occasions this week in which they can "say a good word about Jesus the Son."

Jesus Is Speaking!

A key affirmation the Hebrews writer makes to us is that "in these last days [God] has spoken to us by his Son" (Hebrews 1:2). The four Gospels record much that Jesus said to us about God's will. Even his very presence and actions among humans also speaks volumes of God's character. In each of the following thought balloons, use Scripture to determine what God is saying to us in each action.

Jesus' sacrificial death on the cross

Jesus' life of selfless service

Jesus' humble birth

Jesus' association with sinners

Jesus' use of his divine powers

Jesus' dealings with enemies

Jesus' prayer life

Jesus Is Superior!

Hebrews 1 describes Jesus' superiority in several ways. See how many of these lines you can fill in.

Jesus is superior to _____ because _____.

Jesus is superior to _____ because _____.

Jesus is superior to _____ because _____.

Jesus is superior to _____ because _____.

ONLY INTERCESSOR

LESSON 2

WHY TEACH THIS LESSON?

No one likes to feel lonely. We try to shake loneliness, but sometimes we can't. Our hearts ache, yet often we cannot find someone with whom to share our burdens. Even when we do find someone, we still don't give away our secrets easily. Something inside of us insists that others won't understand or that they will think less of us. Too often we have received a "spiritual band-aid" in the form of a hollow sounding "I'll pray for you" response. So we are tempted to "self-medicate" our pain by experimenting with worldly fixes such as alcohol and entertainment.

The sense of being alone begins to change when we understands that Jesus is always available. He understands and cares about our needs. This is important: Jesus stands ready to communicate to our Father the deepest longings of our hearts. Jesus lived to make intercession for us on the cross. As he lives now, he continues to make intercession for us daily.

These truths can radically change your students' lives. They can discover that worldly fixes that temporarily change one's mood fade to unimportance when compared with Jesus' ability to intercede. He will never fail us.

INTRODUCTION

A. "I AM THE GREATEST!"

The famous world champion boxer Muhammad Ali is known for many memorable sound bites. But none is better known than his claim to be the greatest boxer of all time. It is impossible to find out whether he was truly better than all those who came before him. Neither is it clear that he could have beaten all the boxers that have come since his heyday. The fact that Ali lost five fights clouds the issue.

This is the way of all humanity; someone will always come along to take your place. The author of Hebrews proves to the reader that Jesus, the Son of God, is different in this respect. Jesus is truly and absolutely the greatest of all eternity. There has been no one before him who was greater, and there will be no one after. There will be no one to take his place, because there will never be any need for anyone to do so.

B. LESSON BACKGROUND

In last week's lesson we learned that the original readers of Hebrews were Jewish believers who were under persecution. As a result, they were beginning to doubt whether faith in Jesus was really better than their previous beliefs. Our author addressed one aspect for his readers by proving from Scripture that Jesus is infinitely better than the angels.

Today's passage falls in the middle of a lengthy discussion covering the priesthood. The larger section includes Hebrews 4:14–10:25; we note the repetition of "great high priest" and "great priest" in 4:14 and 10:21, marking off

---

DEVOTIONAL READING:
JEREMIAH 31:31-34
BACKGROUND SCRIPTURE:
HEBREWS 7
PRINTED TEXT:
HEBREWS 7:20-28

LESSON AIMS

After participating in this lesson, each student will be able to:

1. Compare and contrast Jesus' priesthood with the Old Testament Levitical priesthood.

2. Explain why it is better for us to live under Jesus' priesthood than under a continued Levitical priesthood.

3. Prepare a response to the assertion that living under the Jewish system is just as good as being a Christian.

KEY VERSE

He is able to save completely those who come to God through him, because he always lives to intercede for them.
—Hebrews 7:25

the beginning and ending of this large unit. The Old Testament role of high priest was that of a mediator between God and people to make peace (Hebrews 5:1). It is as though the Jewish believers in Christ were wondering, "Is Jesus' priesthood better than the Levitical priesthood set up in the law of Moses?"

In Hebrews 5, our author began to establish proof of Jesus' superior priesthood by describing the nature of that priesthood. In 5:1-4, the author lists the universal qualities of a priest. In 5:5-10, the author shows Jesus' relation to high priesthood by quoting Psalm 110:4, which compares the Son's priesthood to that of Melchizedek.

The author interrupts the argument at Hebrews 5:11 to warn the readers about falling away. After proving that Melchizedek's priesthood was greater than that of the Levites (the descendants of Abraham, 7:1-10), the author shows that Scripture describes the Son's priesthood as superior even to Melchizedek's (7:11-28). The fact that Jesus' priesthood is superior to even that of Melchizedek is the immediate backdrop to today's lesson (7:13-19).

I. GREATEST IN APPOINTMENT (HEBREWS 7:20-22)

A. EXISTENCE OF OATH (v. 20a)

20a. And it was not without an oath!

The negative *was not without an oath* is a literary way of emphasizing that an oath was involved in making Jesus a priest. The author of Hebrews will finish this thought in verse 22, but first there is a pause in verses 20b, 21 for some clarification.

B. PRIEST BY OATH (vv. 20b, 21)

20b, 21. Others became priests without any oath, but he became a priest with an oath when God said to him:

    "The Lord has sworn
       and will not change his mind:
    'You are a priest forever.'"

One of the qualities of priesthood the author has already mentioned is that of being called, or appointed, by God (Hebrews 5:4). Although Aaron was called to be a priest by the Lord, all those who were high priests after him succeeded him by birth rather than by a direct call from God. Jesus, the Son, however, was made priest by a direct oath of the Lord. This was predicted in Psalm 110:4, which is quoted here.

Understanding how various words are used in the original context of Psalm 110 requires a bit of patience. In Hebrew, the language in which the Old Testament was written, the personal name of God is *Yahweh*. Most versions render this in English as LORD, with small capital letters. There is a different word that translations render *Lord* or *lord*, which often signifies "master," "owner," or "sir."

When we turn to Psalm 110:1, we see that David (the author) identifies the speaker as "the LORD" and the one being spoken to as "my Lord." The author of Hebrews clearly understands that in Psalm 110:4 the speaker is still "the LORD" (Yahweh) and the one being spoken to is "the Lord," meaning the Son. *Has sworn* refers to an oath or vow. God is not going to *change his mind* about appointing the Son as high priest.

David quotes the actual words of Yahweh: "You are a priest forever, in the order of Melchizedek." *You* refers to the addressee. To whom is Yahweh referring? It must refer to the Son, the Messiah, Jesus. Thus, Psalm 110:4 is the oath of God that the Son will be a priest forever.

WHAT DO YOU THINK?

What impact does the fact that Jesus is priest forever have on your life? How should that fact help you grow spiritually?

C. RESULT OF OATH (v. 22)

22. Because of this oath, Jesus has become the guarantee of a better covenant.

The words *because of this* pick up on what was started in verse 20. The Levitical priests of the Old Testament had no oath to establish their appointment to priesthood, but Jesus did. The difference between having that oath and not is as great as the difference between the old Mosaic covenant and the new covenant in Christ.

The Greek word translated *guarantee* occurs only once in the New Testament (right here) and only twice in the nonbiblical Jewish works written before the New Testament. However, it is common enough elsewhere. *Guarantee* may be understood either impersonally or personally. Impersonally, it may be the collateral "thing" that is put up to guarantee repayment of a loan. If the figure of speech is used in this way, Jesus himself is collateral, put up by the Father, who offers the *better covenant.*

On the other hand, the word may be used for "a guarantor," meaning the person legally responsible for repayment. If this is the sense here, it means that Jesus is the one responsible to pay for the *better covenant* by offering himself.

The latter idea is better, since Jesus' own sacrifice became the payment. The gravity of the role of guarantor is illustrated from the nonbiblical wisdom passage Sirach (Ecclesiasticus) 29:15: "Do not forget the kindness of your guarantor, for he has given his life for you." This is exactly what the Son has done for us—given his life.

The *better covenant* is the new agreement that God has made with humanity. This covenant is better to the degree that the trustworthiness of God's Son as guarantor is better than that of the earthly, Levitical priests. This is all based on the oath from the Lord himself.

II. GREATEST IN DURATION (HEBREWS 7:23-25)

A. LEVITICAL PRIESTS DIED (v. 23)

23. Now there have been many of those priests, since death prevented them from continuing in office;

The reason the Levitical priests were *many* is that they kept dying. Death *prevented* Aaron and his descendants from *continuing* as priests.

B. JESUS LIVES FOREVER (vv. 24, 25)

24. . . . but because Jesus lives forever, he has a permanent priesthood.

In contrast, the Son abides forever. He is eternal. The author of Hebrews has just made a significant point of this in 7:16.

Numbers 35:9-28 lists laws regarding killing and the cities of refuge. If a person kills someone without malice aforethought, the law says that the killer is bound to the city of refuge only until the high priest dies. After that, the person is free to return home without any fear from the kinsman-redeemer. In Hebrews 7:12, our author makes the point that where there is a change of priest, there is necessarily a change in law. Since the Old Testament priesthood with its long succession of priests has been replaced by the new priesthood of Jesus, the old law and priesthood are over and a new law and a new priesthood are in place.

The original audience of Jewish believers can take comfort that Jesus is that new priest. But lest any reader wonder if there is yet another, better priesthood and covenant coming, our author focuses on the word *"forever"* in that oath of Psalm 110:4. As a result of his immortality, Jesus *has a permanent priesthood.* In

DAILY BIBLE READINGS

Monday, June 2—*Preparing for a New Covenant (Jeremiah 31:31-34)*

Tuesday, June 3—*The Old Order of Priests (Hebrews 7:1-3)*

Wednesday, June 4—*King Melchizedek (Genesis 14:17-20)*

Thursday, June 5—*Introduction of a New Order (Hebrews 7:4-17)*

Friday, June 6—*The Permanent Priesthood (Hebrews 7: 18-24)*

Saturday, June 7—*Interceding for All Who Approach God (Hebrews 7:25, 26)*

Sunday, June 8—*Perfect Forever (Hebrews 7:27, 28)*

HOW TO SAY IT

Aaron. AIR-un.
Abraham. AY-bruh-ham.
Ecclesiasticus. Ik-LEEZ-ee-AS-teh-kus.
Eucharist. YOU-kar-ist.
Hebrews. HEE-brews.
Jesuit. JEH-zhu-it.
Levites. LEE-vites.
Levitical. Leh-VIT-ih-kul.
Leviticus. Leh-VIT-ih-kus.
Melchizedek. Mel-KIZ-eh-dek.
Muhammad Ali. Mow-HAH-med Ah-LEE.
Sirach. SIGH-rak.
transubstantiation. tran-sub-stan-she-A-shun.

Visual for Lesson 2. *Point to this visual as you ask, "Why is it appropriate to speak of Jesus as a bridge?"*

this context, Jesus' priesthood is permanent in that he has no successors and no need of any. Therefore, there never will be any other priesthood to replace him. There will never come another covenant to supersede the one of which Jesus is the guarantor.

FOREVER

People often have different notions of an elapse of time. Some people say, "I'll be ready in a minute," when it actually takes about 10 minutes. "Just a second," someone once told me; I waited for several minutes. I have a dear friend whom I often do things with. But I have learned to double his estimate of time. If he says he will be ready in 10 minutes, I know it will be 20; if he says 15, I know it will be 30.

Children are known to say repeatedly, "Are we there yet?" on car trips. When told that they have not yet arrived, they often say, "It's taking forever!" Indeed, *forever* is another interesting word. In the eighteenth century, the Roman Catholic Church received many criticisms about the Jesuit order because of its alleged political interference in various Catholic countries. Under pressure from several Catholic monarchs, Pope Clement XIV dissolved the Jesuit order "forever" in 1773. However, a new political climate emerged early in the nineteenth century, and the Jesuits were reactivated in 1814—just 41 years after they were dissolved "forever." I suppose that means, then, that "forever" lasts 41 years.

In spite of such variations and unpredictability, there is assurance in knowing that when God says *forever,* he means it. He refers to the new high priest as continuing, ever and ever living. God's assertions will not be changed by a new political climate. They are sure and "forever."   —J. B. N.

25. Therefore he is able to save completely those who come to God through him, because he always lives to intercede for them.

Because Jesus is an eternal priest, the guarantor of an eternal, irreplaceable covenant, he alone is able *to save* people. *Completely* means that there is no limit to Jesus' ability to save—neither to the depth of sin nor to the number of sinners.

The object of Jesus' saving, though, serves as a condition: *those who come to God through him* means that God turns away no one who comes to him. But each must come on God's terms. The only way to come to God is through the Son (John 14:6). The Son is able to save all because he *lives* eternally for the purpose of making eternal intercession (Romans 8:34; 1 John 2:1).

This message strengthened the faith of the original readers (Jewish Christians) as they began to realize the greatness of their Savior and their salvation. But this message is no less valuable today. How many lost people fear coming to God because they doubt that he will forgive them? How many Christians doubt their salvation because they dwell on their sin? Can Jesus save even though we still sin? Yes, Jesus saves now and forever, if we trust in his priestly work.

III. GREATEST IN EXALTATION (HEBREWS 7:26-28)
A. JESUS IS HOLY (v. 26)
26. Such a high priest meets our need—one who is holy, blameless, pure, set apart from sinners, exalted above the heavens.

The Son is the kind of priest that is suitable to meet *our need* because of five qualities.

First, he is *holy.* The Greek word translated *holy* is not the usual word referring to God's holiness. The word that the author of Hebrews employs has various

---

WHAT DO YOU THINK?

What would you say to a fellow believer who says that he has sins in his life that not even Jesus could forgive?

uses in the old Greek translation of the Old Testament, depending on context. "Innocent of wrongdoing" is what the author of Hebrews means here.

Second, he is *blameless*. This word occurs in only a few other places in the New Testament. In modern English, it carries the idea of being "without fault" in a moral sense. Third, he is *pure*. This means "without blemish." See Hebrews 13:4 and James 1:27, which describe other things that are pure.

Fourth, the phrase *set apart from sinners* does not mean that Jesus has no association with us (see Hebrews 2:11-17), but that he is utterly without sin. Fifth, *exalted above the heavens* refers to Jesus' rightful place as divine ruler over the universe (Ephesians 1:20-22; Philippians 2:9-11; 1 Peter 3:22).

B. JESUS SANCTIFIED HIMSELF (v. 27)

27. Unlike the other high priests, he does not need to offer sacrifices day after day, first for his own sins, and then for the sins of the people. He sacrificed for their sins once for all when he offered himself.

As priests, both the Son and the Levitical *high priests* had to *offer sacrifices* for the people. However, before the Levitical high priests could offer sacrifice for the people, they first had to offer sacrifice for their *own sins*. There were two specific occasions when priests had to sacrifice for themselves before they could sacrifice for the people: the annual Day of Atonement (Leviticus 16:6) and the occasions when the anointed priest had sinned (Leviticus 4:3).

However, there is no Mosaic law requiring the priests to sacrifice *daily* for themselves. F. F. Bruce suggests that Leviticus 4:3 is what the author has in mind in using the word *daily*. Leviticus 4:2 talks about sins being committed "unintentionally." Even though they had more knowledge of the law than anyone else, priests would need to atone for such unintentional sins. But because the Son is absolutely and completely innocent of anything sinful, he has no need of any of those sacrifices. The Son is a priest who is ever a suitable intercessor on our behalf.

We are all sinful. The best of us is ugly to the core with sin. As intercessors, earthly high priests offered an important service to the Old Testament Israelites. But ultimately they were poor representatives for the people, since they were sinful too. What makes the Son exactly suitable as a priest for us is his sinlessness. He is just the one we need to go to the Father on our behalf. He is the only one we need to do that, and he is the only one who can do that.

HE DID IT ONCE

One of the most bitterly disputed issues among the leaders of the sixteenth-century Protestant Reformation was the difference in understanding regarding the Lord's Supper. But the major leaders of that movement all agreed on one thing: they all disagreed with the Roman Catholic understanding. Catholicism taught the doctrine of *transubstantiation*—the idea that the bread and fruit of the vine actually turn into Jesus' flesh and blood at the time of the mass.

This ties in with Catholic teaching that the Lord's Supper is a repetition of the sacrifice of Christ on Calvary. According to this idea, the benefit of the mass comes from offering up Christ again and again to God as a sacrifice for our sins—every time a Catholic priest celebrates the Eucharist. The alleged result is an unending supply of God's grace that comes from the repeated and constant sacrificing of his Son. This also the Protestant leaders rejected.

The writer of Hebrews tells us that Christ is offered up once—not perpetually and not even daily, as the Old Testament high priests offered up their sacrifices.

WHAT DO YOU THINK?

How do you (or should you) respond to the fact that Jesus is "set apart from sinners" (utterly without sin)?

WHAT DO YOU THINK?

What is the danger of not recognizing the sinfulness of earthly leaders?

PRAYER

Loving Father, we thank you that you gave us just the right priest, who is really able to remove our sins and make us presentable to you. We offer our thanks in the name of the one who is your appointee, eternal and utterly perfect, Jesus your Son, amen.

WHAT DO YOU THINK?

What do you appreciate most about having Jesus as your high priest?

THOUGHT TO REMEMBER
No fear!

This adds to the foundational theme of Hebrews that Christ is superior in every way to the Old Testament dispensation. Christ's sacrifice was necessary only once.

—J. B. N.

C. JESUS IS THE GREATEST (v. 28)

28. For the law appoints as high priests men who are weak; but the oath, which came after the law, appointed the Son, who has been made perfect forever.

This verse not only summarizes the idea of Jesus' having the greatest perfection, but also the entire first half of the argument begun in Hebrews 4:14: Jesus' high priesthood is superior because of his superior appointment. The kind of weakness that the author of Hebrews has in mind here is both physical (the old priests die) and spiritual (they sin, even the most holy of them). These are the best that the Mosaic law could provide.

The oath refers to what God said in Psalm 110:4, which we saw quoted in Hebrews 7:21 earlier. Since this oath in Psalm 110 came after the law, it superseded it. Therefore, the Son's priesthood superseded the Levitical priesthood and lasts *forever*. The Greek for "forever" here in verse 28 is identical to the "forever" in verse 21; so the author of the book of Hebrews is once again drawing from Psalm 110:4.

Under the Old Testament system (to which the original Jewish-Christian readers of Hebrews were tempted to return), the important role of priest as intercessor was carried out by flawed men. The contrast with the high priest Son could not be sharper. All humanity is sinful and in need of someone to make us acceptable to the holy one.

Thanks be to God that he has provided the very kind of intercessor high priest that we desperately need: one who is appointed by the Father himself, one who is immortal with an eternal priestly intercession, and one who is absolutely perfect. The earthly, Levitical priests descended from Aaron had none of those characteristics.

CONCLUSION

Do you remember a time when you were overcome by a sudden sense of dread? Perhaps it happened when you were young, out on a playground. For some reason, an older, bigger kid threatened you. When he turned his back, you stuck your tongue out at him. But he saw you and came back at you. Sudden dread!

Later as an adult you see in your rearview mirror those flashing blue lights while you are driving. You look down; you are speeding. A ticket means inconvenience, a fine, and higher insurance rates. If you are just barely making ends meet, how will you make it now? Sudden dread!

When we become aware of our sinful standing before God, the only sensible emotion to have is a sense of dread. The realization that our sin against God makes us his enemy ought to give us an overwhelming sense of dread. We puny humans have no chance of standing up against the wrath of the infinitely powerful God of the universe. Our only chance is if we have an intercessor.

Jesus is the only suitable one to stand up for us. If we come to God through the blood of Jesus, we can be saved to the uttermost. Because God himself has appointed the Son to be our eternal, perfect high priest, we can have confidence of being accepted by God. God's acceptance is not based on our own righteousness, but on the perfection and obedience of the Son. We can live our lives today with no dread, no fear.

Discovery Learning

This page contains an alternative lesson plan emphasizing learning activities. Some of these activities are also found in the helpful student book, NIV Bible Student. *The next page is a reproducible activity page to further enhance discovery learning.*

INTO THE LESSON

Invite a class member (or someone outside the class) who enjoys drama to prepare and present the following monologue on the Old Testament person Melchizedek. In today's text (and in the whole section of Hebrews related to this subject), Jesus' priesthood is shown to be relatively more like that of Melchizedek than that of Aaron. Ask your actor to "dress the part," if appropriate ancient dress is available. Otherwise, let your actor wear a big name label around his neck.

Melchizedek Monologue

"I see you have come to study the one who is the seed of my friend Abraham. Yes, that seed is Jesus; he is my Lord as well as yours. His Father anointed me to his priesthood long before Levi was a twinkle in his earth-ly father's eyes.

"It was my city of Salem (which you now call Jeru-salem) that would one day become the city of the great king. And I don't mean David. My Lord would later sit on the mountain east of my city and bemoan its rejec-tion of his kingship. They never understood how he would or could mediate for them in dying.

"You see that I am shrouded in both priestly garb and kingly regalia. They are both appropriate. Our Lord is both King of kings and high priest of Heaven itself. My own origin and ordination are shrouded in mystery. Can you comprehend the ordination of Christ Jesus to be high priest? Do you understand forever?

"Can you fathom the power of an indestructible life? You will hardly understand who I am or whence I came. But that does not matter. Your great high priest, Christ Jesus—understand him. Understand his offering of his own blood to cover your sins. Who am I, Melchizedek? Only a shadow of the Lord who was and is and is to be. Understand him. See him in the words you study today.

"Now, Abraham did not hesitate to provide a tithe of all that he had to me. He knew it would be used only in worship of God Most High. It has always been true. God expects the honor of our gifts—not simply material offerings, but lives. What will you give him?"

Alternative: To introduce the lesson, let students complete the Bad Priest, Good Priest, Best Priest activity from the Reproducible Page. Place copies in students' chairs to work on as they arrive.

INTO THE WORD

Prepare and distribute copies of the following word-search puzzle.

```
I N T N A N E V O C T E V E
R D E T T A W U C N E N H R
P E R M A N E N T S C Y T U
S G O R I N X N T H T E E P
E U R C E S A S U K O S R R
I A N T E M L N M R S I Z C
E R S S T B T R O E E R O I
N A T S E J E T L S E R S C
E N E T A X D E T Y O A T H
S T T B N S M O L T R I O T
N E L O T A E X R E C L E A
R E C E L S A S O R Y R I E
N T E B R D R E V E R O F D
S A C R I F I C E S I N T E
```

Tell your class that the challenge is to find 14 words from today's text. To add excitement, you can have your learners work in small groups or pairs to see which can finish first. The 14 words to be found are *oath, priest, for-ever, guarantee, covenant, death, permanent, holy, blame-less, pure, sacrifices, once, better, exalted.* Point out that most verses from today's text have at least one word represented in the puzzle. To add difficulty, do not give your learners the list of 14 words they are to find.

INTO LIFE

Ask the class, "If we were still living under the Old Testament system of the Levitical priesthood, how would our daily lives be different?" Answers may include the needed trips to a central location for the sac-rificial work to be accomplished, the purchase of ani-mals to be offered, the necessity of tithes for support of the priesthood and the worship rituals, the required separation of males and females in worship assembly, and the lesser role each of us would play in the media-tion process with God.

Jot responses on the board. Conclude with a simple comment: "Aren't you glad we have Jesus as our high priest, our sacrifice, and our intercessor?" Ask three class members to word prayers of thanksgiving, one each for those three areas of your comment. Distrib-ute copies of the Good You, Better You, Best You activity from the Reproducible Page as take-home work.

Bad Priest, Good Priest, Best Priest

Look at the following Bible texts. All deal with priests. Decide if each is a reference to a bad priest (B), a good priest (G), or the best priest (Jesus).

		_____ Genesis 14:18-20
_____ Exodus 3:1	_____ Exodus 29:1-9	_____ 1 Samuel 2:12-17
_____ Psalm 110:1-4	_____ Amos 7:10-13	_____ Matthew 26:3-5
_____ Luke 1:5-10	_____ Acts 14:13	_____ Ephesians 5:2
_____ Hebrews 8:1, 2	_____ Hebrews 9:11-14	_____ 1 Peter 2:5

Good You, Better You, Best You

From the list below, select your two most important must-do actions that you think your great high priest (Jesus) expects of you this week. Trade your list with someone else and pray for each other's choices.

Push Myself

Be Content

Stick with It

Read the Bible

Repent

Give Proportionally

Ask Forgiveness

Pray Longer

Do What the Bible Says

Ask BIG

Get a Grip on Reality

Be Confident

Reconcile with Someone

Get Help

Look Up

Hold On

Give Sacrificially

Be Joyful

Lend a Hand

Pray More Specifically

PERFECT REDEEMER

| LESSON 3 |

WHY TEACH THIS LESSON?

I convinced Ruby to read the Bible. Instead of starting with the Gospel of John, she insisted on starting with Genesis. When she got to the book of Leviticus, she exclaimed, "This Bible is a bloody book!" Her assessment was correct.

I explained that humans have a problem: despite our best efforts, we cannot shed the guilt of sin by our own efforts. We need help in ridding ourselves of the shameful deeds of the past. When I explained the precious sacrifice of Christ, she nodded in agreement. "I never understood the crucifixion before," she said. "God doesn't see a Christian's sin anymore," she continued. "He only sees the blood of his Son. Without Christ's blood, there is no forgiveness."

Ruby discovered that truth at age 86. She confessed her faith in Jesus and was baptized the following Sunday. The truth of today's lesson can change lives!

INTRODUCTION

A. USING FREQUENT FLIER MILES

Because I fly often, I am careful to get credit for every flight in the various "frequent flier" programs. The system is simple. You accumulate points based on the miles of the flights you take. When you have enough points, you can use them to obtain free tickets or upgrades to first class. When you cash in your points for travel, some programs refer to it as "redeeming" your miles. Redeeming miles is not always so simple, though. Most airlines restrict the use of mileage programs with blackout dates. These are high-demand times when the planes will be full anyway, so airlines hesitate to issue free tickets. Another problem comes when you have many miles accumulated on Airline XYZ, but XYZ doesn't fly to where you want to go. Redeeming frequent flier miles can be a frustrating process.

When the Bible talks about redemption, it intends us to understand something far removed from the imperfect "redemption" programs of modern airlines. To have Christ as our redeemer does not involve unexpected glitches or surprises. The most important difference is that with Christ we have not earned anything we can redeem. He is redeeming us!

B. LESSON BACKGROUND

The theme of *redemption* runs throughout the Bible. In the Old Testament it usually has the idea of saving someone from peril. Thus, a *redeemer* is nearly synonymous with a *deliverer*. By delivering the Israelites from the slavery of Egypt, God redeemed them (see Exodus 15:13; Deuteronomy 15:15). On the human-to-human level, the law allowed family property to be repurchased (redeemed) by a kinsman if it had been sold under distress (Leviticus 25:25).

In other places, the Old Testament authors use the concept of redemption to express personal deliverance (see 2 Samuel 4:9; Job 19:25; compare Psalm 19:14). In general, the Old Testament teaches the principle that God redeems those who serve him (Psalm 34:22).

DEVOTIONAL READING:
JOHN 4:21-26
BACKGROUND SCRIPTURE:
HEBREWS 9:11–10:18
PRINTED TEXT:
HEBREWS 9:11-18; 10:12-18

LESSON AIMS

After participating in this lesson, each student will be able to:

1. Summarize the nature and effects of Christ's sacrifice.

2. Explain how the animal sacrifices of the Old Testament foreshadow the sacrifice of Christ.

3. Write a prayer of gratitude for Christ's sacrifice.

KEY VERSE

He did not enter by means of the blood of goats and calves; but he entered the Most Holy Place once for all by his own blood, having obtained eternal redemption.
—Hebrews 9:12

The later history of Israel saw oppression and exile by foreign nations. In these periods, the Jewish people looked forward to a time when God would redeem them again (see Micah 4:10). This expectation continued into the Israel of Jesus' day. Many Jews looked for deliverance from the Romans (see Luke 2:38; 24:21).

While these ideas of national and personal redemption are important themes in the Bible, the social world of the New Testament understood the language of redemption from the context of the institution of slavery. Redemption was related to the concept of ransom (see Mark 10:45). This was the price paid for a slave who was purchased and then set free.

The New Testament often uses slavery or bondage as an image to express spiritual realities. Paul speaks of three great spiritual tyrants: sin, death, and the law. For example, Paul sees us as being servants (slaves) of sin while in the sinful state of unbelief, unable to do genuine acts of righteousness. Faith in Christ saves/redeems us from this slavery, giving us the freedom to serve Christ (see Romans 6:16-19; 8:2). Christ has truly freed us (Galatians 5:1; compare John 8:32).

The book of Hebrews exhibits both an abundant Old Testament background and an awareness of the social structures of the first-century Roman world. When Hebrews speaks of Christ as the redeemer, it draws upon both worlds. The book's original readers looked to God as Israel's redeemer and deliverer in both past and future senses.

The book of Hebrews also understands the realities of the world of freed slaves, with the gratitude and devotion they felt for the one who rescued them. When it comes to sin, we can never redeem ourselves. Our redemption can be purchased only by the blood of the Son of God, our Savior (Colossians 1:14). This is forgiveness and freedom to live as true servants of our Lord.

I. ETERNAL REDEMPTION (HEBREWS 9:11-14)

The previous sections of Hebrews established Christ as the all-sufficient high priest for the people of God. He is not subject to the failings of the Jewish Levitical priesthood, which amounted to sinful men making continual sin sacrifices for themselves and others. Jesus is presented as the ideal, sinless priest who is not subject to death. Consequently, he will never need to be replaced (see Hebrews 2:17; 7:26-28). The primary function of the Jewish high priest was to offer sacrifices that would atone for the sins of the nation. These sacrifices were offered at the central place of worship for Israel: first the semiportable tabernacle and then the Jerusalem temple. The author of Hebrews draws upon the image of the tabernacle to explain the nature of Christ's sacrifice for our sins.

A. NOT IN THE EARTHLY TABERNACLE (v. 11)
11. When Christ came as high priest of the good things that are already here, he went through the greater and more perfect tabernacle that is not man-made, that is to say, not a part of this creation.

In keeping with his theme of comparing Christianity with the Mosaic covenant, the author uses the ancient tabernacle (rather than the Jerusalem temple) for the point of comparison. The tabernacle was understood to be an earthly representation of the eternal dwelling place of God.

The true tabernacle, however, is in Heaven (Revelation 15:5). God did not dwell in the earthly tabernacle or in the Jerusalem temple (Acts 7:48; 17:24). These merely served as specific locations for the Israelites to perform various offerings for sin. Jesus' work *as a high priest* was not in Jerusalem, but in Heaven at the *greater and more perfect tabernacle* (compare Hebrews 8:2).

Monday, June 9—"I Am He" (John 4:21-26)

Tuesday, June 10—Mediator of a New Covenant (Hebrews 9: 11-15)

Wednesday, June 11—On Our Behalf (Hebrews 9:16-24)

Thursday, June 12—Once for All Time (Hebrews 9:25-28)

Friday, June 13—A One-Time Sacrifice (Hebrews 10: 1-10)

Saturday, June 14—For Our Sanctification (Hebrews 10: 11-14)

Sunday, June 15—Forgiveness Forever (Hebrews 10:15-18)

B. Not by the Blood of Animals (vv. 12-14)

12. He did not enter by means of the blood of goats and calves; but he entered the Most Holy Place once for all by his own blood, having obtained eternal redemption.

One of the high priest's duties was to offer an annual sacrifice for the people on the Day of Atonement (Yom Kippur). This involved the sacrifice of a young bull and a goat, plus the sprinkling of their *blood* on the mercy seat within the Holy of Holies, the innermost chamber of the tabernacle (see Leviticus 16:14, 15). In the Christian system there is no more need for sacrificial animals, because Christ has offered *his own* perfect *blood* for this function. Christ's sacrificial death purchased our *eternal redemption*.

Quantity and Quality

I am always slightly amazed that people have so much difficulty distinguishing between *quantity* and *quality*. In the college classes I teach, I often have students ask if they can turn in "extra credit" work to raise their grade. I always say *no*.

I believe it is not fair to judge some students on the basis of 100 percent of their work and judge others on the basis of 125 percent of their work. Besides, how many *C* papers does it take to raise a grade to a *B*? *C* work should get a grade of *C*; turning in additional work does not raise its quality.

The same principle applies in other areas as well. How many junior high band concerts does it take to equal the quality of a single professional symphony orchestra? How many cans of baked beans does it take to equal an expertly prepared filet mignon? How much blood of bulls and goats does it takes to equal the redeeming value of the blood of the Son of God?

Quantity and *quality* are different things. It is Jesus' sinless quality that makes his blood effective for earning our eternal redemption.   —J. B. N.

13. The blood of goats and bulls and the ashes of a heifer sprinkled on those who are ceremonially unclean sanctify them so that they are outwardly clean.

The author now adds *a heifer* (young cow) to the list of sacrificial animals, an animal whose *blood* and *ashes* were also used in a rite of purification for the people of Israel (see Numbers 19:1-10). The author's point is that these animal sacrifices had an effect, even if only temporarily. If they had been totally ineffective, then God would not have commanded the people of Israel to use them. This does not nullify the author's main point, however, that the animal sacrifices were short-term fixes offered by earthly priests, who had their own sin problems.

14. How much more, then, will the blood of Christ, who through the eternal Spirit offered himself unblemished to God, cleanse our consciences from acts that lead to death, so that we may serve the living God!

This verse contains an important indication regarding the nature of Christ's sacrifice. While the author uses the rich imagery of the tabernacle to help us understand this process, he is not saying that there was an actual ceremony in Heaven at which the ascended and glorified Christ entered Heaven's temple.

Christ's offering was done spiritually (*through the eternal Spirit*). It was done on the physical cross. That was where his perfect *blood* was sprinkled for our purification. Jesus' atoning death was a fulfillment of the intent of the entire sacrificial system of the Old Testament (see Hebrews 12:2).

The author now brings this home to the readers. Christ's death makes human actions of sacrificing animals for sin unnecessary, so any ritualistic behavior has become superfluous. We cannot feel secure by going through the traditional motions of religion. We must *serve the living God*, worshiping him with our lives

What Do You Think?

Jesus' death on the cross is referred to as the substitutionary atonement. What usually comes to your mind when you think of the word substitute? *How is that different from the idea of Jesus being a substitute?*

What Do You Think?

Why do some believers find it hard to understand and accept the sacrifice of Christ for their sins? What would you say to someone having trouble in this area? [Hint: be sure to consider Romans 5:7, 8.]

What Do You Think?

What are some of the "acts that lead to death" you have done instead of being involved in active service? How did you put this behind you?

of obedience. We don't sacrifice bulls, goats, or heifers. We give the Lord our "sacrifice of praise" (Hebrews 13:15), the full expression of our lives of devotion.

II. ETERNAL INHERITANCE (HEBREWS 9:15-18)

The Old Testament is a record of covenants—agreements that included promises of future blessings for those who obeyed and served God. We can distinguish specific covenants with Abraham, Moses, David, and others—thus the plural phrase "covenants of the promise" (Ephesians 2:12). The authors of the New Testament tend to lump all of the pre-Christ covenants together as the "old covenant" or "old testament." This idea of an old covenant became synonymous with the Scriptures of the Jewish people, what Christians now call the Old Testament (see 2 Corinthians 3:14).

The word translated *covenant* has a dual meaning. It can carry the sense of a binding agreement between two parties. It can also have the sense of a person's will, one's instructions for disposing of possessions after death. Here, Hebrews uses both senses in that a new covenant begins with the death of the covenant maker.

A. New Covenant (v. 15)

15. For this reason Christ is the mediator of a new covenant, that those who are called may receive the promised eternal inheritance—now that he has died as a ransom to set them free from the sins committed under the first covenant.

A *mediator* is one who brings two sides together into an agreement. Jesus did this by his death. Jesus' sacrificial blood makes possible and begins the *new covenant* (see Luke 22:20). The *first covenant* is not so much nullified as it is now fulfilled completely.

God redeems his chosen people in an eternal, spiritual way. This is much more important to him than defeating the national enemies of Israel like the Roman Empire. The Lord has brought about a redemption that frees men and women from the curse of sin and gives them an *eternal inheritance,* meaning eternal life (see John 3:16).

B. Enforceable Will (vv. 16-18)

16, 17. In the case of a will, it is necessary to prove the death of the one who made it, because a will is in force only when somebody has died; it never takes effect while the one who made it is living.

Hebrews emphasizes the importance of the death of Jesus. From the context of the Old Testament and its sacrificial system, there had to be a *death* for sins. From the context of a last *will* and testament, the terms of the will are not valid until *the one who* makes the will is dead. Then the will comes into *force*.

18. This is why even the first covenant was not put into effect without blood.

Animal sacrifice is a bloody business. Altars are made with drainage systems so that the *blood* can be collected and removed. It has been speculated that the city of Jerusalem in Jesus' day must have had a terrible stench from the continual burning of animal flesh. The smell of spoiling blood is repulsive in and of itself. To the residents of the city, this pervasive odor is a constant reminder of their sin.

We, as Christians, are reminded of this bloody requirement every time we participate of the Lord's Supper. We remember the precious blood of Jesus that was shed for our sins. We should never forget that sin is not forgiven by God without the shedding of blood (Hebrews 9:22).

How to Say It

Hebrews. HEE-brews.
Israel. IZ-ray-el.
Jerusalem. Juh-ROO-suh-lem.
Levitical. Leh-VIT-ih-kul.
Leviticus. Leh-VIT-ih-kus.
Melchizedek. Mel-KIZ-eh-dek.
Micah. MY-kuh.
Mosaic. Mo-ZAY-ik.
Moses. MO-zes or MO-zez.
Yom Kippur. Yom Kih-PUR.

III. ETERNAL FORGIVENESS (HEBREWS 10:12-18)

We Christians know we are saved, but we may forget what we are saved *from*: eternal punishment by God. Unless our sin problem is taken care of in a permanent way, we always live under the threat of the future wrath of God being poured out on us. This section of Hebrews lifts up the eternal nature of our forgiveness through the blood of our Savior, Jesus Christ.

A. CHRIST SITS AT GOD'S RIGHT HAND (vv. 12, 13)

12, 13. But when this priest had offered for all time one sacrifice for sins, he sat down at the right hand of God. Since that time he waits for his enemies to be made his footstool,

The author draws upon the Melchizedek psalm (Psalm 110) once again to help explain the current position of Jesus. Christ has been enthroned with God and now awaits the full submission of all creation to his sovereignty. This is expressed symbolically as having his *enemies* made into a *footstool* (see Hebrews 1:13; compare 1 Peter 3:22). Even though Christ reigns in Heaven, there is a sense that not all things have become subject to him just yet (Hebrews 2:8). One thing that remains is the final destruction of death itself (1 Corinthians 15:26).

B. CHRIST PERFECTS THE SANCTIFIED (v. 14)

14. . . . because by one sacrifice he has made perfect forever those who are being made holy.

We are not *holy* through our own efforts, but because Christ's atoning death has taken away the taint of sin in our lives. The author does not mean that we have eliminated sin from daily life, but that in God's eyes we are *made perfect* because our sins are forgiven. We don't need to seek out a temple and slaughter animals as a proxy sacrifice.

C. CHRIST REMITS OUR SINS (vv. 15-18)

15, 16. The Holy Spirit also testifies to us about this. First he says:
"This is the covenant I will make with them
after that time, says the Lord.
I will put my laws in their hearts,
and I will write them on their minds."

The author continues the method of using the Old Testament promises to help the readers understand the wonders of forgiveness in Christ. In this case, the author repeats some of the words of Jeremiah 31, which Hebrews 8 discusses extensively. This should cause us to remember that while the sacrificial system of the old covenant has been superseded in Christ, the Old Testament is still a valid Word of God, a witness from the *Holy Spirit.*

This verse serves as a warning against legalism. We do not follow a detailed written code, nor may we impose such a thing on others. Instead, we are controlled by the internal witness of the written Word through the power of the Holy Spirit. We are controlled by the great ethical principles taught by Jesus: to love God fully and to think of others more highly than ourselves.

HEARTS AND MINDS

One of the greatest emperors in ancient history was Justinian, who ruled the Byzantine Empire from AD 527 to 565. He revitalized the empire in numerous ways—reconquering half of the old western Roman Empire, reorganizing the government, and restructuring the army and the finances.

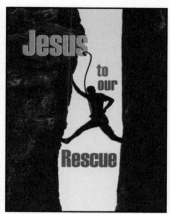

Visual for Lesson 3. *Point to this visual as you ask, "What attitude is necessary on our part to allow Jesus to rescue us?"*

WHAT DO YOU THINK?

What gives you confidence in the promise of your eternal inheritance? How do you live out this confidence?

PRAYER

Lord God, who reigns in majesty from Heaven, we offer our thanks for our redemption through Jesus Christ. May we live as people who are not under the threat of punishment, but as those who have been redeemed. We pray this in the name of our Redeemer, Jesus, amen.

WHAT DO YOU THINK?

Since our works are not an offering made for the forgiveness of our sins, why bother doing good works? How have you grown in your motives in this regard?

THOUGHT TO REMEMBER

The perfect Christ perfects us.

But one of his greatest achievements was codifying the laws of the empire. For centuries, the old Roman Empire had adopted various laws, but it had been a long time since they were organized. The result was that often various legal enactments contradicted each other. Justinian saw the problems with this and made legal revision a high priority for his reign. The revisions became the basis of law codes for much of the rest of western civilization.

Others have followed Justinian's precedent of organizing (or attempting to organize) laws. Some years ago the U.S. Congress revised the Internal Revenue Code into over a thousand bewildering pages. And that became the problem! The common report is that even agents of the Internal Revenue Service are not consistent in applying the code. All those laws, written on paper, are hard to remember and even more difficult to understand. God has a better plan: he writes the laws of the new covenant on our hearts and in our minds. —J. B. N.

17. Then he adds:
   "Their sins and lawless acts
      I will remember no more."

Under certain circumstances, a bank may be willing to "forgive" a debt through bankruptcy proceedings. But we may rest assured that the unpaid debt is not forgotten. It will be included on credit reports for many years and may make future loans impossible. The promise in this verse is truly astounding. Through Christ, our *sins* have not just been moved from the *unforgiven* column to the *forgiven* side of the ledger. They have been blotted out completely (see Acts 3:19).

18. And where these have been forgiven, there is no longer any sacrifice for sin.

Because of the all-sufficient and eternal nature of our forgiveness through the blood of Jesus, the old sacrificial system (which was so integral to the Judaism of Jesus' day) is rendered redundant and unnecessary. We need not worry about a temple in Jerusalem, for our eternal high priest is in Heaven. His sacrifice for sins has been accepted once for all time.

CONCLUSION

Tradition says that when Roman gladiators entered the Coliseum for their contests, they would address the emperor's box by saying, "We who are about to die salute you!" These brutal men lived their last days with the knowledge that they had survived only to provide a spectacle in their deaths.

A Christian believer's acknowledgement of the Lord should be the flip side of the gladiator salute. Daily we could say, "We who have been rescued from death serve you!" We should celebrate our redemption. We must never forget that our salvation has been accomplished by the sacrificial blood of Jesus, not by our own efforts. We are not part of a team that has developed a successful strategy to avoid the consequences of sin. We are all, individually and as a whole, utterly beholden to Jesus for delivering us from eternal death.

Understanding this has a leveling effect in the church. Some church members may be more prominent and have more authority than other members. Some believers may be more mature in the faith or more learned in the Word than others. Some may have inspiring stories of persecution endured or hardship overcome. But every Christian, young or old, male or female, black or white, rich or poor, has exactly the same status before God. He or she is a sinner who has been granted redemption through the work of our eternal high priest, Jesus Christ.

There is no room for comparisons or boasting here, for we are all equally winners (see Ephesians 2:9). The church is the community of those redeemed from the slavery of sin to live in joyful service to our king.

Discovery Learning

This page contains an alternative lesson plan emphasizing learning activities. Some of these activities are also found in the helpful student book, NIV Bible Student. The next page is a reproducible activity page to further enhance discovery learning.

INTO THE LESSON

Display a grid with the word *ETERNAL* running horizontally. Have three blank spaces above the first *E* and six spaces below (for the word *REDEMPTION*). Have two blank spaces above the *R* and eight spaces below (for the word *FORGIVENESS*). Have seven blank spaces above the *A* and three spaces below (for the word *INHERITANCE*). When completed per the following, you will have on display the outline of today's text: I. Eternal Redemption; II. Eternal Inheritance; III. Eternal Forgiveness.

To fill in the blanks, say to your learners, "Three words will complete this grid and provide an outline of our study today. What letters do you think belong in the blanks? Give me one at a time." As learners suggest letters, fill in the ones that are correct. Continue until all are complete. Note to the class, "Here we have the writer's outline of our study today."

To verify your group's understanding of the concept of redemption, ask them in what ways the term is used today. Expect such responses as "redeeming airline frequent flier miles," "redeeming bonus points at banks or other businesses," and in the sense of someone having "a redeeming quality" that helps cancel out more obvious negative qualities. Introduce the writer's explanation of the concept in the first-century Roman world and thus, in many respects, the New Testament usage.

INTO THE WORD

Divide your class into two groups, a *Hebrews 9 Group* and a *Hebrews 10 Group* for an antiphonal reading. The readings will be Hebrews 9:11-18 and Hebrews 10:12-18. Direct the groups to alternate verses: the *Hebrews 10 Group* begins by reading 10:12, then the *Hebrews 9 Group* reads 9:11; the *Hebrews 10 Group* reads 10:13, the *Hebrews 9 Group* reads 9:12; and so forth. Though these texts are not perfectly parallel, reading them in this back-and-forth manner will work, and several interesting pairings will be seen.

Next, give your learners the following list of Bible verses with this direction: "Look up each of these verses and relate each to a specific verse in today's text. Decide which is the best match for each. You may change your mind as you look up more verses." (This activity may be done as a group activity, or you may allow time for

individuals to make matches before the class as a whole looks at decisions.)

References: Exodus 27:1, 2; Numbers 19:9; Numbers 27:8-11; 1 Chronicles 6:49; Psalm 110:1; Isaiah 59:20, 21; Jeremiah 31:33; Jeremiah 31:34; Luke 24:46, 47; John 2:19; John 5:36; 2 Timothy 2:21; Hebrews 7:27; 1 Peter 3:22.

Consider these to be appropriate matches: Exodus 27:1, 2 with Hebrews 9:18 (in the sense that the Hebrew worship required an altar for sacrifice; it required blood); Numbers 19:9 with Hebrews 9:13; Numbers 27:8-11 with Hebrews 9:16, 17 (in that it speaks of inheritances being given at the death of a person); 1 Chronicles 6:49 with Hebrews 9:12 (both having to do with entering the Holy of Holies); Psalm 110:1 with Hebrews 10:12; Isaiah 59:20, 21 with Hebrews 9:15; Jeremiah 31:33 with Hebrews 10:16; Jeremiah 31:34 with Hebrews 10:17; Luke 24:46, 47 with Hebrews 10:18 (as both deal with forgiveness of sins by sacrifice); John 2:19 with Hebrews 9:11, 12 (former deals with the heavenly tabernacle, the other with the tabernacle of Christ's body); John 5:36 with Hebrews 10:15 (as each refers to the testimony of the Spirit); 2 Timothy 2:21 with Hebrews 9:14 (both deal with individuals cleansed for service to God); Hebrews 7:27 with Hebrews 10:14 (each emphasizes the once-for-all sacrifice of Christ); 1 Peter 3:22 with Hebrews 10:12.

Expect other matches as well; ask for reasons why.

INTO LIFE

Distribute copies of the following, with a suggestion that your learners fill it in as their personal reflection on the redemptive grace of God.

"Lord, I sold myself to _____; You bought me back at _____. I sold myself for _____; You bought me back in _____. I sold myself by _____; You bought me back by _____. I sold myself too _____; You bought me back with _____. Thank You, Lord, for Your redeeming love in Christ."

Alternative: The Reproducible Page includes the words to the hymn-poem "Redeemed, How I Love to Proclaim It!" Have someone lead the class in singing this hymn before your learners complete the Do I Love to Proclaim It? activity. Distribute the Redeemed from Slavery activity as a take-home exercise.

Do I Love to Proclaim It?

Fanny Crosby's classic hymn-poem below is a beautiful personal exclamation of full appreciation for the redemption we have received in Christ's death. Make personal notes to the right of the lines that reflect your own gratitude for God's gift in Christ's blood.

Redeemed, how I love to proclaim it!
Redeemed by the blood of the Lamb;
Redeemed through His infinite mercy,
His child and forever I am.

Redeemed and so happy in Jesus,
No language my rapture can tell;
I know that the light of His presence
With me doth continually dwell.

I think of my blessed Redeemer,
I think of Him all the day long:
I sing, for I cannot be silent;
His love is the theme of my song.

I know I shall see in His beauty
The King in whose law I delight;
Who lovingly guardeth my footsteps,
And giveth me songs in the night.

REFRAIN
Redeemed, redeemed,
Redeemed by the blood of the Lamb;
Redeemed, redeemed,
His child and forever I am.

Redeemed from Slavery

Jesus affirmed it clearly: "I tell you the truth, everyone who sins is a slave to sin" (John 8:34). But on the same occasion, he joyfully announces, "If the Son sets you free, you will be free indeed" (John 8:36) On the chain links below write in some of the sins that—at one time earlier and even today—enslaved you. On each link that is no longer binding you, superimpose a cross. For those links yet unbroken, consider what you need to do to allow the Son to set you free.

TRUSTWORTHY LEADER

LESSON 4

WHY TEACH THIS LESSON?

People gravitate toward leaders who live what they believe. Unfortunately, even the greatest of heroes can disappoint us. What do you do when you have been disappointed so many times that you are fearful of trusting again?

Christians will imitate a life that is authentic. An authentic person is one who has received the discipline of God and has responded by living a self-disciplined life. We are thankful for the example we see in the lives of the great heroes of the faith (Hebrews 11). Even so, they all had their moments of failure.

Jesus is the only perfect example of faith. Those who put their trust in him will never be disappointed. This lesson shows us how and why to "fix our eyes on Jesus" (Hebrews 12:2).

INTRODUCTION

A. CHEATING TO WIN

Cheating scandals seem to confront us on a continual basis in the world of professional sports. Baseball players take illegal performance-enhancing supplements to make themselves stronger and faster. Hockey players alter their sticks to give an advantage the rules do not allow. Race car drivers violate their sport's regulations by installing hidden equipment to improve their cars' performance.

Cheating is rampant in other areas of life too. Business leaders "cook the books" to create the illusion of more profit in order to secure bigger performance bonuses. Scientists engage in fraudulent or misleading research in order to make a name for themselves. Students freely admit to cheating on exams, claiming that this behavior is necessary to give them a competitive advantage over other students and thereby gain admission to the best colleges or graduate schools. Too often, people are living under the impression that cheating is the only way to win.

In every area of life, then, society is forced to set up ever tougher enforcement agencies. We must catch those cheaters! We have moved to a cat-and-mouse game in which some say, "I will cheat unless there is a substantial risk of being caught." The onus for cheating prevention is now on those enforcing the rules, not on the cheaters themselves. We have moved a long way from having most participants simply say, "I won't cheat."

All of this is a matter of discipline. A *disciplined* person is one who abstains from cheating and resolves to follow the rules. This person submits to discipline, even when doing things the right way is doing things the hard way. This person is more concerned about living within the rules than questioning the fairness of the rules. True discipline and cheating are incompatible and irreconcilable. In the end, avoiding discipline by cheating is for losers. Winning by cheating is a hollow, empty victory. This lesson looks at some of the key elements of the disciplined life of a Christian, a life where there is no place for cheating.

DEVOTIONAL READING:
PROVERBS 3:5-12
BACKGROUND SCRIPTURE:
HEBREWS 12:1-13
PRINTED TEXT:
HEBREWS 12:1-13

Jun
22

LESSON AIMS

After participating in this lesson, each student will be able to:

1. Describe the role and the importance of discipline in the training of an athlete and in rearing a child.

2. Compare and contrast human discipline with God's discipline.

3. Identify one area where he or she needs to submit to divine discipline.

KEY VERSES

Let us throw off everything that hinders and the sin that so easily entangles, and let us run with perseverance the race marked out for us. Let us fix our eyes on Jesus, the author and perfecter of our faith.
—Hebrews 12:1, 2

LESSON 4 NOTES

B. LESSON BACKGROUND

Today's lesson text follows one of the most famous chapters in the New Testament, Hebrews 11. That chapter is known as the "Faith Hall of Fame." It is a rehearsal of the lives of several key Old Testament saints, showing how they lived by faith in God. Yet the chapter ends by noting, "These were all commended for their faith, yet none of them received what had been promised" (11:39).

The Old Testament faithful could only look ahead to the blessings enjoyed by Christians. The original community receiving the letter to the Hebrews was facing hardship (Hebrews 10:32-34), even persecution. The author of Hebrews did not want his readers to think that they were alone in enduring hardships; the earlier people of God had it rough too. A frequent exhortation in the book is to "hold," "hold firmly," or "hold unswervingly" to the precious faith in Christ (see Hebrews 3:6, 14; 4:14; 10:23).

Chapter 12, this lesson's focus, gets down to some of the nitty-gritty details of this "holding firmly." Not only will there be hardships imposed on the believers from the outside, there will be hardships that come from God himself. This is the chastening of God. As the author clearly portrays, it is discipline designed for the benefit of the believer. The central principle in this chapter is that such discipline is part of his love.

Discipline could be harsh in the ancient world. The success of the Roman army was built on ruthless discipline within the legions. Apprentices learning a trade were forced to work long hours. Yet there was another side to discipline in this era too. To be *a disciple* meant that you were a student. You had attached yourself to a teacher and allowed him to be your master in all things.

This relationship was more than tutoring once or twice a week. The teacher-disciple arrangement was often a "24/7" situation, where the teacher was in total control of the student's life. This is the way the book of Hebrews pictures the relationship of Christians to God. God is concerned with every aspect of our lives and uses corrective discipline to bring us to advanced levels of godliness and holiness.

I. PREPARING TO RUN WITH JESUS (HEBREWS 12:1, 2)

At the end of chapter 11, we are told that the great faith heroes of the Old Testament could not be "made perfect" (Hebrews 11:40). This expression was sometimes used of runners who could not finish a race. The author of Hebrews continues this race analogy into chapter 12, now applying it to Christians.

A. DISCARDING OUR BAGGAGE (v. 1)

1. *Therefore, since we are surrounded by such a great cloud of witnesses, let us throw off everything that hinders and the sin that so easily entangles, and let us run with perseverance the race marked out for us.*

This verse paints a marvelous picture. Imagine the premier running *race* in all the world: the marathon at the Olympic games. A handful of runners, the world's finest, are at the starting line. Thousands of spectators await the starting gun. But this crowd is magnified to perhaps two or three billion people via worldwide television. That would be *a great cloud of witnesses!*

The runners are wearing the barest of essential clothing. They have shed their warm-up suits. They are not carrying their duffle bags. Some have even shaved their bodies to rid themselves of a tiny amount of weight. Their training has increased their endurance and eliminated excess body fat. They have thrown *off everything* that might slow them down.

The analogy to the Christian life has to do with personal sin. The author's point is that sin slows us down in our pursuit of godliness. We know the race-course. We want to finish the race. Sin hinders our success. Unchecked sin in our lives may slow us down, get us off course, or even stop us dead in our tracks. We want to be like Paul, who at the end of his life was able to say, "I have finished the race, I have kept the faith" (2 Timothy 4:7).

B. DISCERNING OUR GOAL (v. 2)

2. Let us fix our eyes on Jesus, the author and perfecter of our faith, who for the joy set before him endured the cross, scorning its shame, and sat down at the right hand of the throne of God.

The text continues the race analogy, now with a slight shift. The author speaks of *Jesus* as the runner, and *the cross* as the race. Jesus was willing to accept the hard things of his run. He was not deterred by the *shame* of his scandalous death, a gruesome execution befitting the worst criminal. He was a finisher, not a quitter. In this Jesus has shown us the way, the way of *our faith*, the way we too should run the course of our lives in submission to his leadership.

We also see the great reward Jesus has gained. It is more than an Olympic gold medal or a huge signing bonus for the next season. Jesus has been recognized once and for all by being given a seat *at the right hand of the throne of God*. There is no higher honor available.

II. TRAINING TO RUN WITH JESUS (HEBREWS 12:3-11)

The author of Hebrews continues to describe the Christian life in terms of athletic competition. The author uses the metaphor of the oldest competition known to humans: running races. The intent is for us to see this race as a lifelong event, not a short sprint. We run and learn how to run better at the same time. We are in the race of our lives!

A. STRIVING AGAINST SIN (vv. 3, 4)

3. Consider him who endured such opposition from sinful men, so that you will not grow weary and lose heart.

Distance runners know that in the race there comes a time when the runner wants to quit. The body screams, "Enough!" Lungs are burning. Legs are rubbery. The runner feels *weary*, oh so weary!

The race that Jesus ran was made tortuous because of the *opposition from sinful men*, meaning the resistance he encountered from the leadership of the Jews in his day. He *endured* public denunciations, name-calling, threats of death, attempts to dissuade his disciples from following him, and eventually arrest and crucifixion. While this atoning death made our salvation possible, the life of Jesus also serves as an example and inspiration to those who follow him.

4. In your struggle against sin, you have not yet resisted to the point of shedding your blood.

For the book of Hebrews, to live by faith is to *struggle against sin*. The life of faith engages in a constant fight against sin, for "everything that does not come from faith is sin" (Romans 14:23).

The great faith heroes of chapter 11 were surely beset by doubts. They had opportunities to disobey God and serve themselves. The author reminds us that although living the Christian life can be challenging, most of us do not suffer death (resist *to the point of shedding [our] blood*) in our efforts to resist temptation and avoid falling to sin. Our efforts, no matter how great, will not equal the sacrifices made by our leader, Jesus.

B. DEALING WITH DISCIPLINE (vv. 5-11)

5, 6. And you have forgotten that word of encouragement that addresses you as sons:

> *"My son, do not make light of the Lord's discipline,*
> *and do not lose heart when he rebukes you,*
> *because the Lord disciplines those he loves,*
> *and he punishes everyone he accepts as a son."*

A frequent theme in the Old Testament is that God's corrective punishment of Israel is motivated from God's love for Israel (see Deuteronomy 8:5; compare Revelation 3:19). One of the ways in which God is our "Father" is in this matter of discipline. The author uses Proverbs 3:11 to make a point: hardship in life is not a sign of God's disfavor. It may be a manifestation of God's love through corrective *discipline*.

A hard lesson of parenthood is that love for a child is sometimes expressed in the form of discipline. The coddled child who is never told *no* and never experiences parental punishment will be ill equipped to live with the harsh realities of the adult world. Those parents who avoid the painful task of correction and discipline are really thinking more of themselves than of their children.

7, 8. Endure hardship as discipline; God is treating you as sons. For what son is not disciplined by his father? If you are not disciplined (and everyone undergoes discipline), then you are illegitimate children and not true sons.

Sometimes when we are discouraged by the turn of events in our lives, we want to ask, "Where is God in all of this?" The answer is that God may be right in the middle of it. God takes no joy in seeing his children suffer. He is not a masochist. Our pain does not bring him pleasure. Yet God never abdicates his role as our corrective parent (compare 2 Samuel 7:14).

The author reminds us that we should not fear the hardships that God allows into our lives. We should fear the day when the hardships cease, for that would be the time when we are *not true sons*. That would be a day when God truly abandons us, a day when we become God-forsaken. That would be a time when God gives us up to the depraved lusts of our passions (see Romans 1:26, 27).

9. Moreover, we have all had human fathers who disciplined us and we respected them for it. How much more should we submit to the Father of our spirits and live!

From an adult perspective it is easier to understand that discipline given by our parents was for our own benefit. This principle, however, is not a justification for the cruel, abusive behavior practiced by some parents. Firm and consistent guidelines in the formative years give children the possibility of being self-disciplined as adults.

In the normal course of life, then, we do not hold a grudge against the parent who taught us self-discipline. Instead, we respect that effort, and we are blessed by it. Likewise, we should understand that God's discipline in our lives is motivated by God's concern for us. We give him the respect he deserves, even in the most trying of times.

10. Our fathers disciplined us for a little while as they thought best; but God disciplines us for our good, that we may share in his holiness.

Discipline by human parents is never perfect. Parents use their best judgment (*as they* think *best*) when administering discipline. Some parents are too harsh; some are too lenient. But God's discipline is always just right. The Lord has no

---

WHAT DO YOU THINK?

What was a time when you believe you were chastened or rebuked by the Lord? How did you grow spiritually as a result?

WHAT DO YOU THINK?

How can you show reverence to God when he corrects your behavior?

need to relieve his frustrations through brutality or abuse. His goal is our perfection, our attainment of *holiness*. On the practical level, holiness is not achieved in one fell swoop. It is more commonly the process of conquering one sinful behavior at a time. In this, God's firm hand of discipline is pushing us along in our faithful, lifelong pursuit of holiness.

11. No discipline seems pleasant at the time, but painful. Later on, however, it produces a harvest of righteousness and peace for those who have been trained by it.

One oft-repeated phrase in many disciplines is *no pain, no gain.* We do not become smarter by taking a smart pill. We do not become accomplished musicians by merely buying a guitar. We do not become skilled athletes by watching games on television.

This verse continues the athletic training analogy by saying that our trials are ways in which we are *trained*. The Greek word behind *trained* is also the root for our word *gymnasium*. This word is drawn from the athletic terminology of the ancient Greeks. The gymnasium was (and still is) a place where athletes practiced wrestling, did strength-building exercises, and participated in other activities to develop their abilities. Perhaps we can view life as God's gymnasium: the place where we receive ongoing training in our faithful pursuit of holiness in order to produce *a harvest of righteousness* (compare James 3:17, 18).

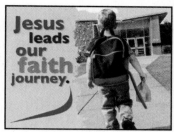

Visual for Lesson 4. *Point to this visual as you ask for volunteers to describe some important parts of their faith journeys.*

CHASTENING

Some yeas ago, I had a friend who had instructed his son on how to mow the lawn. He showed him all that was to be done—not only cutting the grass, but also trimming around the trees and sweeping up the clippings. For this task, the father promised five dollars (a goodly sum in those days!).

Accordingly, the son cut the grass and swept up the clippings, but he neglected trimming around the trees. When his dad came home and inspected the job, he said that the son had failed to fulfill his assignment and there would be no pay. The son pleaded for the opportunity for a second chance to trim around the trees properly. But his dad refused. Because the job was not done right, there was no financial reward.

The boy was disappointed, but the next time he was asked to mow the grass, he did a thorough job and got paid. In fact, he got so good at it he was soon asked to mow other people's lawns. He worked his way through college by doing yard work. If his dad had let him off the hook on his first assignment, perhaps he never would have learned the lesson of doing a job right the first time. As it was, the father's chastisement resulted in a valuable lesson for the future. Such is true in the Christian life as well.   —J. B. N.

III. HEALING TO RUN WITH JESUS (HEBREWS 12:12, 13)

The tone changes in this section to one of exhortation. The readers are encouraged not to be deterred by the prospect of God's chastening.

A. ADJUSTING ATTITUDE (v. 12)

12. Therefore, strengthen your feeble arms and weak knees.

The idea of the athlete in training is continued. Toward the end of a basketball game, coaches remind fatigued players to keep their *arms* up and keep moving their feet when playing defense. Here, the exhortation is to *strengthen* arms and *knees*. The underlying idea is that we must grow strong again and not be overcome by weariness. We cannot let fatigue defeat us. We claim God's promise that we may "run and not grow weary . . . walk and not be faint" (Isaiah 40:31; compare 35:3).

How to Say It
Barak. BAIR-uk.
Enoch. E-nock
Jephthah. JEF-thuh.
marathon. MEHR-uh-thon.

What are some signs that we have reached a plateau in our faith because of spiritual fatigue? How do we correct course?

This is not athletic training advice, however. It is spiritual instruction. We cannot be satisfied with reaching a certain level in our walk with God, or "plateauing." We must continue to employ our hands to work for God. We must stay on our feet and continue our spiritual journey, even if our knees are aching.

ENCOURAGING THE WEARY

Encouraging the discouraged sometimes can be done with gentle words of support; sometimes it has to be done with harsh words of censure. Consider the case of Eddie Rickenbacker (1890–1973).

Rickenbacker was a U.S. World War I Air Corps hero. He was credited with 26 victories, the highest number of any American. After the war he became a pioneer in commercial aviation. During World War II he offered his civilian services to the government, touring air bases and doing public relations work for the military.

He found himself on a tour of bases in the Pacific in October of 1942. Flying west from Hawaii in a B-17, the pilot missed Canton Island, and the plane had to ditch in the Pacific. Rickenbacker and the crew floated on the sea for 24 days, staying alive by eating the occasional fish or captured bird and drinking rainwater.

Rickenbacker became the unofficial encourager of the group, occasionally resorting to browbeating and caustic remarks. He never let them give up. Sometimes he made them hate him, hopefully giving them enough reason to continue to live, if for no other reason than to kill and eat him at the right time.

Throughout the ordeal, Rickenbacker's intention was to strengthen the "feeble arms and weak knees." Hopefully, our encouragement can be done in ways more polite than some that Rickenbacker had to use! But whatever the method, the ultimate purpose is the eternal rescue of others.   —J. B. N.

PRAYER

Lord God, we know that our lives are not always journeys of joy. May we not forget that pain and trials are not signs of your lack of love, and that you will never abandon us. Please help us turn times of trial into opportunities to trust you more. We pray this in the name of our leader in the faith, Jesus Christ, your beloved Son, amen.

B. KEEPING ON COURSE (v. 13)

13. "Make level paths for your feet," so that the lame may not be disabled, but rather healed.

The section ends by giving a leadership principle. Why must we continue to work and walk with God? Because there are people following us. There are those who are spiritually *disabled*, the *lame*, who need a strong leader walking in *level paths*. If leaders sit down or turn aside, these will never be *healed*. We should not forget that traveling the paths of righteousness is not a solo journey. There is no place for spiritual selfishness in the church. The spiritually strong are expected to help the weak (see Acts 20:35). Parents will want to make sure their children are walking with the Lord. Teachers should be leading their students to the throne of God. Elders and ministers must never forget the flock they are leading.

CONCLUSION

We refer to subject areas that are learned or skills that are mastered as *disciplines*. We become accomplished in these areas by watching others who have already mastered the discipline. Sometimes we submit to the tutelage of teachers who are experienced in developing raw ability into proficiency. Whether this be in athletics, music, acting, or writing, no one is a complete "natural" with a full array of inherited skills. Even those with physical gifts and inclinations in a certain area become true masters through disciplined practice.

Why should we think the most important "skill" in the world, living the Christian life, is any different? It likewise is not something we are born with. It is a discipline that we learn by observing our master, Jesus Christ, and by submitting to his teachings. This is not always an easy road, as our lesson today has shown. But eternity will make it all worthwhile.

Discovery Learning

This page contains an alternative lesson plan emphasizing learning activities. Some of these activities are also found in the helpful student book, NIV Bible Student. The next page is a reproducible activity page to further enhance discovery learning.

INTO THE LESSON

Prepare colorful labels for each of the following names and groups, all found in the "Faith Hall of Fame" in Hebrews 11: Abel; Enoch; Noah; Abraham; Isaac; Jacob; Joseph; Moses' Parents; Moses; the Hebrews of the Exodus; Rahab; Gideon; Barak; Samson; Jephthah; David; Samuel; the Prophets. Post these randomly around your assembly space.

As class begins, ask, "Who can tell me what all these people had in common?" The key responses are "faith in God" and "each is honored as an example in Hebrews 11." If the group hesitates, have someone read Hebrews 12:1 to elicit the responses.

Turn to today's text and say, "Seeing that we are surrounded by such a large number of those exemplifying faith in God, let's talk about our need for their discipline, patience, and perseverance, to follow their example."

INTO THE WORD

Tell your learners that you are going to present some "Principles of Discipline" based on today's text in Hebrews 12. Ask them to identify verses that justify or contradict the principles you are stating. Suggested verses are given here after each statement, but those should not be read with the statements.

1. Jesus is the ideal example of a disciplined person (v. 2); 2. The rigors of discipline hardly ever seem pleasant (v. 11a); 3. The good parent will correct and direct the child he or she loves (v. 7); 4. Good things result in the life of the disciplined one (v. 11b); 5. It is possible that physical and mental weariness will interfere with commitment (v. 3b); 6. Opposition is to be expected when one has worthy personal goals (v. 3); 7. External discipline should be respected, not rejected (v. 9); 8. Discipline from God should be considered punishment, not a matter of holiness demanded (v. 10); 9. Those who have achieved success are worthy models for the one trying to do right (v. 1); 10. Some parents discipline children for the feelings of power it gives them (v. 10a). 11. God is wiser than human parents; he knows what discipline will help us most (v. 9); 12. Holding on to old habits makes forming new habits more difficult (v. 1); 13. "No pain, no gain" may be true in the spiritual disciplines as well, but few die in their striving for godliness (v. 4); 14. The Christian should consider life to be God's gymnasium, a place to work out in righteousness (v. 11; *see writer's notes*); 15. The one who stays on God's level path sets an example for the weaker who follow (v. 13); 16. When arms flop at one's sides and knees wobble in fatigue, that is the time for extra effort for self or encouragement of others (vv. 12, 13).

Today's lesson demonstrates that the discipline in life that characterized the Lord in his journey to the cross will give success to any who follow him. Give your class the following two lists, one from ideas in the text in Hebrews 12 and one of other biblical texts. Ask students to match the elements in the first with the incidents and/or quotes in the second.

List A: 1. The good leader is fully aware of those watching his or her progress with interest and support. 2. The good leader realizes some things have to be left behind in order to make progress. 3. The good leader knows that the example of a successful life is important to those who follow. 4. The good leader can foresee the results of success. 5. The good leader expects opposition, both fair and unfair. 6. The good leader knows that any goal worth pursuing will involve some setbacks and disappointments. 7. The good leader is sensitive to God's correction of his or her plans. 8. The good leader experiences both joy and grief. 9. The good leader stops to help those who flag in the process.

List B: a. Matthew 8:19-22; b. Matthew 14:28-32; c. Matthew 16:24-28; d. Matthew 17:1-3; e. Mark 14:35, 36; f. Luke 22:3-5; g. John 6:61-68; h. John 11:33-35, 43, 44; i. Acts 7:55, 56.

Matches: 1-d, 2-a, 3-c, 4-i, 5-f, 6-g, 7-e, 8-h, 9-b.

INTO LIFE

Children often know when they deserve and need correction. The same is true of the child of God. Remind your class of these truths.

Suggest that your learners examine themselves and make a commitment of submission to God's discipline in one needed aspect in their lives. This is an area where having an accountability partner can help. (You can use either The Weighted Runner or the Teach Me, Lord activity from the Reproducible Page at this point. Distribute the other as a take-home exercise.)

The Weighted Runner

Some try to live the Christian life with lots of "baggage" from their earlier, ungodly lifestyle. This baggage can take the form of sins and distractions that the believer won't release.

On the weights to the right, list what some of these sins and distractions might be. One example is given to get you started.

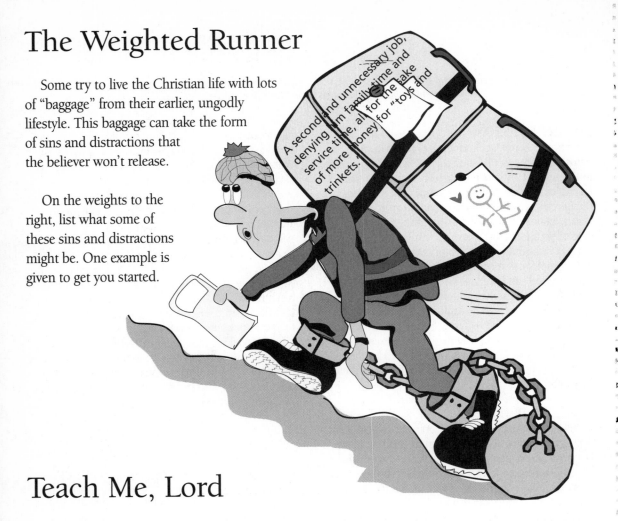

A second and unnecessary job, denying him family time and service time, all for the sake of more money for "toys and trinkets."

Teach Me, Lord

Have you "forgotten that word of encouragement that addresses you as sons"? Do you "make light of the Lord's discipline"? Do you "lose heart when he rebukes you"? Do you "endure hardship as discipline"? Do you sense his love in discipline? (See Hebrews 12:5-11.) Look at your Christian life and fill in the following with your prayer of submission.

Lord, teach me . . .

ETERNAL CHRIST

LESSON 5

WHY TEACH THIS LESSON?

Nothing has been quite the same since September 11, 2001. The wars in Afghanistan and Iraq have unsettled the lives of thousands of people. Hurricane Katrina devastated the Mississippi Delta region and upended the lives of many Americans. Earthquakes have shaken Hawaii. Wildfires have consumed thousands of acres in California. Politics, economics, disease, and countless other variables threaten our stability. Where is the sense of stability and permanence that every person longs for?

A lack of a sense of stability and permanence can be followed by physical and/or mental illness. The ultimate solution is to look to the eternal Christ. That's what this lesson will help your learners do. Christ is our bedrock! With him we will not be shaken by physical or spiritual disasters.

INTRODUCTION

A. THE ETERNAL GOD

Mathematicians use a symbol for infinity that looks like this: ∞. The idea is that if you were to travel around a track shaped like this, you would never reach the end. Instead, you would continue endlessly around the track.

Some religions view eternity in this way, as an endless treadmill from which we never escape. Yet this is not the view of the Bible. The biblical perspective is that eternity is a projection into the future that has no end point. Likewise, eternity looks to the past and sees no beginning point. It is not a repetitive cycle. A prayer of Moses expresses it like this: "Before the mountains were born or you brought forth the earth and the world, from everlasting to everlasting you are God" (Psalm 90:2).

Many biblical teachings are tied to this core belief in the everlasting nature of God. God made an everlasting covenant with David that was cemented through Jesus, the Messiah (2 Samuel 23:5). God's love and mercy toward us "endures forever" (Psalm 118:1-4; compare Isaiah 54:8). We, as Christians, are partakers in an "eternal gospel" (Revelation 14:6).

Therefore, we can take great comfort in the eternal nature of God. God is not like the boss at work who changes his mind on a daily basis. God is not like human governments that rise and fall, come and go. God is not subject to human fads, whims, or trends. As the psalmist wrote about God, "But you remain the same, and your years will never end" (Psalm 102:27). We cannot overestimate the value to us of God's eternal nature.

B. LESSON BACKGROUND

The book of Hebrews compares the new covenant of the Christian faith with the old covenant of the Jewish faith. Throughout the book, the author shows that Jesus has inaugurated a new relationship with God that is both a fulfillment of the old covenant patterns and is superior at every point to them. In the final

DEVOTIONAL READING:
PSALM 118:5-9
BACKGROUND SCRIPTURE:
HEBREWS 13:1-16
PRINTED TEXT:
HEBREWS 13:1-16

Jun
29

LESSON AIMS

After participating in this lesson, each student will be able to:

1. List some of the sacrifices with which the writer of Hebrews says God is pleased.

2. Explain the significance of our giving God the sacrifices mentioned in verse 16 in light of Christ's once-for-all sacrifice.

3. Express one sacrifice of praise for Christ and his work.

KEY VERSE

Jesus Christ is the same yesterday and today and forever.
—Hebrews 13:8

chapter of the book, chapter 13, the author moves to practical matters: relationships between believers. The backdrop of this final section is twofold.

First, there is the strong recognition of the moral expectations that come from the Old Testament. The book of Deuteronomy is an explanation of God's requirements for Israel. Moses uses the image of the Lord as a "consuming fire" (Deuteronomy 4:24) shortly before he gets to the very basics of human relationships: the Ten Commandments (Deuteronomy 5:6-22). Similarly, the author of Hebrews moves from the picture of God as judge to God's expectations for humans in relationship with each other. This may be seen in the admonition of Hebrews 12:29: "For our 'God is a consuming fire,'" which comes immediately before today's text.

The second element of background is that of God's eternal nature, found in both Deuteronomy and Hebrews. One of the key standards of God's relationship with his people is that it is more than a temporary arrangement. It is intended to last forever (see Deuteronomy 5:29; 29:29).

I. UNCHANGING ACTIONS (HEBREWS 13:1-6)

The members of the first-century church need to have a good reputation in their communities (1 Timothy 2:2; 3:2). The gospel message will never be heard if Christians are a bunch of bickering malcontents with questionable integrity. The author of Hebrews is well aware of this issue and uses the final section of the book to give practical advice on how to live a Christlike life in the community.

A. BE LOVING (vv. 1-3)

1. Keep on loving each other as brothers.

A hallmark of the Christian community is that Christ's disciples are to be known by their genuine concern for one another. This was commanded by Jesus (John 13:34), and the author of Hebrews reminds the readers that the command has not been rescinded. Jesus set the example in his own life. They were to love each other in the same manner that Jesus had loved them (John 15:12). This love of Jesus was strong enough to cause him to die for his beloved, and we should not be satisfied with any lesser attitude (John 15:13).

So, what does this mean in terms of showing concern for everyone in our church? How do we love the unlovely? How do we act with love toward those who seem to be ornery and mean-spirited? It is not an easy task, and the author does not claim that it is. He simply reminds us to *keep on loving.*

2. Do not forget to entertain strangers, for by so doing some people have entertained angels without knowing it.

The literal meaning of *entertain strangers* here is to "love outsiders." It is the same idea as in verse 1, but now applied to a different group. We are to love our Christian brothers and sisters, and we are to love visitors to our community too.

In the ancient world, there isn't much in the way of accommodations for travelers. To camp out in the public square is dangerous. To stay in an inn is to put oneself at the mercy of criminals and to endure filthy conditions. Travelers, therefore, usually stay in private homes. The churches in the various cities are used as a network for providing hospitality for fellow believers. This can become a burdensome task, and there are other places in the New Testament where believers are reminded of their responsibilities in this area (see 3 John 5-8).

The author reminds the readers that there have been instances when the strangers seeking lodging were *angels* traveling incognito (see Genesis 18:2-10). The author of Hebrews is not telling the readers to take care of travelers in the

HOW TO SAY IT

Corinthians. Ko-RIN-thee-unz.

Deuteronomy. Due-ter-AHN-uh-me.

Galatians. Guh-LAY-shunz.

Golgotha. GAHL-guh-thuh.

Hebrews. HEE-brews.

Isaiah. Eye-ZAY-uh.

Jerusalem. Juh-ROO-suh-lem.

Leviticus. Leh-VIT-ih-kus.

Moses. MO-zes or MO-zez.

hopes they might get lucky and entertain an angel. Rather, the idea is that caring for strangers may result in unexpected blessings, such as meeting new brothers and sisters and learning from them.

3a. Remember those in prison as if you were their fellow prisoners,

The author does not qualify those remembered in terms of whether the imprisonment is the result of justice or injustice. God still loves those people, and we should too. They should receive support from their brothers and sisters outside (Matthew 25:36; Hebrews 10:34).

Prisons in the ancient world offer little in the way of care for *prisoners*. To visit a prisoner is more than just for encouragement. It is up to a prisoner's family and friends to bring food and clothes and to dress wounds from floggings or fights. Family might be expected to give money to the jailer in return for a higher level of protection for the prisoner.

3b. . . . and those who are mistreated as if you yourselves were suffering.

The idea of *suffering* likely refers to those in prison. It carries the idea of being tortured. It is not uncommon for prisoners to be *mistreated* by brutal and sadistic jailers. This is enhanced by the crude security methods of Roman jails, including heavy manacles and leg irons; these restrictive stocks clamp down on feet and hands. If a fellow Christian is in jail for his faith, the other believers should realize that such a fate could easily be theirs in the future.

B. BE PURE (v. 4)

4. Marriage should be honored by all, and the marriage bed kept pure, for God will judge the adulterer and all the sexually immoral.

The traditional *marriage* ceremony includes the well-known statement, "Marriage is an honorable estate." There is nothing shameful about being married. But marriages of Christian believers must be protected. Husbands and wives must treat each other with "brotherly love" and show the highest degree of respect for one another.

There is nothing more damaging to a couple's reputation and to the health and longevity of a marriage than to have *the marriage bed* become impure. To engage in sex outside of marriage is not just an act of selfish gratification, it is a disrespectful slap in the face of the marriage partner.

The ancient world of the Greeks and Romans does not hold to these standards. For them, it is not considered dishonorable if a man is an *adulterer* (that is, has sex with other men's wives) or otherwise *sexually immoral*. Loose sexual morality is not to be tolerated within the Christian community of the first century and should not be acceptable today (1 Corinthians 5; Galatians 5:19).

C. BE CONTENT (v. 5)

5. Keep your lives free from the love of money and be content with what you have, because God has said,

    "Never will I leave you;

        never will I forsake you."

Covetousness relates to materialism, the burning desire to have more possessions. If we have a heart of covetousness, we are in a constant state of jealousy against those who have nicer stuff. To guard against this consuming desire has been a long-standing responsibility of the people of God (see Exodus 20:17; compare Proverbs 21:26).

A deeper motive behind materialism is insecurity: we want more wealth so that we don't have to depend on anyone else. The author reminds the readers

---

WHAT DO YOU THINK?

What are some blessings you think you may have missed by not practicing hospitality? How have you matured spiritually in this regard?

WHAT DO YOU THINK?

What are some practical ways to express sympathy for those in adversity?

WHAT DO YOU THINK?

What can you do this week to help maintain marriage as an honorable institution, even if you're not married?

WHAT DO YOU THINK?

What has caused you to be more covetous than content over the years? How have you made progress in overcoming this tendency?

that this insecurity is really a lack of faith in God, because God has promised *never* to *leave* or *forsake* us (Deuteronomy 31:8; Joshua 1:5).

WITHOUT COVETOUSNESS

Some years ago I read of a sales manager who was very successful in challenging his sales representatives to increase their sales. Every year he had an end-of-summer party at his house and invited all his sales reps and their wives. Also every year, he had a new luxurious addition to his home. One year it was a swimming pool. Another year it was a glass-enclosed patio room. Another year it was a backyard barbecuing unit. When the sales reps came over, their wives would *ooh* and *ahh* over the newest feature. It was all part of his plan.

When the party ended and everyone went home, the wives began to "work on" their husbands. "It sure would be nice if we had a _____ like that," they would say. The wives pestered their husbands until they gave in. That meant, of course, that the men would have to push the sales routine even harder to get the money. That's exactly what the sales manager wanted. By planning on the wives' covetousness, he was successful in keeping his sales reps motivated. Thus they continued to push hard and make more sales, enhancing his own position in the process. Covetousness can be an insidious enemy to our contentment. —J. B. N.

D. BE UNAFRAID (v. 6)

6. *So we say with confidence,*
   "The Lord is my helper; I will not be afraid.
   What can man do to me?"

If we were to be stripped of all possessions, we would still have the most important thing: our relationship with *the Lord*. No one can ever take this away from us. The author explains that this should embolden us to trust the Lord for all things. If we are being helped or supported by the Lord, we may ask with the psalmist, "of whom shall I *be afraid*?" (Psalm 27:1; compare 118:6).

II. UNCHANGING BELIEFS (HEBREWS 13:7-14)

The foundation of godly relationships within the church is the body of teachings that has been passed on from the apostles. Earlier, the author of Hebrews traced these basic doctrines directly back to Jesus himself (see Hebrews 2:3, 4).

A. WHAT TO EMBRACE (vv. 7, 8)

7, 8. *Remember your leaders, who spoke the word of God to you. Consider the outcome of their way of life and imitate their faith. Jesus Christ is the same yesterday and today and forever.*

These verses have been interpreted two ways. Some think that it is the teaching of the church leaders that doesn't change. In other words, they have taught *Jesus Christ* as Lord and will continue to do so. To be sure, we Christians should respect the guidance of our church *leaders*. At the same time, we should measure their teachings by the standard of God's Word. There is nothing more central than a focus on Jesus Christ.

A more common interpretation, though, is that the core of their teaching is the eternal nature of Christ. In other words, it is Jesus himself who is *the same yesterday and today and forever.* This is a strong statement of the divinity of Jesus.

B. WHAT TO REJECT (vv. 9, 10)

9, 10. *Do not be carried away by all kinds of strange teachings. It is good for our hearts to be strengthened by grace, not by ceremonial foods, which are of no value*

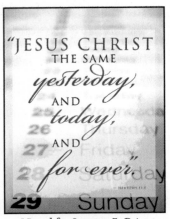

Visual for Lesson 5. *Point to this visual as you begin the* Into the Word *section on page 375.*

to those who eat them. We have an altar from which those who minister at the tabernacle have no right to eat.

Sometimes we think that false teaching is a new problem in the church. But even the apostles have to deal with teachers who want to introduce false doctrine into the church. For example, within two decades of Jesus' resurrection, a decision is made to condemn the teaching propagated by some that Gentiles are required to be circumcised in order to be saved (see Acts 15:1). Peter warns the church to be on guard for those who bring in "destructive heresies" (2 Peter 2:1).

The author warns against any dependence on *ceremonial foods,* meaning sacrificial animals. Such activities have no value to the Christian. Our salvation is not tied to the Jewish system of sacrifices but is *strengthened by grace.*

C. WHAT TO REMEMBER (vv. 11-14)

11, 12. The high priest carries the blood of animals into the Most Holy Place as a sin offering, but the bodies are burned outside the camp. And so Jesus also suffered outside the city gate to make the people holy through his own blood.

The author draws an interesting contrast between the Jewish sacrificial system and the sacrifice of Jesus. How did the priests dispose of the leftovers—the "holy trash"—of the daily animal sacrifices? The answer is that they were *burned outside* the temple or tabernacle precincts. What seemed holy and special in the ceremony of sacrifice became a common nuisance in the aftermath (see Leviticus 16:27).

The author plays on these disposal practices to illustrate the irony of Jesus' sacrifice. In effect, he was thrown away as being unworthy, but he became the greatest, perfect sacrifice. He was able to *make us holy through his own blood.*

The author includes a historical detail that is only implied in the Gospels: the site of Jesus' crucifixion (Golgotha) was outside the gates and walls of Jerusalem (see John 19:17). This detail was important in determining the location of the Church of the Holy Sepulcher in the fourth century AD and continues to be important for biblical archeologists today.

13, 14. Let us, then, go to him outside the camp, bearing the disgrace he bore. For here we do not have an enduring city, but we are looking for the city that is to come.

This is the author's parting shot at those who want to leave the church and return to their Jewish roots. He says, "We must leave the earthly Jerusalem behind." Christians are not tied to the temple and its system of sacrifice for sins. We have forgiveness through the blood of Jesus. We look forward to the perfect city of God, the New Jerusalem that will be established with Christ's second coming (see Revelation 3:12; 21:10; compare Galatians 4:26).

III. UNCHANGING WORSHIP (HEBREWS 13:15, 16)

The break with the Jewish system has implications for how Christians understand worship. The Jerusalem temple can no longer be a focus for worship, but neither does it need to be.

A. SACRIFICE OF PRAISE (v. 15)

15. Through Jesus, therefore, let us continually offer to God a sacrifice of praise— the fruit of lips that confess his name.

The author offers us an astoundingly simple yet rich way to worship: *a sacrifice of praise.* We don't have to be in a temple or church building to do this. We don't have to wait for a certain day or hour to begin. Although we are not to

DAILY BIBLE READINGS

Monday, June 23—Take Refuge in God (Psalm 118:5-9)

Tuesday, June 24—Christ as Supreme and Eternal (Colossians 1:15-20)

Wednesday, June 25— Show Hospitality and Courage (Hebrews 13:1-6)

Thursday, June 26—True Leaders to Imitate (Hebrews 13: 7-9)

Friday, June 27—Confess Christ's Name (Hebrews 13: 10-16)

Saturday, June 28—A Leader Who Professes Christ (Philippians 3:12-16)

Sunday, June 29—A Leader Looking to Christ Eternal (Philippians 3:17-21)

WHAT DO YOU THINK?

What are some of your own sacrifices of praise?

Eternal Father, it is beyond our abilities to comprehend your eternal nature, so we must simply believe it. We have trouble knowing what tomorrow will be, but your Word says you inhabit eternity. May we offer to you our sacrifice of praise, our humble words of reverence and adoration. We pray this in the name of our Lord Jesus Christ, amen.

"give up meeting together" (Hebrews 10:25), we can worship God at any time and in any place by pausing to give him thanks.

This book has been rich in telling us what we have to be thankful for. We have a wonderful Savior. We have an eternal Father who will never abandon us. We have freedom from the limits of the Jewish system. We have promises that even the greatest heroes of the faith only looked forward to. We are surely blessed.

CONTINUAL PRAISE

On February 3, 1970, students and faculty of Asbury College in Wilmore, Kentucky, gathered at 10 AM for what they assumed would be a typical chapel service. Instead, revival broke out. The service, originally scheduled for 50 minutes, did not let up for 185 hours.

The meeting was nonstop, 24 hours a day, for that interval. Students and faculty started by giving testimonies and were soon weeping, praying, and singing. Many asked forgiveness from those they had wronged. The meeting was marked by orderliness. Attendees did not become loud, speak out of turn, or fall to the floor in ecstasy.

News of the event soon reached local newspapers and television stations. The revival was highlighted in large cities, some clear across the country. Off-campus people were soon coming to Wilmore to witness and participate in the event.

After the revival had run its course, churches invited speakers from Asbury College to come and talk about the experience. By the summer of 1970 the revival had spread to 130 other campuses and scores of churches, both in America and abroad. One church in Anderson, Indiana, had a spontaneous revival that lasted for 50 nights. The church became so packed that services had to be moved to a school gymnasium for the crowds of up to 2,500 people.

The Asbury experience is obviously not the standard experience. But it is a witness to what can happen when people offer continual praise.   —J. B. N.

B. SACRIFICE OF DOING GOOD (v. 16)

16. And do not forget to do good and to share with others, for with such sacrifices God is pleased.

The encouragement *to share with others* means sharing our possessions. The author finishes this section by reminding the believers that they have a responsibility *to do good* by taking care of the needy.

God is no longer interested in animal sacrifices. He wants the sacrifice of a humble heart that cares for the less fortunate. It is not enough to listen to the teaching of church leaders and walk around humming praise songs. We must demonstrate our love by assisting our brothers and sisters in their time of need (Hebrews 13:1).

CONCLUSION

Jesus shares God's eternal nature. This is why he can serve as a "high priest forever" (Hebrews 6:20). This is why his sacrifice for sins is effective forever (Hebrews 10:12). This is why faith in Jesus gives us the promise of eternal life (John 3:15, 16), for Jesus alone has the words of eternal life (John 6:68). If we have named Jesus as Lord (Romans 10:9), we have believed in his eternal nature. Why else would we place our faith in a person who lived 2,000 years ago?

Jesus' eternal nature should spur us to praise of his name and into doing good deeds for his sake. We continue his work of caring about the poor and the downtrodden of the earth. If the truth of the eternal reign of Christ makes no impact on our lives, we either have not understood it or have not believed it.

Jesus Christ doesn't change. Neither do his expectations.

Discovery Learning

*This page contains an alternative lesson plan emphasizing learning activities. Some of these activities
are also found in the helpful student book, NIV Bible Student. The next page
is a reproducible activity page to further enhance discovery learning.*

INTO THE LESSON

Fill your room with as many timepieces as you can accumulate. (Perhaps invite your class members to bring "spare" ones from home.) Include clocks with an audible ticking sound to be plugged in, if not battery powered. Include one old, nonworking clock with the hands removed; post this one prominently.

As class begins, ask, with your hand cupped to your ear, "What is that you hear?" Accept answers, such as "time," "life passing by," and others, but suggest that it is only a man-imposed mechanical sound designed to reflect the measure of that which is truly immeasurable.

Direct the attention of the group to your clock with no hands. Ask, "In what way does this timepiece represent eternity?" Comment on the fact that today's study relates to the eternality of Christ and the necessity of right living while we are still caught by time.

INTO THE WORD

On a poster board, display this key truth from today's text: "Jesus Christ is the same yesterday and today and forever" (Hebrews 13:8). As the learners are watching, write on the poster, *Therefore, I . . .* Lead your class in seeing the implications for Christian living that are a part of the timelessness of Christ's person and power. Ask them to suggest some *therefores* they immediately see. If response is slow, give them an example, such as, "Therefore, I can still believe what he said a long time ago," or "Therefore, I will expect him to return as he said he would."

Once you have several responses from the class, say, "Look at today's text in Hebrews 13:1-16 and see if you can identify the expected results the writer includes as parts of these truths." Read 12:28, 29, then use a series of questions based on 13:1-16 to elicit discussion.

1. "How does our need to continue in love for one another relate to God's character and Christ's constant being?" (v. 1)

2. "How does Jesus' continuing sameness require us to be hospitable to strangers?" (v. 2)

3. "How does Jesus' life and present ministry indicate our need to remember those in bonds and adversity?" (v. 3)

4. "In what sense does Jesus' eternality demand faithfulness and purity in marriage?" (v. 4)

5. "How does God's consistent presence negate the need for covetousness and discontent?" (v. 5)

6. "How is fear inappropriate if Father and Son and Spirit remain constant and true?" (v. 6)

7. "In what way does honoring your leaders show your honor of Christ?" (v. 7)

8. "How does being attracted to 'new' doctrines deny the power and authority of the 'old' Christ?" (v. 9)

9. "In what way does an attraction to the former system of sacrifices minimize the sacrifice that Christ made?" (vv. 9b-12)

10. "How does our shame for the shame of Christ's death dishonor him?" (v. 13)

11. "In what instances does our focus on either material things or our earthly lives make no sense at all?" (v. 14)

12. "If Jesus were not the same yesterday, today, and forever, why would praising him with our lips be foolish?" (v. 15)

13. "What does doing good deeds and sharing materially with others have to do with believing Jesus is eternal God, unchanged and unchangeable?" (v. 16)

Help your learners see the relationship between their behaviors as they live within the constraints of time and the unconstrained, eternal person and power of Christ Jesus.

INTO LIFE

Verses 9-16 of today's text deal with the contrast between the sacrifices of the Old Testament system and the sacrifice of Jesus that is the perfection in the New. Ask the class to identify the specifics of God's work in Christ that are revealed and recalled in this text.

After each is noted, ask a class member to offer a brief prayer of thanksgiving—a sacrifice of praise—for that work. For example, as someone notes the truth that "God will judge," from verse 4, ask a learner to express thanks that God will one day make everything right and just. As you wind up this activity, suggest that learners copy your list and use items from it this week in their personal times of "sacrifice of praise" with their lips.

Alternative or additional exercise: Have learners complete the Time and Eternity activity on the Reproducible Page. Distribute copies of the A Forever Reminder as your learners depart.

Time and Eternity

On the clock face to the left write in some of the godly obligations we have in this life in the light of Jesus' once-for-all sacrifice for our sins. Consider elements of behavior and attitudes highlighted in today's text in Hebrews 13.

On the infinity symbol to the right, write a personal expression of the delights you are anticipating for the eternal life to come. Today's text mentions at least two: being face-to-face with the eternal Jesus (v. 8) and a continuing city of glory (v. 14).

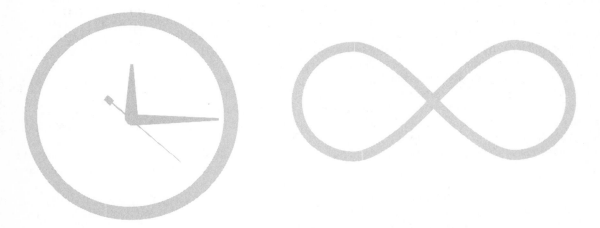

How do your two sets of observations match up or intersect?

A Forever Reminder

Cut off the strip at the bottom of this page and attach it end to end after making one twist to create a Möbius strip. Hang it over a door knob or car mirror this week so that every time you see it you will be reminded of the grand truth printed on it. Let it remind you also of the practical implications discussed in today's study.

Jesus Christ is the same yesterday and today and forever.

MASTER TEACHER

LESSON 6

WHY TEACH THIS LESSON?

My wife is a Certified Diabetes Educator. She is highly sought after as a teacher in that regard. Without question, other instructors have as much knowledge as she does. My wife is different, however, because she doesn't just tell people how to treat diabetes, she *shows* them. Mary is not a diabetic, yet she gladly gives herself countless numbers of saline injections. She doesn't flinch. She wants her students, especially children, to know that they have nothing to fear. Her credentials are not just her knowledge, but her actions too.

Jesus backed up his teaching with actions—indeed, miraculous actions. That's why Jesus is to be believed and followed as the Son of God. Your students will discover in today's lesson that Jesus has all the right credentials to be our master teacher.

INTRODUCTION

A. QUESTION AUTHORITY

The slogan *Question Authority* may conjure up vague memories of a bumper sticker on the back of a 1960s VW microbus. The slogan may be interpreted as the ravings of an anarchist who cares little for the norms of conventional thought. It may reflect a rebellious spirit that is self-centered and listens only to the voices in one's own head.

But is it ever right to question authority? to stand up to conventional thinking? to challenge the majority view? Albert Einstein (1879–1955) remarked, "Unthinking respect for authority is the greatest enemy of truth." If someone pounded on your door and demanded entry, it would be the better part of wisdom to question the basis for his or her authoritative demand. If it's the police with a search warrant, the command to open the door requires compliance.

Jesus' voice of authority was accepted by some and questioned by others. But his credentials were available for all honest seekers to examine. Unbelief can start as a matter of evidence. But after the evidence is established, continued unbelief becomes a matter of the heart.

B. LESSON BACKGROUND

Luke identifies the beginning of Jesus' Galilean ministry with summary statements in Luke 4:14, 15. The one who had been empowered as God's Son (Luke 3:22) and tested concerning the nature of his sonship (Luke 4:1-13) now comes to Galilee "in the power of the Spirit" and teaches "in their synagogues."

The scenes comprising Luke 4:14-44 illustrate Jesus' authoritative power and teachings in the "synagogues of Judea" (see Luke 4:44). In the synagogue in Nazareth (Luke 4:16-30), Jesus explained his authoritative powers by identifying himself as one empowered by the Spirit and one who announced the good news of God's saving presence (Luke 4:16-20). Those claims resulted in rejection and hostility (Luke 4:28, 29).

DEVOTIONAL READING:
ISAIAH 11:1-3
BACKGROUND SCRIPTURE:
LUKE 4:14-37; 20:1-47
PRINTED TEXT:
LUKE 4:31-37; 20:1-8

Jul
6

LESSON AIMS

After participating in this lesson, each student will be able to:

1. Tell how today's texts reveal Jesus' authority.

2. Compare and contrast the impact of Jesus' authoritative presence in his day with the impact it has today.

3. Identify one area of life where he or she should allow Jesus to have more authority.

KEY VERSE

They were amazed at his teaching, because his message had authority. —Luke 4:32

I. JESUS' ACTION, PEOPLE'S REACTION (LUKE 4:31-37)

In the next synagogue scene, Jesus has moved about 20 miles northeast of Nazareth to the fishing community of Capernaum. Here his authoritative words and deeds are received more favorably. Unlike the Nazareth experience, where people sought to throw him off a cliff (Luke 4:29), the residents of Capernaum seek him eagerly (4:42). Yet it is not clear that they grasp Jesus' true identity, although the demons definitely do (4:34).

Throughout Luke's story, the one empowered by the Holy Spirit shatters the tyrannical grip of diabolical forces as the kingdom of God is manifested powerfully. Later, the same power will be extended to the 12 disciples as they are called to participate in Jesus' authoritative mission (9:1).

A. AUTHORITY (vv. 31, 32)

31. Then he went down to Capernaum, a town in Galilee, and on the Sabbath began to teach the people.

Jesus' movement from Nazareth to *Capernaum* is definitely a descent (*went down to*), since Nazareth is some 1,800 feet above Capernaum. Capernaum is a relatively large fishing village with a population perhaps between 1,000 and 1,500. This site is Jesus' place of residence early in his ministry (Matthew 4:13; John 2:12). Later, Capernaum will be one of the towns singled out for its stubborn refusal to be moved to repentance by Jesus' mighty deeds of power (Matthew 11:20-24).

By custom, male Jews may read from the Scriptures and offer comments in the synagogue *on the Sabbath* (see Acts 13:15, 42; 14:1; 17:2). Although the content of Jesus' teaching is not specified, the previous scene in the Nazareth synagogue (4:17-21) is probably a backdrop to Jesus' teaching in Capernaum. We also learn from Luke 4:43 that Jesus preached the kingdom of God. The announcement that God has drawn near to reign over his people surely stirs hearts—one way or another.

32. They were amazed at his teaching, because his message had authority.

Jesus' ongoing *teaching* is matched by continual amazement at the *authority* inherent in his words. Luke connects the authoritative value of Jesus' words to their visible effects. The approach in Mark 1:22 at this point is to contrast Jesus' authoritative words with those of the scribes. Luke, however, chooses to emphasize the inherent power of Jesus' words. What is experienced in Nazareth as "gracious words" (Luke 4:22) is experienced in Capernaum as words of powerful authority. Jesus speaks as one with an awareness of the will of his Father.

B. RECOGNITION (vv. 33, 34)

33, 34. In the synagogue there was a man possessed by a demon, an evil spirit. He cried out at the top of his voice, "Ha! What do you want with us, Jesus of Nazareth? Have you come to destroy us? I know who you are—the Holy One of God!"

Luke does not provide an explanation of how a demonized man comes to be present *in the synagogue*. Even so, it is clear that the authoritative presence of *the Holy One of God*, who is empowered by the Holy Spirit (Luke 4:14), means the demise of evil forces and the cleansing of the unclean. Indeed, the time has come for the tyrannical hold of Satan to be shattered by the advance of God's powerful reign (see Matthew 12:28, 29). While the forces of evil may appear to run rampant, Jesus' exorcisms clearly announce "our God reigns."

The demons immediately recognize Jesus' identity, and the implications are understood in terms of their inevitable destruction. We recall from the testing of

WHAT DO YOU THINK?

If you were to ask "the man on the street" to express his understanding of the kingdom of God, how might he answer? Why is this question important?

Jesus in the desert that Satan recognized Jesus' identity as the Son of God (Luke 4:3, 9). While humans may dispute the claim, evil cosmic forces have no doubt concerning Jesus' divine nature and authority! This is suggested by the two questions they raise: *What do you want with us?* and *Have you come to destroy us?* The first acknowledges that the demons have nothing in common with the holy presence of Jesus. The second concedes their fate and Jesus' power to destroy them.

C. COMMAND (v. 35)

35. "Be quiet!" Jesus said sternly. "Come out of him!" Then the demon threw the man down before them all and came out without injuring him.

This is the first of numerous accounts of miracles in Luke's Gospel. The exorcisms highlight that the Spirit-empowered Jesus exudes a cleansing and liberating power, rescuing humanity from evil forces. Jesus' authoritative rebuke of *the demon* indicates his refusal to give credence to demonic resistance or protest. Thus with two brief commands Jesus silences the demon and forces him to depart from *the man.*

As a result, the demon is compelled to release his power and turn the man over to Jesus. This is a concession to Jesus' superior authority. Amazingly, the demon's violent response in throwing the man down results in no injury.

D. AMAZEMENT (vv. 36, 37)

36. All the people were amazed and said to each other, "What is this teaching? With authority and power he gives orders to evil spirits and they come out!"

Both Jesus' *teaching* and deeds evoke amazement. Like his authoritative teaching, Jesus' command resulting in the demon's expulsion is recognized as a concrete expression of *authority* and *power.* The reader knows from Luke 4:14 that Jesus' authoritative power is derived from the Holy Spirit. Jesus' words and deeds can restore, cleanse, and "release the oppressed" (Luke 4:18). Luke is careful to link Jesus' authority to both his words and his deeds. Jesus' words are continually validated by the power of his deeds.

37. And the news about him spread throughout the surrounding area.

Jesus' fame spreads throughout Galilee, even to those regions where he has yet to visit (compare Luke 4:14). The effect of his reputation spreading throughout the *area* can be seen in Luke 4:40. Later, his fame will spread even farther (Luke 5:15), eventually even "throughout Judea" (Luke 7:17). Luke will use similar summaries in the book of Acts, his second volume, to describe the growing impact of the early church (see Acts 2:47; 5:11; 6:7; 8:4; 9:31).

But Jesus does not seek the fame of a miracle worker or an exorcist (compare Luke 5:14). His acts of power are almost like parables: they must be interpreted and understood in light of the entire drama unfolding in his ministry. This is why the city of Capernaum stands condemned. Even though the residents are amazed by his deeds of power, they do not interpret those deeds properly. Thus they are not moved to repentance (Matthew 11:23, 24).

II. LEADERS' CHALLENGE, JESUS' RESPONSE (LUKE 20:1-8)

More than two years have now elapsed since the exorcism of Luke 4. The issue of Jesus' authority surfaces again when he travels to Jerusalem and confronts the city with his staggering claims and deeds. Jesus' actions involving the temple elicit questions from Israel's leadership regarding the nature and source of his authority. We learn from Luke 19:47 that the Jewish leaders are seeking his demise, so the questioning of 20:1-8 has only hostile intentions.

WHAT DO YOU THINK?

In what ways have you witnessed the power of God at work in people's lives?

HOW TO SAY IT

Baal. BAY-ul.
Capernaum. Kuh-PER-nay-um.
Elijah. Ee-LYE-juh.
Galilean. Gal-uh-LEE-un.
Galilee. GAL-uh-lee.
Judea. Joo-DEE-uh.
Nazareth. NAZ-uh-reth.
Sanhedrin. SAN-huh-drun or San-HEED-run.
synagogue. SIN-uh-gog.

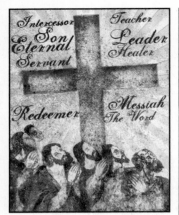

Visual for Lessons 1, 6, & 10. *Point to this visual as you ask, "What do these titles and descriptions say about Jesus' authority?"*

A. QUESTION (vv. 1, 2)

1. One day as he was teaching the people in the temple courts and preaching the gospel, the chief priests and the teachers of the law, together with the elders, came up to him.

This is Jesus' final public ministry in Jerusalem before his crucifixion. It appears that Jesus is daily assuming the role of teacher in *the temple* precincts. His *preaching* of *the gospel* undoubtedly includes his earlier teaching about God's in-breaking kingdom (compare Luke 4:18, 19, 43; 8:1; 9:6; 16:16). However, the religious leaders are perturbed by Jesus as he assumes a role reserved for those having official standing. They are outraged by this upstart Galilean's presumption to position himself as a teacher in the shadow of Israel's most sacred site.

These leaders, the *chief priests and the teachers of the law* and *elders*, undoubtedly are members of the Jerusalem Sanhedrin. The Sanhedrin is comprised of 71 members and is the "supreme court" for resolving Jewish legal disputes. They have come to see Jesus as a formidable threat to their leadership authority, and thus this threat must be neutralized.

AT HOME?

There is an old proverb, "Home is where the heart is." We assume that where a person's emotions are attached marks his or her "real" home. Professional athletes spend a lot of time in arenas and gymnasiums. Devoted mothers spend many hours with their children. Academicians spend time with their books. Religious people spend time in religious activities. All are comfortably "at home" with their primary interests.

The same could be said of Jesus. Early in his Gospel, Luke records Jesus' words, "I had to be in my Father's house" (2:49). Jesus came to bring a message of salvation and hope, so he was constantly among the people—preaching, teaching, healing. Whether it was during the Sermon on the Mount, with a crowd along the beach, or with people accompanying him as he walked from place to place, he was "at home" bringing the gospel to the people.

The religious authorities we see in today's text were "at home" primarily at the temple. But their attachment to it (see John 11:48) was not the same as that of Jesus (see John 2:13-17). Jesus challenges us to reexamine where we are most "at home" and make any and all adjustments necessary (see Luke 14:26; 18:18-30). The religious leaders of his day were not willing to do this. Are we?   —J. B. N.

2. "Tell us by what authority you are doing these things," they said. "Who gave you this authority?"

Jesus' earlier actions in the temple (Luke 19:45, 46) and his assumed role as teacher are enough to alarm the religious leaders. They understand that such actions constitute a claim of *authority* that openly challenges their own authoritative status.

So the established leaders interrogate Jesus regarding the basis and the source of his authority. They understand that Jesus' actions necessitate authorization from a superior source. Yet Jesus has no formal rabbinic or priestly credentials that might warrant his actions and validate his right to teach. So how can he presume to speak with authority about temple proceedings?

The leaders of the Sanhedrin can claim legal and religious jurisdiction as well as their political authorization from Rome. But what does Jesus bring to the table? Thus their questions are intended to discredit Jesus by shaming him before the people. But the result of their questioning undermines their own authority, as we shall see.

WHAT DO YOU THINK?

The Sanhedrin members who confronted Jesus were clearly more interested in their own credentials than they were in the content of Jesus' message. What are some examples of misplaced priorities in religious circles today?

B. COUNTERQUESTION (vv. 3, 4)

3, 4. He replied, "I will also ask you a question. Tell me, John's baptism—was it from heaven, or from men?"

Notice that Jesus does not challenge the legitimacy of the inquiry. In fact, Jesus will inform his disciples that "the teachers of the law and the Pharisees sit in Moses' seat. So you must obey them and do everything they tell you" (Matthew 23:2, 3). Obviously a new teacher who calls into question what has been taken for granted in Israel (as Jesus has done) should be investigated. Yet while there is no problem with the religious leaders' questions as such, they are not motivated by an honest pursuit of truth.

So instead of responding directly, Jesus counters with a *question* of his own. He does not do this to be evasive, but to expose the motives behind their inquiry. The ministry of John foreshadowed and is in continuity with Jesus' own ministry. Thus an assessment of John is critical to any understanding of Jesus' authority. There are only two options: either John's authority to initiate a cleansing ritual (*baptism*) was divine in origin or it was a mere human invention.

The answer to Jesus' counterquestion will demonstrate where these religious leaders stand. Like Jesus, John (now dead) lacked the sort of credentials they demand; yet he is widely regarded among the people as having had prophetic status. If the leaders interpret John's ministry correctly, then they will have their answer concerning Jesus' authority. But that also means going "on record" in front of everyone listening!

C. RESPONSE (vv. 5-7)

5, 6. They discussed it among themselves and said, "If we say, 'From heaven,' he will ask, 'Why didn't you believe him?' "But if we say, 'From men,' all the people will stone us, because they are persuaded that John was a prophet."

The implications of Jesus' question are not lost on the religious leaders. You don't get to be a member of the Sanhedrin by being unintelligent! But their intelligence has limits, since their deliberations indicate that they are more concerned with their own agenda than with truth.

Thus the deliberations center not on the spiritual implications of Jesus' question, but upon the earthly consequences of their answer. If they acknowledge that John was backed by divine authority, their hypocrisy will be exposed for not believing and acting upon the implications of John's ministry. John's baptism forms a serious challenge to their authority and their view of God's redemptive purpose (Luke 3:1-20). On the other hand, if the religious leaders openly repudiate John's baptism, then they run the risk of alienating *the people*. The leaders thus would put themselves in danger of severe retaliation. Their lack of integrity puts them on the defensive.

LOGIC

We don't normally consider the Bible to be a textbook of logic, but there are numerous examples of pure logic found in its pages. One of the most interesting categories is *the dilemma*. The basic form of a dilemma is this:

1. If A, then B; if C, then D.
2. Either A or C;
3. Therefore, either B or D.

A classic case is found in 1 Kings 18:21. There Elijah confronts the people on Mount Carmel about choosing between the Lord and Baal. The form of his argument is this:

DAILY BIBLE READINGS

Monday, June 30—*Spirit-Anointed Teacher (Isaiah 11:1-3)*

Tuesday, July 1—*Filled with God's Spirit (Luke 4:14, 15)*

Wednesday, July 2—*With Authority (Luke 4:31-37)*

Thursday, July 3—*Blessed Are You (Luke 6:17-23)*

Friday, July 4—*Woe to Them (Luke 6:24-26)*

Saturday, July 5—*Love Your Enemies (Matthew 5:38-45)*

Sunday, July 6—*Authority Questioned (Luke 20:1-8)*

WHAT DO YOU THINK?

Give an example of a serious spiritual discussion whose major purpose was to "prove a point" rather than arrive at the truth. How did the discussion turn out?

[Use this question with extreme caution! If your church has had problems in this area, you don't want to pour gasoline on smoldering embers.]

1. If (A) the Lord is God, then (B) serve him; if (C) Baal is God, then (D) serve him.
2. Either (A) the Lord is God or (C) Baal is God.
3. Therefore, either (B) serve the Lord or (D) serve Baal.

It is presumed that a person cannot serve both the Lord and Baal—one must
choose. Sometimes a dilemma is framed in such a way that both options are unpal-
atable, but it forces us to choose and commit to one idea or the other. This is what
Jesus does in Luke 20:5, 6, and the chief priests, scribes, and elders knew it.

1. If we say John's baptism is from Heaven, then why did we reject it? If we say it's
   from men, then the people will stone us.
2. John's baptism is either from Heaven or men.
3. Either we admit we sinned by rejecting it, or the people will stone us.

They did not like either outcome, so they refused to answer. Jesus then used
their unwillingness to answer to justify his own unwillingness to answer the questions as to the origin of his authority. He had caught them on the classic "horns of
a dilemma."   —J. B. N.

7. So they answered, "We don't know where it was from."

Ironically, by their claim of ignorance the religious leaders admit their incom-
petence to discern spiritual matters! Thus they forfeit their own claim to authority. If they, the religious scholars, cannot determine what is from God and what is
of mere human origin in John's case, then how can they possibly stand in judgment concerning Jesus?

What begins as an effort to discredit Jesus results in a self-condemnation of
the scholars. They are more concerned about maintaining and protecting their
privileged position than they are in recognizing divine intervention. "If we let him
go on like this, everyone will believe in him, and then the Romans will come and
take away both our place and our nation" (John 11:48).

D. COUNTERRESPONSE (v. 8)

8. Jesus said, "Neither will I tell you by what authority I am doing these things."

Notice that Jesus doesn't try to "make nice" with his opponents. He refuses
to play their game. The motives of the chief priests, scribes, and elders in asking
their question followed by their admitted ignorance concerning the authority of
John mean that any further discussion will go nowhere.

Nevertheless, Jesus has implicitly answered their question by connecting his
ministry to the divinely authorized ministry of John. While Jesus does refuse a
direct response to their question regarding his *authority*, the parable to follow
(Luke 20:9-18) and subsequent discussions leave no doubt about the nature and
source of that authority.

CONCLUSION

Jesus' authoritative teachings and deeds cannot be ignored. They must be
evaluated in terms of the nature and basis of his authoritative claims. Jesus'
claims are validated by his deeds, which point to his divine status. This is the evidence of the miracles (John 14:11).

But such conclusions are determined by a heart that honestly seeks the truth.
As we observed with the religious leaders, sometimes a hidden agenda or personal
ambitions blunt the force of divine truth. The truth of Jesus' authority challenges
assumptions that are grounded on earthly foundations. The question we must ask
is, "Who has ultimate authority to direct our lives?" The alternatives always have
been the same: human authority or divine authority. What is your choice?

Discovery Learning

This page contains an alternative lesson plan emphasizing learning activities. Some of these activities are also found in the helpful student book, NIV Bible Student. *The next page is a reproducible activity page to further enhance discovery learning.*

INTO THE LESSON

Write the following on the board in large letters: *Teachers Transform Lives!* Point to the poster as you say, "A teacher's transforming power may come through the content of a class, the personality of the teacher, personal exchanges with the teacher, or even just a single comment from the teacher. The transformations teachers bring are seen in changed values, an enlarged vision for the future, career selection, changed behaviors, etc."

Remind the class that influential teachers may surface in a school setting, seminars, churches, or other environments. Then ask for two people to share the names and circumstances of teachers who have been significant influences on their lives or the lives of family members.

Make the transition to Bible study by saying, "The authority of a teacher is foundational to influencing student lives. That's why it is important to view the authority of one who has been called the world's greatest teacher—our Savior. We may be angry with Jesus' antagonists. However, we are blessed by this questioning as we find that our own confidence in his authority soars to new heights."

INTO THE WORD

Early in the week, ask two students to prepare five-minute presentations for this portion of the lesson. Ask one student to prepare a background for the study; the issue for the presentation is *The Authority of Jesus.* Give him or her a copy of the Lesson Background from the lesson commentary. The student should highlight the issue(s) at stake and the result(s) of each of Jesus' visits. The following outline may be helpful:

       I. Synagogue Scene #1: Nazareth.
      II. Synagogue Scene #2: Capernaum.
     III. Temple Scene: Jerusalem.

The second student will prepare and deliver a presentation on *Demon or Spirit Possession* in the Bible. Give the student copies of articles about demons from Bible dictionaries and Bible handbooks. The presentation should address these questions: "Who or what are demons?" "What do they do or represent?" and "How did they work in human beings in the Bible?"

Introduce the first speaker by telling the class, "First, let's look at the issue of Jesus' authority from circumstances arising in Luke's Gospel. To begin our study I have asked [name of student] to give us some background."

Then distribute photocopies of Luke 4:31-37 and Luke 20:1-8. Read Luke 4:31-37 from it. Students will be asked to write on these copies in a later activity.

Next, introduce the second speaker by saying, "Demon possession is strange to us. Therefore, I have asked [name of student] to give us some background on demon possession."

After the presentation, ask students to underline every word or phrase of Luke 4:31-37 on their photocopies that deals with Jesus' authority. Then ask the following discussion questions: 1. What does your underlining exercise tell you about Jesus' authority? 2. What in this passage seems to give credibility to Jesus' authority?

Then read Luke 20:1-8 from the handout. Again, ask class members to underline every word, phrase, question, or statement that has to do with Jesus' authority. Then, ask the following discussion questions: 1. What does verse 2 refer to when the Jewish leaders mention "these things"? 2. How is the response to Jesus different from the previous passage we studied? Why do you suppose it is so different? 3. What does this say to you about questioning or searching for the source of Jesus' authority? 4. Why do you think Jesus refused to answer their question about his authority?

Option: time permitting, have learners complete the Jesus' Power and Authority exercise from the Reproducible Page. The Satan's Attacks exercise can follow this, or you can distribute copies as a take-home activity.

INTO LIFE

Ask students how they view the authority of Jesus relative to human authority on these five issues: 1. Sanctity of human life (abortion and embryonic stem cell research). 2. Monetary decisions. 3. Family issues and goals. 4. Career attitudes and values. 5. Life after death.

Ask, "Are there areas that you think Jesus doesn't really care that much about because you think other things 'must be' more important to him?" After discussion, ask, "What is one area of life where you will allow Jesus to have more authority? How will you pray in this regard?"

Jesus' Power and Authority

Jesus often spoke about his authority. Some accepted it while others chose to reject it. Below are just a few Scriptures that address the issue of the power and/or authority of Jesus. Read each one. Then list the circumstance or setting for the account at hand. Also, note the power or the authority that was demonstrated. (Hint: power is the *ability* to do something; authority is the *right* to do something.)

SCRIPTURE	CIRCUMSTANCE OR SETTING	POWER OR AUTHORITY DEMONSTRATED
Matthew 7:29		
Matthew 9:1-8		
Matthew 28:18		
Mark 2:10		
Luke 4:31-34		
Luke 5:17-24		
John 2:18-22		
John 10:14-18		
John 17:2		

Satan's Attacks

Satan will always try to undermine the authority of Jesus. What are some ways you see him at work today? (Example: Satan promotes postmodernism, which has created a climate where people have no basis for moral authority in life.)

1.

2.

3.

POWERFUL HEALER

LESSON 7

WHY TEACH THIS LESSON?

Some people receive healing from their infirmities, and some die from them. I wish I knew why. I imagine you do too. It doesn't make sense to us. When decent people suffer terribly, it seems so unfair. John the Baptist was left in prison where he was executed (Mark 6:14-29), but Peter was miraculously delivered from prison (Acts 12:1-19). Why did God allow them to be treated differently? Haven't you asked yourself that kind of question?

Jesus healed many, but he didn't heal everyone. This lesson is important partly because we all struggle with the question, "Why?" But we dare not lose focus on the fact that the healings that Jesus *did* perform prove his identity. Ultimately, that fact is more important than whatever physical healing we may or may not receive personally. The proof of Jesus' identity should cause your learners to make a renewed commitment to glorify God. He is always worthy of our praise.

INTRODUCTION

A. ARE MIRACLES CREDIBLE?

There are many miracle episodes in Mark's story. For some folks, miracles are impossible because they do not conform to known natural laws. Thus the skeptics discount the historical reliability of the Gospels. Skeptics cut away those portions of the story they find offensive to the "reasonable" secular mind. But the miraculous is so embedded in the story line of the gospel that a radically different picture emerges if the miraculous is removed (see 1 Corinthians 15:13-17).

Jesus' story is a continuation of Old Testament Israel's story. That story looked forward to a time when a compassionate king would reign in righteousness and justice. His reign would result in the oppressed being set free, the eyes of the blind being opened, the ears of the deaf being healed, the lame leaping like a deer, and the mute tongue shouting for joy (see Isaiah 32:3, 4; 35:5, 6; 58:6; 61:1, 2). Jesus embodied that vision as his power and authority were manifested in acts of mercy and compassion to victims of various afflictions.

We caution ourselves that Jesus' miracles must not be misinterpreted. The Jewish authorities admitted that Jesus had miraculous powers, but rather than repent they attributed the source of the miracles to the demonic (Mark 3:22). Cities where Jesus performed many mighty deeds of power were rebuked because his miracles did not result in repentance and recognition of his authoritative status (Matthew 11:20-24).

Jesus had no interest in being perceived as a mere wonder-worker. A theme dominant in Mark's Gospel is Jesus' repeated efforts to deter recipients of his healing powers from speaking publicly about healings (Mark 1:44; 5:43; 7:36). The message of the gospel is primarily "repent" (Mark 1:15), not "come and get your physical problems fixed." Thus the miraculous healings are proof of a greater spiritual reality of the in-breaking kingdom of God. The miracles are to be understood as proof of this (John 14:11).

DEVOTIONAL READING:
ISAIAH 61:1-4

BACKGROUND SCRIPTURE:
MARK 1:14-45

PRINTED TEXT:
MARK 1:29-45

LESSON AIMS

After participating in this lesson, each student will be able to:

1. Describe Jesus' early ministry in and around Capernaum.

2. Tell what Jesus' healing ministry reveals to us today about who Jesus is.

3. Articulate one way to share the good news of Jesus' healing presence.

Jul
13

KEY VERSE

Jesus healed many who had various diseases. He also drove out many demons. —Mark 1:34

B. LESSON BACKGROUND

Mark, the briefest of the four Gospels, is a book of action. After an introduction of only three verses, the record is that "John came, baptizing . . . and preaching" (Mark 1:4). The action continues at a brisk pace when Mark records only five verses later that "Jesus came." Next we see that "the Spirit sent him" (v. 12) and "Jesus went into Galilee, proclaiming" (v. 14). The other three Gospels give us more details at various points, but Mark likes to keep the action moving with his condensed style. After the call of the first disciples (1:16-20), Mark records a series of scenes in and around Capernaum (1:21-39). That's where we pick up today's lesson.

Before moving into the lesson proper, we should take note of first-century Judaism as the backdrop of Jesus' healing ministry. Foundational for Judaism is the profound commitment to God as the healer and sustainer of all life (see Exodus 15:26; Deuteronomy 32:39; Isaiah 6:10; Jeremiah 8:15). Sickness and various infirmities are often viewed as signs of God's disfavor resulting from one's sinful condition, although Jesus does not necessarily endorse this view (see John 9:2, 3). The miracles demonstrate the advancement of the kingdom because they demonstrate God's power to accomplish his will.

I. JESUS HEALS (MARK 1:29-34)

A. PETER'S MOTHER-IN-LAW (vv. 29-31)

29, 30. As soon as they left the synagogue, they went with James and John to the home of Simon and Andrew. Simon's mother-in-law was in bed with a fever, and they told Jesus about her.

Mark gives some clues that the events between verses 29 and 38 take place over a 24-hour period of time. After going to the synagogue in Capernaum on the Sabbath (v. 21), Jesus and his disciples *left the synagogue*. Events then move forward to the time of "that evening after sunset" (v. 32), then to "the morning" (v. 35). This movement of the scenes takes the reader from a public gathering in the synagogue (v. 21) to the privacy of a home (v. 29) and ultimately to a "solitary place" where Jesus seeks his Father in prayer (v. 35).

Thus it is clear that the movement from the synagogue (v. 21) *to the home of Simon and Andrew* is intended to continue a recount of events that take place on one particular Sabbath. It appears that Simon and Andrew have moved from Bethsaida (John 1:44) to take up residence in Capernaum. The presence of Simon, Andrew, *James,* and *John* reminds us of their earlier calling (see Mark 1:16-20). We also learn that Peter is married when he is called to follow Jesus (compare 1 Corinthians 9:5).

The fact that Peter's *mother-in-law* resides with Peter implies that she is a widow with no living sons. In the ancient world, illness is often described in terms of the symptoms (compare John 4:52; Acts 28:8). Leviticus 26:16 and Deuteronomy 28:22 list divine punishment as one cause of *fever,* although there is no indication of such punishment here. The disciples have seen Jesus' power exhibited in the synagogue, thus they do not hesitate to draw his attention to her condition.

31. So he went to her, took her hand and helped her up. The fever left her and she began to wait on them.

In the previous scene, Jesus drove out the demon with an authoritative word (v. 25). Here *the fever* is expelled by Jesus' authoritative touch. There is no need for convalescence, for her cure is instantaneous. Peter's mother-in-law models a fundamental aspect of discipleship by responding to healing with grateful service.

WHAT DO YOU THINK?

What limits do people place on their faith in what God can do? How do we go about helping them remove those limitations?

WHAT DO YOU THINK?

Think of a time when you or a loved one prayed for physical healing. What motivated the request? How was the motivation like or unlike that of those who sought healing from Jesus?

B. TOWN'S SICK PEOPLE (vv. 32-34)

32, 33. *That evening after sunset the people brought to Jesus all the sick and demon-possessed. The whole town gathered at the door,*

Following the specific healing of Peter's mother-in-law, Mark moves to the broader contours of Jesus' ministry. Jesus' reputation is growing. The interim summaries in Mark 1:39; 3:10-12; and 6:53-56 provide overviews of the scope and impact of Jesus' messianic activity. The way these are told indicates that they are only samples of what is generally characteristic of Jesus' ministry.

While Mark's language *that evening after sunset* may sound redundant, it stresses that sunset marks the end of Sabbath and the restrictions associated with it. Thus the people can now bring *to Jesus all the sick and demon-possessed.*

Notice that Mark makes a distinction between those who are *sick* and those who are *demon-possessed.* Thus it is not accurate to conclude that ancient people confuse medical conditions such as schizophrenia with demon possession. While occasionally those possessed by demons do exhibit certain forms of physical afflictions (Mark 9:17, 18), it is simply not the case that all people of antiquity attribute every medical condition to demonic possession. See also Mark 6:13 for a clear distinction between the two.

Not only are the conditions distinguished, but also the methods used to remedy the situations are different. Exorcisms are performed with an authoritative command, while healings usually involve Jesus' touch. The note that *the whole town* is *gathered at the door* underscores Jesus' growing popularity. The word has gotten out!

Jesus' healings have important restorative value, socially in addition to physically. The debilitating effects of unclean spirits and the contaminating results of various illnesses have shattered social networks and community involvement (compare Leviticus 13:45, 46). Jesus' healing powers restore people to a valued state.

34. . . . *and Jesus healed many who had various diseases. He also drove out many demons, but he would not let the demons speak because they knew who he was.*

Jesus' ministry of healing is comprehensive. This is indicated by the terms translated *various diseases.* There are no conditions that Jesus cannot remedy. The only incident where Jesus' power was limited was back in Nazareth (Mark 6:5). But the limitation there was from a lack of faith on the part of the Nazarenes (Matthew 13:58).

We note that the demons are silenced once again (compare Mark 1:25). In this case the reason is given: *because they knew who he was.* The fact that Jesus is able to silence the demons demonstrates who is really in charge here. It appears that Jesus does not want the demons' knowledge to be revealed, at least at this time. In the Gospel of Mark, Jesus' identity as God's Son is understood only later. Confession by a human that Jesus is "the Son of God" in Mark's Gospel doesn't come until 15:39; a demon makes this confession much earlier (Mark 3:11).

Jesus' sonship includes a sacrificial commitment to the will of his Father, and Jesus' identity can be appreciated fully only in the light of his redemptive message. That's a reality no demon can possibly understand.

II. JESUS PRAYS (MARK 1:35-37)

A. ALONE (v. 35)

35. *Very early in the morning, while it was still dark, Jesus got up, left the house and went off to a solitary place, where he prayed.*

Visual for Lesson 7. *Point to this visual as you ask, "In what ways has Jesus healed your brokenness?"*

The reference to time (*very early in the morning*) indicates that the 24-hour period begun in verse 21 now comes to a close. The movement is away from the crowds and toward a place of solitude. Before the next phase of his ministry, Jesus needs a time of extended prayer. Mark, unlike Luke, does not record many scenes depicting Jesus' prayer habits. Yet Mark does note often that Jesus retreats from the public arena and the pressure of the crowds (Mark 1:45; 3:13; 6:31, 32, 46; 7:24; 9:2, 30).

It is critical that Jesus remain focused on the will of his Father and not get caught up in the expectations of the crowds. How many popular Christian teachers and preachers today make a mistake in this area?

B. FOUND (vv. 36, 37)

36, 37. Simon and his companions went to look for him, and when they found him, they exclaimed: "Everyone is looking for you!"

The disciples, led by *Simon*, embark on an urgent mission in pursuit of Jesus. They are not content to wait until Jesus returns on his own. Apparently, they think that Jesus in his isolation is failing to take advantage of his growing popularity. They would have Jesus accommodate his surge of popularity by returning to Capernaum and building on his newfound fame.

But Jesus has no interest in pursuing the fleeting adulations of the crowds. He will not have the plans of other people thrust upon him. Simon's statement to Jesus is certainly true: *Everyone is looking for you!* But it apparently is not Jesus' teaching and preaching they want, but his miracles.

III. JESUS PREACHES (MARK 1:38, 39)

A. DESIRE (v. 38)

38. Jesus replied, "Let us go somewhere else—to the nearby villages—so I can preach there also. That is why I have come."

Jesus will not be distracted from his divine mission to proclaim the good news of God's kingdom (Mark 1:14, 15). The disciples are invited to accompany him in his itinerant ministry (*let us go*) that will take him into the neighboring towns and *villages*. Evidently Jesus' time in prayer has led him to conclude that it is now time to bring the message to other areas of Galilee. He has not been sent to be a mere local healer or folk hero.

SENT TO PREACH

John Knox (1513–1572) was the central figure in the Protestant Reformation in Scotland. Probably converted to Protestantism sometime in the 1540s, Knox moved into the castle of St. Andrews in Edinburgh in 1546. Protestant leaders there invited Knox to come among them to preach; he did so realizing that he was putting himself at serious risk.

Indeed, the castle was captured by Catholic forces in 1547, and Knox spent the next 19 months on a prison ship. He was released only at the request of the English government. He served churches in England over the next few years, and it was there that he uttered his famous prayer, "Lord, give me Scotland or I die." His life's interest was to convert the Scots to Protestantism.

Knox later went to the Continent, served in several churches there, and returned permanently to Scotland in 1559. His preaching of evangelical doctrines and his opposition to the Catholic practices of the queen often got him into trouble, but he never wavered from his commitment to preach the truth as he understood it. Preaching the gospel to his people was his life's ambition. Do we have this kind of courage today?   —J. B. N.

WHAT DO YOU THINK?

What are some ways that people try to gain the approval of others? How are those ways like or unlike the way Jesus dealt with crowds?

B. Action (v. 39)

39. So he traveled throughout Galilee, preaching in their synagogues and driving out demons.

What Jesus did in the Capernaum synagogue he now does in *synagogues* throughout all *Galilee*. Jesus both teaches the message of God's kingdom and reinforces its reality by overthrowing the agents of Satan.

IV. JESUS HINDERED (MARK 1:40-45)

A. Request (v. 40)

40. A man with leprosy came to him and begged him on his knees, "If you are willing, you can make me clean."

Following the general description of Jesus' itinerant ministry (v. 39), Mark now focuses on one particular *man* who makes a request. He has *leprosy*, a general term in the ancient world for someone who has some kind of skin disease (not necessarily leprosy in the modern sense). The priests are charged with determining the severity of such problems along with the necessary course of action (Leviticus 13:1-46; 14:1-32). If the condition is diagnosed as contagious, the afflicted person is excluded from social contact and forced to warn all who come near with the words "Unclean! Unclean!" (Leviticus 13:45, 46).

The banishment is not rooted in a medical concern of spreading infection, but rather in the religious impurity and uncleanness attached to such afflictions. Like touching a corpse, any contact with a leper means religious contamination.

The description of the leper's approach to Jesus forms a positive picture of genuine faith and confidence in Jesus' power to remedy the situation. Unlike the scene at Mt. Sinai, where the holiness of God called for the creation of distance between God and the people, God's presence in Jesus does not call for the avoidance of those deemed untouchable.

B. Response (vv. 41, 42)

41, 42. Filled with compassion, Jesus reached out his hand and touched the man. "I am willing," he said. "Be clean!" Immediately the leprosy left him and he was cured.

The rules for ritual cleanness warn against touching that which is unclean (Leviticus 5:2, 3). Yet Jesus touches those whom others avoid (Mark 1:41; 5:41; 7:32, 33; 8:25). His touch results not in contamination of himself, but in the leper's cleansing.

C. Sent (vv. 43, 44)

43, 44. Jesus sent him away at once with a strong warning: "See that you don't tell this to anyone. But go, show yourself to the priest and offer the sacrifices that Moses commanded for your cleansing, as a testimony to them."

After the healing, Jesus emphatically tells the man precisely what he is to do and not do. Three imperatives highlight Jesus' request. The first imperative *See that you don't tell this to anyone* is intended to counter a misplaced enthusiasm that would draw others to Jesus as a miracle worker.

The second and third imperatives are that the man is to present himself before a *priest* and comply with the Mosaic legislation. This indicates Jesus' respect for the provisions of the law. The procedure also assures that the one formerly excluded from society can now be restored to full communal and spiritual life. We note that the man's healing is not the same as his being declared clean. To be declared clean requires the action of a priest according to Leviticus 14:2-31.

The actions of the leper are also intended as *a testimony to them*. Probably the pronoun *them* refers to the priests before whom the man will present himself. The leper's sacrifice and healed state are to become powerful witnesses to Jesus' restorative powers. The word out of Galilee will be that God has drawn near in the form of Jesus.

SHOW A TESTIMONY

The 1938 film *The Adventures of Robin Hood* was a milestone production. Costing two million dollars, it was the most expensive investment in a film that Warner Brothers had made to that point. The film tells the story of Robin Hood, the legendary nobleman-turned-outlaw, who was trying to save the Saxon peasants from oppression. In one episode, Robin has captured Maid Marian, who was repulsed by the outlaw with his disreputable ways. He tried to tell her that he was working for justice, but she did not believe him.

Then he introduced her to the peasants who were around his camp. For the first time she saw citizenry that was oppressed by Prince John's taxation policies. In contrast, she also saw Robin's kindness to the poor and the outcast. She heard their expressions of gratitude to him. As she returned to the castle, she became a convert to the justice of his cause and fell in love with him as well (after all, it was a Hollywood version).

Actions become a better explanation than words. When Jesus dismissed the healed leper, he told him to show himself to the priests and present the normal offerings required by the Law of Moses. Those were the actions that Jesus wanted to do the speaking and testifying. How do our actions witness for Christ today?

—J. B. N.

D. SOUGHT (v. 45)

45. Instead he went out and began to talk freely, spreading the news. As a result, Jesus could no longer enter a town openly but stayed outside in lonely places. Yet the people still came to him from everywhere.

Did the man ever go to the priest as Jesus instructed? We don't know. What is clear, however, is that the man disobeyed Jesus' instructions not to tell anyone. No doubt it would be extremely difficult to contain oneself after experiencing such a remarkable event. Nevertheless, the man's disobedience means that Jesus is hindered from going freely to the towns throughout Galilee, which is his intent (v. 38). Now even *lonely places* offer no reprieve from the crush of the crowd.

Certainly Jesus wants the message and power of the kingdom to get out. But the frenzied excitement of the crowds only exalts him to celebrity status as a miracle worker. Jesus prefers to walk the path of unpretentious service and humility rather than fulfill the aspirations of the crowds.

The episode involving the leper also prepares us for the series of negative responses to Jesus' ministry that we see in Mark 2:6, 7, 16, 18, 24; 3:2, 6. The leper should be a visible witness confronting Israel's leadership with the unprecedented dimensions of Jesus' ministry. But as the scenes comprising Mark 2:1–3:6 indicate, a growing antagonism results in their decision to seek Jesus' destruction.

CONCLUSION

Jesus' display of healing powers catapulted him to instant fame. Yet Jesus showed no interest in seeking the headlines or even remaining in the public eye. The adulation of the crowds rang hollow without their understanding and repentance. In the final analysis, *complete physical healing* plus *no repentance* equals *nothing*. This should cause us to reflect on how we approach Jesus today.

Discovery Learning

This page contains an alternative lesson plan emphasizing learning activities. Some of these activities are also found in the helpful student book, NIV Bible Student. *The next page is a reproducible activity page to further enhance discovery learning.*

INTO THE LESSON

Arrange chairs to accommodate small groups of two to five as students enter. You will need a minimum of three groups, so construct your group sizes accordingly. Large classes may duplicate the assignments that will be given below. Post the following discussion assignment: *Do you believe in the potential for supernatural physical healings in 2008? Discuss your beliefs. (Option:* have small groups complete the Faith and Healing activity on the Reproducible Page instead of or in addition to the above.)

After a few minutes of discussion, make a transition to Bible study by saying, "While we usually associate physical healing with prescriptions, doctors, and lifestyle changes, we must recognize that God still has the power to intervene. Otherwise, our prayers at the time of illness and before surgeries are useless. Today we'll view Jesus' supernatural power at work and catch another glimpse of his authority and compassion."

INTO THE WORD

Give groups copies of the discussion questions below, along with a photocopy of the lesson commentary on the assigned passages. After an appropriate amount of group study time, allow each group to report its findings.

Group #1: Read Mark 1:29-34 and answer the following questions: A. Describe the issues concerning Sabbath activity in this account. What were the potential problems and resolutions? B. Why do you think Jesus silenced the demons? C. What does this passage tell you about the nature or character of Jesus?

Group #2: Read Mark 1:35-39 and answer the following questions: A. Describe the setting and events in this passage. Why did Jesus say, "Let us go . . . to the nearby villages"? What were the implications of that directive? B. What does this passage tell you about the nature or character of Jesus? C. What disciplines do you see modeled by Jesus for believers in 2008? Why are they important?

Group #3: Read Mark 1:40-45 and answer the following questions: A. What was the setting of the events? Be sure to discuss the concerns of physical contact with lepers and Jesus' response. B. Why do you think Jesus commanded the leper to tell no one about his healing?

C. What does this passage tell you about the nature or character of Jesus?

INTO LIFE

Again, give written copies of assignments to the groups as follows:

Group #1: Discuss the lessons we learn from how people react to leprosy and apply them to our reactions to modern afflictions. What do you think are appropriate Christian responses and attitudes toward modern afflictions? How should our reactions differ between contagious and non-contagious afflictions, if at all?

Group #2: Remembering our discussion about God's power to intervene in healing in our world, how would you counsel in the following situation? A young wife was reared by Christian parents who disapproved of blood transfusions and allowed only limited doctor's care. The husband is a new Christian. Their one-year-old daughter has certain nonlife-threatening birth defects, and the doctor wants to do surgery. However, the couple is experiencing tensions in deciding how much faith to place in the doctor and how much to place in God's hands.

What Scriptures can you draw upon in counseling this couple? How do you avoid coming across as "a Bible thumper"? How will your counseling be different if this couple seeks you out as opposed to your seeking them out? How do you "counsel" without "giving advice"?

Group #3: Remembering our discussion about God's power to intervene in healing in our world, what advice would you give to this couple in their 60s? Both have become Christians in the last couple of months. The husband has been a smoker all of his adult life and has just been diagnosed with lung cancer. Both are frightened as they await the doctor's recommendation for a course of action. They ask you, "Does God really intervene in health issues in today's world?"

How do you respond? What Scriptures can you draw upon in counseling this couple? How would you pray with them?

Alternative: if you used the Faith and Healing activity from the Reproducible Page in the Into the Lesson segment, you can now have each of your small groups complete the What to Pray activity instead of the three group exercises above. Compare groups' conclusions.

Faith and Healing

Adults seek healing through many different vehicles. List as many possible ways you can recall how modern people seek cures. Place a check mark out to the left beside those you consider to be biblically legitimate.

- ☐ _____
- ☐ _____
- ☐ _____
- ☐ _____
- ☐ _____
- ☐ _____
- ☐ _____
- ☐ _____

What to Pray

Did you include the healing power of a compassionate Christ in the above list? Christians often wrestle with balancing or combining faith in the power of the supernatural God and faith in the blessings of modern medical care. Imagine you are a friend or minister visiting the people below. What would you consider to be an appropriate prayer for each circumstance?

1. A 59-year-old Sunday school teacher has been prepped and is awaiting cardiac bypass surgery. What would be the theme of your prayer for this man?

2. A believer has been praying for healing from her Lupus disease for many years. Now she is wondering why God has not given her healing. She has invited you to her house to pray. What will be the theme of your prayer?

3. You accompany your neighbor to the hospital emergency room as she takes her 8-year-old daughter, who just fell and broke her wrist. How would you pray with this young mother as her daughter waits to be examined?

Images of Christ
Unit 2: Images of Christ in the Gospels
(Lessons 6–9)

EXEMPLARY SERVANT

LESSON 8

WHY TEACH THIS LESSON?

One harried housewife exclaimed, "Jesus washed the disciples' feet, and I can't even get my husband to wash the dishes!" Though we identify with her, we know that aid that is coerced is not true service.

There are many factors that might motivate us to serve our Lord, the church, or others. When we think, "If I don't do it, nobody will," we are motivated by guilt. If someone manipulates us into serving, we may serve, but with resentment. The only appropriate motivation for service is love. Jesus modeled love when he washed the disciples' feet. This is the model your learners need in a "me first" world.

INTRODUCTION

A. UNDERSTANDING CULTURAL SYMBOLS

An early misconception held by the Romans was that Christians engaged in cannibalism. This misunderstanding was based on the "eating of the body" and the "drinking of the blood" of the Lord's Supper. The charge, of course, was unfounded and even a little ironic because the leaders who met in Jerusalem in Acts 15 explicitly forbade the drinking of blood (v. 20).

This issue does illustrate, however, that understanding symbols and symbolic language can be a tricky business. First, one has to understand that something is meant to be a symbol and not to be taken literally. Thankfully, the literary and historical contexts usually provide the information necessary to make this determination.

In today's passage, Jesus washes the disciples' feet. This act of service was viewed as menial by the Greco-Roman culture of the first century. As a task for low-level servants, it was not a job that anyone would embrace voluntarily and eagerly. Yet in so doing Jesus created for the church a symbol of loving service.

B. LESSON BACKGROUND

The Passover was one of the great pilgrimage festivals of Jewish antiquity. Its observance recalled God's first deliverance of (what would become) the nation of Israel from slavery (Exodus 12). By Jesus' day, several symbols were used to commemorate the original deliverance: bitter herbs, unleavened bread, etc. Unlike the other Gospel accounts of Jesus' last supper, John's doesn't elaborate on any of these symbols (compare Matthew 26:17-30; Mark 14:12-26; Luke 22:7-23). However, by mentioning the Feast of the Passover, John probably seeks to evoke the symbolic meaning of the total Passover event itself in the light of Christ.

Jesus took two of these symbols—unleavened bread and fruit of the vine— in instituting the Lord's Supper. But that is not the subject of today's lesson. Instead, we will focus on an additional imagery that Christ created on that fateful night: an imagery of service.

DEVOTIONAL READING:
ISAIAH 53:4-6
BACKGROUND SCRIPTURE:
JOHN 13:1-20
PRINTED TEXT:
JOHN 13:1-20

LESSON AIMS

After participating in this lesson, each student will be able to:

1. Summarize the account of Jesus' washing his disciples' feet.

2. Explain the principle that Jesus established when he washed his disciples' feet.

3. Suggest one practical way to apply the principle above in his or her church.

Jul
20

KEY VERSE

I have set you an example that you should do as I have done for you.   —John 13:15

LESSON 8 NOTES

I. SPECIAL FEAST (JOHN 13:1-3)

A. PASSOVER (v. 1)

1. It was just before the Passover Feast. Jesus knew that the time had come for him to leave this world and go to the Father. Having loved his own who were in the world, he now showed them the full extent of his love.

This verse begins the second half of John's Gospel. As such, it serves as an interpretive introduction to this foot-washing passage and also to Jesus' pending death. The first half of John's Gospel deals with Jesus' public ministry. The second half focuses on Jesus' concern for his disciples and his last week and passion.

The drama for Jesus' passion has already been set. The Jewish leaders have conspired to kill him (John 11:46-53). Jesus has made his triumphal entrance into Jerusalem and predicted his own death (John 12:12-15, 23-33). Now Jesus teaches his disciples privately by performing a simple act of foot-washing. However, this act intends to communicate something profound, as we shall see.

B. PROMPTING (v. 2)

2. The evening meal was being served, and the devil had already prompted Judas Iscariot, son of Simon, to betray Jesus.

The *evening meal* we are reading about is the same one indicated in the other Gospel accounts (Matthew 26:17-30; Mark 14:12-26; Luke 22:7-23). We know this because of the similar references to *Judas* (Matthew 26:21-23; Mark 14:18-20; John 13:18 [below]). The Passover meal is an important Jewish ceremony with a defined set of ritual steps or stages. That Jesus would add something to its sequence to wash the disciples' feet shows how important this event is for him. This is even more evident because usually feet are washed upon entering a household before any meal is served. But in this case the meal is in progress.

The devil here is of course Satan (see John 13:27). The two terms occur in the New Testament about an equal amount of times in the Greek and refer to the same individual. In the Old Testament, the Hebrew word *satan* refers to an adversary or wicked opponent (examples: 2 Samuel 19:22; 1 Kings 11:25). The heavenly being Satan first appears in Job 1, where Satan seeks to accuse God's righteous servant Job. Satan opposes God and the salvation he brings to his people (Matthew 13:19-21; John 8:41-44; Revelation 12:9, 17).

A great evil is about to happen: the betrayal of Jesus. Although Satan is the instigator here, he is not ultimately the one in control—God is. God will use this betrayal to advance his greater purposes (see Acts 4:27, 28; etc.). Even though the devil has *already prompted Judas Iscariot, son of Simon, to betray Jesus,* this shouldn't be taken to mean that Judas isn't responsible for what is about to happen. Peter acknowledges this in Acts 1:15-25. Even Judas himself eventually comes to realize this (Matthew 27:4, 5). By deciding to betray Jesus, Judas joins his will with the devil and makes himself one with him (compare John 6:70, 71). What a contrast this is with what Jesus is about to do!

Incidentally, true followers of Christ should find nothing to fear in this verse. Satan may tempt us, but God has said that he will not allow his people to be tempted beyond what they can handle (1 Corinthians 10:13).

BETRAYAL

Benedict Arnold (1741–1801) was an American war hero. He had served with distinction in the French and Indian War and had fought in the Revolutionary War with valor. For his courage in the invasion of Canada, he was promoted to brigadier general. Promotion to major general came in 1777. He led a series of naval battles at Lake Champlain that delayed the British invasion of New York. His actions at the Battle of Saratoga earned the admiration of George Washington as well as the common soldiers.

But Arnold was bitter that he had not received the recognition that he felt he deserved. In addition, he was seriously in debt. So he negotiated with the British to hand over the American fort at West Point, which he controlled. He was to be paid a large bounty and receive an appointment as brigadier general in the British army.

As a result, Benedict Arnold's name has become synonymous in American history with treason. The name Judas carries similar overtones. The very words betrayal and traitor carry deep connotations of unpleasantness and disgust. We expect the devil to resist Jesus; we do not expect betrayal from one of his friends. What will eternity say about how your friendship with Jesus turned out?   —J. B. N.

C. POWER (v. 3)

3. *Jesus knew that the Father had put all things under his power, and that he had come from God and was returning to God;*

Jesus is fully aware of his own status as God the Son and creator (John 1:1-3). He is confidently awaiting glorification. It is with this full awareness that he now undertakes to wash his disciples' feet.

II. SYMBOLIC SERVICE (JOHN 13:4-17)

A. ACTION (vv. 4, 5)

4. *. . . so he got up from the meal, took off his outer clothing, and wrapped a towel around his waist.*

By removing his outer garment and tying *a towel around* himself, Jesus categorizes himself as a servant.

5. *After that, he poured water into a basin and began to wash his disciples' feet, drying them with the towel that was wrapped around him.*

In the Mediterranean world of the time, people wear open sandals as they walk along dusty streets. Feet thus get dirty quickly. For people to *wash* their own *feet* is a common practice. Cultural hospitality includes providing *water* (and sometimes servants) for guests to get their feet clean. This is typical and even somewhat expected (see Luke 7:44).

Perhaps the reason that no one has washed anyone's feet already is that this supper may be taking place in a wealthier, more sanitary part of Jerusalem. This is just a guess. Yet if this is the case, then the need to wash may not be as great as it would be if it were to take place in a less sanitary part of town where animal waste, etc., is present on the streets. In any case, Jesus takes the initiative, availing himself of the opportunity to model an important lesson.

B. INTERACTION (vv. 6-11)

6. *He came to Simon Peter, who said to him, "Lord, are you going to wash my feet?"*

To appreciate Peter's astonishment, it is helpful to understand the social dynamics involved. The normal expectation is that foot-washing is to be performed by the lowest-level of servant or slave. In fact, this particular task is thought to be so demeaning that some Jews see foot-washing as a task that is off-limits for male Jewish slaves to perform.

Given these societal taboos, Peter's response *Lord, are you going to wash my feet?* is understandable. If any of the party is going to wash someone else's feet, it should be one of the disciples. *Simon Peter* is well aware of just how far Jesus is humbling himself with respect to normal cultural expectations.

WHAT DO YOU THINK?

In what ways can Christians take the initiative in providing humble service to others?

WHAT DO YOU THINK?

In what areas of your life has Jesus performed a "role reversal" by taking care of your needs?

How to Say It

Corinthians. Ko-RIN-thee-unz.

Deuteronomy. Due-ter-AHN-uh-me.

Ezekiel. Ee-ZEEK-ee-ul or Ee-ZEEK-yul.

Isaiah. Eye-ZAY-uh.

Judas Iscariot. JOO-dus Iss-CARE-ee-ut.

7. Jesus replied, "You do not realize now what I am doing, but later you will understand."

Jesus intends his action to become a symbolic example of humble service in general. The disciples do not yet *understand* this. But they will understand it *later*, in the future context of Jesus' death and resurrection.

This act of humble service serves as a precursor to Jesus' death on the cross as his ultimate service to humankind. We may pause to note that this is not the first time that people fail to grasp the significance of Jesus' words, nor will it be the last (John 7:37; 12:16; 20:9).

You'll Understand Later

Some years ago, a friend of mine bought a bicycle for his young daughter. She had outgrown her tricycle, and she desperately wanted a bike. So my friend bought one, complete with training wheels.

His little girl was very happy. She rode her bike all around the yard and the neighborhood. She got comfortable riding because the training wheels saw to it that she never overturned. She often sat still on the bike, keeping her feet on the pedals. The training wheels kept her upright, and she enjoyed the experience. Then one day my friend took off the training wheels. His daughter was now terrified. She soon discovered she couldn't just sit on the bike any more. Without the training wheels it would fall. Not only that, it was more of a challenge to get going because she had to have a certain amount of speed before the bike would remain upright.

Now she was responsible to get some speed, get on, keep pedaling, and maintain her balance—all at the same time! She almost gave up on the bike, thinking her dad had destroyed her enjoyment of it. But her dad encouraged her, and ultimately she got it all together. At first she didn't understand why her dad had removed the training wheels. Only later did she realize how much more freedom and enjoyment this gave her. Many things in life are like that. At first we don't understand; the understanding comes later.   —J. B. N.

8. "No," said Peter, "you shall never wash my feet."
Jesus answered, "Unless I wash you, you have no part with me."

We can almost feel the shock of Peter's reply *you shall never wash my feet*. The words *no part with me* is an expression used among Jews for having part in either a physical inheritance, such as land or goods (Numbers 18:20; Deuteronomy 14:27; Luke 15:12), or a spiritual inheritance, bad or good (Matthew 24:51; Revelation 20:6). In this context it is clearly the spiritual that Jesus has in mind. The Lamb of God's blood washes away sin and prepares his disciples to share in his inheritance (John 1:29; 14:2, 3).

9. "Then, Lord," Simon Peter replied, "not just my feet but my hands and my head as well!"

Peter is not even grasping the first level of meaning of this foot-washing: an example of loving service. However, Jesus will delay further explaining its first level of meaning until verses 12-17. For now, Jesus will continue to allude to its prefiguring of his loving service of death on a cross. Whatever the exact cause and nature of Peter's misunderstanding, Jesus is able to use it to develop the discourse in the direction he wants it to go. He is able to take advantage of misunderstandings for this purpose (see John 3:1-5; 4:7-26).

10, 11. Jesus answered, "A person who has had a bath needs only to wash his feet; his whole body is clean. And you are clean, though not every one of you." For he knew who was going to betray him, and that was why he said not every one was clean.

What Do You Think?

What was a time in your life when you allowed Jesus to take full control? What brought that on? What was the result?

Up to this point, Jesus has used what he is doing in the foot-washing to point, in part, toward his coming work of atonement on the cross. Most of the disciples are already *clean* through the word they received (John 15:3). Permanent cleansing will come via the work on the cross. That act of cleansing will never be repeated, nor need it be. True spiritual cleansing will come through both Jesus' word and his sacrifice on the cross.

C. INTERPRETATION (vv. 12-17)

12. When he had finished washing their feet, he put on his clothes and returned to his place. "Do you understand what I have done for you?" he asked them.

Verses 12-17 interpret the significance of the foot-washing, especially at the first level of meaning noted in verse 9, above. The master stoops to perform a slave's task in order to illustrate, by a specific cultural action, a memorable example of general service for his disciples to follow.

13. "You call me 'Teacher' and 'Lord,' and rightly so, for that is what I am.

The word *Teacher* equates to *Rabbi* according to John 1:38. Service to one's teacher/rabbi is considered quite praiseworthy. Jesus affirms the disciples' assessment of him in this regard. The word *Lord* takes on different meanings, depending on context. Sometimes it is merely a polite term of respect, such as "sir." The word *Lord* takes a much deeper meaning after the resurrection (Acts 2:36).

14. "Now that I, your Lord and Teacher, have washed your feet, you also should wash one another's feet.

Social rank and status are as important and as exaggerated in the ancient world as they are in ours. But Jesus counts that ranking less important than love and service. Up to this point in John's Gospel the focus has been on the disciples' relation to Jesus. Now in anticipation of his death, Jesus calls for them to serve one another.

15. "I have set you an example that you should do as I have done for you.

Some Christians put foot-washing on the same plane as the Lord's Supper and baptism, all three to be practiced on a regular basis. But is that really what Jesus is saying? By referring to the foot-washing as *an example,* Jesus indicates that he is not just asking for disciples to wash feet. Jesus' historical act is embedded in an arid, dusty culture where this particular kind of humble service is appropriate. It would be less appropriate in other climates. And unlike the Lord's Supper, which according to the other Gospel accounts and 1 Corinthians 11:23-29 was instituted at this last supper, foot-washing is not mentioned again as an established, institutionalized New Testament worship practice. Notice again the word *example.*

The only other time foot-washing is mentioned in the New Testament is in 1 Timothy 5:10. There it is listed as one of several good deeds that characterize certain kinds of widows. It's not that there is anything wrong with washing each other's feet as a reminder of humble service. But humble, loving service is too important to be restricted merely to an occasional act of foot-washing.

16. "I tell you the truth, no servant is greater than his master, nor is a messenger greater than the one who sent him.

Notice that in verses 13 and 14 Jesus takes the phrase "Teacher and Lord," (v. 13) and inverts it to "Lord and Teacher," (v. 14). This places *Lord* at the center of emphasis. Thus he has been building to the verse before us because the word *master* in Greek is also translated "lord." He wants to emphasize that if their Lord would do such service, so must his servants. What kind of servant would think that he or she was "too good" to do something that the Lord himself has

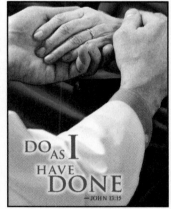

Visual for Lesson 8. *Use this visual to introduce either the first question on page 395 or the question just above the visual on this page.*

already done? If Jesus intends to include a deeper level of meaning here, he also may be alluding to his plan to endure the cross (John 18:11; Matthew 26:39; compare Luke 9:23; 14:27).

17. "Now that you know these things, you will be blessed if you do them.

John 13:1 begins what has been called *Jesus' farewell discourse.* It is noteworthy that this discourse begins with an action. True discipleship has to understand God's words, but the disciple hasn't fully learned from Christ until the understanding translates into action. A disciple not only *hears* the Word of God, he or she *does* the things of God (see also Matthew 7:24). Note the importance of keeping the Word in John 8:51; 14:23; 17:6.

III. SOBERING DECLARATIONS (JOHN 13:18-20)

A. BETRAYAL IS COMING (v. 18)

18. "I am not referring to all of you; I know those I have chosen. But this is to fulfill the scripture: 'He who shares my bread has lifted up his heel against me.'

Fulfilled prophecies are proof of God's sovereignty (Ezekiel 24:20-24). The reference here is to Psalm 41:9, which speaks of betrayal by friends. The tragedy of the betrayal is that it is by one who has eaten *bread* with Jesus. Sharing a meal is an activity of friends, not enemies.

B. BELIEF IS EXPECTED (v. 19)

19. "I am telling you now before it happens, so that when it does happen you will believe that I am He.

Jesus' knowledge of the future should help his disciples to continue to *believe* in him through this trying time (see John 14:29). Telling the disciples of the forthcoming betrayal proves that the crucifixion is not an unexpected development that thwarts the Messiah's intention. Rather, in the providence of God the betrayal will help bring his intentions to pass. The disciples need to know that God is still in control throughout the forthcoming events.

I am He is a clear allusion to Christ's deity here as it is in John 8:24, 28, 58 (compare Exodus 3:14; Isaiah 43:10). Being a prophet doesn't require that one be God. In fact no one else who spoke God's prophecies was deity. Yet Jesus wants to emphasize his deity here. It is God himself who comes down to offer salvation for all who will believe (John 1:1, 14). It is God's love that motivates him to do so (John 3:16). It is the God who "is love" (1 John 4:8) who wants his people to reach out and serve each other in love.

C. MINISTRY IS TRANSFERRED (v. 20)

20. "I tell you the truth, whoever accepts anyone I send accepts me; and whoever accepts me accepts the one who sent me."

Jesus' statement reflects the closeness between God's will and that of Jesus that has already been stated more fully in John 5:19-30. The verse before us establishes the disciples' forthcoming ministry after Jesus' death. As such, it anticipates their commission in John 20:21. Jesus has the authority of the Father.

CONCLUSION

Why don't more Christians take up humble service? Is it the work involved? Work can be hard, but we go to work for pay every day. Is it time constraints? We all seem to find time for many other things. Is our time just too "valuable"? Jesus' time was overwhelmed with his ministry (Matthew 4:23-25; John 6:24; 8:2). But he found time to do even a servant's job. Should we do any less?

Discovery Learning

This page contains an alternative lesson plan emphasizing learning activities. Some of these activities
are also found in the helpful student book, NIV Bible Student. *The next page*
is a reproducible activity page to further enhance discovery learning.

INTO THE LESSON

Prepare a poster with the heading *The Worst Household Chore Is . . .* Under the heading, make a horizontal list of the following chores: repair plumbing, clean toilets, mow lawn, carry out garbage, scrub floors, change diapers, wash dishes, prepare meals, vacuum floors, wash windows, other (please specify).

As class members enter the room, give each two colored adhesive dots (available at office supply stores or some discount stores). Ask them to vote by placing the dot underneath what they think are the two worst household chores. An alternative is to use colored push pins if the poster is mounted on a bulletin board. Make the transition to Into the Word by saying, "The household chores that make lists like this are usually dirty, messy, or thankless jobs. Today, we'll see how Jesus uses a dirty and thankless job to teach a lesson on greatness."

Alternative introduction: put a copy of the Word Search activity from the Reproducible Page in each student's chair before class begins. Your learners naturally will begin working on it as they arrive.

INTO THE WORD

Activity #1. Give each class member a photocopy of today's printed text. Ask learners to listen as you read the text. They are to circle words or phrases that give clues to the nature or character of Jesus.

Then ask your learners to share audibly the words and phrases that they circled. You will write them on the board as they do so. Words and phrases may include "loved his own," "showed them the full extent of his love," "the Father had put all things under his power," "he had come from God and was returning to God," "began to wash his disciples' feet," "Lord," "Teacher," "set you an example," "servant," etc.

Ask, "What curious question seems to jump out at us in this list of words and phrases?" (Expected response: *Why does the eternal God wash feet?*) Make the transition to the next activity by saying that you're going to unpack some of these words and concepts that teach us so much about God's values and our values.

Activity #2. Pose the following questions to the class:

1. What were the cultural or practical issues that led to the practice of washing feet during Jesus' days on earth? Who usually did the service of foot-washing?

2. Why do you think Jesus washed the disciples' feet? What lessons did they learn (or should they have learned)?

3. Is there value in Christians washing one another's feet today? Would you recommend it as a regular or periodic practice? Why, or why not?

4. What twenty-first century practices of humble service could be seen as parallel to the first century practice of foot-washing? (*One possible response: washing one another's cars.*)

5. As Jesus washed the disciples' feet as an example of serving, do you think he belittled his authority or power as the Son of God? Why, or why not? What does this example tell you about Christian vs. secular leadership?

INTO LIFE

Give poster boards and markers to teams of two to four people. Each team is to make bullet lists in answering these questions:

1. Why is the lesson of servanthood important for Christians?

2. Why is the lesson of servanthood important for the world?

3. What values can you list for acting as a servant? Remember, there will be values both for the servant and for those being served.

Next, your groups are to make lists on the back of the poster boards of ways that Christians can demonstrate servanthood. Assign teams different target groups to serve. Potential areas of focus include the elderly, neighbors, employees, coworkers, neighborhood "latchkey" children, church life. Allow each team to report from each of the above assignments. How will their service differ for Christians and unbelievers?

To make the lesson personal, ask each learner to target someone to encourage in the week ahead by serving that person. Ask learners to share the name of the individual (if appropriate) or the category of that person (elderly, neighbor, etc.) whom he or she plans to serve. Ask learners to share ideas on how to serve that person.

Groups will close with each member praying for the person to his or her right. If some feel threatened by praying in public, ask for a volunteer from each group to pray for the plans that have just been stated.

Word Search: "Lessons from a Basin"

In the blanks below, write God's words from John 13:4-17 that teach values and behavior for life today. Then locate these words in the grid below.

So he got up from the _____, took off his outer clothing, and _____ a _____ around his waist. After that, he poured water into a _____ and began to _____ his _____ _____, drying them with the towel that was wrapped around him. He came to Simon _____, who said to him, "_____, are you going to wash my feet?" Jesus replied, "You do not _____ now what I am doing, but later you will understand." "No," said Peter, "you shall _____ wash my feet." Jesus answered, "Unless I wash you, you have no part with me." "Then, Lord," Simon Peter replied, "not just my feet but my _____ and my _____ as well."

Jesus answered, "A person who has had a bath needs only to wash his feet; his whole body is _____ . And you are clean, though not every one of you." For he knew who was going to _____ him, and that was why he said not every one was clean.

When he had _____ washing their feet, he put on his clothes and returned to his place. "Do you _____ what I have done for you?" he asked them. "You call me '_____' and 'Lord,' and rightly so, for that is what I am. Now that I, your Lord and Teacher, have washed your feet, you also should wash one _____ feet. I have set you an _____ that you should do as I have done for you. I tell you the _____, no _____ is greater than his _____, nor is a _____ greater than the one who sent him. Now that you know these things, you will be _____ if you do them."

```
J R D U S E R V A N T Y D N H X B Y K
M E U T F Z T S B U N D E R S T A N D
Z H K V T I O T R U T H F W A I P Y Z
F C A J D L W H Z J G F I V W O C X Z
V A N A E A E M E A L E P W P T X C V
A E O I S E L P M A X E Q U G T A G J
C T T S S R E T E P D T Q O K M D Z Z
E L H D E A P N D E P P A R W S E Q K
K Q E N L Z B E T R A Y M P G Q U K G
P V R A B Y F S L P O I M B U Z K K Q
Y N S H N E V E R G Y L F W V Z K I Q
D T S E L P I C S I D B F Z B H R X O
F I N I S H E D C N P G E C A C D W X
I Q B M A S T E R F I U Z Z V P G X Q
W V X R E G N E S S E M Z R Z B J D K
H J L A Y C M Z I W G B N U I V P Q K
G X C R A Q D Y H D J A G B B F Y H X
G D G K B J V O Q O D I O X D Q Y L K
Q O Z X Z Q G Y Z Y Y Y V K O X Z Q V
```

Answers: another's; basin; betray; blessed; clean; disciples; example; feet; finished; hands; head; Lord; master; meal; messenger; never; Peter; realize; servant; Teacher; towel; truth; understand; wash; wrapped

PROMISED MESSIAH

LESSON 9

WHY TEACH THIS LESSON?

Sometimes we confuse *what we do* with *who we are*. When asked, "Who are you?" a woman might say, "I'm a mother" or "I'm a wife." She might say, "I'm an accountant" or "I'm a Sunday school teacher." She hasn't described the essence of herself, but she has described herself relationally and vocationally. Some people today would describe Jesus as a prophet or miracle worker. Some might say he was a teacher or a preacher. He filled all of those functions, but they don't describe his essence. We don't want to confuse *what he did* with *who he is*, although the two are related (that is, *what he did* proves *who he is*).

To Jesus' question "Who do you say I am?" Peter answered correctly. But each person must answer that question for himself or herself. This lesson will help your learners to "get it right." Eternity is at stake!

INTRODUCTION

A. WHO DO PEOPLE SAY JESUS IS?

Who do people say Jesus is? The answers vary. That has always been true. And an answer will be heavily influenced by a person's other beliefs. For example, Enlightenment thinkers of the eighteenth century, having discounted miracles, primarily saw Jesus as a commonsense teacher of morality. Some theologians today whose main concern is social justice see in Christ a great liberator of the economic poor, rather than primarily the "poor in spirit."

People tend to make Jesus fit their cultural expectations. The people of the first century AD were no different. It is not that the preceding understandings are totally incorrect. Getting the right answer regarding Jesus' person and work must include an emphasis on what he actually did. The divine revelation we have in the Bible is our starting point in that regard. Our focus on this divine disclosure will help keep us from reducing Jesus to fit our own cultural mold.

B. LESSON BACKGROUND

The events in today's lesson take place in the regions of Caesarea Philippi. That city was located in the northeast region of Palestine. The *Caesarea* part of the name was to honor Caesar, the Roman emperor. The *Philippi* part of the name refers to Herod Philip II. Pagan influence is evident in the fact that the city contained a temple for Pan, a Greek nature deity. The area's massive rock cliffs may help suggest the imagery for Matthew 16:18 in today's text. We should be careful not to confuse Caesarea Philippi with the other Caesarea mentioned several times in Acts.

As Jesus and his disciples traveled to the area of Caesarea Philippi in today's lesson, we find Jesus in the third year of his public ministry. Jesus already had performed many miracles and provoked much opposition. It's time for people—or at least the disciples—to come to a conclusion on an important question: Who is Jesus?

DEVOTIONAL READING:
ISAIAH 43:1-7
BACKGROUND SCRIPTURE:
MATTHEW 16:13-28
PRINTED TEXT:
MATTHEW 16:13-23

LESSON AIMS

After participating in this lesson, each student will be able to:

1. Describe Peter's confession and the circumstances surrounding it.

2. Explain the importance of Peter's confession.

3. Acknowledge Peter's confession to be his or her own.

Jul
27

KEY VERSE

Simon Peter answered, "You are the Christ, the Son of the living God." —Matthew 16:16

I. PROBING QUESTIONS (MATTHEW 16:13-15)

A. Jesus' First Question (v. 13)

13. When Jesus came to the region of Caesarea Philippi, he asked his disciples, "Who do people say the Son of Man is?"

Having completed the major part of his Galilean ministry (Matthew 4:12–16:12), Jesus is now alone with his 12 *disciples*. Notice that Jesus does not pose the question *Who do people say the Son of Man is?* to the crowds. Rather, he asks this question of his disciples in private.

The disciples are allowed to know the deeper realities about Jesus (see Matthew 13:11). Now the time has come to reflect on the various responses to Jesus that his Galilean ministry has evoked. It is time to clarify Jesus' true identity.

The Jewish people of first-century Palestine, including the 12 disciples, have an expectation of a coming Messiah. They also hold certain concepts of what the Messiah will be like. They primarily think of him in terms of a coming triumphant king, after the model of King David. Further, they think this king will begin his reign on earth by liberating Israel and judging her enemies. If Jesus does not meet those expectations, then who is he?

We can pause to point out that Jesus uses the phrase *the Son of Man* to refer to himself more than two dozen times in Matthew's Gospel alone. It is a title with messianic associations, based primarily on Daniel 7:13, 14. Jesus probably favors this title because it is a subtler claim to his messiahship. It is also not as directly tied to, nor limited by, mere earthly kingship. Earlier in his ministry, Jesus could not be too explicit about his messiahship because of misunderstandings about the nature of his kingdom. Claims of kingship also would draw unwelcome attention from the Roman Empire (compare Matthew 27:11).

B. Various Wrong Answers (v. 14)

14. They replied, "Some say John the Baptist; others say Elijah; and still others, Jeremiah or one of the prophets."

The crowds are generally well-disposed toward Jesus. They are amazed by his deeds, but many have no deep understanding or abiding commitment to him. It is understandable that some think him to be *one of the prophets* because of his preaching and miracles. But the fact that they do not recognize or acknowledge him as the Messiah shows in part how successful the Jewish leaders have been in creating doubts about Jesus.

The two Old Testament prophets specifically mentioned are connected with the Messiah. *Jeremiah* predicted Messiah's coming reign (Jeremiah 23:5; 33:15, 16). Discussions about the importance of Jeremiah appear in the nonbiblical 2 Maccabees 2:1-8; 15:14, 15, written during the time between the Old and New Testaments. The reappearance of *Elijah* is expected to precede the messianic age (Malachi 4:5, 6). Those who think Jesus to be *John the Baptist* may be reflecting Herod's concern (Matthew 14:1, 2).

C. Jesus' Second Question (v. 15)

15. "But what about you?" he asked. "Who do you say I am?"

Jesus' follow-up question presses for personal commitment from all the disciples, since the *you* is plural. The question tests their present level of understanding and faith. Jesus is not interested in mere academic or knee-jerk speculation about who they think he is. The nature of his work demands a more thoughtful and personal response.

What Do You Think?

What is the difference between the questions Who is Jesus? *and* Who is Jesus to you? *How should our understanding of who Jesus is affect our daily living?*

II. IMPORTANT ANSWER (MATTHEW 16:16, 17)

A. PETER'S BELIEF (v. 16)

16a. Simon Peter answered, "You are the Christ,

Combined with Peter's confession, the link of Jesus to Abraham and David in Matthew 1:1 identifies Jesus as the promised Messiah who has come to "save his people from their sins" (Matthew 1:21). This messianic hope began with God's promise to Abraham that through his seed "all peoples on earth will be blessed" (Genesis 12:3; 17:4; 22:18).

God maintained his faithfulness to this promise through Jacob (Genesis 28:14), then through David (2 Samuel 7:12, 16), and then ultimately through Jesus (Galatians 3:8, 16). *The Christ* is the Greek equivalent of the Jewish title *Messiah* (compare John 1:41; 4:25). Both mean "the anointed one." Many psalms and prophecies point to Messiah's arrival and reign (see Psalms 2:7; 110; Isaiah 11; Micah 5:2; Zechariah 9:9). In so doing, they point to Jesus.

16b. "... the Son of the living God."

In a certain sense, Jesus is the obedient *Son of God* whom God wanted Israel to be, but never was because of sin (see Exodus 4:22; Jeremiah 31:9). In a more profound sense, Jesus is the only eternally preexistent Son of God; that is something that has never been true for either Old Testament Israel as a whole or any other human being individually.

There are other clear indications of Jesus' deity recorded in Matthew. For example, Matthew has already identified Jesus as "'Immanuel'—which means, 'God with us'" (Matthew 1:23). Jesus teaches on his own authority (5:17-20; 21:23-27; 28:18-20; etc.). It is he who will judge humanity (7:21-23). When Jesus forgives sin, he is accused of blasphemy because the Jewish leaders rightly understand that this is the prerogative of God alone (9:2-6). Jesus' enemies recognize clearly who Jesus claims to be (26:63-65). The demonic spirits also testify that Jesus is God's Son (8:29). Only the actual, divine Son of God can live the sinless life that the perfect sacrifice required to redeem humankind (Hebrews 10:11-14).

B. FATHER'S REVELATION (v. 17)

17. Jesus replied, "Blessed are you, Simon son of Jonah, for this was not revealed to you by man, but by my Father in heaven."

This verse explicitly states that Peter's recognition of Jesus' true identity is because of divine revelation. This fact is also emphasized in this verse by referring to Peter formally as *Simon son of Jonah* coupled with the phrase *not revealed to you by man*.

It is not Peter the mere man who figures this out, but Peter the recipient of the Father's revelation. Peter is *blessed* because he is privileged to receive this revelation and because he expresses it and does not reject it. But how much does Peter really understand at this point? As we will see in Matthew 16:21-23 (below), Peter's understanding of Jesus' divine nature and mission is not yet as deep as it could be.

III. RESULTING PROMISE (MATTHEW 16:18, 19)

A. THE ROCK AND THE CHURCH (v. 18a)

18a. "And I tell you that you are Peter, and on this rock I will build my church,

The proper interpretation of this verse has been the subject of much discussion throughout church history. The main issue is to determine to what or to whom *this rock* refers.

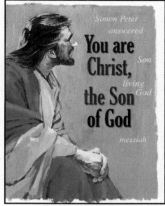

Visual for Lesson 9. *Use this visual to introduce the question on page 402.*

HOW TO SAY IT

Aramaic. AIR-uh-MAY-ik.
Caesar. SEE-zur.
Caesarea Philippi. Sess-uh-REE-uh Fih-LIP-pie or FIL-ih-pie.
Cephas (Aramaic). SEE-fus.
Elijah. Ee-LYE-juh.
Galilean. Gal-uh-LEE-un.
Gentiles. JEN-tiles.
Maccabees. MACK-uh-bees.
Messiah. Meh-SIGH-uh.
petra (Greek). PEH-trah.
petros (Greek). PEH-tross.

Is the rock Jesus himself? When we consider this idea, we recall that Jesus refers to himself as the capstone in Matthew 21:42 (compare 1 Corinthians 10:4; 1 Peter 2:4-8). However, the imagery in the text before us would be rather odd if Jesus were referring to himself as both the foundation (*rock*) of the church and the church's builder (*I will build*) in the same sentence.

We also need to realize that the Bible is flexible in its imagery, depending on what needs to be stressed in various contexts. For instance, Jesus is the builder here, while Paul is "an expert builder" in 1 Corinthians 3:10, with Jesus as the foundation in 1 Corinthians 3:11. But in Ephesians 2:19, 20, God's household is "built on the foundation of the apostles and prophets, with Christ himself as the chief cornerstone" (compare Revelation 21:14).

This flexibility in figurative language means that the context will determine how words and phrases are to be understood. The context does not seem to require the reader to see Jesus himself as the *rock* in this particular case.

Is Peter himself the rock? The word *Peter* is Greek for "rock" or "stone"; in the Aramaic language, the same word is *Cephas,* which we see at John 1:42; 1 Corinthians 1:12; 3:22; 9:5; etc. Those who think Peter himself to be the rock thus see Jesus using a play on words between Peter's name and *this rock.*

This reading seems natural enough, but it has some difficulties. First, there is Peter's mixed historical record. His failings make some think that he is too unreliable to have the church built on him (v. 23, below; also Matthew 14:31; 26:69-75; Galatians 2:11). Furthermore, Peter's name in the Greek (which is *Petros*) naturally is masculine in gender while the word for *rock* (which is *petra*) is feminine; thus there is a mismatch in the gender of the two words. Some students also see a mismatch in the sizes of a smaller stone (*petros*) and a larger rock (*petra*) in the Greek language.

Is Peter's confession the rock? The Bible tells us that confession of Jesus as Savior and Lord is vital to the growth of the church (Matthew 10:32; Romans 10:9; 1 John 4:15; etc.). After denying the Lord before the crucifixion, Peter himself "re-confessed" Christ many times (John 21:15-17; Acts 2:14-40; 4:8-12; etc.). As he did, he was building the church. This leads many students to believe that Peter's confession is the rock upon which Jesus builds his church.

In response, those who think that Peter himself is the rock point out that the play on words between his name and *rock* is unmistakable, despite the fact that one word is masculine and the other is feminine. They also note that any supposed difference in size between a smaller stone (*petros*) and a larger rock (*petra*) in the Greek language becomes meaningless when Peter's Aramaic name *Cephas* is considered; that word is used for both a proper name and a rock without such a distinction.

Before concluding our lengthy discussion of this verse, we point out that this is the first time Matthew uses the word *church* in his Gospel. Jesus himself is the one who inaugurates this community of God's people. They are to be committed to him and submit to his rule. The church is not an innovation created by his disciples after his death.

BUILT ON ROCK

Some years ago, I visited the town of Salzburg, Austria, with members of my family. There were many sights to see, including various locations used for the filming of *The Sound of Music.* One of my daughters was particularly interested in the house where Mozart was born. My wife was fascinated by the beautiful floral displays in Mirabell Gardens. My other daughter was interested in the abbey where Maria resided before she became governess to the von Trapp children.

But I must admit, the high point for me (pardon the pun!) was the "High Salzburg" Fortress overlooking the city. The well-preserved fortress, built by the archbishop of Salzburg in 1077, stands atop a rocky hill called, in English, *Monks' Mountain*. I was fascinated to see that the walls of the fortress rest solidly on bare rock. Although the castle is over 900 years old, I saw no evidence of cracks due to settling or shifting. The castle is anchored firmly to the outcropping of rock.

Buildings anchored this way are on the firmest of foundations. Jesus says that the church will be anchored just as firmly. There will be no shifting in the foundation that undergirds God's people.   —J. B. N.

B. THE GATES OF HADES (v. 18b)

18b. *". . . and the gates of Hades will not overcome it.*

Nothing can harm Christ's church! *Gates* can mean "fortifications" as in Psalm 127:5. It doesn't matter how strong those fortifications are, Jesus is stronger.

C. THE GRANTED AUTHORITY (v. 19)

19a. *"I will give you the keys of the kingdom of heaven;*

Peter preaches the first sermon after Christ's resurrection. This opens the doors of the church to the Jews first (Acts 2:14-41). Later Peter is the one to open those doors to the Gentiles (Acts 10:34-48) after again receiving and submitting to God's revelation (Acts 10:15, 28; 11:18).

19b. *". . . whatever you bind on earth will be bound in heaven, and whatever you loose on earth will be loosed in heaven."*

This is another one of those passages that has drawn many different interpretations. The binding and loosing have to do with the preaching and teaching of the gospel and the authority inherent in it. Peter has an important role in this, as much of the book of Acts reveals. This authority is not exclusive to Peter, however. It is also given to church leaders (Matthew 18:17, 18). Peter probably stands as representative here, especially of apostolic authority. We could say that he is "first among equals." The most important thing about this authority is that it is ultimately Heaven's authority. It is only legitimately exercised on earth when it is consistent with all of God's revelation.

IV. NECESSARY MISSION (MATTHEW 16:20-23)

A. IMPORTANT WARNING (v. 20)

20. *Then he warned his disciples not to tell anyone that he was the Christ.*

Jesus finds it necessary to withhold this good news to avoid misunderstandings about his messiahship (compare John 6:15). As we learn from the first-century Jewish historian Josephus and Acts 5:36, 37, there were Jewish insurrectionists in and around the time of Jesus who led revolts that were suppressed. Jesus undoubtedly does not want either the people or the Roman Empire to confuse him with one of those revolutionaries.

We also remember that Herod the Great had attempted to keep this new king from arising (Matthew 2:3-12). When the disciples limit their "God talk" about Jesus at this point in time, it will help ensure that people come to Jesus for the right reasons. Faith, not an expectation of the overthrow of the Romans, is the basis on which people need to approach Jesus.

B. DIRE PREDICTION (v. 21)

21. *From that time on Jesus began to explain to his disciples that he must go to Jerusalem and suffer many things at the hands of the elders, chief priests and teachers of the law, and that he must be killed and on the third day be raised to life.*

WHAT DO YOU THINK?

When we see boarded up church buildings, how do we relate that sad fact to Jesus' statement in Matthew 16:18b?

[Hint: make sure Revelation 2:5 is part of your answer.]

WHAT DO YOU THINK?

When have you noticed the church struggling with the concept of authority? What is the solution to this struggle?

PRAYER

Father, give us grateful hearts to recognize our Savior's love. May we ever confess Jesus as our Messiah. May we renounce our sins to his lordship. It's in his holy name that we pray, amen.

WHAT DO YOU THINK?

In what ways are we guilty of rebuking Jesus today? How do we reverse this problem?

WHAT DO YOU THINK?

What are some of "the things of men" that you have valued over the things of God in the past? How did you turn this problem around?

From now on Jesus will use allusions that are less veiled to show his disciples more directly what are the necessary aspects of his mission. It is clear that he is the Messiah (v. 16, above). Now his real redemptive mission as Messiah must also be set forth clearly.

Jesus begins by explaining the sequence of events in the final phase of his earthly ministry. The fact that he *must go* indicates that there is a divine plan behind this imperative. It also signals that Jesus understands that he is fulfilling prophecy (compare Isaiah 42:1 with Matthew 3:16, 17; Isaiah 61:1-3 with Luke 4:18, 19; etc.).

The Messiah's mission must involve suffering (Isaiah 52:13–53:12). It is both ironic and tragic that it is at the hands of the elders, chief priests, and scribes that this suffering comes. These Jewish leaders should be among the ones most open to welcoming him.

C. MISGUIDED REBUKE (v. 22)

22. Peter took him aside and began to rebuke him. "Never, Lord!" he said. "This shall never happen to you!"

Peter's attempted *rebuke* is a strong one. It contrasts sharply with his confession in verse 16 in implying that Peter knows better than Jesus does! The word *began* implies that Jesus does not wait for *Peter* to finish his misguided attempt. Jesus interrupts with a rebuke of his own.

D. STERN RESPONSE (v. 23)

23. Jesus turned and said to Peter, "Get behind me, Satan! You are a stumbling block to me; you do not have in mind the things of God, but the things of men."

A very harsh response, indeed! By interfering with God's plan and tempting Jesus to an easier road, Peter, like *Satan* (Matthew 4:8, 9), is making himself into Jesus' adversary.

PRIORITIES

Certain U.S. national parks pride themselves on attracting many tourists. In fact, the more tourists, the more reasonable are the requests for increased governmental funding. Better funding means more financial resources to improve the park, which in turn will attract more tourists.

Unfortunately, some parks have attracted "too many" tourists, and the sheer volume of visitors creates a negative ecological impact. Too many people are walking on the grass, climbing on the rocks, and disrupting the vegetation and wildlife. The result is a park in decline. That will lead to a loss of tourists and a decrease in revenue that could redress the devastation wrought by so many visitors. One suggestion is to make some parks "drive-through only." But the result still will be fewer tourists. Sometimes we don't know enough to set the right priorities!

Peter had the same problem. His priority was to defend Jesus from harm, not realizing that harm was the reason for Jesus' coming into the world. He minded the things of man, not the things of God. This should cause us to be especially prayerful before reaching conclusions about what *is* and *is not* the will of God.

—J. B. N.

CONCLUSION

In today's world, people look for security in many places. They place their hope in democratic freedom, finances, military security, etc. In effect, these things become false messiahs. But today's lesson makes clear that God has provided only one true Savior: Jesus the Christ.

THOUGHT TO REMEMBER

Make Peter's confession your own.

Discovery Learning

This page contains an alternative lesson plan emphasizing learning activities. Some of these activities are also found in the helpful student book, NIV Bible Student. *The next page is a reproducible activity page to further enhance discovery learning.*

INTO THE LESSON

As learners enter the room, give each a piece of paper with the heading *Confession* and a subheading *Four Kinds of Confession.* Include the following four kinds of confession as bullets down the left side of the page:

- An act of disclosing one's personal guilt in a crime.
- An act of disclosing one's sins.
- A formal statement of religious beliefs.
- An organized religious body having a common belief system.

Ask learners to work in pairs to think of one or two examples of each of the four kinds of confession. Allow the pairs to share their examples with the class as a whole. Make the transition to the Into the Word segment by saying, "As you see, the word *confession* has different meanings. Today I'm going to allow you to make a confession. However, I'm not going to tell you what type of confession it is until later, and I won't put you on the spot."

INTO THE WORD

Before class, put the following identities (real and imagined) of Jesus in bold letters on seven letter-sized pieces of paper, with one name per sheet: *Son of Man, John the Baptist, Elijah, Jeremiah, one of the prophets, Christ, Son of God.* Begin this segment by reading the printed text and asking learners to watch for the identities attributed to Jesus. After the reading, ask people to call out the names or titles as you list them on the board.

Activity #1: "What's in a name?" Create four study teams of two to five people each. Teams will interpret the significance of each name and title attributed to Jesus in the lesson. (Smaller classes may make individual assignments.) Give each team a photocopy of the lesson commentary on verses Matthew 16:13-16 and one or more of the appropriate identity signs you prepared earlier. Each team is to prepare a brief report on the names and/or identities assigned. Team A: *Son of Man,* verse 13. Also give this team a Bible dictionary as a resource. Tell them that the designation *Son of Man* is often listed under *Jesus* or *Christ Jesus.* Team B: This team has several names to explore from verse 14. Each will require only a very brief report. The names and

designations are *John the Baptist, Elijah, Jeremiah,* and *one of the prophets.* Team C: *Christ,* verse 16. Team D: *Son of the living God,* verse 16. Ask each team to report. During the reports, a team member can hold up the appropriate sign displaying the name or designation of Jesus as that name or designation is discussed.

Activity #2: Mini-lectures and whole-class discussion questions. 1. What do you think is the significance of Peter's answer in verse 16? Why do we call it *the Good Confession?* Considering 1 Timothy 6:13, is that an appropriate name for it? 2. Using the lesson commentary as a resource, give a mini-lecture on the significance of verses 19b and 20. 3. Tell the class that the lesson commentary on verse 21 makes the following statement, "It is both ironic and tragic that it is at the hands of the elders, chief priests, and scribes that this suffering comes." Ask, "Why would the writer say this is 'ironic and tragic'"? 4. Give a mini-lecture on verse 23.

Activity #3: Confusion and Clarity. Create study teams or discussion pairs to complete this exercise from the Reproducible Page. Ask each team or pair to report.

INTO LIFE

Remind the learners that one definition of *confession* is "A formal statement of religious beliefs." Peter made his confession. But individuals must decide to accept or reject Jesus as Christ. Many musicians have already done that as they set their feelings about Jesus to music. Brainstorm and list song titles or phrases that make statements about Jesus' divinity. Examples: "Hallelujah! What a Savior" and "He Is Lord."

Remind learners that you promised they would have an opportunity to make a confession. Ask each to write his or her own statement on an index card, answering that probing question, "Who is Jesus?" Give learners a few minutes, then ask for volunteers to read their confessions of faith. Do not put anyone on the spot to read his or her card.

After hearing a confession of Jesus' deity, ask how the learner will live out that confession. Have a gracious, low-key reply ready for "non-deity" confessions. *Option:* use the Who Do They Say He Is? activity from the Reproducible Page as a lead-in to this segment. Time allowing, you may also wish to use the Christ for Me activity from the Reproducible Page.

Confusion and Clarity

Imagine the disciples' possible reactions to Jesus' comments after Peter declares Jesus' identity. Some things were becoming clearer, but not everything. What thoughts or questions could have been running through the minds of the other disciples? Write the possibilities in the balloons.

Who Do They Say He Is?

If Jesus were to ask "Who do people say that I am?" in 2008, what answers might people give? Would or should the answer be clearer than the possible questions in the minds of the disciples? Why?

Christ for Me

People look for security in many places, but Christians find it in knowing that Jesus is God's Son and Savior. Write a testimony about experiences with Jesus that have brought peace and security to your life.

_____

_____

_____

Images of Christ
Unit 3: Images of Christ in Us
(Lessons 10–14)

DOERS OF THE WORD

LESSON 10

WHY TEACH THIS LESSON?

"I don't like Bible studies," groused an elderly gentleman. I knew that he had been attending Sunday school for years, so his declaration caught me off guard. "Then why do you come?" I asked. "I enjoy the fellowship," he answered.

James, the author of today's Bible text, undoubtedly thought that Bible study, fellowship, etc., were good things. But his issue was that of ensuring that Bible knowledge was put into practice. His concern was for *knowing* the Word of God in a way that would enable a Christian to *do* the will of God. And being a doer goes far beyond pleasant fellowship with other Christians. That's something my elderly gentleman didn't seem to grasp. Today's lesson will ensure that your learners understand where their knowledge and study of the Word should lead.

INTRODUCTION

A. GAG GIFTS

Some gifts are given simply for the fun of the moment. Gag gifts used for a "white elephant" exchange fit this category. Everyone rummages in the basement or attic, goes to the dollar store, or recycles gifts from the last white elephant exchange in order to provide an item that will be the worst (and most hilarious) gift at the party. Bad art, ridiculous hats, and ugly cups—such gifts are worthless in and of themselves.

Other gifts have real, lasting value. The gift talked about in today's passage is foremost of these. In fact, it is the only truly eternal gift.

B. LESSON BACKGROUND

The epistle of James was written by James, the brother of Jesus (Galatians 1:19; 2:9). James did not believe Jesus to be the Christ until after Jesus' resurrection (John 7:5; 1 Corinthians 15:7). James was present with those gathered just before the Day of Pentecost (Acts 1:14). By the time of the Jerusalem council in Acts 15, James had emerged as one of the principal leaders of the church. James was noteworthy enough for the historian Josephus to record his murder, which happened in about AD 62.

The epistle of James is his only work in the New Testament. Unlike books from Paul, which often are concerned about the place of Gentiles in the church, James writes primarily to Jewish Christians. They were in a tough situation (James 1:1-3). Some even had fled Jerusalem following the persecution by Herod Agrippa that occurred in the time period of Stephen's stoning and the execution of James, the son of Zebedee (Acts 11:19–12:2).

I. GIFTS FROM GOD (JAMES 1:17, 18)

In the verses preceding those for this lesson (James 1:1-16), James challenges believers to have the kind of mature faith that can stand up to life's disasters and disappointments. He seems worried about their eternal future. He is concerned

DEVOTIONAL READING:
PSALM 92:1-8

BACKGROUND SCRIPTURE:
JAMES 1

PRINTED TEXT:
JAMES 1:17-27

LESSON AIMS

After participating in this lesson, each student will be able to:

1. Summarize James's teaching on hearing and doing and on making one's religion real.

2. Explain how God's Word should lead to active discipleship.

3. Make a plan to correct one area of life in which he or she needs to move from being a mere hearer to being a doer.

Aug
3

KEY VERSE

Do not merely listen to the word, and so deceive yourselves. Do what it says. —James 1:22

that many Christians believe—wrongly—that God is tempting them when the opposite is true (1:13). God wants all believers to succeed! In fact, rather than throwing hazards at us, he continually strews our paths with gifts to encourage us as we go.

A. The Best Gifts (v. 17)

17. Every good and perfect gift is from above, coming down from the Father of the heavenly lights, who does not change like shifting shadows.

James describes God in three ways: as the one *from above,* as the *Father of the heavenly lights,* and as the one *who does not change like shifting shadows.* The first phrase is a common expression of ancient Jews that is based on their understanding of God's location. The second phrase connects God with the creation of light (Genesis 1:3, 14).

This sets the stage for James's third observation. This is an issue of the constancy of God's character, which contrasts with that of people, who are described as "double-minded" and "unstable" in James 1:8. The image *does not change like shifting shadows* brings to mind the lengthening of shadows as created by the interference of the sun's light by buildings and trees. God's character is like a sun that never sets and that has nothing to block its light. With God, it is always high noon. With this correct understanding of God, it is easy to grasp the idea that he wants only the best for us in life.

GEOSTATIONARY

I grew up with the knowledge of satellites as a new science. I still remember the thrill and concern that greeted the news that Sputnik I was in orbit. Of course, we Americans could not let the Russians get ahead of us in the space race, so we soon had our own satellites. They have been increasing in number ever since.

I remember driving out into the country on a summer night in 1960 to watch a satellite moving across the sky. That was the problem with satellites of the time: they moved. There were some advantages to that movement, but the disadvantage was that they didn't give a constant report because their location continually changed. Since then, a new generation of satellites has arrived—satellites that are geostationary. That means they remain in one place over the surface of the earth. This is an improvement over the way the older satellites operate. Because geostationary satellites move in exact synchronous movement with the rotation of the earth, their location and report are constant—they do not vary.

James didn't have geostationary satellites in his day to use to illustrate God's unchanging nature, so James used images of lights and shadows to make his point: with God there is no change. We sinful mortals shift constantly—in our morals, our actions, our priorities, our physical locations, and our attitudes. It is convenient—even vital—to have a point of reference that never changes. That "satellite reference" is the unchanging God.   —J. B. N.

B. The Eternal Gift (v. 18)

18. He chose to give us birth through the word of truth, that we might be a kind of firstfruits of all he created.

As in verse 17 above, this verse first draws on creation ideas from Genesis. The creation of humankind by God's *word* is implied as the absolute best result of all his creation activities.

The major concern of this passage is not to talk about that life-giving word in Genesis, but to use its language as a stepping-stone to talk about God's perfect gift: *the word of truth.* This word gives birth to life of a different order: eternal life.

What Do You Think?

Every good thing is from God! Given this fact, what should you thank him for at this very moment?

This *birth* takes place at the spiritual level and is propelled by a specific word, the message of the gospel. Christians are the *firstfruits* of humanity. This is apparent because (1) the *we* and *us* refer to believers, (2) becoming a Christian is commonly referred to as birth in the New Testament (John 3:3; 1 Peter 1:3), and (3) *word of truth* refers to the gospel (see also Ephesians 1:13).

II. LESSONS FROM A PROVERB (JAMES 1:19-27)

At first the following verses don't seem to connect very well to the previous ones. However, 1:22, 23 will again talk about "the word." It can be presumed that this word is the perfect gift, the word of truth from 1:17, 18.

A. THE PROVERB (v. 19)

19. My dear brothers, take note of this: Everyone should be quick to listen, slow to speak and slow to become angry,

Proverbs are carefully crafted, memorable sayings. This one not only provides a keen perception about the relationship between listening and outbursts of anger, it also provides the framework for the immediate verses that follow. Verses 20, 21 expand on the third part of the proverb, verses 22-25 on the first, and verse 26 on the second. Not only that, the three parts of verse 19 introduce the broad concerns of the entire book of James: correctly hearing the word (chapter 2), the difficulty of controlling the tongue (chapter 3), and the damaging effect angry speech has on the church (chapter 4).

The primary observation of this proverb is that careful attention to what someone else is saying is the gateway to disciplining one's own talk. Then disciplining one's own talk leads to breaking the bad habit of angry, uncontrolled, emotion-laden outbursts. Though every human being occasionally speaks like this, control of this human weakness is a virtue. Such outbursts usually result in our saying things that hurt others whom we really don't wish to hurt.

The teaching of each of the three concerns of this verse is found in the book of Proverbs. Proverbs 5:1, 2; 15:31; 19:20; 22:17, 18; etc., extol the virtue of listening. Proverbs 10:8, 10, 19; 13:3; and 18:2 deal with controlling our speech. Also see Proverbs 12:16; 14:17; 15:18; 16:32; 17:27; 20:3; 29:11, 20, 22.

RASH SPEECH

When I was a freshman in college, I had not yet learned some of the subtleties of interpersonal communication. On one occasion I asked a fellow student a question about a rather controversial situation. When she began to explain her view on the issue, I immediately realized her opinion was different from mine. So I jumped in, arguing with her. She let me rattle on for a couple of minutes, then she softly observed, "I thought you were asking for my opinion; I didn't realize you just wanted to argue."

I was abashed, but she was right. It was obvious I really didn't care for her opinion; I just wanted to present my own and argue against hers. I learned over the process of time that she was a thoughtful person, quite bright about a lot of things. But at the time I was a presumptuous freshman, more interested in arguing than in intelligent discussion.

First of all, it probably would have been better if I had never initiated a controversial confrontation. But even then it would have been much smoother if I had waited for her to explain her view so we could then calmly discuss our different viewpoints. In other words, it would have been much better for me to be swift to hear, slower to speak. But, of course, I'm the only one who has ever had to learn that lesson the hard way, right? —J. B. N.

HOW TO SAY IT

Ezekiel. Ee-ZEEK-ee-ul or Ee-ZEEK-yul.

Gentiles. JEN-tiles.

Herod Agrippa. HAIR-ud Uh-GRIP-puh.

Isaiah. Eye-ZAY-uh.

Jerusalem. Juh-ROO-suh-lem.

Josephus. Jo-SEE-fus.

Pentecost. PENT-ih-kost.

Zebedee. ZEB-eh-dee.

Zechariah. ZEK-uh-RYE-uh.

Visual for Lessons 1, 6, & 10. *Point to this visual as you ask, "How will lifting our eyes to the cross help us control our speech?"*

B. CONTROLLING ANGER (vv. 20, 21)

20. . . . for man's anger does not bring about the righteous life that God desires.

The word *anger* in other contexts can refer to the emotional feelings people have when they are upset. But here it represents the unregulated, hurtful words people shout at others when they are angry. This type of behavior is unacceptable to God. Angry words that aim to do harm are always wrong. They are vindictive. However, the emotion of anger itself is in many ways a natural, human way of coping with stressful, unfair things that happen to us in our lives. God himself gets angry (see Zechariah 10:3; Mark 3:5).

The human virtue that is crucial to pleasing God is *control.* How a person deals with his or her anger is the difference between righteous and unrighteous character. A person can use anger as the impetus to solving problems in productive ways. Mean-spirited, emotional outbursts are not helpful to these ends and are therefore displeasing to God.

21. Therefore, get rid of all moral filth and the evil that is so prevalent and humbly accept the word planted in you, which can save you.

An uncontrolled display of angry words is only one of many unrighteous— and therefore unacceptable—things that people do. By using the word *filth,* James pictures people covered in something disgustingly smelly that they need to wash off. With the phrase *evil that is so prevalent,* the picture switches to that of overgrown weeds that need to be cut back so that righteousness can flourish.

Rather than continue to allow unrighteous behavior (such as angry speech) to dominate our behavior, we are to cultivate *the word* we were given when we believed. That precious gift is the word of truth (1:18, above), the gospel. James pictures this word as a seed that has been *planted* in the soil of our lives. That seed needs to be nurtured so it will bloom and grow, replacing the weeds of evil and the sinful nature within us. This seed and only this seed enables people to develop the righteous character that God desires. However, only Christians have received this seed. God has created every human being with a cultivated spot in his or her life to receive this seed, the word of the gospel. But he does not force anyone to accept it. Rather, each one upon hearing the gospel may accept this seed as a welcome guest into his or her life, just as the believers James is writing about have done (compare Matthew 13:23).

Humility, easily overlooked in verse 21, is a key component for generating the kind of Christian lives that James demands. Certainly, its opposite (namely, arrogance) cannot be present when a person first accepts the gospel, repents of sin, and fully relies on the graciousness of God. Arrogance also impedes the growth of that gospel seed implanted in our lives. Full reliance on God for strength to overcome our unrighteous character is the only way we can become the excellent kind of people God desires. Clearly, the believers James writes to have accepted the implanted word, but they have dampened its growth by their pride. This stands as a warning to us not to do the same.

C. HEARING GOD'S WORD (vv. 22-25)

22. Do not merely listen to the word, and so deceive yourselves. Do what it says.

The interest now turns to spiritual matters. *The word* mentioned here is still the "word of truth," the gospel planted by God as the eternal gift taking root in the lives of believers.

As most evident in children, there is a big difference between merely hearing and really listening. Poor listening (in terms of "in one ear and out the other") decreases our ability to perform well. Yet we are to be excellent listeners, focusing

WHAT DO YOU THINK?

What situations present the greatest danger for you to speak out inappropriately? What tips have you found helpful for keeping your tongue in check?

WHAT DO YOU THINK?

How can an attitude of humility help keep our tempers in check?

intently on what God is saying to us through his gospel, which is now a permanent part of our lives. If we *listen* well, we will perform well. Our lives will demonstrate the righteous character that pleases God. We will *do what* the word *says* (compare Matthew 7:26).

23, 24. Anyone who listens to the word but does not do what it says is like a man who looks at his face in a mirror and, after looking at himself, goes away and immediately forgets what he looks like.

What will happen if we refuse to listen attentively to *the word*? Suppose that one morning we look at the *face* in the *mirror* and we don't recognize ourselves. We ask, "Is that really me?" What a frightening thought! Something would be terribly wrong if this were to happen. After all, this is our very own face.

Yet, that's what the case would be if we had forgotten what we looked like. Someone who uses a mirror then *immediately forgets what he looks like* won't recognize himself the next time he uses a mirror. In this case, previously known flaws would go ungroomed.

25. But the man who looks intently into the perfect law that gives freedom, and continues to do this, not forgetting what he has heard, but doing it—he will be blessed in what he does.

The mirror analogy applies to the issue of a believer's behavior, or doing. In this the term *word* of verse 23 is replaced by the term *law*. Laws are supposed to be enforceable rules intended to curtail criminal behavior so law-abiding citizens are free from the fear of criminals. Good idea, but whose law is perfect? Not any in human society.

The law at issue here is described as *perfect* and as giving *freedom*. It is that part of the word of truth that God has planted in believers. It is perfect because it is the eternal gift of God (1:17). It provides freedom because it is not like any normal human law. Rather than an external rule to enforce behavior by punishment, this law (or word) changes people at their core, releasing them to live out God's desires because enacting his word comes naturally. It is the fulfillment of Jeremiah 31:33, "I will put my law in their minds and write it on their hearts." This *law* is best represented by "love your neighbor as yourself" (Matthew 19:19). This is a positive principle for determining what God's desire is from one situation to the next. James probably has this in mind because he refers to it in James 2:8 as the royal law. It is the key law instituted by Jesus for the kingdom of God.

D. CONTROLLING SPEECH (v. 26)

26. If anyone considers himself religious and yet does not keep a tight rein on his tongue, he deceives himself and his religion is worthless.

This verse deepens the importance of the second part of the proverb of James 1:19. The matter of the control of the *tongue* is underlined in dire, spiritual terms. James draws a straight line that connects this virtue of speech control to the genuineness of one's religious experience, and then to the validity of the *religion* one claims to be true.

James believes at the very least that any religion worth anything should make its devotees better people in ways that others can observe. As applied to Christianity, the communication of its truth to others is utterly dependent on the way Christians behave. The way we talk is one of the best and easiest ways for people to experience the value of Christianity, not only to them as individuals but also to society at large.

Surprisingly, verse 26 uses the word *religious* like we would today. For the sake of his argument, James views Christianity as one of many religions that

WHAT DO YOU THINK?

Have you ever listened to a sermon and thought to yourself, "This is exactly what so-and-so needs to hear"? How can we focus on letting God's Word affect us personally rather than worrying about others?

DAILY BIBLE READINGS

Monday, July 28—The Full Effect of Endurance (James 1:1-4)

Tuesday, July 29—Ask in Faith (James 1:5-8)

Wednesday, July 30—How to Boast (James 1:9-11)

Thursday, July 31—Endure Temptation (James 1:12-15)

Friday, Aug. 1—Everything Is from God (James 1:16-21)

Saturday, Aug. 2—Blessed in Doing (James 1:22-27)

Sunday, Aug. 3—How Great Are Your Works (Psalm 92:1-8)

Author of all good gifts and provider of the gift of life eternal through the gospel, thank you for your generous demonstration of love toward us. Help us return our love to you by loving others in all we do and say. In Jesus' name, amen.

people follow. Of course, Christianity is the only completely true religion, since only it incorporates the full, direct revelation from God in Jesus Christ. However, the concern here is not with defending Christianity in terms of its truth claims. Rather, the issue is helping us know that when we fail to control our speech, we exhibit to the world that Christianity has no power to change people for the better. This is devastating to Christianity. We are to let the implanted word blossom into things like honest, uplifting, and genuine words. Compare Psalm 34:13; 39:1; and 141:3.

E. PRACTICAL APPLICATION (v. 27)

27. Religion that God our Father accepts as pure and faultless is this: to look after orphans and widows in their distress and to keep oneself from being polluted by the world.

James explicitly extends the observations about the importance of a believer's controlled speech to general behavior. Not only should a valid *religion* affect our speech, it should bring about observable improvements in the way we live our lives.

When this verse speaks of true religion as *pure* and *faultless,* everyone in the ancient world—Greeks and Jews—would think that what is at issue is ritual sacrifice in a temple. Pure religion in this perspective involves how one goes about selecting the best animals and performing proper prayers and rituals. It is probably shocking to the first readers of James that a connection is made to *widows* and *orphans,* since they are at the very bottom of life economically and socially.

However, God's consistent concern for their welfare is inscribed in Hebrew law. Deuteronomy 24:17 provides that they should be allowed to take a share from the stored produce of Israel; it warns that anyone who deprives them should be cursed. Prophets condemn Israel for mistreating orphans and widows (Isaiah 1:10-17; Jeremiah 5:28; Ezekiel 22:7; Zechariah 7:10).

This verse emphasizes that believers should *look after* those widows and orphans. This does not imply that merely writing out a check exhibits the behavior that pleases God. Rather, what is at issue is caring enough to be involved personally. This is intended to be an example of many observable behaviors in believers that are the result of the word of truth becoming fruitful in our lives.

A second example lies in how believers behave generally. Having cleaned up our lives to allow the implanted word to grow, we no longer want to exhibit behavior that looks like our old lives. To *keep oneself from being polluted by the world* does not imply that we are to retreat somehow from the world, keeping ourselves apart from unbelievers. Rather, it implies that believers are no longer to be influenced by the ideas and priorities that motivate unbelievers. We are to show them what Christianity looks like "in the flesh." We can't do that if we don't associate with them.

WHAT DO YOU THINK?

What keeps us from assisting needy people today? How do we overcome this?

CONCLUSION

Gifts come in all sizes and shapes—and purposes. Blouses, shirts, and ties are to be worn. Cookies and candy are to be eaten. Books are to be read, CDs listened to. Artwork and photos are to be admired. Many gifts are intended to be used and used and used. Tools like drills and screwdrivers fit this category. So do appliances such as can openers, coffee makers, and microwaves.

The gift of salvation is intended to be used too. Its use, however, involves allowing Christ's principle of loving others to transform every word and deed of our lives into object lessons of God's love for men and women everywhere.

THOUGHT TO REMEMBER

Live out the gift of the gospel in word and deed.

Discovery Learning

This page contains an alternative lesson plan emphasizing learning activities. Some of these activities are also found in the helpful student book, NIV Bible Student. The next page is a reproducible activity page to further enhance discovery learning.

INTO THE LESSON

Bring a variety of mirrors to class and place them around the room. Then ask your learners whether they particularly like or dislike mirrors, and why. Expect humorous answers such as, "The mirror is too honest!"

Ask the men, "If you've been shaving all these years, why do you still need a mirror? Don't you know the contours of your own face by now?" Ask the women, "If you've been putting on make-up all these years, why do you still need a mirror? Don't you know the contours of your own face by now?" Expect more humorous answers. After a few minutes, point out the error in your logic if no one already has: the need for shaving and make-up mirrors isn't an issue of forgetting the contours of our own faces; rather, it's an issue of knowing precisely where to take something off of or put something onto our faces.

Say, "In today's lesson, our Bible author also points out a logic error. The error is being a *hearer* of God's Word and not a *doer* of God's Word. James says that's like someone looking in a mirror, then forgetting what he or she looks like after turning away." Refer to James 1:23-25.

INTO THE WORD

Next, divide the class into groups of four or five. Provide each group with a blank sheet of paper. Ask your learners to turn the paper so that the longest side is across the top (landscape position). Leaving a 1" margin on each side, have them create three columns labeled as follows: *Verse* (left column, about 1" wide), *Action* (middle column, about 4" wide), and *Reason* (right column, about 4" wide). Instead of handing out blank sheets of paper, you may wish to prepare photocopies of the above to save class time.

Have each group review James 1, looking for the specific ways that James tells his readers to be doers of the word. They are to fill in the chart with the verse reference, the action James describes, and the reason for the action. *Example: Verses: 2, 3; Action: rejoice in temptations. Reason: develops perseverance.*

After a few minutes of discussion, have each group share its discoveries. If time permits, compile a composite chart on the board that includes each group's findings.

Optional activity: One way to learn a passage is to paraphrase it, using modern terminology and examples. Have each student write a paraphrase of James 1. You can offer the following paraphrase as an example for James 1:1. "This e-mail is from James@Jerusalem.org. I want to be known as a servant of God and of the Lord Jesus Christ. I am writing to you my fellow Jews who have been scattered all over the world."

Challenge your learners to capture the meaning without being overly casual or flippant. To keep this activity from dragging out, assign only one or two verses per learner. Have learners read their paraphrases aloud.

INTO LIFE

A week before class, ask learners to visit a nursing home, a hospice situation, or a shut-in during the week. Ask for volunteers to tell about their experiences. If they do not have the opportunity to do this in the week before class, ask for volunteers to discuss a time in the past when they visited one of these places or situations.

A follow-up activity that puts the lesson into practice is for one person to make arrangements for the entire class to visit a caregiving institution. If your church sponsors or supports a specific agency, that can be the first choice. After the visit, discuss a class project that would benefit the residents of that institution.

An alternative is to find a way for the class to help a specific person or family in your congregation who has some special need. When visiting this person or family, don't take "too many" of your class members along lest the ones being visited feel intimidated. These activities provide a practical way for the class to experience the challenge "to look after orphans and widows in their distress" (James 1:27). It is doing what they hear from God's Word. If you have someone in your church who is experienced in visiting hospitals, nursing homes, etc., you can ask that person to do some visitation role-playing activities with your class in advance of their own visits. This will help keep your learners from making avoidable mistakes or saying and doing inappropriate things during their visits.

Options: use the Doers of the Word exercise from the Reproducible Page as a precursor to the above activities; distribute the Pausing to Reflect exercise as a take-home activity.

Doers of the Word

James 1:22 tells us, "Do not merely listen to the word, and so deceive yourselves. Do what it says." Find the specific actions that James 1 instructs Christians to do. One example is given to get you started.

Verse(s)	Action	Reason
2, 3	Consider trials a joy	Develops perseverance

Pausing to Reflect

Describe your physical qualities (good and bad) on this mirror.

Describe your spiritual qualities (good and bad) on this mirror.

Which set of reflections concerns you the most?

Which set concerns Jesus the most? Why are these questions important?

IMPARTIAL DISCIPLES

LESSON 11

WHY TEACH THIS LESSON?

I didn't like what I saw at a youth convention recently. One young man who took the stage had earrings and a tattoo. To me he looked like a "biker," not a preacher. I stayed, but only because I was the sponsor of the teens. I felt sure that this young man had nothing to say to me. The chip on my shoulder disappeared as he communicated God's truth. Young people responded publicly to his heartfelt invitation. My prejudice had nearly prevented me from experiencing a "once in a lifetime" moment.

We often make value judgments about people based upon their appearance or economic status. James's students came to realize that there was to be no such discrimination. This lesson will allow your own students to come to the same life-changing conclusion.

INTRODUCTION

A. A STAIN UPON HUMANITY

The U.S. Declaration of Independence boldly declares "all men are created equal, that they are endowed by their Creator with certain unalienable Rights." By incorporating a biblically influenced view of human dignity, those who wrote this struck a knockout blow against the perceived right of nobility to rule over the faceless hordes of commoners. Yet the writers' own prejudices prevented them from seeing how excluding equal rights and dignity to slaves, women, and others contradicted their bold plan.

Callous disregard for people of different races, tribes, and religious convictions is not just an American problem. It has played itself out against the backdrop of human history and continues today. One need think no further than the Nazi oppression of the Jews or Sunnis versus Shiites in Iraq. The Bible stands firmly against discrimination and prejudicial mistreatment of others for any reason. The lesson today is a key text in this regard.

B. LESSON BACKGROUND

Today's text expands on James 1:17-27 (last week) to show how vital it is for Christians to give words and feet to the gospel that is planted in their lives. An embarrassing feature of early Christian gatherings was that the wealthy were given preferential treatment. It is surprising that Christianity attracted any interest at all from the socially advantaged, since first-century Christianity was not a dominant world religion as it is today. By all historical accounts, Christianity was viewed as an obscure sect that attracted an odd assortment of Jews, Gentiles, women, slaves, etc. Christianity did not emerge out of the shadow of Judaism until almost the second century AD.

Though a few people of advantage did attach themselves to Christianity, early Christianity was primarily a religion of people outside of power. "The crowd," the nameless in Jewish society, were the ones who followed Jesus from place to

DEVOTIONAL READING:
MATTHEW 25:31-46
BACKGROUND SCRIPTURE:
JAMES 2
PRINTED TEXT:
JAMES 2:1-13

LESSON AIMS

After participating in this lesson, each student will be able to:

1. Recount James's admonition to follow the royal law rather than show favoritism.

2. Compare and contrast the effects of following the royal law with what happens when an individual or church does not follow it.

3. Suggest one specific way to implement the royal law more fully in his or her life or church.

Aug
10

KEY VERSE

Listen, my dear brothers: Has not God chosen those who are poor in the eyes of the world to be rich in faith and to inherit the kingdom he promised those who love him? —James 2:5

place. He openly and compassionately associated with those "at the bottom": tax collectors, widows, children, lepers, the demon-possessed, Samaritans, Gentiles.

Mary's song at Jesus' birth prophesied the reversal of social positions that he would bring (Luke 1:52, 53). The reversal of position in Jesus' kingdom is addressed in James 1:9-11 and is assumed to be the backdrop to 2:1-13. Here, language similar to Jesus' teaching as found in the Gospels is evident.

I. UNHOLY DISCRIMINATION (JAMES 2:1-7)

Discrimination and favoritism in the time of James were relative to one's position. This remains true today. People tend to mistreat those below them in the social pecking order and grovel at the feet of people above them. Thus, the vast majority experiences both social mistreatment as well as social superiority. Both are wrong.

A. WITHIN THE CHURCH (vv. 1-4)

1. My brothers, as believers in our glorious Lord Jesus Christ, don't show favoritism.

The phrase *show favoritism* describes what people do when they size others up based only on what they can see—the other person's attractiveness, skin color, clothing, house, etc. In the Old Testament, the equivalent Hebrew idea is applied to personal relationships as well as to the administration of civil justice. Leviticus 19:15 instructs the people of Israel "Do not show partiality to the poor or favoritism to the great" (see also Deuteronomy 1:17; Psalm 82:2; Proverbs 18:5).

Deuteronomy 10:17 explains that God himself is not partial. God's impartiality is foundational to New Testament instruction too. This is clearest in Acts 10:34, 35. See also Galatians 3:28; Ephesians 6:9; Colossians 3:25; Philemon; 1 Peter 2:13-25.

The verse before us bases its appeal for impartial relationships on its readers' faith *as believers*. Their common commitment to Christ makes this obvious. However, the verse draws attention to this by naming *Jesus Christ* specifically, the only mention of that name in this letter other than in James 1:1. He is *our glorious Lord*. For Jews in the New Testament period, glory has a particular reference to the presence or manifestation of God in all his grandeur. For Christians, glory is associated with the resurrection splendor of Christ. It corresponds with his highest position of exaltation at the right hand of God (Colossians 3:1).

But we should be sure to remember, as 1 Peter 2:21-24 does, that Christ came to his exalted position after abject humiliation, mistreatment, and suffering on the cross. His experience of discrimination was one of being wrongfully convicted, and his position is now reversed! God made him judge even over those who condemned him (Mark 14:62; Revelation 1:7).

2, 3. Suppose a man comes into your meeting wearing a gold ring and fine clothes, and a poor man in shabby clothes also comes in. If you show special attention to the man wearing fine clothes and say, "Here's a good seat for you," but say to the poor man, "You stand there" or "Sit on the floor by my feet,"

Verses 2, 3 tell a story of discrimination in the early church. We know it is a hypothetical story because it begins with *suppose*, yet we could say that it is based on reality. James tells of a person entering a group of believers. The term used for *meeting* is actually the word *synagogue* in Greek, normally expressing the regular gathering of Jews primarily for teaching and prayer.

The problem in this hypothetical event is exaggerated to be sure we "get it." Two men from opposite ends of the social and economic spectrum enter the meeting. One is extremely rich, and the other is very *poor*. One is a man of immense influence—perhaps a landowner, nobleman, or politician; the other is someone everyone wants to avoid. One wears *a gold ring*, symbolizing power. He also has an impressive outer cloak, his best of many selections. The other has none of this. He simply comes in "off the street," smelly, unwashed, unkempt.

Almost everyone, then and now, would do the same thing James describes with this situation: pander to the rich guy and ignore or insult the smelly guy. The poor man is sent to *sit on the floor*. The rich man receives a *seat* of honor. Yet these seating arrangements have nothing to do with character or faith conviction. The host has only looked at the men superficially.

Only a person of extraordinary conviction could possibly treat them the same or even reverse their positions. Yet to do so would model the central tenets of Christianity. In God's kingdom the position of the rich and poor will be reversed. Why not begin eliminating favoritism in the church now?

GOODLY APPAREL

In the musical *My Fair Lady*, Alfred P. Doolittle is the charming but irreverent dustman. Often unemployed, he comes to Professor Henry Higgins and asks him for a mere five pounds—that's British currency—in exchange for Alfred's daughter, Eliza. When Higgins offers more, Doolittle refuses. He explains that too much money will only corrupt everything, including himself. Later when Higgins communicates with a wealthy American philanthropist regarding the need for a lecturer on morality, Higgins suggests Alfred P. Doolittle, common dustman.

Doolittle is shocked when he later is informed that the philanthropist has left him a fund guaranteeing an income of 5,000 pounds per year. Just as Doolittle had feared, now everyone comes to him asking for money. His common-law wife demands marriage. All this happens because he has become wealthy and "respectable." He himself has not changed, but his new financial status changes how other people react to him.

When Doolittle had nothing, the wealthy ignored him and the poor treated him as an equal. After ending up with all that money, the poor responded with deference, and the wealthy treated him as an equal. That's a fictional story, but doesn't art often imitate life? Today, people still ignore the Doolittles who are dustmen, but they bow to the Doolittles who have status. Christians dare not embrace such discrimination.   —J. B. N.

4. . . . have you not discriminated among yourselves and become judges with evil thoughts?

Verse 4 moves beyond the hypothetical scenario to a blunt accusation. It accuses the readers of behaving in ways comparable to the pattern of verse 3. In doing so, they have become *judges with evil thoughts*. See Matthew 7:1.

B. AGAINST THE CHURCH (vv. 5-7)

5. Listen, my dear brothers: Has not God chosen those who are poor in the eyes of the world to be rich in faith and to inherit the kingdom he promised those who love him?

Verses 5-7 ask four rhetorical questions that assume a *yes* response. They are intended to draw attention to matters that the church already knows but has not applied to the issue of discrimination among themselves.

The first question reminds the church that God remains the champion of the *poor*. This truth assumes the teaching in the Old Testament (examples: Job 34:25-29; Proverbs 14:31). The situation of these poor, who will *inherit the kingdom*, causes us to think of one of the most memorable sayings of Jesus: "Blessed are the poor in spirit, for theirs is the kingdom of heaven" (Matthew 5:3).

WHAT DO YOU THINK?

What kind of clothing do you choose to wear to church? What motivates your choices? What should *motivate* your choices?

DAILY BIBLE READINGS

Monday, Aug. 4—Sheep or Goats? (Matthew 25:31-46)

Tuesday, Aug. 5—Acts of Favoritism? (James 2:1-4)

Wednesday, Aug. 6—God's Favored (James 2:5-7)

Thursday, Aug. 7—The Royal Law (James 2:8-11)

Friday, Aug. 8—The Law of Freedom (James 2:12-17)

Saturday, Aug. 9—Faith and Works (James 2:18-20)

Sunday, Aug. 10—An Active Faith (James 2:21-26)

Visual for Lesson 11. *You can use this visual aid to introduce several of the questions in the margins of this lesson.*

Neither Jesus nor James is suggesting that the poor are somehow automatically saved because of their economic condition. Yet the poor are more inclined than the rich to develop trust in God for his care of them. Despite being at a cultural disadvantage, the poor are at an advantage over the rich when it comes to spiritual development and kingdom potential.

6. But you have insulted the poor. Is it not the rich who are exploiting you? Are they not the ones who are dragging you into court?

Just before asking a second and third rhetorical question, James accuses the church of mistreating *the poor.* If they are treating the poor in any way like the picture in verses 3, 4, then they certainly have *insulted* them.

Using questions, James goes on to remind his readers of the social and economic realities of the time. Many of the readers are poor themselves; as such, they surely have experienced the strong arm of exploitation wielded by the *rich* and powerful. Then as now the wealthy have the advantage in court; they know the law, the judges, and the politicians. They own land, and their interests often affect the jobs and development of communities. Thus, they are pictured colorfully as being able to drag the poor *into court* against their will.

What is imagined here is not criminal court, but civil court. There the rich seek debt repayment or seek to extend property rights.

7. Are they not the ones who are slandering the noble name of him to whom you belong?

The fourth rhetorical question asks the church to recall that not only do the wealthy exploit them in court, but also by doing so they besmirch *the noble name of him to whom* they *belong.* Although his name is not mentioned specifically, there can be no doubt that the name at issue here is *Jesus.* It is possible that the verse thinks of the social harassment or taunting of Christians, but what James is more likely pointing out is the harm done to Jesus' name itself.

This text is written in a social world that contains only two classes of people: poor and rich. Of these, perhaps 90 percent are poor. In today's world, those in the middle class of Western democracies do not consider themselves to be "rich." Yet from the broader standpoint of world economics, they are. Anyone studying these verses must not only consider how he or she is treated by the rich but should also consider that they may well be among those who are exploiting the poor in their culture, whether in business or personally.

II. ROYAL LAW (JAMES 2:8-13)

Our next section shows that discrimination against another person is a violation of the love-for-neighbor principle. Those who violate this principle put themselves at a major disadvantage at judgment, since this is the measure that will be applied.

A. PRINCIPLE FOR APPLICATION (vv. 8-11)

8. If you really keep the royal law found in Scripture, "Love your neighbor as yourself," you are doing right.

The *law* of loving one's *neighbor* is found in Leviticus 19:18. Jesus elevated this law to a position above all other laws, except the command to love God (Matthew 22:36-40; Mark 12:28-31). The impact of this teaching on the early church can be observed in Romans 13:9; Galatians 5:14; and in the verses before us, which seek to evaluate behavior based on this principle.

James specifically connects this principle of neighbor love to Jesus' teaching about his kingdom by describing it as *royal.* This law was referred to earlier in

HOW TO SAY IT

Beguines. BAY-genes.

Deuteronomy. Due-ter-AHN-uh-me.

Gentiles. JEN-tiles.

Leviticus. Leh-VIT-ih-kus.

Philemon. Fih-LEE-mun or Fye-LEE-mun.

Samaritans. Suh-MARE-uh-tunz.

Shiites. SHE-ites.

Sunnis. SUE-nees.

synagogue. SIN-uh-gog.

James as "the word of truth" (James 1:18) and as "the perfect law that gives freedom" (1:25). Later it will be called simply the "law that gives freedom" (2:12). It is the standard that declares judging others to be wrong (4:12). It is a law unlike any other law!

9. But if you show favoritism, you sin and are convicted by the law as lawbreakers.

James now takes the microscope of the love-for-neighbor principle and uses it to look at the issue of discriminating against others. Treating others positively or negatively based on superficial cues demonstrates a failure to love them as our neighbors. Within the ethical principles established by Jesus for those in his kingdom, this is blatant *sin*. To discriminate is to break *the law* of Jesus.

No Respecters of Persons

The Beguines was an interesting social institution of the Middle Ages. There is much about this movement that is not well understood today, but we know enough to form an intriguing picture of them. The Beguines were women who had formed a semimonastic organization. That is, they were not nuns living under vows; they were free to own private property and could leave the group and marry if they wished. Organized first in the Netherlands in the twelfth century, they soon spread to other countries.

Their primary consideration was social works, particularly the care of the poor, the sick, and other needy. In an age of growing urbanization, they normally were associated with urban communities, providing some social relief to those who were caught in the transition from peasantry to urban life, but did not have skills to provide a decent living. The movement reached its height in the thirteenth century.

The Beguines served a useful function, tending to the needs of a downtrodden portion of the population. They were not respecters of persons and did not discriminate. They were simply women trying to be Christian servants in a changing culture. Do they have anything to teach us today? —J. B. N.

10. For whoever keeps the whole law and yet stumbles at just one point is guilty of breaking all of it.

Here James recites a truism that Jewish teachers commonly applied to Jewish law. It is still a valid legal principle. Specific legal regulations generally are grouped under categories. In Jewish teaching, for instance, one can walk only a certain distance on the Sabbath. To go farther than that is to transgress the regulation; but in transgressing the regulation, a person also breaks the law against working on the Sabbath. The parallel this verse draws is that not to discriminate is a regulation under the broader principle of loving our neighbor as ourselves. Thus to discriminate breaks the *law* of love.

11. For he who said, "Do not commit adultery," also said, "Do not murder." If you do not commit adultery but do commit murder, you have become a lawbreaker.

James offers an example of the truism of verse 10. The Ten Commandments is a unit of law provided in the Old Testament by God (Exodus 20; Deuteronomy 5). Violating 1 of the 10 specific rules makes a person guilty of breaking the wider unit of law. The regulations against *adultery* and *murder* may be chosen as examples because Jesus brought them up himself when he talked with the rich young ruler (Matthew 19:18, 19).

B. Principle for Judgment (vv. 12, 13)

12. Speak and act as those who are going to be judged by the law that gives freedom,

The law that gives freedom is the standard by which our lives will be measured. It is a guideline in all things. Although we may tend to think of our lives

What Do You Think?

What are some ways we can follow the "royal law" of loving our neighbors as we love ourselves?

What Do You Think?

What kinds of favoritism are there?

PRAYER

Father of us all, who created us to flourish in the world you made, give us the courage to live out our lives with the unrestricted love you have shown us in Jesus Christ. Enable us to display to the world a community of faith that dignifies all people, even as Christ did. In his name, amen.

WHAT DO YOU THINK?

If showing love and mercy to others is what builds up our "spiritual bank accounts," what words, attitudes, and actions can you change to build up your balance?

THOUGHT TO REMEMBER

Uphold the dignity of every person, both inside and outside the church.

primarily as a sequence of right or wrong actions, this verse brings the way we talk into the equation.

This is important because people probably have more opportunity to do more harm or good by what they say than by what they do. This verse picks up on an issue that becomes a full-blown concern in James 3. Jesus says in Matthew 15:11 that it is what comes "out of his mouth" that contaminates people.

Both words and behavior will be *judged*, then. But judged for what purpose? Aren't Christians already saved from judgment for their sins by the cross and the grace of God? The New Testament is very clear that although believers escape condemnation through the blood of Christ, they do not escape unevaluated. Second Corinthians 5:10 tells us that this evaluation is to be done by Christ and that everything we have done—our entire lives—will be surveyed. What verse 12 clarifies is that this judgment will include what we say and that it will be based upon Christ's law of freedom, or loving our neighbor.

13. . . . because judgment without mercy will be shown to anyone who has not been merciful. Mercy triumphs over judgment!

In this verse James picks up the teaching of Jesus found in Matthew 5:7: "Blessed are the merciful, for they will be shown *mercy.*" Within this beatitude is the kernel of Christ's law of neighbor love, but also the threat of *judgment*. Everyone wants to be given the benefit of the doubt by their coworkers, family, and friends. We need the forgiveness and forbearance of others when we mess up. This need should be the spark that makes us want to do the same for others.

To add to our motivation, this verse develops the beatitude to promise judgment on those who fail to show mercy, on those who do not live their lives on the basis of Christ's law of love. In his Parable of the Unforgiving Servant, Jesus likewise depicted severe punishment for the man who was forgiven a large debt he owed but would not forgive a smaller one owed to him (Matthew 18:21-35).

Verse 13 ends with a proverbial saying that promises safe passage through Christ's seat of judgment for those who live their lives in ways that consciously implement Christ's law of love. They do this by exercising mercy to others. The word *triumphs* depicts more than just "getting through." It pictures celebration in the face of anticipated victory, dancing with joy into our eternal reward. If we live our lives under the rule of love, we can enter judgment with supreme confidence that we have pleased Christ and that he will say, "Well done, good and faithful servant!" (Matthew 25:21).

If we live this way, it also is good news for the people around us. Among other things we won't be showing contempt for those "below" us in the social and economic orders of our culture. Nor will we give undue deference to those "above" us. We will not discriminate on such superficial things, just as God does not. We will be the impartial disciples whom Christ desires.

CONCLUSION

The last two verses sound a warning. Whereas Israel was judged on the degree to which they observed the law God gave them through Moses, those who form the church will be evaluated on their implementation of Christ's law for his kingdom. Israel was sent into exile for breaking their covenant with God. What will happen to those in the church? We must look closely at our lives and be fully aware of how well we are loving our neighbor. As Christians, not to live with this principle at the forefront of all our behavioral decisions is to invite God's condemnation.

Discovery Learning

This page contains an alternative lesson plan emphasizing learning activities. Some of these activities are also found in the helpful student book, NIV Bible Student. *The next page is a reproducible activity page to further enhance discovery learning.*

INTO THE LESSON

Bring a copy of the U.S. Declaration of Independence to class (easy to find on the Internet). Have someone read aloud just the first two sentences, ending with the words *and the pursuit of happiness.* Discuss the author's view of individual worth that the document proposes. Also discuss who was omitted in this document because of common practices of the time. Answers may include African-Americans (slaves), women (couldn't vote), etc.

Ask, "Why did the author feel—theoretically, at least—that it was important to declare that 'all men are created equal, that they are endowed by their Creator with certain unalienable rights'?" After some discussion time, point out that today's study will show that God has never been a respecter of persons as we have been.

INTO THE WORD

Before class, write the following Scripture references across the top of 14 sheets of paper, one per paper: Proverbs 14:31; Proverbs 28:3; Matthew 7:1, 2; Matthew 19:24; Matthew 22:39; Acts 10:34; James 2:1; James 2:2-4; James 2:5; James 2:6, 7; James 2:8; James 2:10, 11; James 2:13; 1 John 3:4.

Shuffle the sheets and distribute. Each learner should look up the passage given to him or her and write it out on the paper. Then ask the person with the reference to James 2:1 to read that text. Then ask, "Who has the text closest in meaning to this that is not from James?" Have that person read his or her text. Move through the passages from James 2 in sequence this way. The expected matches are *James 2:1 to Acts 10:34; James 2:2-4 to Proverbs 14:31; James 2:5 to Matthew 19:24; James 2:6, 7 to Proverbs 28:3; James 2:8 to Matthew 22:39; James 2:10, 11 to 1 John 3:4; James 2:13 to Matthew 7:1, 2.*

If you have fewer than 14 students, you can give learners more than one passage each (but give each either texts only from James or only not from James). If considering 14 texts is not practical given the constraints of time, use fewer texts.

Optional activity #1. Read the Key Verse, James 2:5. Ask for discussion about why James said that God chose the poor of this world to be rich in faith. Why are the poor more likely to have a strong faith? Why is it difficult for the rich to depend on God's gracious gifts? Passages such as Matthew 19:23, 24 and James 5:1 can enrich your discussion.

Optional activity #2. Have some class members pantomime the scene in James 2:2, 3. Select learners who have a flair for the dramatic for this demonstration. You can ask your actors a week ahead of time so they have time to practice.

Optional activity #3. Continue paraphrasing the book of James from last week, this time having learners paraphrase James 2. Again, challenge your learners to capture the meaning without being overly casual or flippant. To keep this activity from dragging out too long, assign only one or two verses per learner. After a few minutes, have learners read their paraphrases aloud in sequence. To extend this learning activity, encourage your learners to paraphrase the entire lesson text each week at home. Comment that this is an excellent way to focus on and understand God's Word.

INTO LIFE

Assemble your class into four small groups. Ask them to discuss the following sets of questions. Write these questions on the board or make copies of them for each group. Depending on the time available, you can have each group either discuss only one set of questions each or all four sets of questions.

1. What was a time when you felt discrimination directed at you? Do you think you reacted biblically? Why, or why not?

2. With what group of people do you find yourself feeling uncomfortable? Is *lack of comfort* the same as *discrimination*? Why, or why not?

3. Does our congregation show partiality or discriminate? If so, how do we fix this as God would want? What are some specific steps that this church can take to make all people feel welcome here?

4. A secular definition of discrimination is "unequal treatment without a rational basis." Does this definition harmonize with the Bible? Why, or why not?

To wrap up, have one person from each group summarize his or her group's conclusions for the class. Discuss as time allows. *Optional:* if time allows, have learners complete and discuss the My Inner Circle exercise from the Reproducible Page. As class concludes, distribute Rich Man, Poor Man as a take-home exercise.

My Inner Circle

In the innermost circle, write names of your family and closest friends. In the next circle, write names of two people whose company you enjoy but who are not in the innermost circle. In the third, outer circle write the names of two others whom you would like to know better and who are not in the first two circles. To the sides write a plan of action to get to know the four people in the outside two circles better.

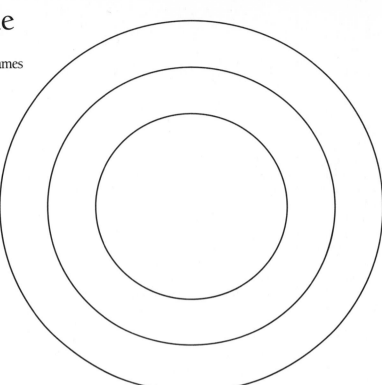

Rich Man, Poor Man

This is a take-home activity. List all the "categories" of people in your congregation. Include the categories of race, economic status, age, and gender.

Go back through your list and put a check mark beside the groups of people you enjoy and feel comfortable with. Circle the ones who make you uncomfortable for any reason. Use a one- or two-word identifier with each explaining why you feel comfortable or uncomfortable. Now read James 2 (the entire chapter). What is your plan of action to overcome your discomfort?

WISE SPEAKERS

LESSON 12

WHY TEACH THIS LESSON?

Some Native Americans believe that when a word is spoken it begins to live that day, and that no word spoken will ever die. There is a ring of truth to this. Careless, thoughtless remarks and their effects seem to live on and on, don't they? All of us have experienced the lingering pain caused by unkind words. We'd like to take back some of the words we've spoken. Though we apologize, we know that damage has already been done.

Each day we have an opportunity to glorify Christ with our tongues or give victory to the devil. Your learners don't control their tongues as well as they should—none of us do. This lesson will help all of us do better in this regard.

INTRODUCTION

A. A WORLD FULL OF WORDS

Talk fills our lives. Family, friends, coworkers, neighbors, salespeople, teachers, politicians, and preachers knit together the fabric of life with talk. Talk has tremendous impact that often goes unnoticed. We believed in the power of words when were little—that *abracadabra* could bring a rabbit out of a hat and that saying "There's no place like home" could transport a person from Oz to Kansas. But as we grew older and cast aside a "magical" view of words, we seem to forget that words still have a lot of power.

Most of us utter harmful, dangerous words every day. Our desire to be right, to get ahead, to gain control, to be heard, or to defend ourselves can motivate us to say all kinds of things at the expense of others. Fortunately, with sincere words we can also apologize. However, catching ourselves before we sin with our speech is tough. Still, we can do better, as this lesson will teach.

B. LESSON BACKGROUND

The epistle of James sits on the shoulders of a large body of literature that both collects and develops wise sayings to help people succeed. Bible readers will be most familiar with this type of literature, called *wisdom literature,* from reading Proverbs or Ecclesiastes. This style of literature was very popular in the ancient world.

Speech habits are one of the most predominant themes of these collections of wisdom. Proverbs 18:21 says, "The tongue has the power of life and death, and those who love it will eat its fruit." Jesus said, "But I tell you that men will have to give account on the day of judgment for every careless word they have spoken. For by your words you will be acquitted, and by your words you will be condemned" (Matthew 12:36, 37). Such is the importance of this issue!

After offering a brief warning to be "slow to speak" in James 1:19 and then reinforcing this with the advice in 1:26, James unleashes in chapter 3 his entire arsenal of reasons why the tongue must be controlled. Though it begins as a mandate to teachers in the church, it applies to everyone.

DEVOTIONAL READING:
PROVERBS 15:1-4; 16:21-24
BACKGROUND SCRIPTURE:
JAMES 3
PRINTED TEXT:
JAMES 3

LESSON AIMS

After participating in this lesson, each student will be able to:

1. Restate some of James's illustrations of an untamed tongue.

2. Distinguish between wholesome and unwholesome use of the tongue.

3. Make a plan to improve his or her use of the tongue in one specific way.

Aug
17

KEY VERSE

Out of the same mouth come praise and cursing. My brothers, this should not be. —James 3:10

LESSON 12 NOTES

I. POWER OF THE TONGUE (JAMES 3:1-5a)

A. WARNING ABOUT JUDGMENT (vv. 1, 2)

1. Not many of you should presume to be teachers, my brothers, because you know that we who teach will be judged more strictly.

Teachers are highly respected in the ancient world. Given the large number of people entering into the first-century church as new disciples, the importance of having good teachers to guide them in faith, understanding, and behavior is crucial.

Teachers in the first-century church share leadership at the local level with the prophets and apostles (see 1 Corinthians 12:28; Ephesians 4:11). Then as now, however, people sometimes desire to be teachers for the prestige of it without fully recognizing the enormous responsibility involved. James discourages unqualified people from seeking to be teachers with the warning that teachers are under a special scrutiny by Christ. James includes himself as a teacher, indicated by *we*, and accepts this greater risk of judgment he places over all teachers in the church.

The responsibility of nurturing Christian disciples is immense. The fact that this often was not done that well in the first-century church is seen in the New Testament epistles, which address troubling concerns about the influence of false teachers in the churches. This is still a problem today as evidenced by the "Christian" cults that continue to pop up.

2. We all stumble in many ways. If anyone is never at fault in what he says, he is a perfect man, able to keep his whole body in check.

The primary tool of teachers is the tongue. They talk in order to instruct people. This puts them at risk, because the tongue, or speech, cannot be controlled 100 percent of the time. Only a *perfect* person could stop the sinful tongue every time it is about to do damage. Since no one is perfect, we cannot keep our speech absolutely pure at all times.

Good teachers impart the truth from God and are entrusted to nurture their students to growth and maturity with that truth. This is so at all levels of Christian maturity, from nursery age to seniors in the church. Good teachers work hard to prepare and understand what they are teaching and to be sure it is based on Scripture. Bad teachers are sloppy in their preparation and don't work to develop their understanding of Christianity. Their students will not be provided the foundation they need and may become stagnant or may even rebel from their faith. It's no wonder the warning in these first two verses is so threatening!

OFFENDING IN WORD

A friend of mine was ministering with a church some years ago. His wife, whom he had recently married, was not always discreet in the use of her tongue. Soon after her husband was called to be the minister of that church, the chairman of the elders was showing them the parsonage where they would live. As they walked into the kitchen, she noted the new cabinets and remarked, "Wow, what ugly cabinets. Who chose these?" The cabinets had been chosen by the wife of the chairman of the elders—the very man who was showing them around the parsonage.

On another occasion her husband was at a meeting with the elders, and she became irritated that she had to change yet another one of her infant daughter's diapers. So she marched across the road to the church, walked into the elders' meeting, thrust the baby into her husband's arms, and said, "Here, you take her; it's your turn to change her diaper." Her lack of control over her tongue (which was based in an improper sense of propriety) was a constant impediment to her husband's ministry. It was not long before the elders asked for his resignation.

WHAT DO YOU THINK?

Of the words you heard yesterday, what percentage was helpful? What percentage was neutral? What percentage was negative or hurtful? How do you keep negative or hurtful words from influencing your own speech patterns?

Indeed, as James states, it is difficult to control the tongue. Someone who has the self-discipline to control his or her tongue can control just about anything. On the other hand, failure to control the tongue can lead to a downfall, in spite of numerous other good qualities. —J. B. N.

B. SMALL BUT MIGHTY (vv. 3-5a)

3. When we put bits into the mouths of horses to make them obey us, we can turn the whole animal.

James now moves on to some poignant examples of the power of the tongue. Once a small bit with bridle is placed properly, a rider can harness a horse's enormous power for the task at hand. This is no less true today.

4. Or take ships as an example. Although they are so large and are driven by strong winds, they are steered by a very small rudder wherever the pilot wants to go.

The second example makes an analogy between the tongue and the *rudder* of a ship. This analogy is more elaborate than the one involving the horse in verse 3, since James adds the *winds* and the ship's *pilot*. In first-century seafaring, the only source of power for ships (other than muscle power on the oars) is the wind. The rudder is controlled by the pilot on deck. The pilot makes decisions not only about what general direction to go but also how best to negotiate dangerous waters. This is a positive picture only if the pilot knows how to control the ship to its optimum.

This picture of the ship is particularly appropriate to accent both the mighty power of the human tongue over the body and the danger of the tongue with a poor pilot. This is the way verse 5 (next) is able to slip into a negative perspective on the human tongue, which is not so readily possible with the illustration involving the horse and bit.

5a. Likewise the tongue is a small part of the body, but it makes great boasts.

The tongue is portrayed as boasting, one of the many ways people sin when their speech is not under control. Boasting seeks attention to make up for deficiencies. It is a form of lying and deception as it exaggerates the truth or at least the significance of something.

Having set the stage by bringing up the speech sin of boasting, the verses to follow focus on the dangerous threat the tongue poses. For its relatively small size, the tongue is mighty. It can build people up or tear them down. It can launch nations into war or sit them down to peace.

II. DANGER OF THE TONGUE (JAMES 3:5b-12)

A. CAPABLE OF DESTRUCTION (vv. 5b, 6)

5b, 6. Consider what a great forest is set on fire by a small spark. The tongue also is a fire, a world of evil among the parts of the body. It corrupts the whole person, sets the whole course of his life on fire, and is itself set on fire by hell.

Fire is one of the most frightening forces people experience. People in the ancient world are exposed to the ravages of fire more routinely than people who live in modern democracies. Cooking and heating homes with open flame makes house fires more common in the first century.

These verses thus convey the image of the massive destruction that fire is capable of inflicting. Unlike the horse and the ship, whose images are mostly positive, the image turns decidedly negative here. Forest fires always begin at some specific point and then spread wildly. Even today, they are notoriously difficult to stop. And so the human *tongue* through gossip, slander, etc., can sweep

WHAT DO YOU THINK?

What was a time when someone else's words sparked a major decision for you? What was a time when you were surprised with the impact your words had on someone else?

HOW TO SAY IT

Corinth. KOR-inth.
Corinthians. Ko-RIN-thee-unz.
Ecclesiastes. Ik-LEEZ-ee-AS-teez.
Ephesians. Ee-FEE-zhunz.
epistles. ee-PIS-uls.
Galatians. Guh-LAY-shunz.
Marah. MAH-ruh.
menagerie. meh-NAJ-ree.

DAILY BIBLE READINGS

Monday, Aug. 11—The Tongue of the Wise (Proverbs 15:1-4)

Tuesday, Aug. 12—With Greater Strictness (James 3:1-4)

Wednesday, Aug. 13—Taming the Tongue (James 3:5-9)

Thursday, Aug. 14—Purity of One's Words (James 3:10-12)

Friday, Aug. 15—Born of Wisdom (James 3:13-16)

Saturday, Aug. 16—Sown in Peace (James 3:17, 18)

Sunday, Aug. 17—Wise and Pleasant Speech (Proverbs 16:21-24)

WHAT DO YOU THINK?

Since no one can tame the tongue, what hope do we have? [Hint: use Matthew 15:17-19; Mark 10:27; and Galatians 5:22, 23 to frame your answer.]

---

through a community just as quickly, just as uncontrollably, and with just as much emotional devastation.

Verse 6 sketches four dimensions of just how corrupt the human tongue is. The first dimension is that the tongue is *a world of evil* within a person. This description looks at the tongue as the most evil part of the body—more evil than the hand that steals, for instance. The tongue is the point from which more evil comes forth than anywhere else. It is the "command center" for those despicable sins that are so harmful.

The second dimension of the tongue's destructiveness is its corruption of the rest of the *parts of the* human *body.* The tongue that offers someone smooth flattery may be "setting up" the hand to commit theft.

The third dimension of the tongue's destructiveness is the damage it inflicts on society. This is expressed by the use of the phrase *course of his life,* or literally, "wheel of birth." This is a well-known phrase among ancient philosophers for the concept of fate: those external social and cultural forces that affect our lives and over which we have no control. When the sins of speech enter this sphere, then those sins can have devastating results on the lives of people we don't even know.

The fourth dimension of the tongue's destructiveness is its source. This is called *hell,* but that is a roundabout way of referring to Satan. The human tongue is Satan's point of access into our lives—a frightening thought that should make us want to keep that door shut as much as possible.

B. IMPOSSIBLE TO CONTROL (vv. 7, 8)

7, 8. All kinds of animals, birds, reptiles and creatures of the sea are being tamed and have been tamed by man, but no man can tame the tongue. It is a restless evil, full of deadly poison.

No longer speaking of the human *tongue* in analogies, these verses label it specifically as hopelessly *evil.* A sad irony in God's creation is detected: people can tame *animals,* but they can't control their own tongues.

The term *tame* should be taken very broadly, not just in terms of domesticating pets but also in terms of dominating all other living creations (Genesis 1:26, 28; 2:20). The verses before us depict the human tongue itself as a dangerous creature, perhaps the most dangerous. This is the one creature that humans do not seem to rule over.

The tongue's description as poisonous makes us think of a snake, an identification made in the Old Testament (see Job 20:12-16; Psalm 58:3, 4; 140:3). However, from the perspective of Genesis 3:1-6 this description connects to the serpent in the Garden of Eden, who deceived Adam and Eve with his conniving words. The result was their being thrust out of the garden.

UNTAMED

Wilbert Behn is a self-taught animal tamer. He lives in Aniwa, Wisconsin, where he hosts Behn's Game Farm. Now into his 80s, he still has a menagerie of lions, tigers, and dogs. He opens his shows with an outdoor presentation of performing dogs, leaping and barking, before he moves into his inside arena for the lions and tigers. Visitors are protected by a hurricane fence, but Behn works alone inside the fence.

The animals are trained to respond to music. Behn cracks his whip and lions jump up on barrels. A tiger walks a high-wire. Another large cat jumps through a flaming hoop, snarling menacingly. A tiger falls "dead" at the shot of a pistol loaded with blanks. Behn puts his head in the mouth of a lion. All provide a good show.

Ferocious animals can be tamed, but James says no one can tame the tongue. It's exciting to watch wild animals do tricks under the hands of a daring tamer. How much more useful it would be to see a person in total control of his or her speech!
—J. B. N.

C. Inclined to Evil (vv. 9-12)

9, 10. With the tongue we praise our Lord and Father, and with it we curse men, who have been made in God's likeness. Out of the same mouth come praise and cursing. My brothers, this should not be.

The next four verses observe some disheartening truths when it comes to the tongue. Though the human *tongue* can reach its zenith in belting out heartfelt *praise* for its creator, it reveals the depths of its degradation in its *cursing* the very best of God's creation: men and women created in his image (Genesis 1:27). The fact that verse 10 says this *should not be* holds out a bit of hope that the tongue's evil nature can be controlled with God's help.

11, 12. Can both fresh water and salt water flow from the same spring? My brothers, can a fig tree bear olives, or a grapevine bear figs? Neither can a salt spring produce fresh water.

The rhetorical questions acknowledge that we expect certain, predictable things from natural springs and plants. *Water* that is gloriously drinkable is described with the word *fresh* or sweet. (The Greek word behind this gives us our English word *glucose.*) The undrinkable water is *salty.* Even today, we know that a natural spring does not produce both kinds of water at once. And we would be quite puzzled to talk to someone who expected to harvest *figs* from his *grapevine!*

What "harvest" do we expect from our tongues? A dual harvest of blessing God and cursing others is as improper as expecting both salty and fresh water to come from the same source. Perhaps through the power of God's Word the bitter water can become sweet, as when Israel was at Marah (Exodus 15:22-25).

III. THOUGHTS ON WISDOM (JAMES 3:13-18)

A. Wisdom Shown by Life (v. 13)

13. Who is wise and understanding among you? Let him show it by his good life, by deeds done in the humility that comes from wisdom.

After thinking so much about the tongue with its follies and failures, it is fitting to turn our thoughts to wisdom. Wisdom is what every tongue needs to restrain and guide it. If asked, each one of us would like to state with confidence, "I am a person who is *wise and understanding.*" But James wants an answer in the form of our *deeds.* A person who does foolish things is not wise.

A person's *life* includes one's entire manner of living (Galatians 1:13; Ephesians 4:22). If a person is wise, his or her lifestyle is *good,* unselfish, helpful. That good lifestyle is the stage on which each individual work is done. Further, it is done with wise *humility* (compare Matthew 5:5). Now, how wise are you?

B. Wisdom from Below (vv. 14-16)

14. But if you harbor bitter envy and selfish ambition in your hearts, do not boast about it or deny the truth.

Imagine a popular leader in a certain church. Perhaps he is a handsome man with a ready smile and charming manners. With his pleasant ways and flattering words he wins followers easily, but this fellow is winning them for himself rather than for Christ. His heart is full of *bitter envy* of other leaders. Instead of cooperating with them, he belittles them, their opinions, and their plans. In

think, then speak...

Visual for Lesson 12. *Point to this visual as you introduce the question on page 430.*

What Do You Think?

What helps you maintain gracious speech under stressful circumstances?

[Hint: Ephesians 4:29-32 and Colossians 4:6 are important to consider.]

so doing, he generates strife (factionalism) instead of unified fellowship. James warns such a one not to *boast*—don't brag, don't be proud of yourself and your accomplishments. Speak well of others rather than praising yourself. (This is part of the humility of v. 13.) Don't exaggerate your own goodness, your own wisdom, your own accomplishments, because when you do, you *deny the truth.*

15. Such "wisdom" does not come down from heaven but is earthly, unspiritual, of the devil.

The *wisdom* that glorifies self is not God-given. It arises out of *earthly* ambition, selfishness, and the prompting of *the devil* (compare 1 Corinthians 1:20; 2:5, 6). One who asks God for wisdom (Proverbs 2:6; James 1:5) is rewarded with the kind described in verse 17 (below).

16. For where you have envy and selfish ambition, there you find disorder and every evil practice.

If *envy* and *selfish ambition* are prompted by evil (v. 15), we can be sure they are not good for us. This kind of disorder infected the church at Corinth (2 Corinthians 12:20). But confusion and *every evil practice* please no one but Satan and some victims of his deceit.

C. WISDOM FROM ABOVE (vv. 17, 18)

17. But the wisdom that comes from heaven is first of all pure; then peace-loving, considerate, submissive, full of mercy and good fruit, impartial and sincere.

Paul lists the "fruit of the Spirit" in Galatians 5:22, 23. Here, James lists what may be called the "fruit of *wisdom.*" Wisdom that is *pure* has no trace of the phoniness that is earthly, sensual, and devilish. *Peace-loving* wisdom will not produce strife, as selfishness and pride often do. A person of *considerate* wisdom does not try to overpower others and force opinions on them.

A wise person stands firm for truth and righteousness. In matters of opinion, however, this kind of person is *submissive.* This means such a person listens to reason and compromises when appropriate. A wise person shows *mercy* by being kind, helpful, and quick to forgive. Wisdom is evident in a person's *good* fruits or deeds to others, especially to fellow Christians (Galatians 6:10). Partiality and a lack of sincerity are baser things that have no place in wisdom that is pure.

18. Peacemakers who sow in peace raise a harvest of righteousness.

Envying and strife provide the soil where confusion grows along with "every evil practice" (v. 16). But wise people who make peace find in that peace the soil where they can plant the seeds that grow into the fruit *of righteousness,* their own and that of others. (See also 2 Corinthians 9:10; Philippians 1:11.)

CONCLUSION

One day I learned an important lesson about being more careful about what I say. While my 10-year-old son was preparing his gear for a Little League baseball game that I couldn't attend, I wanted to send him off with some encouraging words. Jokingly, I said, "Don't hit any home runs tonight, OK?"

Little did I know the positive—and negative—effect this would have on him. After the game, I was both delighted and dismayed when I was told that he hit a ball so far he could have walked to home base, but instead he held up at third and would not budge no matter what the third-base coach said. The coach told me, "He didn't want to break his promise to you."

The power of words goes far beyond what we can imagine at the time we say them. We must be careful and as wise as we can be. We can all do better if we try, and we will make the world a better place for Christ.

Discovery Learning

This page contains an alternative lesson plan emphasizing learning activities. Some of these activities are also found in the helpful student book, NIV Bible Student. The next page is a reproducible activity page to further enhance discovery learning.

INTO THE LESSON

As an attention-getter, bring in lots of pictures of people talking; display them round the room. You can find on the Internet a wide variety of people talking in various situations: on cell phones with friends, in angry confrontations on the street, of parents correcting their children, etc. *Alternative #1:* make a recording of a few choice minutes of the TV show *The View* and bring it to class for your learners to watch. This show is notable for the four cohosts all talking at the same time and nobody doing much listening. *Alternative #2:* to work on as learners begin arriving, place in chairs copies of the Watch Your Words exercise from the Reproducible Page.

Ask learners how talk affects their daily lives, both good and bad. Prompt class discussion by mentioning talk radio, 24-hour news programs, sermons, arguments, encouragement from friends and family, sound bites, etc. After a few minutes, ask learners to react to this phrase: *too many words!*

INTO THE WORD

Ask the class to identify figures of speech and comparisons in James 3. Have one person write them on the board. Ask class members to explain very briefly what each illustrates; tell them that you will go back for fuller analysis later.

Taking the above list in order, discuss each illustration more thoroughly, beginning with the warning regarding teachers. Note that this may not have been listed by the class as a figure of speech. However, it is the first topic listed by James in verse 1 as a use of the tongue.

Divide your class into discussion pairs or five small groups. Give each pair or group a copy of the following list of five passages: Luke 12:48; 1 Corinthians 12:28, 29; 2 Timothy 4:3; Titus 2:3; Hebrews 5:12. Ask groups to discern what is taught about teachers in each passage, and then compare the conclusions with James 3:1.

Each group should formulate a one- or two-sentence summary of the results of the comparison. After groups have finished, have a spokesperson from each group read its summary. (To make this part of the lesson go faster, assign each group or discussion pair only one of the five passages.)

Each of your five discussion pairs or small groups will then analyze one of these five segments from James 3: verses 2-6; verses 7, 8; verses 9-12; verses 13-16; and verses 17, 18. Provide the following written instructions:

Group #1, James 3:2-6. Let those in your group who have experience with either horses or ships explain how a small part guides the whole. What parallels are there in modern technology? How do those parallels apply to the tongue? Give personal experiences regarding the destructiveness of fire; how is the tongue like this?

Group #2, James 3:7, 8. Who in your group has ever had an exotic or unusual pet? How was that pet tamed? Discuss James's assertion that the tongue cannot be tamed.

Group #3, James 3:9-12. Look at the "impossibilities" of verses 11 and 12; paraphrase this using imagery from modern technology. Relate your paraphrase back to verses 9 and 10.

Group #4, James 3:13-16. Discuss how the secular world decides who is "wise" and who is not. Compare and contrast that viewpoint with God's view of wisdom.

Group #5, James 3:17, 18. Look at the descriptions of wisdom's characteristics in verse 17; then think of some ways to describe secular, earthly wisdom. Compare and contrast your two lists; relate your conclusions to verse 18.

Give each group about 10 minutes to work before you call for conclusions. There is a lot of ground to cover with 18 verses, so keep things moving briskly.

INTO LIFE

Distribute blank sheets of paper. Have each learner make a list down the left side of places where his or her words will have influence in the coming week. After a few minutes, allow some time for silent prayer about the use of the tongue in those situations.

Ask learners to take their lists home with them. They are to use the lists to make notes during the week of whether the words spoken were beneficial or harmful in various interactions. Encourage learners to have a time of prayer at the end of every day during the week ahead. The prayer will be specifically about words spoken that day and words to be spoken the next day. Also encourage those learners who have chosen to do so to continue paraphrasing James chapter by chapter. Finally, distribute as a take-home exercise copies of the A Letter to the Wise activity from the Reproducible Page.

Watch Your Words

List destructive uses of the tongue:

_____

_____

_____

_____

_____

_____

_____

_____

List beneficial uses of the tongue:

_____

_____

_____

_____

_____

_____

_____

_____

A Letter to the Wise

Write a letter to a person who has used his or her tongue to influence you in a positive way at a vulnerable time in your life. Tell the person why this was significant to you.

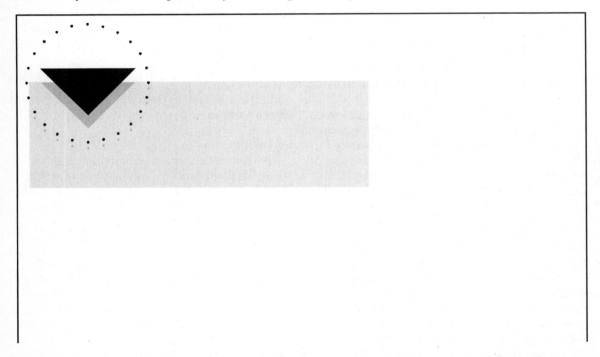

GODLY SERVANTS

LESSON 13

WHY TEACH THIS LESSON?

There are times when we are challenged to justify our questionable actions. If our justification in word or thought is "I'm not so bad! Just look at that guy!" then we need to heed this lesson from James.

We must not judge ourselves by the standard of imperfect people. Our standard for Christian life must be the standard of Christ! When we examine our thoughts and deeds against Christ's perfection, we will instantly see that we fall short. Seeing Christ clearly and seeing ourselves truthfully should be a humbling experience. When our arrogance is revealed in his presence, we have an opportunity to become more like him. As we learn to come humbly into God's presence, we have his assurance that he will come near to us.

Most Christians want to become more like Jesus. This lesson should help us to make an honest assessment regarding our flaws without making judgmental rationalizations that include others.

INTRODUCTION

A. YOU'VE GOT A FRIEND

James Taylor's popular song "You've Got a Friend" touches a chord in everyone. We all need friends. We tend to want lots of friends, to be popular. This kind of casual friendship, however, does not really satisfy our intense longing for deep, lasting friendship—the kind of friendship that is mutual, intimate, unswerving. We will be very blessed to find this kind of friendship in one or two people in the course of our lives.

Today's lesson poses the attractive idea that God wants to be this kind of friend to us. In bonding with God in this way, Christians should be prepared for their lives to be revolutionized with regard to the world and with regard to other believers.

B. LESSON BACKGROUND

In James 4:1-12, the epistle's criticism of its audience comes to a climax. James's readers expose the inadequacy of their Christian faith by the mean-spirited way they treat one another in the community of the church. This leads to the demand made in 4:7-10 for repentance and recommitment to God.

When we look back at what was said earlier in the epistle, we see a carefully laid path to this point. In 3:13-18, the characteristics of true wisdom that come from God are described in contrast to "wisdom" that comes from Satan. This amounts to being a peacemaker who restores community relationships rather than a self-promoter who divides a community. James 4:1-3 accuses the church of being driven by Satan's wisdom, and James 4:4-6 declares that this makes them enemies of God, whom they claim to serve.

In James 4:1-3 the readers are accused of various kinds of harmful speech, probably relating to anger, and in 4:11, 12 they are accused of slander. Concern

DEVOTIONAL READING:
PROVERBS 3:13-18
BACKGROUND SCRIPTURE:
JAMES 4
PRINTED TEXT:
JAMES 4:1-12

LESSON AIMS

After participating in this lesson, each student will be able to:

1. Summarize James's teaching about fighting, humility, and judging others.

2. Explain how fighting, humility, and judging others are related and what impact they have on the church today.

3. Plan a specific way to say or do something encouraging for someone in his or her church.

KEY VERSE

Come near to God and he will come near to you. Wash your hands, you sinners, and purify your hearts, you double-minded.

—James 4:8

Aug
24

for such speech sins and lack of control in this area of behavior was developed in 3:1-13 and emphasized in 1:19 and 1:26.

In James 4:4 friendship is held up as the highest expression of relationship with God. Earlier, in 2:23, Abraham was called "God's friend." He was God's friend in that he trusted God implicitly. Abraham demonstrated this even to the point of being prepared to sacrifice Isaac, his son of promise. Similarly, James's readers are to demonstrate their trusting relationship with God by living in the way he asks and applying Christ's law of neighbor love to those who hold in common a true faith in Jesus Christ.

I. CREATING ENEMIES (JAMES 4:1-6)

People can hardly claim to be God's servants when they portray attitudes and behaviors that attack other servants of God. To put God's house into such disarray is disgraceful. Those who conduct themselves in this way not only alienate themselves from others, they make any kind of genuine relationship with God impossible.

A. WITHIN THE CHURCH (vv. 1-3)

1. What causes fights and quarrels among you? Don't they come from your desires that battle within you?

This verse asks two questions, the second one (with its assumed affirmative response) being the answer to the first. The first question, interestingly, does not ask whether or not the church members are fighting among themselves; James already knows that they are! Rather, James wants to get Christians to probe the reasons *why* they are fighting and to consider the truthfulness of the second question to explain this.

The second question turns the conflict language inward to each individual's private, spiritual war. It challenges Christians to recognize that behavior is determined by whether or not we are able to win the internal war with our *desires*.

The Greek word behind *desires* comes into English as *hedonism*. This points to a lifestyle that is committed to indulging in worldly pleasures. This passage says that believers have within themselves cravings for these self-indulgent pleasures. If not controlled, this will result in destructive behavior toward the others in the church.

2. You want something but don't get it. You kill and covet, but you cannot have what you want. You quarrel and fight. You do not have, because you do not ask God.

How all this works itself out is startling. Coveting happens when a person wants something that belongs to someone else. The desire can become so strong that a person will do anything to satisfy it, including *kill*. We can see how this might describe a drug addict or a thief, but how can these verses say such a thing about Christians?

To understand this, it is necessary to look at how closely the Bible equates harmful words with harmful actions. In Matthew 5:21, 22, Jesus teaches that anger that leads to destructive words is equivalent to the anger that leads to murder.

Extremely mean words can be launched against others in the heat of verbal battle: ridicule, insults, cursing, slander. James 3:8 already spoke of the tongue as capable of inflicting death, and this simply follows a trail of horrific images of the tongue in the Old Testament. "Evil is sweet in [the wicked person's] mouth and he hides it under his tongue" (Job 20:12). "[The] tongue [of the Israelites] is a

What negative motives do you see in nonbelievers that have the potential to cause problems between you and your brothers and sisters in Christ? What action will you take to prevent this from happening?

deadly arrow; it speaks with deceit. With his mouth each speaks cordially to his neighbor, but in his heart he sets a trap for him" (Jeremiah 9:8). "The words of the wicked lie in wait for blood" (Proverbs 12:6). See also Psalm 10:7-10; 64:3.

YOU CANNOT HAVE

The 1968 film *Oliver!* is a musical adaptation of Charles Dickens's outstanding novel *Oliver Twist*. In the musical, the part of Fagin, a rather menacing figure in the original, is changed into an almost charming, comic character. A trainer of adolescent pickpockets, Fagin provides food and shelter in exchange for the stolen items the children bring him. He also acts as a "fence," disposing of stolen items for Bill Sikes, a former student of his, who is now a notorious thief and villain. But Fagin is also concerned about building up his own financial reserves. While giving Sikes his share of the proceeds, Fagin also keeps back certain items in order to provide for his own later financial security.

Toward the end of the movie, the police follow Sikes to the warehouse where Fagin and his boys live. In their desperate attempt to get away, Fagin gathers up his loot. But in moving across the dilapidated boardwalks in their hurried dash to escape, Fagin stumbles, and all his precious items fall into the muddy ooze which is the backwaters of the Thames River. His precious store of gold, silver, jewels, etc., quickly disappears into the slime, lost forever.

James talks about those who lust after worldly possessions and even kill in order to obtain them. But ultimately they are just as unsuccessful as Fagin was. Such self-centered materialism will always come to no good end. Fagin's loss is typical of all those who use unethical methods to gain worldly goods.   —J. B. N.

3. When you ask, you do not receive, because you ask with wrong motives, that you may spend what you get on your pleasures.

Verses 2 and 3 describe a tension between wanting what does not belong to us (coveting, as in Exodus 20:17) and simply asking God for what we want. This is a genuine spiritual tension because when we *ask* God for something, we know—regardless of what we ask for—that he wants to give us only what is best for us. He is the giver of good gifts, not bad, as James 1:17 states.

We insult God if we ask him for something we know to begin with is not good for us or, as in these verses, breaks God's law because it belongs to someone else. The instruction here should be understood to apply to the panorama of situations for which we ask God's help. In each instance, though, we need to remember the holy and good nature of the one to whom we are talking.

B. WITH GOD (vv. 4-6)

4. You adulterous people, don't you know that friendship with the world is hatred toward God? Anyone who chooses to be a friend of the world becomes an enemy of God.

These verses open by addressing the readers in a way that instantly conveys their condemnation in the manner of an Old Testament prophet. Accusations of adultery were reserved for the people of Israel when they had betrayed God by openly cavorting with other gods. "'But like a woman unfaithful to her husband, so you have been unfaithful to me, O house of Israel,' declares the Lord" (Jeremiah 3:20; see also Ezekiel 23; Hosea 2:2-5).

Ephesians 5:22-33 depicts the church as Christ's bride. We may compare that image with the concern here in James that people who call themselves Christian are conducting themselves in ways that show an intimate relationship with the pleasures of *the world* rather than with the holiness of God.

WHAT DO YOU THINK?

What steps will you take to make sure you are not inflicting pain on other believers? When you cross the line with unkind words, what will you do to initiate the healing process?

[Make sure to review Matthew 5:23, 24 and Romans 12:15, 16 as you consider your answer.]

DAILY BIBLE READINGS

Monday, Aug. 18—Understanding and Peace (Proverbs 3: 13-18)

Tuesday, Aug. 19—Ask Rightly (James 4:1-3)

Wednesday, Aug. 20—Yearn for God's Spirit (James 4:4-7)

Thursday, Aug. 21—Humble Yourselves (James 4:8-10)

Friday, Aug. 22—Do Not Judge (James 4:11-14)

Saturday, Aug. 23—Seek God's Wishes (James 4:15-17)

Sunday, Aug. 24—Living in the Light of God (Ephesians 5:8-11)

The public confession of belief in Christ can be understood to be comparable to wedding vows. This confession of Christ is not simply a statement of belief. It is a commitment to a relationship that Christ matches with his own promise of eternal life and the presence of the Holy Spirit. To consort with the world as our soul mate in making decisions about how we are going to conduct our lives is to betray our relationship with Christ.

FRIENDSHIP WITH THE WORLD

Thomas More (1478–1535) was certainly one of the most stimulating individuals in England in the days of King Henry VIII, who reigned 1509–1547. More served as the chancellor in Henry's government and was favored by the king, until he opposed the king's divorce from Katherine of Aragon in order to marry Anne Boleyn.

Still an adherent of papal policy, More was unwilling to sign a statement that acknowledged Henry as the "Head of the Church of England." More resigned from his office as chancellor and for a while lived quietly. But his opponents wanted to get rid of him, and he was charged with treason against the king by refusing to accept one of the king's titles. More believed he could escape by not admitting anything.

However, Richard Rich brought evidence into the court that he had heard More deny the king's title. More knew that Rich's testimony was false and that Rich had been granted the position as Governor of Wales as payment for his false testimony. In court More chastised Rich for his false testimony and suggested that Wales was but poor payment for the spiritual damnation of his lies.

James makes a similar point. "Friendship with the world"—represented in Rich's avarice, greed, and betrayal—"is hatred toward God" (4:4). Coveting the things of this world can lead to a more serious spiritual rebellion against God.

—J. B. N.

5. Or do you think Scripture says without reason that the spirit he caused to live in us envies intensely?

James now offers a *Scripture* quotation whose exact biblical reference is uncertain. This quotation most likely intends to express the intense desire God placed in people that makes us want to have a close relationship with him. The best Old Testament expressions of this thought are "As the deer pants for streams of water, so my soul pants for you, O God. My soul thirsts for God, for the living God. When can I go and meet with God?" (Psalm 42:1, 2) and "My soul yearns, even faints, for the courts of the Lord; my heart and my flesh cry out for the living God" (Psalm 84:2).

6. But he gives us more grace. That is why Scripture says:
  "God opposes the proud
    but gives grace to the humble."

The Greek (Septuagint) version of Proverbs 3:34 is quoted as testimony to God's abundant *grace*. It shows that when we come to him in true humility, even after living in prideful arrogance and self-promotion that insults him, he will accept us. To have this relationship with God, we must turn our backs on harmful envy and bad attitudes that are part of our lives.

II. CREATING FRIENDS (JAMES 4:7-12)

If people who are God's servants have made enemies among fellow servants in the church, a remedy for their situation exists. This remedy calls first for abject repentance before God. Next comes reformation in how people are treat-